Lecture Notes in Computer Science 8714

Commenced Publication in 1973
Founding and Former Series Editors:
Gerhard Goos, Juris Hartmanis, and Jan van Leeuwen

Manolis Koubarakis   Giorgos Stamou
Giorgos Stoilos   Ian Horrocks
Phokion Kolaitis   Georg Lausen
Gerhard Weikum (Eds.)

Reasoning Web

Reasoning on the Web in the Big Data Era

10th International Summer School 2014
Athens, Greece, September 8-13, 2014
Proceedings

 Springer

Volume Editors

Manolis Koubarakis
National and Kapodistrian University of Athens, Greece
E-mail: koubarak@di.uoa.gr

Giorgos Stamou
Giorgos Stoilos
National Technical University of Athens, Zografou, Greece
E-mail: gstam@cs.ntua.gr; gstoil@image.ntua.gr

Ian Horrocks
University of Oxford, UK
E-mail: ian.horrocks@cs.ox.ac.uk

Phokion Kolaitis
University of California, Santa Cruz, CA, USA
E-mail: kolaitis@soe.ucsc.edu

Georg Lausen
University of Freiburg, Germany
E-mail: lausen@informatik.uni-freiburg.de

Gerhard Weikum
Max Planck Institute for Informatics, Saarbrücken, Germany
E-mail: weikum@mpi-inf.mpg.de

ISSN 0302-9743   e-ISSN 1611-3349
ISBN 978-3-319-10586-4   e-ISBN 978-3-319-10587-1
DOI 10.1007/978-3-319-10587-1
Springer Cham Heidelberg New York Dordrecht London

Library of Congress Control Number: 2014946916

LNCS Sublibrary: SL 3 – Information Systems and Application,
incl. Internet/Web and HCI

Typesetting: Camera-ready by author, data conversion by Scientific Publishing Services, Chennai, India

Printed on acid-free paper

Springer is part of Springer Science+Business Media (www.springer.com)

Preface

This volume contains tutorial papers prepared for the 10th Reasoning Web Summer School (RW 2014) held during September 8–13, 2014, in Athens, Greece.

The Reasoning Web series of annual summer schools started in 2005 by the European Network of Excellence REWERSE. Since 2005, the school has become the prime educational event in the field of reasoning techniques on the Web, attracting both young and established researchers. The 2014 edition of the school was organized by the Department of Informatics and Telecommunications, National and Kapodistrian University of Athens (Prof. Manolis Koubarakis) and the Institute for Communication and Computer Systems of the National Technical University of Athens (Prof. Giorgos Stamou and Dr. Giorgos Stoilos). As with previous editions, this year's summer school was co-located with the 8th International Conference on Web Reasoning and Rule Systems (RR 2014).

The research area of the Semantic Web and Linked Data has been covered comprehensively by recent editions of the Reasoning Web Summer School since many advanced capabilities required by Semantic Web and Linked Data application scenarios call for reasoning. In 2014, the theme of the school was:

"Reasoning on the Web in the Big Data Era."

The invention of new technologies such as sensors, social networks platforms, and smart phones has enabled organizations to tap a huge amount of data that traditionally has not been available to them, and to combine it with in-house proprietary data. At the same time, enabling technologies (e.g., elastic cloud computing platforms) have made strong progress enabling the implementation of data management and knowledge discovery techniques that work on terabytes or petabytes of data. In 2014, the lecture program of the Reasoning Web school reflected this industrial reality, and introduced students to recent advances in Big Data aspects of Semantic Web and Linked Data, and the fundamentals of reasoning techniques that can be used to tackle Big Data applications.

The tutorial papers are in-depth surveys of the research topics covered in lectures by the distinguished invited speakers of the school. They have been written as accompanying material for the students of the summer school, to deepen their understanding and to serve as a reference for further detailed study.

The accompanying lecture slides of all tutorials are available on the summer school web-site: http://rw2014.di.uoa.gr/.

We would like to thank everybody who made this event possible. First and foremost, the presenters of the lectures and their co-authors. Secondly, the members of our scientific advisory board (Profs. Ian Horrocks, Phokion Kolaitis, Georg Lausen, and Gerhard Weikum) and our reviewers. We are thankful for their advice and feedback and their timely reviews of the papers. Furthermore, we would like to thank the local organization team at the National and Kapodistrian University of Athens and the Institute for Communication and Computer

Systems, especially Kalliroi Dogani, Maria Karpathiotaki, Lydia Themeli, and Eleni Iskou. We would also like to thank our sponsors: the *Artificial Intelligence* journal, the European project Optique (`http://www.optique-project.eu/`), the National Science Foundation (NSF), the Institut national de recherche en informatique et en automatique (Inria), the Hellenic Artificial Intelligence Society (EETN), ORACLE Greece, Siemens, and Google Inc.

Last but not least, we would like to thank the chairs of RR 2014, Prof. Axel Polleres, Dr. Roman Kontchakov, Prof. Marie-Laure Mugnier, and Prof. Francesco Ricca for a great collaboration in putting together all the details of the two events.

June 2014

Manolis Koubarakis
Giorgos Stamou
Giorgos Stoilos

Organization

Organizing Chairs

Manolis Koubarakis   National Kapodistrian University of Athens, Greece

Giorgos Stamou   National Technical University of Athens, Greece

Giorgos Stoilos   National Technical University of Athens, Greece

Scientific Advisory Board

Ian Horrocks   University of Oxford, UK

Phokion Kolaitis   University of California, Santa Cruz, USA

Georg Lausen   University of Freiburg, Germany

Gerhard Weikum   Max Planck Institute for Informatics, Germany

Website Administrators

Kalliroi Dogani   National Kapodistrian University of Athens, Greece

Maria Karpathiotaki   National Kapodistrian University of Athens, Greece

Local Organization

Lydia Themeli   National Kapodistrian University of Athens, Greece

Eleni Iskou   National Technical University of Athens, Greece

Additional Reviewers

Giannakopoulou, Asimina   Tsalapati, Eleni

Trivela, Despoina

Sponsors

Artificial
Intelligence

www.elsevier.com/locate/artint

Google

ORACLE

Optique

EETN

SIEMENS

Inria

Table of Contents

Introduction to Linked Data and Its Lifecycle
on the Web

Axel-Cyrille Ngonga Ngomo, Sören Auer, Jens Lehmann, and Amrapali Zaveri

AKSW, Institut für Informatik, Universität Leipzig, Pf 100920, 04009 Leipzig
lastname@informatik.uni-leipzig.de
http://aksw.org

Abstract. With Linked Data, a very pragmatic approach towards achieving the vision of the Semantic Web has gained some traction in the last years. The term Linked Data refers to a set of best practices for publishing and interlinking structured data on the Web. While many standards, methods and technologies developed within by the Semantic Web community are applicable for Linked Data, there are also a number of specific characteristics of Linked Data, which have to be considered. In this article we introduce the main concepts of Linked Data. We present an overview of the Linked Data life-cycle and discuss individual approaches as well as the state-of-the-art with regard to extraction, authoring, linking, enrichment as well as quality of Linked Data. We conclude the chapter with a discussion of issues, limitations and further research and development challenges of Linked Data. This article is an updated version of a similar lecture given at Reasoning Web Summer School 2013.

1 Introduction

One of the biggest challenges in the area of intelligent information management is the exploitation of the Web as a platform for data and information integration as well as for search and querying. Just as we publish unstructured textual information on the Web as HTML pages and search such information by using keyword-based search engines, we are already able to easily publish structured information, reliably interlink this information with other data published on the Web and search the resulting data space by using more expressive querying beyond simple keyword searches. The Linked Data paradigm has evolved as a powerful enabler for the transition of the current document-oriented Web into a Web of interlinked Data and, ultimately, into the Semantic Web. The term Linked Data here refers to a set of best practices for publishing and connecting structured data on the Web. These best practices have been adopted by an increasing number of data providers over the past three years, leading to the creation of a global data space that contains many billions of assertions – the Web of Linked Data (cf. Figure 1).

In this chapter we give an overview of recent development in the area of Linked Data management. The different stages in the linked data life-cycle [11] are depicted in Figure 2. Information represented in unstructured form or adhering to other structured or semi-structured representation formalisms must be mapped to the RDF data model (*Extraction*). Once there is a critical mass of RDF data, mechanisms have to be in place to store, index and query this RDF data efficiently (*Storage & Querying*). Users must

M. Koubarakis et al. (Eds.): Reasoning Web 2014, LNCS 8714, pp. 1–99, 2014.

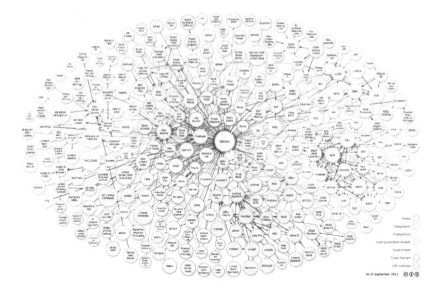

Fig. 1. Overview of some of the main Linked Data knowledge bases and their interlinks available on the Web. (This overview is published regularly at `http://lod-cloud.net` and generated from the Linked Data packages described at the dataset metadata repository `ckan.net`.)

have the opportunity to create new structured information or to correct and extend existing ones (*Authoring*). If different data publishers provide information about the same or related entities, links between those different information assets have to be established (*Linking*). Since Linked Data primarily comprises instance data we observe a lack of classification, structure and schema information. This deficiency can be tackled by approaches for enriching data with higher-level structures in order to be able to aggregate and query the data more efficiently (*Enrichment*). As with the Document Web, the Data Web contains a variety of information of different quality. Hence, it is important to devise strategies for assessing the quality of data published on the Data Web (*Quality Analysis*). Once problems are detected, strategies for repairing these problems and supporting the evolution of Linked Data are required (*Evolution & Repair*). Last but not least, users have to be empowered to browse, search and explore the structure information available on the Data Web in a fast and user friendly manner (*Search, Browsing & Exploration*).

These different stages of the linked data life-cycle do not exist in isolation or are passed in a strict sequence, but support each other. Examples include the following:

– The detection of mappings on the schema level support instance-level matching and vice versa.
– Ontology schema mismatches between knowledge bases can be compensated for by learning which concepts of one are equivalent to which concepts of the other knowledge base.
– Feedback and input from end users can be taken as training input (i.e., as positive or negative examples) for machine-learning techniques to perform inductive reasoning

on larger knowledge bases, whose results can again be assessed by end users for iterative refinement.

– Semantically-enriched knowledge bases improve the detection of inconsistencies and modelling problems, which in turn results in benefits for linking, fusion, and classification.

– The querying performance of the RDF data management directly affects all other components and the nature of queries issued by the components affects the RDF data management.

As a result of such interdependence, we envision the Web of Linked Data to realize an improvement cycle for knowledge bases, in which an improvement of a knowledge base with regard to one aspect (e.g., a new alignment with another interlinking hub) triggers a number of possible further improvements (e.g., additional instance matches).

The use of Linked Data offers a number of significant benefits:

– *Uniformity.* All datasets published as Linked Data share a uniform data model, the RDF statement data model. With this data model all information is represented in facts expressed as triples consisting of a subject, predicate and object. The elements used in subject, predicate or object positions are mainly globally unique identifiers (IRI/URI). Literals, i.e., typed data values, can be used at the object position.

– *De-referencability.* URIs are not just used for identifying entities, but since they can be used in the same way as URLs they also enable locating and retrieving resources describing and representing these entities on the Web.

– *Coherence.* When an RDF triple contains URIs from different namespaces in subject and object position, this triple basically establishes a link between the entity

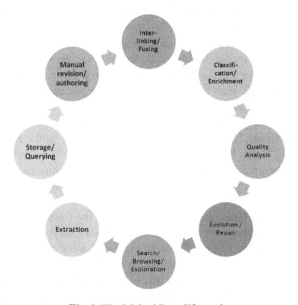

Fig. 2. The Linked Data life-cycle

identified by the subject (and described in the source dataset using namspace A) with the entity identified by the object (described in the target dataset using namespace B). Through the typed RDF links, data items are effectively interlinked.

– *Integrability.* Since all Linked Data sources share the RDF data model, which is based on a single mechanism for representing information, it is very easy to attain a syntactic and simple semantic integration of different Linked Data sets. A higher level semantic integration can be achieved by employing schema and instance matching techniques and expressing found matches again as alignments of RDF vocabularies and ontologies in terms of additional triple facts.

– *Timeliness.* Publishing and updating Linked Data is relatively simple thus facilitating a timely availability. In addition, once a Linked Data source is updated it is straightforward to access and use the updated data source, since time consuming and error prune extraction, transformation and loading is not required.

Table 1. Juxtaposition of the concepts Linked Data, Linked Open Data and Open Data

Representation \ degree of openness	Possibly closed	Open (cf. `opendefinition.org`)
Structured data model (i.e. XML, CSV, SQL etc.)	**Data**	**Open Data**
RDF data model (published as Linked Data)	**Linked Data** (LD)	**Linked Open Data** (LOD)

The development of research approaches, standards, technology and tools for supporting the Linked Data lifecycle data is one of the main challenges. Developing adequate and pragmatic solutions to these problems can have a substantial impact on science, economy, culture and society in general. The publishing, integration and aggregation of statistical and economic data, for example, can help to obtain a more precise and timely picture of the state of our economy. In the domain of health care and life sciences making sense of the wealth of structured information already available on the Web can help to improve medical information systems and thus make health care more adequate and efficient. For the media and news industry, using structured background information from the Data Web for enriching and repurposing the quality content can facilitate the creation of new publishing products and services. Linked Data technologies can help to increase the flexibility, adaptability and efficiency of information management in organizations, be it companies, governments and public administrations or online communities. For end-users and society in general, the Data Web will help to obtain and integrate required information more efficiently and thus successfully manage the transition towards a knowledge-based economy and an information society.

Structure of this chapter. This chapter aims to explain the foundations of Linked Data and introducing the different aspects of the Linked Data lifecycle by highlighting particular approaches and providing references to related work and further reading. We start by briefly explaining the principles underlying the Linked Data paradigm in Section 2. The first aspect of the Linked Data lifecycle is the extraction of information from unstructured, semi-structured and structured sources and their representation according to the RDF data model (Section 3). We present the user friendly authoring and manual revision aspect of Linked Data with the example of Semantic Wikis in Section 4. The interlinking aspect is tackled in Section 5 and gives an overview on the LIMES framework. We describe how the instance data published and commonly found on the Data Web can be enriched with higher level structures in Section 6. We present an overview of the various data quality dimensions and metrics along with currently existing tools for data quality assessment of Linked Data in Section 7. Due to space limitations we omit a detailed discussion of the evolution as well as search, browsing and exploration aspects of the Linked Data lifecycle in this chapter. The chapter is concluded by several sections on promising applications of Linked Data and semantic technologies, in particular Open Governmental Data, Semantic Business Intelligence and Statistical and Economic Data. Overall, this is an updated version of a similar lecture given at Reasoning Web Summer School 2013 [13].

2 The Linked Data Paradigm

In this section we introduce the basic principles of Linked Data. The section is partially based on the Section 2 from [79]. The term Linked Data refers to a set of best practices for publishing and interlinking structured data on the Web. These best practices were introduced by Tim Berners-Lee in his Web architecture note Linked Data[1] and have become known as the Linked Data principles. These principles are:

- Use URIs as names for things.
- Use HTTP URIs so that people can look up those names.
- When someone looks up a URI, provide useful information, using the standards (RDF, SPARQL).
- Include links to other URIs, so that they can discover more things.

The basic idea of Linked Data is to apply the general architecture of the World Wide Web [95] to the task of sharing structured data on global scale. The Document Web is built on the idea of setting hyperlinks between Web documents that may reside on different Web servers. It is built on a small set of simple standards: Uniform Resource Identifiers (URIs) and their extension Internationalized Resource Identifiers (IRIs) as globally unique identification mechanism [22], the Hypertext Transfer Protocol (HTTP) as universal access mechanism [56], and the Hypertext Markup Language (HTML) as a widely used content format [88]. Linked Data builds directly on Web architecture and applies this architecture to the task of sharing data on global scale.

2.1 Resource Identification with IRIs

To publish data on the Web, the data items in a domain of interest must first be identified. These are the things whose properties and relationships will be described in the data, and may include Web documents as well as real-world entities and abstract concepts. As Linked Data builds directly on Web architecture, the Web architecture term *resource* is used to refer to these *things of interest*, which are in turn identified by HTTP URIs.

---

[1] http://www.w3.org/DesignIssues/LinkedData.html

Linked Data uses only HTTP URIs, avoiding other URI schemes such as URNs [136] and DOIs[2]. The structure of HTTP URIs looks as follows:

[scheme:][//authority][path][?query][#fragment]

A URI for identifying Shakespeare's 'Othello', for example, could look as follows:

http://de.wikipedia.org/wiki/Othello#id

HTTP URIs make good names for two reasons:

1. They provide a simple way to create globally unique names in a decentralized fashion, as every owner of a domain name or delegate of the domain name owner may create new URI references.
2. They serve not just as a name but also as a means of accessing information describing the identified entity.

2.2   De-referencability

Any HTTP URI should be de-referencable, meaning that HTTP clients can look up the URI using the HTTP protocol and retrieve a description of the resource that is identified by the URI. This applies to URIs that are used to identify classic HTML documents, as well as URIs that are used in the Linked Data context to identify real-world objects and abstract concepts. Descriptions of resources are embodied in the form of Web documents. Descriptions that are intended to be read by humans are often represented as HTML. Descriptions that are intended for consumption by machines are represented as RDF data. Where URIs identify real-world objects, it is essential to not confuse the objects themselves with the Web documents that describe them. It is therefore common practice to use different URIs to identify the real-world object and the document that describes it, in order to be unambiguous. This practice allows separate statements to be made about an object and about a document that describes that object. For example, the creation year of a painting may be rather different to the creation year of an article about this painting. Being able to distinguish the two through use of different URIs is critical to the consistency of the Web of Data.

The Web is intended to be an information space that may be used by humans as well as by machines. Both should be able to retrieve representations of resources in a form that meets their needs, such as HTML for humans and RDF for machines. This can be achieved using an HTTP mechanism called content negotiation [56]. The basic idea of content negotiation is that HTTP clients send HTTP headers with each request to indicate what kinds of documents they prefer. Servers can inspect these headers and select an appropriate response. If the headers indicate that the client prefers HTML then the server will respond by sending an HTML document If the client prefers RDF, then the server will send the client an RDF document.

There are two different strategies to make URIs that identify real-world objects de-referencable [179]. Both strategies ensure that objects and the documents that describe them are not confused and that humans as well as machines can retrieve appropriate representations.

---

[2] http://www.doi.org/hb.html

303 URIs. Real-world objects can not be transmitted over the wire using the HTTP protocol. Thus, it is also not possible to directly de-reference URIs that identify real-world objects. Therefore, in the 303 URI strategy, instead of sending the object itself over the network, the server responds to the client with the HTTP response code 303 See Other and the URI of a Web document which describes the real-world object. This is called a *303 redirect.* In a second step, the client de-references this new URI and retrieves a Web document describing the real-world object.

Hash URIs. A widespread criticism of the 303 URI strategy is that it requires two HTTP requests to retrieve a single description of a real-world object. One option for avoiding these two requests is provided by the hash URI strategy. The hash URI strategy builds on the characteristic that URIs may contain a special part that is separated from the base part of the URI by a hash symbol (#). This special part is called the fragment identifier. When a client wants to retrieve a hash URI the HTTP protocol requires the fragment part to be stripped off before requesting the URI from the server. This means a URI that includes a hash cannot be retrieved directly, and therefore does not necessarily identify a Web document. This enables such URIs to be used to identify real-world objects and abstract concepts, without creating ambiguity [179].

Both approaches have their advantages and disadvantages. Section 4.4. of the W3C Interest Group Note *Cool URIs for the Semantic Web* compares the two approaches [179]: Hash URIs have the advantage of reducing the number of necessary HTTP round-trips, which in turn reduces access latency. The downside of the hash URI approach is that the descriptions of all resources that share the same non-fragment URI part are always returned to the client together, irrespective of whether the client is interested in only one URI or all. If these descriptions consist of a large number of triples, the hash URI approach can lead to large amounts of data being unnecessarily transmitted to the client. 303 URIs, on the other hand, are very flexible because the redirection target can be configured separately for each resource. There could be one describing document for each resource, or one large document for all of them, or any combination in between. It is also possible to change the policy later on.

2.3 RDF Data Model

The RDF data model [1] represents information as sets of statements, which can be visualized as node-and-arc-labeled directed graphs. The data model is designed for the integrated representation of information that originates from multiple sources, is heterogeneously structured, and is represented using different schemata. RDF can be viewed as a *lingua franca*, capable of moderating between other data models that are used on the Web.

In RDF, information is represented in statements, called RDF triples. The three parts of each triple are called its subject, predicate, and object. A triple mimics the basic structure of a simple sentence, such as for example:

```
Burkhard Jung    is the mayor of    Leipzig
  (subject)        (predicate)       (object)
```

The following is the formal definition of RDF triples as it can be found in the W3C RDF standard [1].

Definition 1 (RDF Triple). *Assume there are pairwise disjoint infinite sets I, B, and L representing IRIs, blank nodes, and RDF literals, respectively. A triple $(v_1, v_2, v_3) \in (I \cup B) \times I \times (I \cup B \cup L)$ is called an RDF triple. In this tuple, v_1 is the subject, v_2 the predicate and v_3 the object. We call $T = I \cup B \cup L$ the set of RDF terms.*

The main idea is to use IRIs as identifiers for entities in the subject, predicate and object positions in a triple. Data values can be represented in the object position as literals. Furthermore, the RDF data model also allows in subject and object positions the use of identifiers for unnamed entities (called blank nodes), which are not globally unique and can thus only be referenced locally. However, the use of blank nodes is discouraged in the Linked Data context as we discuss below. Our example fact sentence about Leipzig's mayor would now look as follows:

```
<http://leipzig.de/id>
            <http://example.org/p/hasMayor>
                                        <http://Burkhard-Jung.de/id> .
    (subject)           (predicate)             (object)
```

This example shows that IRIs used within a triple can originate from different namespaces thus effectively facilitating the mixing and mashing of different RDF vocabularies and entities from different Linked Data knowledge bases. A triple having identifiers from different knowledge bases at subject and object position can be also viewed as an typed link between the entities identified by subject and object. The predicate then identifies the type of link. If we combine different triples we obtain an RDF graph.

Definition 2 (RDF Graph). *A finite set of RDF triples is called RDF graph. The RDF graph itself represents an resource, which is located at a certain location on the Web and thus has an associated IRI, the graph IRI.*

An example of an RDF graph is depicted in Figure 3. Each unique subject or object contained in the graph is visualized as a node (i.e. oval for resources and rectangle for literals). Predicates are visualized as labeled arcs connecting the respective nodes. There are a number of synonyms being used for RDF graphs, all meaning essentially the same but stressing different aspects of an RDF graph, such as *RDF document* (file perspective), *knowledge base* (collection of facts), *vocabulary* (shared terminology), *ontology* (shared logical conceptualization).

Problematic RDF features in the Linked Data Context. Besides the features mentioned above, the RDF Recommendation [1] also specifies some other features. In order to make it easier for clients to consume data only the subset of the RDF data model described above should be used. In particular, the following features are problematic when publishing RDF as Linked Data:

- *RDF reification* (for making statements about statements) should be avoided if possible, as reified statements are rather cumbersome to query with the SPARQL query

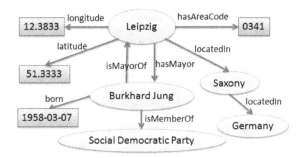

Fig. 3. Example RDF graph describing the city of Leipzig and its mayor

language. In many cases using reification to publish metadata about individual RDF statements can be avoided by attaching the respective metadata to the RDF document containing the relevant triples.

- *RDF collections* and *RDF containers* are also problematic if the data needs to be queried with SPARQL. Therefore, in cases where the relative ordering of items in a set is not significant, the use of multiple triples with the same predicate is recommended.
- The scope of *blank nodes* is limited to the document in which they appear, meaning it is not possible to create links to them from external documents. In addition, it is more difficult to merge data from different sources when blank nodes are used, as there is no URI to serve as a common key. Therefore, all resources in a data set should be named using IRI references.

2.4   RDF Serializations

The initial official W3C RDF standard [1] comprised a serialization of the RDF data model in XML called *RDF/XML*. Its rationale was to integrate RDF with the existing XML standard, so it could be used smoothly in conjunction with the existing XML technology landscape. However, RDF/XML turned out to be difficult to understand for the majority of potential users because it requires to be familiar with two data models (i.e., the tree-oriented XML data model as well as the statement oriented RDF datamodel) and interactions between them, since RDF statements are represented in XML. As a consequence, with *N-Triples*, *Turtle* and *N3* a family of alternative text-based RDF serializations was developed, whose members have the same origin, but balance differently between readability for humans and machines. Later in 2009, *RDFa* (RDF Annotations, [3]) was standardized by the W3C in order to simplify the integration of HTML and RDF and to allow the joint representation of structured and unstructured content within a single source HTML document. Another RDF serialization, which is particularly beneficial in the context of JavaScript web applications and mashups is the serialization of RDF in JSON. In the sequel we present each of these RDF serializations in some more detail. Figure 5 presents an example serialized in the most popular serializations.

N-Triples.   This serialization format was developed specifically for RDF graphs. The goal was to create a serialization format which is very simple. N-Triples are easy to

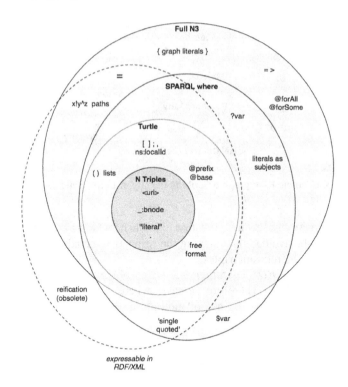

Full N3

{ graph literals }

=

=>

SPARQL where

x!y^z paths

@forAll
@forSome

?var

Turtle

[ ] ;,
ns:localId

( ) lists

@prefix
@base

literals as
subjects

N Triples

<uri>

_:bnode

"literal"

free
format

reification
(obsolete)

'single
quoted'

$var

*expressable in
RDF/XML*

Fig. 4. Various textual RDF serializations as subsets of N3 (from [170])

parse and generate by software. An N-Triples document consists of a set of triples, which are separated '.' (lines 1-2, 3-4 and 5-6 in Figure 5 contain one triple each). URI components of a triple are written in full and enclosed by '<' and '>'. Literals are enclosed in quotes, datatypes can be appended to a literal using 'g (line 6), language tags using '@' (line 4). They are a subset of *Notation 3* and *Turtle* but lack, for example, shortcuts such as CURIEs. This makes them less readable and more difficult to create manually. Another disadvantage is that N-triples use only the 7-bit US-ASCII character encoding instead of UTF-8.

Turtle. Turtle (Terse RDF Triple Language) is a subset of Notation 3 (and is consequently compatible with Notation 3)and a superset of the minimal N-Triples format (cf. Figure 4). The goal was to use the essential parts of Notation 3 for the serialization of RDF models and omit everything else. Turtle became part of the SPARQL query language for expressing graph patterns. Compared to N-Triples, Turtle introduces a number of shortcuts, such as namespace definitions (lines 1-5 in Figure 5), the semicolon as a separator between triples sharing the same subject (which then does not have to be repeated in subsequent triples) and the comma as a separator between triples sharing the same subject and predicate. Turtle, just like Notation 3, is human-readable, and can handle the "%" character in URIs (required for encoding special characters) as well as IRIs due to its UTF-8 encoding.

Notation 3. N3 (Notation 3) was devised by Tim Berners-Lee and developed for the purpose of serializing RDF. The main aim was to create a very human-readable serialization. Hence, an RDF model serialized in N3 is much more compact than the same model in RDF/XML but still allows a great deal of expressiveness even going beyond the RDF data model in some aspects. Since the encoding for N3 files is UTF-8, the use of IRIs is natively supported by this format.

RDF/XML. The RDF/XML syntax [130] is standardized by the W3C and is widely used to publish Linked Data on the Web. However, the syntax is also viewed as difficult for humans to read and write, and therefore consideration should be given to using other serializations in data management and curation workflows that involve human intervention, and to the provision of alternative serializations for consumers who may wish to eyeball the data. The MIME type that should be used for RDF/XML within HTTP content negotiation is `application/rdf+xml`.

RDFa. RDF in Attributes (RDFa, [3]) was developed for embedding RDF into XHTML pages. Since it is an extension to the XML based XHTML, UTF-8 and UTF-16 are used for encoding. The "%" character for URIs in triples can be used because RDFa tags are not used for a part of a RDF statement. Thus IRIs are usable, too. Because RDFa is embedded in XHTML, the overhead is higher compared to other serialization technologies and also reduces the readability. The basic idea of RDFa is enable an RDFa processor to extract RDF statements from an RDFa enriched HTML document. This is achieved by defining the scope of a certain resource description, for example, using the 'about' attribute (cf. line 10 in Figure 5). Within this scope, triples can now be extracted from links having an additional 'rel' attribute (line 13) or other tags having a 'property attribute' (lines 11 and 14).

JSON-LD. JavaScript Object Notation (JSON) was developed for easy data interchange between applications. JSON, although carrying JavaScript in its name and being a subset of JavaScript, meanwhile became a language independent format which can be used for exchanging all kinds of data structures and is widely supported in different programming languages. Compared to XML, JSON-LD requires less overhead with regard to parsing and serializing. JSON-LD has been developed by the JSON for Linking Data Community Group and been transferred to the RDF Working Group for review, improvement, and publication along the Recommendation track. JSON-LD's design goals are simplicity, compatibility, expressiveness, terseness, zero edits and one-pass processing. As a result, JSON-LD documents are basically standard attribute-value JSON documents with an additional context section (lines 2-7 in Figure 5) establishing mappings to RDF vocabularies. Text in JSON and, thus, also RDF resource identifiers are encoded in Unicode and hence can contain IRIs.

3 Extraction

Information represented in unstructured form or adhering to a different structured representation formalism must be mapped to the RDF data model in order to be used within the Linked Data life-cycle. In this section, we give an overview on some relevant approaches for extracting RDF from unstructured and structured sources.

N-Triples

```
1   <http://dbpedia.org/resource/Leipzig> <http://dbpedia.org/property/hasMayor>
2       <http://dbpedia.org/resource/Burkhard_Jung> .
3   <http://dbpedia.org/resource/Leipzig> <http://www.w3.org/2000/01/rdf-schema#label>
4       "Leipzig"@de .
5   <http://dbpedia.org/resource/Leipzig> <http://www.w3.org/2003/01/geo/wgs84_pos#lat>
6       "51.333332"^^<http://www.w3.org/2001/XMLSchema#float> .
```

Turtle

```
1   @prefix rdf: <http://www.w3.org/1999/02/22-rdf-syntax-ns#> .
2   @prefix rdfs="http://www.w3.org/2000/01/rdf-schema#> .
3   @prefix dbp="http://dbpedia.org/resource/> .
4   @prefix dbpp="http://dbpedia.org/property/> .
5   @prefix geo="http://www.w3.org/2003/01/geo/wgs84_pos#> .
6
7   dbp:Leipzig   dbpp:hasMayor   dbp:Burkhard_Jung ;
8                 rdfs:label      "Leipzig"@de ;
9                 geo:lat         "51.333332"^^xsd:float .
```

RDF/XML

```
1   <?xml version="1.0"?>
2   <rdf:RDF xmlns:rdf="http://www.w3.org/1999/02/22-rdf-syntax-ns#"
3                   xmlns:rdfs="http://www.w3.org/2000/01/rdf-schema#"
4            xmlns:dbpp="http://dbpedia.org/property/"
5                   xmlns:geo="http://www.w3.org/2003/01/geo/wgs84_pos#">
6    <rdf:Description rdf:about="http://dbpedia.org/resource/Leipzig">
7     <property:hasMayor rdf:resource="http://dbpedia.org/resource/Burkhard_Jung" />
8     <rdfs:label xml:lang="de">Leipzig</rdfs:label>
9     <geo:lat rdf:datatype="http://www.w3.org/2001/XMLSchema#float">51.3333</geo:lat>
10   </rdf:Description>
11  </rdf:RDF>
```

RDFa

```
1   <?xml version="1.0" encoding="UTF-8"?>
2   <!DOCTYPE html PUBLIC "-//W3C//DTD XHTML+RDFa 1.0//EN"
3       "http://www.w3.org/MarkUp/DTD/xhtml-rdfa-1.dtd">
4   <html version="XHTML+RDFa 1.0" xml:lang="en" xmlns="http://www.w3.org/1999/xhtml"
5          xmlns:rdf="http://www.w3.org/1999/02/22-rdf-syntax-ns#"
6               xmlns:rdfs="http://www.w3.org/2000/01/rdf-schema#"
7          xmlns:dbpp="http://dbpedia.org/property/"
8               xmlns:geo="http://www.w3.org/2003/01/geo/wgs84_pos#">
9    <head><title>Leipzig</title></head>
10   <body about="http://dbpedia.org/resource/Leipzig">
11     <h1 property="rdfs:label" xml:lang="de">Leipzig</h1>
12     <p>Leipzig is a city in Germany. Leipzig's mayor is
13        <a href="Burkhard_Jung" rel="dbpp:hasMayor">Burkhard Jung</a>. It is located
14           at latitude <span property="geo:lat" datatype="xsd:float">51.3333</span>.</p>
15   </body>
16  </html>
```

JSON-LD

```
1   {
2    "@context": {
3     "rdfs": "http://www.w3.org/2000/01/rdf-schema#",
4     "hasMayor": { "@id": "http://dbpedia.org/property/hasMayor", "@type": "@id" },
5     "Person": "http://xmlns.com/foaf/0.1/Person",
6     "lat": "http://www.w3.org/2003/01/geo/wgs84_pos#lat"
7    },
8    "@id": "http://dbpedia.org/resource/Leipzig",
9    "rdfs:label": "Leipzig",
10   "hasMayor": "http://dbpedia.org/resource/Burkhard_Jung",
11   "lat": { "@value": "51.3333", "@type": "http://www.w3.org/2001/XMLSchema#float"
12  }
```

Fig. 5. Different RDF serializations of three triples from Figure 3

3.1 From Unstructured Sources

The extraction of structured information from unstructured data sources (especially text) has been a central pillar of *natural language processing* (NLP) and *Information Extraction* (IE) for several decades. With respect to the extraction of RDF data from unstructured data, three sub-disciplines of NLP play a central role: *Named Entity Recognition* (NER) for the extraction of entity labels from text, *Keyword/Keyphrase Extraction* (KE) for the recognition of central topics and *Relationship Extraction* (RE, also called relation mining) for mining the properties which link the entities and keywords described in the data source. A noticeable additional task during the migration of these techniques to Linked Data is the extraction of suitable IRIs for the discovered entities and relations, a requirement that was not needed before. In this section, we give a short overview of approaches that implement the required NLP functionality. Then we present a framework that applies machine learning to boost the quality of the RDF extraction from unstructured data by merging the results of NLP tools.

Named Entity Recognition. The goal of NER is to discover instances of a predefined classes of entities (e.g., persons, locations, organizations) in text. NER tools and frameworks implement a broad spectrum of approaches, which can be subdivided into three main categories: dictionary-based, rule-based, and machine-learning approaches. The first systems for NER implemented dictionary-based approaches, which relied on a list of NEs and tried to identify these in text [199,6]. Following work that showed that these approaches did not perform well for NER tasks such as recognizing proper names [178], rule-based approaches were introduced. These approaches rely on hand-crafted rules [42,189] to recognize NEs. Most rule-based approaches combine dictionary and rule-based algorithms to extend the list of known entities. Nowadays, handcrafted rules for recognizing NEs are usually implemented when no training examples are available for the domain or language to process [141].

When training examples are available, the methods of choice are borrowed from supervised machine learning. Approaches such as Hidden Markov Models [213], Maximum Entropy Models [47] and Conditional Random Fields [57] have been applied to the NER task. Due to scarcity of large training corpora as necessitated by machine learning approaches, semi-supervised [162,140] and unsupervised machine learning approaches [142,53] have also been used for extracting NER from text. [140] gives an exhaustive overview of approaches for NER.

Keyphrase Extraction. Keyphrases/Keywords are multi-word units (MWUs) which capture the main topics of a document. The automatic detection of such MWUs has been an important task of NLP for decades but due to the very ambiguous definition of what an appropriate keyword should be, current approaches to the extraction of keyphrases still display low F-scores [99]. From the point of view of the Semantic Web, the extraction of keyphrases is a very similar task to that of finding tags for a given document. Several categories of approaches have been adapted to enable KE, of which some originate from research areas such as summarization and information retrieval (IR). Still, according to [98], the majority of the approaches to KE implement combinations of statistical, rule-based or heuristic methods [60,157] on mostly document [128], keyphrase [192] or term cohesion features [161]. [99] gives a overview of current tools for KE.

Relation Extraction. The extraction of relations from unstructured data builds upon work for NER and KE to determine the entities between which relations might exist. Most tools for RE rely on pattern-based approaches. Some early work on pattern extraction relied on supervised machine learning [72]. Yet, such approaches demanded large amount of training data, making them difficult to adapt to new relations. The subsequent generation of approaches to RE aimed at bootstrapping patterns based on a small number of input patterns and instances. For example, [35] presents the Dual Iterative Pattern Relation Expansion (DIPRE) and applies it to the detection of relations between authors and titles of books. This approach relies on a small set of seed patterns to maximize the precision of the patterns for a given relation while minimizing their error rate of the same patterns. Snowball [4] extends DIPRE by a new approach to the generation of seed tuples. Newer approaches aim to either collect redundancy information from the whole Web [160] or Wikipedia [201,208] in an unsupervised manner or to use linguistic analysis [75,156] to harvest generic patterns for relations.

URI Disambiguation. One important problem for the integration of NER tools for Linked Data is the retrieval of IRIs for the entities to be manipulated. In most cases, the URIs can be extracted from generic knowledge bases such as DBpedia [118,112] by comparing the label found in the input data with the `rdfs:label` or `dc:title` of the entities found in the knowledge base. Furthermore, information such as the type of NEs can be used to filter the retrieved IRIs via a comparison of the `rdfs:label` of the `rdf:type` of the URIs with the name of class of the NEs. Still in many cases (e.g., Leipzig, Paris), several entities might bear the same label.

The FOX Framework

Several frameworks have been developed to implement the functionality above for the Data Web including OpenCalais[3] and Alchemy[4]. Yet, these tools rely mostly on one approach to perform the different tasks at hand. In this section, we present the FOX (Federated knOwledge eXtraction) framework[5]. FOX differs from the state of the art by making use of several NER algorithms at once and combining their results by using ensemble learning techniques. FOX's NED is implemented by the AGDISTIS framework[6], which combines graph search with the HITS algorithm to detect resources that match a set of strings.

Named Entity Recognition in FOX. The basic intuition behind the FOX framework is that while manifold approaches have been devised for the purpose of NER, they

---

[3] http://www.opencalais.com
[4] http://www.alchemyapi.com
[5] http://aksw.org/projects/fox
[6] http://aksw.org/projects/agdistis

mostly rely on one algorithm. However, it is known that each algorithm has intrinsic limitations by virtue of the model that it relies on. For example, polynomial classifiers cannot model decision planes that are non-polynomial. FOX makes use of the diversity of the algorithms available for NER approaches by combining their results within the ensemble learning setting. Formally, the idea is the following: Let $C_1 \ldots C_n$ be classifiers that values between 0 and 1 when given a string s and an entity type t as input, i.e., $C_i(s, t) \in [0, 1]$. Then, we can always train a novel classifier C that performs at least as well as any of the C_i on an training dataset D. To this end, we consider the supervised ensemble learning problem where the input data for C is the vector $V = (v_i)_{i=1\ldots n}$ with $v_i = C_i(s, t)$ and the output must be the expected score for (s, t). Learning the classifier C can be carried by using any supervised machine-learning approach that can deal with non-binary data.

The architecture of FOX consists of *three main layers* as shown in Figure 6. The *machine learning* layer implements interfaces for accommodating ensemble learning techniques such as simple veto algorithms but also neural networks. It consists of *two main modules*. The *training module* allows to load training data so as to enable FOX to learn the best combination of tools and categories for achieving superior recall and precision on the input training data. Depending on the training algorithm used, the user can choose to tune the system for either precision or recall. When using neural networks for example, the user can decide to apply a higher threshold for the output neurons, thus improving the precision but potentially limiting the recall. The *prediction module* allows to run FOX by loading the result of a training session and processing the input data according to the tool-category combination learned during the training phase. Note that the same learning approach can by applied to NER, KE, RE and URI lookup as they call all be modelled as classification tasks. The second layer of FOX is the *controller*, which coordinates the access to the modules that carry out the language processing. The controller is aware of each of the modules in its backend and carries out the initialisation of these modules once FOX is started. Furthermore, it collects the results from the backend modules and invokes the results of a training instance to merge the results of these tools. The final layer of FOX is the *tool layer*, wherein all NLP tools and services integrated in FOX can be found. It is important to notice that the tools per se are not trained during the learning phase of FOX. Rather, we learn of the models already loaded in the tools to allow for the best prediction of named entities in a given domain.

Currently, FOX includes Stanford NER, Illinois NER, Balie and OpenNLP. In an effort to quantify the gain in accuracy of FOX, we integrated the Waikato Environment for Knowledge Analysis (Weka) [74] and the implemented classifiers with default parameters: AdaBoostM1 (ABM1) [61] and Bagging (BG) [32] with J48 [165] as base classifier, Decision Table (DT) [101], Functional Trees (FT) [65,105], J48 [165], Logistic Model Trees (LMT) [105], Logistic Regression (Log) [106], Additive Logistic Regression (LogB) [63], Multilayer Perceptron (MLP), Naïve Bayes [96], Random Forest (RF) [33], Support Vector Machine (SVM) [38] and Sequential Minimal Optimization (SMO) [78]. In addition, we used voting at entity level (CVote) and a simple voting (Vote) approach [206] with equal weights for all NER tools. CVote selects the NER tool with the highest prediction performance for each type according to the evaluation and uses that particular tool for the given class. Vote as naive approach combines the

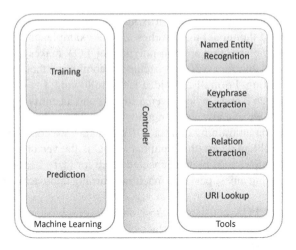

Fig. 6. FOX Architecture

results of the NER tools with the Majority Vote Rule [100] and was the baseline ensemble learning technique in our evaluation. In Table 2, the comparison of fifteen different types of classifiers in a ten-fold cross validation over a dataset extracted from online newspapers and containing 150 locations, 139 organizations and 178 persons is shown. Like in previous works [150], these results suggest that multi-layer perceptrons tend to perform well on this task. Interestingly, learning on this small dataset already pushes the overall F-measure of FOX to 95.23% while the best single algorithm achieves 91.01% F-measure.

Named Entity Disambiguation: AGDISTIS. The goal of AGDISTIS is to detect correct resources from a KB K for a vector N of n a-priori determined named entities $N_1, \ldots, N_n$ extracted from a certain input text T. In general, several resources from a given knowledge base K can be considered as candidate resources for a given entity N_i. For the sake of simplicity and without loss of generality, we will assume that each of the entities can be mapped to m distinct candidate resources. Let C be the matrix which contains all candidate-entity mappings for a given set of entities. The entry C_{ij} stands for the jth candidate resource for the ith named entity. Let μ be a family of functions which maps each entity N_i to exactly one candidate C_{ij}. We call such functions *assignments*. The output of an assignment is a vector of resources of length $|N|$ that is such that the ith entry of the vector maps with N_i.

Let ψ be a function which computes the similarity between an assignment $\mu(C, N)$ and the vector of named entities N. The *coherence* function ϕ calculates the similarity of the knowledge base K and an assignment μ [169] to ensure the topical consistency of μ. The coherence function ϕ is implemented by the HITS algorithm, which calculates the most pertinent entities while the similarity function ψ is, e.g., string similarity. Given this formal model, the goal is to find the assignment $\mu^\star$ with

$$\mu^\star = \arg\max_{\mu} \left(\psi(\mu(C, N), N) + \phi(\mu(C, N), K) \right).$$

Table 2. The News data set

S	Recall	Precision	F_1	error	MCC
MLP	**95.19**	**95.28**	**95.23**	**0.32**	**0.951**
RF	95.15	**95.28**	95.21	**0.32**	**0.951**
ABM1.J48	94.82	95.18	95.00	0.33	0.948
SVM	94.86	95.09	94.97	0.33	0.948
BG.J48	94.76	94.93	94.84	0.34	0.947
J48	94.78	94.98	94.88	0.34	0.947
DT	94.63	94.95	94.79	0.34	0.946
LMT	94.68	94.95	94.82	0.34	0.946
FT	94.30	95.15	94.72	0.35	0.945
LogB	93.54	95.37	94.44	0.37	0.943
Log	94.05	94.75	94.40	0.37	0.942
SMO	94.01	94.37	94.19	0.39	0.940
Naïve Bayes	94.61	92.64	93.60	0.42	0.934
Stanford	92.36	91.01	91.68	0.53	0.914
CVote	92.02	90.84	91.42	0.54	0.911
Vote	89.98	82.97	85.92	0.94	0.857
Illinois	82.79	87.35	84.95	0.92	0.845
OpenNLP	71.42	90.47	79.57	1.13	0.797
Balie	77.68	82.05	79.8	1.21	0.792

The formulation of the problem given above has been proven to be NP-hard [46]. Thus, for the sake of scalability, AGDISTIS computes an approximation μ^+ by using HITS, a fast graph algorithm which runs with an upper bound of $\Theta(k \cdot |V|^2)$ with k the number of iterations and $|V|$ the number of nodes in the graph. Furthermore, using HITS leverages 1) scalability, 2) well-researched behaviour and 3) the ability to explicate semantic authority.

For each named entity, candidates resources from the input knowledge base can be detected by the labels of the resources in the knowledge base with the named entity. Here, resources such as surface forms can also be used. Given a set of candidate nodes, we begin the computation of the optimal assignment by constructing a disambiguation graph G_d with search depth d. To this end, we regard the input knowledge base as a directed graph $G_K = (V, E)$ where the vertices V are resources of K, the edges E are properties of K and $x, y \in V, (x, y) \in E \Leftrightarrow \exists p : (x, p, y)$ is an RDF triple in K. Given the set of candidates C, we begin by building an initial graph $G_0 = (V_0, E_0)$ where V_0 is the set of all resources in C and $E_0 = \emptyset$. Starting with G_0 we extend the graph in a breadth-first search manner. Therefore, we define the extension of a graph $G_i = (V_i, E_i)$ to a graph $\rho(G_i) = G_{i+1} = (V_{i+1}, E_{i+1})$ where $i = 0, \ldots, d$ as follows:

$$V_{i+1} = V_i \cup \{y : \exists x \in V_i \wedge (x, y) \in E\} \tag{1}$$

$$E_{i+1} = \{(x, y) \in E : x, y \in V_{i+1}\} \tag{2}$$

We iterate the ρ operator d times on the input graph G_0 to compute the initial disambiguation graph G_d.

After constructing the disambiguation graph G_d we need to identify the correct candidate node for a given named entity. Using the graph-based HITS algorithm we calculate authoritative values x_a, y_a and hub values x_h, y_h for all $x, y \in V_d$. We initialize the authoritative and hub values as follows:

$$\forall x \in V_d, x_a = x_h = \frac{1}{|V_d|}. \tag{3}$$

Afterwards, we iterate k times the following equations:

$$x_a \longleftarrow \sum_{(y,x) \in E_d} y_h, \quad y_h \longleftarrow \sum_{(y,x) \in E_d} x_a. \tag{4}$$

We choose $k = 20$ iterations, which suffices to achieve convergence in general. Afterwards we identify the most authoritative candidate C_{ij} among the set of candidates C_i as correct disambiguation for a given named entity N_i. When using DBpedia as KB and C_{ij} is a redirect AGDISTIS uses the target resource. As can be seen, we calculate μ^+ solely by using algorithms with a polynomial time complexity. The evaluation of AGDISTIS shown in Table 3 on datasets by [45] shows clearly that AGIDISTIS outperforms the state of the art in 3 out of 4 cases.

Table 3. Performance of AGDISTIS, DBpedia Spotlight and TagMe2 on four different datasets using micro F-meassure

Dataset	Approach	F_1	Precision	Recall
	TagMe 2	0.565	0.58	0.551
AIDA/CO-NLL-TestB	DBPedia Spotlight	0.341	0.308	0.384
	AGDISTIS	**0.596**	**0.642**	**0.556**
	TagMe 2	0.457	0.412	**0.514**
AQUAINT	DBPedia Spotlight	0.26	0.178	0.48
	AGDISTIS	**0.547**	**0.777**	0.422
	TagMe 2	0.408	0.416	0.4
IITB	DBPedia Spotlight	**0.46**	0.434	**0.489**
	AGDISTIS	0.31	**0.646**	0.204
	TagMe 2	0.466	0.431	0.508
MSNBC	DBPedia Spotlight	0.331	0.317	0.347
	AGDISTIS	**0.761**	**0.796**	**0.729**

3.2   From Structured Sources

Structured knowledge, e.g. relational databases and XML, is the backbone of many (web) applications. Extracting or converting this knowledge to RDF is a long-standing research goal in the Semantic Web community. A conversion to RDF allows to integrate the data with other sources and perform queries over it. In this lecture, we focus on the conversion of relational databases to RDF (see Figure 7). In the first part, we summarize

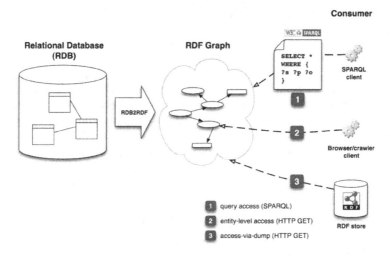

Fig. 7. Illustration of RDB to RDF conversion. Source: `http://www.w3.org/2001/sw/rdb2rdf/use-cases/`.

Approach	Automation (a)	Domain or database semantics-driven (b)	Access paradigm (c)	Mapping language (d)	Domain reliance (e)
Dartgrid [17]	Manual	Domain	SPARQL	Visual Tool	dependent
Hu et al. [11]	Auto	Both	ETL	intern	dependent
Tirmizi et al. [16]	Auto	DB	ETL	FOL	general
Li et al. [12]	Semi	DB	ETL	n/a	general
DB2OWL[10]	Semi	DB	SPARQL	R2O	general/dependent
RDBToOnto [6]	Semi	DB+M	ETL	Visual Tool	general
Sahoo et al. [15]	Manual	Domain	ETL	XSLT	dependent
R2O[13]	Manual	DB+M	SPARQL	R2O	dependent
D2RQ[4]	Auto	DB+M	LD, SPARQL	D2RQ	general
Virtuoso RDF View [5, 9]	Semi	DB+M	SPARQL	own	general
Triplify	Manual	Domain	LD	SQL	general

Table 4: An integrated overview of mapping approaches. Criteria for classification were merged, some removed, fields were completed, when missing. DB+M means that the semi-automatic approach can later be customized manually

Fig. 8. Table comparing relevant approaches from [8]

material from a recent relational database to RDF (RDB2RDF) project report. After that, we describe the mapping language R2RML, which is a language for expressing database to RDF conversion mappings. While we focus on relational date, we also want to note that extraction from CSV files is also highly important as illustrated in use cases in the financial [127] and health sector [211].

Triplify and RDB2RDF Survey Report. The table displayed in Figure 8 is taken from the Triplify WWW paper [8]. The survey report [177] furthermore contained a chart(see Figure 9) showing the reference framework for classifying the approaches and an extensive table classifying the approaches (see Figure 10). Another recent survey is [187].

The following criteria can be extracted:

Automation Degree. Degree of mapping creation automation.
Values: Manual, Automatic, Semi-Automatic.

Domain or Database Semantics Driven. Some approaches are tailored to model a do-main, sometimes with the help of existing ontologies, while others attempt to extract domain information primarily from the given database schema with few other resources used (domain or database semantics-driven). The latter often results in a table-to-class, column-to-predicate mapping. Some approaches also use a (semi) automatic approach based on the database, but allow manual customization to model domain semantics.
Values: Domain, DB (database), DB+M (database and later manual customisation), Both (Domain and DB)

Access Paradigm. Resulting access paradigm (ETL [extract transform load], Linked Data, SPARQL access). Note that the access paradigm also determines whether the resulting RDF model updates automatically. ETL means a one time conversion, while Linked Data and SPARQL always process queries versus the original database.
Values: SPARQL, ETL, LD

Mapping Language. The used mapping language as an important factor for reusability and initial learning cost.
Values: Visual Tool, intern (internal self-designed language), FOL, n/a (no information available), R2O, XSLT, D2RQ, proprietary, SQL

Domain reliance. Domain reliance (general or domain-dependent): requiring a pre-defined ontology is a clear indicator of domain dependency.
Values: Dependent, General

Type. Although not used in the table the paper discusses four different classes:
Values: Alignment, Database Mining, Integration, Languages/Servers

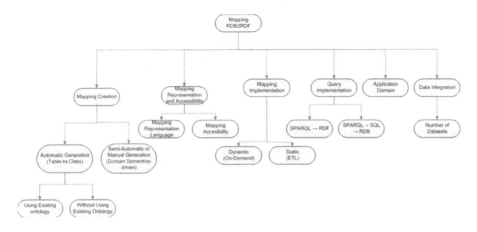

Fig. 9. Reference framework by [177]

PROJECTS	MAPPING CREATION	MAPPING REPRESENTATION AND ACCESSIBILITY		MAPPING IMPLEMENTATION	QUERY IMPLEMENTATION	APPLICATION DOMAIN	DATA INTEGRATION	
	Automatic (Table-to-Class) or Manual/Semi-Automatic (Domain Semantics-driven)	Representation Language	Mapping Access	Static (ETL) or Dynamic	SPARQL → RDF or SPARQL→SQL→ RDB		Yes/No	Number of Datasets
1. Hu et. al, 2007	Automatic (with use of existing ontology)	First Order Logic formulae or Horn Clauses	Files	None Specified	None Specified	Generic	Enables (through contextual mappings)	Potentially Multiple
2. Kashyap et al, 2007	Manual/Semi-Automatic (Domain Semantics-driven)	Mediator Framework Classes	Mapping mediator	Dynamic	SPARQL→SQL→ RDB	Life Sciences	Enables	Potentially Multiple
3. DB2OWL (Cullot et al, 2007)	Automatic (Table to Class)	R2O language	R2O mapping document		SPARQL→SQL→ RDB	Generic	Enables	Potentially Multiple
4. Tirmizi et. al 2008	Automatic (Table to Class, SQL-DDL to RDF)	First Order Logic	None specified	Static	None Specified	Generic	No	None
5. SOAM (Li et al, 2005)	Automatic (Table to Class) with user input	Logic Rules	Implemented as part of system	Static	Potentially SPARQL (on generated populated ontology)	Generic (Case Study: Economics)	No	None
6. Sahoo et al, 2008	Manual/Semi-Automatic (Domain Semantics-driven)	XPath expressions	XSLT document	Static	SPARQL	Life Sciences	Yes	Test included five (Gene, Biological Pathway)
7. Byrne, 2008	Manual/Semi-Automatic (Domain Semantics-driven)	SKOS vocabulary	RDF document	Static	SPARQL	Cultural Heritage	No	None
8. Green et. al, 2008	Manual/Semi-Automatic (Domain Semantics-driven)	D2RQ language	D2RQ mapping file	Dynamic	SPARQL→SQL→ RDB	Ordnance Survey	Yes	Multiple
9. Virtuoso RDF View (Blakeley, 2007)	Both (user-specified)	SPASQL-based Meta Schema Language	Quad Storage	Both	Both	Generic	Enables	Potentially Multiple
10. D2RQ (Bizer et al, 2007)	Both (user-specified)	D2RQ language	D2RQ mapping file	Both	Both	Generic	Enables	Potentially Multiple
11. R2O (Barras a et al, 2006)	Both (user-specified)	R2O language	R2O mapping document	Both	Both	Generic	Enables	Potentially Multiple
12. Dartgrid (Wu et al, 2006)	Automatic (Table to Class)	XML File	Visualized Mapping tool	Dynamic	SPARQL→SQL→ RDB (Provide search and query interface)	Life Science (Traditional Chinese Medicine, TCM)	Yes	Test included databases for herb, compound formulas, disease, drug, TCM treatment.
13. RDBtoOnto (Cerbah, 2008)	Automatic (Table to Class, allows user intervention)	Constraint rules	Not explicitly stored	Static	Potentially SPARQL (on generated populated ontology)	Generic	No	None
14. Asio Tools	Automatic (Table to	OWL Full based language	File based	Both	SPARQL→SQL→ RDB	Generic	Enables	Potentially Multiple

Fig. 10. Comparison of approaches from [177]

R2RML - RDB to RDF Mapping Language. The R2RML W3C recommendation[7] specifies an RDF notation for mapping relational tables, views or queries into RDF. The primary area of applicability of this is extracting RDF from relational databases, but in special cases R2RML could lend itself to on-the-fly translation of SPARQL into SQL or to converting RDF data to a relational form. The latter application is not the primary intended use of R2RML but may be desirable for importing linked data into relational stores. This is possible if the constituent mappings and underlying SQL objects constitute updateable views in the SQL sense.

Data integration is often mentioned as a motivating use case for the adoption of RDF. This integration will very often be between relational databases which have logical entities in common, each with its local schema and identifiers.Thus, we expect to see relational to RDF mapping use cases involving the possibility of a triple coming from multiple sources. This does not present any problem if RDF is being extracted but does lead to complications if SPARQL queries are mapped into SQL. In specific, one will end up with potentially very long queries consisting of joins of unions. Most of the joins between terms of the unions will often be provably empty and can thus be optimized away. This capability however requires the mapping language to be able to express metadata about mappings, i.e. that IRIs coming from one place are always disjoint from IRIs coming from another place. Without such metadata optimizing SPARQL to SQL translation is not possible, which will significantly limit the possibility of querying collections of SQL databases through a SPARQL end point without ETL-ing the mapped RDF into an RDF store.

RDF is emerging as a format for interoperable data publishing. This does not entail that RDF were preferable as a data warehousing model. Besides, for large warehouses, RDF is not cost competitive with relational technology, even though projects such as LOD2 and LDBC expect to narrow this gap (see, e.g., [137,138] for recent SPARQL benchmarks). Thus it follows that on the fly mapping of SPARQL to SQL will be important. Regardless of the relative cost or performance of relational or RDF technology, it is not a feasible proposition to convert relational warehouses to RDF in general, rather existing investments must be protected and reused. Due to these reasons, R2RML will have to evolve in the direction of facilitating querying of federated relational resources.

Supervised Extraction Example: Sparqlify. The challenges encountered with large scale relational data sources LinkedGeoData [12,188] indicate that ETL style approaches based on the conversion of all underlying data to RDF have severe deficiencies. For instance, the RDF conversion process is very time consuming for large-scale, crowdsourced data. Furthermore, changes in data modelling require many changes in the extracted RDF data or the creation of a completely new dump. In summary, the ETL approach is not sufficiently flexible for very large and frequently changing data. It seems preferable to establish virtual RDF views over the existing relational database. In contrast to other tools, such as *D2R* and *Virtuoso RDF views*, Sparqlify converts each SPARQL query to a single SQL query. This allows all optimisations of the underlying database to be applied and can lead to better scalability.

---

[7] http://www.w3.org/TR/r2rml/

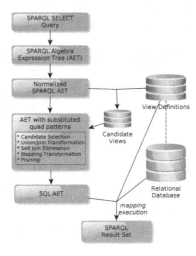

Fig. 11. The Sparqlify concepts and query rewriting workflow

Figure 11 shows the query rewriting workflow in Sparqlify. The rationale of Sparqlify is to leave the schema of the underlying relational database schema unmodified and define RDF views over it. SPARQL queries can then be written against those views, which are expressed in the *Sparqlify-ML* (mapping language). Sparqlify-ML is easy to learn for users, who are experienced in SPARQL and SQL and more compact than other syntactic variants such as R2RML. The left part of Figure 11 shows all steps, which are performed to answer a query. First, the query is converted into an algebra expression. This expression is subsequently converted to a normal form. Given the query patterns, relevant Sparqlify-ML views need to be detected. After this is done, the algebra expression is rewritten to include those relevant views. In a next step, optimisations on the algebra expression are performed to improve efficiency. Finally, this algebra expression can be transformed to an SQL algebra expression. For accomplishing this, we define a general relational algebra for RDB-to-RDF mappings. The SQL query, which was obtained, is executed against the relational database. Using the defined mappings, the SQL result set returned by the relational database can be converted to a SPARQL result set.

All of the above steps are explained in detail throughout the next sections. The main contribution of the Sparqlify project is a formalization, which goes beyond previous work by being capable to push the complete query execution using a single SQL query into the DBMS.

4   Authoring with Semantic Wikis

Semantic Wikis are an extension to conventional, text-based Wikis. While in conventional Wikis pages are stored as blocks of text using a special Wiki markup for structuring the display of the text and adding links to other pages, semantic Wikis aim at adding rich structure to the information itself. To this end, two initially orthogonal approaches

Table 4. Conceptual differences between Semantic MediaWiki and OntoWiki

	Semantic MediaWiki	OntoWiki
Managed entities	Articles	Resources
Editing	Wiki markup	Forms
Atomic element	Text blob	Statement

have been used: a) extending the markup language to allow semantic annotations and links with meaning or b) building the Wiki software directly with structured information in mind. Nowadays, both approaches have somewhat converged, for instance Semantic MediaWiki [103] also provides forms for entering structured data (see Figure 12). Characteristics of both approaches are summarized in Table 4 for the two prototypical representatives of both approaches, i.e. Semantic MediaWiki and OntoWiki.

Extending Wikis with Semantic Markup. The benefit of a Wiki system comes from the amount of interlinking between Wiki pages. Those links clearly state a relationship between the linked-to and the linking page. However, in conventional Wiki systems this relationship cannot be made explicit. Semantic Wiki systems therefore add a means to specify typed relations by extending the Wiki markup with semantic (i.e. typed) links. Once in place, those links form a knowledge base underlying the Wiki which can be used to improve search, browsing or automatically generated lists and category pages. Examples of approaches for extending Wikis with semantic markup can be found in [103,180,15,159,186]. They represent a straightforward combination of existing Wiki systems and the Semantic Web knowledge representation paradigms. Yet, we see the following obstacles:

Usability: The main advantage of Wiki systems is their unbeatable usability. Adding more and more syntactic possibilities counteracts ease of use for editors.
Redundancy: To allow the answering of real-time queries to the knowledge base, statements have to be additionally kept in a triple store. This introduces a redundancy, which complicates the implementation.
Evolution: As a result of storing information in both Wiki texts and triple store, supporting evolution of knowledge is difficult.

Wikis for Editing Structured Data. In contrast to text-based systems, Wikis for structured data – also called Data Wikis – are built on a structured model of the data being edited. The Wiki software can be used to add instances according to the schema or (in some systems) edit the schema itself. One of those systems is OntoWiki[8] [9] which bases its data model on RDF. This way, both schema and instance data are represented using the same low-level model (i.e. statements) and can therefore be handled identically by the Wiki.

---

[8] Available at: `http://ontowiki.net`

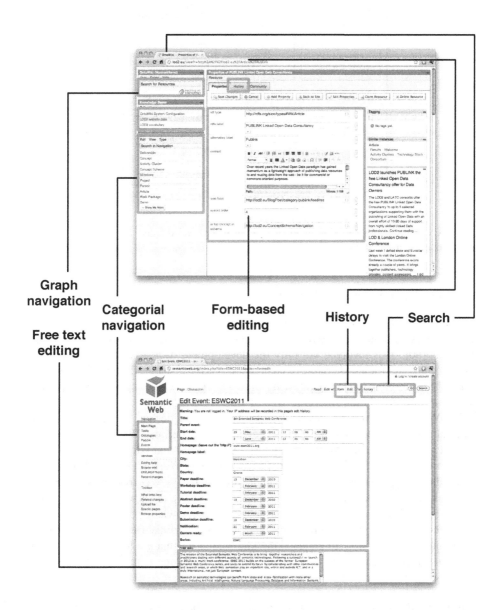

Graph navigation

Free text editing

Categorical navigation

Form-based editing

History

Search

Fig. 12. Comparison of Semantic MediaWiki and OntoWiki GUI building blocks

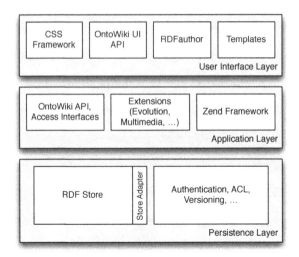

Fig. 13. Overview of OntoWiki's architecture with extension API and Zend web framework (modified according to [80])

4.1 OntoWiki - A Semantic Data Wiki

OntoWiki started as an RDF-based data wiki with emphasis on collaboration but has meanwhile evolved into a comprehensive framework for developing Semantic Web applications [80]. This involved not only the development of a sophisticated extension interface allowing for a wide range of customizations but also the addition of several access and consumption interfaces allowing OntoWiki installations to play both a provider and a consumer role in the emerging Web of Data.

OntoWiki is inspired by classical Wiki systems, its design, however, (as mentioned above) is independent and complementary to conventional Wiki technologies. In contrast to other semantic Wiki approaches, in OntoWiki text editing and knowledge engineering (i. e. working with structured knowledge bases) are not mixed. Instead, OntoWiki directly applies the Wiki paradigm of "making it easy to correct mistakes, rather than making it hard to make them" [121] to collaborative management of structured knowledge. This paradigm is achieved by interpreting knowledge bases as *information maps* where every node is represented visually and interlinked to related resources. Furthermore, it is possible to enhance the knowledge schema gradually as well as the related instance data agreeing on it. As a result, the following requirements and corresponding features characterize OntoWiki:

Intuitive display and editing of instance data should be provided in generic ways, yet enabling domain-specific presentation of knowledge.

Semantic views allow the generation of different views and aggregations of the knowledge base.

Versioning and evolution provides the opportunity to track, review and roll-back changes selectively.

Semantic search facilitates easy-to-use full-text searches on all literal data, search results can be filtered and sorted (using semantic relations).

Community support enables discussions about small information chunks. Users are encouraged to vote about distinct facts or prospective changes.

Online statistics interactively measures the popularity of content and activity of users.

Semantic syndication supports the distribution of information and their integration into desktop applications.

OntoWiki enables the easy creation of highly structured content by distributed communities. The following points summarize some limitations and weaknesses of OntoWiki and thus characterize the application domain:

Environment: OntoWiki is a Web application and presumes all collaborators to work in a Web environment, possibly distributed.

Usage Scenario: OntoWiki focuses on knowledge engineering projects where a single, precise usage scenario is either initially (yet) unknown or not (easily) definable.

Reasoning: Application of reasoning services was (initially) not the primary focus.

4.2 Generic and Domain-Specific Views

OntoWiki can be used as a tool for presenting, authoring and managing knowledge bases adhering to the RDF data model. As such, it provides generic methods and views, independent of the domain concerned. Two generic views included in OntoWiki are the resource view and the list view. While the former is generally used for displaying all known information about a resource, the latter can present a set of resources, typically instances of a certain concept. That concept must not necessarily be explicitly defined as `rdfs:Class` or `owl:Class` in the knowledge base. Via its faceted browsing, OntoWiki allows the construction of complex concept definitions, with a pre-defined class as a starting point by means of property value restrictions. These two views are sufficient for browsing and editing all information contained in a knowledge base in a generic way. For domain-specific use cases, OntoWiki provides an easy-to-use extension interface that enables the integration of custom components. By providing such a custom view, it is even possible to hide completely the fact that an RDF knowledge base is worked on. This permits OntoWiki to be used as a data-entry frontend for users with a less profound knowledge of Semantic Web technologies.

4.3 Workflow

With the use of RDFS [34] and OWL [163] as ontology languages, resource definition is divisible into different layers: a terminology box for conceptual information (i. e. classes and properties) and an assertion box for entities using the concepts defined (i. e. instances). There are characteristics of RDF which, for end users, are not easy to comprehend (e. g. *classes* can be defined as *instances* of `owl:Class`). OntoWiki's user interface, therefore, provides elements for these two layers, simultaneously increasing usability and improving a user's comprehension for the structure of the data. After starting and logging in into OntoWiki with registered user credentials, it is possible to select one of the existing ontologies. The user is then presented with general information about the ontology (i. e. all statements expressed about the knowledge base as a resource) and a list of defined classes, as part of the conceptual layer.

After starting and logging in into OntoWiki with registered user credentials, it is possible to select one of the existing knowledge bases. The user is then presented with general information about the ontology (i. e. all statements expressed about the knowledge base as a resource) and a list of defined classes, as part of the conceptual layer. By selecting one of these classes, the user obtains a list of the class' instances. OntoWiki applies basic `rdfs:subClassOf` reasoning automatically. After selecting an instance from the list – or alternatively creating a new one – it is possible to manage (i. e. insert, edit and update) information in the details view.OntoWiki focuses primarily on the assertion layer, but also provides ways to manage resources on the conceptual layer. By enabling the visualization of schema elements, called *System Classes* in the OntoWiki nomenclature, conceptional resources can be managed in a similar fashion as instance data.

4.4 Authoring

Semantic content in OntoWiki is represented as resource descriptions. Following the RDF data model representing one of the foundations of the Semantic Web vision, resource descriptions are represented (at the lowest level) in the form of *statements*. Each of these statements (or triples) consist of a *subject* which identifies a resource as well as a *predicate* and an *object* which together represent data about said resource in a fashion reminiscent of key-value pairs. By means of RDFa [3], these statements are retained in the HTML view (i.e. user interface) part and are thus accessible to client-side techniques like JavaScript.

Authoring of such content is based on said client-side representation by employing the RDFauthor approach [191]: views are declared in terms of the model language (RDF) which allows the underlying model be restored. Based on this model, a user interface can be generated with the model being providing all the domain knowledge required to do so. The RDFauthor system provides an extensible set of authoring widgets specialized for certain editing tasks. RDFauthor was also extended by adding capabilities for automatically translating literal object values between different languages. Since the semantic context is known to the system, these translation functionality can be bound to arbitrary characteristics of the data (e. g. to a certain property or a missing language).

Versioning & Evolution. As outlined in the wiki principles, keeping track of all changes is an important task in order to encourage user participation. OntoWiki applies this concept to RDF-based knowledge engineering in that all changes are tracked on the statement level [10]. These low-level changes can be grouped to reflect application- and domain-specific tasks involving modifications to several statements as a single versioned item. Provenance information as well as other metadata (such as time, user or context) of a particular changeset can be attached to each individual changeset. All changes on the knowledge base can be easily reviewed and rolled-back if needed. The loosely typed data model of RDF encourages continuous evolution and refinement of

Fig. 14. OntoWiki views: (background) A tabular list view, which contains a filtered list of resources highlighting some specific properties of those resources and (foreground) a resource view which allows to tag and comment a specific resource as well as editing all property values

knowledge bases. With *EvoPat*, OntoWiki supports this in a declarative, pattern-based manner (see section on evolution).

4.5   Access Interfaces

In addition to human-targeted graphical user interfaces, OntoWiki supports a number of machine-accessible data interfaces. These are based on established Semantic Web standards like SPARQL or accepted best practices like publication and consumption of Linked Data.

SPARQL Endpoint. The SPARQL recommendation not only defines a query language for RDF but also a protocol for sending queries to and receiving results from remote endpoints[9]. OntoWiki implements this specification, allowing all resources managed in an OntoWiki be queried over the Web. In fact, the aforementioned RDFauthor authoring interface makes use of SPARQL to query for additional schema-related information, treating OntoWiki as a remote endpoint in that case.

---

[9] http://www.w3.org/TR/rdf-sparql-protocol/

Linked Data. Each OntoWiki installation can be part of the emerging Linked Data Web. According to the Linked Data publication principles (cf. section 2), OntoWiki makes all resources accessible by its IRI (provided, the resource's IRI is in the same namespace as the OntoWiki instance). Furthermore, for each resource used in OntoWiki additional triples can be fetches if the resource is de-referenceable.

Semantic Pingback. Pingback is an established notification system that gained wide popularity in the blogsphere. With Semantic Pingback [190], OntoWiki adapts this idea to Linked Data providing a *notification mechanism* for resource usage. If a Pingback-enabled resource is mentioned (i. e. linked to) by another party, its pingback server is notified of the usage. Provided, the Semantic Pingback extension is enabled all resources used in OntoWiki are pinged automatically and all resources defined in OntoWiki are Pingback-enabled.

4.6   Exploration Interfaces

For exploring semantic content, OntoWiki provides several exploration interfaces that range from generic views over search interfaces to sophisticated querying capabilities for more RDF-knowledgable users. The subsequent paragraphs give an overview of each of them.

Knowledge base as an information map. The compromise between, on the one hand, providing a generic user interface for arbitrary RDF knowledge bases and, on the other hand, aiming at being as intuitive as possible is tackled by regarding knowledge bases as *information maps*. Each node at the information map, i. e. RDF resource, is represented as a Web accessible page and interlinked to related digital resources. These Web pages representing nodes in the information map are divided into three parts: a left sidebar, a main content section and a right sidebar. The left sidebar offers the selection of content to display in the main content section. Selection opportunities include the set of available knowledge bases, a hierarchical browser and a full-text search.

Full-text search. The full-text search makes use of special indexes (mapped to proprietary extensions to the SPARQL syntax) if the underlying knowledge store provides this feature, else, plain SPARQL string matching is used. In both cases, the resulting SPARQL query is stored as an object which can later be modified (e. g. have its filter clauses refined). Thus, full-text search is seamlessly integrated with faceted browsing (see below).

Content specific browsing interfaces. For domain-specific use cases, OntoWiki provides an easy-to-use extension interface that enables the integration of custom components. By providing such a custom view, it is even possible to hide completely the fact that an RDF knowledge base is worked on. This permits OntoWiki to be used as a data-entry frontend for users with a less profound knowledge of Semantic Web technologies.

Faceted-browsing. Via its faceted browsing, OntoWiki allows the construction of complex concept definitions, with a pre-defined class as a starting point by means of property value restrictions. These two views are sufficient for browsing and editing all information contained in a knowledge base in a generic way.

Query-builder. OntoWiki serves as a SPARQL endpoint, however, it quickly turned out that formulating SPARQL queries is too tedious for end users. In order to simplify the creation of queries, we developed the *Visual Query Builder*[10] (VQB) as an OntoWiki extension, which is implemented in JavaScript and communicates with the triple store using the SPARQL language and protocol. VQB allows to visually create queries to the stored knowledge base and supports domain experts with an intuitive visual representation of query and data. Developed queries can be stored and added via drag-and-drop to the current query. This enables the reuse of existing queries as building blocks for more complex ones.

4.7 Applications

Catalogous Professorum. The World Wide Web, as an ubiquitous medium for publication and exchange, already significantly influenced the way historians work: the online availability of catalogs and bibliographies allows to efficiently search for content relevant for a certain investigation; the increasing digitization of works from historical archives and libraries, in addition, enables historians to directly access historical sources remotely. The capabilities of the Web as a medium for collaboration, however, are only starting to be explored. Many, historical questions can only be answered by combining information from different sources, from different researchers and organizations. Also, after original sources are analyzed, the derived information is often much richer, than can be captured by simple keyword indexing. These factors pave the way for the successful application of knowledge engineering techniques in historical research communities.

In [172] we report about the application of an adaptive, semantics-based knowledge engineering approach using OntoWiki for the development of a prosopographical knowledge base. In prosopographical research, historians analyze common characteristics of historical groups by studying statistically relevant quantities of individual biographies. Untraceable periods of biographies can be determined on the basis of such accomplished analyses in combination with statistically examinations as well as patterns of relationships between individuals and their activities.

In our case, researchers from the historical seminar at Universität Leipzig aimed at creating a prosopographical knowledge base about the life and work of professors in the 600 years history of Universität Leipzig ranging from the year 1409 till 2009 - the *Catalogus Professorum Lipsiensis* (CPL). In order to enable historians to collect, structure and publish this prosopographical knowledge an ontological knowledge model was developed and incrementally refined over a period of three years. The community of historians working on the project was enabled to add information to the knowledge base using an adapted version of OntoWiki. For the general public, a simplified user interface[11] is dynamically generated based on the content of the knowledge base. For access and exploration of the knowledge base by other historians a number of access interfaces was developed and deployed, such as a graphical SPARQL query builder, a relationship finder and plain RDF and Linked Data interfaces. As a result, a group of

---

[10] http://aksw.org/Projects/OntoWiki/Extension/VQB
[11] Available at: http://www.uni-leipzig.de/unigeschichte/professorenkatalog/

10 historians supported by a much larger group of volunteers and external contributors collected information about 1,300 professors, 10,000 associated periods of life, 400 institutions and many more related entities.

The benefits of the developed knowledge engineering platform for historians are twofold: Firstly, the collaboration between the participating historians has significantly improved: The ontological structuring helped to quickly establish a common understanding of the domain. Collaborators within the project, peers in the historic community as well as the general public were enabled to directly observe the progress, thus facilitating peer-review, feedback and giving direct benefits to the contributors. Secondly, the ontological representation of the knowledge facilitated original historical investigations, such as historical social network analysis, professor appointment analysis (e.g. with regard to the influence of cousin-hood or political influence) or the relation between religion and university. The use of the developed model and knowledge engineering techniques is easily transferable to other prosopographical research projects and with adaptations to the ontology model to other historical research in general. In the long term, the use of collaborative knowledge engineering in historian research communities can facilitate the transition from largely individual-driven research (where one historian investigates a certain research question solitarily) to more community-oriented research (where many participants contribute pieces of information in order to enlighten a larger research question). Also, this will improve the reusability of the results of historic research, since knowledge represented in structured ways can be used for previously not anticipated research questions.

OntoWiki Mobile. As comparatively powerful mobile computing devices are becoming more common, mobile web applications have started gaining in popularity. An important feature of these applications is their ability to provide *offline functionality* with local updates for later synchronization with a web server. The key problem here is the reconciliation, i. e. the problem of potentially *conflicting updates* from *disconnected clients*. Another problem current mobile application developers face is the plethora of mobile application development platforms as well as the incompatibilities between them. *Android* (Google), *iOS* (Apple), *Blackberry OS* (RIM), *WebOS* (HP/Palm), *Symbian* (Nokia) are popular and currently widely deployed platforms, with many more proprietary ones being available as well. As a consequence of this fragmentation, realizing a special purpose application, which works with many or all of these platforms is extremely time consuming and inefficient due to the large amount of duplicate work required.

The W3C addressed this problem, by enriching HTML in its 5th revision with access interfaces to local storage (beyond simple cookies) as well as a number of devices and sensors commonly found on mobile devices (e. g. GPS, camera, compass etc.). We argue, that in combination with semantic technologies these features can be used to realize a *general purpose*, mobile collaboration platform, which can support the long tail of mobile special interest applications, for which the development of individual tools would not be (economically) feasible.

In [51] we present the *OntoWiki Mobile* approach realizing a mobile semantic collaboration platform based on the OntoWiki. It comprises specifically adopted user interfaces for browsing, faceted navigation as well as authoring of knowledge bases. It allows users to collect instance data and refine the structured knowledge bases on-the-go. OntoWiki Mobile is implemented as an *HTML5 web application*, thus being completely mobile device platform independent. In order to allow offline use in cases with restricted network coverage (or in order to avoid roaming charges) it uses the novel HTML5 local storage feature for replicating parts of the knowledge base on the mobile device. Hence, a crucial part of OntoWiki Mobile is the advanced conflict resolution for RDF stores. The approach is based on a combination of the EvoPat [173] method for data evolution and ontology refactoring along with a versioning system inspired by distributed version control systems like Git. OntoWiki Mobile is a generic, application domain agnostic tool, which can be utilized in a wide range of very different usage scenarios ranging from instance acquisition to browsing of semantic data on the go. Typical OntoWiki Mobile usage scenarios are settings where users need to author and access semantically structured information on the go or in settings where users are away from regular power supply and restricted to light-weight equipment (e. g. scientific expeditions).

Semantics-Based Requirements Engineering. Semantic interoperability, linked data, and a shared conceptual foundation become increasingly important prerequisites in software development projects that are characterized by spatial dispersion, large numbers of stakeholders, and heterogeneous development tools. The SoftWiki OntoWiki extension [124] focuses specifically on semantic collaboration with respect to requirements engineering. Potentially very large and spatially distributed groups of stakeholders, including developers, experts, managers, and average users, shall be enabled to collect, semantically enrich, classify, and aggregate software requirements. OntoWiki is used to support collaboration as well as interlinking and exchange of requirements data. To ensure a shared conceptual foundation and semantic interoperability, we developed the SoftWiki Ontology for Requirements Engineering (SWORE) that defines core concepts of requirement engineering and the way they are interrelated. For instance, the ontology defines frequent relation types to describe requirements interdependencies such as details, conflicts, related to, depends on, etc. The flexible SWORE design allows for easy extension. Moreover, the requirements can be linked to external resources, such as publicly available domain knowledge or company-specific policies. The whole process is called semantification of requirements. It is envisioned as an evolutionary process: The requirements are successively linked to each other and to further concepts in a collaborative way, jointly by all stakeholders. Whenever a requirement is formulated, reformulated, analyzed, or exchanged, it might be semantically enriched by the respective participant.

5   Linking

The fourth Linked Data Principle, i.e., "Include links to other URIs, so that they can discover more things" (cf. section 2) is the most important Linked Data principle as it enables the paradigm change from data silos to interoperable data distributed across the

Web. Furthermore, it plays a key role in important tasks such as cross-ontology question answering [23,125], large-scale inferences [194,131] and data integration [126,21]. Yet, while the number of triples in Linked Data sources increases steadily and has surpassed 31 billions[12], links between knowledge bases still constitute less than 5% of these triples. The goal of linking is to tackle this sparseness so as to transform the Web into a platform for data and information integration as well as for search and querying.

5.1 Link Discovery

Linking can be generally defined as *connecting things that are somehow related*. In the context of Linked Data, the idea of linking is especially concerned with establishing typed links between entities (i.e., classes, properties or instances) contained in knowledge bases. Over the last years, several frameworks have been developed to address the lack of typed links between the different knowledge bases on the Linked Data web. Overall, two main categories of frameworks that aim to achieve this goal can be differentiated. The first category implements *ontology matching* techniques and aims to establish links between the ontologies underlying two data sources. The second and more prominent category of approaches, dubbed *instance matching* approaches (also called linking or link discovery approaches), aims to discover links between instances contained in two data sources. It is important to notice that while ontology and instance matching are similar to schema matching [167,166] and record linkage [205,50,27] respectively (as known in the research area of databases), linking on the Web of Data is a more generic and thus more complex task, as it is not limited to finding equivalent entities in two knowledge bases. Rather, it aims at finding semantically related entities and establishing typed links between them, most of these links being imbued with formal properties (e.g., transitivity, symmetry, etc.) that can be used by reasoners and other application to infer novel knowledge. In this section, we will focus on the discovery of links between instances and use the term link discovery as name for this process. An overview of ontology matching techniques is given in [54].

Formally, link discovery can be defined as follows:

Definition 3 (Link Discovery). *Given two sets S (source) and T (target) of instances and a relation R, find the set $M \subseteq S \times T$ that is such that $\forall (s,t) \in M : R(s,t)$.*

Solving this problem is obviously not trivial. Declarative frameworks thus reduce this problem to a similarity computation problem and try to approximate M by a set $\tilde{M}$ for which the following holds:

Definition 4 (Link Discovery as Similarity Computation). *Given two sets S (source) and T (target) of instances, a (complex) semantic similarity measure $\sigma : S \times T \to [0,1]$ and a threshold $\theta \in [0,1]$, the goal of link discovery task is to compute the set $\tilde{M} = \{(s,t), \sigma(s,t) \geq \theta\}$.*

In general, the similarity function used to carry out a link discovery task is described by using a *link specification* (sometimes called *linkage decision rule* [91]).

---

[12] http://lod-cloud.net/

5.2 Challenges

Two key challenges arise when trying to discover links between two sets of instances: the computational complexity of the matching task *per se* and the selection of an appropriate link specification. The first challenge is intrinsically related to the link discovery process. The time complexity of a matching task can be measured by the number of comparisons necessary to complete this task. When comparing a source knowledge base S with a target knowledge base T, the completion of a matching task requires a-priori $O(|S||T|)$ comparisons, an impractical proposition as soon as the source and target knowledge bases become large. For example, discovering duplicate cities in DBpedia [7] alone would necessitate approximately 0.15×10^9 similarity computations. Hence, the provision of time-efficient approaches for the reduction of the time complexity of link discovery is a key requirement to instance linking frameworks for Linked Data.

The second challenge of the link discovery process lies in the selection of an appropriate link specification. The configuration of link discovery frameworks is usually carried out manually, in most cases simply by guessing. Yet, the choice of a suitable link specification measure is central for the discovery of satisfactory links. The large number of properties of instances and the large spectrum of measures available in literature underline the complexity of choosing the right specification manually[13]. Supporting the user during the process of finding the appropriate similarity measure and the right properties for each mapping task is a problem that still needs to be addressed by the Linked Data community. Methods such as supervised and active learning can be used to guide the user in need of mapping to a suitable linking configuration for his matching task. In the following, we give a short overview of existing frameworks for Link Discovery on the Web of Data. Subsequently, we present a time-efficient framework for link discovery in more detail and show how it can detect link specifications using active learning.

5.3 Approaches to Link Discovery

Current frameworks for link discovery can be subdivided into two main categories: *domain-specific* and *universal* frameworks. Domain-specific link discovery frameworks aim at discovering links between knowledge bases from a particular domain. One of the first domain-specific approaches to carry out instance linking for Linked Data was implemented in the *RKBExplorer*[14] [69] with the aim of discovering links between entities from the domain of academics. Due to the lack of data available as Linked Data, the RKBExplorer had to extract RDF from heterogeneous data source so as to populate its knowledge bases with instances according to the AKT ontology[15]. Especially, instances of persons, publications and institutions were retrieved from several major metadata websites such as ACM and DBLP. The linking was implemented by the so-called Consistent Reference Service (CRS) which linked equivalent entities by comparing properties including their type and label. So far, the CRS is limited to linking

---

[13] The SimMetrics project (`http://simmetrics.sf.net`) provides an overview of strings similarity measures.

[14] `http://www.rkbexplorer.com`

[15] `http://www.aktors.org/publications/ontology/`

objects in the knowledge bases underlying the RKBExplorer and cannot be used for other tasks without further implementation.

Another domain-specific tool is GNAT [168], which was developed for the music domain. It implements several instance matching algorithms of which the most sophisticated, the online graph matching algorithm (OGMA), applies a similarity propagation approach to discover equivalent resources. The basic approach implemented by OGMA starts with a single resource $s \in S$. Then, it retrieves candidate matching resources $t \in T$ by comparing properties such as foaf:name for artists and dc:title for albums. If $\sigma(s, t) \geq \theta$, then the algorithm terminates. In case a disambiguation is needed, the resourced related to s and t in their respective knowledge bases are compared and their similarity value is cumulated to recompute $\sigma(s, t)$. This process is iterated until a mapping resource for s is found in T or no resource matches.

Universal link discovery frameworks are designed to carry out mapping tasks independently from the domain of the source and target knowledge bases. For example, RDF-AI [181], a framework for the integration of RDF data sets, implements a five-step approach that comprises the preprocessing, matching, fusion, interlinking and post-processing of data sets. RDF-AI contains a series of modules that allow for computing instances matches by comparing their properties. Especially, it contains translation modules that allow to process the information contained in data sources before mapping. By these means, it can boost the precision of the mapping process. These modules can be configured by means of XML-files. RDF-AI does not comprise means for querying distributed data sets via SPARQL[16]. In addition, it suffers from not being time-optimized. Thus, mapping by using this tool can be very time-consuming.

A time-optimized approach to link discovery is implemented by the LIMES framework [148,147,153] (Link Discovery Framework for metric spaces) .[17] The idea behind the LIMES framework is to use the mathematical characteristics of similarity and distance measures to reduce the number of computations that have to be carried out by the system without losing any link. For example, LIMES can make use of the fact that the edit distance is a distance metric to approximate distances without having to compute them [148]. Moreover, it implements the reductio-ratio-optimal space tiling algorithm $\mathcal{HR}^3$ to compute similarities in affine spaces with Minkowski measures [146]. In contrast to other frameworks (of which most rely on blocking), LIMES relies on time-efficient set operators to combine the results of these algorithms efficiently and has been shown to outperform the state of the art by these means [147]. Moreover, LIMES implements unsupervised and supervised machine learning approaches for detecting high-quality link specifications [153,154].

Another link discovery framework is SILK [198]. SILK implements several approaches to minimize the time necessary for mapping instances from knowledge bases. In addition to implementing rough index pre-matching to reach a quasi-linear time-complexity, SILK also implements a lossless blocking algorithm called MultiBlock [92] to reduce its overall runtime. The approach relies on generating overlapping blocks of instances and only comparing pairs of instances that are located in the same block.

---

[16] http://www.w3.org/TR/rdf-sparql-query/

[17] http://limes.sf.net. A graphical user interface can be found at
http://saim.aksw.org

Moreover, SILK provides supervised machine learning approaches for link discovery [93].

It is important to notice that the task of discovering links between knowledge bases is related with record linkage [205,50] and de-duplication [27]. The database community has produced a vast amount of literature on efficient algorithms for solving these problems. Different blocking techniques such as standard blocking, sorted-neighborhood, bigram indexing, canopy clustering and adaptive blocking [20,24,102] have been developed to address the problem of the quadratic time complexity of brute force comparison methods. The idea is to filter out obvious non-matches efficiently before executing the more detailed and time-consuming comparisons. In the following, we present a state-of-the-art framework that implements lossless instance matching based on a similar idea in detail.

5.4 The LIMES Algorithm

The original LIMES algorithm described in [148] addresses the scalability problem of link discovery by utilizing the *triangle inequality* in metric spaces to compute pessimistic estimates of instance similarities. Based on these approximations, LIMES can filter out a large number of instance pairs that cannot suffice the matching condition set by the user. The real similarities of the remaining instances pairs are then computed and the matching instances are returned.

Mathematical Framework. In the remainder of this section, we use the following notations:

1. A is an affine space,
2. m, m_1, m_2, m_3 symbolize metrics on A,
3. x, y and z represent points from A and
4. α, β, γ and δ are scalars, i.e., elements of $\mathbb{R}$.

Definition 5 (Metric space). *A metric space is a pair (A, m) such that A is an affine space and $m : A \times A \to \mathbb{R}$ is a function such that for all x, y and $z \in A$*

1. $m(x, y) \geq 0$ (M_1) *(non-negativity)*,
2. $m(x, y) = 0 \Leftrightarrow x = y$ (M_2) *(identity of indiscernibles)*,
3. $m(x, y) = m(y, x)$ (M_3) *(symmetry) and*
4. $m(x, z) \leq m(x, y) + m(y, z)$ (M_4) (triangle inequality).

Note that the definition of a matching based on a similarity function σ can be rewritten for metrics m as follows:

Definition 6 (Instance Matching in Metric Spaces). *Given two sets S (source) and T (target) of instances, a metric $m : S \times T \to [0, \infty[$ and a threshold $\theta \in [0, \infty[$, the goal of instance matching task is to compute the set $M = \{(s, t) | m(s, t) \leq \theta\}$.*

Example of metrics on strings include the Levenshtein distance and the block distance. However, some popular measures such as JaroWinkler [204] do not satisfy the

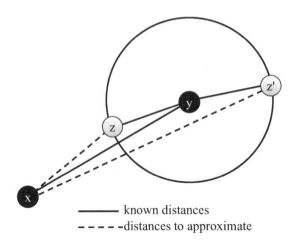

known distances
- - - - -distances to approximate

Fig. 15. Approximation of distances via exemplars. The lower bound of the distance from x to z can be approximated by $m(x, y) - m(y, z)$.

triangle inequality and are consequently not metrics. The rationale behind the LIMES framework is to make use of the boundary conditions entailed by the triangle inequality (TI) to reduce the number of comparisons (and thus the time complexity) necessary to complete a matching task. Given a metric space (A, m) and three points x, y and z in A, the TI entails that

$$m(x, y) \leq m(x, z) + m(z, y). \tag{5}$$

Without restriction of generality, the TI also entails that

$$m(x, z) \leq m(x, y) + m(y, z), \tag{6}$$

thus leading to the following boundary conditions in metric spaces:

$$m(x, y) - m(y, z) \leq m(x, z) \leq m(x, y) + m(y, z). \tag{7}$$

Inequality 7 has two major implications. The first is that the distance from a point x to any point z in a metric space can be approximated given the distance from x to a reference point y and the distance from the reference point y to z. Such a reference point is called an *exemplar* following [62]. The role of an exemplar is to be used as a sample of a portion of the metric space A. Given an input point x, knowing the distance from x to an exemplar y allows to compute lower and upper bounds of the distance from x to any other point z at a known distance from y. An example of such an approximation is shown in Figure 20. In this figure, all the points on the circle are subject to the same distance approximation. The distance from x to z is close to the lower bound of inequality 7, while the distance from x to z' is close to the upper bound of the same inequality.

The second implication of inequality 7 is that the distance from x to z can only be smaller than θ if the lower bound of the approximation of the distance from x to z via *any exemplar y* is also smaller than θ. Thus, if the lower bound of the approximation of the distance $m(x, z)$ is larger than θ, then $m(x, z)$ itself must be larger than θ. Formally,

$$m(x, y) - m(y, z) > \theta \Rightarrow m(x, z) > \theta. \tag{8}$$

Supposing that all distances from instances $t \in T$ to exemplars are known, reducing the number of comparisons simply consists of using inequality 8 to compute an approximation of the distance from all $s \in S$ to all $t \in T$ and computing the real distance only for the (s, t) pairs for which the first term of inequality 8 does not hold. This is the core of the approach implemented by LIMES.

Computation of Exemplars The core idea underlying the computation of exemplars in LIMES is to select a set of exemplars in the metric space underlying the matching task in such a way that they are distributed uniformly in the metric space. One way to achieve this goal is by ensuring that the exemplars display a high dissimilarity. The approach used by LIMES to generate exemplars with this characteristic is shown in Algorithm 1.

Algorithm 1. Computation of Exemplars

Require: Number of exemplars n
Require: Target knowledge base T
  1. Pick random point $e_1 \in T$
  2. Set $E = E \cup \{e_1\}$;
  3. Compute the distance from e_1 to all $t \in T$
while $|E| < n$ **do**
    4. Get a random point e' such that $e' \in argmax_t \sum_{t \in T} \sum_{e \in E} m(t, e)$
    5. $E = E \cup \{e'\}$;
    6. Compute the distance from e' to all $t \in T$
end while
  7. Map each point in $t \in T$ to one of the exemplars $e \in E$ such that $m(t, e)$ is minimal
return E

Let n be the desired number of exemplars and E the set of all exemplars. In step 1 and 2, LIMES initializes E by picking a random point e_1 in the metric space (T, m) and setting $E = \{e_1\}$. Then, it computes the similarity from the exemplar e_1 to every other point in T (step 3). As long as the size of E has not reached n, LIMES repeats steps 4 to 6: In step 4, a point $e' \in T$ such that the sum of the distances from e' to the exemplars $e \in E$ is maximal (there can be many of these points) is chosen randomly. This point is chosen as new exemplar and consequently added to E (step 5). Then, the distance from e' to all other points in T is computed (step 6). Once E has reached the size n, LIMES terminates the iteration. Finally, each point is mapped to the exemplar to which it is most similar (step 7) and the exemplar computation terminates (step 8). This algorithm has a constant time complexity of $O(|E||T|)$.

An example of the results of the exemplar computation algorithm ($|E| = 3$) is shown in Figure 16. The initial exemplar was the leftmost exemplar in the figure.

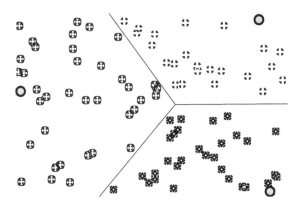

Fig. 16. Mapping of points to three exemplars in a metric space. The exemplars are displayed as gray disks.

Matching Based on Exemplars. The instances associated with an exemplar $e \in E$ in step 7 of Algorithm 1 are stored in a list L_e sorted in descending order with respect to the distance to e. Let $\lambda_1^e \ldots \lambda_m^e$ be the elements of the list L_e. The goal of matching an instance s from a source knowledge base to a target knowledge base w.r.t. a metric m is to find all instances t of the target knowledge source such that $m(s, t) \leq \theta$, where θ is a given threshold. LIMES achieves this goal by using the matching algorithm based on exemplars shown in Algorithm 2.

LIMES only carries out a comparison when the approximation of the distance is less than the threshold. Moreover, it terminates the similarity computation for an exemplar e as soon as the first λ^e is found such that the lower bound of the distance is larger than θ. This break can be carried out because the list L_e is sorted, i.e., if $m(s, e) - m(e, \lambda_i^e) > \theta$ holds for the ith element of L_e, then the same inequality holds for all $\lambda_j^e \in L_e$ with $j > i$. In the worst case, LIMES' matching algorithm has the time complexity $O(|S||T|)$, leading to a total worst time complexity of $O((|E| + |S|)|T|)$, which is larger than that of brute force approaches. However, as the results displayed in Figure 17 show, a correct parameterization of LIMES leads to significantly smaller numbers of comparisons and runtimes.

5.5 The $\mathcal{HR}^3$ Algorithm

Let S resp. T be the source and target of a Link Discovery task. One of the key ideas behind time-efficient Link Discovery algorithms $\mathcal{A}$ is to reduce the number of comparisons that are effectively carried out to a number $C(\mathcal{A}) < |S||T|$. The reduction ratio RR of an algorithm $\mathcal{A}$ is given by

$$RR(\mathcal{A}) = 1 - \frac{C(\mathcal{A})}{|S||T|}. \qquad (9)$$

$RR(\mathcal{A})$ captures how much of the Cartesian product $|S||T|$ was not explored before the output of $\mathcal{A}$ was reached. It is obvious that even an optimal lossless solution which performs only the necessary comparisons cannot achieve a RR of 1. Let C_{min} be the

---

Algorithm 2. LIMES' Matching algorithm

Require: Set of exemplars E
Require: Instance $s \in S$
Require: Metric m
Require: threshold θ
  1. $M = \emptyset$
  for $e \in |E|$ **do**
    if $m(s, e) \leq \theta$ **then**
      2. $M = M \cup \{e\}$
      for $i = 1...|L_e|$ **do**
        if $(m(s, e) - m(e, \lambda_i^e)) \leq \theta$ **then**
          if $m(s, \lambda_i^e) \leq \theta$ **then**
            3. $M = M \cup \{(s, \lambda_i^e)\}$
          end if
        else
          break
        end if
      end for
    end if
  end for
  return M

---

minimal number of comparisons necessary to complete the Link Discovery task without losing recall, i.e., $C_{min} = |\mathcal{M}|$. The relative reduction ratio $RRR(\mathcal{A})$ is defined as the portion of the minimal number of comparisons that was carried out by the algorithm $\mathcal{A}$ before it terminated. Formally

$$RRR(\mathcal{A}) = \frac{1 - \frac{C_{min}}{|S||T|}}{1 - \frac{C(\mathcal{A})}{|S||T|}} = \frac{|S||T| - C_{min}}{|S||T| - C(\mathcal{A})}. \qquad (10)$$

$RRR(\mathcal{A})$ indicates how close $\mathcal{A}$ is to the optimal solution with respect to the number of candidates it tests. Given that $C(\mathcal{A}) \geq C_{min}$, $RRR(\mathcal{A}) \geq 1$. Note that the larger the value of $RRR(\mathcal{A})$, the poorer the performance of $\mathcal{A}$ with respect to the task at hand.

The main observation that led $\mathcal{HR}^3$ is that while most algorithms aim to optimize their RR (and consequently their RRR), most approaches do not provide any guarantee with respect to the RR (and consequently the RRR) that they can achieve. The approach is the first mathematically optimal algorithm w.r.t the reduction ratio that it can achieve, i.e., the first approach such that given any relative reduction ratio r, there is always a setting that leads $\mathcal{HR}^3$ achieving a relative reduction ratio r' with $r' \leq r$. To achieve this goal $\mathcal{HR}^3$ relies on space tiling as introduced by the HYPPO algorithm [145].

Space Tiling for Link Discovery. HYPPO addresses the problem of efficiently mapping instance pairs $(s, t) \in S \times T$ described by using exclusively numeric values in a n-dimensional metric space and has been shown to outperform the state of the art in previous work [145]. The observation behind space tiling is that in spaces (Ω, δ) with

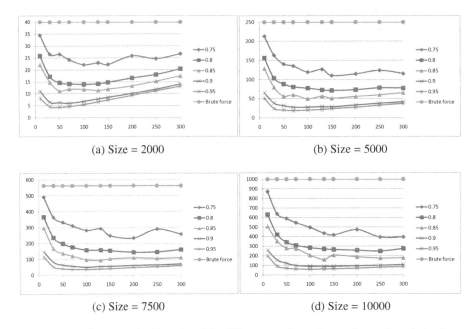

(a) Size = 2000   (b) Size = 5000

(c) Size = 7500   (d) Size = 10000

Fig. 17. Comparisons required by LIMES for different numbers of exemplars on knowledge bases of different sizes. The x-axis shows the number of exemplars, the y-axis the number of comparisons in multiples of 10^5.

orthogonal, (i.e., uncorrelated) dimensions[18], common metrics for Link Discovery can be decomposed into the combination of functions $\phi_{i,i\in\{1...n\}}$ which operate on exactly one dimension of Ω : $\delta = f(\phi_1, ..., \phi_n)$. For Minkowski distances of order p, $\phi_i(x, \omega) = |x_i - \omega_i|$ for all values of i and $\delta(x, \omega) = \sqrt[p]{\sum_{i=1}^{n} \phi_i^p(x, \omega)^p}$. A direct consequence of this observation is the inequality $\phi_i(x, \omega) \leq \delta(x, \omega)$. The basic insight that results this observation is that the hypersphere $H(\omega, \theta) = \{x \in \Omega : \delta(x, \omega) \leq \theta\}$ is a subset of the hypercube V defined as $V(\omega, \theta) = \{x \in \Omega : \forall i \in \{1...n\}, \phi_i(x_i, \omega_i) \leq \theta\}$. Consequently, one can reduce the number of comparisons necessary to detect all elements of $H(\omega, \theta)$ by discarding all elements which are not in $V(\omega, \theta)$ as non-matches. Let $\Delta = \theta/\alpha$, where $\alpha \in \mathbb{N}$ is the *granularity parameter* that controls how fine-grained the space tiling should be (see Figure 18 for an example). We first tile Ω into the adjacent hypercubes (short: cubes) C that contain all the points ω such that

$$\forall i \in \{1...n\}, c_i\Delta \leq \omega_i < (c_i + 1)\Delta \text{ with } (c_1, ..., c_n) \in \mathbb{N}^n. \tag{11}$$

We call the vector $(c_1, ..., c_n)$ the coordinates of the cube C. Each point $\omega \in \Omega$ lies in the cube $C(\omega)$ with coordinates $(\lfloor \omega_i/\Delta \rfloor)_{i=1...n}$. Given such a space tiling, it is obvious that $V(\omega, \theta)$ consists of the union of the cubes such that $\forall i \in \{1...n\} : |c_i - c(\omega)_i| \leq \alpha$.

---

[18] Note that in all cases, a space transformation exists that can map a space with correlated dimensions to a space with uncorrelated dimensions.

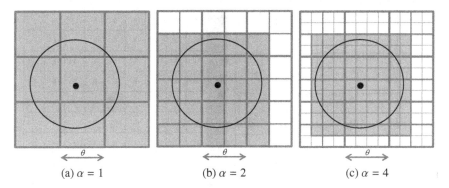

(a) $\alpha = 1$ (b) $\alpha = 2$ (c) $\alpha = 4$

Fig. 18. Space tiling for different values of α. The colored squares show the set of elements that must be compared with the instance located at the black dot. The points within the circle lie within the distance θ of the black dot. Note that higher values of α lead to a better approximation of the hypersphere but also to more hypercubes.

$\mathcal{HR}^3$**'s Indexing Scheme.** Let $\omega \in \Omega = S \cup T$ be an arbitrary reference point. Furthermore, let δ be the Minkowski distance of order p. The *index* function is defined as follows:

$$index(C, \omega) = \begin{cases} 0 \text{ if } \exists i : |c_i - c(\omega)_i| \leq 1 \text{ with } i \in \{1, ..., n\}, \\ \sum_{i=1}^{n} (|c_i - c(\omega)_i| - 1)^p \text{ else,} \end{cases} \quad (12)$$

where C is a hypercube resulting from a space tiling and $\omega \in \Omega$. Figure 19 shows an example of such indexes for $p = 2$ with $\alpha = 2$ (Figure 19a) and $\alpha = 4$ (Figure 19b). Note that the blue square with index 0 contains the reference point ω. All elements of C must only be compared with the elements of cubes C' such that $index(C, C') \leq \alpha^p$. The authors of [146] prove formally that given this approach to space tiling, the following theorem holds:

Theorem 1. $\lim_{\alpha \to \infty} RRR(\mathcal{HR}^3, \alpha) = 1$.

This conclusion is illustrated by Figure 20, which shows the space tiling computed by $\mathcal{HR}^3$ for different values of α with $p = 2$ and $n = 2$. The higher α, the closer the approximation is to a circle. Note that these results allow to conclude that for any *RRR*-value r larger than 1, there is a setting of $\mathcal{HR}^3$ that can compute links with a *RRR* smaller or equal to r.

Evaluation. $\mathcal{HR}^3$ was evaluated against HYPPO w.r.t. to the number of comparisons that it has to carry out in several settings. In the first and second experiments, the goal was to deduplicate DBpedia places by comparing their names (`rdfs:label`), minimum elevation, elevation and maximum elevation. 2988 entities possessed all four properties. The Euclidean metric was applied to the last three values with the thresholds 49 meters resp. 99 meters for the first resp. second experiment. The third and fourth experiments aimed to discover links between Geonames and LinkedGeoData. This experiment was

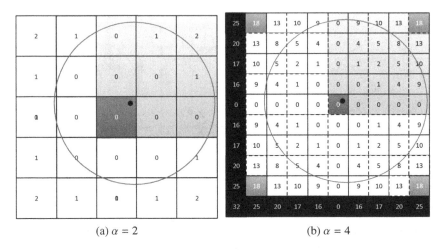

(a) $\alpha = 2$ (b) $\alpha = 4$

Fig. 19. Space tiling and resulting index for a two-dimensional example. Note that the index in both subfigures was generated for exactly the same portion of space. The black dot stands for the position of ω.

of considerably larger scale than the first one, as we compared 74458 entities in Geonames with 50031 entities from LinkedGeoData. Again, the number of comparisons necessary to complete the task by using the Euclidean metric was measured. The distance thresholds were set to 1 resp. 9° in experiment 3 resp. 4. We ran all experiments on the same Windows 7 Enterprise 64-bit computer with a 2.8GHz i7 processor with 8GB RAM. The JVM was allocated 7GB RAM to ensure that the runtimes were not influenced by swapping. Only one of the kernels of the processors was used.

The results (see Figure 21) show that $\mathcal{HR}^3$ can reduce the overhead in comparisons (i.e., the number of unnecessary comparisons divided by the number of necessary comparisons) from approximately 24% for HYPPO to approximately 6% (granularity = 32). In experiment 2, the overhead is reduced from 4.1% to 2%. This difference in overhead reduction is mainly due to the data clustering around certain values and the clusters having a radius between 49 meters and 99 meters. Thus, running the algorithms with a threshold of 99 meters led to only a small a-priori overhead and HYPPO performing remarkably well. Still, even on such data distributions, $\mathcal{HR}^3$ was able to discard even more data and to reduce the number of unnecessary computations by more than 50% relative. In the best case (Exp. 4, $\alpha = 32$, see Figure 21d), $\mathcal{HR}^3$ required approximately 4.13×10^6 less comparisons than HYPPO for $\alpha = 32$. Even for the smallest setting (Exp. 1, see Figure 21a), $\mathcal{HR}^3$ still required 0.64×10^6 less comparisons.

5.6   Active Learning of Link Specifications

The second challenge of Link Discovery is the time-efficient discovery of link specifications for a particular linking task. Several approaches have been proposed to achieve this goal, of which most rely on genetic programming [93,154,152]. The COALA

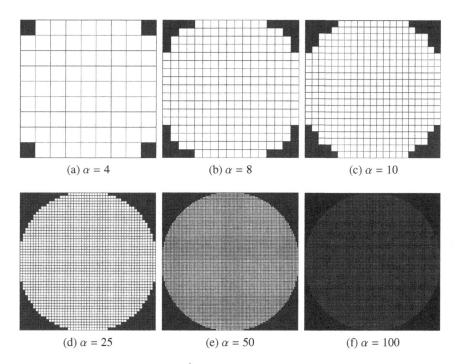

(a) $\alpha = 4$ (b) $\alpha = 8$ (c) $\alpha = 10$

(d) $\alpha = 25$ (e) $\alpha = 50$ (f) $\alpha = 100$

Fig. 20. Space tilings generated by $\mathcal{HR}^3$ for different values of α. The white squares are selected for comparisons with the elements of the square in the middle of the figure whilst the colored ones are discarded.

(Correlation-Aware Active Learning) approach was implemented on top of the genetic programming approach EAGLE [153] with the aim of improving the selection of positive and negative examples during active learning. In the following, we give an overview of COALA.

Intuition. Let $\mathcal{N}$ be the set of most informative negative and $\mathcal{P}$ the set of most informative negative examples w.r.t. an informativeness function ifm (e.g., the distance from the decision boundary).used by a curious classifier [183] The basic insight behind COALA is that the correlation between the features of the elements of $\mathcal{N}$ and $\mathcal{P}$ should play a role when computing the sets $\mathcal{I}^+$ and $\mathcal{I}^-$ of positive resp. negative queries for the oracle. In particular, two main factors affect the information content of a link candidate: its similarity to elements of its presumed class and to elements of the other class. For the sake of simplicity, we will assume that the presumed class of the link candidate of interest is $+1$, i.e., that the link candidate was classified as positive by the current curious classifier. Our insights yet hold symmetrically for link candidates whose presumed class is -1.

Let $A = (s_A, t_A), B = (s_B, t_B) \in \mathcal{P}$ to be two link candidates which are equidistant from C's boundary. Consider Figure 22a, where $\mathcal{P} = \{A, B, C\}$ and $\mathcal{N} = \{D\}$. The link candidate B is on on average most distant from any other elements of $\mathcal{P}$. Thus, it is more

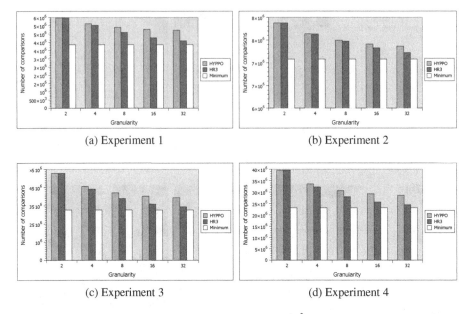

(a) Experiment 1

(b) Experiment 2

(c) Experiment 3

(d) Experiment 4

Fig. 21. Number of comparisons for $\mathcal{HR}^3$ and HYPPO

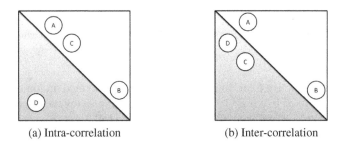

(a) Intra-correlation

(b) Inter-correlation

Fig. 22. Examples of correlations within classes and between classes. In each subfigure, the gray surface represent $\mathcal{N}$ while the white surface stands for $\mathcal{P}$. The oblique line is C's boundary.

likely to be a statistical outlier than A. Hence, making a classification error on B should not have the same impact as an erroneous classification of link candidate A, which is close to another presumably positive link candidate, C. Consequently, B should be considered less informative than A. Approaches that make use of this information are said to exploit the *intra-class correlation*. Now, consider Figure 22b, where $\mathcal{P} = \{A, B\}$ and $\mathcal{N} = \{C, D\}$. While the probability of A being an outlier is the same as B's, A is still to be considered more informative than B as it is located closer to elements of $\mathcal{N}$ and can thus provide more information on where to set the classifier boundary. This information is dubbed *inter-class correlation*. Several approaches that make use of these two types of correlations can be envisaged. In the following, we present two approaches for these purposes. The first makes use of intra-class correlations and relies on graph clustering. The second approach relies on the spreading activation principle in combination with weight decay. We assume that the complex similarity function σ underlying C is computed by combining n atomic similarity functions $\sigma_1, \ldots, \sigma_n$. This combination is most commonly carried out by using metric operators such as min, max or linear combinations.[19] Consequently, each link candidate (s, t) can be described by a vector $(\sigma_1(s, t), \ldots, \sigma_n(s, t)) \in [0, 1]^n$. We define the *similarity of link candidates* $sim : (S \times T)^2 \to [0, 1]$ to be the inverse of the Euclidean distance in the space spawned by the similarities σ_1 to σ_n. Hence, the similarity of two link candidates (s, t) and (s', t') is given by:

$$sim((s, t), (s', t')) = \frac{1}{1 + \sqrt{\sum_{i=1}^{n}(\sigma_i(s, t) - \sigma_i(s', t'))^2}}. \tag{13}$$

Note that we added 1 to the denominator to prevent divisions by 0.

Graph Clustering. The basic intuition behind using clustering for COALA is that groups of very similar link candidates can be represented by a single link candidate. Consequently, once a representative of a group has been chosen, all other elements of the group become less informative. An example that illustrates this intuition is given in Figure 23. We implemented COALA based on clustering as follows: In each iteration, we begin by first selecting two sets $\mathcal{S}^+ \subseteq \mathcal{P}$ resp. $\mathcal{S}^- \subseteq \mathcal{N}$ that contain the positive resp. negative link candidates that are most informative for the classifier at hand. Formally, $\mathcal{S}^+$ fulfills

$$\forall x \in \mathcal{S}^+ \ \forall y \in \mathcal{P}, y \notin \mathcal{S}^+ \to \text{ifm}(y) \leq \text{ifm}(x). \tag{14}$$

The analogous equation holds for $\mathcal{S}^-$. In the following, we will explain the further steps of the algorithm for $\mathcal{S}^+$. The same steps are carried out for $\mathcal{S}^-$.

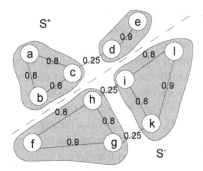

Fig. 23. Example of clustering. One of the most informative single link candidate is selected from each cluster. For example, d is selected from the cluster $\{d, e\}$.

---

[19] See [147] for a more complete description of a grammar for link specifications.

First, we compute the similarity of all elements of S^+ by using the similarity function shown in Equation 13. In the resulting similarity matrix, we set all elements of the diagonal to 0. Then, for each $x \in S^+$, we only retain a fixed number ec of highest similarity values and set all others to 0. The resulting similarity matrix is regarded as the adjacency matrix of an undirected weighted graph $G = (V, E, sim)$. G's set of nodes V is equal to S^+. The set of edges E is a set of 2-sets[20] of link candidates. Finally, the weighted function is the similarity function sim. Note that ec is the minimal degree of nodes in G.

In a second step, we use the graph G as input for a graph clustering approach. The resulting clustering is assumed to be a partition $\mathcal{V}$ of the set V of vertices of G. The informativeness of partition $V_i \in \mathcal{V}$ is set to $\max_{x \in V_i} ifm(x)$. The final step of our approach consists of selecting the most informative node from each of the k most informative partitions. These are merged to generate I^+, which is sent as query to the oracle. The computation of I^- is carried out analogously. Note that this approach is generic in the sense that it can be combined with any graph clustering algorithm that can process weighted graphs as well as with any informativeness function ifm. Here, we use Border-Flow [155] as clustering algorithm because (1) it has been used successfully in several other applications such as the creation of SPARQL benchmarks [137] and the analysis of protein-protein interactions [144]. and (2) it is parameter-free and does not require any tuning.

Spreading Activation with Weight Decay. The idea behind spreading activation with weight decay (WD) is to combine the intra- and inter-class correlation to determine the informativeness of each link candidate. Here, we begin by computing the set $S = S^+ \cup S^-$, where S^+ and S^- are described as above. Let s_i and s_j be the ith and j^{th} elements of S. We then compute the quadratic similarity matrix M with entries $m_{ij} = sim(s_i, s_j)$ for $i \neq j$ and 0 else. Note that both negative and positive link candidates belong to S. Thus, M encodes both inter- and intra-class correlation. In addition to M, we compute the activation vector $\mathcal{A}$ by setting its entries to $a_i = ifm(s_i)$. In the following, $\mathcal{A}$ is considered to be a column vector.

In a first step, we normalize the activation vector $\mathcal{A}$ to ensure that the values contained therein do not grow indefinitely. Then, in a second step, we set $\mathcal{A} = \mathcal{A} + M \times \mathcal{A}$. This has the effect of propagating the activation of each s to all its neighbors according to the weights of the edges between s and its neighbors. Note that elements of S^+ that are close to elements of S^- get a higher activation than elements of S^+ that are further away from S^- and vice-versa. Moreover, elements at the center of node clusters (i.e., elements that are probably no statistical outliers) also get a higher activation than elements that are probably outliers. The idea behind the weight decay step is to update the matrix by setting each m_{ij} to m_{ij}^r, where $r > 1$ is a fix exponent. This is the third step of the algorithm. Given that $\forall i \forall j \, m_{ij} \leq 1$, the entries in the matrix get smaller with time. By these means, the amount of activation transferred across long paths is reduced. We run this three-step procedure iteratively until all non-1 entries of the matrix are less or equal to a threshold $\epsilon = 10^{-2}$. The k elements of S^+ resp. S^- with maximal activation are returned as I^+ resp. I^-. In the example shown in Figure 24, while all nodes from S^+

---

[20] A n-set is a set of magnitude n.

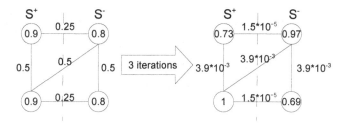

Fig. 24. Example of weight decay. Here r was set to 2. The left picture shows the initial activations and similarity scores while the right picture shows the results after 3 iterations. Note that for the sake of completeness the weights of the edges were not set to 0 when they reached ϵ.

and S^- start with the same activation, two nodes get the highest activation after only 3 iterations.

Evaluation. COALA was evaluated by running weight decay and clustering in combination with EAGLE, an active genetic programming approach for learning link specifications. Throughout the following experiments, EAGLE's mutation and crossover rates were set to 0.6. Individuals were given a 70% chance to get selected for reproduction. The population sizes were set to 20 and 100. We set $k = 5$ and ran our experiments for 10 iterations. Between each iteration we evolved the populations for 50 generations. We ran our experiments on two real-world datasets and three synthetic datasets. The synthetic datasets consisted of the Persons1, Person2 and Restaurants datasets from the OAEI 2010 benchmark[21]. The real-world datasets consisted of the ACM-DBLP and Abt-Buy datasets, which were extracted from websites or databases [102][22]. Given that genetic programming is non-deterministic, all results presented below are the means of 5 runs. Each experiment was ran on a single thread of a server running JDK1.7 on Ubuntu 10.0.4 and was allocated maximally 2GB of RAM. The processors were 2.0GHz Quadcore AMD Opterons. An excerpt of the results is shown in Figure 25. While the results show that COALA outperform EAGLE, it remains unclear whether WD or CL is the best approach to achieving a faster convergence towards the optimal solution.

5.7 Conclusion

We presented and discussed linking approaches for Linked Data and the challenges they face. In addition, we gave an overview of several state-of-the-art approaches for instance matching for Linked Data. We then presented time-efficient approaches for link discovery. Finally, we presented a state-of-the-art approach for the active learning of link specifications. This approach can be easily extended to learn specifications automatically.[23]

---

[21] http://oaei.ontologymatching.org/2010/

[22] http://dbs.uni-leipzig.de/en/research/projects/object_matching/fever/
benchmark_datasets_for_entity_resolution

[23] Such an extension is the basis of the self-configuration algorithm of the SAIM framework.

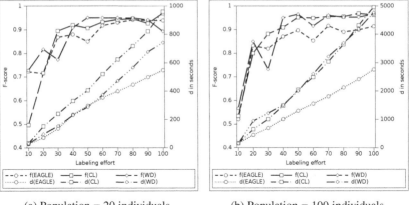

(a) Population = 20 individuals.   (b) Population = 100 individuals.

Fig. 25. F-score and runtime on the ACM-DBLP dataset. f(X) stands for the F-score achieved by algorithm X, while d(X) stands for the total duration required by the algorithm.

Novel challenges that need to be addressed include the automatic management of resources for link specifications. First works on running link discovery in parallel have shown that using massively parallel hardware such as GPUs can lead to better results that using cloud implementations even on considerably large datasets [151]. Detecting the right resources for linking automatically given a hardware landscape is yet still a dream to achieve.

6   Enrichment

The term *enrichment* in this chapter refers to the (semi-)automatic extension of a knowledge base schema. It describes the process of increasing the expressiveness and semantic richness of a knowledge base. Usually, this is achieved by adding or refining terminological axioms.

Enrichment methods can typically be applied in a *grass-roots* approach to knowledge base creation. In such an approach, the whole ontological structure is not created upfront, but evolves with the data in a knowledge base. Ideally, this enables a more agile development of knowledge bases. In particular, in the context of the Web of Linked Data such an approach appears to be an interesting alternative to more traditional ontology engineering methods. Amongst others, Tim Berners-Lee advocates to get "raw data now"[24] and worry about the more complex issues later.

Knowledge base enrichment can be seen as a sub-discipline of ontology learning. Ontology learning is more general in that it can rely on external sources, e.g. written text, to create an ontology. The term knowledge base enrichment is typically used when already existing data in the knowledge base is analysed to improve its schema.

---

[24] http://www.ted.com/talks/tim_berners_lee_on_the_next_web.html

Enrichment methods span several research areas like knowledge representation and reasoning, machine learning, statistics, natural language processing, formal concept analysis and game playing. Considering the variety of methods, we structure this section as follows: First, we give an overview of different types of enrichment and list some typical methods and give pointers to references, which allow the reader to obtain more information on a topic. In the second part, we describe a specific software – the ORE tool – in more detail.

6.1 State of the Art and Types of Enrichment

Ontology enrichment usually involves applying heuristics or machine learning techniques to find axioms, which can be added to an existing ontology. Naturally, different techniques have been applied depending on the specific type of axiom.

One of the most complex tasks in ontology enrichment is to find *definitions* of classes. This is strongly related to Inductive Logic Programming (ILP) [158] and more specifically supervised learning in description logics. Research in those fields has many applications apart from being applied to enrich ontologies. For instance, it is used in the life sciences to detect whether drugs are likely to be efficient for particular diseases. Work on learning in description logics goes back to e.g. [43,44], which used so-called *least common subsumers* to solve the learning problem (a modified variant of the problem defined in this article). Later, [19] invented a refinement operator for $\mathcal{ALER}$ and proposed to solve the problem by using a top-down approach. [52,89,90] combine both techniques and implement them in the YINYANG tool. However, those algorithms tend to produce very long and hard-to-understand class expressions. The algorithms implemented in DL-Learner [115,116,107,117,109] overcome this problem and investigate the learning problem and the use of top down refinement in detail. DL-FOIL [55] is a similar approach, which is based on a mixture of upward and downward refinement of class expressions. They use alternative measures in their evaluation, which take the open world assumption into account, which was not done in ILP previously. Most recently, [111] implements appropriate heuristics and adaptations for learning definitions in ontologies. The focus in this work is efficiency and practical application of learning methods. The article presents plugins for two ontology editors (Protégé and OntoWiki) as well stochastic methods, which improve previous methods by an order of magnitude. For this reason, we will analyse it in more detail in the next subsection. The algorithms presented in the article can also learn *super class axioms*.

A different approach to learning the definition of a named class is to compute the so called *most specific concept* (msc) for all instances of the class. The most specific concept of an individual is the most specific class expression, such that the individual is instance of the expression. One can then compute the *least common subsumer* (lcs) [18] of those expressions to obtain a description of the named class. However, in expressive description logics, an msc does not need to exist and the lcs is simply the disjunction of all expressions. For light-weight logics, such as $\mathcal{EL}$, the approach appears to be promising.

Other approaches, e.g. [122] focus on learning in hybrid knowledge bases combining ontologies and *rules*. Ontology evolution [123] has been discussed in this context. Usually, hybrid approaches are a generalisation of concept learning methods, which enable powerful rules at the cost of efficiency (because of the larger search space). Similar as in knowledge representation, the tradeoff between expressiveness of the target language and efficiency of learning algorithms is a critical choice in symbolic machine learning.

Another enrichment task is *knowlege base completion*. The goal of such a task is to make the knowledge base complete in a particular well-defined sense. For instance, a goal could be to ensure that all subclass relationships between named classes can be inferred. The line of work starting in [174] and further pursued in e.g. [17] investigates the use of *formal concept analysis* for completing knowledge bases. It is promising, although it may not be able to handle noise as well as a machine learning technique. A Protégé plugin [182] is available. [196] proposes to improve knowledge bases through relational exploration and implemented it in the *RELExO framework*[25]. It focuses on simple relationships and the knowledge engineer is asked a series of questions. The knowledge engineer either must positively answer the question or provide a counterexample.

[197] focuses on learning *disjointness* between classes in an ontology to allow for more powerful reasoning and consistency checking. To achieve this, it can use the ontology itself, but also texts, e.g. Wikipedia articles corresponding to a concept. The article includes an extensive study, which shows that proper modelling disjointness is actually a difficult task, which can be simplified via this ontology enrichment method.

Another type of ontology enrichment is schema mapping. This task has been widely studied and will not be discussed in depth within this chapter. Instead, we refer to [41] for a survey on ontology mapping.

There are further more light-weight ontology enrichment methods. For instance, *taxonomies* can be learned from simple tag structures via heuristics [36,195]. Similarly, "properties of properties" can be derived via simple statistical analysis. This includes the detection whether a particular property might be symmetric, function, reflexive, inverse functional etc. Similarly, domains and ranges of properties can be determined from existing data. Enriching the schema with domain and range axioms allows to find cases, where properties are misused via OWL reasoning.

Table 5. Work in ontology enrichment grouped by type or aim of learned structures

Type/Aim	References
Taxonomies	[207,36,195]
Definitions	often done via ILP approaches such as [115,116,117,111,55,52,89,90,19], genetic approaches [107] have also been used
Super Class Axioms	[111,195,36]
Rules in Ontologies	[122,123]
Disjointness	[197]
Properties of properties	[36,58]
Alignment	challenges: [185], recent survey: [41]
Completion	formal concept analysis and relational exploration [17,196,182]

---

[25] http://code.google.com/p/relexo/

In the following subsection, we describe an enrichment approach for learning definitions and super class axioms in more detail. The algorithm was recently developed by the first authors and is described in full detail in [111].

6.2   Class Expression Learning in DL-Learner

The Semantic Web has recently seen a rise in the availability and usage of knowledge bases, as can be observed within the Linking Open Data Initiative, the TONES and Protégé ontology repositories, or the Watson search engine. Despite this growth, there is still a lack of knowledge bases that consist of sophisticated schema information and instance data adhering to this schema. Several knowledge bases, e.g. in the life sciences, only consist of schema information, while others are, to a large extent, a collection of facts without a clear structure, e.g. information extracted from data bases or texts. The combination of sophisticated schema and instance data allows powerful reasoning, consistency checking, and improved querying possibilities. We argue that being able to learn OWL class expressions[26] is a step towards achieving this goal.

Example 1. As an example, consider a knowledge base containing a class Capital and instances of this class, e.g. London, Paris, Washington, Canberra etc. A machine learning algorithm could, then, suggest that the class Capital may be equivalent to one of the following OWL class expressions in Manchester OWL syntax[27]:

```
City and isCapitalOf at least one GeopoliticalRegion
City and isCapitalOf at least one Country
```

Both suggestions could be plausible: The first one is more general and includes cities that are capitals of states, whereas the latter one is stricter and limits the instances to capitals of countries. A knowledge engineer can decide which one is more appropriate, i.e. a semi-automatic approach is used, and the machine learning algorithm should guide her by pointing out which one fits the existing instances better. Assuming the knowledge engineer decides for the latter, an algorithm can show her whether there are instances of the class Capital which are neither instances of City nor related via the property isCapitalOf to an instance of Country.[28] The knowledge engineer can then continue to look at those instances and assign them to a different class as well as provide more complete information; thus improving the quality of the knowledge base. After adding the definition of Capital, an OWL reasoner can compute further instances of the class which have not been explicitly assigned before.

Using machine learning for the generation of suggestions instead of entering them manually has the advantage that 1.) the given suggestions fit the instance data, i.e. schema and instances are developed in concordance, and 2.) the entrance barrier for knowledge engineers is significantly lower, since understanding an OWL class expression is easier than analysing the structure of the knowledge base and creating a

---

[26] http://www.w3.org/TR/owl2-syntax/#Class_Expressions

[27] For details on Manchester OWL syntax (e.g. used in Protégé, OntoWiki) see [87].

[28] This is not an inconsistency under the standard OWL open world assumption, but rather a hint towards a potential modelling error.

class expression manually. Disadvantages of the approach are the dependency on the availability of instance data in the knowledge base and requirements on the quality of the ontology, i.e. modelling errors in the ontology can reduce the quality of results.

Overall, we describe the following in this chapter:

- extension of an existing learning algorithm for learning class expressions to the ontology engineering scenario,
- presentation and evaluation of different heuristics,
- showcase how the enhanced ontology engineering process can be supported with plugins for Protégé and OntoWiki,
- evaluation of the presented algorithm with several real ontologies from various domains.

The adapted algorithm for solving the learning problems, which occur in the ontology engineering process, is called *CELOE (Class Expression Learning for Ontology Engineering)*. It was implemented within the open-source framework DL-Learner.[29] DL-Learner [108,109] leverages a modular architecture, which allows to define different types of components: knowledge sources (e.g. OWL files), reasoners (e.g. DIG[30] or OWL API based), learning problems, and learning algorithms. In this overview, we focus on the latter two component types, i.e. we define the class expression learning problem in ontology engineering and provide an algorithm for solving it.

Learning Problem. The process of learning in logics, i.e. trying to find high-level explanations for given data, is also called *inductive reasoning* as opposed to *inference* or *deductive reasoning*. The main difference is that in deductive reasoning it is formally shown whether a statement follows from a knowledge base, whereas in inductive learning new statements are invented. Learning problems, which are similar to the one we will analyse, have been investigated in *Inductive Logic Programming* [158] and, in fact, the method presented here can be used to solve a variety of machine learning tasks apart from ontology engineering.

In the ontology learning problem we consider, we want to learn a formal description of a class A, which has (inferred or asserted) instances in the considered ontology. In the case that A is already described by a class expression C via axioms of the form $A \sqsubseteq C$ or $A \equiv C$, those can be either refined, i.e. specialised/generalised, or relearned from scratch by the learning algorithm. To define the class learning problem, we need the notion of a *retrieval* reasoner operation $R_{\mathcal{K}}(C)$. $R_{\mathcal{K}}(C)$ returns the set of all instances of C in a knowledge base $\mathcal{K}$. If $\mathcal{K}$ is clear from the context, the subscript can be omitted.

Definition 7 (class learning problem). *Let an existing named class A in a knowledge base $\mathcal{K}$ be given. The* class learning problem *is to find an expression C such that $R_{\mathcal{K}}(C) = R_{\mathcal{K}}(A)$.*

Clearly, the learned expression C is a description of (the instances of) A. Such an expression is a candidate for adding an axiom of the form $A \equiv C$ or $A \sqsubseteq C$ to the

---

[29] http://dl-learner.org
[30] http://dl.kr.org/dig/

knowledge base $\mathcal{K}$. If a solution of the learning problem exists, then the used base learning algorithm (as presented in the following subsection) is complete, i.e. guaranteed to find a correct solution if one exists in the target language and there are no time and memory constraints (see [116,117] for the proof). In most cases, we will not find a solution to the learning problem, but rather an approximation. This is natural, since a knowledge base may contain false class assignments or some objects in the knowledge base are described at different levels of detail. For instance, in Example 1, the city "Apia" might be typed as "Capital" in a knowledge base, but not related to the country "Samoa". However, if most of the other cities are related to countries via a role `isCapitalOf`, then the learning algorithm may still suggest `City and isCapitalOf at least one Country` since this describes the majority of capitals in the knowledge base well. If the knowledge engineer agrees with such a definition, then a tool can assist him in completing missing information about some capitals.

According to Occam's razor [29] simple solutions of the learning problem are to be preferred over more complex ones, because they are more readable. This is even more important in the ontology engineering context, where it is essential to suggest simple expressions to the knowledge engineer. We measure simplicity as the *length* of an expression, which is defined in a straightforward way, namely as the sum of the numbers of concept, role, quantifier, and connective symbols occurring in the expression. The algorithm is biased towards shorter expressions. Also note that, for simplicity the definition of the learning problem itself does enforce coverage, but not prediction, i.e. correct classification of objects which are added to the knowledge base in the future. Concepts with high coverage and poor prediction are said to *overfit* the data. However, due to the strong bias towards short expressions this problem occurs empirically rarely in description logics [117].

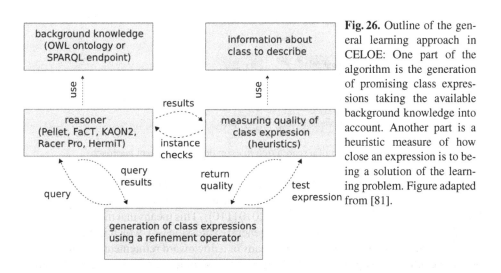

Fig. 26. Outline of the general learning approach in CELOE: One part of the algorithm is the generation of promising class expressions taking the available background knowledge into account. Another part is a heuristic measure of how close an expression is to being a solution of the learning problem. Figure adapted from [81].

Base Learning Algorithm. Figure 26 gives a brief overview of the *CELOE* algorithm, which follows the common "generate and test" approach in ILP. This means that learning is seen as a search process and several class expressions are generated and tested against a background knowledge base. Each of those class expressions is evaluated using a heuristic, which is described in the next section. A challenging part of a learning algorithm is to decide which expressions to test. In particular, such a decision should take the computed heuristic values and the structure of the background knowledge into account. For CELOE, we use the approach described in [116,117] as base, where this problem has already been analysed, implemented, and evaluated in depth. It is based on the idea of *refinement operators*:

Definition 8 (refinement operator). *A* quasi-ordering *is a reflexive and transitive relation. In a quasi-ordered space* $(S, \leq)$ *a downward (upward) refinement operator* ρ *is a mapping from S to* 2^S, *such that for any* $C \in S$ *we have that* $C' \in \rho(C)$ *implies* $C' \leq C$ $(C \leq C')$. C' *is called a* specialisation *(generalisation) of C.*

Refinement operators can be used for searching in the space of expressions. As ordering we can use subsumption. (Note that the subsumption relation $\sqsubseteq$ is a quasi-ordering.) If an expression C subsumes an expression D ($D \sqsubseteq C$), then C will cover all examples which are covered by D. This makes subsumption a suitable order for searching in expressions as it allows to prune parts of the search space without losing possible solutions.

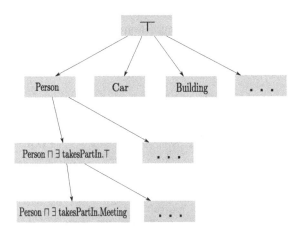

Fig. 27. Illustration of a search tree in a top down refinement approach

The approach we used is a top-down algorithm based on refinement operators as illustrated in Figure 27 (more detailed schemata can be found in the slides[31] of the ontology learning lecture of Reasoning Web 2010 [110]). This means that the first class expression, which will be tested is the most general expression ($\top$), which is then mapped to a set of more specific expressions by means of a downward refinement operator. Naturally, the refinement operator can be applied to the obtained expressions again, thereby

---

[31] http://reasoningweb.org/2010/teaching-material/lehmann.pdf

spanning a *search tree*. The search tree can be pruned when an expression does not cover sufficiently many instances of the class *A* we want to describe. One example for a path in a search tree spanned up by a downward refinement operator is the following ($\rightsquigarrow$ denotes a refinement step):

$$\top \rightsquigarrow \texttt{Person} \rightsquigarrow \texttt{Person} \sqcap \texttt{takesPartinIn}.\top$$
$$\rightsquigarrow \texttt{Person} \sqcap \texttt{takesPartIn.Meeting}$$

The heart of such a learning strategy is to define a suitable refinement operator and an appropriate search heuristics for deciding which nodes in the search tree should be expanded. The refinement operator in the considered algorithm is defined in [117]. It is based on earlier work in [116] which in turn is built on the theoretical foundations of [115]. It has been shown to be the best achievable operator with respect to a set of properties (not further described here), which are used to assess the performance of refinement operators. The learning algorithm supports conjunction, disjunction, negation, existential and universal quantifiers, cardinality restrictions, hasValue restrictions as well as boolean and double datatypes.

6.3   Finding a Suitable Heuristic

A heuristic measures how well a given class expression fits a learning problem and is used to guide the search in a learning process. To define a suitable heuristic, we first need to address the question of how to measure the accuracy of a class expression. We introduce several heuristics, which can be used for *CELOE* and later evaluate them.

We cannot simply use supervised learning from examples directly, since we do not have positive and negative examples available. We can try to tackle this problem by using the existing instances of the class as positive examples and the remaining instances as negative examples. This is illustrated in Figure 28, where $\mathcal{K}$ stands for the knowledge base and *A* for the class to describe. We can then measure accuracy as the number of correctly classified examples divided by the number of all examples. This can be computed as follows for a class expression *C* and is known as *predictive accuracy* in Machine Learning:

$$predacc(C) = 1 - \frac{|R(A) \setminus R(C)| + |R(C) \setminus R(A)|}{n} \quad n = |Ind(\mathcal{K})|$$

Here, $Ind(\mathcal{K})$ stands for the set of individuals occurring in the knowledge base. $R(A) \setminus R(C)$ are the false negatives whereas $R(C) \setminus R(A)$ are false positives. *n* is the number of all examples, which is equal to the number of individuals in the knowledge base in this case. Apart from learning definitions, we also want to be able to learn super class axioms ($A \sqsubseteq C$). Naturally, in this scenario $R(C)$ should be a superset of $R(A)$. However, we still do want $R(C)$ to be as small as possible, otherwise $\top$ would always be a solution. To reflect this in our accuracy computation, we penalise false negatives more than false positives by a factor of t ($t > 1$) and map the result to the interval [0, 1]:

$$predacc(C, t) = 1 - 2 \cdot \frac{t \cdot |R(A) \setminus R(C)| + |R(C) \setminus R(A)|}{(t + 1) \cdot n} \quad n = |Ind(\mathcal{K})|$$

While being straightforward, the outlined approach of casting class learning into a standard learning problem with positive and negative examples has the disadvantage that the number of negative examples will usually be much higher than the number of positive examples. As shown in Table 6, this may lead to overly optimistic estimates. More importantly, this accuracy measure has the drawback of having a dependency on the number of instances in the knowledge base.

Therefore, we investigated further heuristics, which overcome this problem, in particular by transferring common heuristics from information retrieval to the class learning problem:

1. *F-Measure:* F_β-Measure is based on *precision* and *recall* weighted by β. They can be computed for the class learning problem without having negative examples. Instead, we perform a retrieval for the expression C, which we want to evaluate. We can then define precision as the percentage of instances of C, which are also instances of A and recall as percentage of instances of A, which are also instances of C. This is visualised in Figure 28. F-Measure is defined as harmonic mean of precision and recall. For learning super classes, we use F_3 measure by default, which gives recall a higher weight than precision.

2. *A-Measure:* We denote the arithmetic mean of precision and recall as A-Measure. Super class learning is achieved by assigning a higher weight to recall. Using the arithmetic mean of precision and recall is uncommon in Machine Learning, since it results in too optimistic estimates. However, we found that it is useful in super class learning, where F_n is often too pessimistic even for higher n.

3. *Generalised F-Measure:* Generalised F-Measure has been published in [48] and extends the idea of F-measure by taking the three valued nature of classification in OWL/DLs into account: An individual can either belong to a class, the negation of a class or none of both cases can be proven. This differs from common binary classification tasks and, therefore, appropriate measures have been introduced (see [48] for details). Adaption for super class learning can be done in a similar fashion as for F-Measure itself.

4. *Jaccard Distance:* Since $R(A)$ and $R(C)$ are sets, we can use the well-known Jaccard coefficient to measure the similarity between both sets.

We argue that those four measures are more appropriate than predictive accuracy when applying standard learning algorithms to the ontology engineering use case. Table 6 provides some example calculations, which allow the reader to compare the different heuristics.

Efficient Heuristic Computation. Several optimisations for computing the heuristics are described in [111]. In particular, adapted approximate reasoning and stochastic approximations are discussed. Those improvements have shown to lead to order of magnitude gains in efficiency for many ontologies. We refrain from describing those methods in this chapter.

The Protégé Plugin. After implementing and testing the described learning algorithm, we integrated it into *Protégé* and *OntoWiki*. Together with the Protégé developers, we

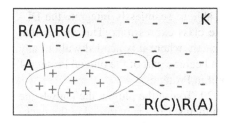 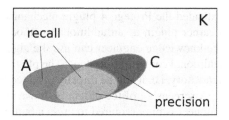

Fig. 28. Visualisation of different accuracy measurement approaches. $\mathcal{K}$ is the knowledge base, A the class to describe and C a class expression to be tested. Left side: Standard supervised approach based on using positive (instances of A) and negative (remaining instances) examples. Here, the accuracy of C depends on the number of individuals in the knowledge base. Right side: Evaluation based on two criteria: recall (*Which fraction of $R(A)$ is in $R(C)$?*) and precision (*Which fraction of $R(C)$ is in $R(A)$?*).

Table 6. Example accuracies for selected cases (eq = equivalence class axiom, sc = super class axiom). The images on the left represent an imaginary knowledge base $\mathcal{K}$ with 1000 individuals, where we want to describe the class A by using expression C. It is apparent that using predictive accuracy leads to impractical accuracies, e.g. in the first row C cannot possibly be a good description of A, but we still get 80% accuracy, since all the negative examples outside of A and C are correctly classified.

illustration	pred. acc.		F-Measure		A-Measure		Jaccard
	eq	sc	eq	sc	eq	sc	
K:1000 C:100 A:100	80%	67%	0%	0%	0%	0%	0%
K:1000 C:200 A:100	90%	92%	67%	73%	75%	88%	50%
K:1000 C:400 A:100	70%	75%	40%	48%	63%	82%	25%
K:1000 10 C:100 10 A:100	98%	97%	90%	90%	90%	90%	82%
K:1000 A:100 C:50	95%	88%	67%	61%	75%	63%	50%

extended the Protégé 4 plugin mechanism to be able to seamlessly integrate the DL-Learner plugin as an additional method to create class expressions. This means that the knowledge engineer can use the algorithm exactly where it is needed without any additional configuration steps. The plugin has also become part of the official Protégé 4 repository, i.e. it can be directly installed from within Protégé.

A screenshot of the plugin is shown in Figure 29. To use the plugin, the knowledge engineer is only required to press a button, which then starts a new thread in the background. This thread executes the learning algorithm. The used algorithm is an *anytime algorithm*, i.e. at each point in time we can always see the currently best suggestions. The GUI updates the suggestion list each second until the maximum runtime – 10 seconds by default – is reached. This means that the perceived runtime, i.e. the time after which only minor updates occur in the suggestion list, is often only one or two seconds for small ontologies. For each suggestion, the plugin displays its accuracy.

When clicking on a suggestion, it is visualized by displaying two circles: One stands for the instances of the class to describe and another circle for the instances of the suggested class expression. Ideally, both circles overlap completely, but in practice this will often not be the case. Clicking on the plus symbol in each circle shows its list of individuals. Those individuals are also presented as points in the circles and moving the mouse over such a point shows information about the respective individual. Red points show potential problems detected by the plugin. Please note that we use closed world reasoning to detect those problems. For instance, in our initial example, a capital which is not related via the property `isCapitalOf` to an instance of `Country` is marked red. If there is not only a potential problem, but adding the expression would render the ontology inconsistent, the suggestion is marked red and a warning message is displayed. Accepting such a suggestion can still be a good choice, because the problem often lies elsewhere in the knowledge base, but was not obvious before, since the ontology was not sufficiently expressive for reasoners to detect it. This is illustrated by a screencast available from the plugin homepage,[32] where the ontology becomes inconsistent after adding the axiom, and the real source of the problem is fixed afterwards. Being able to make such suggestions can be seen as a strength of the plugin.

The plugin allows the knowledge engineer to change expert settings. Those settings include the maximum suggestion search time, the number of results returned and settings related to the desired target language, e.g. the knowledge engineer can choose to stay within the OWL 2 EL profile or enable/disable certain class expression constructors. The learning algorithm is designed to be able to handle noisy data and the visualisation of the suggestions will reveal false class assignments so that they can be fixed afterwards.

The OntoWiki Plugin. Analogous to Protégé, we created a similar plugin for OntoWiki (cf. section 4). OntoWiki is a lightweight ontology editor, which allows distributed and collaborative editing of knowledge bases. It focuses on wiki-like, simple and intuitive authoring of semantic content, e.g. through inline editing of RDF content, and provides different views on instance data.

---

[32] http://dl-learner.org/wiki/ProtegePlugin

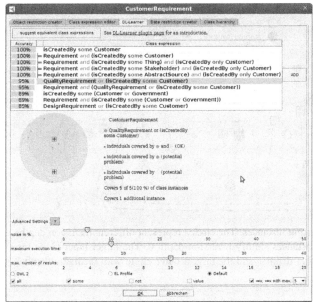

Fig. 29. A screenshot of the DL-Learner Protégé plugin. It is integrated as additional tab to create class expressions in Protégé. The user is only required to press the "suggest equivalent class expressions" button and within a few seconds they will be displayed ordered by accuracy. If desired, the knowledge engineer can visualize the instances of the expression to detect potential problems. At the bottom, optional expert configuration settings can be adopted.

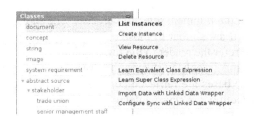

Fig. 30. The DL-Learner plugin can be invoked from the context menu of a class in OntoWiki

Recently, a fine-grained plugin mechanism and extensions architecture was added to OntoWiki. The DL-Learner plugin is technically realised by implementing an OntoWiki component, which contains the core functionality, and a module, which implements the UI embedding. The DL-Learner plugin can be invoked from several places in OntoWiki, for instance through the context menu of classes as shown in Figure 30.

The plugin accesses DL-Learner functionality through its WSDL-based web service interface. Jar files containing all necessary libraries are provided by the plugin. If a user invokes the plugin, it scans whether the web service is online at its default address. If not, it is started automatically.

A major technical difference compared to the Protégé plugin is that the knowledge base is accessed via SPARQL, since OntoWiki is a SPARQL-based web application. In Protégé, the current state of the knowledge base is stored in memory in a Java object. As a result, we cannot easily apply a reasoner on an OntoWiki knowledge base. To overcome this problem, we use the DL-Learner fragment selection mechanism described in

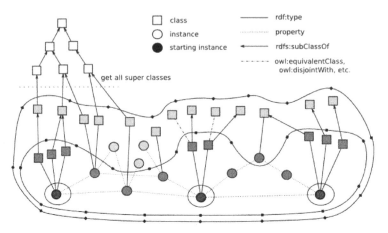

Fig. 31. Extraction with three starting instances. The circles represent different recursion depths. The circles around the starting instances signify recursion depth 0. The larger inner circle represents the fragment with recursion depth 1 and the largest outer circle with recursion depth 2. Figure taken from [81].

[81,82,40]. Starting from a set of instances, the mechanism extracts a relevant fragment from the underlying knowledge base up to some specified recursion depth. Figure 31 provides an overview of the fragment selection process. The fragment has the property that learning results on it are similar to those on the complete knowledge base. For a detailed description we refer the reader to the full article.

The fragment selection is only performed for medium to large-sized knowledge bases. Small knowledge bases are retrieved completely and loaded into the reasoner. While the fragment selection can cause a delay of several seconds before the learning algorithm starts, it also offers flexibility and scalability. For instance, we can learn class expressions in large knowledge bases such as DBpedia in OntoWiki.[33]

Figure 32 shows a screenshot of the OntoWiki plugin applied to the SWORE [171] ontology. Suggestions for learning the class "customer requirement" are shown in Manchester OWL Syntax. Similar to the Protégé plugin, the user is presented a table of suggestions along with their accuracy value. Additional details about the instances of "customer requirement", covered by a suggested class expressions and additionally contained instances can be viewed via a toggle button. The modular design of OntoWiki allows rich user interaction: Each resource, e.g. a class, property, or individual, can be viewed and subsequently modified directly from the result table as shown for "design requirement" in the screenshot. For instance, a knowledge engineer could decide to import additional information available as Linked Data and run the CELOE algorithm again to see whether different suggestions are provided with additional background knowledge.

---

[33] OntoWiki is undergoing an extensive development, aiming to support handling such large knowledge bases. A release supporting this is expected for the first half of 2012.

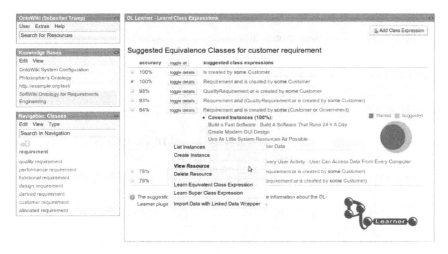

Fig. 32. Screenshot of the result table of the DL-Learner plugin in OntoWiki

Evaluation. To evaluate the suggestions made by our learning algorithm, we tested it on a variety of real-world ontologies of different sizes and domains. Please note that we intentionally do not perform an evaluation of the machine learning technique as such on existing benchmarks, since we build on the base algorithm already evaluated in detail in [117]. It was shown that this algorithm is superior to other supervised learning algorithms for OWL and at least competitive with the state of the art in ILP. Instead, we focus on its use within the ontology engineering scenario. The goals of the evaluation are to 1. determine the influence of reasoning and heuristics on suggestions, 2. to evaluate whether the method is sufficiently efficient to work on large real-world ontologies.

To perform the evaluation, we wrote a dedicated plugin for the Protégé ontology editor. This allows the evaluators to browse the ontology while deciding whether the suggestions made are reasonable. The plugin works as follows: First, all classes with at least 5 inferred instances are determined. For each such class, we run CELOE with different settings to generate suggestions for definitions. Specifically, we tested two reasoners and five different heuristics. The two reasoners are standard Pellet and Pellet combined with approximate reasoning (not described in detail here). The five heuristics are those described in Section 6.3. For each configuration of CELOE, we generate at most 10 suggestions exceeding a heuristic threshold of 90%. Overall, this means that there can be at most 2 * 5 * 10 = 100 suggestions per class – usually less, because different settings of CELOE will still result in similar suggestions. This list is shuffled and presented to the evaluators. For each suggestion, the evaluators can choose between 6 options (see Table 8):

1 The suggestion improves the ontology (improvement),
2 The suggestion is no improvement and should not be included (not acceptable) and
3 Adding the suggestion would be a modelling error (error).

In the case of existing definitions for class A, we removed them prior to learning. In this case, the evaluator could choose between three further options:

Table 7. Statistics about test ontologies

Ontology	#logical axioms	#classes	#object properties	#data properties	#individuals	DL expressivity
SC Ontology[34]	20081	28	8	5	3542	$\mathcal{AL}(\mathcal{D})$
Adhesome[35]	12043	40	33	37	2032	$\mathcal{ALCHN}(\mathcal{D})$
GeoSkills[36]	14966	613	23	21	2620	$\mathcal{ALCHOIN}(\mathcal{D})$
Eukariotic[37]	38	11	1	0	11	$\mathcal{ALCON}$
Breast Cancer[38]	878	196	22	3	113	$\mathcal{ALCROF}(\mathcal{D})$
Economy[39]	1625	339	45	8	482	$\mathcal{ALCH}(\mathcal{D})$
Resist[40]	239	349	134	38	75	$\mathcal{ALUF}(\mathcal{D})$
Finance[41]	16014	323	247	74	2466	$\mathcal{ALCROIQ}(\mathcal{D})$
Earthrealm[42]	931	2364	215	36	171	$\mathcal{ALCHO}(\mathcal{D})$

4 The learned definition is equal to the previous one and both are good (equal +),

5 The learned definition is equal to the previous one and both are bad (equal -) and

6 The learned definition is inferior to the previous one (inferior).

We used the default settings of CELOE, e.g. a maximum execution time of 10 seconds for the algorithm. The knowledge engineers were five experienced members of our research group, who made themselves familiar with the domain of the test ontologies. Each researcher worked independently and had to make 998 decisions for 92 classes between one of the options. The time required to make those decisions was approximately 40 working hours per researcher. The raw agreement value of all evaluators is 0.535 (see e.g. [5] for details) with 4 out of 5 evaluators in strong pairwise agreement (90%). The evaluation machine was a notebook with a 2 GHz CPU and 3 GB RAM.

Table 8 shows the evaluation results. All ontologies were taken from the Protégé OWL[43] and TONES[44] repositories. We randomly selected 5 ontologies comprising instance data from these two repositories, specifically the Earthrealm, Finance, Resist, Economy and Breast Cancer ontologies (see Table 7).

---

[34] http://www.mindswap.org/ontologies/SC.owl
[35] http://www.sbcny.org/datasets/adhesome.owl
[36] http://i2geo.net/ontologies/current/GeoSkills.owl
[37] http://www.co-ode.org/ontologies/eukariotic/2005/06/01/eukariotic.owl
[38] http://acl.icnet.uk/%7Emw/MDM0.73.owl
[39] http://reliant.teknowledge.com/DAML/Economy.owl
[40] http://www.ecs.soton.ac.uk/~aoj04r/resist.owl
[41] http://www.fadyart.com/Finance.owl
[42] http://sweet.jpl.nasa.gov/1.1/earthrealm.owl
[43] http://protegewiki.stanford.edu/index.php/Protege_Ontology_Library
[44] http://owl.cs.manchester.ac.uk/repository/

Table 8. Options chosen by evaluators aggregated by class. FIC stands for the fast instance checker, which is an approximate reasoning procedure.

reasoner/heuristic	improvement	equal quality (+)	equal quality (-)	inferior	not acceptable	error	missed improvements in %	selected position on suggestion list (incl. std. deviation)	avg. accuracy of selected suggestion in %
Pellet/F-Measure	16.70	0.44	0.66	0.00	64.66	17.54	14.95	2.82 ± 2.93	96.91
Pellet/Gen. F-Measure	15.24	0.44	0.66	0.11	66.60	16.95	16.30	2.78 ± 3.01	92.76
Pellet/A-Measure	16.70	0.44	0.66	0.00	64.66	17.54	14.95	2.84 ± 2.93	98.59
Pellet/pred. acc.	16.59	0.44	0.66	0.00	64.83	17.48	15.22	2.69 ± 2.82	98.05
Pellet/Jaccard	16.81	0.44	0.66	0.00	64.66	17.43	14.67	2.80 ± 2.91	95.26
Pellet FIC/F-Measure	36.30	0.55	0.55	0.11	52.62	9.87	1.90	2.25 ± 2.74	95.01
Pellet FIC/Gen. F-M.	33.41	0.44	0.66	0.00	53.41	12.09	7.07	1.77 ± 2.69	89.42
Pellet FIC/A-Measure	36.19	0.55	0.55	0.00	52.84	9.87	1.63	2.21 ± 2.71	98.65
Pellet FIC/pred. acc.	32.99	0.55	0.55	0.11	55.58	10.22	4.35	2.17 ± 2.55	98.92
Pellet FIC/Jaccard	36.30	0.55	0.55	0.11	52.62	9.87	1.90	2.25 ± 2.74	94.07

The results in Table 8 show which options were selected by the evaluators. It clearly indicates that the usage of approximate reasoning is sensible. The results are, however, more difficult to interpret with regard to the different employed heuristics. Using predictive accuracy did not yield good results and, surprisingly, generalised F-Measure also had a lower percentage of cases where option 1 was selected. The other three heuristics generated very similar results. One reason is that those heuristics are all based on precision and recall, but in addition the low quality of some of the randomly selected test ontologies posed a problem. In cases of too many very severe modelling errors, e.g. conjunctions and disjunctions mixed up in an ontology or inappropriate domain and range restrictions, the quality of suggestions decreases for each of the heuristics. This is the main reason why the results for the different heuristics are very close. Particularly, generalised F-Measure can show its strengths mainly for properly designed ontologies. For instance, column 2 of Table 8 shows that it missed 7% of possible improvements. This means that for 7% of all classes, one of the other four heuristics was able to find an appropriate definition, which was not suggested when employing generalised F-Measure. The last column in this table shows that the average value of generalised F-Measure is quite low. As explained previously, it distinguishes between cases when an individual is instance of the observed class expression, its negation, or none of both. In many cases, the reasoner could not detect that an individual is instance of the negation of a class expression, because of the absence of disjointness axioms and negation in the knowledge base, which explains the low average values of generalised F-Measure. Column 4 of Table 8 shows that many selected expressions are amongst the top 5 (out of 10) in the suggestion list, i.e. providing 10 suggestions appears to be a reasonable choice.

In general, the improvement rate is only at about 35% according to Table 8 whereas it usually exceeded 50% in preliminary experiments with other real-world ontologies with fewer or less severe modelling errors. Since CELOE is based on OWL reasoning, it is clear that schema modelling errors will have an impact on the quality of suggestions. As a consequence, we believe that the CELOE algorithm should be combined with ontology debugging techniques. We have obtained first positive results in this direction and plan to pursue it in future work. However, the evaluation also showed that CELOE does still work in ontologies, which probably were never verified by an OWL reasoner.

Summary. We presented the CELOE learning method specifically designed for extending OWL ontologies. Five heuristics were implemented and analysed in conjunction with CELOE along with several performance improvements. A method for approximating heuristic values has been introduced, which is useful beyond the ontology engineering scenario to solve the challenge of dealing with a large number of examples in ILP [203]. Furthermore, we biased the algorithm towards short solutions and implemented optimisations to increase readability of the suggestions made. The resulting algorithm was implemented in the open source DL-Learner framework. We argue that CELOE is the first ILP based algorithm, which turns the idea of learning class expressions for extending ontologies into practice. CELOE is integrated into two plugins for the ontology editors Protégé and OntoWiki and can be invoked using just a few mouse clicks.

7   Linked Data Quality

Linked Open Data (LOD) has provided, over the past several years, an unprecedented volume of structured data currently amount to 50 billion facts, represented as RDF triples. Although publishing large amounts of data on the Web is certainly a step in the right direction, the published data is only as useful as its quality. On the Data Web we have very varying quality of information covering various domains since data is merged together from different autonomous evolving data sources on the Web. For example, data extracted from semi-structured or even unstructured sources, such as DBpedia, often contains inconsistencies as well as mis-represented and incomplete information. Despite data quality in LOD being an essential concept, the autonomy and openness of the information providers makes the web vulnerable to missing, inaccurate, incomplete, inconsistent or outdated information.

Data quality is commonly conceived as *fitness for use* [97,202] for a certain application or use case. However, even datasets with quality problems might be useful for certain applications, as long as the quality is in the required range. For example, in the case of DBpedia the data quality is perfectly sufficient for enriching Web search with facts or suggestions about common sense information, such as entertainment topics. In such a scenario, DBpedia can be used to show related movies and personal information, when a user searches for an actor. In this case, it is rather neglectable, when in relatively few cases, a related movie or some personal fact is missing. For developing a medical application, on the other hand, the quality of DBpedia is probably completely insufficient. It should be noted that even the traditional, document-oriented Web has content of varying quality and is still perceived to be extremely useful by most people.

Consequently, one of the key challenges is to determine the quality of datasets published on the Web and making this quality information explicitly available. Assuring data quality is particularly a challenge in LOD as it involves a set of autonomously evolving data sources. Other than on the document Web, where information quality can be only indirectly (e.g. via page rank) or vaguely defined, there are much more concrete and measurable data quality metrics available for structured information such as accuracy of facts, completeness, adequacy of semantic representation or degree of understandability.

In this chapter, we first define the basic concepts of data quality (subsection 7.1), then report the formal definitions of a set of 18 different dimensions along with their respective metrics identified in [212] (subsection 7.2). Thereafter, we compare a set of currently available tools specially designed to assess the quality of Linked Data (subsection 7.7).

7.1 Data Quality Concepts

In this section, we introduce the basic concepts of data quality to help the readers understand these terminologies in their consequent usage.

Data Quality. The term *data quality* is commonly conceived as a multi-dimensional construct with a popular definition as the "fitness for use" [97]. In case of the Semantic Web, there are varying concepts of data quality such as the semantic metadata on the one hand and the notion of link quality on the other. There are several characteristics of data quality that should be considered i.e. the completeness, accuracy, consistency and validity on the one hand and the representational consistency, conciseness as well as the timeliness, understandability, availability and verifiability on the other hand.

Data Quality Problems. A set of issues that can affect the potentiality of the applications that use the data are termed as data quality problems. The problems may vary from the incompleteness of data, inconsistency in representation, invalid syntax or inaccuracy.

Data Quality Dimensions and Metrics. Data quality assessment involves the measurement of quality *dimensions* (or *criteria*) that are relevant to the user. A data quality assessment *metric* (or *measure*) is a procedure for measuring an information quality dimension [26]. The metrics are basically heuristics designed to fit a specific assessment situation [120]. Since the dimensions are rather abstract concepts, the assessment metrics rely on quality *indicators* that can be used for the assessment of the quality of a data source w.r.t the criteria [59].

Data Quality Assessment Method. A data quality assessment methodology is the process of evaluating if a piece of data meets the information consumers need for a specific use case [26]. The process involves measuring the quality dimensions that are relevant to the user and comparing the assessment results with the users quality requirements.

7.2 Linked Data Quality Dimensions

In [212], a core set of 18 different data quality dimensions were reported that can be applied to assess the quality of Linked Data. These dimensions are divided into the following groups:

- Accessibility dimensions
- Intrinsic dimensions
- Contextual dimensions
- Representational dimensions

Figure 33 shows the classification of the dimensions into these four different groups as well as the relations between them.

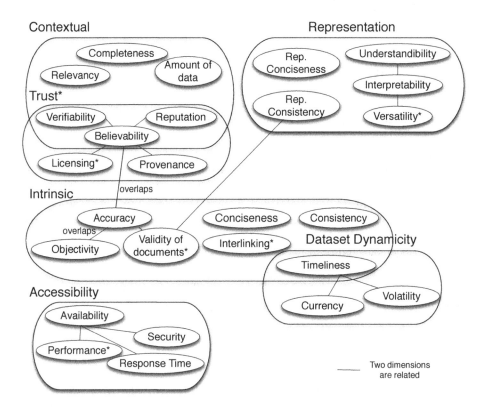

Fig. 33. Linked data quality dimensions and the relations between them [Source: [212].]

Use Case Scenario. Since data quality is conceived as "fitness for use", we introduce a specific use case that will allow us to illustrate the importance of each dimension with the help of an example. The use case is about an intelligent flight search engine, which relies on aggregating data from several datasets. The search engine obtains information about airports and airlines from an airline dataset (e.g. *OurAirports*[45], *OpenFlights*[46]).

---

[45] http://thedatahub.org/dataset/ourairports
[46] http://thedatahub.org/dataset/open-flights

Information about the location of countries, cities and particular addresses is obtained from a spatial dataset (e.g. *LinkedGeoData*[47]). Additionally, aggregators pull all the information related to flights from different booking services (e.g., *Expedia*[48]) and represent this information as RDF. This allows a user to query the integrated dataset for a flight between any start and end destination for any time period. We will use this scenario throughout as an example to explain each quality dimension through a quality issue.

7.3 Accessibility Dimensions

The dimensions belonging to this category involve aspects related to the access, authenticity and retrieval of data to obtain either the entire or some portion of the data (or from another linked dataset) for a particular use case. There are five dimensions that are part of this group, which are *availability, licensing, interlinking, security* and *performance*.

Availability. Bizer [25] adopted the definition of availability from Pipino et al. [164] as "the extent to which information is available, or easily and quickly retrievable". Flemming [59] referred to availability as the proper functioning of all access methods. However, the definition by Pipino et al. is more related to the measurement of available information rather than to the method of accessing the information as implied in the latter explanation by Flemming.

Definition 9 (Availability). *Availability of a dataset is the extent to which data (or some portion of it) is present, obtainable and ready for use.*

Metrics. The metrics identified for availability are:

- A1: checking whether the server responds to a SPARQL query [59]
- A2: checking whether an RDF dump is provided and can be downloaded [59]
- A3: detection of dereferencability of URIs by checking:
  - for dead or broken links [85], i.e. that when an HTTP-GET request is sent, the status code `404 Not Found` is not returned [59]
  - that useful data (particularly RDF) is returned upon lookup of a URI [85]
  - for changes in the URI, i.e. compliance with the recommended way of implementing redirections using the status code `303 See Other` [59]
- A4: detect whether the HTTP response contains the header field stating the appropriate content type of the returned file, e.g. `application/rdf+xml` [85]
- A5: dereferncability of all forward links: all available triples where the local URI is mentioned in the subject (i.e. the description of the resource) [86]

Example. Let us consider the case in which a user looks up a flight in our flight search engine. She requires additional information such as car rental and hotel booking at the destination, which is present in another dataset and interlinked with the flight dataset. However, instead of retrieving the results, she receives an error response code `404 Not Found`. This is an indication that the requested resource cannot be dereferenced and is therefore unavailable. Thus, with this error code, she may assume that either there is no information present at that specified URI or the information is unavailable.

---

[47] linkedgeodata.org
[48] http://www.expedia.com/

Licensing. Licensing is a new quality dimensions not considered for relational databases but mandatory in the data world such as LD. Flemming [59] and Hogan et al. [86] both stated that each RDF document should contain a license under which the content can be (re-)used, in order to enable information consumers to use the data under clear legal terms. Additionally, the existence of a machine-readable indication (by including the specifications in a VoID[49] description) as well as a human-readable indication of a license are important not only for the permissions a licence grants but as an indication of which requirements the consumer has to meet [59]. Although both these studies do not provide a formal definition, they agree on the use and importance of licensing in terms of data quality.

Definition 10 (Licensing). *Licensing is defined as the granting of permission for a consumer to re-use a dataset under defined conditions.*

Metrics. The metrics identified for licensing are:

- L1: machine-readable indication of a license in the VoID description or in the dataset itself [59,86]
- L2: human-readable indication of a license in the documentation of the dataset [59,86]
- L3: detection of whether the dataset is attributed under the same license as the original [59]

Example. Since our flight search engine aggregates data from several existing data sources, a clear indication of the license allows the search engine to re-use the data from the airlines websites. For example, the LinkedGeoData dataset is licensed under the Open Database License[50], which allows others to copy, distribute and use the data and produce work from the data allowing modifications and transformations. Due to the presence of this specific license, the flight search engine is able to re-use this dataset to pull geo-spatial information and feed it to the search engine.

Interlinking. Interlinking is a relevant dimension in LD since it supports data integration. Interlinking is provided by RDF triples that establish a link between the entity identified by the subject with the entity identified by the object. Through the typed RDF links, data items are effectively interlinked. The importance of interlinking, also know as "mapping coherence" can be classified in one of the four scenarios: (i) Frameworks; (ii) Terminological Reasoning; (iii) Data Transformation; (iv) Query Processing, as identified in [133]. Even though the core articles in this survey do not contain a formal definition for interlinking, they provide metrics on how to measure this dimension.

Definition 11 (Interlinking). *Interlinking refers to the degree to which entities that represent the same concept are linked to each other, be it within or between two or more data sources.*

---

[49] http://vocab.deri.ie/void
[50] http://opendatacommons.org/licenses/odbl/

Metrics. The metrics identified for interlinking are:

- I1: detection of:
  - interlinking degree: how many hubs there are in a network[51] [73]
  - clustering coefficient: how dense is the network [73]
  - centrality: indicates the likelihood of a node being on the shortest path between two other nodes [73]
  - whether there are open sameAs chains in the network [73]
  - how much value is added to the description of a resource through the use of sameAs edges [73]
- I2: detection of the existence and usage of external URIs (e.g. using `owl:sameAs` links) [85,86]
- I3: detection of all local in-links or back-links: all triples from a dataset that have the resource's URI as the object [86]

Example. In our flight search engine, the instance of the country "`United States`" in the airline dataset should be interlinked with the instance "`America`" in the spatial dataset. This interlinking can help when a user queries for a flight, as the search engine can display the correct route from the start destination to the end destination by correctly combining information for the same country from both the datasets. Since names of various entities can have different URIs in different datasets, their interlinking can help in disambiguation.

Security. Flemming [59] referred to security as "the possibility to restrict access to the data and to guarantee the confidentiality of the communication between a source and its consumers". Additionally, Flemming referred to the verifiability dimension as the mean a consumer is provided with to examine the data for correctness. Bizer [25] adopted the definition of verifiability from Naumann et al. [143] as the "degree and ease with which the information can be checked for correctness". Without such means, the assurance of the correctness of the data would come from the consumer's trust in that source. It can be observed here that on the one hand Naumann et al. provided a formal definition whereas Flemming described the dimension by providing its advantages and metrics. Thus, security and verifiability point towards the same quality dimension i.e. to avoid alterations of the dataset and verify its correctness.

Definition 12 (Security). *Security is the extent to which data is protected against alteration and misuse.*

Metrics. The metrics identified for security are:

- S1: degree of using digital signatures to sign documents containing an RDF serialization, a SPARQL result set or signing an RDF graph [37,59]
- S2: verifying authenticity of the dataset based on provenance information such as the author and his contributors, the publisher of the data and its sources, if present in the dataset [59]

---

[51] In [73], a network is a set of facts provided by the graph of the Web of Data, excluding the blank nodes.

Example: In our use case, if we assume that the flight search engine obtains flight information from arbitrary airline websites, there is a risk for receiving incorrect information from malicious websites. For instance, an airline or sales agency website can pose as its competitor and display incorrect expensive flight fares. Thus, by this spoofing attack, this airline can prevent users to book with the competitor. In that case, the use of digital signatures for published RDF data allows to verify the identity of the publisher.

Performance. Performance is a dimension that has an influence on the quality of the information system or search engine, however not on the data set itself. Flemming [59] states that "the performance criterion comprises aspects of enhancing the performance of a source as well as measuring of the actual values". Flemming [59] gave a general description of performance without explaining the meaning while Hogan et al. [86] described the issues related to performance. Moreover, Bizer [25], defined response-time as "the delay between submission of a request by the user and reception of the response from the system". Thus, response-time and performance point towards the same quality dimension.

Definition 13 (Performance). *Performance refers to the efficiency of a system that binds to a large dataset, that is, the more performant a data source is the more efficiently a system can process data.*

   Metrics. The metrics identified for performance are:

- P1: checking for usage of slash-URIs where large amounts of data is provided[52] [59]
- P2: low latency[53]: (minimum) delay between submission of a request by the user and reception of the response from the system [25,59]
- P3: high throughput: (maximum) number of answered HTTP-requests per second [59]
- P4: scalability - detection of whether the time to answer an amount of ten requests divided by ten is not longer than the time it takes to answer one request [59]

Example. In our use case, the performance may depend on the type and complexity of the query by a large number of users. Our flight search engine can perform well by considering response-time when deciding which sources to use to answer a query.

Intra-relations. The dimensions in this group are related with each other as follows: performance (response-time) of a system is related to the availability dimension. Only if a dataset is available and has low response time, it can perform well. Also, interlinking is related to availability because only if a dataset is available, it can be interlinked and the interlinks can be traversed. Additionally, the dimensions security and licensing are related since providing a license and specifying conditions for re-use helps secure the dataset against alterations and misuse.

---

[52] http://www.w3.org/wiki/HashVsSlash

[53] Latency is the amount of time from issuing the query until the first information reaches the user [143].

7.4   Intrinsic Dimensions

Intrinsic dimensions are those that are independent of the user's context. There are five dimensions that are part of this group, which are *syntactic validity, semantic accuracy, consistency, conciseness* and *completeness*. These dimensions focus on whether information correctly (syntactically and semantically), compactly and completely represents the real world data and whether information is logically consistent in itself.

Syntactic Validity. Flemming [59] defined the term validity of documents as "the valid usage of the underlying vocabularies and the valid syntax of the documents". Fürber et al. [64] classified accuracy into syntactic and semantic accuracy. He explained that a "value is syntactically accurate, when it is part of a legal value set for the represented domain or it does not violate syntactical rules defined for the domain". We associate the validity of documents defined by Flemming to syntactic validity. We distinguish between the two types of accuracy defined by Fürber et al. and form two dimensions: *Syntactic validity* (syntactic accuracy) and *Semantic accuracy*. Additionally, Hogan et al. [85] identify syntax errors such as RDF/XML syntax errors, malformed datatype literals and literals incompatible with datatype range, which we associate with syntactic validity.

Definition 14 (Syntactic validity). *Syntactic validity is defined as the degree to which an RDF document conforms to the specification of the serialization format.*

Metrics. The metrics identified for syntactic validity are:

- SV1: detecting syntax errors using validators [59,85]
- SV2: detecting use of:
  - explicit definition of the allowed values for a certain datatype [64]
  - syntactic rules (type of characters allowed and/or the pattern of literal values) [64]
- SV3: detection of ill-typed literals which do not abide by the lexical syntax for their respective datatype that can occur if a value is (i) malformed or (ii) is a member of an incompatible datatype [85]

Example. In our use case, let us assume that the ID of the flight between Paris and New York is A123 while in our search engine the same flight instance is represented as A231. Since this ID is included in one of the datasets, it is considered to be syntactically accurate since it is a valid ID (even though it is incorrect).

Semantic Accuracy. Bizer [25] adopted the definition of accuracy from Wang et al. [200] as the "degree of correctness and precision with which information in an information system represents states of the real world". Furthermore, Furber et al. [64] classified accuracy into syntactic and semantic accuracy. He explained that values are semantically accurate when they represent the correct state of an object. Based on this definition, we also considered the problems of *spurious annotation* and *inaccurate annotation* (inaccurate labeling and inaccurate classification) identified in Lei et al. [119] related to the semantic accuracy dimension.

Definition 15 (Semantic accuracy). *Semantic accuracy is defined as the degree to which data values correctly represent the real world facts.*

Metrics. The metrics identified for semantic accuracy are:

- SA1: detection of outliers by using distance-based, deviations-based and distribution-based methods [26]
- SA2: detection of inaccurate values by using functional dependency rules[54] [64,209]
- SA3: detection of inaccurate annotations[55], labellings[56] or classifications[57] using the formula:
  $1 - \frac{\text{inaccurate instances}}{\text{total no. of instances}} * \frac{\text{balanced distance metric}}{\text{total no. of instances}}$[58] [119]
- SA4: verifying correctness of the dataset with the help of unbiased trusted third party (humans) [25]
- SA5: detection of misuse of properties[59] by using profiling statistics, which support the detection of discordant values or misused properties and facilitate to find valid values for specific properties [30]
- SA6: ratio of the number of semantically valid rules[60] to the number of nontrivial rules[61] [39]

Example. In our use case, let us assume that the ID of the flight between Paris and New York is A123 while in our search engine the same flight instance is represented as A231. In this case, the instance is semantically inaccurate since the flight ID does not represent its real-world state i.e. A123.

Consistency. Bizer [25] adopted the definition of consistency from Mecella et al., [132] as when "two or more values do not conflict with each other". Similarly, Hogan et al. [85] defined consistency as "no contradictions in the data". Another definition was given by Mendes et al. [134] where "a dataset is consistent if it is free of conflicting information". Additionally, Böhm et al. [30] and Mostafavi et al. [139] present metrics to assess consistency. However, it should be noted that for some languages such as OWL DL, there are clearly defined semantics, including clear definitions what inconsistency means. In description logics, model based semantics are used: A knowledge base is a

---

[54] Functional dependencies are dependencies between the values of two or more different properties.

[55] where an instance of the semantic metadata set can be mapped back to more than one real world object or in other cases, where there is no object to be mapped back to an instance.

[56] where mapping from the instance to the object is correct but not properly labeled.

[57] in which the knowledge of the source object has been correctly identified by not accurately classified.

[58] Balanced distance metric is an algorithm that calculates the distance between the extracted (or learned) concept and the target concept [129]

[59] Properties are often misused when no applicable property exists.

[60] valid rules are generated from the real data and validated against a set of principles specified in the semantic network

[61] The intuition is that the larger a dataset is, the more closely it should reflect the basic domain principles and the less semantically incorrect rules will be generated.

set of axioms. A model is an interpretation, which satisfies all axioms in the knowledge base. A knowledge base is consistent if and only if it has a model [16].

Definition 16 (**Consistency**). *Consistency means that a knowledge base is free of (logical/formal) contradictions with respect to particular knowledge representation and inference mechanisms.*

Metrics. A straighforward way to check for consistency is to load the knowledge base into a reasoner and check whether it is consistent. However, for certain knowledge bases (e.g. very large or inherently inconsistent ones) this approach is not feasible. For such cases, specific aspects of consistency can be checked individually. Some important metrics identified in the literature are:

- CS1: detection of use of entities as members of disjoint classes using the formula: $\frac{\text{no. of entities described as members of disjoint classes}}{\text{total no. of entities described in the dataset}}$ [85]
- CS2: detection of misplaced classes or properties[62] using entailment rules that indicate the position of a term in a triple [85]
- CS3: detection of misuse of `owl:DatatypeProperty` or `owl:ObjectProperty` through the ontology maintainer[63] [85]
- CS4: detection of use of members of `owl:DeprecatedClass` or `owl:DeprecatedProperty` through the ontology maintainer or by specifying manual mappings from deprecated terms to compatible terms [85]
- CS5: detection of bogus `owl:InverseFunctionalProperty` values by checking the uniqueness and validity of the inverse-functional values [85]
- CS6: detection of the re-definition by third parties of external classes/ properties (ontology hijacking) such that reasoning over data using those external terms is affected [85]
- CS7: detection of negative dependencies/correlation among properties using association rules [30]
- CS8: detection of inconsistencies in spatial data through semantic and geometric constraints [139]

Example. Let us assume a user looking for flights between Paris and New York on the 21st of December, 2013. Her query returns the following results:

```
Flight From  To       Arrival Departure
A123   Paris NewYork 14:50      22:35
A123   Paris London  14:50      22:35
```

The results show that the flight number A123 has two different destinations[64] at the same date and same time of arrival and departure, which is inconsistent with the ontology definition that one flight can only have one destination at a specific time and date. This contradiction arises due to inconsistency in data representation, which is detected by using inference and reasoning.

---

[62] For example, a URI defined as a class is used as a property or vice-a-versa.

[63] For example, attribute properties used between two resources and relation properties used with literal values.

[64] Under the assumption that we can infer that NewYork and London are different entities or, alternatively, make the unique names assumption.

Conciseness. Mendes et al. [134] classified conciseness into schema and instance level conciseness. On the schema level (intensional), "a dataset is concise if it does not contain redundant attributes (two equivalent attributes with different names)". Thus, intensional conciseness measures the number of unique schema elements (i.e. properties and classes) of a dataset in relation to the overall number of schema elements in a schema. On the data (instance) level (extensional), "a dataset is concise if it does not contain redundant objects (two equivalent objects with different identifiers)". Thus, extensional conciseness measures the number of unique objects in relation to the overall number of objects in the dataset. This definition of conciseness is very similar to the definition of 'uniqueness' defined by Fürber et al. [64] as the "degree to which data is free of redundancies, in breadth, depth and scope". This comparison shows that uniqueness and conciseness point to the same dimension. Redundancy occurs when there are *equivalent* schema elements with different names/identifiers (in case of intensional conciseness) and when there are *equivalent* objects (instances) with different identifiers (in case of extensional conciseness) in a dataset.

Definition 17 (Conciseness). *Conciseness refers to the minimization of redundancy of entities at the schema and the data level. Conciseness is classified into (i) intensional conciseness (schema level) which refers to the case when the data does not contain redundant schema elements (properties and classes) and (ii) extensional conciseness (data level) which refers to the case when the data does not contain redundant objects (instances).*

Metrics. The metrics identified for conciseness are:

- CN1: intensional conciseness measured by $\frac{\text{no. of unique properties/classes of a dataset}}{\text{total no. of properties/classes in a target schema}}$ [134]
- CN2: extensional conciseness measured by:
  - $\frac{\text{no. of unique instances of a dataset}}{\text{total number of instances representations in the dataset}}$ [134] or
  - $1 - \frac{\text{total no. of instances that violate the uniqueness rule}}{\text{total no. of relevant instances}}$ [64,119]
- CN3: detection of unambiguous annotations using the formula:
  $1 - \frac{\text{no. of ambiguous instances}}{\text{no. of the instances contained in the semantic metadata set}}$[65] [119]

Example. In our flight search engine, an example of intensional conciseness would be a particular flight, say A123, being represented by two different properties in the same dataset, such as http://flights.org/airlineID and http://flights.org/name. This redundancy ('airlineID' and 'name' in this case) can ideally be solved by fusing the two properties and keeping only one unique identifier. On the other hand, an example of extensional conciseness is when both these identifiers of the same flight have the same information associated with them in both the datasets, thus duplicating the information.

Completeness. Bizer [25] adopted the definition of completeness from Pipino et al. [164] as "the degree to which information is not missing". Fürber et al. [64] further classified completeness into: (i) Schema completeness, which is the degree to which

---

[65] detection of an instance mapped back to more than one real world object leading to more than one interpretation.

classes and properties are not missing in a schema; (ii) Column completeness, which is a function of the missing property values for a specific property/column; and (iii) Population completeness, which refers to the ratio between classes represented in an information system and the complete population. Mendes et al. [134] distinguish completeness on the schema and the data level. On the schema level, a dataset is complete if it contains all of the attributes needed for a given task. On the data (i.e. instance) level, a dataset is complete if it contains all of the necessary objects for a given task. As can be observed, Pipino et al. provided a general definition whereas Fürber et al. provided a set of sub-categories for completeness. On the other hand, the two types of completeness defined in Mendes et al. can be mapped to the two categories (i) Schema completeness and (iii) Population completeness provided by Fürber et al.

Definition 18 (Completeness). *Completeness refers to the degree to which all required information is present in a particular dataset. In terms of LD, completeness comprises of the following aspects: (i) Schema completeness, the degree to which the classes and properties of an ontology are represented, thus can be called "ontology completeness", (ii) Property completeness, measure of the missing values for a specific property, (iii) Population completeness is the percentage of all real-world objects of a particular type that are represented in the datasets and (iv) Interlinking completeness, which has to be considered especially in LD, refers to the degree to which instances in the dataset are interlinked.*

Metrics. The metrics identified for completeness are:

- CM1: schema completeness - no. of classes and properties represented / total no. of classes and properties [25,64,134]
- CM2: property completeness - no. of values represented for a specific property / total no. of values for a specific property [25,64]
- CM3: population completeness - no. of real-world objects are represented / total no. of real-world objects [25,64,134]
- CM4: interlinking completeness - no. of instances in the dataset that are interlinked / total no. of instances in a dataset [73]

It should be noted, that in this case, users should assume a closed-world-assumption where a gold standard dataset is available and can be used to compare against the converted dataset.

Example. In our use case, the flight search engine contains complete information to include all the airports and airport codes such that it allows a user to find an optimal route from the start to the end destination (even in cases when there is no direct flight). For example, the user wants to travel from Santa Barbara to San Francisco. Since our flight search engine contains interlinks between these close airports, the user is able to locate a direct flight easily.

Intra-relations. The dimensions in this group are related to each other as follows: Data can be semantically accurate by representing the real world state but still can be inconsistent. However, if we merge accurate datasets, we will most likely get fewer inconsistencies than merging inaccurate datasets. On the other hand, being syntactically valid does not necessarily mean that the value is semantically accurate. Moreover, if a dataset is complete, syntactic validity, semantic accuracy and consistency checks need to be performed to determine if the values have been completed correctly. Additionally, conciseness is related to completeness since both point towards the dataset having all, however unique (non-redundant) information. However, if data integration leads to duplication of instances, it may lead to contradictory values thus leading to inconsistency [28].

7.5 Contextual Dimensions

Contextual dimensions are those that highly depend on the context of the task at hand. There are four dimensions that are part of this group, namely *relevancy, trustworthiness, understandability* and *timeliness*.

Relevancy. Bizer [25] adopted the definition of relevancy from Pipino et al. [164] as "the extent to which information is applicable and helpful for the task at hand". Additionally, Bizer [25] adopted the definition for the amount-of-data dimension from Pipino et al. [164] as "the extent to which the volume of data is appropriate for the task at hand". Thus, since the amount-of-data dimension is similar to the relevancy dimension, we merge both dimensions. Flemming [59] defined amount-of-data as the "criterion influencing the usability of a data source". While Pipino et al. provided a formal definition, Flemming and Chen et al. explained the dimension by mentioning its advantages.

Definition 19 (Relevancy). *Relevancy refers to the provision of information which is in accordance with the task at hand and important to the users' query.*

Metrics. The metrics identified for relevancy are:

- R1: obtaining relevant data by:
  - counting the occurrence of relevant terms (keywords) within meta-data attributes (e.g. title, description, subject) [25]
  - using a combination of hyperlink analysis and information retrieval methods such as the vector space model that assigns higher weight to terms (keywords) that appear within the meta-data attribuftes [25]
  - ranking (a numerical value similar to PageRank), which determines the centrality of RDF documents and statements [31])
- R2: measuring the coverage (i.e. number of entities described in a dataset) and level of detail (i.e. number of properties) in a dataset to ensure that there exists an appropriate volume of relevant data for a particular task [59]

Example. When a user is looking for flights between any two cities, only relevant information i.e. departure and arrival airports and starting and ending time, duration and cost per person should be provided. Some datasets, in addition to relevant information, also contain much irrelevant data such as car rental, hotel booking, travel insurance etc. and as a consequence a lot of irrelevant extra information is provided. Providing irrelevant data distracts service developers and potentially users and wastes network resources. Instead, restricting the dataset to only flight related information, simplifies application development and increases the likelihood to return only relevant results to users.

Trustworthiness. Trustworthiness is a crucial topic due to the availability and the high volume of data from varying sources on the Web of Data. Bizer [25] adopted the definition of trust from Pipino et al. [164] as "the extent to which information is regarded as true and credible". Jacobi et al. [94], similar to Pipino et al., referred to trustworthiness as a subjective measure of a user's belief that the data is "true". Gil et al. [67] used reputation of an entity or a dataset either as a result from direct experience or recommendations from others to establish trust. Additionally, Bizer [25] adopted the definition of objectivity from Pipino et al. [164] as "the extent to which information is unbiased, unprejudiced and impartial." Thus, reputation as well as objectivity are part of the trustworthiness dimension. Other articles [31,66,68,70,71,76,134,184] provide metrics for assessing trustworthiness.

Definition 20 (Trustworthiness). *Trustworthiness is defined as the degree to which the information is accepted to be correct, true, real and credible.*

Metrics. The metrics identified for trustworthiness are:

- T1: computing statement trust values based on:
  - provenance information which can be either unknown or a value in the interval [-1,1] where 1: absolute belief, -1: absolute disbelief and 0: lack of belief/disbelief [76]
  - opinion-based method, which use trust annotations made by several individuals [68,76]
  - provenance information and trust annotations in Semantic Web-based social-networks [70]
- T2: using annotations for data to encode two facets of information:
  - blacklists (indicates that the referent data is known to be harmful) [31] and
  - authority (a boolean value which uses the Linked Data principles to conservatively determine whether or not information can be trusted) [31]
- T3: using trust ontologies that assigns trust values that can be transferred from known to unknown data [94] using:
  - content-based methods (from content or rules) and
  - metadata-based methods (based on reputation assignments, user ratings, and provenance, rather than the content itself)
- T4: computing trust values between two entities through a path by using:
  - a propagation algorithm based on statistical techniques [184]
  - in case there are several paths, trust values from all paths are aggregated based on a weighting mechanism [184]
- T5: computing trustworthiness of the information provider by:
  - construction of decision networks informed by provenance graphs [66]
  - checking whether the provider/contributor is contained in a list of trusted providers [25]
  - indicating the level of trust for the publisher on a scale of 1 − 9 [67,71]
  - no bias or opinion expressed when a data provider interprets or analyses facts [25]

- T6: checking content trust[66] based on associations (e.g. anything having a relation-ship to a resource such as author of the dataset) that transfer trust from content to resources [67]
- T7: assignment of explicit trust ratings to the dataset by humans or analyzing ex-ternal links or page ranks [134]

Example. In our flight search engine use case, if the flight information is provided by trusted and well-known airlines then a user is more likely to trust the information then when it is provided by an unknown travel agency. Generally information about a product or service (e.g. a flight) can be more trusted, when it is directly published by the producer or service provider (e.g. the airline). On the other hand, if a user retrieves information from a previously unknown source, she can decide whether to believe this information by checking whether the source is well-known or if it is contained in a list of trusted providers.

Understandability. Bizer [25] adopted the definition of understandability from Pipino et al. [164] stating that "understandability is the extent to which data is easily compre-hended by the information consumer". Flemming [59] related understandability also to the comprehensibility of data i.e. the ease with which human consumers can under-stand and utilize the data. Thus, comprehensibility can be interchangeably used with understandability.

Definition 21 (Understandability). *Understandability refers to the ease with which data can be comprehended without ambiguity and be used by a human information consumer.*

Metrics. The metrics identified for understandability are:

- U1: detection of human-readable labelling of classes, properties and entities as well as indication of metadata (e.g. name, description, website) of a dataset [59,86]
- U2: detect whether the pattern of the URIs is provided [59]
- U3: detect whether a regular expression that matches the URIs is present [59]
- U4: detect whether examples of SPARQL queries are provided [59]
- U5: checking whether a list of vocabularies used in the dataset is provided [59]
- U6: checking the effectiveness and the efficiency of the usage of the mailing list and/or the message boards [59]

Example. Let us assume that a user wants to search for flights between Boston and San Francisco using our flight search engine. Data related to Boston in the integrated dataset, for the required flight is represented as follows:

- http://rdf.freebase.com/ns/m.049jnng
- http://rdf.freebase.com/ns/m.043j22x
- "Boston Logan Airport"@en

---

[66] Context trust is a trust judgment on a particular piece of information in a given context [67].

For the first two items no human-readable label is available, therefore the machine is only able to display the URI as a result of the users query. This does not represent anything meaningful to the user besides perhaps that the information is from Freebase. The third entity, however, contains a human-readable label, which the user can easily understand.

Timeliness. Gamble et al. [66] defined timeliness as "a comparison of the date the annotation was updated with the consumer's requirement". The timeliness dimension is motivated by the fact that it is possible to have current data that is actually useless because it reflects a too old state of the real world for a specific usage. According to the timeliness dimension, data should ideally be recorded and reported as frequently as the source values change and thus never become outdated.

Definition 22. *Timeliness measures how up-to-date data is relative to a specific task.*

Metrics. The metrics identified for timeliness are:

- TI1: detecting freshness of datasets based on currency and volatility using the formula:
  $max\{0, 1 - currency/volatility\}$ [77], which gives a value in a continuous scale from 0 to 1, where data with 1 is timely and 0 is unacceptable. In the formula, volatility is the length of time the data remains valid [64] and currency is the age of the data when delivered to the user [134,176].
- TI2: detecting freshness of datasets based on their data source by measuring the distance between last modified time of the data source and last modified time of the dataset [64,135]

Measuring currency of arbitrary documents or statements in LD presents several challenges: (i) it is unlikely that temporal metadata (e.g., the last modification date) are associated with statements; (ii) temporal metadata are not always available and (iii) LD is characterized by *autonomous providers* which use different vocabularies and different patterns for representing temporal metadata. In a recent study [175], the authors described the approaches used for representing temporal metadata associated with statements or documents and also showed the scarce availability of temporal metadata which impact the assessment of currency.

Example. Consider a user checking the flight timetable for her flight from a city A to a city B. Suppose that the result is a list of triples comprising of the description of the resource A such as the connecting airports, the time of arrival, the terminal, the gate, etc. This flight timetable is updated every 10 minutes (volatility). Assume there is a change of the flight departure time, specifically a delay of one hour. However, this information is communicated to the control room with a slight delay. They update this information in the system after 30 minutes. Thus, the timeliness constraint of updating the timetable within 10 minutes is not satisfied which renders the information out-of-date.

Intra-relations. Data is of high relevance if data is current for the user needs. The timeliness of information thus influences its relevancy. On the other hand, if a dataset has current information, it is considered to be trustworthy. Moreover, to allow users to properly understand information in a dataset, a system should be able to provide sufficient relevant information.

7.6   Representational Dimensions

Representational dimensions capture aspects related to the design of the data such as the *representational-conciseness, interoperability, interpretability* as well as the *versatility*.

Representational-conciseness. Bizer [25], adopted the definition of representational-conciseness from Pipino et al. [164] as "the extent to which information is compactly represented". This is the only article that describes this dimension (from the core set of articles included in this survey).

Definition 23 (Representational-conciseness). *Representational-conciseness refers to the representation of the data which is compact and well formatted on the one hand and clear and complete on the other hand.*

Metrics. The metrics identified for representational-conciseness are:

- RC1: detection of long URIs or those that contain query parameters [86]
- RC2: detection of RDF primitives i.e. RDF reification, RDF containers and RDF collections [86]

Example. Our flight search engine represents the URIs for the destination compactly with the use of the airport codes. For example, LEJ is the airport code for Leipzig, therefore the URI is http://airlines.org/LEJ. This short representation of URIs helps users share and memorize them easily.

Interoperability. Bizer [25] adopted the definition of representational-consistency from Pipino et al. [164] as "the extent to which information is represented in the same format". We use the term "interoperability" for this dimension. In addition, the definition of "uniformity", which refers to the re-use of established formats to represent data as described by Flemming [59], can be associated to the interoperability of the dataset. Additionally, as stated in Hogan et al. [86], the re-use of well-known terms to describe resources in a uniform manner increases the interoperability of data published in this manner and contributes towards the interoperability of the entire dataset.

Definition 24 (Interoperability). *Interoperability is the degree to which the format and structure of the information conforms to previously returned information as well as data from other sources.*

Metrics. The metrics identified for interoperability are:

- IO1: detection of whether existing terms from all relevant vocabularies for that particular domain have been reused [86]
- IO2: usage of relevant vocabularies for that particular domain [59]

Example. Let us consider different airline datasets using different notations for representing temporal data, e.g. one dataset uses the time ontology while another dataset uses XSD notations. This makes querying the integrated dataset difficult as it requires users to understand the various heterogeneous schema. Additionally, with the difference in the vocabularies used to represent the same concept (in this case time), the consumers are faced with problem of how the data can be interpreted and displayed. In order to avoid these interoperability issues, we provide data based on the Linked Data principles, which are designed to support heterogeneous description models necessary to handle different formats of data.

Interpretability. Bizer [25] adopted the definition of interpretability from Pipino et al. [164] as the "extent to which information is in appropriate languages, symbols and units and the definitions are clear". This is the only article that describes this dimension (from the core set of articles included in this survey).

Definition 25 (Interpretability). *Interpretability refers to technical aspects of the data, that is, whether information is represented using an appropriate notation and whether the machine is able to process the data.*

Metrics. The metrics identified for interpretability are:

- IN1: identifying objects and terms used to define these objects with globally unique identifiers[67] [25]
- IN2: detecting the use of appropriate language, symbols, units, datatypes and clear definitions [25,164,59]
- IN3: detection of invalid usage of undefined classes and properties (i.e. those without any formal definition) [85]
- IN4: detecting the use of blank nodes[68] [86]

Example. Consider our flight search engine and a user that is looking for a flight from `Mumbai` to `Boston` with a two day stop-over in `Berlin`. The user specifies the dates correctly. However, since the flights are operated by different airlines, thus different datasets, they have a different way of representing the date. In the first leg of the trip, the date is represented in the format `dd/mm/yyyy` whereas in the other case, date is represented as `mm/dd/yy`. Thus, the machine is unable to correctly interpret the data and cannot provide an optimal result for this query. This lack of consensus in the format of the date hinders the ability of the machine to interpret the data and thus provide the appropriate flights.

Versatility. Flemming [59] defined versatility as the "alternative representations of the data and its handling." This is the only article that describes this dimension (from the core set of articles included in this survey).

Definition 26 (Versatility). *Versatility refers to the availability of the data in an internationalized way and alternative representations of data.*

---

[67] `www.w3.org/TR/webarch/`

[68] Blank nodes are not recommended since they cannot be externally referenced.

Metrics. The metrics identified for versatility are:

- V1: checking whether data is available in different serialization formats [59]
- V2: checking whether data is available in different languages [14,59,104]

Example. Consider a user who does not understand English but only Spanish and wants to use our flight search engine. In order to cater to the needs of such a user, the dataset should provide labels and other language-dependent information in Spanish so that any user has the capability to understand it.

Intra-relations. The dimensions in this group are related as follows: Interpretability is related to the the interoperability of data since the consistent representation (e.g. re-use of established vocabularies) ensures that a system will be able to interpret the data correctly [49]. Versatility is also related to the interpretability of a dataset as the more versatile forms a dataset is represented in (e.g. in different languages), the more interpretable a dataset is. Additionally, concise representation of the data allows the data to be interpreted correctly.

7.7   Data Quality Assessment Frameworks

In Table 9, we compare the tools proposed by eight of the 21 core articles, identified in the survey, based on eight different attributes. These tools implement the methodologies and metrics defined in the respective approaches.

Table 9. Comparison of quality assessment tools according to several attributes

	Trellis, Gil et al., 2002	TrustBot, Golbeck al., 2003	tSPARQL, et Hartig, 2008	WIQA, Bizer et al., 2009	ProLOD, Böhm et al., 2010	Flemming, al., 2010	LinkQA, Gueret et al., 2012	Sieve, Mendes et al., 2012
Accessibility/ Availability	–	–	✓	–	–	✓	✓	✓
Licensing	Open-source	–	GPL v3	Apache v2	–	–	Open-source	Apache
Automation	Semi-automated	Semi-automated	Semi-automated	Semi-automated	Semi-automated	Semi-automated	Automated	Semi-automated
Collaboration	Allows users to add observations and conclusions	No	No	No	No	No	No	No
Customizability	✓	✓	✓	✓	✓	✓	No	✓
Scalability	–	No	Yes	–	–	No	Yes	Yes
Usability/ Documentation	2	4	4	2	2	3	2	4
Maintenance (Last updated)	2005	2003	2012	2006	2010	2010	2011	2012

Accessibility/Availability. In Table 9, only the tools marked with a tick are available to be used for quality assessment. The other tools are either available only as a demo or screencast (Trellis, ProLOD) or not available at all (TrustBot, WIQA).

Licensing. Each of the tools is available using a particular software license, which specifies the restrictions with which it can be redistributed. The Trellis and LinkQA tools are open-source and as such by default they are protected by copyright which is *All Rights Reserved.* Also, WIQA and Sieve are both available with open-source license: the Apache Version 2.0[69] and Apache licenses respectively. tSPARQL is distributed under the GPL v3 license[70]. However, no licensing information is available for TrustBot, ProLOD and Flemming's tool.

Automation. The automation of a system is the ability to automatically perform its intended tasks thereby reducing the need for human intervention. In this context, we classify the eight tools into semi-automated and automated approaches. As seen in Table 9, all the tools are semi-automated except for LinkQA, which is completely automated as there is no user involvement. LinkQA automatically selects a set of resources, information from the Web of Data (i.e. SPARQL endpoints and/or dereferencable resources) and a set of new triples as input and generates the respective quality assessment reports.

On the other hand, the WIQA and Sieve tools require a high degree of user involvement. Specifically in Sieve, the definition of metrics has to be done by creating an XML file which contains specific configurations for a quality assessment task. Although it gives the users the flexibility of tweaking the tool to match their needs, it requires much time for understanding the required XML file structure and specification. The other semi-automated tools, Trellis, TrurstBot, tSPARQL, ProLOD and Flemming's tool require a minimum amount of user involvement. For example, Flemming's Data Quality Assessment Tool requires the user to answer a few questions regarding the dataset (e.g. existence of a human-readable license) or they have to assign weights to each of the pre-defined data quality metrics.

Collaboration. Collaboration is the ability of a system to support co-operation between different users of the system. None of the tools, except Trellis, support collaboration between different users of the tool. The Trellis user interface allows several users to express their trust value for a data source. The tool allows several users to add and store their observations and conclusions. Decisions made by users on a particular source are stored as annotations, which can be used to analyze conflicting information or handle incomplete information.

Customizability. Customizability is the ability of a system to be configured according to the users' needs and preferences. In this case, we measure the customizability of a tool based on whether the tool can be used with any dataset that the user is interested in. Only LinkQA cannot be customized since the user cannot add any dataset of her choice. The other seven tools can be customized according to the use case. For example, in TrustBot, an IRC bot that makes trust recommendations to users (based on the trust network it builds), the users have the flexibility to submit their own URIs to the bot at any time while incorporating the data into a graph. Similarly, Trellis, tSPARQL, WIQA, ProLOD, Flemming's tool and Sieve can be used with any dataset.

---

[69] http://www.apache.org/licenses/LICENSE-2.0
[70] http://www.gnu.org/licenses/gpl-3.0.html

Scalability. Scalability is the ability of a system, network, or process to handle a growing amount of work or its ability to be enlarged to accommodate that growth. Out of the eight tools only three, the tSPARQL, LinkQA and Sieve, tools are scalable, that is, they can be used with large datasets. Flemming's tool and TrustBot are reportedly not scalable for large datasets [71,59]. Flemming's tool, on the one hand, performs analysis based on a sample of three entities whereas TrustBot takes as input two email addresses to calculate the weighted average trust value. Trellis, WIQA and ProLOD do not provide any information on the scalability.

Usability/Documentation. Usability is the ease of use and learnability of a human-made object, in this case the quality assessment tool. We assess the usability of the tools based on the ease of use as well as the complete and precise documentation available for each of them. We score them based on a scale from 1 (low usability) – 5 (high usability). TrustBot, tSPARQL and Sieve score high in terms of usability and documentation followed by Flemming's data quality assessment tool. Trellis, WIQA, ProLOD and LinkQA rank lower in terms of ease of use since they do not contain useful documentation of how to use the tool.

Maintenance/Last Updated. While TrustBot, Trellis and WIQA have not been updated since they were first introduced in 2003, 2005 and 2006 respectively, ProLOD and Flemming's tool have been updated in 2010. The recently updated tools are LinkQA (2011), tSRARQL (2012) and Sieve (2012) and are currently being maintained.

8   Outlook and Future Challenges

Although the different approaches for aspects of the Linked Data life-cycle as presented in this chapter are already working together, more effort must be done to further integrate them in ways that they mutually fertilize themselves. The discovery of new links or the authoring of new resource descriptions, for example, should automatically trigger the enrichment of the linked knowledge bases. The enrichment in turn can trigger the application of inconsistency detection and repair techniques. This leads to recognizing data quality problems and their consequent assessment and improvement. The browsing and exploration paths followed by end-users can be taken into account for machine learning techniques to refine the knowledge bases etc. Ultimately, when the different aspects of Linked Data management are fully integrated we envision the Web of Data becoming a washing machine for knowledge. A progress in one particular aspect will automatically trigger improvements in many other ones as well. In the following we outline some research challenges and promising research directions regarding some of the Linked Data management aspects.

Extraction. One promising research direction with regard to the extraction from unstructured sources is the development of standardized, LOD enabled integration interfaces between existing NLP tools. An open question is whether and how efficient bidirectional synchronization between extraction source and target knowledge base can be established. With regard to the extraction from structured sources (e.g. relational, XML) we need a declarative syntax and semantics for data model transformations.

Some orthogonal challenges include the use of LOD as background knowledge and the representation and tracing of provenance information.

Authoring. Current Semantic Wikis still suffer from a lack of scalability. Hence, an important research and development target are large-scale Semantic Wikis, which include functionality for access control and provenance. In order to further flexibilize and simplify the authoring an adaptive choreography of editing widgets based on underlying data structures is needed. Also, the joint authoring of unstructured and structured sources (i.e. HTML/RDFa authoring) and better support for the integrated semantic annotation of other modalities such as images, audio, video is of paramount importance.

Natural Language Queries. One of the future challenges for Linked Data is to create user interfaces, which are able to hide the complexity of the underlying systems. A possible path towards this goal is question answering, e.g. converting natural language queries to SPARQL [193,114]. In order to allow users to interact with such systems, there is ongoing work on converting the created SPARQL queries back to natural language [149] and employ feedback mechanisms [113,83]. Ultimately, a goal is to provide users enhanced functionality without the need to adapt to different kinds of interface.

Automatic Management of Resources for Linking. With the growth of the Cloud and of the datasets that need to be interlinked, the use of parallel hardware has been studied over the last few years [84,151]. The comparative study of parallel hardware for link discovery yet shows surprising results and suggests that the use of massively parallel yet local hardware can lead to tremendous runtime improvements. Still, when result sets go beyond sizes of 10^{10}, the higher amount of resources available on remote devices in the Cloud is still to be used. Devising automatic solutions for selecting the right hardware to run a linking task is one of the most interesting research areas pertaining to the efficient execution of link specifications. In addition, developing reduction-ratio optimal algorithms for spaces other than Minkowski spaces promises to ensure the best possible use of available hardware. Finally, devising more efficient means to combine single algorithms is the third open area of research in this domain. The challenges faces with regard to learning link specifications are also manifold and include devising approaches that can efficiently detected most informative positive and negative examples as well even running in a fully unsupervised manner on properties that are not one-to-one relations.

Linked Data Visualization. The potential of the vast amount of Linked Data on the Web is enormous but in most cases it is very difficult *and* cumbersome for users to visualize, explore and use this data, especially for lay users without experience with Semantic Web technologies. Visualizations are useful for obtaining an overview of the datasets, their main types, properties and the relationships between them. Compared to prior information visualization strategies, we have a unique opportunity on the Data Web. The unified RDF data model being prevalent on the Data Web enables us to bind data to visualizations in an *unforeseen* and *dynamic* way. An information visualization technique requires certain data structures to be present. When we can derive and generate these data structures automatically from reused vocabularies or semantic representations, we are able to realize a largely automatic visualization workflow. Ultimately, various visualizations techniques can develop an ecosystem of data extractions and visualizations, which can be bound together in a dynamic and unforeseen way. This will enable users to explore datasets even if the publisher of the data does not provide any exploration or visualization means. Yet, most existing work related to visualizing RDF is focused on concrete domains and concrete datatypes.

Linked Data Quality. With the amount of Linked Data on the Web growing at an exponential rate, assessing the quality of the datasets is of utmost importance in order to ensure reliability of the applications built using that data. However, currently there are few methodologies in place to perform this assessment. Also, the tools currently available are either not scalable for large datasets or do not cover all the data quality aspects for assessing the quality of Linked Data, in particular. Moreover, these tools provide results that are difficult to interpret, in certain cases do not allow a user to choose the input dataset or require considerable amount of user involvement. Currently, crowdsourcing based approaches for quality assessment are being explored, which prove to be cost-effective and accurate when used in combination with semi-automated approaches [210,2]. Thus, one of the main challenges is to device such a methodology supported by a tool to perform quality assessment for large datasets. Additionally, the tools should provide features that allow dataset owners to amend the quality aspects that are detected during the quality assessment.

Acknowledgments. We would like to thank our colleagues from the AKSW research group in Leipzig as well as the LOD2, GeoKnow and BioASQ project consortia, without whom writing this chapter would not have been possible. In particular, we would like to thank Christian Bizer and Tom Heath, whose Chapter 2 of the book 'Linked Data – Evolving the Web into a Global Data Space' [79] served as a blueprint for section 2; Sebastian Hellmann, Claus Stadler, René Speck, Jörg Unbehauen and Ricardo Usbeck for their contributions to section 3, Sebastian Tramp, Michael Martin, Norman Heino, Phillip Frischmuth and Thomas Riechert for their contributions to the development of OntoWiki as described in section 4. This work was supported by a grant from the European Union's 7th Framework Programme provided for the projects LOD2 (GA no. 257943), GeoKnow (GA no. 318159) and BioASQ (GA no. 318652).

References

1. Resource description framework (RDF): Concepts and abstract syntax. Technical report, W3C, 2 (2004)
2. Acosta, M., Zaveri, A., Simperl, E., Kontokostas, D., Auer, S., Lehmann, J.: Crowdsourcing linked data quality assessment. In: Alani, H., Kagal, L., Fokoue, A., Groth, P., Biemann, C., Parreira, J.X., Aroyo, L., Noy, N., Welty, C., Janowicz, K. (eds.) ISWC 2013, Part II. LNCS, vol. 8219, pp. 260–276. Springer, Heidelberg (2013)
3. Adida, B., Birbeck, M., McCarron, S., Pemberton, S.: RDFa in XHTML: Syntax and processing – a collection of attributes and processing rules for extending XHTML to support RDF. W3C Recommendation (October 2008), `http://www.w3.org/TR/rdfa-syntax/`

4. Agichtein, E., Gravano, L.: Snowball: Extracting relations from large plain-text collections. In: ACM DL, pp. 85–94 (2000)
5. Agresti, A.: An Introduction to Categorical Data Analysis, 2nd edn. Wiley-Interscience (1997)
6. Amsler, R.: Research towards the development of a lexical knowledge base for natural language processing. SIGIR Forum 23, 1–2 (1989)
7. Auer, S., Bizer, C., Kobilarov, G., Lehmann, J., Cyganiak, R., Ives, Z.: Dbpedia: A nucleus for a web of open data. In: Aberer, K., et al. (eds.) ISWC/ASWC 2007. LNCS, vol. 4825, pp. 722–735. Springer, Heidelberg (2007)
8. Auer, S., Dietzold, S., Lehmann, J., Hellmann, S., Aumueller, D.: Triplify: Light-weight linked data publication from relational databases. In: Quemada, J., León, G., Maarek, Y.S., Nejdl, W. (eds.) Proceedings of the 18th International Conference on World Wide Web, WWW 2009, Madrid, Spain, April 20-24, pp. 621–630. ACM (2009)
9. Auer, S., Dietzold, S., Riechert, T.: OntoWiki – A Tool for Social, Semantic Collaboration. In: Cruz, I., Decker, S., Allemang, D., Preist, C., Schwabe, D., Mika, P., Uschold, M., Aroyo, L.M. (eds.) ISWC 2006. LNCS, vol. 4273, pp. 736–749. Springer, Heidelberg (2006)
10. Auer, S., Herre, H.: A versioning and evolution framework for RDF knowledge bases. In: Virbitskaite, I., Voronkov, A. (eds.) PSI 2006. LNCS, vol. 4378, pp. 55–69. Springer, Heidelberg (2007)
11. Auer, S., Lehmann, J.: Making the web a data washing machine - creating knowledge out of interlinked data. Semantic Web Journal (2010)
12. Auer, S., Lehmann, J., Hellmann, S.: LinkedGeoData: Adding a spatial dimension to the web of data. In: Bernstein, A., Karger, D.R., Heath, T., Feigenbaum, L., Maynard, D., Motta, E., Thirunarayan, K. (eds.) ISWC 2009. LNCS, vol. 5823, pp. 731–746. Springer, Heidelberg (2009)
13. Auer, S., Lehmann, J., Ngonga Ngomo, A.-C., Zaveri, A.: Introduction to linked data and its lifecycle on the web. In: Rudolph, S., Gottlob, G., Horrocks, I., van Harmelen, F. (eds.) Reasoning Weg 2013. LNCS, vol. 8067, pp. 1–90. Springer, Heidelberg (2013)
14. Auer, S., Weidl, M., Lehmann, J., Zaveri, A.J., Choi, K.-S.: I18n of semantic web applications. In: Patel-Schneider, P.F., Pan, Y., Hitzler, P., Mika, P., Zhang, L., Pan, J.Z., Horrocks, I., Glimm, B. (eds.) ISWC 2010, Part II. LNCS, vol. 6497, pp. 1–16. Springer, Heidelberg (2010)
15. Aumüller, D.: Semantic Authoring and Retrieval within a Wiki (WikSAR). In: Demo Session at the Second European Semantic Web Conference (ESWC 2005) (May 2005), http://wiksar.sf.net
16. Baader, F., Diageo, C., McGuinness, D., Nardi, D., Patel-Schneider, P. (eds.): The Description Logic Handbook, Cambridge (2003)
17. Baader, F., Ganter, B., Sattler, U., Sertkaya, B.: Completing description logic knowledge bases using formal concept analysis. In: IJCAI 2007. AAAI Press (2007)
18. Baader, F., Sertkaya, B., Turhan, A.-Y.: Computing the least common subsumer w.r.t. a background terminology. J. Applied Logic 5(3), 392–420 (2007)
19. Badea, L., Nienhuys-Cheng, S.-H.: A refinement operator for description logics. In: Cussens, J., Frisch, A.M. (eds.) ILP 2000. LNCS (LNAI), vol. 1866, pp. 40–59. Springer, Heidelberg (2000)
20. Baxter, R., Christen, P., Churches, T.: A comparison of fast blocking methods for record linkage. In: KDD 2003 Workshop on Data Cleaning, Record Linkage, and Object Consolidation (2003)

21. Ben-David, D., Domany, T., Tarem, A.: Enterprise data classification using semantic web technologies. In: Patel-Schneider, P.F., Pan, Y., Hitzler, P., Mika, P., Zhang, L., Pan, J.Z., Horrocks, I., Glimm, B. (eds.) ISWC 2010, Part II. LNCS, vol. 6497, pp. 66–81. Springer, Heidelberg (2010)

22. Berners-Lee, T., Fielding, R.T., Masinter, L.: Uniform resource identifiers (URI): Generic syntax. Internet RFC 2396 (August 1998)

23. Bhagdev, R., Chapman, S., Ciravegna, F., Lanfranchi, V., Petrelli, D.: Hybrid search: Effectively combining keywords and semantic searches. In: Bechhofer, S., Hauswirth, M., Hoffmann, J., Koubarakis, M. (eds.) ESWC 2008. LNCS, vol. 5021, pp. 554–568. Springer, Heidelberg (2008)

24. Bilenko, M., Kamath, B., Mooney, R.J.: Adaptive blocking: Learning to scale up record linkage. In: ICDM 2006, pp. 87–96. IEEE (2006)

25. Bizer, C.: Quality-Driven Information Filtering in the Context of Web-Based Information Systems. PhD thesis, Freie Universität Berlin (March 2007)

26. Bizer, C., Cyganiak, R.: Quality-driven information filtering using the wiqa policy framework. Web Semantics 7(1), 1–10 (2009)

27. Bleiholder, J., Naumann, F.: Data fusion. ACM Comput. Surv. 41(1), 1–41 (2008)

28. Bleiholder, J., Naumann, F.: Data fusion. ACM Computing Surveys (CSUR) 41(1), 1 (2008)

29. Blumer, A., Ehrenfeucht, A., Haussler, D., Warmuth, M.K.: Occam's razor. In: Readings in Machine Learning, pp. 201–204. Morgan Kaufmann (1990)

30. Böhm, C., Naumann, F., Abedjan, Z., Fenz, D., Grütze, T., Hefenbrock, D., Pohl, M., Sonnabend, D.: Profiling linked open data with ProLOD. In: ICDE Workshops, pp. 175–178. IEEE (2010)

31. Bonatti, P.A., Hogan, A., Polleres, A., Sauro, L.: Robust and scalable linked data reasoning incorporating provenance and trust annotations. Journal of Web Semantics 9(2), 165–201 (2011)

32. Breiman, L.: Bagging predictors. Machine Learning 24(2), 123–140 (1996)

33. Breiman, L.: Random forests. Machine Learning 45(1), 5–32 (2001)

34. Brickley, D., Guha, R.V.: RDF Vocabulary Description Language 1.0: RDF Schema. W3C recommendation, W3C (February 2004),
http://www.w3.org/TR/2004/REC-rdf-schema-20040210/

35. Brin, S.: Extracting patterns and relations from the world wide web. In: Atzeni, P., Mendelzon, A.O., Mecca, G. (eds.) WebDB 1998. LNCS, vol. 1590, pp. 172–183. Springer, Heidelberg (1999)

36. Bühmann, L., Lehmann, J.: Universal OWL axiom enrichment for large knowledge bases. In: ten Teije, A., Völker, J., Handschuh, S., Stuckenschmidt, H., d'Acquin, M., Nikolov, A., Aussenac-Gilles, N., Hernandez, N. (eds.) EKAW 2012. LNCS, vol. 7603, pp. 57–71. Springer, Heidelberg (2012)

37. Carroll, J.J.: Signing RDF graphs. In: Fensel, D., Sycara, K., Mylopoulos, J. (eds.) ISWC 2003. LNCS, vol. 2870, pp. 369–384. Springer, Heidelberg (2003)

38. Chang, C.-C., Lin, C.-J.: Libsvm - a library for support vector machines, The Weka classifier works with version 2.82 of LIBSVM (2001)

39. Chen, P., Garcia, W.: Hypothesis generation and data quality assessment through association mining. In: IEEE ICCI, pp. 659–666. IEEE (2010)

40. Cherix, D., Hellmann, S., Lehmann, J.: Improving the performance of the DL-learner SPARQL component for semantic web applications. In: Takeda, H., Qu, Y., Mizoguchi, R., Kitamura, Y. (eds.) JIST 2012. LNCS, vol. 7774, pp. 332–337. Springer, Heidelberg (2013)

41. Choi, N., Song, I.-Y., Han, H.: A survey on ontology mapping. SIGMOD Record 35(3), 34–41 (2006)

42. Coates-Stephens, S.: The analysis and acquisition of proper names for the understanding of free text. Computers and the Humanities 26, 441–456 (1992), doi:10.1007/BF00136985

43. Cohen, W.W., Borgida, A., Hirsh, H.: Computing least common subsumers in description logics. In: AAAI 1992, pp. 754–760 (1992)

44. Cohen, W.W., Hirsh, H.: Learning the CLASSIC description logic: Theoretical and experimental results. In: KR 1994, pp. 121–133. Morgan Kaufmann (1994)

45. Cornolti, M., Ferragina, P., Ciaramita, M.: A framework for benchmarking entity-annotation systems. In: Proceedings of the 22nd International Conference on World Wide Web, pp. 249–260. International World Wide Web Conferences Steering Committee (2013)

46. Cucerzan, S.: Large-scale named entity disambiguation based on wikipedia data. In: EMNLP-CoNLL, pp. 708–716 (2007)

47. Curran, J.R., Clark, S.: Language independent ner using a maximum entropy tagger. In: Proceedings of the Seventh Conference on Natural Language Learning at HLT-NAACL 2003, Morristown, NJ, USA, vol. 4, pp. 164–167. Association for Computational Linguistics (2003)

48. d'Amato, C., Fanizzi, N., Esposito, F.: A note on the evaluation of inductive concept classification procedures. In: Gangemi, A., Keizer, J., Presutti, V., Stoermer, H. (eds.) SWAP 2008. CEUR Workshop Proceedings, vol. 426. CEUR-WS.org (2008)

49. Ding, L., Finin, T.W.: Characterizing the semantic web on the web. In: Cruz, I., Decker, S., Allemang, D., Preist, C., Schwabe, D., Mika, P., Uschold, M., Aroyo, L.M. (eds.) ISWC 2006. LNCS, vol. 4273, pp. 242–257. Springer, Heidelberg (2006)

50. Elmagarmid, A.K., Ipeirotis, P.G., Verykios, V.S.: Duplicate record detection: A survey. IEEE Transactions on Knowledge and Data Engineering 19, 1–16 (2007)

51. Ermilov, T., Heino, N., Tramp, S., Auer, S.: OntoWiki Mobile – Knowledge Management in Your Pocket. In: Antoniou, G., Grobelnik, M., Simperl, E., Parsia, B., Plexousakis, D., De Leenheer, P., Pan, J. (eds.) ESWC 2011, Part I. LNCS, vol. 6643, pp. 185–199. Springer, Heidelberg (2011)

52. Esposito, F., Fanizzi, N., Iannone, L., Palmisano, I., Semeraro, G.: Knowledge-intensive induction of terminologies from metadata. In: McIlraith, S.A., Plexousakis, D., van Harmelen, F. (eds.) ISWC 2004. LNCS, vol. 3298, pp. 441–455. Springer, Heidelberg (2004)

53. Etzioni, O., Cafarella, M., Downey, D., Popescu, A.-M., Shaked, T., Soderland, S., Weld, D.S., Yates, A.: Unsupervised named-entity extraction from the web: an experimental study. Artif. Intell. 165, 91–134 (2005)

54. Euzenat, J., Shvaiko, P.: Ontology matching. Springer, Heidelberg (2007)

55. Fanizzi, N., d'Amato, C., Esposito, F.: DL-FOIL concept learning in description logics. In: Železný, F., Lavrač, N. (eds.) ILP 2008. LNCS (LNAI), vol. 5194, pp. 107–121. Springer, Heidelberg (2008)

56. Fielding, R., Gettys, J., Mogul, J., Frystyk, H., Masinter, L., Leach, P., Berners-Lee, T.: Hypertext transfer protocol – http/1.1 (rfc 2616). Request For Comments (1999), http://www.ietf.org/rfc/rfc2616.txt (accessed July 7, 2006)

57. Finkel, J.R., Grenager, T., Manning, C.: Incorporating non-local information into information extraction systems by gibbs sampling. In: Proceedings of the 43rd Annual Meeting on Association for Computational Linguistics, ACL 2005, pp. 363–370. Association for Computational Linguistics, Morristown (2005)

58. Fleischhacker, D., Völker, J., Stuckenschmidt, H.: Mining RDF data for property axioms. In: Meersman, R., et al. (eds.) OTM 2012, Part II. LNCS, vol. 7566, pp. 718–735. Springer, Heidelberg (2012)

59. Flemming, A.: Quality characteristics of linked data publishing datasources. Master's thesis, Humboldt-Universität zu Berlin (2010)

60. Frank, E., Paynter, G.W., Witten, I.H., Gutwin, C., Nevill-Manning, C.G.: Domain-specific keyphrase extraction. In: Proceedings of the Sixteenth International Joint Conference on Artificial Intelligence, IJCAI 1999, pp. 668–673. Morgan Kaufmann Publishers Inc, San Francisco (1999)

61. Freund, Y., Schapire, R.E.: Experiments with a New Boosting Algorithm. In: International Conference on Machine Learning, pp. 148–156 (1996)

62. Frey, B.J., Dueck, D.: Clustering by passing messages between data points. Science 315, 972–976 (2007)

63. Friedman, J., Hastie, T., Tibshirani, R.: Additive logistic regression: a statistical view of boosting. Technical report, Stanford University (1998)

64. Fürber, C., Hepp, M.: SWIQA - a semantic web information quality assessment framework. In: ECIS (2011)

65. Gama, J.: Functional trees 55(3), 219–250 (2004)

66. Gamble, M., Goble, C.: Quality, trust, and utility of scientific data on the web: Towards a joint model. In: ACM WebSci, pp. 1–8 (June 2011)

67. Gil, Y., Artz, D.: Towards content trust of web resources. Web Semantics 5(4), 227–239 (2007)

68. Gil, Y., Ratnakar, V.: Trusting information sources one citizen at a time. In: Horrocks, I., Hendler, J. (eds.) ISWC 2002. LNCS, vol. 2342, p. 162. Springer, Heidelberg (2002)

69. Glaser, H., Millard, I.C., Sung, W.-K., Lee, S., Kim, P., You, B.-J.: Research on linked data and co-reference resolution. Technical report, University of Southampton (2009)

70. Golbeck, J.: Using trust and provenance for content filtering on the semantic web. In: Workshop on Models of Trust on the Web at the 15th World Wide Web Conference (2006)

71. Golbeck, J., Parsia, B., Hendler, J.: Trust networks on the semantic web. In: Klusch, M., Omicini, A., Ossowski, S., Laamanen, H. (eds.) CIA 2003. LNCS (LNAI), vol. 2782, pp. 238–249. Springer, Heidelberg (2003)

72. Grishman, R., Yangarber, R.: Nyu: Description of the Proteus/Pet system as used for MUC-7 ST. In: MUC-7. Morgan Kaufmann (1998)

73. Guéret, C., Groth, P., Stadler, C., Lehmann, J.: Assessing linked data mappings using network measures. In: Simperl, E., Cimiano, P., Polleres, A., Corcho, O., Presutti, V. (eds.) ESWC 2012. LNCS, vol. 7295, pp. 87–102. Springer, Heidelberg (2012)

74. Hall, M., Frank, E., Holmes, G., Pfahringer, B., Reutemann, P., Witten, I.H.: The weka data mining software: An update. SIGKDD Explor. Newsl. 11(1), 10–18 (2009)

75. Harabagiu, S., Bejan, C.A., Morarescu, P.: Shallow semantics for relation extraction. In: IJCAI, pp. 1061–1066 (2005)

76. Hartig, O.: Trustworthiness of data on the web. In: STI Berlin and CSW PhD Workshop, Berlin, Germany (2008)

77. Hartig, O., Zhao, J.: Using web data provenance for quality assessment. In: Freire, J., Missier, P., Sahoo, S.S. (eds.) SWPM. CEUR Workshop Proceedings, vol. 526, CEUR-WS.org (2009)

78. Hastie, T., Tibshirani, R.: Classification by pairwise coupling. In: Jordan, M.I., Kearns, M.J., Solla, S.A. (eds.) Advances in Neural Information Processing Systems, vol. 10, MIT Press (1998)

79. Heath, T., Bizer, C.: Linked Data - Evolving the Web into a Global Data Space. Synthesis Lectures on the Semantic Web:Theory and Technology, vol. 1. Morgan & Claypool (2011)

80. Heino, N., Dietzold, S., Martin, M., Auer, S.: Developing semantic web applications with the ontoWiki framework. In: Pellegrini, T., Auer, S., Tochtermann, K., Schaffert, S. (eds.) Networked Knowledge - Networked Media. SCI, vol. 221, pp. 61–77. Springer, Heidelberg (2009)

81. Hellmann, S., Lehmann, J., Auer, S.: Learning of OWL class descriptions on very large knowledge bases. Int. J. Semantic Web Inf. Syst. 5(2), 25–48 (2009)

82. Hellmann, S., Lehmann, J., Auer, S.: Learning of OWL class expressions on very large knowledge bases and its applications. In: Interoperability Semantic Services and Web Applications: Emerging Concepts, ch. 5, pp. 104–130. IGI Global (2011)

83. Hellmann, S., Lehmann, J., Unbehauen, J., Stadler, C., Lam, T.N., Strohmaier, M.: Navigation-induced knowledge engineering by example. In: Takeda, H., Qu, Y., Mizoguchi, R., Kitamura, Y. (eds.) JIST 2012. LNCS, vol. 7774, pp. 207–222. Springer, Heidelberg (2013)

84. Hillner, S., Ngomo, A.-C.N.: Parallelizing limes for large-scale link discovery. In: I'Semantics (2011)

85. Hogan, A., Harth, A., Passant, A., Decker, S., Polleres, A.: Weaving the pedantic web. In: LDOW (2010)

86. Hogan, A., Umbrich, J., Harth, A., Cyganiak, R., Polleres, A., Decker, S.: An empirical survey of linked data conformance. Journal of Web Semantics (2012)

87. Horridge, M., Patel-Schneider, P.F.: Manchester syntax for OWL 1.1. In: OWLED 2008 (2008)

88. HTML 5: A vocabulary and associated APIs for HTML and XHTML. W3C Working Draft (August 2009), http://www.w3.org/TR/2009/WD-html5-20090825/

89. Iannone, L., Palmisano, I.: An algorithm based on counterfactuals for concept learning in the semantic web. In: Ali, M., Esposito, F. (eds.) IEA/AIE 2005. LNCS (LNAI), vol. 3533, pp. 370–379. Springer, Heidelberg (2005)

90. Iannone, L., Palmisano, I., Fanizzi, N.: An algorithm based on counterfactuals for concept learning in the semantic web. Applied Intelligence 26(2), 139–159 (2007)

91. Inan, A., Kantarcioglu, M., Bertino, E., Scannapieco, M.: A hybrid approach to private record linkage. In: ICDE, pp. 496–505 (2008)

92. Isele, R., Jentzsch, A., Bizer, C.: Efficient multidimensional blocking for link discovery without losing recall. In: WebDB (2011)

93. Isele, R., Jentzsch, A., Bizer, C.: Active learning of expressive linkage rules for the web of data. In: Brambilla, M., Tokuda, T., Tolksdorf, R. (eds.) ICWE 2012. LNCS, vol. 7387, pp. 411–418. Springer, Heidelberg (2012)

94. Jacobi, I., Kagal, L., Khandelwal, A.: Rule-based trust assessment on the semantic web. In: Bassiliades, N., Governatori, G., Paschke, A. (eds.) RuleML 2011 - Europe. LNCS, vol. 6826, pp. 227–241. Springer, Heidelberg (2011)

95. Jacobs, I., Walsh, N.: Architecture of the world wide web, vol. one. World Wide Web Consortium, Recommendation REC-Webarch-20041215 (December 2004)

96. John, G.H., Langley, P.: Estimating continuous distributions in bayesian classifiers. In: Eleventh Conference on Uncertainty in Artificial Intelligence, San Mateo, pp. 338–345. Morgan Kaufmann (1995)

97. Juran, J.: The Quality Control Handbook. McGraw-Hill, New York (1974)

98. Kim, S.N., Kan, M.-Y.: Re-examining automatic keyphrase extraction approaches in scientific articles. In: Proceedings of the Workshop on Multiword Expressions: Identification, Interpretation, Disambiguation and Applications, MWE 2009, pp. 9–16. Association for Computational Linguistics, Stroudsburg (2009)

99. Kim, S.N., Medelyan, O., Kan, M.-Y., Baldwin, T.: Semeval-2010 task 5: Automatic keyphrase extraction from scientific articles. In: Proceedings of the 5th International Workshop on Semantic Evaluation, SemEval 2010, pp. 21–26. Association for Computational Linguistics, Stroudsburg (2010)

100. Kittler, J., Hatef, M., Duin, R.W., Matas, J.: On combining classifiers. IEEE Transactions on Pattern Analysis and Machine Intelligence 20(3), 226–239 (1998)

101. Kohavi, R.: The power of decision tables. In: Lavrač, N., Wrobel, S. (eds.) ECML 1995. LNCS, vol. 912, pp. 174–189. Springer, Heidelberg (1995)

102. Köpcke, H., Thor, A., Rahm, E.: Comparative evaluation of entity resolution approaches with fever. Proc. VLDB Endow. 2(2), 1574–1577 (2009)
103. Krötzsch, M., Vrandecic, D., Völkel, M., Haller, H., Studer, R.: Semantic wikipedia. Journal of Web Semantics 5, 251–261 (2007)
104. Gayo, J.E.L., Kontokostas, D., Auer, S.: Multilingual linked open data patterns. Semantic Web Journal (2012)
105. Landwehr, N., Hall, M., Frank, E.: Logistic model trees. Machine Learning 95(1-2), 161–205 (2005)
106. le Cessie, S., van Houwelingen, J.C.: Ridge estimators in logistic regression. Applied Statistics 41(1), 191–201 (1992)
107. Lehmann, J.: Hybrid learning of ontology classes. In: Perner, P. (ed.) MLDM 2007. LNCS (LNAI), vol. 4571, pp. 883–898. Springer, Heidelberg (2007)
108. Lehmann, J.: DL-Learner: learning concepts in description logics. Journal of Machine Learning Research (JMLR) 10, 2639–2642 (2009)
109. Lehmann, J.: Learning OWL Class Expressions. PhD thesis, University of Leipzig, PhD in Computer Science (2010)
110. Lehmann, J.: Ontology learning. In: Proceedings of Reasoning Web Summer School (2010)
111. Lehmann, J., Auer, S., Bühmann, L., Tramp, S.: Class expression learning for ontology engineering. Journal of Web Semantics 9, 71–81 (2011)
112. Lehmann, J., Bizer, C., Kobilarov, G., Auer, S., Becker, C., Cyganiak, R., Hellmann, S.: DBpedia - a crystallization point for the web of data. Journal of Web Semantics 7(3), 154–165 (2009)
113. Lehmann, J., Bühmann, L.: AutoSPARQL: Let users query your knowledge base. In: Antoniou, G., Grobelnik, M., Simperl, E., Parsia, B., Plexousakis, D., De Leenheer, P., Pan, J. (eds.) ESWC 2011, Part I. LNCS, vol. 6643, pp. 63–79. Springer, Heidelberg (2011)
114. Lehmann, J., et al.: DEQA: Deep web extraction for question answering. In: Cudré-Mauroux, P., et al. (eds.) ISWC 2012, Part II. LNCS, vol. 7650, pp. 131–147. Springer, Heidelberg (2012)
115. Lehmann, J., Hitzler, P.: Foundations of refinement operators for description logics. In: Blockeel, H., Ramon, J., Shavlik, J., Tadepalli, P. (eds.) ILP 2007. LNCS (LNAI), vol. 4894, pp. 161–174. Springer, Heidelberg (2008)
116. Lehmann, J., Hitzler, P.: A refinement operator based learning algorithm for the $\mathcal{ALC}$ description logic. In: Blockeel, H., Ramon, J., Shavlik, J., Tadepalli, P. (eds.) ILP 2007. LNCS (LNAI), vol. 4894, pp. 147–160. Springer, Heidelberg (2008)
117. Lehmann, J., Hitzler, P.: Concept learning in description logics using refinement operators. Machine Learning Journal 78(1-2), 203–250 (2010)
118. Lehmann, J., Isele, R., Jakob, M., Jentzsch, A., Kontokostas, D., Mendes, P.N., Hellmann, S., Morsey, M., van Kleef, P., Auer, S., Bizer, C.: DBpedia - a large-scale, multilingual knowledge base extracted from wikipedia. Semantic Web Journal (2014)
119. Lei, Y., Uren, V., Motta, E.: A framework for evaluating semantic metadata. In: 4th International Conference on Knowledge Capture, K-CAP 2007, vol. (8), pp. 135–142. ACM (2007)
120. Pipino, D.K.L., Wang, R., Rybold, W.: Developing Measurement Scales for Data-Quality Dimensions, vol. 1. M.E. Sharpe, New York (2005)
121. Leuf, B., Cunningham, W.: The Wiki Way: Collaboration and Sharing on the Internet. Addison-Wesley Professional (2001)
122. Lisi, F.A.: Building rules on top of ontologies for the semantic web with inductive logic programming. Theory and Practice of Logic Programming 8(3), 271–300 (2008)
123. Lisi, F.A., Esposito, F.: Learning SHIQ+log rules for ontology evolution. In: SWAP 2008. CEUR Workshop Proceedings, vol. 426, CEUR-WS.org (2008)

124. Lohmann, S., Heim, P., Auer, S., Dietzold, S., Riechert, T.: Semantifying requirements engineering – the softwiki approach. In: Proceedings of the 4th International Conference on Semantic Technologies (I-SEMANTICS 2008), pp. 182–185. J.UCS (2008)

125. Lopez, V., Uren, V., Sabou, M.R., Motta, E.: Cross ontology query answering on the semantic web: an initial evaluation. In: K-CAP 2009, pp. 17–24. ACM, New York (2009)

126. Ma, L., Sun, X., Cao, F., Wang, C., Wang, X., Kanellos, N., Wolfson, D., Pan, Y.: Semantic enhancement for enterprise data management. In: Bernstein, A., Karger, D.R., Heath, T., Feigenbaum, L., Maynard, D., Motta, E., Thirunarayan, K. (eds.) ISWC 2009. LNCS, vol. 5823, pp. 876–892. Springer, Heidelberg (2009)

127. Martin, M., Stadler, C., Frischmuth, P., Lehmann, J.: Increasing the financial transparency of european commission project funding. Semantic Web Journal, Special Call for Linked Dataset Descriptions (2), 157–164 (2013)

128. Matsuo, Y., Ishizuka, M.: Keyword Extraction From A Single Document Using Word Co-Occurrence Statistical Information. International Journal on Artificial Intelligence Tools 13(1), 157–169 (2004)

129. Maynard, D., Peters, W., Li, Y.: Metrics for evaluation of ontology-based information extraction. In: Workshop on Evaluation of Ontologies for the Web (EON) at WWW (May 2006)

130. McBride, B., Beckett, D.: Rdf/xml syntax specification. W3C Recommendation (February 2004)

131. McCusker, J., McGuinness, D.: Towards identity in linked data. In: Proceedings of OWL Experiences and Directions Seventh Annual Workshop (2010)

132. Mecella, M., Scannapieco, M., Virgillito, A., Baldoni, R., Catarci, T., Batini, C.: Managing data quality in cooperative information systems. In: Meersman, R., Tari, Z. (eds.) CoopIS/DOA/ODBASE 2002. LNCS, vol. 2519, pp. 486–502. Springer, Heidelberg (2002)

133. Meilicke, C., Stuckenschmidt, H.: Incoherence as a basis for measuring the quality of ontology mappings. In: 3rd International Workshop on Ontology Matching (OM) at the ISWC (2008)

134. Mendes, P., Mühleisen, H., Bizer, C.: Sieve: Linked data quality assessment and fusion. In: LWDM (March 2012)

135. Mendes, P., Bizer, C., Miklos, Z., Calbimonte, J.-P., Moraru, A., Flouris, G.: D2.1: Conceptual model and best practices for high-quality metadata publishing. Technical report, PlanetData Deliverable (2012)

136. Moats, R.: Urn syntax. Internet RFC 2141 (May 1997)

137. Morsey, M., Lehmann, J., Auer, S., Ngonga Ngomo, A.-C.: DBpedia SPARQL Benchmark – Performance Assessment with Real Queries on Real Data. In: Aroyo, L., Welty, C., Alani, H., Taylor, J., Bernstein, A., Kagal, L., Noy, N., Blomqvist, E. (eds.) ISWC 2011, Part I. LNCS, vol. 7031, pp. 454–469. Springer, Heidelberg (2011)

138. Morsey, M., Lehmann, J., Auer, S., Ngomo, A.-C.N.: Usage-Centric Benchmarking of RDF Triple Stores. In: Proceedings of the 26th AAAI Conference on Artificial Intelligence, AAAI 2012 (2012)

139. Mostafavi, M.A., Edwards, G., Jeansoulin, R.: Ontology-based method for quality assessment of spatial data bases. In: International Symposium on Spatial Data Quality, vol. 4, pp. 49–66 (2004)

140. Nadeau, D.: Semi-Supervised Named Entity Recognition: Learning to Recognize 100 Entity Types with Little Supervision. PhD thesis, University of Ottawa (2007)

141. Nadeau, D., Sekine, S.: A survey of named entity recognition and classification. Linguisticae Investigationes 30(1), 3–26 (2007)

142. Nadeau, D., Turney, P.D., Matwin, S.: Unsupervised named-entity recognition: Generating gazetteers and resolving ambiguity. In: Lamontagne, L., Marchand, M. (eds.) Canadian AI 2006. LNCS (LNAI), vol. 4013, pp. 266–277. Springer, Heidelberg (2006)

143. Naumann, F.: Quality-Driven Query Answering for Integrated Information Systems. LNCS, vol. 2261. Springer, Heidelberg (2002)
144. Ngomo, A.-C.N.: Parameter-free clustering of protein-protein interaction graphs. In: Proceedings of Symposium on Machine Learning in Systems Biology (2010)
145. Ngomo, A.-C.N.: A time-efficient hybrid approach to link discovery. In: Proceedings of OM@ISWC (2011)
146. Ngonga Ngomo, A.-C.: Link discovery with guaranteed reduction ratio in affine spaces with minkowski measures. In: Cudré-Mauroux, P., et al. (eds.) ISWC 2012, Part I. LNCS, vol. 7649, pp. 378–393. Springer, Heidelberg (2012)
147. Ngomo, A.-C.N.: On link discovery using a hybrid approach. Journal on Data Semantics 1, 203–217 (2012)
148. Ngomo, A.-C.N., Auer, S.: Limes - a time-efficient approach for large-scale link discovery on the web of data. In: Proceedings of IJCAI (2011)
149. Ngomo, A.-C.N., Bühmann, L., Unger, C., Lehmann, J., Gerber, D.: Sorry, i don't speak sparql — translating sparql queries into natural language. In: Proceedings of WWW (2013)
150. Ngonga Ngomo, A.-C., Heino, N., Lyko, K., Speck, R., Kaltenböck, M.: Scms - semantifying content management systems. In: Aroyo, L., Welty, C., Alani, H., Taylor, J., Bernstein, A., Kagal, L., Noy, N., Blomqvist, E. (eds.) ISWC 2011, Part II. LNCS, vol. 7032, pp. 189–204. Springer, Heidelberg (2011)
151. Ngomo, A.-C.N., Kolb, L., Heino, N., Hartung, M., Auer, S., Rahm, E.: When to reach for the cloud: Using parallel hardware for link discovery. In: Cimiano, P., Corcho, O., Presutti, V., Hollink, L., Rudolph, S. (eds.) ESWC 2013. LNCS, vol. 7882, pp. 275–289. Springer, Heidelberg (2013)
152. Ngomo, A.-C.N., Lehmann, J., Auer, S., Höffner, K.: Raven: Active learning of link specifications. In: Proceedings of the Ontology Matching Workshop (co-located with ISWC) (2011)
153. Ngonga Ngomo, A.-C., Lyko, K.: Eagle: Efficient active learning of link specifications using genetic programming. In: Simperl, E., Cimiano, P., Polleres, A., Corcho, O., Presutti, V. (eds.) ESWC 2012. LNCS, vol. 7295, pp. 149–163. Springer, Heidelberg (2012)
154. Ngomo, A.-C.N., Lyko, K., Christen, V.: Coala – correlation-aware active learning of link specifications. In: Cimiano, P., Corcho, O., Presutti, V., Hollink, L., Rudolph, S. (eds.) ESWC 2013. LNCS, vol. 7882, pp. 442–456. Springer, Heidelberg (2013)
155. Ngonga Ngomo, A.-C., Schumacher, F.: Border flow – a local graph clustering algorithm for natural language processing. In: Gelbukh, A. (ed.) CICLing 2009. LNCS, vol. 5449, pp. 547–558. Springer, Heidelberg (2009)
156. Nguyen, D.P.T., Matsuo, Y., Ishizuka, M.: Relation extraction from wikipedia using subtree mining. In: AAAI, pp. 1414–1420 (2007)
157. Nguyen, T., Kan, M.-Y.: Keyphrase Extraction in Scientific Publications, pp. 317–326 (2007)
158. Nienhuys-Cheng, S.-H., de Wolf, R. (eds.): Foundations of Inductive Logic Programming. LNCS, vol. 1228. Springer, Heidelberg (1997)
159. Oren, E.: SemperWiki: A Semantic Personal Wiki. In: Decker, J., Park, D., Quan, L. (eds.) roc. of Semantic Desktop Workshop at the ISWC, Galway, Ireland, vol. 175 (November 6, 2005)
160. Pantel, P., Pennacchiotti, M.: Espresso: Leveraging generic patterns for automatically harvesting semantic relations. In: ACL, pp. 113–120. ACL Press (2006)
161. Park, Y., Byrd, R.J., Boguraev, B.K.: Automatic glossary extraction: beyond terminology identification. In: Proceedings of the 19th International Conference on Computational Linguistics, COLING 2002, vol. 1, pp. 1–7. Association for Computational Linguistics, Stroudsburg (2002)

162. Pasca, M., Lin, D., Bigham, J., Lifchits, A., Jain, A.: Organizing and searching the world wide web of facts - step one: the one-million fact extraction challenge. In: Proceedings of the 21st National Conference on Artificial Intelligence, vol. 2, pp. 1400–1405. AAAI Press (2006)

163. Patel-Schneider, P.F., Hayes, P., Horrocks, I.: OWL Web Ontology Language - Semantics and Abstract Syntax. W3c:rec, W3C (February 10, 2004), http://www.w3.org/TR/owl-semantics/

164. Pipino, L.L., Lee, Y.W., Wang, R.Y.: Data quality assessment. Communications of the ACM 45(4) (2002)

165. Quinlan, J.R.: C4.5: Programs for Machine Learning. Morgan Kaufmann Publishers Inc., San Francisco (1993)

166. Rahm, E.: Schema Matching and Mapping. Springer, Heidelberg (2011)

167. Rahm, E., Bernstein, P.A.: A survey of approaches to automatic schema matching. The VLDB Journal 10, 334–350 (2001)

168. Raimond, Y., Sutton, C., Sandler, M.: Automatic interlinking of music datasets on the semantic web. In: 1st Workshop about Linked Data on the Web (2008)

169. Ratinov, L., Roth, D., Downey, D., Anderson, M.: Local and global algorithms for disambiguation to wikipedia. In: Proceedings of the 49th Annual Meeting of the Association for Computational Linguistics: Human Language Technologies, Portland, Oregon, USA, pp. 1375–1384. Association for Computational Linguistics (2011)

170. Röder, M., Usbeck, R., Hellmann, S., Gerber, D., Both, A.: N3 - a collection of datasets for named entity recognition and disambiguation in the nlp interchange format. In: Language Resources and EvaluationConference, 9th edn., Reykjavik, Iceland, May 26-31 (2014)

171. Riechert, T., Lauenroth, K., Lehmann, J., Auer, S.: Towards semantic based requirements engineering. In: Proceedings of the 7th International Conference on Knowledge Management, I-KNOW (2007)

172. Riechert, T., Morgenstern, U., Auer, S., Tramp, S., Martin, M.: Knowledge engineering for historians on the example of the catalogus professorum lipsiensis. In: Patel-Schneider, P.F., Pan, Y., Hitzler, P., Mika, P., Zhang, L., Pan, J.Z., Horrocks, I., Glimm, B. (eds.) ISWC 2010, Part II. LNCS, vol. 6497, pp. 225–240. Springer, Heidelberg (2010)

173. Rieß, C., Heino, N., Tramp, S., Auer, S.: EvoPat – Pattern-Based Evolution and Refactoring of RDF Knowledge Bases. In: Patel-Schneider, P.F., Pan, Y., Hitzler, P., Mika, P., Zhang, L., Pan, J.Z., Horrocks, I., Glimm, B. (eds.) ISWC 2010, Part I. LNCS, vol. 6496, pp. 647–662. Springer, Heidelberg (2010)

174. Rudolph, S.: Exploring relational structures via FLE. In: Wolff, K.E., Pfeiffer, H.D., Delugach, H.S. (eds.) ICCS 2004. LNCS (LNAI), vol. 3127, pp. 196–212. Springer, Heidelberg (2004)

175. Rula, A., Palmonari, M., Harth, A., Stadtmüller, S., Maurino, A.: On the Diversity and Availability of Temporal Information in Linked Open Data. In: Cudré-Mauroux, P., et al. (eds.) ISWC 2012, Part I. LNCS, vol. 7649, pp. 492–507. Springer, Heidelberg (2012)

176. Rula, A., Palmonari, M., Maurino, A.: Capturing the Age of Linked Open Data: Towards a Dataset-independent Framework. In: IEEE International Conference on Semantic Computing (2012)

177. Sahoo, S.S., Halb, W., Hellmann, S., Idehen, K., Thibodeau Jr., T., Auer, S., Sequeda, J., Ezzat, A.: A survey of current approaches for mapping of relational databases to rdf (January 2009)

178. Sampson, G.: How fully does a machine-usable dictionary cover english text. Literary and Linguistic Computing 4(1) (1989)

179. Sauermann, L., Cyganiak, R.: Cool uris for the semantic web. W3C Interest Group Note (December 2008)

180. Schaffert, S.: Ikewiki: A semantic wiki for collaborative knowledge management. In: Proceedings of the 1st International Workshop on Semantic Technologies in Collaborative Applications, STICA (2006)

181. Scharffe, F., Liu, Y., Zhou, C.: Rdf-ai: an architecture for rdf datasets matching, fusion and interlink. In: Proc. IJCAI, IR-KR Workshop (2009)

182. Sertkaya, B.: OntocomP system description. In: Grau, B.C., Horrocks, I., Motik, B., Sattler, U. (eds.) Proceedings of the 22nd International Workshop on Description Logics (DL 2009), Oxford, UK, July 27-30. CEUR Workshop Proceedings, vol. 477. CEUR-WS.org. (2009)

183. Settles, B.: Active Learning. Synthesis Lectures on Artificial Intelligence and Machine Learning. Morgan & Claypool Publishers (2012)

184. Shekarpour, S., Katebi, S.D.: Modeling and evaluation of trust with an extension in semantic web. Web Semantics: Science, Services and Agents on the World Wide Web 8(1), 26–36 (2010)

185. Shvaiko, P., Euzenat, J.: Ten challenges for ontology matching. Technical report (August 01, 2008)

186. Souzis, A.: Building a Semantic Wiki. IEEE Intelligent Systems 20(5), 87–91 (2005)

187. Spanos, D.-E., Stavrou, P., Mitrou, N.: Bringing relational databases into the semantic web: A survey. Semantic Web 3(2), 169–209 (2012)

188. Stadler, C., Lehmann, J., Höffner, K., Auer, S.: Linkedgeodata: A core for a web of spatial open data. Semantic Web Journal 3(4), 333–354 (2012)

189. Thielen, C.: An approach to proper name tagging for german. In: Proceedings of the EACL-95 SIGDAT Workshop (1995)

190. Tramp, S., Frischmuth, P., Ermilov, T., Auer, S.: Weaving a Social Data Web with Semantic Pingback. In: Cimiano, P., Pinto, H.S. (eds.) EKAW 2010. LNCS (LNAI), vol. 6317, pp. 135–149. Springer, Heidelberg (2010)

191. Tramp, S., Heino, N., Auer, S., Frischmuth, P.: RDFauthor: Employing RDFa for collaborative Knowledge Engineering. In: Cimiano, P., Pinto, H.S. (eds.) EKAW 2010. LNCS (LNAI), vol. 6317, pp. 90–104. Springer, Heidelberg (2010)

192. Peter, D.: Turney. Coherent keyphrase extraction via web mining. In: Proceedings of the 18th International Joint Conference on Artificial Intelligence, pp. 434–439. Morgan Kaufmann Publishers Inc., San Francisco (2003)

193. Unger, C., Bühmann, L., Lehmann, J., Ngomo, A.-C.N., Gerber, D., Cimiano, P.: Template-based question answering over rdf data. In: Proceedings of the 21st International Conference on World Wide Web, pp. 639–648 (2012)

194. Urbani, J., Kotoulas, S., Maassen, J., van Harmelen, F., Bal, H.: Owl reasoning with webpie: calculating the closure of 100 billion triples. In: Aroyo, L., Antoniou, G., Hyvönen, E., ten Teije, A., Stuckenschmidt, H., Cabral, L., Tudorache, T. (eds.) ESWC 2010, Part I. LNCS, vol. 6088, pp. 213–227. Springer, Heidelberg (2010)

195. Völker, J., Niepert, M.: Statistical schema induction. In: Antoniou, G., Grobelnik, M., Simperl, E., Parsia, B., Plexousakis, D., De Leenheer, P., Pan, J. (eds.) ESWC 2011, Part I. LNCS, vol. 6643, pp. 124–138. Springer, Heidelberg (2011)

196. Völker, J., Rudolph, S.: Fostering web intelligence by semi-automatic OWL ontology refinement. In: Web Intelligence, pp. 454–460. IEEE (2008)

197. Völker, J., Vrandečić, D., Sure, Y., Hotho, A.: Learning disjointness. In: Franconi, E., Kifer, M., May, W. (eds.) ESWC 2007. LNCS, vol. 4519, pp. 175–189. Springer, Heidelberg (2007)

198. Volz, J., Bizer, C., Gaedke, M., Kobilarov, G.: Discovering and maintaining links on the web of data. In: Bernstein, A., Karger, D.R., Heath, T., Feigenbaum, L., Maynard, D., Motta, E., Thirunarayan, K. (eds.) ISWC 2009. LNCS, vol. 5823, pp. 650–665. Springer, Heidelberg (2009)

199. Walker, D., Amsler, R.: The use of machine-readable dictionaries in sublanguage analysis. In: Analysing Language in Restricted Domains (1986)

200. Wand, Y., Wang, R.Y.: Anchoring data quality dimensions in ontological foundations. Communications of the ACM 39(11), 86–95 (1996)

201. Wang, G., Yu, Y., Zhu, H.: Pore: Positive-only relation extraction from wikipedia text. In: Aberer, K., et al. (eds.) ISWC/ASWC 2007. LNCS, vol. 4825, pp. 580–594. Springer, Heidelberg (2007)

202. Wang, R.Y., Strong, D.M.: Beyond accuracy: what data quality means to data consumers. Journal of Management Information Systems 12(4), 5–33 (1996)

203. Watanabe, H., Muggleton, S.: Can ILP be applied to large dataset? In: De Raedt, L. (ed.) ILP 2009. LNCS (LNAI), vol. 5989, pp. 249–256. Springer, Heidelberg (2010)

204. Winkler, W.: The state of record linkage and current research problems. Technical report, Statistical Research Division, U.S. Bureau of the Census (1999)

205. Winkler, W.: Overview of record linkage and current research directions. Technical report, Bureau of the Census - Research Report Series (2006)

206. Wu, D., Ngai, G., Carpuat, M.: A stacked, voted, stacked model for named entity recognition. In: Proceedings of the Seventh Conference on Natural Language Learning at HLT-NAACL 2003, CONLL 2003, vol. 4, pp. 200–203. Association for Computational Linguistics, Stroudsburg (2003)

207. Wu, H., Zubair, M., Maly, K.: Harvesting social knowledge from folksonomies. In: Proceedings of the Seventeenth Conference on Hypertext and Hypermedia, HYPERTEXT 2006, pp. 111–114. ACM, New York (2006)

208. Yan, Y., Okazaki, N., Matsuo, Y., Yang, Z., Ishizuka, M.: Unsupervised relation extraction by mining wikipedia texts using information from the web. In: ACL 2009, pp. 1021–1029 (2009)

209. Yu, Y., Heflin, J.: Extending functional dependency to detect abnormal data in RDF Graphs. In: Aroyo, L., Welty, C., Alani, H., Taylor, J., Bernstein, A., Kagal, L., Noy, N., Blomqvist, E. (eds.) ISWC 2011, Part I. LNCS, vol. 7031, pp. 794–809. Springer, Heidelberg (2011)

210. Zaveri, A., Kontokostas, D., Sherif, M.A., Bühmann, L., Morsey, M., Auer, S., Lehmann, J.: User-driven quality evaluation of dbpedia. To appear in Proceedings of 9th International Conference on Semantic Systems, I-SEMANTICS 2013, Graz, Austria, September 4-6, pp. 97–104. ACM (2013)

211. Zaveri, A., Lehmann, J., Auer, S., Hassan, M.M., Sherif, M.A., Martin, M.: Publishing and interlinking the global health observatory dataset. Semantic Web Journal, Special Call for Linked Dataset Descriptions (3), 315–322 (2013)

212. Zaveri, A., Rula, A., Maurino, A., Pietrobon, R., Lehmann, J., Auer, S.: Quality assessment methodologies for linked open data. Under review, http://www.semantic-web-journal.net/content/quality-assessment-methodologies-linked-open-data

213. Zhou, G., Su, J.: Named entity recognition using an hmm-based chunk tagger. In: Proceedings of the 40th Annual Meeting on Association for Computational Linguistics, ACL 2002, pp. 473–480. Association for Computational Linguistics, Morristown (2002)

An Introduction to Question Answering over Linked Data

Christina Unger[1], André Freitas[2], and Philipp Cimiano[1]

[1] CITEC, Bielefeld University, Inspiration 1, 33615 Bielefeld
[2] Insight, National University of Galway (NUIG), Galway

Abstract. While the amount of knowledge available as linked data grows, so does the need for providing end users with access to this knowledge. Especially question answering systems are receiving much interest, as they provide intuitive access to data via natural language and shield end users from technical aspects related to data modelling, vocabularies and query languages. This tutorial gives an introduction to the rapidly developing field of question answering over linked data. It gives an overview of the main challenges involved in the interpretation of a user's information need expressed in natural language with respect to the data that is queried. The paper summarizes the main existing approaches and systems including available tools and resources, benchmarks and evaluation campaigns. Finally, it lists the open topics that will keep question answering over linked data an exciting area of research in the years to come.

1 Introduction

The amount of structured knowledge available on the web is growing steadily. The linked data cloud, consisting of a large amount of interlinked RDF (*Resource Description Framework*[1]) datasets, now comprises more than 30 billion RDF triples[2]. Knowledge bases such as Freebase[3] and DBpedia[4] are huge and become more and more popular for various applications. Structured data is by now also collected and exploited by search engines such as Google, e.g. in the form of knowledge graphs[5] that are used to enhance search results.

As the amount of available structured knowledge keeps growing, intuitive and effective paradigms for accessing and querying this knowledge become more and more important. Over the past years, there has been a growing amount of research on interaction paradigms that allow end users to profit from the expressive power of Semantic Web standards while at the same time hiding their complexity behind an intuitive and easy-to-use interface. Especially natural language interfaces such as question answering systems have received wide attention [30], as

---

[1] http://www.w3.org/TR/rdf-primer/
[2] http://www4.wiwiss.fu-berlin.de/lodcloud/state/
[3] http://www.freebase.com/
[4] http://dbpedia.org/
[5] http://www.google.com/insidesearch/features/search/knowledge.html

M. Koubarakis et al. (Eds.): Reasoning Web 2014, LNCS 8714, pp. 100–140, 2014.

they allow users to express arbitrarily complex information needs in an intuitive fashion and, at least in principle, in their own language. In contrast to traditional search engines, question answering systems allow users to pose a (possibly complex) full fledged question, instead of merely a list of keywords, and return precise answers, instead of documents in which the answer can be potentially found. Prominent examples of question answering systems are Wolfram Alpha[6] and IBM's Watson[7], which won the game show Jeopardy! in 2011 against two of the best human players.

Originally, question answering had a strong focus on textual data sources to find answers, relying mostly on information retrieval techniques. In the early 70's, question answering then started to incorporate structured data, developing natural language interfaces to databases [1]. Nowadays, with the growing amount of knowledge in the linked open data cloud, interest in question answering over structured data is quickly regaining interest.

The key challenge for question answering over linked data is to translate the users' information needs into a form such that they can be evaluated using standard Semantic Web query processing and inferencing techniques. Over the past years, a range of approaches have been developed to address this challenge, showing significant advances towards answering natural language questions with respect to large, heterogeneous sets of structured data. In this tutorial, we give an introduction to this exciting, growing field of research.

We start with an overview of the challenges involved in answering questions over linked data in Section 2. Then, Section 3 provides the anatomy of a typical question answering system over linked data, presenting the components that most systems implement in one way or another. Equipped with this general architecture, Section 4 summarizes some of the prominent approaches to question answering over linked data, describing existing systems that are representative for these approaches in more detail. In Section 5 we then list tools and resources that proved useful for question answering over linked data and that can get you started in building your own system. Next, Section 6 mentions measures for evaluating question answering systems and points to some important benchmarking campaigns. Finally, Section 7 reviews the open topics and challenges for future research.

Throughout the tutorial we assume that you have a working knowledge of RDF and its query language SPARQL. For an introduction or refresher, we recommend the W3C primers http://www.w3.org/TR/rdf11-primer/ and http://www.w3.org/TR/rdf-sparql-query/.

2   Main Challenges

If a common web end user wanted to access information in the linked data cloud, he would face two obstacles. First, the amount of available datasets is huge and it is by no means trivial to identify and find those datasets that contain the

---

[6] https://www.wolframalpha.com/

[7] http://researcher.ibm.com/researcher/view_project.php?id=2099

information he is looking for. Second, once he found a relevant dataset, he would need to formulate a query that retrieves the information, e.g. in SPARQL[8], the standard query language for RDF data. To this end, he needs to speak SPARQL and he needs to know the vocabulary and schema underlying the dataset he wants to query.

Since the common web user is usually not familiar with Semantic Web languages or the structure of the linked data cloud and the available datasets, question answering systems aim to bridge the gap between the user and the (structure of the) data, by translating between an information need expressed in natural language on the one hand side and structured queries and answers on the other hand side. In the following, we describe the major challenges in doing so.

2.1   Bridging the Gap between Natural Language and Linked Data

The major task for question answering systems is to interpret the user's information need expressed in natural language with respect to the data that is queried. Consider a simple example: With respect to DBpedia, the question 1a can be expressed by means of the SPARQL query 1b:[9]

1. (a) What is the currency of the Czech Republic?

   (b) ```
       SELECT DISTINCT ?uri
       WHERE {
           res:Czech_Republic dbo:currency ?uri .
       }
       ```

In order to get from the question to the query, we need to know that the name the Czech Republic corresponds to the resource res:Czech_Republic, that the expression currency corresponds to the property dbo:currency, and we need to know the structure of the query, i.e. that the entity res:Czech_Republic is the subject of the property and that the object is to be returned as answer.

While constructing the SPARQL query from the question is (relatively) straightforward in this particular example, very often the process is much more involved. In most cases it involves two challenges: mapping natural language expressions to the vocabulary elements used by the data, accounting for lexical and structural mismatches in doing so, and handling meaning variations introduced by ambiguous and vague expressions, anaphoric expressions, and so on. Let us look at both challenges in turn.

**Mapping Natural Language Expressions to Vocabulary Elements.** URIs are language-independent identifiers. Although they usually bear mnemonic

---

[8] http://www.w3.org/TR/rdf-sparql-query/

[9] Throughout the tutorial, we will use the following prefixes: dbo for http://dbpedia.org/ontology/, dbp for http://dbpedia.org/property/, and res for http://dbpedia.org/resource/
       ```

names, their only actual connection to natural language is by the labels that are attached to them. These labels often provide a canonical way to refer to the URI, but usually do not account for lexical variation. The class dbo:Film, for example, has the English label film but does not capture other variants such as movie. Similarly, the property dbo:spouse bears the English label spouse, while natural language knows a wide varierty of ways of expressing this relationship, among them wife of, husband of, and to be married to, which are more likely to occur in a user question than the somewhat more formal term spouse.

So although the vocabulary of natural language and the vocabulary used by the data overlap, the expressions a user uses often differ from the labels attached to the data. Bridging the resulting *lexical gap* is thus one of the challenges that a question answering system needs to address. The following example 2 illustrates vocabulary similarities and differences.

2. (a) Which Greek cities have more than 1 million inhabitants?

   (b)
```
SELECT DISTINCT ?uri
WHERE {
     ?uri rdf:type dbo:City .
     ?uri dbo:country res:Greece .
     ?uri dbo:populationTotal ?p .
     FILTER (?p > 1000000)
}
```

It is more or less straightforward to match the expression cities to the class dbo:City having the label city. Less straightforward is matching have inhabitants to the property populationTotal; here the similarity between both exists only on the semantic level but not on the string level. Furthermore, Greek needs to be matched with the property dbo:country with fixed object Greece. This already points to another difficulty: differences in the structure of the question and the query.

Structural differences are due to the fact that the conceptual granularity of language does often not coincide with that of the schema underlying a particular dataset. On the one hand side it can be that natural language is more granular than the data, as in the following example 3, where the structure of the natural language questions suggests a relation join that relates two entities, Germany and the EU, while the required property is dbp:accessioneudate, relating a country to the date when it joined the EU.

3. (a) When did Germany join the EU?

   (b)
```
SELECT DISTINCT ?date
WHERE {
     res:Germany dbp:accessioneudate ?date .
}
```

On the other hand side it can be that the data is more granular than natural language. In the following example 4, there is one natural language expressions great-grandchildren that corresponds to a property chain consisting of three times the property dbo:child.

4. (a) Who are the great-grandchildren of Bruce Lee?

   (b)
```
SELECT DISTINCT ?uri
WHERE {
      res:Bruce_Lee dbo:child ?c1 .
                    ?c1 dbo:child ?c2 .
                    ?c2 dbo:child ?uri .
}
```

In addition to mapping natural language expressions to vocabulary elements underlying a particular dataset, there are expressions that do not correspond to any vocabulary element but rather have a fixed, dataset-independent meaning. Examples are quantifiers like the most (see example 5), comparative expressions like more than (see example 6) and less than, cardinals and superlatives (see example 7). These expressions correspond to aggregation operations in SPARQL, such as filtering, ordering and limits.

5. (a) Who produced the most films?

   (b)
```
SELECT DISTINCT ?uri
WHERE {
      ?x rdf:type dbo:Film .
      ?x dbo:producer ?uri .
}
ORDER BY DESC(COUNT(?x))
LIMIT 1
```

6. (a) Which cities have more than three universities?

   (b)
```
SELECT DISTINCT ?uri
WHERE {
      ?x rdf:type dbo:University .
      ?x dbo:city ?uri .
}
HAVING (COUNT(?x) > 3)
```

7. (a) What is the second highest mountain on Earth?

   (b)
```
SELECT DISTINCT ?uri
WHERE {
          ?uri rdf:type dbo:Mountain .
          ?uri dbo:elevation ?x .
}
ORDER BY DESC(?x)
OFFSET 1 LIMIT 1
```

Meaning Variation. Question answering systems involve processing natural language and thus inherit the challenges involved in processing natural language in general. On of these challenges is dealing with ambiguities. Ambiguity covers all cases in which a natural language expression can have more than one meaning, in our case can map to more than one vocabulary element in the target dataset. For instance, different vocabularies usually offer different ways of answering an information need. In 8, having adopted the Euro can be expressed either by means of the property dbo:currency with the object resource res:Euro, or by means of the property dbp:currency with the object literal 'EUR'. In this case, both mappings are appropriate; we thus constructed a query taking the union of the results of both mappings.

8. (a) Which countries adopted the Euro?

   (b) ```
SELECT DISTINCT ?uri
WHERE {
    ?uri rdf:type dbo:Country .
    { ?uri dbo:currency res:Euro . }
    UNION
    { ?uri dbp:currencyCode 'EUR'@en . }
}
```

In other cases only one mapping is appropriate, often depending on the context. For example, to retrieve the mayor of a city from DBpedia, the corresponding property is dbo:mayor in the case of Lyon, dbo:leader in the case of Berlin, and dbo:leaderName in the case of Tel Aviv.

A more extreme form of ambiguity arises from semantically light expressions, such as the verbs to be and to have, and prepositions like of, with, etc. What vocabulary element they need to be mapped to strongly depends on the linguistic context they occur in. Consider the verb to have. In 9, have corresponds to the property dbo:exhibits, while in 10, have corresponds to the property dbo:location. The only difference between both questions is that the former is about museums and painting, and the latter is about countries and caves.

9. (a) Which museum has the most paintings?

   (b) ```
SELECT DISTINCT ?uri
WHERE {
    ?uri rdf:type dbo:Museum .
    ?x   rdf:type dbo:Painting .
    ?uri dbo:exhibits ?x .
}
ORDER BY DESC(COUNT(?x))
LIMIT 1
```

10. (a) Which country has the most caves?

   (b) ```
SELECT DISTINCT ?uri
WHERE {
    ?uri rdf:type dbo:Country .
    ?x   rdf:type dbo:Cave .
    ?x   dbo:location ?uri .
```
```

```
}
ORDER BY DESC(COUNT(?x))
LIMIT 1
```

Of course, semantically light expressions can in one context also be mapped to different vocabulary elements, as the preposition in in the following example.

11. (a) Give me all companies in Munich.

(b)
```
SELECT DISTINCT ?uri
WHERE {
    ?uri rdf:type dbo:Company .
    { ?uri dbo:location res:Munich . }
    UNION
    { ?uri dbo:headquarter res:Munich . }
    UNION
    { ?uri dbo:locationCity res:Munich . }
}
```

2.2 Multilinguality

Multilinguality has become an issue of major interest for the Semantic Web community, as both the number of actors creating and publishing data in languages other than English, as well as the amount of users that access this data and speak native languages other than English is growing substantially. In order to achieve the goal that users from all countries have access to the same information, there is an impending need for systems that can help in overcoming language barriers by facilitating multilingual access to semantic data originally produced for a different culture and language.

In principle, the Semantic Web is very well suited for multilinguality, as URIs are language-independent identifiers. However, in order to access and use these identifiers in different language contexts, it is important to have labels in these languages. But adding multilingual labels is not common practice. A recent study [21] has shown that the majority of datasets is monolingual: Less than a quarter of the RDF literals have language tags, and most of those tags are in English.

In the context of question answering over linked data, a challenge is to interpret questions in multiple languages. For example, all the questions in 12 taken from the QALD-4 benchmarking dataset express the same information need and thus should be mapped to the same SPARQL query 13.

12. – *English:* Which German cities have more than 250000 inhabitants?
    – *German:* Welche deutschen Städte haben mehr als 250000 Einwohner?
    – *Spanish:* ¿Qué ciudades alemanas tienen más de 250000 habitantes?
    – *Italian:* Quali città tedesche hanno più di 250000 abitanti?
    – *French:* Quelles villes allemandes ont plus de 250000 habitants?

– *Dutch:* Welke Duitse steden hebben meer dan 250000 inwoners?
– *Romanian:* Ce oraşe germane au mai mult de 250000 de locuitori?

```
13. PREFIX dbo: <http://dbpedia.org/ontology/>
    PREFIX res: <http://dbpedia.org/resource/>
    PREFIX rdf: <http://www.w3.org/1999/02/22-rdf-syntax-ns#>
    SELECT DISTINCT ?uri
    WHERE {
            { ?uri rdf:type dbo:City . }
            UNION
            { ?uri rdf:type dbo:Town . }
            ?uri dbo:country res:Germany .
            ?uri dbo:populationTotal ?population .
            FILTER ( ?population > 250000 ) }
```

2.3 Data Quality and Data Heterogeneity

Strong requirements on question answering systems are completeness and accuracy (wrong answers are often worse than no answers). In the context of linked data, this especially requires a system to deal with heterogeneous and imperfect data. First of all, the knowledge available on the linked data cloud is incomplete, so question answering systems should be able to detect when the queried data sources do not contain the answer. Second, the datasets sometimes contain duplicate information, with different datasets using different vocabularies even when talking about the same things. Possibly, datasets also contain conflicting information and inconsistencies, which have to be dealt with.

2.4 Performance and Scalability

The temporal performance of question answering systems over linked data is rarely reported in the literature. In [28], FREyA is reported to require 36 seconds on average to answer questions over DBpedia, while Aqualog reports an average of 20 seconds on the same dataset, and these are figures for one dataset only. This shows that yielding performant systems that provide timely answers is challenging. The challenge here is to cope with large datasets comprising billions of triples. Performance in real time, which we regard as processing a question in under a second, can only be obtained by using appropriate index structures, search heuristics and possibly adopting distributed computing principles. Also, systems are often considered scalable only if the response time is not proportional to the size of data being accessed.

2.5 Coping with Distributed and Linked Datasets

Only few systems yet address the fact that the structured data available nowadays is distributed among a large collection of interconnected datasets, and that answers to questions can often only be provided if information from several sources are combined. In fact, the issue of how to evaluate natural language questions of distributed but linked datasets has not been investigated extensively yet. Exceptions are PowerAqua (see Section 4.1) and the system by Ngonga et al. [34], which builds on federation and attempts to decompose a question into several parts that can be answered with respect to different datasets.

Consider the example query *What are side effects of drugs used for the treatment of Tuberculosis?* (taken in modified form from [34]), which can be answered using three different (linked) datasets, i.e. the Sider dataset[10] (containing information about drugs and their side effects), the Diseasome dataset[11] (containing information about diseases and genes associated with these diseases) and Drugbank [12] (containing comprehensive knowledge base containing information about drugs, drug target (i.e. protein) information, interactions and enzymes, etc.).

2.6 Integrating Structured and Unstructured Data

In addition, a lot of information is still available only in textual form, both on the web and in the form of labels and abstracts in linked data sources. Therefore approaches are needed that can not only deal with the specific character of structured data but also with finding information in several sources, processing both structured and unstructured information, and combining such gathered information into one answer.

An example for a question requiring both structured and unstructured data when being answered over DBpedia is the following one. Here, the information that needs to be extracted from free text is marked by the prefix `text`.

14. (a) Where did the first man in space die?

    (b)
```
SELECT DISTINCT ?uri
WHERE {
    ?x text:"is" text:"first man in space" .
    ?x dbo:deathPlace ?uri .
}
```

Identifying the person that was the first man in space is possible only by means of the free text abstract, while his death place is encoded only in the RDF data.

Approaches that exploit both structured and unstructured data are very rare so far. A notable exception is the system by Fader et al. [14].

3   The Anatomy of a Question Answering System

All approaches to question answering over linked data share the challenges mentioned in the previous section, and most of the systems rely on the same kind of

---

[10] http://sideeffects.embl.de/
[11] http://diseasome.kobic.re.kr/
[12] http://www.drugbank.ca/

components to address them, although they often differ in their particular implementation. This section introduces the subtasks involved in the overall task of answering questions, and then presents the general architecture of a prototypical question answering system over linked data, explaining the components that most existing systems employ.

3.1   Dimensions of Question Answering

Question answering is a complex and multi-dimensional task. Categorizing the different dimensions of question answering is fundamental for understanding the different phenomena and challenges involved in a question answering task. Additionally, the categorization helps in the definition of the scope of a question answering system and to set up a proper evaluation. This section describes the most important dimensions involved in question answering and their associated elements, including types of questions and answers, data source types, and key functionalities.

Question and Answer Type. Question classification is often done based on a categorization of the answers that are expected, based either on their *form* or their *type*. Classifying questions with respect to the answer form results in a question taxonomy roughly along the following lines:

- *Factoid questions*, including
    Predicative questions, e.g.
        Who was the first man in space?
        What is the highest mountain in Korea?
        How far is it from Earth to Mars?
        When did the Jurassic Period end?
        Where is Taj Mahal?
    List questions, e.g.
        Give me all cities in Germany.
    Yes/No questions, e.g.
        Was Margaret Thatcher a chemist?
- *Definition questions*, e.g.
        Who was Tom Jobim?
- *Evaluative or comparative questions*, e.g.
        What is the difference between impressionism and expressionism?
- *Association questions*, e.g.
        What is the connection between Barack Obama and Indonesia?
- *Explanation/Justification questions*, e.g.
        Why did the revenue of IBM drop?
- *Process questions*, e.g.
        How do I make a cheese cake?
- *Opinion question*, e.g.
        What do most Americans think of gun control?

Question answering systems often focus on factoid and definition questions. In the context of the linked data cloud this is mainly due to this being the kind of information represented in the available datasets.

Classifying questions with respect to the type of the expected answer leads to answer taxonomies such as the one proposed by Li & Roth [26]. The following list gives their five high-level categories together with examples of the more fine-grained subcategories:

- *Abbreviation*
- *Entity:* event, color, animal, plant,...
- *Description:* definition, manner, reason,...
- *Human:* group, individual,...
- *Location:* city, country, mountain,...
- *Numeric:* count, date, distance, size,...

In addition to the form or type of answer, a more fine-grained question classification is possible by means of *question focus* and *topic*, representing what the question is about. For example, in the question What is the height of Mount Everest?, the focus is the property height, and the topic is, more generally, geography. In the question What is the best height increasing drug?, the focus looks similar, while the topic is medicine.

Data Sources. Question answering systems differ with respect to the data source(s) they are able to process to derive an answer. On the one hand side, they usually consume a specific type of data:

- *Structured data*, e.g. relational databases and linked data
- *Semi-structured data*, e.g. XML documents
- *Unstructured data*, e.g. text documents

Hybrid question answering systems are able to process a combination of two or more of the types of data mentioned above.

On the other hand side, question answering systems differ with respect to the number of data sources they consider:

- a *single* dataset
- an enumerated list of *multiple*, distributed datasets
- all datasets available on a *large scale*, i.e. considering all datasets of a certain kind (e.g. structured or text) available on the web or in the linked data cloud

Furthermore, a question answering system can be either *domain-specific*, addressing very specific knowledge in a particular domain, e.g. the biomedical or financial domain, or *open-domain*, addressing general knowledge, especially encylopaedic knowledge, common-sense knowledge, news or trivia.

Finally, the modality of the data that is considered is often text or structured knowledge, but can also include other modalities such as images, sound, and video.

Complexity of the Question Answering Task. The complextiy of the question answering task can be classified according to different dimensions involved in interpreting the question and processing the data, such as the following ones:

- *Semantic tractability* [32], specifying the closeness between the natural language question and the formal query or answer in terms of lexical and structural similarity
- *Semantic complexity*, comprising the level of complexity of the domain, the amount of ambiguity and vagueness in the question, as well as data heterogeneity
- *Answer locality*, specifying whether the answer is wholly contained in one dataset, or snippets from which the answer can be composed are distributed across different datasets
- *Derivability*, specifying whether the answer is explicit or implicit, in the latter case, e.g., requiring additional reasoning

3.2 Components of a Question Answering System

Despite the architectural particularities of different question answering systems, there are high-level functionalities and components which are present in most of them. These components are depicted in Figure 1 and described in the following.

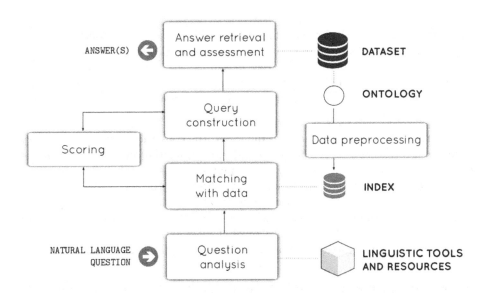

Fig. 1. High-level components of question answering systems over linked data

Data Preprocessing: Preprocessing the information present in a dataset helps to reduce the runtime of a system. For example, systems often rely on an index of the dataset in order to match natural language expressions with labels of vocabulary elements. This also speeds up processing.

Question Analysis: The first step of a question answering system often consists in the linguistic analysis of the question, as well as the detection and extraction of question features. The linguistic analysis can involve both a syntactic and a semantic analysis, commonly relying on tools such as part-of-speech taggers and parsers, on resources such as dictionaries, e.g. WordNet or Wiktionary, and possibly some logical representation formalism to capture the meaning of a question. It also involves steps like Named Entity Recognition. In addition, a question can be analysed with respect to the categories mentioned above, in particular detecting the question type, the focus and the expected answer type.

Data Matching: In order to deal with the lexical and structural differences between the question vocabulary and the dataset elements, a component is required that matches question terms with the dataset terminology. It can range from simple term look-up to more sophisticated semantic matching strategies.

Query Construction: Based on the results of the first two components, the input question is transformed into a structured query.

Scoring: Usually, both the data matching and the query construction components output several candidates that need to be scored and ranked. Criteria for scoring can include different similarity measures (e.g. string similarity and semantic relatedness), popularity of data elements (e.g. based on their frequency), and coherence of the candidates and their combinations with the data schema.

Answer Retrieval and Assessment: Next, the constructed structured query needs to be executed over the database, extracting the answer to the input question. This component possibly also comprises an assessment of the answers, e.g. checking whether the type of the answer fits the expected answer type.

Especially if several datasets are queried that provide either different parts of an answer or overlapping and conflicting answers, the scoring and integration of answers becomes crucial, taking into account information provenance and reliability, i.e. how trust-worthy the source is from which the answer was extracted.

Answer Presentation: Finally, the answer needs to be presented to the user. Especially for question answering systems over linked data aiming at making structured data accessible for common end users not familiar with Semantic Web languages, it is important to not return answers as URIs or triples but in a more comprehensible format, e.g. in natural language or as a visual graph.

4   Overview of State-of-the-Art Systems

There is a range of approaches to meeting the challenges we described in Section 2. They vary in several aspects, e.g. being domain-specific or schema-agnostic, relying on a deep linguistic analysis, on statistical methods, or on graph exploration algorithms, and involving different resources. In general, approaches to question answering over linked data can be classified into the following types of systems.

Approaches Based on Controlled Natural Languages. Approaches based on controlled natural languages, e.g. GiNSENG [3], typically consider a well-defined restricted subset of natural language that can be unambiguously interpreted by a given system.

Approaches Based on Formal Grammars: Systems based on formal grammars, such as ORAKEL and Pythia (see Section 4.2 below), typically rely on linguistic grammars that assign a syntactic and semantic representation to lexical units, and exploit the principle of compositional semantics to compute an overall semantic representation of a question by combining the meaning of the parts as specified in the grammar. The benefit of such systems is that, if the corresponding constructs are covered by the grammar, they can deal with questions of arbitrary complexity. The clear drawback is their brittleness, as they fail if a certain question can not be parsed by the grammar.

Approaches Based on Mapping Linguistic Structures to Ontology-Compliant Semantic Structures: Systems such as Aqualog and PowerAqua (see Section 4.1 below) in contrast adopt a more shallow strategy and try to directly match linguistic structures to semantic triples. To this end, they rely on a measure of similarity that determines the similarity between elements in the query and predicates, subjects or objects in the knowledge base, more or less aiming at computing a bijective mapping between the elements of the query and resources or predicates. QAKIS [5], for instance, tries to establish a match between fragments in the natural language question and textual patterns that were automatically collected from Wikipedia. Other systems along these lines are FREyA [10] and Querix [23]. While such approaches are more robust than approaches based on formal grammars, they suffer from the fact that there needs to be a one-to-one correspondence between the syntactic structure of the question and the semantic representation. An approach aims to remedy this is [40], which generates relaxed query variants that cover the user question to different extents, especially leaving out intractable parts and instead adding them as textual conditions that are then used in determining mappings from natural language expressions to URIs and for disambiguation.

Template-Based Approaches. Template-based approaches, such as LODQA and TBSL (see Section 4.3 below) implement a two-stage process for transforming a natural language question into a SPARQL query. First, they construct a template (or pseudo-query) on the basis of a linguistic analysis of the input question. Second, this template is instantiated by matching the natural language expressions occuring in the question with elements form the queried dataset. The main weakness of such approaches is that often the templates closely correspond to the linguistic structure of the question, thus failing in cases of structural mismatches between natural language and the dataset. While structural variations can be included in the templates, this usually explodes the number of possible queries to build and score.

Graph Exploration Approaches. Graph exploration approaches, such as Treo (see Section 4.4 below), Top-k exploration [35] and the approach by Ngonga et al. [34], interpret a natural language question by mapping elements of the question to entities from the knowledge base, and then proceeding from these pivot elements to navigate the graph, seeking to connect the entities to yield a connected query. The main bottleneck of graph-based approaches is that an exhaustive search of the graph is unfeasible, so that approaches typically explore the graph up to a certain depth or implement some heuristics to make the search over the graph more efficient. This is particularly relevant when the data is not available locally but needs to be explored via HTTP-requests, as is the case for linked data. Treo for example implements a heuristic search over linked data, relying on spreading activation guided by a measure of semantic relatedness. Another drawback of graph-based approaches is that more complex queries involving aggregation, e.g. *Which researcher has written the most papers in the Semantic Web area?* cannot be answered as they do not have a one-to-one correspondence to a path in the graph.

Machine Learning Approaches. A number of recent approaches consider question answering as a machine learning problem. Examples are [33], who propose a model for joint query interpretation and response ranking, [2] and [25], who aim at learning semantic parsers given a knowledge base and a set of question/answer pairs, and [6], who combine a standard supervised algorithm for learning semantic parsers with an algorithm for matching natural language expressions and ontology concepts, and an algorithm for storing matches in a parse lexicon.

In the following, we will discuss a subset of the above mentioned systems in more detail, in particular PowerAqua, one of the first question answering systems for RDF knowledge bases, our own systems Pythia, TBSL, and Treo, as well as the DeepQA approach developed by IBM Watson.

4.1   Aqualog and PowerAqua: Querying on a Semantic Web Scale

PowerAqua [27] is a question answering system focusing on querying multiple datasets on the Semantic Web. PowerAqua is an evolution of the AquaLog

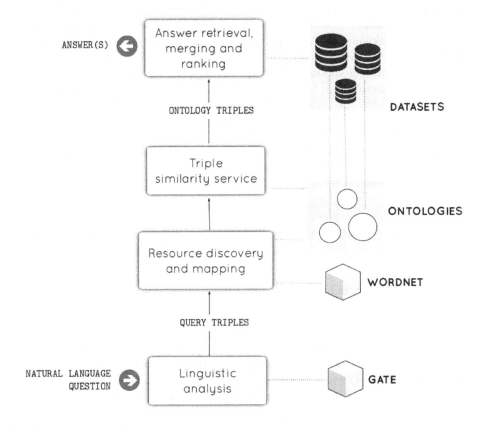

Fig. 2. Architecture of PowerAqua

system [29], one of the first question answering systems targeting Semantic Web data.

Figure 2 depicts the high-level architecture of the PowerAqua system, described in more detail in the following. The first step consists in a linguistic analysis of the question using GATE[13], in order to detect the question type and to translate the natural language question into a triple-based representation, into so-called *query triples*. Here are two examples of question and the corresponding query triples that are generated:

15. Give me actors starring in movies directed by Clint Eastwood.
    – ⟨actors, starring, movies⟩
    – ⟨actors/movies, directed, Clint Eastwood⟩
16. Find me university cities in Japan.
    – ⟨university cities, ?, Japan⟩

---

[13] https://gate.ac.uk/

The subject of the second triple in 15, actors/movies, represents an ambiguity with respect to which of both terms fulfil the role. The property in 16, on the other hand, is unknown, as it stems from the semantically light preposition in.

The second step then searches for candidate instantiations of the occurring terms. This involves detecting ontologies on the Semantic Web that are likely to contain the information requested in the question, and finding vocabulary elements that match the terms. Matching natural language terms and vocabulary elements relies both on string-based similarity measures, allowing for exact matches (Japan) and approximate matchings (CountryJapan), and on WordNet synonyms, hypernyms and hyponyms as well as on owl:sameAs links. Moreover, this component uses word sense disambiguation techniques to disambiguate different interpretations of the question terms across ontologies. The output is a set of tables containing matching semantic elements for each term occurring in the query triples. These mappings can be used to turn query triples into *ontology triples*. For example, given the mappings found in DBpedia for the terms in the first query triple in 15, this triple can be transformed into the following ontology triples:

- ⟨Actor, starring, Film⟩
- ⟨Actor, starring, American_movie⟩

Next, the relation similarity service (RSS) component determines the most likely interpretation both of the terms in the query triples and the question as a whole, on the basis of the linguistic analysis of the question and the ontological context. This can also involve modifying query triples, e.g. by splitting compound terms. The term university cities, for example, can be split, yielding a new query triple:

17. ⟨cities/universities, ?, Japan⟩

Finally, given a ranked list of ontology triples, answers are retrieved from the involved data sources. Since these can be multiple different sources, this step also involves identifying semantically equivalent or overlapping information in the answer set, in order to avoid duplicate results, a ranking of answers, as well as integrating answer fragments from different sources.

PowerAqua's main strength is that it locates and integrates information from different, heterogeneous semantic resources, relying on query disambiguation, ranking and fusion of answers. Its main weakness, on the other hand, is that due to limitations in GATE it cannot cope with aggregation, i.e. questions involving counting (e.g. how many), comparisons (such as higher than or more than), and superlatives (such as the highest and the most).

4.2   ORAKEL and Pythia: Ontology-Specific Question Answering

ORAKEL [9] and Pythia [38] are ontology-based question answering systems. This means that ontologies play a central role in interpreting user questions.

For example, ontological knowledge is used for drawing inferences, e.g. in order to resolve ambiguities or to interpret semantically light expressions. But most importantly, user questions are interpreted with respect to an ontology underlying the dataset that is queried. Unlike systems that first construct general, dataset-independent meaning representations (like the triple representations built by PowerAqua) and only subsequently try to match this with the target data, ORAKEL and Pythia construct meaning representations whose vocabulary is already aligned to the vocabulary of the ontology. To this end, they rely on ontology-lexica that make the possible linguistic realizations of ontology concepts in a particular language explicit, e.g. in *lemon* [31] format. *lemon* is a model for the declarative specification of multilingual, machine-readable lexica in RDF that capture syntactic and semantic aspects of lexical items relative to some ontology. The meaning of a lexical item is given by reference to an ontology element, i.e. a class, property or individual, thereby ensuring a clean separation between the ontological and lexical layer. Since *lemon* abstracts from specific linguistic theories and grammar formalisms, all linguistic categories such as part of speeches, syntactic roles and frames have to be defined in an external linguistic ontology, such as *LexInfo* [8].

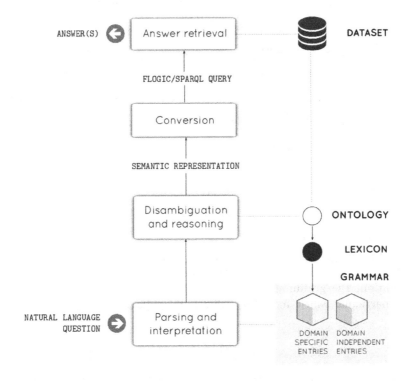

Fig. 3. Architecture of ORAKEL and Pythia

Both ORAKEL and Pythia implement the architecture depicted in Figure 3. First, the ontology lexicon is used to automatically construct principled linguistic representations. ORAKEL relies on *Logical Description Grammars* (LDG) as syntactic formalism and an extended version of lambda calculus for specifying semantic representations; Pythia builds on *Lexicalized Tree Adjoining Grammars* [36] (LTAG) as syntactic formalism and *Dependency-based Underspecified Discourse Representation Structures* [7] (DUDES) for specifying semantic representations. Those linguistic representations – together with domain-independent representations, e.g. for determiners and auxiliary verbs – constitute the grammar that is used for parsing and interpreting an input question. Syntactic and semantic analysis work in parallel. In particular, the interpretation process is compositional, meaning that the semantic representation of the input is recursively computed on the basis of the meaning of the words in the input as well as the way the words are connected syntactically. Finally, the resulting meaning representations are transformed into formal queries, in particular F-Logic and SPARQL queries.

For instance, for the question Which cities have more than three universities?, the following processing would take place. First of all, ORAKEL and Pythia require an ontology-lexicon. This lexicon would specify the English lexicalizations university and alma mater for the ontology class University, the lexicalization city for the ontology class City, and, for example, the lexicalization located in for the ontology property city. On the basis of these lexicalization, syntactic and semantic representations are constructed. Here we only show the ones that are relevant for the interpretation of the questions:

18. a.
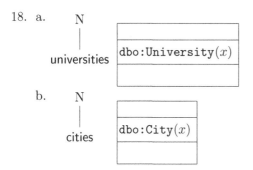

The meaning representations can be viewed as first-order logic like representation. Note that they already use the vocabulary of the ontology.

In addition, the grammar contains entries for domain-independent expressions, in particular which, more than, three, and to have:

19. a.

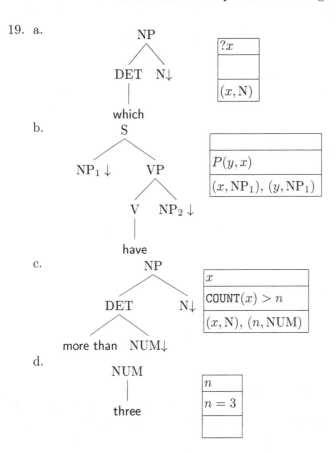

Tree nodes marked with ↓ constitute so-called substitution nodes, which can be replaced by a tree having a root node of the specified category. The meaning representations consist of three parts: a set of variables (where variables marked with a question mark will be returned by the final SPARQL query), a set of first-order logic like conditions, and a set of pairs specifying the role that the meaning contributions of the arguments play (e.g. (x, N) means that the meaning of the N node will be unified with x). The meaning repesentation of the semantically light verb to have moreover contains a predicate variable P, which will need to be resolved with respect to the ontology vocabulary later. Both the lexicon and the generated domain-specific grammar entries as well as the domain-independent grammar entries are constructed offline and then used during the run-time of the systems. Using the trees in 18 and 19 for parsing yields the tree shown in 20a. In parallel to the syntactic analysis, the semantic representations in 18 and 19 are combined into the resulting meaning given in 20b.

20. (a)

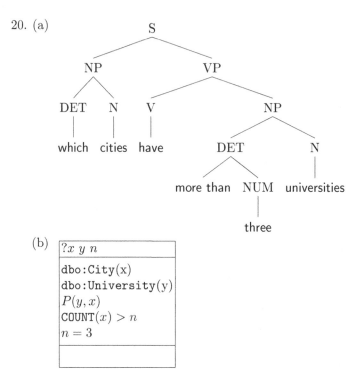

(b)

?x y n
dbo:City(x)
dbo:University(y)
$P(y, x)$
COUNT(x) > n
n = 3

In order to resolve P, the disambiguation and reasoning steps retrieve all those properties from the ontology that are compatible with domain University and range City. In the case of DBpedia, these are the properties city, location, and a few more. At this point, Pythia would assume that all of them are valid instantiations of P, and it would retrieve answers for all possible interpretations. So one of the queries resulting from converting the meaning representation of the question into SPARQL would be the following one:

21.
```
SELECT DISTINCT ?x
   WHERE {
       ?x rdf:type dbo:City .
       ?y rdf:type dbo:University .
       ?y dbo:city ?x .
   }
   GROUP BY ?y
   HAVING (COUNT(?y) > 3)
```

Implementing a principled, deep linguistic analysis allows ORAKEL and Pythia to construct formal queries even for complex natural language questions, e.g. involving quantification and superlatives. Moreover, since the resulting meaning representations are built from atomic building blocks that were generated from an ontology lexicon, they use a vocabulary that is aligned to the vocabulary of the ontology. This ensures a precise and correct mapping of natural language terms to corresponding ontology concepts. The use of an ontology lexicon therefore offers a very precise way of matching natural expressions with ontology concepts.

ORAKEL and Pythia thus are in this sense question answering systems specific for a given ontology that require an ontology lexicon for the ontology that models the data that is queried. The bottleneck here consists in the effort required for building such lexica, either manually or semi-automatically [39]. And although a grammar-based interpretation process offers high precision, systems relying on domain grammars usually suffer from limited coverage.

4.3   TBSL and LODQA: Template-Based Question Answering

TBSL [37] and LODQA [24] are template-based approaches that rely on a parse of the user question to produce a query template. This template mirrors the linguistic structure of the question and is, in a second step, instantiated by mapping the occurring natural language expressions to the domain vocabulary. The main intuition is that the linguistic structure of a question together with expressions like more than and the most already determine part of the query that is needed in order to retrieve answers. This part is domain-independent and provides a skeleton structure of the query that then needs to be filled in with domain-specific vocabulary elements.

More specifically, TBSL implements the architecture depicted in Figure 4. For linguistic analysis, TBSL relies on a parsing and interpretation step just like Pythia (described above). The only difference is that no domain-specific lexicon is required. Instead, the input question is first processed by a part-of-speech tagger. The resulting part-of-speech tags are used to create general linguistic representations on the fly. These representations are underspecified in the sense that their meaning with respect to the queried data is still unknown. Like in the case of Pythia, these representations are, together with pre-defined domain-independent representations, used for parsing, which leads to an underspecified semantic representation of the natural language question (still without specific domain vocabulary elements) that is then converted into a SPARQL query template. This conversion relies on heuristic rules specifying that verbs usually correspond to properties, that nouns and adjectives correspond to classes or properties, and that proper names correspond to resources.

The query templates that TBSL builds for the question Who produced the most films, for example, are given in 22. They consist of a SPARQL query containing slots for all missing elements that need to be filled based on the domain vocabulary. The slots contain information about the type of missing element (class, property or resource) and the natural language expressions it should correspond to. The latter are the words that are contained in the input question together with synonyms retrieved from WordNet.

22. (a) SELECT DISTINCT ?x
         WHERE {
             ?y rdf:type ?c .
             ?y ?p ?x .

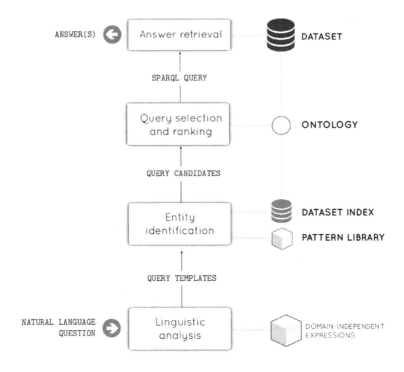

Fig. 4. Architecture of TBSL

```
}
ORDER BY DESC(COUNT(?y))
LIMIT 1
```
  - (?c,Class,[films])
  - (?p,Property,[produced])

```
SELECT DISTINCT ?x
WHERE {
  ?x ?p ?y .
}
ORDER BY DESC(COUNT(?y))
LIMIT 1
```
(b)   - (?p,Property,[films])

In order to obtain URIs that fill the slots, TBSL uses an index to look up entities that match with the required class and given natural language expressions. The matching relies on string similarity, matching with WordNet synonyms, and on an existing collection of natural language patterns, BOA [19]. The basic idea behind BOA is to use the instance knowledge available in a dataset to compute natural language expressions that stand for properties from the underlying ontology. To this end, for any given property, BOA first retrieves pairs of those entities that the property relates. The labels of those entities are then used to search a text corpus for sentences in which they occur, from which possible natural language verbalizations of the property are extracted. Similarly, an ontology-lexicon as used by ORAKEL and Pythia could be employed as pattern collection.

The result of the entity identification step is a list of URI candidates for filling the slots, ranked regarding their string similarity values and prominence values (i.e. their frequency in the dataset). For our example question and considering DBpedia as dataset, candidates for filling the class slot would include the classes `Film` and `FilmFestival`, and candidates for filling the property slot would include the properties `producer` and `wineProduced`, among a range of others.

These candidates are used to construct all possible query instantiations, representing potential translations of the input question. These queries are ranked with respect to the rank of the entities occurring in them. Moreover, TBSL performs a schema conformance check, in particular checking whether the types of the occuring entities are compatible with the domain and range of those properties that relate the entities. For example, the class candiates `Film` and `FilmFestival` are incomaptible with the property candidate `wineProduced`, as the domain of the latter is `WineRegion`.

Finally, the highest ranked queries are tested against the underlying triple store and the best answer is returned to the user. For the question Who produced the most films, for example, the highest ranked query is the following one (with a score of 0.76).

```
23. SELECT DISTINCT ?x
    WHERE {
    ?x <http://dbpedia.org/ontology/producer> ?y .
    ?y rdf:type <http://dbpedia.org/ontology/Film> .
    }
    ORDER BY DESC(COUNT(?y))
    LIMIT 1
```

An enhancement of TBSL and LODQA is the question answering system platform developed in the context of the OKBQA hackathon[14] in 2014, open and freely accessible on GitHub: `https://github.com/okbqa`. Some of the main improvements concern the template generation component, which relies on a more robust linguistic analysis using dependency parsing and semantic role labeling instead of grammars. Also, the main problem that TBSL faces is that the constructed query templates are too fixed. In order to cover all possible template structures as well as all possibilities of filling the slots of those templates with all possible entity candidates, a huge set of candidate queries needs to be considered. Instead, it is desirable not to fix the triple structured of the query body but rather determine it by means of dataset exploration, e.g. relation finding.

---

[14] `http://www.okbqa.org`

4.4   Treo: Schema-agnostic Querying Using Distributional Semantics

Addressing the vocabulary mismatch problem for databases is central to querying large schema and heterogeneous linked datasets. One of the main challenges in addressing the vocabulary mismatch problem is its dependency on large-scale common-sense or domain-specific knowledge. As an example, suppose we want to interpret the question Is Chelsea Clinton married? to the associated data (:`Chelsea_Clinton` :`spouse` :`Marc_Mezvinsky`). Mapping the query to the data depends on semantically matching married to spouse. Representing common-sense knowledge using structured large-scale knowledge bases comes with the price of data acquisition (manually or through automated information extraction methods), data representation and reasoning over large-scale knowledge bases. These are on their own right major challenges in artificial intelligence research. Existing structured resources such as WordNet do not fully address the vocabulary problem [16].

The Treo approach focuses on addressing this challenge using *distributional semantic models*. Distributional semantics is defined upon the assumption that the context surrounding a given word in a text provides important information about its meaning [22]. Distributional semantics focuses on the automatic construction of a semantic model based on the statistical distribution of word co-occurrence in texts, allowing the creation of an associational and quantitative model which captures the degree of semantic relatedness between words. Distributional semantic models are represented by Vector Space Models (VSMs), where the meaning of a word is represented by a weighted vector which captures the patterns of co-occurrence with other words in the corpus. Distributional models focus on complementing approaches such as WordNet and ontology-based approaches, trading structure for volume of commonsense knowledge [18] and automatic construction capabilities. In the Treo system, a distributional semantic model is used as a core element to address the query-dataset vocabulary gap together with a compositional model based query patterns.

Figure 5 depicts the high-level workflow behind Treo using the question Who is the daughter of Bill Clinton married to? as example. The first step (step 1) is the construction of a distributional semantic model based on the extraction of co-occurrence patterns from large corpora, which defines a distributional semantic vector space. The distributional semantic vector space uses concept vectors to semantically represent data and queries, by mapping dataset elements and query terms to concepts in the distributional space. Once the space is built, the RDF graph data is embedded into the space (step 2), defining the $\tau - Space$, a structured distributional semantic vector space. The alignment between structured data and the distributional model allows the use of the large-scale common-sense information embedded in the distributional model (extracted from text) to be used in the *semantic matching/approximation* process.

After the data is indexed into the $\tau - Space$, it is ready to be queried. The query processing starts with the analysis of the natural language question, from which a set of query features and a semi-structured query representation is extracted (step 3). After the query is analyzed, a *query processing plan* is

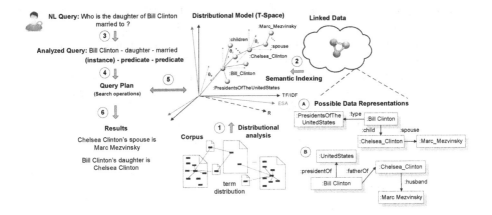

Fig. 5. Example of the vocabulary gap between query and data representation

generated, which maps the set of features and the semi-structured query into a set of search, navigation and transformation operations (step 5) over the data graph embedded in the $\tau - Space$. These operations define the semantic matching between the query and the data, using the distributional semantic information. This corresponds to the compositional model associated to the distributional model.

Question Analysis. The question analysis step consists in recognizing and classifying entities and operations in the question, as well as in mapping the natural language question into a *partial and ordered dependency structure* (PODS), a triple-like pattern, and a set of query features, see Figure 6. The specific question analysis operations are the following ones.

- **Question parsing** consists in the parsing of the question according to its dependency structure and the occurring parts of speech, see Figure 6.
- **Question/answer feature detection and classification** consists in the detection of the query focus and answer type based on rules over part-of-speech tags.
- **Entity detection and classification** uses part-of-speech tag pattern rules to determine the type of detected entity candidates (instances, classes and properties). Examples of those rules ares the following ones:
  - NNP+ → Instance
  - {RB* JJ*} NN(S)* {IN NNP}* → Class OR Property
  - BE* VB {IN NN}* → Property
- **Operation detection** uses part-of-speech tags and keyword patterns to detect operations and associated parameters in the question. While the lexical and structural variation for dataset elements is large, the vocabulary for typical database operations can be enumerated in a knowledge base of lexical expressions of operations Op.

- **Triple-pattern ordering** reduces the dependency structure constructed when parsing the input question to a set of PODS by applying two sets of operations: the removal of stopwords and their associated dependencies, and the re-ordering of the dependencies based on the core entity position in the query (where the core entity becomes the first query term and the topological relations given by the dependencies are preserved). For the example question, the PODS is Bill Clinton – daughter – married to. A detailed description of the triple-pattern processing rules can be found in [17].
- **Query classification** classifies the query according to query features that represent database primitives on the schema level (instances, properties, classes), on the operational level (e.g. aggregation and ordering), and on the structural level (conjuction, disjunction, property composition). The query features for the example question are shown in Figure 6.

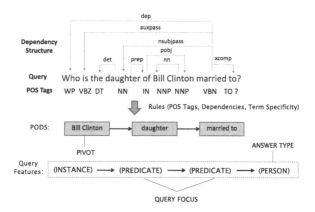

Fig. 6. Question analysis features for the example queries

After the query analysis, the PODS and the query features are sent to the *query planner*, which generates a query processing plan, involving the application of a sequence of search, navigation and transformation operations over the τ-Space:

- **Search operations** consist of keyword and distributional search operations over the data graph in the $\tau - Space$, in particular instance term search (over a term space), distributional class search, and property search.
- **Graph navigation and transformation operations** consist of graph composition and on the application of ordering, user feedback, aggregation and conditional operators.

The query planning algorithm, described in [15], orchestrates the search and graph navigation and transformation operations defined above. A query plan defines multiple operations over the index.

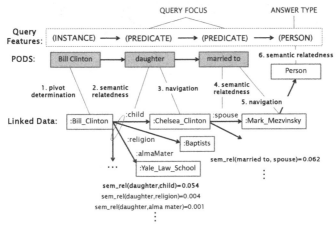

Fig. 7. Execution of a query processing plan for the query Who is the daughter of Bill Clinton married to?

With the PODS and the query features, the query processing approach starts by resolving the *core (pivot) entity* in the query (in this case Bill Clinton) to the corresponding database entity (`res:Bill_Clinton`), see Figure 7. The pivot determination depends on heuristics which take into account the query features and target the element which is less vague or ambiguous, and consequently presents a higher probability of a correct matching.

After Bill Clinton is resolved, the subspace of the entity `res:Bill_Clinton` is selected, constraining the search space to elements associated with this entity, and the next term in the PODS (daughter) is used as a query term for a distributional semantic search over the neighboring elements of `res:Bill_Clinton`. The distributional semantic search is equivalent to computing the distributional semantic relatedness between the query term (daughter) and all predicates associated with res:Bill_Clinton (`dbo:religion`, `dbo:child`, `dbo:almaMater`, etc). The semantic equivalence between daughter and `dbo:child` is determined by using corpus-based distributional common-sense information, capturing that the words daughter and child occur in similar contexts. A threshold filters out unrelated relations. After daughter and `dbo:child` have been aligned, the query processing navigates to the entity associated with the property `dbo:child`, `res:Chelsea_Clinton`, and the next query term, i.e. married in our example, is considered. At this point the entity `res:Chelsea_Clinton` defines the search subspace (properties associated with `res:Chelsea_Clinton`) and a semantic search for predicates which are semantically related to married is conducted. The query term married is matched to `dbo:spouse` and the answer to the query is found: the entity `dbpedia:Mark_Mezvinsky`. Figure 7 depicts the query processing steps for the example question. The high-level workflow and main components for the query approach are given in Figure 8.

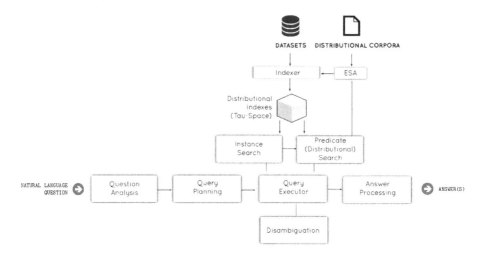

Fig. 8. High-level components diagram of the vocabulary-independent query approach and distributional inverted index structure

4.5   IBM Watson's DeepQA

The IBM Watson DeepQA system is a question answering system designed to be a machine contestant in the Jeopardy! quiz show, where three contestants compete against each another on answering open domain questions. The information sources for the DeepQA system are both unstructured and structured data. Despite the fact that the DeepQA approach focuses on extracting and scoring evidence from unstructured data, structured data sources (in particular in RDF format) play an important role. This section provides a high-level overview of the DeepQA system, focusing on the role of structured data in its question answering pipeline.

The DeepQA system is a massively parallel probabilistic evidence-based architecture which uses more than 100 different techniques for analyzing natural language, finding, merging scoring and ranking hypotheses. Below we describe the main components of the DeepQA platform, as depicted in Figure 9.

- **Question analysis:** consists of a mixture of question analysis methods including shallow and deep parsing, extraction of logical forms, semantic role labelling, coreference resolution, relation extraction, named entity recognition, among others.
- **Question decomposition:** consists in the decomposition of the question into separate phrases, which will generate constraints that need to be satisfied by evidence from the data.
- **Hypothesis generation:** consists of two steps: *primary search* and *candidate answer generation*. The primary search step focuses on finding all content that can support the question (maximizing recall). Different information retrieval techniques for document and passage retrieval are used over

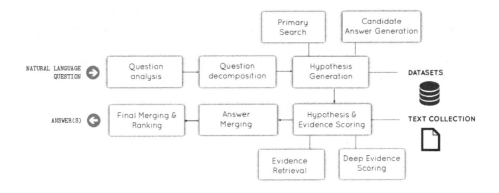

Fig. 9. Architecture of the IBM Watson DeepQA system

unstructured data sources and SPARQL queries are used over triple stores. Triple store queries in the primary search step are based on detected named entities, relations or lexical answer types in the question. The second step consists of the candidate answer generation, where information extraction techniques are applied to the search results to generate candidate answers (for example, for document search results from 'title-oriented' resources, the title is extracted as a candidate answer).

- **Soft filtering:** Consists in the application of lightweight (less resource intensive) scoring algorithms to a larger set of initial candidates to prune the list of candidates before the more intensive scoring components [13].
- **Hypothesis and evidence scoring:** consists of two steps: *supporting evidence retrieval* and *deep evidence scoring*. The supporting evidence retrieval step seeks additional evidence for each candidate answer from the data sources while the deep evidence scoring step determines the degree of certainty that the retrieved evidence supports the candidate answers. The system uses more than 50 scoring components that produce scores which range from probabilities and counts to categorical features. Scores are then combined into an overall evidence profile [13] which groups individual features into aggregate evidence dimensions.
- **Answer merging:** is a step that merges answer candidates (hypotheses) with different surface forms but with related content, combining their scores.
- **Ranking and confidence estimation:** is the last step, in which the system ranks the hypotheses and estimates their confidence based on the scores, using machine learning approaches over a training set. Multiple trained models cover different question types.

All of the components in DeepQA are implemented as Apache UIMA annotators. Apache UIMA[15] is a framework implementation of the *Unstructured Information Management Architecture*. UIMA also supports the parallelization of the pipeline components using asynchronous messages.

---

[15] http://uima.apache.org

Despite the fact that most of the evidence analysis in the IBM Watson DeepQA system is based on unstructured data, different components of the system rely on structured and semi-structured data and certain question types are answered by structured data sources. In particular, the DeepQA system uses three types of structured data sources:

- structured data available online (entity and associated types, movie databases)
- specific structured data extracted from unstructured data
- curated data providing additional information to the system (e.g. question and answer types)

RDF datasets such as DBpedia, Freebase and YAGO are used in the system. DBpedia is used to support the integration between unstructured and structured data and to assist information extraction tasks such as entity disambiguation and relation detection. Data cleaning techniques are used to normalize geospatial and temporal data in DBpedia into a common format. Freebase is used for geospatial data and YAGO as an entity type system. Disjointness properties are manually assigned at the higher level types in the YAGO taxonomy.

The DeepQA system processes a large set of questions that depend on temporal or geospatial evidence. Structured data sources play a fundamental role to provide geospatial and temporal evidence to the system. For example, temporal references detected at the question analysis step can be used to target specific temporal evidence over structured data sources. Structured data is also used for taxonomic reasoning and type coercion [12], checking whether a particular candidate answer's type matches the lexical answer type of the question [13].

Finally, structured data is also used in a separate complementary pipeline, for questions which require a more narrow but more precise answer, providing an incremental improvement in accuracy on the very small subset of questions for which it is applicable [12].

4.6   Other Approaches

Exploring user interaction techniques, FREyA [10], an extension of the QuestIO system [11], is a question answering system which employs feedback and clarification dialogs to resolve ambiguities and improve the domain lexicon with the help of users. User feedback is used to enrich the semantic matching process by allowing manual query-vocabulary mappings.

RTV [20] is a system that integrates lexical semantic modelling and statistical inferences within an architecture that exploits Hidden Markov Models to select ontological triples matching the input question. The natural language interpretation task is decomposed into three different stages. First, salient linguistic information from the question, such as predicates, their arguments and properties, are extracted from the question. Second, this salient information is located in the ontology through joint disambiguation of all candidates. In particular, for each query a Hidden Markov Model is produced whose Viterbi solution is the comprehensive joint disambiguation across the sentence elements. Finally, the final query is executed against the RDF dataset. A similar system along these lines is the one by Ngonga et al. [34].

5 Do-It-Yourself: Resources and Tools

The following datasets play an import role for question answering over linked data, as they provide large amounts of cross-domain knowlegde:

- DBpedia
  http://dbpedia.org/
- Freebase
  http://www.freebase.com/
- YAGO and YAGO2
  http://www.mpi-inf.mpg.de/yago-naga/yago/
- Wikipedia dumps
  http://dumps.wikimedia.org/

Prominent tools for indexing and searching such datasets and text collections are the following ones:

- Lucene and Solr
  http://lucene.apache.org/
  http://lucene.apache.org/solr/
- Terrier
  http://terrier.org/

Building question answering systems is a complex task; it thus helps to exploit high-level tools for component integration as well as existing architectures for question answering systems:

- Apache UIMA
  http://uima.apache.org
- Open Advancement of Question Answering Systems (OAQA)
  http://oaqa.github.io
- Open Knowledgebase and Question Answering (OKBQA)
  http://www.okbqa.org
  https://github.com/okbqa

In the remainder of the section we provide a list of resources and tools that can be exploited especially for the linguistic analysis of a question and the matching of natural language expressions with vocabulary elements from a dataset.

Lexical Resources

- WordNet
  http://wordnet.princeton.edu/

- Wiktionary
  http://www.wiktionary.org/
  API: https://www.mediawiki.org/wiki/API:Main_page
- BabelNet
  http://babelnet.org/
- FrameNet
  https://framenet.icsi.berkeley.edu/fndrupal/
- VerbNet
  http://verbs.colorado.edu/~mpalmer/projects/verbnet.html
- English lexicon for DBpedia 3.8 (in *lemon*[16] format)
  http://lemon-model.net/lexica/dbpedia_en/
- PATTY (collection of semantically-typed relational patterns)
  http://www.mpi-inf.mpg.de/yago-naga/patty/

Text Processing Tools

- GATE (General Architecture for Text Engineering)
  http://gate.ac.uk/
- NLTK (Natural Language Toolkit)
  http://nltk.org/
- Stanford NLP
  http://www-nlp.stanford.edu/software/index.shtml
- LingPipe
  http://alias-i.com/lingpipe/index.html

Dependency Parsers

- MALT
  http://www.maltparser.org/
  Languages (pre-trained): English, French, Swedish
- Stanford parser
  http://nlp.stanford.edu/software/lex-parser.shtml
  Languages: English, German, Chinese, and others
- CHAOS
  http://art.uniroma2.it/external/chaosproject/
  Languages: English, Italian

Named Entity Recognition

- NERD (Named Entity Recognition and Disambiguation)
  http://nerd.eurecom.fr/
- Stanford Named Entity Recognizer
  http://nlp.stanford.edu/software/CRF-NER.shtml
- FOX (Federated Knowledge Extraction Framework)
  http://fox.aksw.org
- DBpedia Spotlight
  http://spotlight.dbpedia.org

---

[16] http://lemon-model.net

String Similarity and Semantic Relatedness

- Wikipedia Miner
  http://wikipedia-miner.cms.waikato.ac.nz/
- WS4J (Java API for several semantic relatedness algorithms)
  https://code.google.com/p/ws4j/
- SecondString (string matching)
  http://secondstring.sourceforge.net
- EasyESA (semantic relatedness)
  http://treo.deri.ie/easyESA

Textual Entailment

- DIRT
  Paraphrase Collection: http://aclweb.org/aclwiki/index.php?title=DIRT_Paraphrase_Collection
  Demo: http://demo.patrickpantel.com/demos/lexsem/paraphrase.htm
- PPDB (The Paraphrase Database)
  http://www.cis.upenn.edu/~ccb/ppdb/

6 Evaluation Campaigns

The two most prominent criteria for assessing the quality of an answer that a question answer system provides are:

- *Correctness*, i.e. whether the answer is factually correct.
- *Completeness*, i.e. whether the answer is complete (especially in the context of list or definition questions).

The following evaluation campaigns provide benchmarks for evaluating and comparing question answering systems over linked data with respect to these two criteria.

QALD. The *Question Answering over Linked Data* (QALD) challenge[17] [28] aims to bring together researchers and developers from different communities, including NLP, Semantic Web, human-computer interaction, and databases. The core task of QALD is multilingual question answering over linked data, targeting all question answering systems that mediate between a user, expressing his or her information need in natural language, and semantic data. Given an RDF dataset and a natural language question or set of keywords in one of several languages (in QALD-4: English, Spanish, German, Italian, French, Dutch, and Romanian), participating systems are required to return either the correct answers or a SPARQL query that retrieves these answers.

For the first instantiations of the challenge, the answers were to be retrieved from a single RDF dataset, in particular DBpedia and (although attracting a

---

[17] http://www.sc.cit-ec.uni-bielefeld.de/qald/

bit less interest) MusicBrainz. The fourth installment of the challenge, QALD-4, started to extend the task also to multiple, interlinked datasets, including questions that can only be answered by aggregating information from different biomedical RDF datasets, as well as hybrid question answering, including questions that require information from both structured RDF data and free text in order to be answered.

QALD evaluates systems with respect to a manually constructed gold standard that specifies SPARQL queries for each question. The answers a participating system provides are compared to the answers that the gold standard query retrieves. For each question q, precision, recall and F-measure are computed as follows:

$$Recall(q) = \frac{\text{number of correct system answers for } q}{\text{number of gold standard answers for } q}$$

$$Precision(q) = \frac{\text{number of correct system answers for } q}{\text{number of system answers for } q}$$

$$F\text{-}Measure(q) = \frac{2 * Precision(q) \times Recall(q)}{Precision(q) + Recall(q)}$$

On the basis of these measures, overall precision and recall values as well as an overall F-measure value is computed as the average mean of the precision, recall and F-measure values for all questions.

INEX Linked Data. The goal of the Linked Data track of INEX[18] is to investigate retrieval techniques over a combination of textual and structured data, aiming to close the gap between key word search exploited in information retrieval and the reasoning techniques available for Semantic Web data. INEX Linked Data thus focuses on typical information retrieval questions, where structured data can be exploited to improve retrieval performance, e.g. because RDF properties provide additional information about semantic relations among objects that cannot be captured by keywords alone.

BioASQ. The BioASQ project[19] organizes a challenge on biomedical semantic indexing and question answering. This includes a variety of tasks from different areas, such as hierarchical text classification, machine learning, information retrieval, question answering from text as well as structured data, and multi-document summarization.

Although the scope is much wider than just question answering over linked data, a lot of the assessed functionalities play an either directly or indirect role for question answering, such as large-scale classification of biomedical documents and questions with respect to relevant ontology concepts, retrieval of relevant document snippets, concepts and knowledge base triples, as well as delivery of the retrieved information in a concise and user-understandable form.

---

[18] https://inex.mmci.uni-saarland.de/tracks/lod/
[19] http://www.bioasq.org/

Joint Question Answering Lab at CLEF 2014. The above mentioned challenges – QALD, BioASQ and INEX Linked Data – recently joined forces in a joint question answering lab[20] at CLEF 2014. They all start from an information need expressed in natural language and build on the insight that the data sources required to answer that question could differ. Some questions might need to query structured data, especially if aggregations or logical inferences are required, whereas other questions might need querying free text and drawing textual inferences, and some questions may need both. By joining challenges on these different aspects, they aim to foster the general vision that question answering systems can find, process and integrate information from all available sources, no matter how diverse.

7 Trends and Open Topics

We showed the challenges involved in question answering over linked data as well as how state-of-the-art approaches address them. Despite the significant advances achieved in recent years, there is still a wide range of open topics that require future research.

Querying Distributed Linked Data. In the context of the Web, it can not be assumed that all relevant data is available on one site, so that answers to questions have to be found in scenarios where the data is distributed. While there are first approaches to this, they still assume that data is integrated locally and there is a central index that can be used to query data (e.g. Poweraqua). First approaches to federated and distributed querying exist (Treo, Ngonga et al), but the question of how to scale QA to the distributed Web of (linked) data is unanswered. A further challenge is related to yielding near real-time query processing, which state-of-the-art systems are still quite far away from.

Integration of Structured and Unstructured Data. A lot of information is still available only in textual form, both on the web and in the form of labels and abstracts in linked data sources. Therefore approaches are needed that can not only deal with the specific character of structured data but also with extracting information from several sources, processing both structured and unstructured information and combining such gathered information into one answer. Systems such as IBM's Watson have largely benefited from the integration of diverse data sources, including both unstructured and structured data [13,14].

The integration of structured and unstructured data can benefit from both structured and unstructured resources and approaches. For example, named entities from linked RDF datasets can be used to support named entity recognition approaches over text sources by providing a first level structure for the domain, serving as a kind of indexing mechanism for unstructured resources in the context of question answering. From the opposite perspective, the information scale

---

[20] http://nlp.uned.es/clef-qa/

of unstructured data can make question answering systems over linked data much more useful in the short term and in industrial settings. Additionally, using structured resources to support more sophisticated information extraction approaches (such relation extraction) in the context of question answering can support the enrichment of structured datasets from unstructured data.

User Interaction and Context Mechanisms. Some of the question answering tasks can benefit from an interaction between the user and the system. For example, when interpreting the user's information need with respect to a particular dataset, user feedback can be used to remove ambiguity and vagueness, or to support co-reference resolution. In addition, allowing for a question answering dialog instead of single questions and answers would allow users to pose questions in a dialog context, e.g. referring to previous questions or answers, as in the following example:

- *User:* Who killed Martin Luther King?
- *System:* James Earl Ray.
- *User:* Was he captured?
- *System:* Yes.

Furthermore, the investigation of different interaction modalities may improve the efficiency of the question answering process, in particular in a dialog context. For example, speech recognition and synthesis may complement the text input, pointing gestures may provide specific references (see e.g. [4]) and cues, and data visualization techniques can provide data consumers with a more efficient interpretation of the answer.

Incorporating Reasoning. Despite the support of Semantic Web standards for deductive reasoning by grounding RDF graph data in Description Logics, logical reasoning is still very dependent on logically consistent knowledge bases, which is an unfeasible constraint for most datasets in the linked data cloud. However, allowing reasoning over inconsistent knowledge bases can strongly improve question answering over linked data. Additionally, investigating the role and the impact of different reasoning approaches (deductive, inductive, abductive, counterfactual, among others) under the question answering task is a long term and high impact research direction.

Moreover, the integration of common-sense knowledge external to the target datasets can be beneficial for addressing vocabulary variations and for supporting the reasoning behind the answer processing. The use of structured and unstructured common-sense resources such as Cyc[21], ConceptNet[22] and Wikipedia[23] in question answering is a fundamental component to improve the semantic flexibility of question answering systems.

---

[21] http://www.cyc.com/platform/opencyc
[22] http://conceptnet5.media.mit.edu/
[23] http://www.wikipedia.org/

Measuring Confidence and Answer Uncertainty. The complexity of the question answering task is associated with the variability and openness of the questions and the data. Providing confidence or uncertainty measures at each step of the question answering processing allows for an estimation of the quality of the final answer and can be used as a heuristic for the selection of different query processing strategies.

Multilinguality. Current question answering systems over linked data are typically monolingual and there are so far no systems that are able to answer questions in more than one language. Extending QA systems over linked data to work for multiple languages involves bridging a severe vocabulary gap, as adding additional languages other than English exacerbates the lexical gap. In order to process questions in multiple languages, lexical knowledge about how a certain data property or class is expressed in the relevant languages is needed, capturing all the intra-lingual and inter-lingual variance in how a vocabulary element can be expressed. A further bottleneck is that most QALD system require some preprocessing that is language-specific. Aqualog for example relies on JAPE-grammars that work for English only and extending the system to other languages requires the availability of grammars in multiple languages. Similar comments apply to Pythia and ORAKEL, as they rely both on language-specific grammars. The templates used by TBSL are also to some extent language-specific. Overall, all the systems discussed here are thus in general language-specific and substantial effort would be required to extend them to other languages. Treo would require semantic relatedness measures in different languages. Overall, developing systems that can answer questions in different languages is indeed a challenge which currently remains at the research frontier and has not been yet tackled.

Machine Learning. A new field dubbed *semantic parsing* has emerged recently that applies machine learning techniques to learn the mapping from natural language to semantics from training data. It is thinkable that such approaches are also applicable to the task of learning to map natural language questions to a SPARQL query, but so far Semantic Parsing approaches have not been thoroughly investigated in this setting. This remains for future work.

8 Conclusion

In this tutorial overview paper, we have introduced the problem of question answering over linked data. We have further presented the main challenges involved in the task and presented the typical architecture or anatomy of systems addressing the task. We have further provided an overview of state-of-the-art approaches to the problem, highlighting their features and drawbacks. Finally, we have described a selected set of systems, comprising those developed by ourselves, in more detail and concluded with a summary of open issues that need to be addressed in future research.

References

1. Androutsopoulos, L.: Natural language interfaces to databases – an introduction. Journal of Natural Language Engineering 1(1), 29–81 (1995)
2. Berant, J., Chou, A., Frostig, R., Liang, P.: Semantic parsing on Freebase from question-answer pairs. In: Proceedings of the 2013 Conference on Empirical Methods in Natural Language Processing, EMNLP (2013)
3. Bernstein, A., Kaufmann, E., Kaiser, C.: Querying the semantic web with GiNSENG: A guided input natural language search engine. In: 15th Workshop on Information Technologies and Systems, Las Vegas, NV, pp. 112–126 (2005)
4. Bringert, B., Cooper, R., Ljunglöf, P., Ranta, A.: Multimodal dialogue system grammars. In: Proceedings of DIALOR 2005, Ninth Workshop on the Semantics and Pragmatics of Dialogue, pp. 53–60 (2005)
5. Cabrio, E., Cojan, J., Aprosio, A.P., Magnini, B., Lavelli, A., Gandon, F.: QAKiS: an open domain QA system based on relational patterns. In: Proceedings of the ISWC 2012 Posters & Demonstrations Track. CEUR Workshop Proceedings, vol. 914 (2012)
6. Cai, Q., Yates, A.: Large-scale semantic parsing via schema matching and lexicon extension. In: Proceedings of the Annual Meeting of the Association for Computational Linguistics, ACL (2013)
7. Cimiano, P.: Flexible semantic composition with DUDES. In: Proceedings of the 8th International Conference on Computational Semantics, IWCS 2009 (2009)
8. Cimiano, P., Buitelaar, P., McCrae, J., Sintek, M.: LexInfo: A declarative model for the lexicon-ontology interface. Web Semantics: Science, Services and Agents on the World Wide Web 9(1), 29–51 (2011)
9. Cimiano, P., Haase, P., Heizmann, J., Mantel, M., Studer, R.: Towards portable natural language interfaces to knowledge bases – the case of the ORAKEL system. Data & Knowledge Engineering 65(2), 325–354 (2008)
10. Damljanovic, D., Agatonovic, M., Cunningham, H.: FREyA: an interactive way of querying linked data using natural language. In: García-Castro, R., Fensel, D., Antoniou, G. (eds.) ESWC 2011 Workshops. LNCS, vol. 7117, pp. 125–138. Springer, Heidelberg (2012)
11. Damljanovic, D., Tablan, V., Bontcheva, K.: A text-based query interface to OWL ontologies. In: 6th Language Resources and Evaluation Conference, LREC 2008 (2008)
12. Kalyanpur, A., et al.: Structured data and inference in DeepQA. IBM Journal of Research & Development 56(3/4) (2012)
13. Ferrucci, D., et al.: Building Watson: an overview of the DeepQA project. AI Magazine 31(3), 59–79 (2010)
14. Fader, A., Zettlemoyer, L., Etzioni, O.: Open question answering over curated and extracted knowledge bases. In: Proceedings of the International Conference on Knowledge Discovery and Data Mining, KDD (to appear, 2014)
15. Freitas, A., Curry, E.: Natural Language Queries over Heterogeneous Linked Data Graphs: A Distributional-Compositional Semantics Approach. In: 18th International Conference on Intelligent User Interfaces, IUI 2014 (2014)
16. Freitas, A., Curry, E., O'Riain, S.: A Distributional Approach for Terminology-Level Semantic Search on the Linked Data Web. In: 27th ACM Symposium on Applied Computing (SAC 2012). ACM Press (2012)

17. Freitas, A., Oliveira, J.G., O'Riain, S., Curry, E., Pereira da Silva, J.C.: Querying linked data using semantic relatedness: a vocabulary independent approach. In: Muñoz, R., Montoyo, A., Métais, E. (eds.) NLDB 2011. LNCS, vol. 6716, pp. 40–51. Springer, Heidelberg (2011)

18. Gabrilovich, E., Markovitch, S.: Computing semantic relatedness using Wikipedia-based Explicit Semantic Analysis. In: Proceedings of the 20th International Joint Conference on Artifical Intelligence (IJCAI 2007), pp. 1606–1611 (2007)

19. Gerber, D., Ngomo, A.-C.N.: Bootstrapping the linked data web. In: Proceedings of the 10th International Semantic Web Conference, ISWC (2011)

20. Giannone, C., Bellomaria, V., Basili, R.: A HMM-based approach to question answering against linked data. In: Proceedings of the Question Answering over Linked Data lab (QALD-3) at CLEF 2013. LNCS. Springer (2013) (to appear)

21. Gómez-Pérez, A., Vila-Suero, D., Montiel-Ponsoda, E., Gracia, J., de Cea, G.A.: Guidelines for multilingual linked data. In: Proceedings of the 3rd International Conference on Web Intelligence, Mining and Semantics (WIMS 2013), pp. 3:1–3:12. ACM (2013)

22. Harris, Z.: Distributional structure. Word 10(2-3), 146–162 (1954)

23. Kaufmann, E., Bernstein, A., Zumstein, R.: A natural language interface to query ontologies based on clarification dialogs. In: Proceedings of the 5th International Semantic Web Conference, ISWC (2006)

24. Kim, J.-D., Cohen, K.B.: Natural language query processing for SPARQL generation: A prototype system for SNOMED-CT. In: Proceedings of BioLINK SIG (2013)

25. Kwiatkowski, T., Choi, E., Artzi, Y., Zettlemoyer, L.: Scaling semantic parsers with on-the-fly ontology matching. In: Proceedings of the 2013 Conference on Empirical Methods in Natural Language Processing (EMNLP), pp. 1545–1556 (2013)

26. Li, X., Roth, D.: Learning question classifiers. In: Proceedings of the 19th International Conference on Computational Linguistics (COLING 2002), pp. 556–562 (2002)

27. Lopez, V., Fernández, M., Motta, E., Stieler, N.: PowerAqua: supporting users in querying and exploring the Semantic Web. Semantic Web 3(3), 249–265 (2012)

28. Lopez, V., Unger, C., Cimiano, P., Motta, E.: Evaluating question answering over linked data. Journal of Web Semantics 21 (2013)

29. Lopez, V., Uren, V., Motta, E., Pasin, M.: Aqualog: An ontology-driven question answering system for organizational semantic intranets. Journal of Web Semantics 5(2), 72–105 (2007)

30. Lopez, V., Uren, V., Sabou, M., Motta, E.: Is question answering fit for the semantic web? a survey. Semantic Web Journal 2, 125–155 (2011)

31. McCrae, J., Aguado de Cea, G., Buitelaar, P., Cimiano, P., Declerck, T., Gomez-Perez, A., Garcia, J., Hollink, L., Montiel-Ponsoda, E., Spohr, D.: Interchanging lexical resources on the Semantic Web. Language Resources and Evaluation 46(4), 701–719 (2012)

32. Popescu, A.-M., Armanasu, A., Etzioni, O., Ko, D., Yates, A.: Modern natural language interfaces to databases: Composing statistical parsing with semantic tractability. In: Proceedings of the 20th International Conference on Computational Linguistics, COLING 2004. Association for Computational Linguistics (2004)

33. Sawant, U., Chakrabarti, S.: Learning joint query interpretation and response ranking. In: Proceedings of the 22nd International Conference on World Wide Web (WWW 2013), pp. 1099–1110 (2013)

34. Shekarpour, S., Ngomo, A.-C.N., Auer, S.: Question answering on interlinked data. In: Proceedings of the 22nd International World Wide Web Conference (WWW), pp. 1145–1156 (2013)
35. Tran, T., Wang, H., Rudolph, S., Cimiano, P.: Top-k exploration of query candidates for efficient keyword search on graph-shaped (RDF) data. In: Proceedings of the 25th International Conference on Data Engineering (ICDE), pp. 405–416 (2009)
36. Unger, C., Hieber, F., Cimiano, P.: Generating LTAG grammars from a lexicon-ontology interface. In: Bangalore, S., Frank, R., Romero, M. (eds.) 10th International Workshop on Tree Adjoining Grammars and Related Formalisms, TAG+10 (2010)
37. Unger, C., Bühmann, L., Lehmann, J., Ngomo, A.-C.N., Gerber, D., Cimiano, P.: Template-based question answering over RDF data. In: Proceedings of the 21st International Conference on World Wide Web, pp. 639–648. ACM (2012)
38. Unger, C., Cimiano, P.: Pythia: Compositional meaning construction for ontology-based question answering on the semantic web. In: Muñoz, R., Montoyo, A., Métais, E. (eds.) NLDB 2011. LNCS, vol. 6716, pp. 153–160. Springer, Heidelberg (2011)
39. Walter, S., Unger, C., Cimiano, P.: A corpus-based approach for the induction of ontology lexica. In: Métais, E., Meziane, F., Saraee, M., Sugumaran, V., Vadera, S. (eds.) NLDB 2013. LNCS, vol. 7934, pp. 102–113. Springer, Heidelberg (2013)
40. Yahya, M., Berberich, K., Elbassuoni, S., Weikum, G.: Robust question answering over the web of linked data. In: Proceedings of the 22nd ACM International Conference on Information & Knowledge Management, pp. 1107–1116. ACM (2013)

Query Processing for RDF Databases

Zoi Kaoudi[1] and Anastasios Kementsietsidis[2]

[1] IMIS, Athena Research Center, Athens, Greece
`zoi@imis.athena-innovation.gr`
[2] Google Research, Mountain View, USA
`akement@google.com`

Abstract. RDF has become recently a very popular data model used in a variety of applications and use cases in both academia and industry. Query processing and evaluation is a central component in data management in general and is, thus, unsurprisingly one of the most active areas of research in the field of RDF data management. In this chapter we provide an overview of query processing techniques for the RDF data model using different system architectures. We survey techniques for both centralized and distributed RDF stores, including peer-to-peer, federated and cloud-based systems.

1 Introduction

Query processing and evaluation is such a central component of data management that unsurprisingly is one of the most active areas of research in this field. As databases evolve and new architectures or models emerge, efficient query processing becomes probably the most pressing problem to address in these new environments. One has to just consider the move from centralized to distributed [59] or streaming [24] sources, or the emergence of new models like XML [60] or RDF [62] and notice the corresponding jump in research works in conferences and workshops on this topic. In spite of this large body of past works, there is always room for improvement or for the generation of new techniques. Each new environment (be it an architecture or a model) carries its own set of assumptions and requirements that necessitate a revision of past query processing techniques, or in the worst case lead to the development of new ones.

In what follows, we provide an overview of query processing techniques in the context of the RDF data model and the SPARQL query language [31]. To put things in perspective and present techniques and architectures in an organized fashion, we are going to use the virtual system overview of Figure 1 as a guide to our presentation. Our system consists of two layers, a *decentralized* layer and a *individual source* layer. There are many architectures that one can use to build a decentralized layer for RDF sources, and in the figure we list the three we are covering in this chapter, namely, *federated*, *peer-to-peer*, and *cloud* systems. Any of these system architectures assumes that it is built on top of a set of RDF sources where each source in the set provides, as a minimum requirement, a data access entry, e.g., a SPARQL endpoint service. Now, internally each individual

M. Koubarakis et al. (Eds.): Reasoning Web 2014, LNCS 8714, pp. 141–170, 2014.
© Springer International Publishing Switzerland 2014

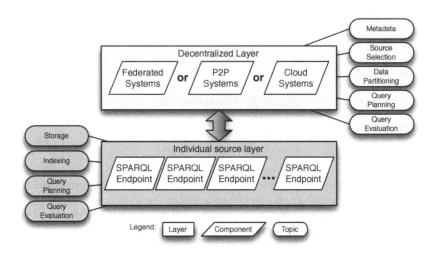

Fig. 1. Virtual RDF system overview

RDF source can have its own architecture which can range from a native RDF store, to a relational store appropriately configured to store RDF data, or even to a relational store with relational data served as RDF through a front-end. Irrespectively of the particular architecture used in either layer, there are a number of research topics that are common across the architectures within each layer, and we list those adjacent to each layer in the figure. Though this is clearly not an exhaustive list of topics, they constitute the minimal topics a system should address to have a workable solution in this space. We briefly review the relevance and importance of each topic in the following paragraphs.

1.1 Decentralized Layer Topics

– Metadata: In decentralized systems, there is a well-known trade-off between query performance and source autonomy. At one end of the spectrum, one can consider a system where the sources only provide a SPARQL endpoint service and no other metadata (e.g., statistics, indexes) is known about them [75]. Since query processing relies heavily on knowledge about such metadata, when no such information is available to a decentralized system, the system must try to dynamically compute the necessary metadata. This process is bound to have an impact on end-to-end query performance since additional work must be performed before the processing of the actual query is initiated. At the other end of the spectrum, one can consider a system with tighter control of the sources where each source is required to generate appropriate metadata and provide them to the decentralized system [4, 28]. This clearly facilitates query processing but requires that the sources themselves are willing to do work for the decentralized system (in addition to query answering) by regularly updating their metadata to reflect the changes in their data.

– Source selection: Not all sources in a decentralized system contain data that are relevant to the query at hand. Figuring out which sources are relevant is another factor affecting query performance since incorrectly identified sources might incur additional costs (both in terms of processing time and communication overhead) without contributing to the end result. There is a close relationship between the topic of source selection and that of metadata, since often the latter is used to provide an answer for the former.

– Data partitioning: Another area where source autonomy is a key factor is in the distribution of data across the decentralized system. At one extreme one can envision a federated system in which data partitioning comes naturally as sources join the federation with their own data. At the other extreme, one can envision a P2P-style system in which sources join the system and it is the decentralized layer that is responsible for assigning which source is going to store which data. While there is not much to be said about partitioning in the former scenario, in the latter scenario partitioning requires an algorithm to partition and distribute the data evenly across the sources. Ideally, other than data load, the algorithm should aim to minimize communication costs during query evaluation.

– Query planning: Once the sources relevant for a query have been identified, and relevant metadata have been computed or retrieved, query planning is a common next step. The type of planning available to a decentralized system also depends on the level of autonomy of the underlying sources. In one extreme case, one can think of a system with fairly uncooperative sources where the sources only provide a SPARQL endpoint service. In such a setting, the results from individual sources must be sent to a central location where the actual query evaluation takes place. It is not hard to see that in such a setting the communication cost may far outweigh actual query evaluation costs. In a more collaborative setting, the sources of the decentralized system might be willing to cooperate in performing distributed query evaluation. Query planning becomes more central at this setting since it specifies the order (as in the centralized case) with which results would be computed and propagated.

– Query evaluation: More often than not, there are multiple ways to combine results from different sources to compute an answer to an input query. Each of these ways generates its own plan and results in a query. All these queries must be evaluated to guarantee the *completeness* of query answers (i.e., that all the results of the query are retrieved and none is *missed*). Executing all these queries (and in parallel) poses its own challenges. Clearly, one can evaluate each of these queries independently, but when there is sharing of sub-queries across the different queries, there is the potential for optimization [50] (e.g., by executing these common sub-queries only once and sharing their results across the different plans).

1.2 Individual Source Layer Topics

– Storage: The storage strategy, or how an individual RDF source decides to internally represent RDF data, is a central topic which influences every aspect of the source, from indexing, to planning and evaluation. There are multiple alternatives here with some sources using novel *native* representations for RDF data (e.g., Jena TDB [39], RDF-3X [58]), while others using relational databases as the back-end (e.g., Jena SDB [39], DB2RDF [17], C-Store [1]) and designing appropriate schemas to store the RDF data.
– Indexing: Indexing plays a key role in query evaluation in general but in the context of RDF this role becomes even more central since indexes sometimes morph into an actual storage strategy (e.g., Jena TDB uses a custom implementation of B+-trees as central component of its storage strategy). This interplay between storage and indexes results in some novel strategies in terms of query evaluation (e.g., [58]).
– Query planning: Unlike query planning in the decentralized setting which focuses on reducing communication costs (mostly through join ordering), planning at the individual source level is typically more complex and has a larger search space of alternatives to consider. One reason for this added complexity comes from the multitude of access methods that are usually available to the planner, which opens up the way for accessing source data and combining intermediate query results using a host of techniques.
– Query evaluation: In traditional DBMSs, there is a tight coupling between the planner and the query evaluation module in the sense that they are both part of the same system (and are often developed by the same group of people). However, this is not always the case with RDF sources, and especially with those that use relational databases as the back-end. In such sources, the RDF query planner might be built as a separate component on top of any existing relational back-end (e.g., see Jena SDB [39] or DB2RDF [17]). Since planning happens outside the relational engine, the planner can dictate the order with which different sub-queries are executed, but it has little control over the actual evaluation by the back-end. Therefore, in such settings, the efficiency of query evaluation is largely determined by how well the planner can predict the efficiency of queries before these are evaluated by the underlying relational store.

Using Figure 1 as a guide for our presentation, we organize the remainder of this chapter in the following manner. For completeness, the next section presents some necessary preliminaries in terms of the RDF model and the SPARQL query language. Then in Section 3, we provide an overview of existing single-source systems that constitute our building blocks in Figure 1 towards constructing any of the decentralized systems shown there. Sections 4, 5 and 6 present respectively existing P2P, federated and cloud-based systems. Not all the topics we covered briefly in the introduction are of equal importance for each presented system and not all systems provide novel solutions across all the topics. Therefore throughout the sections as we describe a (single-source or decentralized) system we make certain that we highlight the topics that are of most notable and novel about the system. The paper concludes with a summary of the work and a short discussion regarding open research directions in the field of RDF query processing.

2   Preliminaries

In this section we introduce the Resource Description Framework (RDF) together with its accompanying schema language RDFS. In addition, we present SPARQL, the standardized query language for querying RDF and RDFS data.

2.1   RDF

The emergence of RDF originated from the Semantic Web vision, where anything in the Web can be interpreted by machines, converting the *Web of documents* to a *Web of data*. RDF is the main data model used to achieve this goal.

RDF offers the following basic constructs:

- *URIs*: Universal Resource Identifiers are used to represent *resources*, e.g., a Web page, a book, an author, a paper or a computer file. In addition, URIs are used to identify *properties*, which are the attributes of a resource or connect two resources. For example, `hasName` may be used for describing the name of an author or `isAuthorOf` may be used to connect a book resource with an author resource.
- *Literals*: Literals are constant values of any property. For example, `"John Doe"` may be the value of the property `hasName`.
- *Blank nodes*: Blank nodes are anonymous resources which are not expressed by a URI but in the form of `_:bnodeID`. The purpose of blank nodes is to encode n-ary relationships and/or to make statements about resources that might not have global URIs but can be described in terms of their relationship with other resources.

Facts in RDF are represented by sets of *triples*. Each triple consists of the resource the fact is about (subject), the property of the resource the statement refers to (predicate), and the value of that property (object). Another representation of RDF data is that of *labelled graphs* where the subject and object is depicted as a *node* and the property as a *directed labelled edge* from the subject node to the object node labelled by the predicate name. More formally:

Definition 1 (RDF triple). *Let U, L and B denote three pairwise disjoint sets of URIs, literals, and blank nodes, respectively. A* triple *is a tuple (s, p, o) from $(U \cup B) \times U \times (U \cup L \cup B)$, where s is the subject, p is the predicate (a.k.a. property) and o is the object of the triple.*

Definition 2 (RDF term and element). *An RDF* term *is any value from $(U \cup L \cup B)$ and an RDF* element *is any among the subject, predicate and object of an RDF triple.*

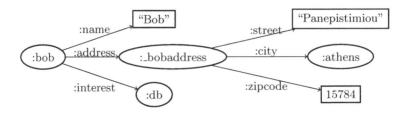

Fig. 2. RDF graph example

Definition 3 (RDF graph). *An RDF graph is a set of RDF triples.*

For example, the following set of triples state that the resource `http://tiny/bob` named `"Bob"` has as research interest databases and lives in a specified address in the city of Athens. The constant `:_bobaddress` denotes a blank node to describe the address of Bob.

```
http://tiny/bob http://tiny/name "Bob" .
http://tiny/bob http://tiny/interest http://tiny/db .
http://tiny/bob http://tiny/address :_bobaddress .
:_bobaddress http://tiny/street "Panepistimiou" .
:_bobaddress http://tiny/postalCode 15784 .
:_bobaddress http://tiny/city http://tiny/athens .
```

Figure 2 shows the same RDF information in an RDF graph. We depict a resource with an oval circle and a literal with a rectangle. The labeled arcs represent the properties of the RDF graph. For clarity reasons, we attach the empty prefix ':' for all URIs to distinguish them from the corresponding literals.

2.2   RDF Schema (RDFS)

The RDF data model offers a simple way for describing relationships among resources in terms of named properties and values, but does not provide mechanisms for declaring these properties, nor does it provide ways for defining the relationships between these properties and other resources. This is the role of RDF Schema (RDFS) [18]. RDFS is the vocabulary of RDF; it provides the means to a user to define terms that will be used in RDF statements and give specific meaning to them. RDFS defines not only the properties of a resource (e.g., title, author, subject etc.) but also the kinds of resources being described (people, paper, Web pages, books etc.). Resources having similar characteristics can be divided into groups called RDFS *classes*. We will refer to both RDF and RDFS information with the term RDF(S).

Figure 3 shows an RDF(S) graph which defines the relationships between classes and assigns the resource `http://tiny/bob` to a certain class. The property `rdfs:subClassOf` is a predefined property in RDFS and denotes a specialization relationship between two classes. For example, `http://tiny/graduateStudent` is a

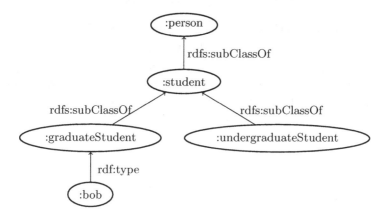

Fig. 3. An RDF(S) graph example

class which defines a specialized type of class `http://tiny/student`. Another pre-defined property commonly used in RDF is `rdf:type`. This property defines the members of a certain class. For example, resource `http://tiny/bob` is a member of class `http://tiny/graduateStudent`. The members of a class are also known as *instances* of the class. Namespaces `rdf` and `rdfs` are the namespaces of the core RDF and RDFS vocabulary defined by the URIs `http://www.w3.org/1999/02/22-rdf-syntax-ns#` and `http://www.w3.org/2000/01/rdf-schema#` respectively.

Another feature of RDFS is that it also provides vocabulary for describing how properties and classes are intended to be connected in an RDF(S) graph. The most important information of this kind is supplied by using the RDF Schema properties `rdfs:domain` and `rdfs:range`. The `rdfs:domain` property is used to indicate that a particular property applies to a specific class. The `rdfs:range` property is used to indicate that the values of a particular property are instances of a specific class or are types of specific literals. For example, in the RDF graph of Figure 2 we could add the following RDFS triples for properties `http://tiny/name` and `http://tiny/interest`:

```
http://tiny/name rdfs:domain http://tiny/person .
http://tiny/interest rdfs:domain http://tiny/student .
http://tiny/name rdfs:range string .
```

This means that the property `http://tiny/name` applies to instances of class `http://tiny/person`, while the property `http://tiny/interest` applies to instances of class `http://tiny/student`. In addition, the last triple states that property `http://tiny/name` takes values that are strings.

The most important functionality of RDFS is the ability to make inferences using the RDFS entailment rules [32]. This means that one can *infer new triples* from an RDF schema and the set of rules. Such triples are often called *implicit or inferred* triples. For example, the RDFS property `rdfs:subClassOf` is defined as a transitive property in the rule *rdfs*11 of the RDFS Semantics [32]:

$$\frac{\text{(a, rdfs:subClassOf, b), (b, rdfs:subClassOf, c)}}{\text{(a, rdfs:subClassOf, c)}}$$

This rule says that if class a is a subclass of class b and class b is a subclass of class c, then we infer that class a is a subclass of class c. Thus, in the example of Figure 3, we can infer that class :graduateStudent is a subclass of class :person. Then, using this inferred triple and rule *rdfs9* from [32]:

$$\frac{\text{(a, rdfs:subClassOf, b), (r, rdf:type, a)}}{\text{(r, rdf:type, b)}}$$

we infer that http://tiny/bob in Figure 3 is also an instance of http://tiny/person. The complete set of the RDFS entailment rules can be found in [32].

2.3 SPARQL

SPARQL [31] is the standard query language for RDF recommended by W3C and has the ability to extract information about both the data and the schema. A core concept of SPARQL is that of a triple pattern, which is a triple with the possibility of a variable in any of the subject, predicate or object positions. A query that contains a conjunction of triple patterns is called *basic graph pattern* (BGP) query, and is the conjunctive fragment of SPARQL allowing to express the core select-project-join queries. More formally:

Definition 4 (Triple pattern). *Let U, L, B and V denote the pairwise disjoint sets of URIs, literals, blank nodes, and variables respectively. A triple pattern is a tuple (s, p, o) from $(U \cup B \cup V) \times (U \cup V) \times (U \cup L \cup B \cup V)$.*

Definition 5 (Basic Graph Pattern). *A basic graph pattern query is a conjunction of triple patterns.*

A basic graph pattern matches a subgraph of the RDF data when RDF terms from the subgraph can be substituted with the variables of the graph pattern.

The syntax of SPARQL follows an SQL-like select-from-where paradigm. The select clause specifies the variables that should appear in the query results. Each variable in SPARQL is prefixed with ?. The from clause specifies the RDF(S) graph that should be used for answering the query. If not used, the query runs over the whole RDF(S) triples stored in the system. The graph patterns of the query are set in the where clause. The following SPARQL query asks for all resources which have a name and a research interest.

Listing 1.1. A simple SPARQL query

```
SELECT *
WHERE {
    ?x http://tiny/name ?y .
    ?x http://tiny/interest ?z
}
```

The answer of a SPARQL query with a `select` clause is a bag of variable bindings. If the above SPARQL query is posed over the RDF graph of Figure 2, the variable bindings of the answer would be:

?x	?y	?z
http://tiny/bob	"Bob"	http://tiny/db

SPARQL also supports more complex queries than simple BGPs with features such as the `OPTIONAL` operation. The *optional* functionality allows for patterns that might not match for every part in an RDF graph. In this case, the optional part creates no bindings but does not eliminate the entire solution. Keyword `OPTIONAL` is used with a graph pattern such as the ones in the `WHERE` clause.

In addition, one can use filter expressions with operators such as $<$, $=$, and $>$ for numerical values (range constraints) and string functions such as regular expressions. Multiple BGPs can be combined through a `UNION` operation. Order constraints are also possible through `ORDERBY` and `LIMIT` operators.

Apart from the `SELECT` clause, SPARQL also allows `CONSTRUCT`, `DESCRIBE` and `ASK` clauses. In the case of a `SELECT` query, the result set is a set of variables and their possible bindings. On the other hand, if we have a `CONSTRUCT` query, the result is an RDF graph constructed by substituting variables in a set of triple templates. Finally, a `DESCRIBE` query returns an RDF graph that describes the resources found and an `ASK` query returns yes or no depending on whether a query pattern matches or not. In this chapter, we focus only on `SELECT` queries.

The latest SPARQL 1.1 proposal [31] also supports property paths, negation, aggregates etc. We do not consider these features in the present chapter since most existing works focus on BGP queries. The formal semantics of SPARQL can be found in [63].

3   Single-Source RDF Stores

The storage strategy is probably the defining component of a single-source RDF store, and therefore we structure this section around the storage strategies used by existing stores. Clearly, there are several alternatives to store RDF data, and at a high level we can classify existing strategies into two categories, namely, those using novel *native* representations for RDF data (e.g., Jena TDB [39], RDF-3X [58]), and those using relational databases as the back-end (e.g., Jena SDB [39], DB2RDF [17], C-Store [1]). While there is usually little information available regarding the internals of the former type of stores, the representations used by the latter stores is commonly explained in detail, and this is where we are going to focus our attention in this section.

3.1   "Monolithic" Triple Stores

The simplest and most straightforward representation of RDF data into a relational store is to create a single SPO relation with columns to store the subject,

Dictionary	
id	uri-literal
1	http://tiny/me
2	http://tiny/name
3	"Tasos"
4	http://tiny/attend
5	"RW 2014"
6	http://tiny/you
7	"Zoi"
8	http://tiny/friend

SPO

subj	pred	obj
http://tiny/me	http://tiny/name	"Tasos"
http://tiny/me	http://tiny/attend	"RW 2014"
http://tiny/you	http://tiny/name	"Zoi"
http://tiny/me	http://tiny/friend	http://tiny/you

(a) One version of the "monolithic" store

SPO

subj	pred	obj
1	2	3
1	4	5
6	2	7
1	8	6

(b) A second version

Fig. 4. The "monolithic" store

predicate and object of each triple. There are multiple ways to *implement* such a store (e.g., see [7]) and Figure 4 shows two alternative versions. In the first version, the URIs and literals are stored directly into the single relation. In the second version, we create a "dictionary" in which we assign an id to each URI or literal. Then, in the *main* relation we store triples created out of these ids, instead of the actual URIs or literals. It is not hard to see that the second version requires less storage space since multiple occurrences of a URI are replaced by a reference to a single id. However, the second version incurs additional costs during query processing since it requires joining the dictionary and SPO relations in order to (re-)establish at query time the relationship between ids and URIs or literals.

Both versions of the store have the desirable characteristic that the schema of the store does not change as we encounter new (types of) triples (in the following sections, we see that this is not a characteristic shared by all the relational representations of RDF). On the negative side, it is clear that the size of the relation storing the triples increases linearly with the number of triples and can very quickly include millions (or billions) of triples/tuples. Managing such a huge relation is bound to have an impact on the evaluation of queries and indeed in "monolithic" stores query performance and scalability do not go hand-in-hand [17]. Therefore, multiple indexes [58] over the single SPO relation are often necessary to support efficient query evaluation.

3.2 Property-Table Stores

The idea behind property tables [83] is the simple observation that entities that are of the same (or similar) type(s) share similar sets of predicates. So, for example, all book entities whose information is represented in RDF are expected to have at least the predicates title, author, and year of copyright. Similarly, all compact-disc entities are expected to also have the predicates of title, artist and year of copyright. Therefore, while designing a schema to store the RDF data for these entities, one can take advantage of these common predicates to create appropriate tables with columns for these common predicates. Figure 5 shows the basic idea through an example. On the left of the figure, we show some sample RDF data pertaining to books, CD's and DVD's. Then, in Figure 5(b) we show an *implementation* of the property tables idea, called *property-class tables*, where given a type in the RDF data we create a table with all the common predicates that appear in the instances of this type. So, one table is created in the figure for the BookType entities, and one table is created for the CDType entities. Notice that the *common* predicates among the instances of these types are selected and become the columns of the created tables. Inspired by the monolithic approach, the schema also contains an SPO relation storing the remaining less common predicates for the various entities.

An alternative way to implement property tables is shown in Figure 5(c), through the use of *cluster property tables*. In a nutshell, in this implementation we create a table that contains common predicates between entities, irrespectively of their types. In our example, these are the title and copyright predicates which seem to be present across all BookType, CDType and DVDType entities. Predicates that are not part of the cluster in this example end up in a monolithic SPO table, as it is shown.

Notice that unlike the monolithic schema which is independent of the data being stored, for the creation of property tables we rely heavily on characteristics of the data. However, as the data change through time, so do their characteristics. For example, a predicate that was not as common at some stage in a dataset, it might end up becoming extremely common later on. This would necessitate a change in the schema of the property tables to reflect the fact. However, such data reorganization is usually extremely costly and undesirable. One might consider the monolithic and property table designs as being the two ends of the design spectrum. At one end, we create schemas that closely fit the data and have an associated high cost of periodic reorganization but also hold the promise of efficient query processing. At the other end, we create schemas that are generic and unchanged but are not as efficient in terms querying. There is an interesting challenge here in figuring out whether there are alternative designs where the schema is both unchanged and does not require reorganization, but efficient query processing is not sacrifice. Indeed, in the following sections we show that such designs are possible.

3.3 Vertically Partitioned Stores

The advent of column-oriented DBMS (e.g., see C-store [49], or more recently the BLU feature of IBM DB2 [66]) gave rise to another alternative representation of RDF data, one in which separate tables are created for each predicate appearing in the RDF data. Figure 6 shows the result of vertically partitioning the data of Figure 5(a).

One of the advantages of vertically partitioned stores is efficient query processing. Since SPARQL queries often bind the predicates of triple patterns, during the evaluation of SPARQL queries over vertically partitioned stores the optimizer only accesses the tables corresponding to the predicates mentioned in the query. So, for example if a SPARQL query requires the entities (subjects) that have a copyright predicate, the optimizer only needs to perform a select-* query over the copyright relation of Figure 6. In contrast to this approach, in the

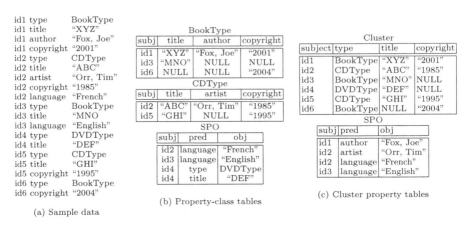

(a) Sample data

(b) Property-class tables

(c) Cluster property tables

Fig. 5. Property tables

Fig. 6. Vertically partitioned data

evaluation of the same query over a monolithic store all the triples in the mono-lithic relation must be accessed, unless an index on the pred column is provided to avoid a sequential scan. On the negative side, the strongest point of the ver-tically partitioned store is also its weakest. If SPARQL queries do not bind the predicate of triple patterns, then all the relations in the store might need to be accessed to evaluate the query. At the same time, this type of RDF representa-tion suffers from the same shortcoming as the one observed in property tables. As the data evolve over time and, say, a new predicate is added in some entity that was never seen before, the schema of the underlying store must change and a new table must be created. This, coupled with the need to often create indexes for the new tables results in a potentially costly operation.

3.4   Entity-Oriented Stores

The last part of this section covers a novel representation for RDF data that attempts to address the shortcomings of past representations [17]. In more detail, the entity-oriented store uses a representation that similar to the monolithic store does not change over the lifetime of the data. However, unlike the monolithic store and like the property and vertically-partitioned stores, it supports efficient evaluation of SPARQL queries across a wide spectrum of queries.

entity	spill	$pred_1$	val_1	$pred_2$	val_2	$pred_3$	val_3
id1	1	title	"XYZ"	type	BookType	author	"Fox, Joe"
id1	1	copyright	"2001"	NULL	NULL	NULL	NULL
id2	1	title	"ABC"	type	CDType	artist	"Orr, Tim"
id2	1	copyright	"1985"	NULL	NULL	language	"French"
id3	0	title	"MNO"	type	BookType	language	"English"
id4	0	title	"DEF"	type	DVDType	NULL	NULL
id5	1	title	"GHI"	type	CDType	NULL	NULL
id5	1	copyright	"1995"	NULL	NULL	NULL	NULL
id6	0	copyright	"2004"	type	BookType	NULL	NULL

Fig. 7. Entity-oriented store

Figure 7 shows the entity-oriented representation for the data shown in Figure 5(a). The first thing to observe in this representation is that unlike any of the previous representations the columns of the relation has no pre-assigned semantics. That is, the table in the particular example has 3 pairs of $(pred_i, val_i)$ without specifying which predicate-object pairs are to be stored there. Indeed, the assignment of predicate-object pairs to $(pred_i, val_i)$ columns happens dynamically by the system, during data loading, and is one of the distinguishing characteristics of the representation. During this assignment, a predicate will always be *hashed* to the same column. So, predicate title is always hashed to column $pred_1$ for any entity having this predicate, while predicate artist is always hashed to column $pred_3$. However, notice that multiple predicates can be hashed to the same column. For example, predicate author is also hashed to $pred_3$. The entity oriented store provides a host of alternative strategies so as to optimize this assignment of predicates to columns with the main objective to avoid *collisions* (i.e., multiple predicates being hashed to the same column for the same entity) while at the same time maximizing compression (i.e., allowing multiple predicates to be hashed to the same column when these predicates are not co-occurring in entities). The end result is a representation that has both a small footprint in terms of space requirements and offers superior query performance when compared with other representations (for more details see [17]).

4   P2P-Based RDF Stores

Peer-to-peer (P2P) networks had initially emerged as a natural way for file sharing in a decentralized manner. Popular systems such as Napster[1], Gnutella[2], Freenet[3], Kazaa[4], Morpheus[5] had made this model of interaction popular. In P2P systems a very large number of autonomous computing nodes (the *peers*) pool together their resources and rely on each other for *data* and *services*. In contrast with a client-server architecture, P2P nodes serve as both a provider

---

[1] http://www.napster.com

[2] There are various clients implementing the Gnutella protocol or variations. See for example, http://www.limewire.com.

[3] http://freenet.sourceforge.net

[4] http://www.kazaa.com

[5] http://www.musiccity.com

and a consumer of resources. P2P networks are typically distinguished into three different classes according to their topology: *unstructured, structured* and *hierarchical* networks.

In unstructured networks all peers are equal and form an overlay network with no restrictions on topology and no centralized source of information. Such systems are highly resilient to churn, i.e., when peers join and leave the network. However, they flood the network with messages to find a piece of data and cannot guarantee to find it in a reasonable amount of hops. Gnutella and Kazaa form examples of such networks. On the contrary, structured networks have a regular topology, e.g., rings or hypercubes, and were devised as a remedy for the routing and object location inefficiencies of unstructured networks. A very popular class of structured networks is the distributed hash tables (DHTs). Hierarchical networks partition the nodes into two categories: super-peers and clients. In such a network, all super-peers are equal and have the same responsibilities: serving a fraction of the clients and keeping indices of the resources of those clients. Super-peers interact by following a protocol of their choice (e.g., a symmetric one like Gnutella, a structured one like Napster or a DHT protocol). Clients can run on user computers and are equal to each other running the same software. Clients learn about resources by querying super-peers and downloading resources directly from other clients.

The combination of Semantic Web technologies (i.e., RDF, RDFS and ontologies) and P2P systems provided accurate data retrieval and efficient search in distributed application scenarios, thus, it has been the focus of many research works the past few years. In the following, we present representative works in this research area where peers are organized in a *structured overlay network* or a *schema-based network*. We mainly focus on how query processing is performed in such distributed settings. The local data access at each peer can be achieved by the various techniques proposed in the previous section. A more comprehensive survey of on P2P-based RDF management can be found in [79].

4.1 Structured Overlay Networks

Distributed hash tables (DHTs) is a prominent class of structured overlays that attempt to solve the object *lookup problem*: given a data item x, find the node which holds x. Each node and each data item is assigned a unique m-bit identifier by using a hashing function such as SHA-1 [76]. The identifier of a node can be computed by hashing its IP address. For data items, we first have to compute a *key* and then hash this key to obtain an identifier *id*. The node with identifier that is numerically closest to *id* is responsible for storing the data item x. The lookup problem is then solved in $O(log(n))$ hops in a network of n peers by providing a simple interface of two requests: PUT(id, x) and GET(id).

We focus on representative RDF stores that use an underlying DHT to store and query RDF data. These include RDFPeers [22], Atlas [40], BabelPeers [15], UniStore [43], RDFCube [53] and GridVine [3].

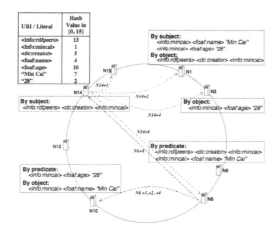

Fig. 8. RDFPeers data partitioning example from [20]

Data Partitioning. In the distributed environment of a DHT, one has to decide how to partition the RDF data. A commonly used data partitioning scheme in DHT-based systems is achieved through the hashing of some or all RDF elements of the triples. RDFPeers [20,22] is the first system that came up with this partitioning scheme and has influenced significantly many follow-up works. RDFPeers is implemented on top of MAAN [21], a self-organized DHT network which extends the well-known DHT protocol of Chord [81] to efficiently answer multi-attribute and range queries.

In RDFPeers, each node uses the RDF data model to create descriptions of resources that it wants to make available to the rest of the network nodes. Each RDF triple in RDF document is indexed to three different network nodes: it is stored once in the node responsible for the identifier that is computed by hashing the subject value of the triple, and twice more by using the predicate and object values of the triple. The SHA-1 hash function [76] is used if the value is a string. If the value is a numeric one then an order preserving hash function is used, which allows efficient evaluation of range queries. Figure 8 shows the indexing of some triples in a network of 8 nodes with a 4-bit identifier space.

GridVine uses P-Grid [2], a structured overlay network based on the principles of DHTs with lexicographic key ordering. Peers in GridVine are able to publish available resources by creating RDF triples (metadata). An RDF triple is stored three times in the network using three different keys based on its subject, predicate and object values, as in [22]. In addition, prefix indexing, e.g., on the beginning of a string representing an object value, can be easily supported using P-Grid routing mechanisms.

BabelPeers [15,33,34] and Atlas [40,41], two more recent systems built on top of Pastry [70] and BambooDHT [68] respectively, also use the triple indexing scheme, storing each triple three times in the network once for each RDF element, as initially proposed in [22]. Unistore [43,44] can index each triple multiple times, using different (combinations of) triple elements in P-Grid [2].

Metadata and Source Selection. In structured overlay networks, and specifically in DHTs, there is no need to keep metadata about identifying which piece of data is located in which node. This is implicitly done by the distributed index they provide for the lookup problem. The problem of source selection is then tackled easily and efficiently by the use of hash functions: the hash value of a key is used to retrieve the node that keeps the data item with this key. DHT-based RDF stores use the constant part(s) of triple patterns involved in the query to compute the identifiers that lead to the nodes storing matching triples.

Query Planning and Evaluation. After the peers that contain matching triples for a triple pattern have been identified, a single triple pattern query can be easily answered by contacting this peer and retrieving the triples that match the triple pattern. Single triple pattern queries require $O(log(n))$ routing hops in a network of n peers, except for the triple pattern without any constant, i.e., (?x, ?y, ?z), where all n peers need to be contacted.

RDFPeers [20] support single triple pattern queries, disjunctive and range queries and conjunctive multi-predicate queries, i.e., conjunctive queries with the join variable on the subject value and the predicate constant. Query execution is performed sequentially at the peers that contain matching triples for the triple patterns of the query and the results are returned to the peer that posed the query. The algorithm finds candidate subjects on each triple pattern recursively and intersects the candidate subjects found at the peer with the found candidate sets for the previously evaluated triple patterns, before returning the search results to the query requestor.

In Atlas [40] the query processing algorithm, QC, works sequentially at the peers containing matching triples, extending the one proposed in [20] for any kind of conjunctive query. With QC the query is evaluated by a chain of nodes. Intermediate results flow through the nodes of this chain and finally the last node in the chain delivers the result back to the node that submitted the query. In [52], an additional query processing algorithm, SBV, is described where the values found to match a triple pattern are used to rewrite the following patterns. SBV achieves a better distribution of the query processing load. It does not create a single chain for a query as QC, but by exploiting the values of matching triples found while processing the query incrementally, it rewrites the query and distributes the responsibility of evaluating it to more nodes than QC (in other words, SBV is constructing multiple chains for each query). Obviously, the order in which the triple patterns are evaluated affects the query performance and in [41] some query optimization techniques are proposed to achieve better query response times.

In BabelPeers [15, 33, 34], query planning and evaluation is performed at a single peer, the one that receives the query request, and includes two phases. In the first phase, all candidate sets for all triples and variables are retrieved from the various nodes of the network to the node that receives the query request. The second phase of the query evaluation, includes local processing of the candidate sets to find the actual answer to the query. The disadvantage of this approach is that the node that receives the query request has to do all the computation and suffers a lot of query processing load. In addition, the candidate sets transferred through the network might contain results that will never be used in the final answer of the query. This causes unnecessary traffic to the network. The authors of [33,34] propose some methods to remove the amount of the useless information from the candidate sets using Bloom filters. Finally, [14] addresses the problem of uneven load among the nodes of BabelPeers due to the skewness of the RDF datasets and proposes several techniques for load balancing.

GridVine [3] follows the principles of data independency and separates the logical from the physical layer. The logical layer consists of the semantic overlay for managing and mapping data and metadata schemas, while the physical layer consists of a structured P2P overlay network that efficiently routes messages. The latter is used to implement various functions at the logical layer, like attribute-based search, schema management and schema mapping management. GridVine allows peers to derive new schemas from well-known base schemas (using RDFS), providing schema inheritance. Each peer has also the possibility to create a mapping between two schemas, in which case translation links among network peers are created (using OWL). In this way, queries are propagated from one semantic domain to another. There are two approaches used for resolving translation links, the iterative and the recursive resolution. With iterative resolution, the peer issuing an RDF query tries to find and process all translation links by itself, while with recursive resolution more than one peers are involved by delegating the query and its translations.

In Unistore [43,44] each query is transformed into a logical query plan which is in turn transformed into a physical query plan using operators defined in [43]. Query planning is performed dynamically at each peer involved in the query evaluation. Unistore uses a cost-based optimizer which estimates the cost of physical operators in terms of the number of hops and messages required for each operator.

4.2   Schema-Based P2P Architectures

In contrast to the RDF stores based on a structured overlay architecture, where data is partitioned among the peers in a specific way and a distributed index is used to locate data, in schema-based P2P systems peers keep the data they have locally and they work collaboratively by exploiting their schemas to tackle the query processing problem. Two influential schema-based P2P for storing and querying RDF data are Edutella [55–57] and SQPeer [46].

Edutella [55–57] is built on top of a super-peer topology, where there are two kind of peers: the super-peers and the clients. The super-peers are organized under the HyperCup topology [74], while clients are connected to super-peers in a star-like fashion. Each client connects to one super-peer only, while a super-peer can have multiple clients and is used to efficiently handle all the requests of clients.

SQPeer [46, 47, 78] is a middleware for routing and planning complex queries in P2P database systems, exploiting the schemas of peers. SQPeer has two different architecture alternatives: it can be organized in a super-peer network or in DHT-based one. Peers that employ the same RDFS schema belong to the same semantic overlay network (SON) [82] and queries posed by peers should conform to the RDFS schema of the SON they belong.

Metadata and Source Selection. In Edutella [26], when a peer joins the network, it provides its super-peer with its metadata information, i.e., a description of the metadata that has been created by this client (supported schema, used values etc.). The actual metadata remains in the client peer. Each super-peer employs two routing indices: The super-peer/peer (SP/P) indices that contain information about each peer that is connected to the super-peer, and the super-peer/super-peer (SP/SP) indices that are extracted summaries from all local SP/P indices. The SP/P indices keep information about peers at different granularities: schemas, schema properties, property value ranges and individual property values. Both types of indices also contain statistics for optimization purposes (size of documents, network characteristics, etc.). This information is used to efficiently route queries only to super-peers and clients that may contain an answer to the query.

In SQPeer, each peer provides the RDFS about the resources that wants to make available in the network. Peers that employ the same schema belong essentially to the same semantic overlay network (SON) [82]. Each peer *advertises* the content (the data values or the schema) of its local database. The RDF Schema defining a SON may contain numerous classes and properties not necessarily populated in a peer's database. For this reason, a peer uses virtual or materialized views to specify the fragment of the schema for which all classes and properties are (in the materialized scenario) or can be (in the virtual scenario) described in a peer's local database. These views may be broadcast to (or requested by) other peers, thus informing the rest of the P2P system of the information available in the peers' databases.

The view propagation in SQPeer depends on the underlying architecture (super-peer or DHT). In the super-peer architecture, a peer that connects to a super-peer forwards its corresponding view and all super-peers are aware of each other. This enables the processing of queries expressed in terms of different RDFS schemata (or fragments). Source selection in a DHT-based SQPeer is done as follows. Unique keys are assigned to each view pattern and hence peers, whose hash values match those keys, are aware of the peer bases that are populated with data answering of a specific schema fragment. An appropriate key assignment and hash function is used for neighbor peers to hold successive view patterns with respect to the class/property hierarchy defined in the employed RDF Schema.

Query Planning and Evaluation. Query planning in Edutella is performed dynamically and not at a single site because super-peers have a very limited view of the whole P2P network (only the neighbors are known), and thus, no comprehensive static plan in the traditional sense can be produced. The query plan chosen by the optimizer is split into a local plan and multiple remote query plans. The remote plans are shipped to the referenced hosts where the optimization process continues on the smaller query plans. The local query plan is instantiated and combines the results of the remote query plans.

Queries in SQPeer are formulated according to the RDF schema that the requester peer supports. The proposed query routing and query processing algorithm can find the relevant peers that actually answer each query and generate query plans by taking into account statistics on data distributions. SQPeer supports two kinds of query optimization for query planning, i.e., compile-time and run-time optimization. The former uses heuristics and statistics to push as much as possible processing to the same peers and decide at compile time among data, query or hybrid shipping execution strategies. On the other hand, run-time optimization includes deciding at execution time on altering the data or query shipping decision or discovering alternative peers for answering a certain part of a query plan.

5   Federated RDF Stores

Probably one of the most distinguishing characteristics of a federated RDF store is that the system is built in a *bottom-up* fashion. That is, existing pre-populated stores come together in order to provide a way to evaluate queries across all of them. Therefore, in federated systems data partitioning is essentially a non-issue and the system has no control as to where data will reside.

Although, there is a considerable number of systems in this category, we are going to limit our presentation to only a subset of them and try to highlight the main design choices through them. So, in the following paragraphs we focus our presentation to a handful of systems including FedX [75], SPLENDID [28] and ANAPSID [4]. For a more extended and in-depth description of the systems, including an evaluation of their performance the reader is encourage to consider related surveys in this space [65, 72].

Metadata and Source Selection. Federated systems have no control or *a priori* knowledge as to where data reside. Still, this information is critical for the evaluation of queries since the system must be able to locate the data that is relevant to the query at hand. In a nutshell, given a query there are two alternative approaches in acquiring the necessary metadata and guiding source selection. The first approach is to determine the metadata at *query time*. This is mostly done by forming appropriate *polling* queries, usually in the form of SPARQL ASK (boolean) queries and using the results of these queries to determine sources that are relevant to a query. The clear benefit of this approach is that no additional metadata are maintained by the federated system (which may need to be updated/maintained as the data in the underlying source change). On the negative side, end-to-end query evaluation time might increase since in addition to the actual query, metadata computation happens at query time and the cost of evaluating ASK queries is not negligible. FedX [75] is an example of a system that maintains no metadata and uses query-time determination of sources (though the system does provide an option for caching to avoid some of the query time costs).

The second approach relies on actually maintaining in the federation some form of description for the contents of the underlying sources. Such metadata can take the form of voiD [6] descriptions used by SPLENDID [28], and can include from high level information like the location of a dataset, to low level information like statistics about the number of triples in a dataset or the number of instances of a property in the data. Other metadata representations, like the one used by ANAPSID [4], are inspired by work in relational databases and employ Local-as-View (LAV) definitions [30] to describe the data stores in individual sources. Yet another alternative includes building summarized indexes [51] describing the contents of the underlying RDF sources, and using such indexes to guide query evaluation [35].

What metadata is available to each system, and how well the system takes advantage of the available metadata are both factors that influence the effectiveness of a source selection strategy. In more detail, using the available metadata, the objective of a source selection strategy is to be both *sound* and *complete*. In this context, completeness is used to denote the desirable property that a source selection strategy identifies *all* the sources that contain data relevant to the query (and thus does not miss any query results). Unfortunately, not all systems are complete with FedX being probably one of the few popular systems having this property [72]. In terms of soundness, the term denotes the desirable property that a source selection strategy should ideally involve *only* the sources that contain data relevant to the query, and no other *irrelevant* sources. Soundness is a property that is closely tied to performance. If a system is not sound then it is bound to contact a lot of irrelevant sources, which results in unnecessary work and prolongs query evaluation time. Not surprisingly, it is particularly hard to achieve soundness in a federated environment and indeed all of the systems do some amount of unnecessary work. Therefore, in the context of soundness, the objective in most systems is minimizing this amount of work, ideally without sacrificing completeness (see [72] for a study of how well existing systems perform in terms of soundness).

Query Planning and Evaluation. Similarly to the centralized setting where once we identify the relations that participate in a query we have to decide the order with which the relations will be joined, in the federated setting once the sources to be involved in the query evaluation are selected, the order with which these sources will be processed needs to be determined. One of the main objectives while deciding the proper ordering is to minimize the intermediate results computed as the results from different sources are correlated (joined). The available metadata, as well as statistics from the evaluated ASK queries during source selection are commonly used to decide this ordering. As the ordering is determined, each system must also decide the join strategy to be used. Bind joins [29], hash joins and nested loop joins are typical strategies used across a variety of systems, with many systems offering more than one strategy. For example, while FedX supports bind joins, SPLENDID supports both hash and bind joins.

As the last step, the actual evaluation of the query takes place. There are still several challenges to be addressed even at this point in the process. For example, a single input query might *spawn* multiple sub-queries over the federated data. Some of these sub-queries might retrieve the same result and therefore one of the challenges is whether the federated system can actually detect these duplicate answers. As another example, being by nature a distributed system, the federation should be able to handle source failures. So, if in the middle of a query evaluation one of the sources leaves the federation (by choice or due to a crash), the system should be able to detect this failure and inform the remaining sources that participate in the federated query.

6   Cloud-Based RDF Stores

The recent explosion in the size of data that is generated and used in various applications, also termed as *big data*, has led to the emergence of new technologies that (i) can scale to large amounts of data, (ii) provide fault-tolerance, (iii) allow for elastic allocation of machines and (iv) free the developer/user from the burden of hardware and software administration. These technologies enable the easy deployment of distributed architectures and are often termed as *cloud computing*. Example systems offering such features, either as a service in the cloud or in a private cluster, are the reputed *NoSQL key-value stores* [23]. At the same time, interest in massively parallel processing has been renewed by the *MapReduce* proposal [25] and many follow-up works, which aim at solving large-volume data management tasks based in a cloud environment, or more generally-speaking in a large-scale distributed platform. We first briefly describe the functionalities offered by MapReduce and distributed key-value stores.

MapReduce. Interest in massively parallel processing has been renewed recently since the emergence of the MapReduce framework [25] and its open source implementation Hadoop [10]. MapReduce has become popular in various computer-science fields as it provides a simple programming paradigm which frees the developer from the burden of handling parallelization, scalability, load balancing and fault-tolerance. MapReduce processing is organized in *jobs*. Each job consists of a *map* and a *reduce* phase, separated by a *shuffle* (data transfer) phase. The map phase is specified by a user-defined function which takes as input (key, value) pairs, performs some tasks on these (if needed) and outputs intermediate pairs (ikey, ivalue). These pairs are shuffled through the network and are given as input to the reduce phase. The distributed file system (DFS) of Hadoop, HDFS, splits data into blocks and each map task operates on a separate block of data. The nodes of the cluster run in parallel one or more map/reduce tasks. A comprehensive survey on MapReduce and its extensions can be found in [27, 71].

Key-value stores. Distributed key-value stores provide very simple data structures based on the concept of *(key, value)* pairs. Such stores typically handle items, each of which consist of a key and several attributes; in turn, an attribute consists of a name and one or several values. For convenience, most key-value stores also support named collections of items, which are typically called tables. An overview of various key-value stores can be found in [23].

In the rest of the section we give an overview of the most recent advances in cloud-based RDF stores with a focus on systems that store data in the MapReduce file system, in NoSQL key-value stores, in multiple centralized RDF stores or in a commercial cloud. A more detailed survey in this research area can be found in [42].

6.1   RDF Stores on MapReduce and DFS

This category includes works that use MapReduce and its underlying distributed file system. These systems are built to make the most out of the parallel processing capacities provided by the underlying MapReduce paradigm. RDF data is stored in files which are split by the distributed file system in the cluster nodes. Their negative aspect from the perspective of the data store is that they do not have efficient fine-grained data stores to rely on. Representative works include SHARD [69], HadoopRDF [38], RAPID+ [45,67] and PigSPARQL [73]. *Metadata* collection and *source selection* in these systems is handled by the MapReduce framework (the namenode and scheduler) and thus, is a non-issue.

Data Partitioning. In these systems the user specifies how the data is partitioned at the file level: the user/system uploads to the system files which contain the RDF triples. There are two commonly used ways to store the data in a file system. In the first one, the data stored in the files are stored based on the triple model, i.e., one triple per line in each file. The second approach contains works that organize the data in predicate-based files. Each predicate file contains the subjects and objects of triples with a specific predicate. Conceptually the first approach resembles the monolithic approach used in single-source approaches, while the latter resembles the vertical partitioning where one relation is created per predicate (see Section 3). As MapReduce does not provide fine-grained indices, the latter way is preferred because it decreases the amount of data that need to be scanned during query evaluation. [69,73] belong to the first category, while [38,67,86] belong to the second one. Note that the placement of the data blocks is performed by the underlying distributed file system.

A different approach is followed in EAGRE [85] where the goal is to reduce the I/O cost during query processing. First, the RDF graph is compressed to an entity-based graph where entities (subjects of triples) with similar properties are grouped in class entities. Then, the compressed graph is partitioned with METIS [54], a graph partitioning tool, into equal to the size of the cluster partitions. Triples are placed in the partition their entity class belongs to.

Query Planning and Evaluation. Usually query planning takes place at a client node and concerns the query decomposition of a query into subqueries to be processed in parallel. The query decomposition can lead to either left-deep or bushy query plans being built. Bushy query plans are better suited for parallel query evaluation as they can exploit both intra- and inter-operator parallelism. However, their search space is very large compared to the one of left-deep trees and for this reason most works build simple left-deep trees, such as SHARD [69] and PigSPARQL [73], or use a hybrid approach where the leaves of the query plan is in bushy shape while the intermediate results are processed in a left-deep manner such as RAPID+ [67]. The only work that builds fully bushy plans is HadoopRDF [38] using a heuristic approach to minimize the number of MapReduce jobs for pruning the search space.

Then, query evaluation is performed using MapReduce jobs. For left-deep query plans one job is performed per join. Since MapReduce does not provide a join functionality, the system has to implement its own join operators. There is wide literature on how to implement a join in MapReduce with the repartition and broadcast join to be the most common ones. The interested reader may refer to [5, 16].

6.2   RDF Stores on Top of NoSQL Key-Value Stores

There are many works that use NoSQL key-value stores as back-ends for storing and indexing RDF data. These systems benefit from the efficient and fine-grained storage and retrieval of the key-value stores, however, they suffer in more complex functionalities such as joins. Representatives of the second category include systems such as Rya [64] which uses Apache Accumulo [8], Trinity.RDF [84] which is built on top of a in-memory key-value store [77], CumulusRDF [48] based on Apache Cassandra [9], and H_2RDF+ [61] built on top of HBase [11]. Similarly with the previous set of works on MapReduce, *metadata* collection and *source selection* is performed by the key-value store opaquely to the user and we thus, omit any discussion about them.

Data Partitioning. Data partitioning in key-value stores amounts to the choice of indices that will be build by each system. As shown in Section 3, centralized RDF stores usually use extensive indexing schemes that enable fast data access for all triple patterns and efficient performing of merge-joins. This extensive indexing scheme has a significant storage overhead which is amplified in a cloud environment where data is also replicated for fault-tolerance reasons. For this reason, most RDF stores built on top of key-value stores employ a subset of these indices which is sufficient for matching efficiently all possible triple patterns. The three permutations massively used are subject-predicate-object (SPO), predicate-object-subject (POS) and object-subject-predicate (OSP). Typically systems materialize each of one of these indices in a separate table in the key-value store. The choice of the keys and values highly depends on the underlying functionality of the key-value store, e.g., if it provides a range scan over the key space. For instance, each of the subject, predicate, object can be mapped to a key in the key value store, or a concatenation of two or three of the RDF elements can be used as key if a range scan is supported by the key-value store.

Query Planning and Evaluation. As key-value stores do not allow for performing joins on the server-side, query planning and query evaluation is often performed at a single site. This is simply done by fetching the triples from the key-value store that match the individual triple patterns and performing the join locally at the client-side. This approach is followed by most systems, e.g., [48,64]. A hybrid approach is proposed in H_2RDF+ [61] where either a centralized local join is performed at the client side or a MapReduce job is instantiated depending on the selectivity of the join. Trinity.RDF [84] uses a graph-based approach by navigating the RDF graph and finding matches to the query.

6.3   Approaches Using Multiple Centralized RDF Stores

Within the third category, centralized RDF stores distributed among multiple nodes are used to exploit parallelization such as in [36, 37]. These systems are based on a master/slave architecture, where the master partitions and places the RDF triples in the slave nodes. Each slave node stores its local RDF triples in a centralized RDF store such as RDF-3X.

Data Partitioning. The goal is a data partitioning scheme that enables high parallelization during query evaluation while striving to minimize communication among the slave nodes. In [37] a graph partitioning tool, called METIS [54], is used to partition the RDF graph into as many partitions as the number of nodes so that a minimum number of edges is cut, i.e., the minimum number of triples have their subject and object in different partitions. Placement is done by assigning each triple in the partition its subject belongs to, termed as 1-hop directed guarantee, or to the partitions that both the subject and object belongs to, termed as 1-hop undirected guarantee. This leads to replicating the triples that are on the edge cuts. There is also the possibility to allow for further replication of those triples that are at partition boundaries. A directed (undirected) n-hop guarantee is achieved when any triples forming a directed (undirected) path of length n will be located within the same partition. A similar approach is followed in [36] with the difference that replication occurs only in the parts of data that are certain to be accessed for a given query workload.

Metadata and Source Selection. Although data is partitioned following a specific scheme, in [36, 37] there is no metadata information for mapping the triples to the nodes they are stored. Therefore, a subquery is sent to all the sources to be answered.

Query Planning and Evaluation. Query planning and execution is performed by decomposing the query to subqueries that can be completely answered by the underlying RDF store. If a query can be completely answered by the underlying RDF store then no communication is required. The answers of the query is the union of the individual results. In any other case, network communication is necessary to join the intermediate results of the query which is done in the MapReduce framework.

6.4 RDF Stores in Commercial Clouds

The first store that proposed an RDF store built in a commercial cloud is Stratustore [80] which relies on Amazons SimpleDB [13], an early developed key-value store of Amazon Web Services. In Stratustore, RDF data is indexed in the key-value store and query processing is performed at the client side running at an EC2 machine.

In AMADA [12, 19], a cloud-resident RDF store, a different approach is followed. Raw RDF data reside in Amazon's storage service (S3) as simple files and a file index built in Amazon's key-value store keeps *metadata* on which data can be found in which files. *Source selection* is performed by consulting the indices built to retrieve the files that contain triples that match the query. During *query evaluation* the triples contained in the files selected by the index are cached in a centralized RDF store where query answering is performed.

7 Conclusions

We have presented an overview of query processing techniques for RDF databases. We identified a set of tasks that are of great importance for RDF query processing and that a system should address. These include metadata collection, source selection, data partitioning and query planning and execution in a decentralized environment and storage/indexing and query planning and evaluation in a centralized system. We analyzed each one of these tasks in different architectures. We first discussed issues related to single-source RDF stores and then navigated through P2P systems, federated architectures and cloud-based proposals.

There are numerous of open problems that are yet to be solved. These range from more advanced techniques for query optimization (query decomposition, join ordering, etc.), to building more sophisticated indices or materialized views for speeding up query performance. An important aspect that is usually neglected in the works we have presented in this chapter is RDFS reasoning. RDFS reasoning is an essential functionality of the RDF model and should, therefore, be taken into account when building systems for answering SPARQL queries.

References

1. Abadi, D.J., Marcus, A., Madden, S., Hollenbach, K.J.: Scalable Semantic Web Data Management Using Vertical Partitioning. In: VLDB, pp. 411–422 (2007)

2. Aberer, K., Cudre-Mauroux, P., Datta, A., Despotovic, Z., Hauswirth, M., Punceva, M., Schmidt, R.: P-Grid: A Self-Organizing Structured P2P System. SIGMOD Record 32, 29–33 (2003)
3. Aberer, K., Cudre-Mauroux, P., Hauswirth, M., Pelt, T.V.: GridVine: Building Internet-Scale Semantic Overlay Networks. In: Proceedings of the 13th World Wide Web Conference (WWW 2004), New York, USA (2004)
4. Acosta, M., Vidal, M.-E., Lampo, T., Castillo, J., Ruckhaus, E.: Anapsid: An adaptive query processing engine for sparql endpoints. In: Aroyo, L., Welty, C., Alani, H., Taylor, J., Bernstein, A., Kagal, L., Noy, N., Blomqvist, E. (eds.) ISWC 2011, Part I. LNCS, vol. 7031, pp. 18–34. Springer, Heidelberg (2011)
5. Afrati, F.N., Ullman, J.D.: Optimizing Multiway Joins in a Map-Reduce Environment. IEEE Trans. Knowl. Data Eng. 23(9) (2011)
6. Alexander, K., Hausenblas, M.: Describing linked datasets - on the design and usage of void, the vocabulary of interlinked datasets. In: Linked Data on the Web Workshop (LDOW 09), in conjunction with 18th International World Wide Web Conference, WWW 2009 (2009)
7. Alexander, N., Lopez, X., Ravada, S., Stephens, S., Wang, J.: Rdf data model in oracle
8. Apache Accumulo (2012), http://accumulo.apache.org/
9. Apache Cassandra (2012), http://cassandra.apache.org/
10. Apache Hadoop (2012), http://hadoop.apache.org/
11. Apache HBase (2012), http://hbase.apache.org/
12. Aranda-Andújar, A., Bugiotti, F., Camacho-Rodríguez, J., Colazzo, D., Goasdoué, F., Kaoudi, Z., Manolescu, I.: Amada: Web Data Repositories in the Amazon Cloud (demo). In: CIKM (2012)
13. Amazon Web Services (2012), http://aws.amazon.com/
14. Battre, D., Heine, F., Hoing, A., Kao, O.: Load-balancing in P2P based RDF stores. In: Proceedings of the 2nd International Workshop on Scalable Semantic Web Knowledge Base Systems (SSWS 2006, Co-located with ISWC 2006), Athens, Georgia, USA (2006)
15. Battre, D., Heine, F., Hoing, A., Kao, O.: BabelPeers: P2P based Semantic Grid Resource Discovery. High Performance Computing and Grids in Action 16, 288–307 (2008)
16. Blanas, S., Patel, J.M., Ercegovac, V., Rao, J., Shekita, E.J., Tian, Y.: A Comparison of Join Algorithms for Log Processing in MapReduce. In: SIGMOD (2010)
17. Bornea, M.A., Dolby, J., Kementsietsidis, A., Srinivas, K., Dantressangle, P., Udrea, O., Bhattacharjee, B.: Building an efficient RDF store over a relational database. In: SIGMOD Conference, pp. 121–132 (2013)
18. Brickley, D., Guha, R.: RDF Vocabulary Description Language 1.0: RDF Schema. Technical report, W3C Recommendation (2004)
19. Bugiotti, F., Goasdoué, F., Kaoudi, Z., Manolescu, I.: RDF Data Management in the Amazon Cloud. In: DanaC Workshop (in Conjunction with EDBT) (2012)
20. Cai, M., Frank, M.: RDFPeers: A Scalable Distributed RDF Repository based on A Structured Peer-to-Peer Network. In: Proceedings of the 13th World Wide Web Conference (WWW 2004), New York, USA (2004)
21. Cai, M., Frank, M., Szekely, P.: MAAN: A Multi-Attribute Addressable Network for Grid Information Services. In: Proceedings of the 4th International Workshop on Grid Computing (Grid2003), Phoenix, Arizona, USA (2003)
22. Cai, M., Frank, M.R., Yan, B., MacGregor, R.M.: A Subscribable Peer-to-Peer RDF Repository for Distributed Metadata Management. Journal of Web Semantics: Science, Services and Agents on the World Wide Web 2(2), 109–130 (2004)

23. Cattell, R.: Scalable SQL and NoSQL data stores. SIGMOD Record 39(4), 12–27 (2011)
24. Chaudhry, N.A., Shaw, K., Abdelguerfi, M. (eds.): Stream Data Management. Advances in Database Systems, vol. 30. Springer (2005)
25. Dean, J., Ghemawat, S.: Mapreduce: Simplified Data Processing on Large Clusters. In: Proceedings of the USENIX Symposium on Operating Systems Design & Implementation (OSDI), pp. 137–147 (2004)
26. Dhraief, H., Kemper, A., Nejdl, W., Wiesner, C.: Processing and Optimization of Complex Queries in Schema-Based P2P-Networks. In: Ng, W.S., Ooi, B.-C., Ouksel, A.M., Sartori, C. (eds.) DBISP2P 2004. LNCS, vol. 3367, pp. 31–45. Springer, Heidelberg (2005)
27. Doulkeridis, C., Norvag, K.: A survey of large-scale analytical query processing in MapReduce. VLDB Journal (2013)
28. Görlitz, O., Staab, S.: Splendid: Sparql endpoint federation exploiting void descriptions. In: COLD (2011)
29. Haas, L.M., Kossmann, D., Wimmers, E.L., Yang, J.: Optimizing queries across diverse data sources. In: Proceedings of the 23rd International Conference on Very Large Data Bases, VLDB 1997, pp. 276–285 (1997)
30. Halevy, A.Y.: Answering queries using views: A survey. The VLDB Journal 10(4), 270–294 (2001)
31. Harris, S., Seaborne, A.: SPARQL 1.1 Query Language. W3C Recommendation (2013), http://www.w3.org/TR/sparql11-overview/
32. Hayes, P.: RDF Semantics. W3C Recommendation (February 2004), http://www.w3.org/TR/rdf-mt/
33. Heine, F.: Scalable P2P based RDF Querying. In: Proceedings of the 1st International Conference on Scalable Information Systems (Infoscale 2006), Hong Kong (2006)
34. Heine, F., Hovestadt, M., Kao, O.: Processing Complex RDF Queries over P2P Networks. In: Proceedings of Workshop on Information Retrieval in Peer-to-Peer-Networks (P2PIR 2005), Bremen, Germany (2005)
35. Hoffmann, J., Selman, B. (eds.): Proceedings of the Twenty-Sixth AAAI Conference on Artificial Intelligence, Toronto, Ontario, Canada, July 22-26. AAAI Press (2012)
36. Hose, K., Schenkel, R.: WARP: Workload-Aware Replication and Partitioning for RDF. In: DESWEB Workshop (in Conjunction with ICDE) (2013)
37. Huang, J., Abadi, D.J., Ren, K.: Scalable SPARQL Querying of Large RDF Graphs. PVLDB 4(11), 1123–1134 (2011)
38. Husain, M., McGlothlin, J., Masud, M.M., Khan, L., Thuraisingham, B.M.: Heuristics-Based Query Processing for Large RDF Graphs Using Cloud Computing. IEEE Trans. on Knowl. and Data Eng. (2011)
39. Jena: a semantic web framework for java, https://jena.apache.org
40. Kaoudi, Z., Koubarakis, M., Kyzirakos, K., Miliaraki, I., Magiridou, M., Papadakis-Pesaresi, A.: Atlas: Storing, Updating and Querying RDF(S) Data on Top of DHTs. Journal of Web Semantics (2010)
41. Kaoudi, Z., Kyzirakos, K., Koubarakis, M.: SPARQL Query Optimization on Top of DHTs. In: Patel-Schneider, P.F., Pan, Y., Hitzler, P., Mika, P., Zhang, L., Pan, J.Z., Horrocks, I., Glimm, B. (eds.) ISWC 2010, Part I. LNCS, vol. 6496, pp. 418–435. Springer, Heidelberg (2010)
42. Kaoudi, Z., Manolescu, I.: RDF in the Clouds: A Survey. The VLDB Journal (2014)
43. Karnstedt, M.: Query Processing in a DHT-Based Universal Storage - The World as a Peer-to-Peer Database. PhD thesis (2009)

44. Karnstedt, M., Sattler, K.-U., Richtarsky, M., Muller, J., Hauswirth, M., Schmidt, R., John, R.: UniStore: Querying a DHT-based Universal Storage. In: Proceedings of the 23rd International Conference on Data Engineering, ICDE 2007 (Demo paper), Istanbul, Turkey (April 2007)

45. Kim, H., Ravindra, P., Anyanwu, K.: From SPARQL to MapReduce: The Journey Using a Nested TripleGroup Algebra (demo). PVLDB 4(12), 1426–1429 (2011)

46. Kokkinidis, G., Christophides, V.: Semantic Query Routing and Processing in P2P Database Systems: The ICS-FORTH SQPeer Middleware. In: EDBT Workshops, Heraklion, Crete, Greece (March 2004)

47. Kokkinidis, G., Sidirourgos, L., Christophides, V.: Query Processing in RDF/S-based P2P Database Systems. In: Semantic Web and Peer-to-Peer. Springer (2006)

48. Ladwig, G., Harth, A.: CumulusRDF: Linked Data Management on Nested Key-Value Stores. In: SSWS (2011)

49. Lamb, A., Fuller, M., Varadarajan, R., Tran, N., Vandiver, B., Doshi, L., Bear, C.: The Vertica Analytic Database: C-store 7 Years Later. In: Proc. VLDB Endow., vol. 5(12), pp. 1790–1801 (2012)

50. Le, W., Kementsietsidis, A., Duan, S., Li, F.: Scalable multi-query optimization for sparql. In: ICDE, pp. 666–677 (2012)

51. Li, F., Le, W., Duan, S., Kementsietsidis, A.: Scalable Keyword Search on Large RDF Data. IEEE Transactions on Knowledge and Data Engineering 99(PrePrints) (2014)

52. Liarou, E., Idreos, S., Koubarakis, M.: Evaluating Conjunctive Triple Pattern Queries over Large Structured Overlay Networks. In: Cruz, I., Decker, S., Allemang, D., Preist, C., Schwabe, D., Mika, P., Uschold, M., Aroyo, L.M. (eds.) ISWC 2006. LNCS, vol. 4273, pp. 399–413. Springer, Heidelberg (2006)

53. Matono, A., Pahlevi, S.M., Kojima, I.: RDFCube: A P2P-Based Three-Dimensional Index for Structural Joins on Distributed Triple Stores. In: Moro, G., Bergamaschi, S., Joseph, S., Morin, J.-H., Ouksel, A.M. (eds.) DBISP2P 2005/2006. LNCS, vol. 4125, pp. 323–330. Springer, Heidelberg (2007)

54. METIS, http://glaros.dtc.umn.edu/gkhome/views/metis

55. Nejdl, W., Wolf, B., Qu, C., Decker, S., Sintek, M., Naeve, A., Nilsson, M., Palmér, M., Risch, T.: EDUTELLA: A P2P Networking Infrastructure based on RDF. In: Proceedings of the 11th World Wide World Conference (WWW 2002), Honolulu, Hawaii, USA, pp. 604–615 (2002)

56. Nejdl, W., Wolf, B., Staab, S., Tane, J.: Semantic Web Workshop 2002. CEUR Workshop Proceedings, vol. 55 (2002)

57. Nejdl, W., Wolpers, M., Siberski, W., Schmitz, C., Schlosser, M., Brunkhorst, I., Loser, A.: Super-Peer-Based Routing and Clustering Strategies for RDF-Based Peer-To-Peer Networks. In: Proceedings of the 12th WWW Conference, Budapest, Hungary (May 2003)

58. Neumann, T., Weikum, G.: The RDF-3X engine for scalable management of RDF data. VLDB J. 19(1), 91–113 (2010)

59. Özsu, M.T., Valduriez, P.: Principles of Distributed Database Systems, 3rd edn. Springer (2011)

60. Paoli, J., Yergeau, F., Sperberg-McQueen, M., Bray, T., Maler, E.: Extensible markup language (XML) 1.0. W3C recommendation, W3C, 5th edn. (November 2008), http://www.w3.org/TR/2008/REC-xml-20081126/

61. Papailiou, N., Konstantinou, I., Tsoumakos, D., Karras, P., Koziris, N.: H2RDF+: High-performance distributed joins over large-scale RDF graphs. In: BigData Conference (2013)

62. Patel-Schneider, P., Hayes, P.: RDF 1.1 semantics. W3C recommendation, W3C (February 2014), http://www.w3.org/TR/2014/REC-rdf11-mt-20140225/
63. Pérez, J., Arenas, M., Gutierrez, C.: Semantics and Complexity of SPARQL. ACM Transactions on Database Systems 34(3), 16:1–16:45 (2009)
64. Punnoose, R., Crainiceanu, A., Rapp, D.: Rya: A Scalable RDF Triple Store for the Clouds. In: Workshop on Cloud Intelligence (in Conjunction with VLDB) (2012)
65. Rakhmawati, N.A., Umbrich, J., Karnstedt, M., Hasnain, A., Hausenblas, M.: Querying over Federated SPARQL Endpoints - A State of the Art Survey. CoRR, abs/1306.1723 (2013)
66. Raman, V., Attaluri, G.K., Barber, R., Chainani, N., Kalmuk, D., KulandaiSamy, V., Leenstra, J., Lightstone, S., Liu, S., Lohman, G.M., Malkemus, T., Müller, R., Pandis, I., Schiefer, B., Sharpe, D., Sidle, R., Storm, A.J., Zhang, L.: Db2 with blu acceleration: So much more than just a column store. PVLDB 6(11), 1080–1091 (2013)
67. Ravindra, P., Kim, H., Anyanwu, K.: An Intermediate Algebra for Optimizing RDF Graph Pattern Matching on MapReduce. In: Antoniou, G., Grobelnik, M., Simperl, E., Parsia, B., Plexousakis, D., De Leenheer, P., Pan, J. (eds.) ESWC 2011, Part II. LNCS, vol. 6644, pp. 46–61. Springer, Heidelberg (2011)
68. Rhea, S., Geels, D., Roscoe, T., Kubiatowicz, J.: Handling Churn in a DHT. In: USENIX Annual Technical Conference (2004)
69. Rohloff, K., Schantz, R.E.: Clause-Iteration with MapReduce to Scalably Query Datagraphs in the SHARD Graph-Store. In: Workshop on Data-intensive Distributed Computing (2011)
70. Rowstron, A., Druschel, P.: Pastry: Scalable, Distributed Object Location and Routing for Large-Scale- Peer-to-Peer Storage Utility. In: Guerraoui, R. (ed.) Middleware 2001. LNCS, vol. 2218, pp. 329–350. Springer, Heidelberg (2001)
71. Sakr, S., Liu, A., Fayoumi, A.G.: The Family of Mapreduce and Large-scale Data Processing Systems. ACM Comput. Surv. 46(1), 11:1–11:44 (2013)
72. Saleem, M., Khan, Y., Ivan Ermilov, A.H.A.D., Ngomo, A.-C.N.:
73. Schätzle, A., Przyjaciel-Zablocki, M., Lausen, G.: PigSPARQL: Mapping SPARQL to Pig Latin. In: SWIM (2011)
74. Schlosser, M.T., Sintek, M., Decker, S., Nejdl, W.: HyperCuP - Hypercubes, Ontologies and Efficient Search on Peer-to-peer Networks. In: Moro, G., Koubarakis, M. (eds.) AP2PC 2002. LNCS (LNAI), vol. 2530, pp. 112–124. Springer, Heidelberg (2003)
75. Schwarte, A., Haase, P., Hose, K., Schenkel, R., Schmidt, M.: Fedx: Optimization techniques for federated query processing on linked data. In: Aroyo, L., Welty, C., Alani, H., Taylor, J., Bernstein, A., Kagal, L., Noy, N., Blomqvist, E. (eds.) ISWC 2011, Part I. LNCS, vol. 7031, pp. 601–616. Springer, Heidelberg (2011)
76. SHA-1. Secure hash standard. National Institute of Standards and Technology. Publication 180-1 (1995)
77. Shao, B., Wang, H., Li, Y.: The Trinity Graph Engine. Technical report (2012), http://research.microsoft.com/pubs/161291/trinity.pdf
78. Sidirourgos, L., Kokkinidis, G., Dalamagas, T., Christophides, V., Sellis, T.: Indexing Views to Route Queries in a PDMS. Journal of Distributed Parallel Databases 23, 45–68 (2008)
79. Staab, S., Stuckenschmidt, H. (eds.): Semantic Web and Peer-to-Peer: Decentralized Management and Exchange of Knowledge and Information. Springer (2006)
80. Stein, R., Zacharias, V.: RDF On Cloud Number Nine. In: Workshop on New Forms of Reasoning for the Semantic Web: Scalable and Dynamic (May 2010)

81. Stoica, I., Morris, R., Liben-Nowell, D., Karger, D., Kaashoek, M.F., Dabek, F., Balakrishnan, H.: Chord: A Scalable Peer-to-Peer Lookup Protocol for Internet Applications. IEEE/ACM Transactions on Networking 11(1), 17–32 (2003)
82. Triantafillou, P., Xiruhaki, C., Koubarakis, M., Ntarmos, N.: Towards high-performance peer-to-peer content and resource sharing systems. In: Proceedings of the First Biennial Conference on Innovative Data Systems Research (CIDR 2003) (January 2003)
83. Wilkinson, K.: Jena property table implementation. In: SSWS (2006)
84. Zeng, K., Yang, J., Wang, H., Shao, B., Wang, Z.: A Distributed Graph Engine for Web Scale RDF Data. In: PVLDB (2013)
85. Zhang, X., Chen, L., Tong, Y., Wang, M.: EAGRE: Towards Scalable I/O Efficient SPARQL Query Evaluation on the Cloud. In: ICDE (2013)
86. Zhang, X., Chen, L., Wang, M.: Towards Efficient Join Processing over Large RDF Graph Using MapReduce. In: Ailamaki, A., Bowers, S. (eds.) SSDBM 2012. LNCS, vol. 7338, pp. 250–259. Springer, Heidelberg (2012)

Introduction to Graph Databases

Josep Lluís Larriba-Pey[1], Norbert Martínez-Bazán[2],
and David Domínguez-Sal[2]

[1] DAMA-UPC, BarcelonaTech, Barcelona, Spain
`larri@ac.upc.edu`
[2] Sparsity Technologies, Barcelona, Spain
{`nortbert,david`}`@spartisty-technologies.com`

Abstract. The use of graphs in analytic environments is getting more
and more widespread, with applications in many different environments
like social network analysis, fraud detection, industrial management,
knowledge analysis, etc. Graph databases are one important solution
to consider in the management of large datasets. The course will be oriented to tackle four important aspects of graph management. First, to
give a characterization of graphs and the most common operations applied on them. Second, to review the technologies for graph management
and focus on the particular case of Sparksee. Third, to analyze in depth
some important applications and how graphs are used to solve them.
Fourth, to understand the use of benchmarking to make the requirements
of the user compatible with the growth of the technologies for graph
management.

1   Introduction to Graphs

A graph G is an ordered pair $G = (V, E)$ consisting of a set V of nodes (vertices)
together with a set E of relationships (edges), where $E \subseteq V \times V$. In addition to
the plain definition of graph, there are some characteristics that are relevant to
mention and that will be useful for defining graph data models upon which we
develop this paper. We summarize them in the following points.

– **Attributes:** Different types of information may be associated to nodes and
  edges in order to enrich the graph-based representation. Such information is
  typically a string or numerical values, which indicate some properties of the
  nodes or their edges. However any other type of information such as enumerated values or vectors might be also used. For instance, for the particular
  case of edges, some graphs include numerical attributes that quantify the relationship, which is usually interpreted as its corresponding length, weight,
  cost or intensity. Moreover, many applications assign a unique identifier for
  each node and edge of the graph (this could be interpreted as an attribute
  called "ID"), useful for enumeration purposes. The information attached to
  nodes and edges can be very influential in the result of an algorithm or
  analysis, thus taking into account this information is very critical.

M. Koubarakis et al. (Eds.): Reasoning Web 2014, LNCS 8714, pp. 171–194, 2014.

- **Directed:** The relation between two nodes can be symmetric or not, depending on the problem at hand. If the relation is symmetric, it has no particular direction, it is then called *undirected*. On the contrary, if the relation is not symmetric, edges differentiate between the head and the tail. The tail of the edge is the node from which the edge starts, and the head of the edge is the node which the edge points to. In this case the edges are said *directed*. Since an undirected edge can be always represented as two directed edges, each one in a reverse direction of the other, undirected graphs are a particular case of directed graphs. This property will determine some measures over graphs, such as connectivity or path lengths are computed.
- **Labels:** In certain applications, different labels (or types) of nodes and edges may be considered. Such labeling or typing impacts the result of operations. For example, in a social network scenario, friendship relationships may be either "positive" or "negative" [1], drastically changing the outcome of certain algorithms.
- **Multigraphs:** Multigraphs are graphs in which two nodes can be connected by more than one edge. This situation commonly appears when two nodes are connected through different types of relationships. For instance, in a mobile telephone network, where phone numbers are represented by nodes and telephone calls by edges, each call between two phones (nodes) might be represented by a particular edge, thus leading to nodes connected with more than one edge when more than one call exists between two telephone numbers.
- **Hypergraphs:** Hypergraphs are a generalization of graphs, where edges are substituted by hyperedges. In contrast to regular edges, a hyperedge connects an arbitrary number of nodes instead of two. Hypergraphs are used, for example, for building artificial intelligence models [2]. Although Hypergraphs appear commonly along different types of networks, in practice they are usually represented as bipartite networks [3], since it facilitates its representation and posterior treatment by the algorithms.
- **Hypernodes:** A hypernode graph is another graph generalization, where nodes are substituted by hypernodes. A hypernode is an entity that contains a set of nodes and edges (i.e. a graph). A regular node is equivalent to an hypernode that contains a single node and no edges [4]. Hypernodes are used to nest graphs inside graphs. They represent both simple and complex objects such as hierarchical, composite and cyclic objects, as well as mappings and records. A key feature is that they have the inherent ability to encapsulate information.

Hypergraphs and hypernodes are formally well defined, but their popularity is limited because of their additional complexity. Unless otherwise stated, in this paper we will suppose directed attributed multigraphs. We will denote the number of nodes in a graph by n and the number of edges by m.

1.1 Graph Characterization

Real graphs are typically very different from graphs following the Erdös-Renyi model (random graphs) [5]. Leskovec et al. [6], analyzed over 100 real-world networks belonging to the following fields: social networks, information/citation networks, collaboration networks, web graphs, Internet networks, bipartite networks, biological networks, low dimensional networks, actor networks, and product-purchaser networks. The size of those networks varied from a few hundred nodes to millions of nodes, and from hundreds to more than one hundred million edges. We note that although they might seem large, the graph data sets of some current real applications are significantly larger: for example Flickr accounts more than 6 billion photographs that can be tagged and rated [7], and Facebook is publishing more than 25 billion pieces of content each month. For these large graphs, one of the most interesting aspects is that in general most graph metrics (such as the node degree or the edge weight) follow power law distributions [6, 8, 9], and hence some areas of the graph are significantly denser than others.

With respect to the characterization of graphs, we summarize some properties that often appear in these real graphs [10], and that will be useful to characterize the graphs from in the use cases below.

- **Large Component:** This property states that for undirected graphs, there is typically a large component that fills most of the network (usually more than 50% and not infrequently 90%), while the rest of the network is divided into a large number of small components disconnected from the rest. There can be networks where there is only one component filling all the network (for instance Internet, or WWW if acquired from one single crawler). For directed networks, there is usually one large weakly connected component and other small ones in a similar way as in the undirected case. For strongly connected components there is typically one strongly connected component and a selection of small ones (for instance, in WWW network, the largest strongly connected component fills about 25% of the network). Associated with each strongly connected component there is an out-component and an in-component. Acyclic networks do not have strongly connected components. Citation networks for instance, which are considered almost acyclic, have few small strongly connected components of 2-3 nodes but not larger ones.
- **Small-World Property:** A small-world network is a type of network in which most nodes are not neighbors of one another, but most nodes can be reached from every other by a small number of hops or steps. In other words, the average diameter of each connected component is small. That is, from a given node there is a short path to reach the majority of the remaining nodes in the connected component. One interesting property of the small-world networks is that the distance L between two randomly chosen nodes in the same component grows proportionally to the logarithm of the number of nodes n in the network, i.e. $L \propto log(n)$, which means that even for huge networks the diameter remains very low compared to the number of nodes in the network.

- **Scale-Free Networks:** Although the exact connection patterns between nodes may differ between graphs, the macroscopic structure of the degrees is often very regular and fits known statistical distributions. We denote the degree of a node as k, or in other words the number of edges attached to that node. Then, the proportion of nodes of the graph that have degree k is $p_k = \frac{\#\ nodes\ with\ degree\ k}{n}$. Thus, p_k can also be seen as the probability that a randomly chosen node has degree k.
  Degree distributions from graphs typically follow power law distributions, that correlate exponentially the number of nodes with a given degree to its frequency. The most popular statistical distribution is the Zipf that defines $p_k = C \cdot k^{-\alpha}$, where C is a normalization factor. These distributions are often plot in logarithmic scale because they trace a straight line since $ln(p_k) = -\alpha \cdot ln(k) + ln(C)$. The most common values for α are between $2 \leq \alpha \leq 3$ (see [3] for a complete list of networks with the corresponding values of α). We note that, for some graphs, the Zipf distribution does not model well the nodes with few connections (do not fit well the straight line), and an alternate process called Zipf with cut-off is used. This procedure removes the small degree nodes when the α for a Zipf is estimated.
  Networks that follow power-law degree distributions are called scale-free networks because their degree distribution look similar for all graph sizes. To give an example, in the Internet network[3], most of the nodes have small degrees but there is a tail containing some nodes with high degree (the highest degree is 2407, which means that such node is connected to about 12% of the nodes in the network). Such well connected nodes are called hubs.
- **Small Average Degree:** The maximum average degree of a graph is $(n - 1) = O(n)$, which corresponds to a structure called clique that connects all pairs of nodes. These graphs are described as dense because they have many edges. However, the study of real graphs has determined that such dense graphs are not common for real datasets [11]. Graphs that represent real world data have an average degree that is small compared to the number of nodes in the graph. The average degree typically remains in the range between 3 and 100, even for graphs with millions of nodes [12]. For graphs that grow over time, it has been found that the average degree tends to increase slightly faster than the number of nodes [11], but the growth is so slow that it is rare to find real graphs with average degrees over a thousand [12].
  Graphs with small average degree are also referred as sparse graphs. The notion of sparse comes from the matrix representation of the graph, which indicates with one the presence of an edge, and zero otherwise. Sparse matrices are those that have a large number of zeros, and similarly, sparse graphs are those whose matrix representation has a large number of zeroes.
- **Large Clustering Coefficient:** Graphs from real datasets have often a clustering coefficient larger than expected by pure chance. This is an effect of transitive relations among members of the network. In other words, "the friends of my friends are also my friends". Graphs usually have observable communities that are groups of nodes structurally strongly related among them, but not structurally related to the rest of the graph.

1.2   Graph Operations and Queries

A graph operation is a computation on the graph that is directly interpreted by the engine of the GDB. A graph query is a user statement that requests a piece of information from the database, which requires one or more operations to be computed.

There is a set of basic operations that is available in most GDBs, which includes: (i) get atomic information from the graph such as getting a node, getting the value of an attribute of an edge, or getting the neighbor nodes of a specific node; and (ii) create/update/delete the nodes/edges/attributes of the graph.

Then, there are graph queries that are more complex and which are built on top of those basic operations. Some GDBs implement subsets of graph queries, such as graph traversals, as operations that are directly interpreted by the GDB. Therefore, depending on the software under analysis some queries can be referred as operations, too. The most common families of graph queries are the following:

– **Traversals:** Traversals are queries that, given a set of starting nodes, explore recursively the neighborhood of those nodes until a terminating condition, such as a fixed number of steps or the arrival to a target node, is fulfilled. Consider for instance, the computation of the *shortest path* between two nodes, which is the shortest sequence of edges (or the smallest addition of edge weights in the case of weighted graphs) that connects two nodes. In a directed graph the direction is restricted to outgoing edges from the tail to the head. Note that shortest paths may be constrained by the value of some node or edge labels/attributes, as in the case of finding the shortest route from two points, avoiding a certain type of road, for instance. Another typical traversal query is the computation of *k-hops*. That is the query returns all the nodes that are at a distance of k edges given a source node. A particular case that is worth to mention because it is widely used in other queries is the 1-hops (i.e $k = 1$). In this case, the query returns all the neighbors of the source node, also known as the neighbors of the node. Examples of queries using 1-hops include calculating the nearest neighborhood in recommender systems, obtaining a particular user's neighborhood with similar interest, or in web ranking using hubs and authorities.
– **Graph Metrics:** The objective is basically the study of the topology of the graph in order to analyze their complexity and to characterize graph objects. It is used for instance to verify some specific data distributions, to evaluate a potential match of a specific pattern, or to get detailed information of the role of nodes and edges. In several situations graph measurement is the first step of the analytical process and it is widely used in social network analysis and protein interaction analysis. Typical graph metrics include: the *hop-plot*, which, given a source node, measures the rate of increase of the neighborhood depending on the distance to such source node; the *diameter*, that is, the largest distance between any pair of vertices in the graph; the *effective diameter*, which is defined as the minimum number of hops in which

90% of all connected pairs of nodes can reach each other; the *density*, i.e. the portion of all possible edges currently present in the graph; or the *clustering coefficient*, which measures the degree of transitivity of the graph.

- **Component Finding:** A *connected component* is a subgraph of the original graph in which there exists a path between any pair of its nodes. With this definition at hand, it is straightforward to see that a node only belongs to a single connected component of the graph. Finding the connected components of a graph is of capital importance in many queries, and it is usually used during pre-processing steps in order to help further computations. Related to connected components, there are some helpful queries to study the vulnerability of a graph, or the probability to separate a connected component into two other components. For instance, finding *bridges*, that are edges whose removal would imply separating a connected component, is important in many applications. Another example is the *cohesion* of the graph which can be computed by finding the minimum number of nodes that disconnect the component if removed.

- **Community Detection:** A community (or cluster) is generally considered to be a set of nodes densely connected among them and poorly connected to nodes outside the community. This effect has been found in many real-world graphs, especially social networks, where people tend to form compact groups having similar profiles in terms of hobbies, jobs, etc. Algorithms for finding communities include the *minimum-cut* method, dendograms (communities formed through hierarchical clustering), methods based on *clique* detection or other clustering techniques, such as the k-means clustering algorithm.

- **Centrality Calculation:** Within the scope of graph theory and network analysis, centrality measures aim at determining the relative importance of a vertex within the graph, based on how well this node connects the network. For instance, in a social network, the centrality of a node would mean how influential a person is within the social network, or how well-used a road is within an urban network. The most well-known centrality measures are the *degree* (number of links incident upon a node), *closeness* (which measures the mean distance from a vertex to other vertices) and *betweenness* (that quantifies the number of times a node acts as a bridge along the shortest path between two other nodes) centrality.

- **Pattern Matching:** Graph matching is the specific process of evaluating the structural similarity of two graphs, and is usually categorized into *exact* and *approximate* graph matching. Exact matchings may include finding *homomorphisms* or *(subgraph) isomorphisms*. Approximate matchings may include *error-correcting (subgraph) isomorphisms, distance-based matching*, etc. Thus pattern matching queries aim at answering whether a given pattern (graph), matches (in one of the different matching variants) a part of another graph.

- **Graph Anonymization:** The anonymization process generates a new graph with properties similar to the original one, avoiding potential intruders to reidentify nodes or edges. This problem gets more complex when the nodes and edges contain attributes. The anonymization of graphs becomes important when several actors exchange datasets that include personal information. To give a couple of examples, two anonymization procedures are the k-degree anonymity of vertices, or the k-neighborhood anonymity, which guarantees that each node must have k others with the same (one step) neighborhood characteristics.

– **Other Queries:** There are other queries related to the applications presented later in this paper. For instance, finding similarity between nodes in a graph has shown to be very important in social network analysis. An example of this is structural equivalence, which refers to the extent to which nodes have a common set of linkages to other nodes in the system. Also, specially for recommendation systems, ranking the nodes of a graph is an important issue (for instance PageRank).

We summarize the previously described operations and queries in Table 1. We note that these graphs operations and queries are not homogeneous from the computational complexity point of view, because they range from constant time to NP-complete complexity. We observe that applications compute a rich set of complex graph queries, using a small set of basic operations that are shared by all scenarios.

2   Graph Databases

A graph database (GDB) is any storage system that uses graph structures with nodes, edges, and properties to represent and store data. Some graph database industrial projects are, for example, Neo4J[1], a Java-based open-source graph database engine; Sparksee[2], a multi-platform graph database management system for efficient graph management in memory constrained environments; HyperGraphDB[3], an embeddable graph database with generalized hypergraphs; OrientDB[4], an open source document-graph database; or InfiniteGraph[5], a distributed and cloud-enabled graph database. In these systems, data manipulation is performed by means of graph operations and types. Operations are characterized by different aspects ranging from the extension of the graph being accessed to the answer they give.

2.1   Operation Categorization

The computational requirements of graph queries are characterized by their heterogeneity. For instance, some queries may access the full graph, while others may only request the degree of a single node. In this section, we build up a set of categories to classify the different operations that can be issued to a graph database.

---

[1] http://neo4j.org
[2] http://www.sparsity-technologies.com/
[3] http://www.hypergraphdb.org/index
[4] http://www.orientdb.org/index.htm
[5] http://www.infinitegraph.com/

Table 1. Graph operations and queries

Graph Operations		Categorization				
Group	Operation	Analytical	Cascaded	Scale[a]	Attr.[b]	Result[c]
Basic Operations						
Local Information Extraction	Get Node/Edge	✓	✗	N	✗	S
	Get Node/Edge Attribute	✓	✗	N	✗	S
	Get Neighborhood	✓	✗	N	✗	S
	Node degree	✓	✗	N	✗	A
Transformations	Add/delete node/edge	✗	✗	N	✗	S
	Add/delete/update attribute	✗	✗	N	✓	S
Complex operations / Queries						
Traversals	(Constrained) Shortest Path	✓	✓	G	E	G
	k-hops	✓	✓	G/N	✗	G
Graph Metrics	Hop-plot	✓	✗	G	✗	A
	Diameter	✓	✓	G	E	S
	Eccentricity	✓	✓	G	E	A
	Density	✓	✗	G	✗	A
	Clustering coefficient	✓	✓	G	✗	A
Components	Connected components	✓	✓	G	✗	G
	Bridges	✓	✓	G	✗	S
	Cohesion	✓	✓	G	✗	S
Communities	Dendogram	✓	✓	G	✗	G
	Max-flow min-cut	✓	✓	G	E	G
	Clustering	✓	✓	G	✗	G
Centrality Measures	Degree centrality	✓	✗	G	✗	S
	Closeness centrality	✓	✓	G	✗	S
	Betweenness centrality	✓	✓	G	✗	S
Pattern Matching	Graph/subgraph matching	✓	✓	N	✗	G
Graph Anonymization	k-degree anonymization	✓	✗	G	✗	G
	k-neighborhood anonymization	✓	✓	G	✗	G
Other Queries	Structural equivalence	✓	✓	G	✗	G
	PageRank	✓	✗	G	N	S

[a] N=Neighborhood, G=Global

[b] ✓=Node and edge, ✗=Neither nodes nor edges, N=Nodes, E=Edges

[c] S=Set, A=Aggregate, G=Graph

- **Transformation (mutating)/Analysis (non-mutating):** We distinguish between two types of operations to access the database: transformations and analysis operations. The first group comprise operations that alter the graph database: bulk loads of a graph, adding/removing nodes or edges to the graphs, create new types of nodes/edges/attributes or modify the value of an attribute. The rest of queries are considered analysis queries. Although an analysis operation does not modify the graph, it may need access to secondary storage because the graph or the temporary results generated during the operation resolution are too large to fit in memory.
- **Cascaded/Non-cascaded Access:** We differentiate two access patterns to the graph: cascaded and not cascaded. We say that an operation follows a cascaded pattern if the operation performs neighbor operations with a depth at least two. For example, a 2-hop operation follows a cascaded pattern. Thus, a non cascaded operation may access a node, an edge or the neighbors of a node. Besides, an operation that does not request the neighbors of a node, though it may access the full graph, is a non cascaded operation. For instance, an operation that returns the node with the largest value of an attribute accesses all nodes, but since it does not follow the graph structure is a non-cascaded operation.
- **Global/Neighborhood Scale:** Depending on the number of nodes accessed, we distinguish two types of queries: global and neighborhood queries. The former type corresponds to queries that access the complete graph structure. In other words, we consider as global queries those that access to all the nodes and/or the edges of the graph. The latter queries only access to a (small) portion of the graph. Examples of global operations may include finding the node with the highest degree, or the number of edges in the graph. Neighborhood operations may include a k-hop operation from one node, for instance.
- **Attributes Accessed:** Graph databases do not only have to manage the structural information of the graph, but also the data associated to the entities of the graph. Here, we classify the queries according to the attribute set that it accesses: edge attribute set, node attribute set, mixed attribute set or no attributes accessed.
- **Result:** We differentiate three different types of results: graphs, aggregated results, and sets. The most distinctive output for a graph database operation is another graph, which is ordinarily a transformation, a selection or a projection of the original graph, which includes nodes and edges. An example of this type of result is getting the minimum spanning tree of a graph, or finding the minimum length path that connects two nodes. The second type of results build up aggregates, whose most common application is to summarize properties of the graph. For instance, a histogram of the degree distribution of the nodes, or a histogram of the community size are computed as aggregations. Finally, a set is an output that contains either atomic entities or result sets that are not structured as graphs. For example, the selection of one node of a graph or finding the edges with the greatest weight are set results.

3 Case Study: The Sparksee Graph Database

Sparksee[6] is an efficient GDB implementation based on bitmap representations of the entities. It is devised to directly handle labeled and directed multigraphs containing an undetermined number of attributes in both nodes and edges. In [13, 14], the authors propose a logic bitmap-based organization to store a graph that does not fit in memory and has to be handled out-of-core. In this scenario, several aspects must hold:

- Computing an operation should not imply loading the whole graph into memory.
- The graph organization must be as compact as possible in order to fit as many graph structures in memory as possible.
- The most commonly used graph-oriented operations, such as edge navigation, should be executed as efficiently as possible.
- Attributes in the graph should be accessed very fast.

In Sparksee, all the nodes and edges are encoded as collections of objects, each of which has a unique oid that is a logical identifier. Sparksee converts a logical adjacency matrix into multiple small indexes to improve the management of out-of-core workloads, with the use of efficient I/O and cache policies. It encodes the adjacency list of each node in a bitmap, which for the adjacent nodes has the corresponding bit set. Given that bitmaps of graphs are typically sparse, the bitmaps are compressed, and hence are more compact than traditional adjacency matrices.

3.1 Sparksee Structures

The basic logical data structure in Sparksee is a labeled and directed attributed multigraph. In this system, nodes and edges are uniquely identified by a set of ids separated into two disjoint domains (oids and eids), and the whole graph is built using a combination of two different types of structures: bitmaps and maps.

A bitmap or bit-vector is a variable-length sequence of presence bits that denotes which objects are selected or related to other objects. They are essential for speeding-up the query execution and reducing the amount of space required to store and manipulate the graph. In a bitmap, each bit is only set to 1 if the corresponding oid is selected. The first bit in a bitmap is always considered to be in position 1 (the first valid oid) and the last one is the last bit set (the highest oid considered in the bitmap). In order to know the length of the bitmap, the number of actual bits set to 1 in the structure is kept updated. The main advantage of this structure is that it is very easy to manage, operate, compress, iterate, etc.

A map is an inverted index with key values associated to bitmaps, and it is used as an auxiliary structure to complement bitmaps, providing full indexed access to all the data stored in the graph.

---

[6] Available at http://www.sparsity-technologies.com/

These two types of structures are combined to build a more complex one: the link. A link is a binary association between unique identifiers and data values. It provides two basic functionalities: given an identifier, it returns the value; and given a value, it returns all the identifiers associated to it.

3.2 Graph Representation Using Bitmaps

A Sparksee graph is built using a combination of links, maps and bitmaps to provide a logical view of a labeled and directed attributed multigraph.: each node or edge type has a bitmap which contains the oids of all the objects (nodes or edges) that belong to the type; each attribute of a type is a link; and, finally, the edges are decomposed into two different links, one for the tails, where for each node contains all the edges outgoing connected to it, when this node acts as their tail or origin, and in the same way another one for the heads which contains the ingoing edges. Thus, an edge is represented as a double join, one between the tail and the edge, and the other one between the head and the edge. If the edge is undirected, then both nodes of the edge are set as tails and heads for the edge.

All Sparksee graphs are built as a collection of bitmaps: one for each type to store the objects in the database, one for each distinct value of each attribute, one for each node that is the tail of one or more edges, and finally one for each node that is the head of one or more edges. With these bitmaps, solving distinct operations such as selecting all the objects of a type, retrieving the objects that have a specific value for an attribute or finding the number of edges or degree of a node, becomes straightforward.

4   Limitations of Graph Databases

Though graph databases offer a very rich data model and, as illustrated in Section 2.1, support diverse query types, they are not without limitations. The following list highlights the limitations that apply to graph databases (from one or more vendors) today.

- **Declarative interface:** most commercial graph databases can not be queried using a declarative language. All vendors provide an imperative programming interface, often with multiple bindings in different languages, but few also offer a declarative query interface.
- **Vectored operations** (e.g. scatter/gather, map/reduce, etc.): a method of input and output by which a procedure sequentially writes data from multiple buffers to a single data stream or reads data from a data stream to multiple buffers. To horizontally scale it is essential that a database supports this type of data access.

  To our knowledge, no graph databases support vectored operations today. Current graph databases (like relational databases) tend to prioritize low-latency query execution over high-throughput data analytics. As such, the omission of this functionality is likely the result of a conscious design decision.

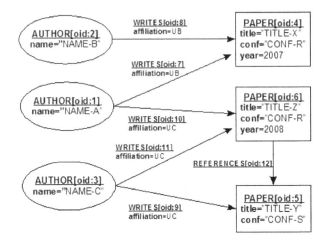

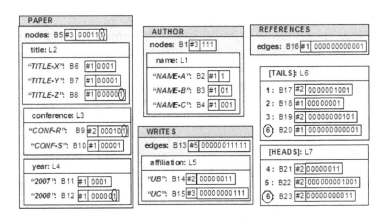

Fig. 1. Sample representation of a graph in Sparksee

Graph analytics frameworks [15–19] - designed for high-throughput process-ing of large data volumes - do offer this functionality. However, these systems are never transactional, rarely persistent, and most often prioritize through-put at the cost of latency - they are therefore not considered graph *databases*.

– **Data partitioning:** most graph databases do not include the functionality to partition and distribute data across multiple networked computers. This is essential for supporting horizontal scalability, too.

There are many reasons for this [20] , including the rapidly reducing cost of main memory, making vertical scaling a viable solution for larger installa-tions than was previously possible. Many of the other reasons can be reduced to the non-functional requirement of providing low-latency query execution.

As, by definition, graph data has a significant amount of data dependencies, it is difficult to partition a graph in a way that would not result in most queries having to access multiple partitions.

In contrast nearly all graph analytics frameworks do have inbuilt support for partitioning. This is largely due to the workloads they target. Whereas graph databases aim to provide low-latency query execution, graph analytics frameworks are optimized for high-throughput processing of massive data volumes, making it significantly easier for the latter to mask the cost of network latency.

- **High throughput data ingestion:** due to lacking support for *vectored operations* and *data partitioning*, the data ingest performance of most graph databases is limited by the write throughput of a single storage device (either a hard drive, a RAID or any distributed storage).

- **Query optimization:** the ability of the system to transparently optimize the execution plan for any given query. Naturally, most graph databases can not do this as they lack a declarative interface.

- **Data schema and constraints:** the schema of a database system is its structure described in a formal language. Schema refers to the organization of data, which describes how the database will be constructed. The formal definition of schema is a set of formulas, a language, which describes the integrity constraints imposed on a database. In effect, a populated database can be considered an instance of its schema.

Schema can make application development a less error-prone task, but is also beneficial as it enables a number of other powerful features, including the ability for the database to perform enhanced query optimization. On the other hand, strict schema enforcement is sometimes considered disadvantageous by those who develop applications for dynamic domains - for example, domains dealing with user-generated content, where the structure of data may change from one day to the next. For precisely this reason, many graph database vendors have opted to either support a weaker notion of schema or to avoid it entirely.

4.1   Sparksee Example

Figure 1 shows an example of a graph extracted from a bibliographic data source (upper side), and the mapping of the previous graph into the internal structures as defined above (lower side).

The graph contains four object types: author (ovals) and paper (boxes) nodes, writes and references edges. These types are represented in the gray boxes at the right, where each type has one bitmap with its collection of objects, represented in the lighter gray frame, and their inner boxes represent the attributes, with one link each. Bitmaps are variable length sequences of 0's and 1's prefixed with the number of bits set. Links have the name, the collection of distinct values and the bitmap for each value. Maps are hidden in this representation because they are only used to index collections, for example the types or the attribute values.

For example, if we look at the node type paper, we can see that there are 3 bits set in bitmap B5, one for each node. There is also a bitmap for each distinct attribute value (L1 to L5 in the example) which indicates the oids of the objects containing this value in the attribute. If an object does not have any value then it will not appear in any bitmap of the attribute. Thus, the union of all the bitmaps of all the values of an attribute is equal to or a subset of the bitmap of the objects of the type. For example, $(B6 \cup B7 \cup B8) = B5$ in attribute title of paper, $(B11 \cup B12) \subset B5$ but because node 5 has no value for the attribute year.

There are two extra links at the rightmost side: one for the tails and the other for the heads. Each one has one value for each node that has edges, with its corresponding bitmap containing the edges where the node is connected. Again, the union of all the bitmaps of each of these links is equal to the union of all the collections of edge types, because all edges have one tail and one head. We can verify that $(B17 \cup B18 \cup B19 \cup B20) = (B21 \cup B22 \cup B23) = (B13 \cup B16)$.

As an example of the meaning of the structures, in the bitmaps we have marked all the occurrences of the oid 6, which identifies the node of the PAPER with title 'TITLE-Z'. These are the value '6' in L6 and L7, and the bit '6' in bitmaps B5, B8, B9 and B12. Note that B5 tells us it is a node PAPER; and B8, B9 and B12 show which are the values for the attributes of this node (title, conference and year respectively). Finally, L6 has the edges where this node is the tail, and L7 which are the edges where it is the head.

As we can see, with these structures now it is very easy to define graph-based operations just by combining one or more bitmap and map operations. For example:

- Number of authors: $|B1| = 3$
- Papers in conference 'CONF-R' of year 2007: $B9 \cap B11 = 4$.
- In-degree of paper 'TITLE-Y': $|B22| = 2$

In conclusion, this representation presents some advantages inherent to the structures and others more subtle that appear as a consequence of how the structures are being used. For example, the use of bitmaps directly provides some statistics without extra penalties, like the number of objects for each type, or the number of objects that have the same value for an attribute, the equivalent of a clustering or a GROUP BY / COUNT(*) operation of the relational model. The out-degree and in-degree of nodes are also the count of a bitmap stored into the tails or heads collections respectively. Also, the capability to add or remove attributes becomes easier because they are independent from the object storage. This is crucial for graph mining algorithms that typically require the creation of temporary attributes like weights or distances.

5   Use Case 1: Social Network Analysis

In this section, we introduce the first of our use cases, the Social Network Analysis (SNA). First, we give a brief introduction about SNA. After that, we characterize the use case, giving the underlying graph model and its characteristics, and introducing the types of operations performed on social networks. This way, we fully characterize the use case in order to better understand which characteristics a benchmark should have when run on this kind of data.

5.1 Introduction

In social networks nodes typically represent people and edges represent some form of social interaction between them, such as friendship, co-authorship, etc. Although the study of the characteristics of social networks known as *Social Networks Analysis* (SNA) (formerly known as *sociometry*), has its starting point in the early 30s, it has become very popular in recent years because of the digital techniques and internet. SNA techniques have been effectively used in several areas of interest like social interaction and network evolution analysis, counterterrorism and covert networks, or even viral marketing. Due to the Web and increasing use of Internet applications, which facilitate interactive collaboration and information sharing, many social networks of different kinds have appeared, like Facebook and LinkedIn for social interaction, or Flickr for multimedia sharing. Other web portals that contain human interactions can also be considered social networks, like in bibliographic catalogs such as Scopus, ACM or IEEE, where the scientific community is sharing information and establishing de facto relationships. In all these cases, there is an increasing interest in the analysis of the underlying networks, to obtain a better knowledge of the patterns and the topological properties. This may be used to improve services to users or even to provide more profit to the information providers in the form of direct advertising or personalized services.

5.2 Graph Model

As we have seen before, there are many different kinds of social networks. Therefore, the nature of the underlying graph model of these networks may differ from one to another. However, the following characteristics are common to many of the existing social networks:

- **Attributed:** Graphs belonging to social networks are attributed graphs. We can find attributes both in the nodes and in the edges. Node attributes may include personal data about the user, their preferences, activity log, comments, etc. Edges may be attributed with the number of times two persons have interacted, comments, etc.
- **Labeled:** Social graphs may be labeled in both the nodes and the edges. For example, interactions between two different users may have different forms, such as like/dislike something, request for something, comments about a post, etc. In the same way, nodes may represent different entities, such as persons or companies in a professional social network.
- **Directed:** Graphs representing social networks are usually directed graphs, since the interactions between the actors in the network are not always symmetric. For instance, a user may like/dislike a comment of another user, and

this is a form of asymmetric or directed interaction, since the user of the comment has no activity in the opposite direction.

- **Multigraph:** Social interactions are usually recurrent. That is, people linked through a social network usually have more than a single interaction, moreover their interactions are unlikely to be limited to the same types. For instance, two friends may have several interactions, some of them being comments about one user post and some of them sending a private message. This multiplicity in the interactions may be represented in a multigraph.

5.3 Statistical Properties

In the following, we summarize the statistical properties that characterizes the graph. Since social networks are essentially evolving networks, we distinguish between static and dynamic properties.

Static Properties: Static properties are those appearing in snapshots of the network at a certain point in time.

- **Community structure:** Real-world social graphs are found to exhibit a modular structure, with nodes forming groups, and possibly groups within groups [21–23]. In addition to that, in [3], it is shown along several social network examples, that in most cases there is a large component which includes more than 80% of the total nodes of the network. An efficient algorithm to locate communities is available in [24].
- **Small-world property:** Social networks exhibit the small-world property. That is, even in the case where the network is composed of millions (or even billions) of nodes, the average geodesic distance between connected vertex pairs is relatively very low, approximately log the number of nodes in the network (around 5 in most of the examples given in [3]).
- **Degree distribution:** The degree distribution of many social networks obey a power law of the form $f(d) \propto d^\beta$, with the exponent $\beta < 0$, and $f(d)$ being the fraction of nodes with degree d. Therefore, they can be considered scale-free networks.
- **Sparse:** Real social networks are almost always sparse, meaning that only a small portion of the total possible number of edges appear in the network. The examples given in [3], show that the portion of existing edges with respect to the total possible edges is less than 1%.

Dynamic Properties: Dynamic properties are those characteristics that the graph exhibits with respect to a change in time. These are typically studied by looking at a series of static snapshots and seeing how measurements of these snapshots compare.

- **Shrinking diameter:** Leskovec. et al. [11] showed that not only the diameter of real social graphs is small, but it also shrinks and then stabilizes along

time [11]. Briefly, at the beginning of time, the network is composed by several small components. As time evolves those small components grow and connections between them lead to bigger connected components and a growing diameter. At some point (the *gelling point*), many of these components merge and the large component emerges and the diameter spikes. After this point, the diameter keeps shrinking until it reaches an equilibrium.
- **Densification power law:** Time-evolving social graphs show the following relation between the number n of nodes and the number m of edges at all time ticks t: $m(t) \propto n(t)^{\beta}$, with $\beta > 1$, which is known as the densification power law. Examples of social networks shown in [3], discover a mean value of β around 1.12.

5.4   Graph Operations and Queries

One characteristic of social networks is that the operations performed on them are extremely diverse, they cover much of the spectrum of operations known to be performed on graphs. Some examples in different workflows are:

- **Transactional:** Insertions, updates and deletions are usually small and affect a few entities (nodes) and relationships (edges). The most usual operation is the insertion of new data, a very frequent action with a high degree of isolation with respect other update operations. Updates are not frequent because the SN grows and information is more evolving than changing. Deletes are also not usual and, in general, information is timestamped when it is deleted to denote the end of its availability instead of begin removed.
- **Lookups:** The basic queries are the most frequent: look for a node, look for the neighbors (1-hop), scan edges in several hops (layers), retrieve an attribute, etc. In general, these operations are small and affect only a few nodes, edges and attributes in the graph. When the graph schema is complex, most of the lookup queries follow a few operation patterns where the underlying lookup operations are in general the same with different arguments. Concurrency is one of the most important issues due to the high amount of small queries executed at the same time in sparse areas of the graph.
- **BI:** While the SN graph data contains a lot of useful information for business intelligence, this is not usually explored due to privacy concerns and restrictions. Aggregate computations or multidimensional analysis using edge adjacencies as dimensions are in general only performed after an anonymization process.
- **Analytics:** Graphs metrics, centrality measures or community finding are tools used to analyze the SN to observe the behavior, predict the evolution or to identify the shape in order to split a very large graph in smaller units, easier to manage. Pattern matching is often used to extract groups of nodes and edges that match a specific pattern, for example for marketing purposes, data cleansing or integrity validation.

6   Use Case 2: Information Technologies Analysis

Organizations use a significant amount of internal and external data to obtain added value information that provides them with an understanding of the positioning of the world in relation to their knowledge and objectives. However, they employ a significant amount of time to complete this search and analysis cycle because of the lack of quality in the data and the lack of flexible technologies to extract and integrate multimedia and multilingual features from the sources, having to use the skills of experts in a slow, error prone and inspiration dependent process.

6.1   Introduction

Knowledge, which sits in the digital core of organizations like SMEs, large companies and public institutions, is not fully exploited because data inside the organization is stored in separate unconnected repositories: the documents written (internal reports, patents filed, meeting minutes, usage manuals, papers published, collaboration reports of funded projects, etc.), strategy reports, financial audits, managerial structure, the electronic mail generated, the relationships with other organizations expressed by means of contracts and agreements and by means of IP ownership and mercantile transactions, the media content produced through courseware and marketing material, and more. Moreover, the international nature of many organizations implies that multiple languages are used in the data they generate. The dispersion and unlinked multimodal nature of those sources leads to a significant lack of corporate self-knowledge[7] that is hidden behind the internal repositories. On the other hand, the Internet offers a huge amount of relevant outside data about the organization: web pages, social networks, product opinions, cloud services... Although organizations usually know which are those interesting data sources, they currently need huge human driven efforts to retrieve and analyse them in the multiple languages and multiple formats they are provided: textual and video blogs and microblogs criticizing or praising their achievements, other companies assessing their performance, newspapers telling stories about them, open data in the form of patents or scientific papers explaining inventions related to their knowledge, videos and images making apparent to the eye events where the organizations are involved, etc. The use of the Internet content in many cases is not only enriching but necessary for the adequate growth of those organizations, and in particular for SMEs.

The integration of inside and outside organization data can merge in a single vision the collection of internal partial perspectives of the company business departments as well as the view of the company in the external world. Corporate data can be analyzed and information can be extracted, interpreted and summarized in the form of added value knowledge and linked relationships among

---

[7] By self-knowledge, we understand the analytical capability that allows an organization to extract added value information from the integrated view of the data in their different applications and repositories.

documents (either textual or media), people in the organization, concepts and keywords in the different languages of the organization providing a network between the sources of knowledge and the actual linked information that describes them. Moreover, from the linked relationships, further analysis can be done to create multilingual ontologies that organize the knowledge of the organization. In all those cases, the relationships and ontologies can be exploited to obtain added value information like, for instance, who knows more and is more reputed within or outside the organization about a topic to find are placement for a person who quit the company, what is the most relevant internal and external IP and how they are related for a specific research being done and who are the most relevant inventors, what internal and external media content is available for the next marketing campaign, what are the documents that describe the products to be announced better and who are the employees with better knowledge for those, etc.

6.2 Dataset Integration

When integrated in a single graph-based framework, the information extracted from the multimedia and multilingual repositories is merged in such a way that the identification of relations and similarities within and across different media will be easier. This way, the internal data sources can be linked, and enriched information is extracted providing added value ground information to increase the ability to detect and exploit meaning from where it was hidden before with analytical queries. The linked information and ontologies created is constantly enriched by the new documents being created within the organization providing a circle of constant improvement of the corporate self-knowledge.

Integration techniques are applied to intelligently aggregate the result sets of the different data providers by means of entity identification techniques [25]. Data linkage typically uses weak identifiers (name, family name, country, etc.) to link data across different data sources. In the case of graphs the integration target are the vertices of the graph, and hence, the entity data linkage deals with finding those vertices that represent the same entity. In order to obtain a perfect recall, the problem becomes quadratic because it is necessary to perform all pairwise comparisons. Since this is prohibitive for large volumes of information one of the main research topics is finding techniques on how to scale them [26]. Some data integration frameworks are available from the research community that facilitate the integration of data. They can be classified in three main groups, based on the interface of the framework: rule, numerical and workflow based. Rule based approaches give users the freedom to state sets of rules that are applied sequentially to integrate datasets [27]. Such rules are not a static set, and can change over time in order to increase the flexibility of the system [28]. Furthermore, such rules can express even exceptions to stated rules, which facilitate the design of the system and the resolution of inconsistencies among previously ingested rules [29]. Numerical approaches compute complex similarity functions based on a set of features among a pair of entities. Those entities with a numerical value over certain threshold are considered as the same entity.

The construction of the numerical function and the threshold setting can be programmed by the users of the system [30], or helped with the aid of a training set [31]. Workflows allow users to define complex data flows where combinations of matchers, conditions and loops [32]. A graph-based framework include functionalities to integrate easily graph features (such as transitive relations or graph patterns among others) during the integration process to compute the similarity of entities that are in a graph. It allows also the scalability of the system in order to support the large graphs coming from different data sources

6.3   Graph Analytics

Once the datasets have been integrated inside a single graph. the goal is to provide a set of techniques to analyze the relationships among the entities. Some examples of self-knowledge services are:

- A document search engine that is be able to return the most relevant documents for a given topic. It allow the analysts to explore the contents of the documental data stored in the graph. The result is a set of documents that had been obtained from outside or inside the information network.
- A reputation algorithm to rank the most relevant persons and organizations in a network according to a search topic. The algorithms take into account that real networks are not hierarchic and consider the cycle shapes to deduce the most reputed individuals. The results are able to return people that are relevant for a query with respect to the information extracted from the graph.
- A sentiment analysis summarization procedure to evaluate multimodal data that talks about a brand name. The query aggregates the sentiment analysis results obtained for a brand name, in order to show to the analysts which is the perception of a product among customers.

In particular, for the different workflows some of the required graph query capabilities are:

- **Transactional:** The graph is built like a large data warehouse of entities and relationships. There are few updates and, in general, all new data is inserted in massive bulk loads of preprocessed, deduplicated and interrelated data. This process can be executed also over a snapshot in such a way that updates are not in conflict with read-only operations. This relaxes the locking and concurrency requirements of the graph database engine.
- **Lookups:** Queries are more analytical than exploratory. Simple lookup queries are used only to validate the content of the generated graph or to generate reports of the data.
- **Analytics:** This represents the most important group of queries for this use case. Analysis is made in several steps by combining different techniques. For example, reputation requires the construction of communities or clusters based on search topic; then the graph is improved with weighted relationships of the involved people; finally, a recommendation algorithm based on connectivity returns the relevant nodes.

7   Graph Database Benchmarking

Early efforts: Popular database benchmarks, such as TPC-C or TPC-H [33], focus on evaluating relational database queries that are typical of a business application. These benchmarks emphasize queries with joins, projections, selections, aggregations and sorting operations. However, since Graph Databases aim at different types of queries, these widespread benchmarks are not adequate for evaluating their performance. Graph use cases often involve recursive steps, e.g. graph neighborhoods within n steps or even an undetermined number of steps. Graph queries may involve structural similarity, e.g. comparing structures of chemical compounds for similarity with a similarity score quantifying the deviations. Graph analytics often produce large intermediate results with complex structure, e.g. edge weights or iteratively calculated ranks (e.g. Page rank). Widespread relational benchmarks do not contain such operations. All those are operations that, in some cases, are difficult to imagine in RDBMSs and that find a good alliance in the RDF area and GDB area since the former adhere to a graph data model.

Object oriented databases (OODB) share some similarities with GDBs. The data of an OODB also conforms a graph structure, where the entities that are represented as objects draw [34] relationships among them. The OO1 benchmark, one of the earliest proposals, is a very simple benchmark that emphasizes three basic operations for OODB: (a) lookup, which finds the set of objects for a given object identifier; (b) traversal, which performs a 7-hop operation starting from a random node; and (c) insertion, which adds a set of objects and relations to the database. OO1 defines a dataset that only contains one type of objects with a fixed number of outgoing edges per object. Since the links mostly go to objects with a similar document identifier, the graphs are very regular. Another popular benchmark for OODB is the OO7 [35] proposed by Carey et al. In OO7, the database contains three types of objects, which are organized as a tree of depth seven. The connectivity of the database is also very regular because objects have a fixed number of relations. The benchmark is made up by a rich set of queries that can be clustered into two groups: (a) traversal queries, which scan one type of objects and then access the nodes connected to them in the tree, and (b) general queries, which mainly perform selections of objects according to certain characteristics.

Graph benchmarking: The graphanalysis.org initiative started a project to evaluate graph performance. After some preliminary benchmark proposals, which refined the queries in the system, the project released the final version of the benchmark as the "HPC Scalable Graph Analysis Benchmark v1.0[36]. The benchmark is compound by four separated operations on a graph that follows a power law distribution generated with the R-MAT generator [37]: (a) insert the graph database as a bulk load; (b) retrieve the set of edges with maximum weight; (c) perform a k-hops operation; and (d) calculate the betweenness centrality of a graph, whose performance is measured as the number of edges traversed per second. However, this benchmark does not evaluate some features expected from a GDB such as object labeling or attribute management. In [38], this benchmark is evaluated on four representative graph data management alternatives (Neo4j, DEX, Jena and HypergraphDB) giving some insights about the strengths and weakness of each system. A recent survey has [39] reviewed some of the main operations and uses cases of graph databases, and thus is a good starting point for the development of graph benchmarks. Other open source initiatives have proposed simple benchmarks to evaluate the performance of graph databases. For instance, Ciglan published a set of traversal oriented queries [40], or Tinkerpop initiated a project (currently stopped) to build a framework for running benchmarks on graph databases [41]. Nevertheless, these initiatives lack a wide acceptance because of their individual approach and limited resources.

Graphs in supercomputers: The performance of supercomputers has been traditionally tested using the Linpack benchmark, which is derived from the Linpack library that computes linear algebra operations. According to the Linpack results, a list of the top 500 computers is published biannually, which determines the most powerful computers in the world. Nevertheless, the use of supercomputers has spread from computationally intensive integer and floating point computation, to memory intensive applications. For such applications, the Linpack is not a good reference and other evaluation methods have been proposed, including graph related computation. Since 2010 an alternative top 500 list is published using the traversed edges per second of a Breadth First Search in a graph [42].

Linked Data Benchmark Council (LDBC): LDBC is a EU funded project that is creating a non profit organization similar to TPC, which will design and support graph database and RDF benchmarks. LDBC benchmarks are innovative because: (i) they will be based on real use cases, and thus be meaningful for users to fairly compare graph databases; (ii) they will motivate graph database vendors to innovate in the development of graph databases to improve its performance and scalability; (iii) they will compile a repository of supporting knowledge for the area of graph database benchmarks that will be used as a reference in the design of benchmarks in this field; and, (iv) they will generate benchmark expertises and rules of fair practice for carrying out and auditing the benchmark of database instances by vendors. The first set of LDBC benchmarks will be published in 2014.

8   Conclusions

We have been describing important aspects of graph charateristics, database implementation, use cases and benchmarking. There is no doubt about the fact that many other aspects concur in the graph area, i.e. graphical representation of large and small graphs, use of graphs in complex systems analysis, etc. However, the objective of this paper was to give a broad overview of the knowledge behind graph management and the technologies around graphs. In the course, we will provide a similar overview with a set of slides provided to the students and the general public through the course web page and through DAMA-UPC web page (www.dama.upc.edu).

References

1. Leskovec, J., Huttenlocher, D.P., Kleinberg, J.M.: Signed networks in social media. In: CHI, pp. 1361–1370 (2010)
2. Goertzel, B.: OpenCogPrime: A cognitive synergy based architecture for artificial general intelligence. In: IEEE ICCI, pp. 60–68 (2009)
3. Newman, M.: Networks: An Introduction. Oxford University Press, Inc., New York (2010)
4. Levene, M., Poulovassilis, A.: The hypernode model: A graph-theoretic approach to integrating data and computation. In: FMLDO, pp. 55–77 (1989)
5. Ërdos, P., Rényi, A.: On random graphs. Mathematicae 6, 290–297 (1959)
6. Leskovec, J., Lang, K.J., Dasgupta, A., Mahoney, M.W.: Statistical properties of community structure in large social and information networks. In: WWW, pp. 695–704 (2008)
7. Flickr Blog: Six billion (retrieved on march 2014), http://blog.flickr.net/en/2011/08/04/6000000000/
8. Faloutsos, M., Faloutsos, P., Faloutsos, C.: On power-law relationships of the internet topology. In: SIGCOMM, pp. 251–262 (1999)
9. McGlohon, M., Akoglu, L., Faloutsos, C.: Weighted graphs and disconnected components: patterns and a generator. In: KDD, pp. 524–532 (2008)
10. Chakrabarti, D., Faloutsos, C.: Graph mining: Laws, generators, and algorithms. ACM Comput. Surv. 38 (2006)
11. Leskovec, J., Kleinberg, J.M., Faloutsos, C.: Graph evolution: Densification and shrinking diameters. TKDD 1 (2007)
12. SNAP: (Stanford large network dataset collection), http://snap.stanford.edu/data/index.html
13. Martínez-Bazan, N., Muntés-Mulero, V., Gómez-Villamor, S., Nin, J., Sánchez-Martínez, M.-A., Larriba-Pey, J.-L.: Dex: high-performance exploration on large graphs for information retrieval. In: CIKM, pp. 573–582 (2007)
14. Martínez-Bazan, N., Aguila-Lorente, M.A., Muntés-Mulero, V., Dominguez-Sal, D., Gómez-Villamor, S., Larriba-Pey, J.-L.: Efficient graph management based on bitmap indices. In: IDEAS, pp. 110–119 (2012)
15. Nelson, J., Myers, B., Hunter, A.H., Briggs, P., Ceze, L., Ebeling, C., Grossman, D., Kahan, S., Oskin, M.: Crunching large graphs with commodity processors. In: HotPar (2011)
16. Malewicz, G., Austern, M.H., Bik, A.J., Dehnert, J.C., Horn, I., Leiser, N., Czajkowski, G.: Pregel: a system for large-scale graph processing. In: SIGMOD, pp. 135–146 (2010)
17. Gonzalez, J.E., Low, Y., Gu, H., Bickson, D., Guestrin, C.: Powergraph: Distributed graph-parallel computation on natural graphs. In: OSDI, pp. 17–30 (2012)
18. Stutz, P., Bernstein, A., Cohen, W.: Signal/Collect: Graph algorithms for the (Semantic) web. In: Patel-Schneider, P.F., Pan, Y., Hitzler, P., Mika, P., Zhang, L., Pan, J.Z., Horrocks, I., Glimm, B. (eds.) ISWC 2010, Part I. LNCS, vol. 6496, pp. 764–780. Springer, Heidelberg (2010)
19. Gupta, P., Goel, A., Lin, J., Sharma, A., Wang, D., Zadeh, R.: Wtf: The who to follow service at twitter. In: WWW, pp. 505–514 (2013)
20. Averbuch, A., Neumann, M.: Partitioning graph databases-a quantitative evaluation. arXiv preprint arXiv:1301.5121 (2013)
21. Flake, G.W., Lawrence, S., Giles, C.L., Coetzee, F.: Self-organization and identification of web communities. IEEE Computer 35(3), 66–71 (2002)

22. Girvan, M., Newman, M.: Community structure in social and biological networks. National Academy of Sciences 99(12), 7821–7826 (2002)
23. Schwartz, M., Wood, D.: Discovering shared interests among people using graph analysis of global electronic mail traffic. Communications of the ACM 36, 78–89 (1992)
24. Prat-Pérez, A., Dominguez-Sal, D., Larriba-Pey, J.-L.: High quality, scalable and parallel community detection for large real graphs. In: To be published in WWW (2014)
25. Bleiholder, J., Naumann, F.: Data fusion. ACM Computing Surveys (CSUR) 41, 1 (2008)
26. Christen, P.: A survey of indexing techniques for scalable record linkage and deduplication. IEEE Trans. on Knowledge and Data Engineering 24, 1537–1555 (2012)
27. Arasu, A., Ré, C., Suciu, D.: Large-scale deduplication with constraints using dedupalog. In: ICDE, pp. 952–963 (2009)
28. Whang, S.E., Garcia-Molina, H.: Entity resolution with evolving rules. PVLDB 3, 1326–1337 (2010)
29. Whang, S.E., Benjelloun, O., Garcia-Molina, H.: Generic entity resolution with negative rules. VLDB Journal 18, 1261–1277 (2009)
30. Leitão, L., Calado, P., Weis, M.: Structure-based inference of xml similarity for fuzzy duplicate detection. In: CIKM, pp. 293–302 (2007)
31. Rastogi, V., Dalvi, N., Garofalakis, M.: Large-scale collective entity matching. PVLDB 4, 208–218 (2011)
32. Thor, A., Rahm, E.: MOMA - A Mapping-based Object Matching System. In: CIDR, pp. 247–258 (2007)
33. Transaction Processing Performance Council (TPC): TPC benchmark website, http://www.tpc.org
34. Cattell, R., Skeen, J.: Object operations benchmark. ACM Trans. Database Syst. 17, 1–31 (1992)
35. Carey, M.J., DeWitt, D.J., Naughton, J.F.: The oo7 benchmark. In: SIGMOD Conference, pp. 12–21 (1993)
36. Bader, D., Feo, J., Gilbert, J., Kepner, J., Koetser, D., Loh, E., Madduri, K., Mann, B., Meuse, T., Robinson, E.: HPC Scalable Graph Analysis Benchmark v1.0. HPC Graph Analysis (2009)
37. Chakrabarti, D., Zhan, Y., Faloutsos, C.: R-mat: A recursive model for graph mining. In: SDM, pp. 442–446 (2004)
38. Dominguez-Sal, D., Urbón-Bayes, P., Giménez-Vañó, A., Gómez-Villamor, S., Martínez-Bazan, N., Larriba-Pey, J.-L.: Survey of graph database performance on the hpc scalable graph analysis benchmark. In: WAIM Workshops, pp. 37–48 (2010)
39. Dominguez-Sal, D., Martinez-Bazan, N., Muntes-Mulero, V., Baleta, P., Larriba-Pey, J.L.: A discussion on the design of graph database benchmarks. In: Nambiar, R., Poess, M. (eds.) TPCTC 2010. LNCS, vol. 6417, pp. 25–40. Springer, Heidelberg (2011)
40. Ciglan, M., Averbuch, A., Hluchý, L.: Benchmarking traversal operations over graph databases. In: ICDE Workshops, pp. 186–189 (2012)
41. Tinkerpop: Open source property graph software stack, http://www.tinkerpop.com
42. Graph 500 Website: The graph 500 list, http://www.graph500.org/

An Introduction to Description Logics and Query Rewriting

Roman Kontchakov and Michael Zakharyaschev

Department of Computer Science and Information Systems,
Birkbeck, University of London, U.K.

Abstract. This chapter gives an overview of the description logics underlying the OWL 2 Web Ontology Language and its three tractable profiles, OWL 2 RL, OWL 2 EL and OWL 2 QL. We consider the syntax and semantics of these description logics as well as main reasoning tasks and their computational complexity. We also discuss the semantical foundations for first-order and datalog rewritings of conjunctive queries over knowledge bases given in the OWL 2 profiles, and outline the architecture of the ontology-based data access system Ontop.

1 Introduction

The first aim of this chapter is to introduce and discuss logic-based formalisms that underpin the OWL 2 Web Ontology Language and its three tractable profiles: RL, EL and QL. OWL 2 is a rather involved language that was designed to represent knowledge about various domains of interest in a machine-accessible form. The diagram in Fig. 1, taken from the official W3C document,[1] shows the general structure of OWL 2. As follows from the diagram, there are (at least) five syntaxes for OWL 2 (various tools can use their own versions). In this chapter, we consider a sixth one, the language of Description Logic (DL). Although not covering all the bells and whistles of the full OWL 2, it will allow the reader to quickly grasp the meaning of the main modelling constructs that OWL 2 provides. The language of DL is elegant and concise because it stems from the formalisms that have been developed in mathematical logic since the middle of the 19th century. It is underpinned by the crystal-clear model-theoretic semantics developed by A. Tarski since the mid 1930s (as shown in the diagram in Fig. 1, OWL 2 has two semantics: RDF-based[2] and Direct Semantics[3]; the latter is based on the model-theoretic semantics of DLs).

We will introduce, in Section 2, most important modelling constructs of OWL 2 and their semantics in terms of the description logics $\mathcal{ALCHI}$ and $\mathcal{SROIQ}$ and the model-theoretic semantics. We then explain fundamental reasoning tasks such as checking consistency (satisfiability), concept and role subsumption, instance checking and conjunctive query answering, and discuss their computational complexity. Our focus in Section 3 is on the DLs underlying the three

---

[1] www.w3.org/TR/owl2-overview
[2] www.w3.org/TR/owl2-rdf-based-semantics
[3] www.w3.org/TR/owl2-direct-semantics

M. Koubarakis et al. (Eds.): Reasoning Web 2014, LNCS 8714, pp. 195–244, 2014.

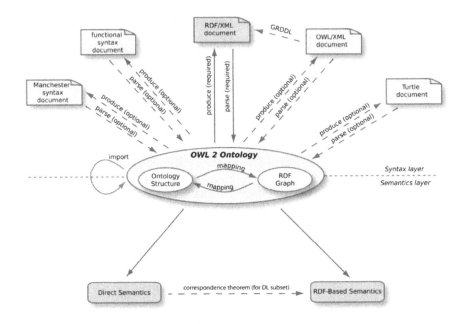

Fig. 1. General structure of OWL 2

profiles (or fragments) of OWL 2 that were identified by the OWL 2 working group to ensure tractability of reasoning at the expense of the expressive power. The Euler diagram in Fig. 2 gives a general overview of the DLs considered in this chapter (RDFS denotes the RDFS fragment of OWL 2 DL under the Direct Semantics).

The second aim of the chapter is to explain, in Section 4, the semantical foundations for first-order and datalog rewritings of conjunctive queries over knowledge bases given in the OWL 2 profiles. Query rewriting is a fundamental technique underlying ontology-based data access: it reduces answering queries over knowledge bases to answering first-order or datalog queries over plain data, which can be done using conventional database management systems or, respectively, datalog engines. For more expressive languages, ontology-based data access will be discussed in Chapter 6.

Finally, in Section 5, we give an overview of the architecture of the ontology-based data access system *Ontop*[4].

2   Description Logics

Description Logic is an area of knowledge representation and reasoning in Artificial Intelligence and the Semantic Web that studies logic-based formalisms whose languages operate with *concepts* to represent classes of individuals in an

---

[4] `ontop.inf.unibz.it`

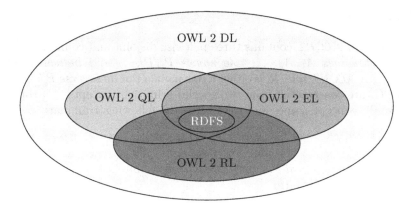

Fig. 2. Relationships between the DL fragments of OWL 2

application domain, and *roles* to represent binary relations between the individuals. Each concrete formalism, called a *description logic* (DL, for short), is characterised by its set of constructs that can be used to build complex concepts and roles from primitive ones.

The zoo of DLs is very big. We begin by defining one particular representative, which goes in the zoo under the moniker of $\mathcal{ALCHI}$. The example below shows a simple knowledge base (or an ontology), which is given in the OWL functional-style syntax (FSS) and the more terse syntax of $\mathcal{ALCHI}$. The reader is invited to decipher the meaning of the knowledge base before consulting the formal definitions.

Example 1. The following three statements are written in the FSS:

$$\text{SubClassOf(ObjectIntersectionOf(Person,} \tag{1}$$
$$\text{ObjectSomeValuesFrom(takesCourse, Course)), Student),}$$
$$\text{SubObjectPropertyOf(mastersDegreeFrom, degreeFrom),} \tag{2}$$
$$\text{SubClassOf(ObjectSomeValuesFrom(} \tag{3}$$
$$\text{ObjectInverseOf(takesCourse), owl:Thing), Course),}$$
$$\text{ClassAssertion(Student, john),} \tag{4}$$
$$\text{ObjectPropertyAssertion(takesCourse, john, sw).} \tag{5}$$

Using the syntax of $\mathcal{ALCHI}$, the same statements can be expressed as follows:

$$\text{Person} \sqcap \exists \text{takesCourse.Course} \sqsubseteq \text{Student,} \tag{1'}$$
$$\text{mastersDegreeFrom} \sqsubseteq \text{degreeFrom,} \tag{2'}$$
$$\text{takesCourse}^{-}.\top \sqsubseteq \text{Course,} \tag{3'}$$
$$\text{Student(john),} \tag{4'}$$
$$\text{takesCourse(john, sw).} \tag{5'}$$

2.1 Syntax

The alphabet of $\mathcal{ALCHI}$ contains three pairwise disjoint and countably infinite sets: *concept names* $A_1, A_2, \ldots$, *role names* $P_1, P_2, \ldots$ and *individual names* $a_1, a_2, \ldots$. An $\mathcal{ALCHI}$ *role*, R, is either a role name P_i or its *inverse* P_i^-. $\mathcal{ALCHI}$ *concepts*, C, are constructed from two special primitive concepts, $\top$ ('top') and $\bot$ ('bottom'), concept names and roles using the following grammar:

$$C ::= A_i \mid \top \mid \bot \mid \neg C \mid C_1 \sqcap C_2 \mid C_1 \sqcup C_2 \mid \exists R.C \mid \forall R.C.$$

An $\mathcal{ALCHI}$ *terminological box* (or TBox), $\mathcal{T}$, is a finite set of *concept* and *role inclusion axioms* of the form

$$C_1 \sqsubseteq C_2 \qquad \text{and} \qquad R_1 \sqsubseteq R_2,$$

where C_1, C_2 are concepts and R_1, R_2 roles. An $\mathcal{ALCHI}$ *assertion box* (or ABox), $\mathcal{A}$, is a finite set of *concept* and *role assertions* of the form

$$C(a) \qquad \text{and} \qquad R(a, b),$$

where C is a concept, R a role and a, b are individual names. Given an ABox $\mathcal{A}$, we denote by $\mathsf{ind}(\mathcal{A})$ the set of individual names that occur in $\mathcal{A}$. Taken together, $\mathcal{T}$ and $\mathcal{A}$ comprise an $\mathcal{ALCHI}$ *knowledge base* (or KB) $\mathcal{K} = (\mathcal{T}, \mathcal{A})$.

Example 1 shows that, in many respects, the DL syntax is simply a less verbose form of the FSS. Thus, $\sqsubseteq$ stands for SubClassOf and SubObjectPropertyOf, and P^- for ObjectInverseOf(P); the correspondences for concept constructs are listed below:

DL	FSS
$\bot$	owl:Nothing
$\top$	owl:Thing
$\neg C$	ObjectComplementOf(C)
$C_1 \sqcap C_2$	ObjectIntersectionOf(C_1, C_2)
$C_1 \sqcup C_2$	ObjectUnionOf(C_1, C_2)
$\exists R.C$	ObjectSomeValuesFrom(R, C)
$\forall R.C$	ObjectAllValuesFrom(R, C)

In Section 2.4, we shall see how most of the OWL constructs can be mapped into the DL syntax. But before that, we need to define the meaning of DL constructs.

2.2 Semantics

As well as all DLs, $\mathcal{ALCHI}$ is equipped with a Tarski-style semantics defined in terms of interpretations (which are a simplified form of interpretations in the Direct Semantics of OWL). An *interpretation* $\mathcal{I}$ is a pair $(\Delta^{\mathcal{I}}, \cdot^{\mathcal{I}})$ that consists of a non-empty *domain of interpretation* $\Delta^{\mathcal{I}}$ and an *interpretation function* $\cdot^{\mathcal{I}}$. The latter assigns

- an element $a_i^{\mathcal{I}} \in \Delta^{\mathcal{I}}$ to each individual name a_i;
- a subset $A_i^{\mathcal{I}} \subseteq \Delta^{\mathcal{I}}$ to each concept name A_i;
- a binary relation $P_i^{\mathcal{I}} \subseteq \Delta^{\mathcal{I}} \times \Delta^{\mathcal{I}}$ to each role name P_i.

(In $\mathcal{ALCHI}$, distinct individuals are usually assumed to be interpreted by distinct domain elements—this is called the *unique name assumption*, or UNA. In this chapter we follow the convention and assume the UNA for all of our DLs, which cannot distinguish between models with and without UNA. Note, however, that OWL 2 and its three profiles *do not* adopt the UNA and use constructs like SameIndividual and DifferentIndividuals instead.) We extend inductively the interpretation function $\cdot^{\mathcal{I}}$ to complex roles and concepts by taking

$$
\begin{aligned}
(P^-)^{\mathcal{I}} &= \{\, (v,u) \mid (u,v) \in P^{\mathcal{I}} \,\}, \\
\top^{\mathcal{I}} &= \Delta^{\mathcal{I}}, \\
\bot^{\mathcal{I}} &= \emptyset, \\
(\neg C)^{\mathcal{I}} &= \Delta^{\mathcal{I}} \setminus C^{\mathcal{I}}, \\
(C_1 \sqcap C_2)^{\mathcal{I}} &= C_1^{\mathcal{I}} \cap C_2^{\mathcal{I}}, \\
(C_1 \sqcup C_2)^{\mathcal{I}} &= C_1^{\mathcal{I}} \cup C_2^{\mathcal{I}}, \\
(\exists R.C)^{\mathcal{I}} &= \{\, u \mid \text{there is } v \in C^{\mathcal{I}} \text{ such that } (u,v) \in R^{\mathcal{I}} \,\}, \\
(\forall R.C)^{\mathcal{I}} &= \{\, u \mid v \in C^{\mathcal{I}}, \text{ for all } v \text{ with } (u,v) \in R^{\mathcal{I}} \,\}.
\end{aligned}
$$

Having fixed the interpretation of individual names, concepts and roles, we now define the *satisfaction relation* $\models$ for inclusions and assertions:

$$
\begin{aligned}
\mathcal{I} \models C_1 \sqsubseteq C_2 &\quad \text{if and only if} \quad C_1^{\mathcal{I}} \subseteq C_2^{\mathcal{I}}, \\
\mathcal{I} \models R_1 \sqsubseteq R_2 &\quad \text{if and only if} \quad R_1^{\mathcal{I}} \subseteq R_2^{\mathcal{I}}, \\
\mathcal{I} \models C(a) &\quad \text{if and only if} \quad a^{\mathcal{I}} \in C^{\mathcal{I}}, \\
\mathcal{I} \models R(a,b) &\quad \text{if and only if} \quad (a^{\mathcal{I}}, b^{\mathcal{I}}) \in R^{\mathcal{I}}.
\end{aligned}
$$

We say that an interpretation $\mathcal{I}$ is a *model* of a knowledge base $\mathcal{K} = (\mathcal{T}, \mathcal{A})$ if it satisfies all concept and roles inclusions of $\mathcal{T}$ and all concept and role assertions of $\mathcal{A}$. In this case we write $\mathcal{I} \models \mathcal{K}$ (and also $\mathcal{I} \models \mathcal{T}$ and $\mathcal{I} \models \mathcal{A}$).

It is to be remembered that (unlike databases) the choice of domains and interpretation functions is not fixed in the DL semantics, so that every knowledge base can have many models. This reflects the *open world assumption*, or OWA, adopted in DL (and OWL), according to which no single agent can possess complete knowledge. Thus, we have to consider all possible assignments of truth-values to assertions—as long as they do not contradict the given knowledge base. (Databases adopt the *closed world assumption*, or CWA, that defines everything unknown as false.)

Example 2. Consider the following knowledge base $\mathcal{K} = (\mathcal{T}, \mathcal{A})$:

$$\mathcal{T} = \{\ \mathsf{GraduateStudent} \sqsubseteq \mathsf{Student},$$
$$\mathsf{GraduateStudent} \sqsubseteq \exists \mathsf{takesCourse}.\mathsf{GraduateCourse}\ \},$$
$$\mathcal{A} = \{\ \mathsf{GraduateStudent}(\mathit{john})\ \}.$$

Denote by $\mathcal{I}_1$ an interpretation with domain $\Delta^{\mathcal{I}_1} = \{\mathit{john}, \mathit{sw}\}$ such that

$$\mathsf{john}^{\mathcal{I}_1} = \mathit{john},$$

$$\mathsf{GraduateStudent}^{\mathcal{I}_1} = \{\mathit{john}\}, \qquad \mathsf{Student}^{\mathcal{I}_1} = \{\mathit{john}\},$$

$$\mathsf{GraduateCourse}^{\mathcal{I}_1} = \{\mathit{sw}\}, \qquad \mathsf{takesCourse}^{\mathcal{I}_1} = \{(\mathit{john}, \mathit{sw})\}.$$

The reader can readily check that $\mathcal{I}_1$ is a model of $\mathcal{K}$; that is, the 'world' described by $\mathcal{I}_1$ satisfies the knowledge and data given in $\mathcal{K}$. Now, take another interpretation $\mathcal{I}_2$ with domain $\Delta^{\mathcal{I}_2} = \{a\}$ in which

$$\mathsf{john}^{\mathcal{I}_2} = a,$$

$$\mathsf{GraduateStudent}^{\mathcal{I}_2} = \{a\}, \qquad \mathsf{Student}^{\mathcal{I}_2} = \{a\},$$

$$\mathsf{GraduateCourse}^{\mathcal{I}_2} = \{a\}, \qquad \mathsf{takesCourse}^{\mathcal{I}_2} = \{(a, a)\}.$$

This interpretation does not make much sense from the modelling point of view (because a takes course a in the world described by $\mathcal{I}_2$). Nevertheless, $\mathcal{I}_2$ satisfies all of the inclusions in $\mathcal{T}$ and assertions in $\mathcal{A}$, and so is a model of $\mathcal{K}$. Yet another interpretation, $\mathcal{I}_3$, with domain $\Delta^{\mathcal{I}_3} = \{\mathit{john}\}$ and

$$\mathsf{john}^{\mathcal{I}_3} = \mathit{john},$$

$$\mathsf{GraduateStudent}^{\mathcal{I}_3} = \{\mathit{john}\}, \qquad \mathsf{Student}^{\mathcal{I}_3} = \{\mathit{john}\},$$

$$\mathsf{GraduateCourse}^{\mathcal{I}_3} = \emptyset, \qquad \mathsf{takesCourse}^{\mathcal{I}_3} = \emptyset$$

satisfies the assertions in $\mathcal{A}$ and the first concept inclusion in $\mathcal{T}$ but fails to satisfy the second concept inclusion, and so is not a model of $\mathcal{K}$.

Intuitively, everything that takes place in *each and every* model of a knowledge base is a logical consequence of the KB, not necessarily explicitly presented in it. Finding logical consequences is usually referred to as *reasoning*.

2.3   Reasoning Problems

A very basic reasoning problem is to decide whether a given knowledge base is *consistent* in the sense that it does not imply mutually contradicting statements. Formally, we can call a knowledge base $\mathcal{K}$ *satisfiable* (or *consistent*) if there exists at least one model of $\mathcal{K}$ (which is obviously enough to guarantee that $\mathcal{K}$ contains no contradictions).

Example 3. Let $\mathcal{T}$ be a TBox containing the following concept inclusions:

$$\text{UndergraduateStudent} \sqsubseteq \forall \text{takesCourse.UndergraduateCourse,}$$
$$\text{UndergraduateCourse} \sqcap \text{GraduateCourse} \sqsubseteq \bot,$$

and $\mathcal{A}$ an ABox with the following assertions:

$$\text{UndergraduateStudent(john),}$$
$$\text{takesCourse(john, sw),}$$
$$\text{GraduateCourse(sw).}$$

If we assume that $(\mathcal{T}, \mathcal{A})$ has a model, then the undergraduate student John in it will only be able to take undergraduate courses that are not graduate courses such as SW. However, according to the ABox, John takes SW, which is a contradiction. Thus, $(\mathcal{T}, \mathcal{A})$ is inconsistent.

Another important reasoning problem is entailment. We say that a concept inclusion $C_1 \sqsubseteq C_2$ is *entailed by* a knowledge base $\mathcal{K}$ and write $\mathcal{K} \models C_1 \sqsubseteq C_2$ if $\mathcal{I} \models C_1 \sqsubseteq C_2$ for all models $\mathcal{I}$ of $\mathcal{K}$ (entailment for role inclusions and concept and role assertions is defined similarly).

Example 4. Consider a TBox $\mathcal{T}$ with the following two concept inclusions:

$$\forall \text{takesCourse.UndergraduateCourse} \sqsubseteq \text{UndergraduateStudent,}$$
$$\text{FirstYearStudent} \sqsubseteq \exists \text{takesCourse.UndergraduateCourse.}$$

In the model $\mathcal{I}_1$ of $\mathcal{T}$ given below, $\text{FirstYearStudent} \sqsubseteq \text{UndergraduateStudent}$ holds true. However, $\mathcal{T}$ *does not entail* this concept inclusion because there is another model, $\mathcal{I}_2$, where it is not satisfied:

$$\Delta^{\mathcal{I}_1} = \{j, s\}, \qquad\qquad \Delta^{\mathcal{I}_2} = \{j, s, \ell\},$$
$$\text{takesCourse}^{\mathcal{I}_1} = \{(j, s)\}, \qquad \text{takesCourse}^{\mathcal{I}_2} = \{(j, s), (j, \ell)\},$$
$$\text{FirstYearStudent}^{\mathcal{I}_1} = \{j\}, \qquad \text{FirstYearStudent}^{\mathcal{I}_2} = \{j\},$$
$$\text{UndergraduateStudent}^{\mathcal{I}_1} = \{j\}, \qquad \text{UndergraduateStudent}^{\mathcal{I}_2} = \emptyset,$$
$$\text{UndergraduateCourse}^{\mathcal{I}_1} = \{s\}, \qquad \text{UndergraduateCourse}^{\mathcal{I}_2} = \{s\}.$$

Intuitively, in $\mathcal{I}_1$, the individual j is a first-year student who takes only one undergraduate course, and so must be an undergraduate student (to satisfy the first concept inclusion). In contrast, in $\mathcal{I}_2$, the individual j also takes another course, ℓ, which is not an undergraduate course, and therefore, j does not have to be an undergraduate student (still satisfying the first concept inclusion); see Fig. 3.

If $C_1 \sqsubseteq C_2$ is entailed by $\mathcal{K}$, then we also say that C_2 *subsumes* C_1 with respect to $\mathcal{K}$ (or that C_1 is *subsumed* by C_2 with respect to $\mathcal{K}$). We note in passing that if $\mathcal{K}$ is inconsistent then any concept is subsumed by any other

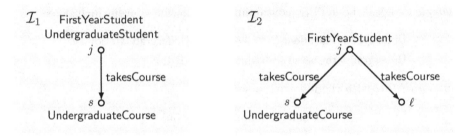

Fig. 3. Interpretations for $\mathcal{T}$ in Example 4

concept: indeed, an arbitrary inclusion $C_1 \sqsubseteq C_2$ is trivially true in every model of $\mathcal{K}$ simply because $\mathcal{K}$ has no models. The following proposition, the proof of which is left to the reader as a simple exercise, shows that concept subsumption is in fact reducible to consistency.

Proposition 5. $(\mathcal{T}, \mathcal{A}) \models C_1 \sqsubseteq C_2$ *if and only if* $(\mathcal{T}, \mathcal{A} \cup \{C_1(a), \neg C_2(a)\})$ *is not satisfiable, for a fresh individual name* a (*not occurring in* $\mathcal{A}$).

(Note as a warning that not every DL allows negation and complex concepts in the ABoxes, in which case the reduction may be not so trivial.)

If $C(a)$ is entailed by $\mathcal{K}$ (that is, $C(a)$ holds in every model of $\mathcal{K}$), then we also say that a is an *instance* of C with respect to $\mathcal{K}$. The problem of checking whether a is an instance of a given C with respect to $\mathcal{K}$ is called *instance checking*. This problem is also reducible to knowledge base consistency (provided that complex concepts are allowed in the ABoxes):

Proposition 6. $(\mathcal{T}, \mathcal{A}) \models C(a)$ *if and only if* $(\mathcal{T}, \mathcal{A} \cup \{\neg C(a)\})$ *is not satisfiable.*

A more general reasoning task is answering conjunctive queries over knowledge bases. A *conjunctive query* (CQ for short) $q(x)$ is an expression of the form $\exists y\, \varphi(x, y)$, where $\varphi(x, y)$ is a conjunction of atoms such as $A(z)$ and $P(z_1, z_2)$, for a concept name A, role name P and terms z, z_1 and z_2, which are individual names or variables from x and y. The variables x_i in $x = (x_1, \dots, x_n)$ are called *answer variables* and the variables in y *existentially quantified variables*. Given a tuple $a = (a_1, \dots, a_n)$ of individual names from $\mathcal{A}$, we denote by $q(a)$ the result of replacing each answer variable x_i in $\exists y\, \varphi(x, y)$ with the respective a_i from a. A tuple a of individual names from $\mathcal{A}$ is a *certain answer* to $q(x)$ over $(\mathcal{T}, \mathcal{A})$ if, for any model $\mathcal{I}$ of $(\mathcal{T}, \mathcal{A})$, the sentence $q(a)$ is true in $\mathcal{I}$ ($\mathcal{I} \models q(a)$, in symbols). We write $(\mathcal{T}, \mathcal{A}) \models q(a)$ to indicate that a is a certain answer to $q(x)$ over $(\mathcal{T}, \mathcal{A})$. A CQ q without answer variables is called *Boolean*, in which case a certain answer to q over $(\mathcal{T}, \mathcal{A})$ is 'yes' if $(\mathcal{T}, \mathcal{A}) \models q$ and 'no' otherwise. The problem of answering Boolean CQs is known as *CQ entailment*.

Example 7. (Andrea's example (Schaerf, 1993)) Suppose a TBox $\mathcal{T}$ contains the inclusions

$$\top \sqsubseteq \mathsf{Male} \sqcup \mathsf{Female}, \qquad\qquad \mathsf{Male} \sqcap \mathsf{Female} \sqsubseteq \bot.$$

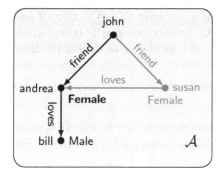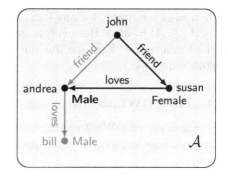

Fig. 4. Two representative models of $(\mathcal{T}, \mathcal{A})$ in Example 7

and an ABox $\mathcal{A}$ contains the assertions

friend(john, susan),   friend(john, andrea),

loves(susan, andrea),   loves(andrea, bill),

Female(susan),   Male(bill).

Consider the CQ

$$q(x) \;=\; \exists y, z \,\big(\mathsf{friend}(x,y) \wedge \mathsf{Female}(y) \wedge \mathsf{loves}(y,z) \wedge \mathsf{Male}(z)\big),$$

which asks to find every individual (in the ABox) with a female friend who is in love with a male. Note that the same CQ can be expressed in the query language SPARQL[5] as follows:

> SELECT $?x$
> WHERE {
> > $?x$:friend $?y$.
> > $?y$ a :Female.
> > $?y$:loves $?z$.
> > $?z$ a :Male.
> }

(Here a is an abbreviation of rdf:type and can be read as 'is a.') We invite the reader to check that the only certain answer to $q(x)$ over $(\mathcal{T}, \mathcal{A})$ is $x \mapsto$ john. (Hint: in every model $\mathcal{I}$ of $(\mathcal{T}, \mathcal{A})$, either andrea$^{\mathcal{I}} \in$ Female$^{\mathcal{I}}$ or andrea$^{\mathcal{I}} \in$ Male$^{\mathcal{I}}$; see Fig. 4.)

Observe that this particular CQ $q(x)$ can also be represented as an *instance query* $C(x)$, where C is the complex concept

$$\exists\mathsf{friend}.(\mathsf{Female} \sqcap \exists\mathsf{loves}.\mathsf{Male}).$$

---

[5] www.w3.org/TR/sparql11-query

It is readily seen that, for any individual name a, we have $(\mathcal{T}, \mathcal{A}) \models C(a)$ if and only if $(\mathcal{T}, \mathcal{A}) \models q(a)$. However, in general, CQs are not necessarily tree-shaped, can contain more than one answer variable, and so are more expressive than instance queries.

2.4   From OWL to DL

The language of OWL 2 contains more constructs than any of the DLs, with many of these constructs being just shortcuts for certain DL expressions. For example,

$$\mathsf{ObjectPropertyDomain(takesCourse, Student)}$$

can be represented as the concept inclusion

$$\exists \mathsf{takesCourse}.\top \sqsubseteq \mathsf{Student}.$$

Similarly,

$$\mathsf{ObjectPropertyRange(takesCourse, Course)}$$

can be represented as

$$\exists \mathsf{takesCourse}^-.\top \sqsubseteq \mathsf{Course}.$$

Note that the latter concept inclusion can only be written in the DLs with *inverse roles* (such as the RL or QL profiles of OWL 2 to be discussed below). If, however, inverse roles are not available in a DL (for instance, $\mathcal{ALC}$), then one can use a universal restriction:

$$\top \sqsubseteq \forall \mathsf{takesCourse}.\mathsf{Course}.$$

One can verify that the two concept inclusions are equivalent in the sense that they are satisfied by precisely the same interpretations. We have collected standard equivalencies of this sort in the following proposition:

Proposition 8. *The following pairs of (sets of) concept inclusions have the same models:*

$$C_1 \sqsubseteq \forall P.C_2 \qquad and \qquad \exists P^-.C_1 \sqsubseteq C_2, \tag{6}$$
$$C_1 \sqcup C_2 \sqsubseteq C \qquad and \qquad \{\, C_i \sqsubseteq C \mid i = 1, 2 \,\}, \tag{7}$$
$$C \sqsubseteq C_1 \sqcap C_2 \qquad and \qquad \{\, C \sqsubseteq C_i \mid i = 1, 2 \,\}, \tag{8}$$
$$C_1 \sqsubseteq \neg C_2 \qquad and \qquad C_1 \sqcap C_2 \sqsubseteq \bot. \tag{9}$$

OWL 2 also has a shortcut for equivalent classes and properties: Equivalent-Classes, EquivalentObjectProperties and EquivalentDataProperties. These can be represented using $\sqsubseteq$: for example,

$$\mathsf{EquivalentClasses}(C_1, C_2, \ldots, C_n)$$

can be written in the DL parlance as n concept inclusions

$$C_1 \sqsubseteq C_2, \quad C_2 \sqsubseteq C_3, \quad \ldots, \quad C_{n-1} \sqsubseteq C_n, \quad C_n \sqsubseteq C_1.$$

Another way is to use a common DL abbreviation $\equiv$, which is defined by taking $A \equiv B$ if and only if $A \sqsubseteq B$ and $B \sqsubseteq A$.

Equivalence (9) provides two alternative ways of expressing *disjointness* of concepts C_1 and C_2 in DL. OWL 2 offers a shortcut for pairwise disjointness of n classes:

$$\text{DisjointClasses}(C_1, C_2, \ldots, C_n),$$

which can be represented in DLs as $n(n-1)/2$ concept inclusions

$$C_i \sqcap C_j \sqsubseteq \bot, \quad \text{for all } i, j \text{ with } 1 \le i < j \le n.$$

Yet another shortcut in OWL 2 allows one to say that class C is the disjoint union of $C_1, \ldots, C_n$:

$$\text{DisjointUnion}(C, C_1, C_2, \ldots, C_n),$$

which combines pairwise disjointness of $C_1, \ldots, C_n$ (see above) with

$$C \equiv C_1 \sqcup \cdots \sqcup C_n.$$

Object properties can be declared symmetric in OWL 2 by using axioms of the form $\text{SymmetricObjectProperty}(P)$. The same effect can be achieved in DLs with the help of the role inclusion

$$P^- \sqsubseteq P.$$

More expressive description logics contain additional constructs such as number restrictions, $\exists R.\text{Self}$, transitive roles, role chains, etc. In particular, the DL subset of OWL 2, known as OWL 2 DL, is based on the description logic called $\mathcal{SROIQ}$ (Horrocks et al., 2006).

2.5   Complexity of Reasoning

Having formulated the reasoning problems, we are facing the following fundamental questions:

- Are these problems *decidable* in the sense that there exist algorithms which always halt and return correct answers?
- How *complex* are such algorithms in terms of the time or memory space they require?
- Are these algorithms (reasonably) *efficient* in real-world applications?

The next theorem, which is a compilation of various results from (Tobies, 2001; Eiter et al., 2009; Horrocks et al., 2006),[6] gives answers to the first two questions:

---

[6] See also the DL Complexity Navigator at `www.cs.man.ac.uk/~ezolin/dl`

Theorem 9. (*i*) *The satisfiability problem is* ExpTime-*complete for* $\mathcal{ALCHI}$ *KBs and* N2ExpTime-*complete for* $\mathcal{SROIQ}$ *KBs.*

(*ii*) *Concept and role subsumption and instance checking are* ExpTime- *and* coN2ExpTime-*complete for, respectively,* $\mathcal{ALCHI}$ *and* $\mathcal{SROIQ}$ *KBs.*

(*iii*) *CQ entailment over* $\mathcal{ALCHI}$ *KBs is* 2ExpTime-*complete.*

Note that full OWL 2 under the RDF-based semantics is undecidable (Motik, 2007), while OWL 2 DL under the direct (model-theoretic) semantics is decidable. There is, however, a price to pay for the additional expressive power of $\mathcal{SROIQ}$ underlying OWL 2 DL: satisfiability is harder than in $\mathcal{ALCHI}$ and CQ entailment is not even known to be decidable.

ExpTime-completeness of satisfiability in $\mathcal{ALCHI}$ means, in particular, two things: first, there exists a satisfiability-checking algorithm that runs in at most exponential time in the size of the input knowledge base and, second, *no* algorithm can check satisfiability of *any* given knowledge base in polynomial time. This complexity-theoretic result does not suggest that reasoning algorithms can be efficient in practice. Fortunately, practical reasoners for OWL 2 DL have been implemented: FaCT++ (Tsarkov and Horrocks, 2006), HermiT (Horrocks et al., 2012), Pellet (Sirin et al., 2007), Konclude (Steigmiller et al., 2014). Their efficiency in typical real-world applications (rather than worst-case scenarios) relies upon sophisticated optimisation techniques and the empirical fact that ontologies designed by humans for such applications are often simple enough for basic reasoning techniques. On the other hand, answering instance queries and, more generally, conjunctive queries over knowledge bases in expressive languages has not become practical so far, especially for large data sets.

3   Description Logics for the OWL Profiles

The current W3C recommendation OWL 2 of the Web Ontology Language identifies three *profiles* (fragments or sub-languages) specifically designed to ensure efficiency (tractability) of reasoning at the expense of expressive power. In this section, we introduce these profiles in the form of DLs (sacrificing some features for the clarity of presentation).

We begin with an observation that in order to ensure tractability of reasoning (that is, the existence of a *deterministic polynomial-time* algorithm for checking consistency) one has to avoid using $\sqcup$ on the right-hand side of concept inclusions. Intuitively, this construct requires (non-deterministic) reasoning about possible cases such as in Example 7 (case 1: Andrea is a female; case 2: Andrea is a male), which can be NP-hard; for an introduction on the computational complexity, consult classical (Garey and Johnson, 1979) or more recent (Kozen, 2006; Arora and Barak, 2009).

We illustrate non-deterministic reasoning by encoding the NP-complete *graph 3-colourability* problem: given an (undirected) graph $G = (V, E)$, decide whether each of its vertices can be painted in one of the given three colours in such a way that no pair of adjacent vertices has the same colour. We represent the input graph G by means of an ABox $\mathcal{A}_G$ comprising assertions

$$\text{edge}(v_1, v_2), \quad \text{for each } \{v_1, v_2\} \in E.$$

Consider a TBox $\mathcal{T}$ containing the following concept inclusions:

$$\top \sqsubseteq C_1 \sqcup C_2 \sqcup C_3,$$
$$C_i \sqcap C_j \sqsubseteq \bot, \qquad\qquad 1 \leq i < j \leq 3,$$
$$C_i \sqcap \exists \text{edge}.C_i \sqsubseteq \bot, \qquad 1 \leq i \leq 3,$$

where C_1, C_2 and C_3 are concept names representing the given three colours. It is not hard to see that each model of $(\mathcal{T}, \mathcal{A}_G)$ gives rise to a 3-colouring of G and, conversely, each 3-colouring of G can be encoded in a model of $(\mathcal{T}, \mathcal{A}_G)$. In other words, $(\mathcal{T}, \mathcal{A}_G)$ is satisfiable if and only if G is 3-colourable. This means that the satisfiability problem for knowledge bases in any DL able to express this TBox is NP-hard (that is, not tractable).

3.1   OWL 2 RL

The OWL 2 RL profile[7] is aimed at applications requiring scalable reasoning that can be done by rule-based implementations (such as datalog engines). Its design was inspired by the so-called Description Logic Programs (Grosof et al., 2003) and pD* (ter Horst, 2005). OWL 2 RL is supported by Oracle Database 11g, OWLIM, BaseVISor, ELLY, Jena and RDFox (for details and references, see www.w3.org/2001/sw/wiki/OWL/Implementations).

A key feature of OWL 2 RL is that it does not allow existential quantifiers on the right-hand side of concept inclusions. Therefore, when reasoning with an OWL 2 RL knowledge base, we do not have to deal with individuals that are not explicitly present in the knowledge base ABox.

In this section, we consider a somewhat simplified version of OWL 2 RL, which will be called *RL*. Concept and role inclusions in *RL* take the form

$$B \sqsubseteq A, \qquad R_1 \sqsubseteq R_2 \quad \text{and} \quad B \sqsubseteq \bot,$$

where R_1 and R_2 are roles (role names or their inverses), A is a concept name and B a concept defined by the following grammar:

$$B \ ::= \ A \ \mid \ \exists R.\top \ \mid \ \exists R.B \ \mid \ B_1 \sqcap B_2.$$

Observe that there is no $\sqcup$ in the syntax, and the existential quantifiers occur only on the left-hand side of concept inclusions. On the other hand, by Proposition 8, universal restrictions, intersection and complement on the right-hand side of concept inclusions and union on the left-hand side of concept inclusions are simply syntactic sugar.

An *RL knowledge base* $(\mathcal{T}, \mathcal{A})$ comprises a finite set $\mathcal{T}$ of inclusions introduced above and a *simple* ABox $\mathcal{A}$, which contains only assertions of the form $A(a)$ and $P(a, b)$, for a concept name A and a role name P.

To understand reasoning in *RL* (and the other two profiles of OWL 2), it is useful to represent its concept and role inclusions as first-order sentences.

---

[7] www.w3.org/TR/owl2-profiles/#OWL_2_RL

Example 10. The RL concept inclusions

$$\exists\mathsf{takesCourse}.\mathsf{UndergraduateCourse} \sqsubseteq \mathsf{UndergraduateStudent},$$
$$\mathsf{UndergraduateStudent} \sqsubseteq \mathsf{Student}$$

are equivalent (have the same models) as the first-order sentences

$$\forall x \forall y \left(\mathsf{takesCourse}(x,y) \wedge \mathsf{UndergraduateCourse}(y) \rightarrow \mathsf{UndergraduateStudent}(x)\right),$$
$$\forall x \left(\mathsf{UndergraduateStudent}(x) \rightarrow \mathsf{Student}(x)\right).$$

More formally, we define a *standard translation* ST of concepts and roles by induction on their structure. First, for any concept name A and any role name P, we set

$$ST_x(A) = A(x),$$
$$ST_{x,y}(P) = P(x,y),$$

where the subscript specifies the variables used as arguments of the predicates. After that, we extend the translation ST to complex roles and concepts by taking

$$ST_{x,y}(P^-) = P(y,x),$$
$$ST_x(\exists R.\top) = \exists y\, ST_{x,y}(R),$$
$$ST_x(\exists R.B) = \exists y\, \left(ST_{x,y}(R) \wedge ST_y(B)\right),$$
$$ST_x(B_1 \sqcap B_2) = ST_x(B_1) \wedge ST_x(B_2).$$

Finally, we translate concept and role inclusions into universally quantified implications:

$$(B \sqsubseteq A)^* = \forall x\, \left(ST_x(B) \rightarrow ST_x(A)\right),$$
$$(R_1 \sqsubseteq R_2)^* = \forall x \forall y\, \left(ST_{x,y}(R_1) \rightarrow ST_{x,y}(R_2)\right),$$
$$(B \sqsubseteq \bot)^* = \forall x\, \left(ST_x(B) \rightarrow \bot\right).$$

As $\exists R.\top$ and $\exists R.B$ can occur only on the left-hand side of concept inclusions, the translation $\cdot^*$ of any RL TBox contains only sentences of the form

$$\forall \boldsymbol{y}\, \left(\gamma_1(\boldsymbol{y}) \wedge \cdots \wedge \gamma_k(\boldsymbol{y}) \rightarrow \gamma_0(\boldsymbol{y})\right),$$
$$\forall \boldsymbol{y}\, \left(\gamma_1(\boldsymbol{y}) \wedge \cdots \wedge \gamma_k(\boldsymbol{y}) \rightarrow \bot\right),$$

where $\gamma_0(\boldsymbol{y}), \ldots, \gamma_k(\boldsymbol{y})$ are unary or binary predicates with variables in $\boldsymbol{y}$. Such sentences are examples of *Horn clauses* (sets of sentences of the first kind are also called *datalog programs*; see e.g., Ceri et al. (1989)). A very important property of Horn clauses known from logic and databases is that everything we may want to know about a knowledge base, whose TBox axioms are Horn clauses, can be found in the canonical model (or chase), which is constructed by 'applying' the clauses to the ABox. We first illustrate the construction by a simple example.

Example 11. Consider the TBox $\mathcal{T}$ from Example 10 and the following ABox:

$$\mathcal{A} \;=\; \{\; \mathsf{takesCourse(john, sp1), UndergraduateCourse(sp1)} \;\}.$$

We begin the construction of the canonical model by representing the ABox as an interpretation $\mathcal{I}_0$ with the domain $\Delta^{\mathcal{I}_0} = \{\mathsf{john, sp1}\}$ and the interpretation function given by

$$\mathsf{takesCourse}^{\mathcal{I}_0} = \{(\mathsf{john, sp1})\},$$
$$\mathsf{UndergraduateCourse}^{\mathcal{I}_0} = \{\mathsf{sp1}\},$$
$$\mathsf{UndergraduateStudent}^{\mathcal{I}_0} = \emptyset,$$
$$\mathsf{Student}^{\mathcal{I}_0} = \emptyset.$$

The interpretation $\mathcal{I}_0$ does not satisfy the first concept inclusion in $\mathcal{T}$ because john is related by takesCourse to sp1, which is an UndergraduateCourse, but john is not an instance of UndergraduateStudent. To repair this 'defect', we apply (as a rule) the first concept inclusion to $\mathcal{I}_0$ and obtain an interpretation $\mathcal{I}_1$ with the same domain, $\Delta^{\mathcal{I}_1} = \Delta^{\mathcal{I}_0}$, and the interpretation function $\cdot^{\mathcal{I}_1}$ that expands $\cdot^{\mathcal{I}_0}$ with

$$\mathsf{UndergraduateStudent}^{\mathcal{I}_1} = \{\mathsf{john}\}$$

(all other symbols have the same interpretation as in $\mathcal{I}_0$). Now, $\mathcal{I}_1$ satisfies the first concept inclusion of $\mathcal{T}$ but fails to satisfy the second one. We repair this defect by 'applying' the second concept inclusion to $\mathcal{I}_1$ and obtaining an interpretation $\mathcal{I}_2$ with the same domain and the interpretation function expanding $\cdot^{\mathcal{I}_1}$ with

$$\mathsf{Student}^{\mathcal{I}_2} = \{\mathsf{john}\}$$

(all other symbols keep their interpretation). It is readily seen that now $\mathcal{I}_2$ is a model of $(\mathcal{T}, \mathcal{A})$. Note that we constructed $\mathcal{I}_2$ by adding to the given ABox $\mathcal{A}$ only those assertions—UndergraduateStudent(john) and Student(john)—that were required by the TBox $\mathcal{T}$. That is why $\mathcal{I}_2$ is referred to as the *minimal model* or *canonical model* of $(\mathcal{T}, \mathcal{A})$.

The procedure used in the example above is known as *forward chaining*. Formally, it can be described as follows. First, a simple ABox can be regarded as an interpretation:

Definition 12. The *standard model* $\mathcal{I}_\mathcal{A}$ of a simple ABox $\mathcal{A}$ is defined by taking

$$\Delta^{\mathcal{I}_\mathcal{A}} = \mathsf{ind}(\mathcal{A}),$$

$a^{\mathcal{I}_\mathcal{A}} = a,$	for $a \in \mathsf{ind}(\mathcal{A})$,
$A^{\mathcal{I}_\mathcal{A}} = \{a \mid A(a) \in \mathcal{A}\},$	for concept name A,
$P^{\mathcal{I}_\mathcal{A}} = \{(a, b) \mid P(a, b) \in \mathcal{A}\},$	for role name P.

Thus, the domain of $\mathcal{I}_{\mathcal{A}}$ is the set of individual names in $\mathcal{A}$, and each individual name is interpreted in $\mathcal{I}_{\mathcal{A}}$ by itself, which is often referred to as the *standard name assumption*.

Next, given an *RL* knowledge base $(\mathcal{T}, \mathcal{A})$, we construct a sequence of interpretations $\mathcal{I}_0, \mathcal{I}_1, \ldots, \mathcal{I}_n$ by setting $\mathcal{I}_0 = \mathcal{I}_{\mathcal{A}}$ and then applying the following rules to each $\mathcal{I}_k$ to obtain $\mathcal{I}_{k+1}$:

(c) if $a \in B^{\mathcal{I}_k}$, $B \sqsubseteq A \in \mathcal{T}$ but $a \notin A^{\mathcal{I}_k}$, then we add a to $A^{\mathcal{I}_{k+1}}$;
(r) if $(a, b) \in R_1^{\mathcal{I}_k}$, $R_1 \sqsubseteq R_2 \in \mathcal{T}$ but $(a, b) \notin R_2^{\mathcal{I}_k}$, then we add (a, b) to $R_2^{\mathcal{I}_{k+1}}$;
(b) if $a \in B^{\mathcal{I}_k}$ and $B \sqsubseteq \bot \in \mathcal{T}$, then the process terminates.

Since the domains of the $\mathcal{I}_k$ are finite and all coincide with the set of individuals in $\mathcal{A}$, the process terminates after a finite number of steps either because neither **(c)** nor **(r)** is applicable or because **(b)** applies. In the former case the resulting interpretation satisfies all the inclusions in $\mathcal{T}$ and all the assertions in $\mathcal{A}$; it is called the *canonical model of* $(\mathcal{T}, A)$ and denoted by $\mathcal{C}_{\mathcal{T}, \mathcal{A}}$. In the latter case, $(\mathcal{T}, \mathcal{A})$ is inconsistent.

Let $\mathcal{T}_+$ be the *positive* part of an *RL* TBox $\mathcal{T}$ that consists of all role inclusions in $\mathcal{T}$ and all concept inclusions of the form $B \sqsubseteq A$ in $\mathcal{T}$. By definition, $(\mathcal{T}_+, \mathcal{A})$ is consistent for any $\mathcal{A}$, and so its canonical model $\mathcal{C}_{\mathcal{T}_+, \mathcal{A}}$ is defined and can be used to check consistency of the full knowledge base (see, e.g., Calì et al. (2012)):

Theorem 13. *An RL knowledge base $(\mathcal{T}, \mathcal{A})$ is consistent if and only if we have* $\mathcal{C}_{\mathcal{T}_+, \mathcal{A}} \models B \sqsubseteq \bot$, *for all* $B \sqsubseteq \bot$ *in* $\mathcal{T}$.

Similar results hold for the other two profiles of OWL 2 (or indeed for any Horn DL), and therefore in the following we do not consider negative concept inclusions (although they are part of both OWL 2 EL and OWL 2 QL).

The canonical model $\mathcal{C}_{\mathcal{T}, \mathcal{A}}$ is *universal* in the sense that it can be homomorphically mapped into any other model of $(\mathcal{T}, \mathcal{A})$ (this notion formalises the minimality mentioned above).

Definition 14. A *homomorphism* h from an interpretation $\mathcal{I}_1$ to an interpretation $\mathcal{I}_2$ is a map from $\Delta^{\mathcal{I}_1}$ to $\Delta^{\mathcal{I}_2}$ such that

- $h(a^{\mathcal{I}_1}) = a^{\mathcal{I}_2}$, for each individual name a,
- $h(u) \in A^{\mathcal{I}_2}$, for any $u \in A^{\mathcal{I}_1}$ and any concept name A,
- $(h(u), h(v)) \in P^{\mathcal{I}_2}$, for any $(u, v) \in P^{\mathcal{I}_1}$ and any role name P.

The universality of the canonical models means, in particular, that checking subsumption and answering CQs over *RL* knowledge bases can be done by analysing their canonical models:

Theorem 15. *Let $(\mathcal{T}, \mathcal{A})$ be a consistent RL knowledge base. Then $\mathcal{C}_{\mathcal{T}, \mathcal{A}} \models (\mathcal{T}, \mathcal{A})$. In addition, we have the following:*

(i) $(\mathcal{T}, \mathcal{A}) \models B \sqsubseteq A$ *if and only if* $\mathcal{C}_{\mathcal{T}, \mathcal{A}} \models B \sqsubseteq A$;
(ii) $(\mathcal{T}, \mathcal{A}) \models R_1 \sqsubseteq R_2$ *if and only if* $\mathcal{C}_{\mathcal{T}, \mathcal{A}} \models R_1 \sqsubseteq R_2$;
(iii) $(\mathcal{T}, \mathcal{A}) \models q(a)$ *if and only if* $\mathcal{C}_{\mathcal{T}, \mathcal{A}} \models q(a)$.

Observe that the forward chaining procedure only requires a polynomial number of steps to construct the canonical model (more precisely, the number of steps is bounded by $O(m^2 \times s)$, where m is the number of individual names in the ABox and s is the number of concept and role names). Therefore, knowledge base consistency, subsumption and instance checking are tractable in RL (the matching lower bound will be discussed in Section 4):

Theorem 16. *The problems of knowledge base consistency, concept and role subsumption and instance checking are* P*-complete in* RL. *The problem of* CQ *entailment in* RL *is* NP*-complete.*

Forward chaining can be regarded as a bottom-up saturation procedure. In datalog, however, more common is the top-down procedure, where a proof is constructed for a given statement; see e.g., (Ceri et al., 1989). We shall return to this topic in Section 4.3.

It is important to note that, since the clauses in the standard translation of RL inclusions contain only universally quantified variables, the canonical model of any RL knowledge base is *finite* (forward chaining does not add any new elements to the individuals in the ABox). We now turn to the profiles where this is not necessarily the case.

3.2   OWL 2 EL

The design of the OWL 2 EL profile[8] of OWL 2 (Baader et al., 2008, 2005) was based on the observation that biomedical ontologies such as SNOMED CT,[9] NCI[10] and GO[11] essentially use only conjunctions and existential quantifiers.

In this section, we consider a somewhat simplified version of OWL 2 EL, which will be called *EL*. Concept and role inclusions in *EL* look as follows:

$$C_1 \sqsubseteq C_2 \qquad \text{and} \qquad P_1 \sqsubseteq P_2,$$

where P_1 and P_2 are role names (role inverses are not allowed in *EL*) and C_1, C_2 are concepts defined by the following grammar:

$$C \quad ::= \quad A \quad | \quad \exists P.\top \quad | \quad \exists P.C \quad | \quad C_1 \sqcap C_2$$

(again, existential restrictions contain only role names). The following are typical concept inclusions from the SNOMED CT ontology:

Pericardium $\sqsubseteq$ Tissue $\sqcap$ containedIn.Heart,

Pericarditis $\sqsubseteq$ Inflammation $\sqcap$ hasLocation.Pericardium,

Inflammation $\sqsubseteq$ Disease $\sqcap$ actsOn.Tissue,

Disease $\sqcap$ hasLocation.containedIn.Heart $\sqsubseteq$ HeartDisease $\sqcap$ NeedsTreatment.

---

[8] www.w3.org/TR/owl2-profiles/#OWL_2_EL

[9] www.ihtsdo.org/snomed-ct

[10] www.obofoundry.org/cgi-bin/detail.cgi?id=ncithesaurus

[11] www.geneontology.org

ABoxes in EL are simple; see Section 3.1. The language we defined above is almost identical to $\mathcal{ELH}$: the only difference is that we do not allow $\top$ to occur outside the scope of existential restrictions. Thus, the EL concepts here are exactly those RL concepts from Section 3.1 that do not contain inverse roles. Note that EL extended with inverse roles is not tractable; moreover reasoning becomes as complex as in $\mathcal{ALCHI}$, that is, ExpTime-complete (Baader et al., 2008).

Since the existential restrictions can also occur on the right-hand side of concept inclusions, the result of translating a given EL TBox into first-order logic (see Section 3.1) is no longer a datalog program. Instead, it belongs to an extension of datalog called datalog$^{\pm}$ (Calì et al., 2012) or existential rules (Baget et al., 2011)[12]; in database theory, this language has been known since the early 1980s under the name of tuple-generating dependencies (Abiteboul et al., 1995). More precisely, EL TBoxes can be translated into sets of sentences of the form

$$\forall \boldsymbol{y} \left(\gamma_1(\boldsymbol{y}) \wedge \cdots \wedge \gamma_k(\boldsymbol{y}) \to \exists \boldsymbol{x}\, \gamma_0(\boldsymbol{x}, \boldsymbol{y})\right),$$

where $\gamma_1(\boldsymbol{y}), \ldots, \gamma_k(\boldsymbol{y})$ contain only universally quantified variables $\boldsymbol{y}$ whereas $\gamma_0(\boldsymbol{x}, \boldsymbol{y})$ contains both universally quantified variables $\boldsymbol{y}$ and existentially quantified variables $\boldsymbol{x}$ (note that the standard translations of EL TBoxes are in fact more restricted than this general form, but it suffices for our explanations). Since these sentences are Horn clauses, we can again apply the forward chaining procedure (chase). However, in the case of EL TBoxes the chase has to 'invent' new domain elements for the existential quantifiers. Following the terminology of database theory, these fresh (previously not existing) domain elements will be called *labelled nulls*. In general, the forward chaining procedure may require infinitely many fresh labelled nulls resulting in a possibly infinite canonical model.

The forward chaining construction of the canonical model for an EL knowledge base $(\mathcal{T}, \mathcal{A})$ can be defined by taking the standard model $\mathcal{I}_\mathcal{A}$ of the ABox as $\mathcal{I}_0$ (see Definition 12) and applying inductively the following rules to obtain $\mathcal{I}_{k+1}$ from $\mathcal{I}_k$:

(c′) if $d \in C^{\mathcal{I}_k}$ and $C \sqsubseteq A \in \mathcal{T}$, then we add d to $A^{\mathcal{I}_{k+1}}$;

(r′) if $(d, d') \in P_1^{\mathcal{I}_k}$ and $P_1 \sqsubseteq P_2 \in \mathcal{T}$, then we add (d, d') to $P_2^{\mathcal{I}_{k+1}}$;

(e) if $d \in C^{\mathcal{I}_k}$ and $C \sqsubseteq \exists P.D \in \mathcal{T}$, where D is a concept name or $\top$, then we take a *fresh* labelled null, d', and add d' to $D^{\mathcal{I}_{k+1}}$ and (d, d') to $P^{\mathcal{I}_{k+1}}$

(here, we assume that only A, $\exists P.A$ and $\exists P.\top$ can occur on the right-hand side of concept inclusions—this restriction is inessential, as we shall see in Theorem 20). Note that rules **(c′)** and **(r′)** are similar to the rules from Section 3.1 except that they are applied without checking whether d and (d, d') are already present in the interpretation of the concept and role, respectively. This modification of the chase procedure is usually called the *oblivious chase* (Johnson and Klug, 1984); see also (Calì et al., 2013).

---

[12] See also Chapter 6 in this volume.

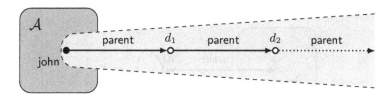

Fig. 5. The infinite canonical model for the KB from Example 17

Example 17. Consider an *EL* TBox $\mathcal{T}$ with the following concept inclusion:

$$\text{Person} \sqsubseteq \exists\text{parent}.\text{Person}.$$

Let us apply the forward chaining procedure to the ABox $\mathcal{A} = \{\text{Person(john)}\}$. We begin by setting $\mathcal{I}_0 = \mathcal{I}_{\mathcal{A}}$:

$$\Delta^{\mathcal{I}_0} = \{\text{john}\}, \quad \text{Person}^{\mathcal{I}_0} = \{\text{john}\} \quad \text{and} \quad \text{parent}^{\mathcal{I}_0} = \emptyset.$$

By the concept inclusion in the TBox, there must be some d_1 that is parent-related to john. So, we expand $\mathcal{I}_0$ to $\mathcal{I}_1$ by taking

$$\Delta^{\mathcal{I}_1} = \{\text{john}, d_1\}, \quad \text{Person}^{\mathcal{I}_1} = \{\text{john}, d_1\} \quad \text{and} \quad \text{parent}^{\mathcal{I}_1} = \{(\text{john}, d_1)\}.$$

Now, the concept inclusion is satisfied for john but fails for d_1, since there must be some d_2 that is parent-related to d_1. So, we expand $\mathcal{I}_1$ to $\mathcal{I}_2$ by taking

$$\Delta^{\mathcal{I}_2} = \{\text{john}, d_1, d_2\}, \quad \text{Person}^{\mathcal{I}_2} = \{\text{john}, d_1, d_2\}, \quad \text{parent}^{\mathcal{I}_2} = \{(\text{john}, d_1), (d_1, d_2)\}.$$

If we take all the newly introduced labelled nulls d_i to be distinct then, clearly, this process will continue *ad infinitum*; see Fig. 5. (A possibility of making some of the d_i identical will be discussed later on in this section.)

Since our simplified definition of *EL* does not involve $\bot$ and $\neg$, every *EL* knowledge base $(\mathcal{T}, \mathcal{A})$ is consistent and the (possibly infinite) forward chaining procedure constructs the canonical model $\mathcal{C}_{\mathcal{T},\mathcal{A}}$ of $(\mathcal{T}, \mathcal{A})$. As in the case of *RL*, the resulting canonical model is universal: it can be homomorphically mapped into any other model of the knowledge base. Note, however, that universal models are not uniquely defined (for instance, one can take two identical fresh labelled nulls instead of one) and, in contrast to *RL*, some knowledge bases may only have *infinite* universal models. For instance, the knowledge base $(\mathcal{T}, \mathcal{A})$ from Example 17 has no finite universal model. Indeed, suppose, for the sake of contradiction, that there is a finite universal model $\mathcal{U}$ of $(\mathcal{T}, \mathcal{A})$. Then $\mathcal{U}$ must contain a sequence of domain elements connected by parent into a cycle. However, the (canonical) model constructed in Example 17 does not contain a homomorphic image of such a cycle, contrary to our assumption.

On the other hand, if we only want to check concept and role subsumption or find answers to instance queries, then we do not have to consider infinite models. The 'folding' construction we are going describe below re-uses the labelled nulls and reminds of the filtration technique known from modal logic; see, e.g., (Chagrov and Zakharyaschev, 1997).

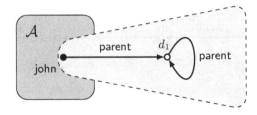

Fig. 6. The small canonical model for the KB from Example 17

Example 18. Consider $(\mathcal{T}, \mathcal{A})$ from Example 17 and suppose that, on step 2 of forward chaining, instead of introducing a fresh labelled null, d_2, we take d_1 instead. This will result in the following interpretation $\mathcal{I}_*$ (see Fig. 6):

$$\Delta^{\mathcal{I}_*} = \{\text{john}, d_1\},$$
$$\text{Person}^{\mathcal{I}_*} = \{\text{john}, d_1\},$$
$$\text{parent}^{\mathcal{I}_*} = \{(\text{john}, d_1), (d_1, d_1)\}.$$

Although the interpretation $\mathcal{I}_*$ makes little sense from the modelling point of view (it states that d_1 is its own parent), it is clearly a model of $(\mathcal{T}, \mathcal{A})$. Moreover, as we shall see below, this small model is good enough for checking subsumption and answering instance queries.

To define such small canonical models (also known as generating models) formally, we first convert *EL* TBoxes to a normal form.

Definition 19. An *EL* TBox is said to be in *normal form* if any of its concept inclusions looks as follows:

$$A_1 \sqcap A_2 \sqsubseteq A, \qquad \exists P.D \sqsubseteq A \quad \text{or} \quad A \sqsubseteq \exists P.D,$$

where P is a role name, A, A_1 and A_2 are concept names and D is either a concept name or $\top$.

By introducing abbreviations for complex concepts, one can transform any *EL* TBox to an equivalent one in normal form.

Theorem 20 (Baader et al. (2005)). *Every EL TBox $\mathcal{T}$ can be transformed into a TBox $\mathcal{T}'$ in normal form such that the size of $\mathcal{T}'$ is linear in the size of $\mathcal{T}$, and $\mathcal{T}$ and $\mathcal{T}'$ are equivalent in the following sense:*

- *every model of $\mathcal{T}$ can be extended to a model of $\mathcal{T}'$ by defining interpretations of the fresh concept names,*
- *every model of $\mathcal{T}'$ is a model of $\mathcal{T}$.*

Example 21. Given a concept inclusion $\exists P.A \sqcap B \sqsubseteq \exists R.\exists P.A$, we first take a fresh concept name C that will stand for $\exists P.A$ and obtain

$$C \sqcap B \sqsubseteq \exists R.C, \qquad \underbrace{\exists P.A \sqsubseteq C, \qquad C \sqsubseteq \exists P.A.}_{\text{`}C \text{ is equivalent to } \exists P.A\text{'}}$$

Next, we take another fresh concept name D to replace $\exists R.C$, which results in the following TBox in normal form:

$$C \sqcap B \sqsubseteq D, \qquad \exists P.A \sqsubseteq C, \qquad C \sqsubseteq \exists P.A, \qquad D \sqsubseteq \exists R.C, \qquad \exists R.C \sqsubseteq D.$$

We are now in a position to define generating models formally. Let $(\mathcal{T}, \mathcal{A})$ be an *EL* knowledge base in normal form. We say that a concept *occurs positively* in $\mathcal{T}$ if it occurs on the right-hand side of a concept inclusion in $\mathcal{T}$. For each concept $\exists S.D$ occurring positively in $\mathcal{T}$ (where D is either a concept name or $\top$), we introduce a *witness* $w_{\exists S.D}$ and define a *generating relation* $\leadsto_{\mathcal{T},\mathcal{A}}$ on the set of these witnesses together with $\mathsf{ind}(\mathcal{A})$ by taking:

$$a \leadsto_{\mathcal{T},\mathcal{A}} w_{\exists S.D} \qquad \text{if} \qquad a \in \mathsf{ind}(\mathcal{A}) \text{ and } (\mathcal{T}, \mathcal{A}) \models (\exists S.D)(a),$$
$$w_{\exists P.A} \leadsto_{\mathcal{T},\mathcal{A}} w_{\exists S.D} \qquad \text{if} \qquad \mathcal{T} \models A \sqsubseteq \exists S.D.$$

The *generating model* $\mathcal{G}_{\mathcal{T},\mathcal{A}}$ for $(\mathcal{T}, \mathcal{A})$ is defined as follows:

$$\Delta^{\mathcal{G}_{\mathcal{T},\mathcal{A}}} = \mathsf{ind}(\mathcal{A}) \;\cup\; \{\, w_{\exists S.D} \mid \exists S.D \text{ occurs positively in } \mathcal{T} \,\},$$
$$a^{\mathcal{G}_{\mathcal{T},\mathcal{A}}} = a, \qquad \text{for } a \in \mathsf{ind}(\mathcal{A}),$$
$$A^{\mathcal{G}_{\mathcal{T},\mathcal{A}}} = \{\, a \in \mathsf{ind}(\mathcal{A}) \mid (\mathcal{T}, \mathcal{A}) \models A(a) \,\} \;\cup$$
$$\{\, w_{\exists S.D} \mid \mathcal{T} \models D \sqsubseteq A \,\}, \qquad \text{for a concept name } A,$$
$$P^{\mathcal{G}_{\mathcal{T},\mathcal{A}}} = \{(a,b) \mid S(a,b) \in \mathcal{A},\ \mathcal{T} \models S \sqsubseteq P\} \;\cup$$
$$\{(w, w_{\exists S.D}) \mid w \leadsto_{\mathcal{T},\mathcal{A}} w_{\exists S.D},\ \mathcal{T} \models S \sqsubseteq P\}, \quad \text{for a role name } P.$$

It should be clear that $\mathcal{G}_{\mathcal{T},\mathcal{A}}$ can be constructed in polynomial number of steps by the modified forward chaining procedure that does not invent fresh labelled nulls for $\exists S.D$ but instead re-uses the existing element $w_{\exists S.D}$ in the domain. The following theorem shows that $\mathcal{G}_{\mathcal{T},\mathcal{A}}$ is indeed a model of $(\mathcal{T}, \mathcal{A})$ and it provides enough information about all concept and role subsumptions and about instance queries.

Theorem 22 (Baader et al. (2005)). *Let $(\mathcal{T}, \mathcal{A})$ be an EL knowledge base. Then $\mathcal{G}_{\mathcal{T},\mathcal{A}} \models (\mathcal{T}, \mathcal{A})$. In addition, we have the following:*

(i) $(\mathcal{T}, \mathcal{A}) \models C_1 \sqsubseteq C_2$ if and only if $\mathcal{G}_{\mathcal{T},\mathcal{A}} \models C_1 \sqsubseteq C_2$;
(ii) $(\mathcal{T}, \mathcal{A}) \models P_1 \sqsubseteq P_2$ if and only if $\mathcal{G}_{\mathcal{T},\mathcal{A}} \models P_1 \sqsubseteq P_2$;
(iii) $(\mathcal{T}, \mathcal{A}) \models C(a)$ if and only if $\mathcal{G}_{\mathcal{T},\mathcal{A}} \models C(a)$;
(iv) $(\mathcal{T}, \mathcal{A}) \models P(a,b)$ if and only if $\mathcal{G}_{\mathcal{T},\mathcal{A}} \models P(a,b)$.

Since the generating model $\mathcal{G}_{\mathcal{T},\mathcal{A}}$ can be constructed in polynomial time in the size of $(\mathcal{T}, \mathcal{A})$, concept and role subsumption are tractable; the same concerns instance checking (matching lower bounds will be discussed in Section 4).

Theorem 23. *The problems of concept and role subsumption and instance checking are* P*-complete in EL.*

However, the following example shows that $\mathcal{G}_{\mathcal{T},\mathcal{A}}$ cannot be directly used to compute answers to conjunctive queries.[13]

Example 24. Consider $(\mathcal{T}, \mathcal{A})$ from Example 17 and the CQ

$$q = \exists x \, \mathsf{parent}(x, x).$$

It should be clear that the answer to q over $(\mathcal{T}, \mathcal{A})$ is 'no' because $\mathcal{C}_{\mathcal{T},\mathcal{A}} \not\models q$; see Fig. 5. On the other hand, since the generating model $\mathcal{G}_{\mathcal{T},\mathcal{A}}$ contains a loop (see Fig. 6), we have $\mathcal{G}_{\mathcal{T},\mathcal{A}} \models q$.

We call $\mathcal{G}_{\mathcal{T},\mathcal{A}}$ generating because the standard canonical model $\mathcal{C}_{\mathcal{T},\mathcal{A}}$ of $(\mathcal{T}, \mathcal{A})$ can be generated by unravelling cycles of the generating relation $\leadsto_{\mathcal{T},\mathcal{A}}$ into infinite trees: for example, $\mathcal{G}_{\mathcal{T},\mathcal{A}}$ in Fig. 6 can be unravelled into $\mathcal{C}_{\mathcal{T},\mathcal{A}}$ in Fig. 5. We remark that the generating model defined here was initially represented as a pair functions by Brandt (2004) and later called the canonical model; see e.g., (Lutz and Wolter, 2007). We prefer the term generating model to avoid confusion with the (possibly infinite) canonical model (the chase).

In Section 4, we shall return to the problem of answering CQs over *EL* knowledge bases and revisit the canonical model construction. In the meantime, we consider the third profile of OWL 2.

3.3   OWL 2 QL

The OWL 2 QL profile[14] of OWL 2 was designed for *ontology-based data access* via query rewriting, where answering CQs over a knowledge base is reduced to answering first-order queries over a database storing the ABox of the KB (this will be discussed in Section 4). OWL 2 QL is based on the logics of the DL-Lite family (Calvanese et al., 2007; Artale et al., 2009).

In this section, we consider a somewhat simplified version of OWL 2 QL, which will be called *QL*. (It is almost identical to what is known as *DL-Lite$_{\mathcal{R}}$* (Calvanese et al., 2007) or *DL-Lite$_{core}^{\mathcal{H}}$* (Artale et al., 2009).) Concept and role inclusions in *QL* are of the form

$$B \sqsubseteq C \qquad \text{and} \qquad R_1 \sqsubseteq R_2,$$

where R_1 and R_2 are roles (role names or their inverses) and B and C are concepts defined by the following grammar:

$$
\begin{array}{llll}
B & ::= & A & | \quad \exists R.\top, \\
C & ::= & A & | \quad \exists R.\top \quad | \quad \exists R.C.
\end{array}
$$

---

[13] The generating model can be used the for answering CQs but the given query has to be modified to take account of identifications of the labelled nulls. This is known as the *combined approach* to query answering, see (Lutz et al., 2009) for the case of *EL* and (Kontchakov et al., 2011) for the case of *QL*. Alternatively, a special procedure has to filter out spurious answers resulting from identification (Lutz et al., 2013).

[14] `www.w3.org/TR/owl2-profiles/#OWL_2_QL`

ABoxes in QL are simple; see Section 3.1. Note that the universal restrictions are not allowed at all and the existential restrictions on the left-hand side of concept inclusions must have $\top$ as their filler (such existential restrictions are called *unqualified* and the $\top$ symbol is often omitted, making $\exists R$ out of $\exists R.\top$); however, the existential restrictions on the right-hand side of concept inclusions can be qualified. Similarly to the case of EL, the standard first-order translations of QL TBoxes require existential quantification, which causes the canonical models to be infinite.

Analogously to EL TBoxes, one can transform any QL TBox to an equivalent one in normal form (see Theorem 20).

Definition 25. A QL TBox is said to be in *normal form* if any concept inclusion in it looks as follows:

$$A' \sqsubseteq A, \qquad \exists R \sqsubseteq A \quad \text{or} \quad A \sqsubseteq \exists R.D,$$

where R is a role, A and A' are concept names and D is either a concept name or $\top$.

Given a QL knowledge base $(\mathcal{T}, \mathcal{A})$ with $\mathcal{T}$ in normal form, we can find all answers to a CQ q over this KB by evaluating q over the (possibly infinite) canonical model $\mathcal{C}_{\mathcal{T},\mathcal{A}}$, which can be constructed using forward chaining (cf. Section 3.2). We begin by taking the standard model $\mathcal{I}_{\mathcal{A}}$ of the ABox as $\mathcal{I}_0$ (see Definition 12) and apply inductively the following rules to obtain $\mathcal{I}_{k+1}$ from $\mathcal{I}_k$:

(c′) if $d \in B^{\mathcal{I}_k}$ and $B \sqsubseteq A \in \mathcal{T}$, then we add d to $A^{\mathcal{I}_{k+1}}$;
(r′) if $(d, d') \in R_1^{\mathcal{I}_k}$ and $R_1 \sqsubseteq R_2 \in \mathcal{T}$, then we add (d, d') to $R_2^{\mathcal{I}_{k+1}}$;
(e) if $d \in B^{\mathcal{I}_k}$ and $B \sqsubseteq \exists R.D \in \mathcal{T}$, where D is a concept name or $\top$, then we take a *fresh* labelled null, d', and add d' to $D^{\mathcal{I}_{k+1}}$ and (d, d') to $R^{\mathcal{I}_{k+1}}$.

(These rules are similar to the rules from Section 3.2 except that they refer to roles with inverses and QL concepts).

The canonical model $\mathcal{C}_{\mathcal{T},\mathcal{A}}$ constructed using rules **(c′)**, **(r′)** and **(e)** in a bottom-up fashion can alternatively be defined by unravelling the generating structure, which is closer to the top-down approach and will be required for query rewriting in Section 4. There are two key observations that lead us to the alternative definition: first, fresh labelled nulls can only be added by applying **(e)**, and, second, if two labelled nulls, d_1 and d_2, are introduced by applying **(e)** with the same concept inclusion $B \sqsubseteq \exists R.D$ then the same rules will be applicable to d_1 and d_2 in the continuation of the forward chaining procedure. So, each labelled null d' resulting from applying **(e)** to some $B \sqsubseteq \exists R.D$ on a domain element d can be identified with a pair of the form $(d, \exists R.D)$. More formally, for each concept $\exists R.D$ that occurs positively in $\mathcal{T}$, we introduce a *witness* $w_{\exists R.D}$ and define a *generating relation* $\leadsto_{\mathcal{T},\mathcal{A}}$ on the set of these witnesses together with $\mathsf{ind}(\mathcal{A})$ by taking:

$$a \leadsto_{\mathcal{T},\mathcal{A}} w_{\exists R.D} \quad \text{if} \quad a \in \mathsf{ind}(\mathcal{A}),\ \mathcal{I}_{\mathcal{A}} \models B(a) \text{ and } \mathcal{T} \models B \sqsubseteq \exists R.D,$$
$$w_{\exists S.B} \leadsto_{\mathcal{T},\mathcal{A}} w_{\exists R.D} \quad \text{if} \quad \mathcal{T} \models \exists S^- \sqsubseteq \exists R.D \quad \text{or} \quad \mathcal{T} \models B \sqsubseteq \exists R.D.$$

A $\leadsto_{\mathcal{T},\mathcal{A}}$-*path* σ is a finite sequence $aw_{\exists R_1.D_1} \cdots w_{\exists R_n.D_n}$, $n \geq 0$, such that $a \in \mathsf{ind}(\mathcal{A})$ and, if $n > 0$, then

$$a \leadsto_{\mathcal{T},\mathcal{A}} w_{\exists R_1.D_1} \quad \text{and} \quad w_{\exists R_i.D_i} \leadsto_{\mathcal{T},\mathcal{A}} w_{\exists R_{i+1}.D_{i+1}}, \text{ for } i < n.$$

Thus, a path of the form $\sigma w_{\exists R.D}$ represents the fresh labelled null introduced by applying **(e)** to some $B \sqsubseteq \exists R.D$ on the domain element σ (and which corresponds to the pair $(\sigma, \exists R.D)$ mentioned above). Denote by $\mathsf{tail}(\sigma)$ the last element in σ; as we noted above, the last element in σ uniquely determines all the subsequent rule applications. The *canonical model* $\mathcal{C}_{\mathcal{T},\mathcal{A}}$ is defined by taking $\Delta^{\mathcal{C}_{\mathcal{T},\mathcal{A}}}$ to be the set of all $\leadsto_{\mathcal{T},\mathcal{A}}$-paths and setting

$$a^{\mathcal{C}_{\mathcal{T},\mathcal{A}}} = a, \qquad \text{for } a \in \mathsf{ind}(\mathcal{A}),$$

$$A^{\mathcal{C}_{\mathcal{T},\mathcal{A}}} = \{a \in \mathsf{ind}(\mathcal{A}) \mid \mathcal{I}_\mathcal{A} \models B(a) \text{ and } \mathcal{T} \models B \sqsubseteq A\} \cup$$
$$\{\sigma w_{\exists R.D} \mid \mathcal{T} \models \exists R^- \sqsubseteq A \text{ or } \mathcal{T} \models D \sqsubseteq A\}, \quad \text{for a concept name } A,$$

$$P^{\mathcal{C}_{\mathcal{T},\mathcal{A}}} = \{(a,b) \mid \mathcal{I}_\mathcal{A} \models R(a,b) \text{ and } \mathcal{T} \models R \sqsubseteq P\} \cup$$
$$\{(\sigma w_{\exists R.D}, \sigma) \mid \mathsf{tail}(\sigma) \leadsto_{\mathcal{T},\mathcal{A}} w_{\exists R.D}, \mathcal{T} \models R \sqsubseteq P^-\} \cup$$
$$\{(\sigma, \sigma w_{\exists R.D}) \mid \mathsf{tail}(\sigma) \leadsto_{\mathcal{T},\mathcal{A}} w_{\exists R.D}, \mathcal{T} \models R \sqsubseteq P\}, \quad \text{for a role name } P.$$

Intuitively, by the definition of rule **(c′)**, an ABox individual a belongs to $A^{\mathcal{C}_{\mathcal{T},\mathcal{A}}}$ just in case there is a sequence of concepts $B_0, B_1, \ldots, B_n$ such that $\mathcal{I}_\mathcal{A} \models B_0(a)$, the $B_{i-1} \sqsubseteq B_i$ are in $\mathcal{T}$, for $1 \leq i \leq n$, and $B_n = A$; in other words, if $\mathcal{I}_\mathcal{A} \models B_0(a)$ and $\mathcal{T} \models B_0 \sqsubseteq A$, for some concept B_0. Similarly, by the definition of rules **(c′)** and **(e)**, a labelled null of the form $\sigma w_{\exists R.D}$ belongs to $A^{\mathcal{C}_{\mathcal{T},\mathcal{A}}}$ just in case $\mathcal{T} \models \exists R^- \sqsubseteq A$ or $\mathcal{T} \models D \sqsubseteq A$. For a role name P, rules **(r′)** and **(e)** provide an analogous argument. More precisely, by the definition of rule **(r′)**, a pair (d, d') of domain elements belongs to $P^{\mathcal{C}_{\mathcal{T},\mathcal{A}}}$ just in case there is a sequence of roles $R_0, \ldots, R_n$ such that $(d, d') \in R_0^{\mathcal{C}_{\mathcal{T},\mathcal{A}}}$, the $R_{i-1} \sqsubseteq R_i$ are in $\mathcal{T}$, for $1 \leq i \leq n$, and $R_n = P$; in other words, $(d, d') \in R_0^{\mathcal{C}_{\mathcal{T},\mathcal{A}}}$ and $\mathcal{T} \models R_0 \sqsubseteq P$, for some role R_0. It then follows from the definition of rule **(e)** that a pair (d, d') belongs to $P^{\mathcal{C}_{\mathcal{T},\mathcal{A}}}$ just in three cases: (i) both elements of the pair are ABox individuals with $\mathcal{I}_\mathcal{A} \models R(d, d')$ and $\mathcal{T} \models R \sqsubseteq P$ (ii) the first component of the pair is created by an application of **(e)** to the second component of the pair: $d = \sigma w_{\exists R.D}$, $d' = \sigma$ and $\mathcal{T} \models R \sqsubseteq P^-$ or (iii) the second component of the pair is created by an application of **(e)** to the first component: $d = \sigma$, $d' = \sigma w_{\exists R.D}$ and $\mathcal{T} \models R \sqsubseteq P$. These three cases are reflected in the three sets in the union in the definition of $P^{\mathcal{C}_{\mathcal{T},\mathcal{A}}}$.

Example 26. Consider a *QL* TBox $\mathcal{T}$ with the following concept and role inclusions:

$$\mathsf{RA} \sqsubseteq \exists\mathsf{worksOn}.\mathsf{Project},$$
$$\mathsf{Project} \sqsubseteq \exists\mathsf{isManagedBy}.\mathsf{Prof},$$
$$\mathsf{worksOn}^- \sqsubseteq \mathsf{involves},$$
$$\mathsf{isManagedBy} \sqsubseteq \mathsf{involves}$$

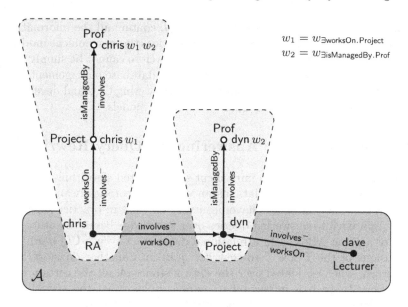

Fig. 7. The canonical model for the knowledge base in Example 26

and an ABox $\mathcal{A}$ comprising the following assertions:

RA(chris),   worksOn(chris, dyn),   Project(dyn),

Lecturer(dave),   worksOn(dave, dyn).

Two concepts occur positively in $\mathcal{T}$: $\exists$worksOn.Project and $\exists$isManagedBy.Prof. For brevity, the witnesses for them will be denoted by w_1 and w_2, respectively. The generating relation $\leadsto_{\mathcal{T},\mathcal{A}}$ is then defined by taking

$$\text{chris} \leadsto_{\mathcal{T},\mathcal{A}} w_1, \qquad \text{dyn} \leadsto_{\mathcal{T},\mathcal{A}} w_2, \qquad w_1 \leadsto_{\mathcal{T},\mathcal{A}} w_2.$$

This gives the following $\leadsto_{\mathcal{T},\mathcal{A}}$-paths:

$$\text{chris}, \qquad \text{chris}\,w_1, \qquad \text{chris}\,w_1\,w_2, \qquad \text{dyn}, \qquad \text{dyn}\,w_2 \quad \text{and} \quad \text{dave}$$

(note that if the graph of $\leadsto_{\mathcal{T},\mathcal{A}}$ contains a cycle then the set of $\leadsto_{\mathcal{T},\mathcal{A}}$-paths is infinite; cf. Example 17). The resulting canonical model $\mathcal{C}_{\mathcal{T},\mathcal{A}}$ is depicted in Fig. 7.

For any QL knowledge base, the defined canonical model is universal, and thus contains all the necessary information for checking concept and role subsumptions, answering instance queries and, more generally, for answering CQs:

Theorem 27. *Let $(\mathcal{T}, \mathcal{A})$ be a QL knowledge base. Then $\mathcal{C}_{\mathcal{T},\mathcal{A}} \models (\mathcal{T}, \mathcal{A})$ and, for any CQ $q(x)$ and any tuple a in* ind$(\mathcal{A})$, *we have*

$$(\mathcal{T}, \mathcal{A}) \models q(a) \quad \text{if and only if} \quad \mathcal{C}_{\mathcal{T},\mathcal{A}} \models q(a).$$

Although the canonical models in *EL* and *QL* contain all the information required to compute answers to conjunctive queries, these canonical models are not necessarily finite (in contrast to *RL*), and therefore cannot be simply materialised, say, by a datalog engine, a triple store or a database management system. In the next section, we analyse the problem of answering CQs and develop practical techniques for dealing with infinite canonical models.

4   Conjunctive Query Answering via Query Rewriting

Database management systems implement sophisticated algorithms for evaluating SQL queries over relational data instances. The (theoretically and empirically supported) fact that databases have been very efficient in practice suggests the following approach to answering queries over knowledge bases. We store the assertions of a given ABox $\mathcal{A}$ in a relational database. Given a CQ $q(x)$, we use the inclusions of the TBox $\mathcal{T}$ to 'rewrite' $q(x)$ into another query $q'(x)$ that would return, when evaluated over the data instance $\mathcal{A}$, all the certain answers to $q(x)$ over $(\mathcal{T}, \mathcal{A})$. It is important to emphasise here that the rewriting $q'(x)$ must only depend on the TBox $\mathcal{T}$ and the given query $q(x)$, and so should work for *all possible* ABoxes $\mathcal{A}$. Thus, we arrive to the following definition.

We call a CQ $q(x)$ and a TBox $\mathcal{T}$ *first-order rewritable* (FO-rewritable, for short) if there exists a first-order formula $q'(x)$ such that, for any ABox $\mathcal{A}$ and any tuple a of individuals in $\mathcal{A}$, we have

$$(\mathcal{T}, \mathcal{A}) \models q(a) \qquad \text{if and only if} \qquad \mathcal{I}_{\mathcal{A}} \models q'(a), \tag{10}$$

where $\mathcal{I}_{\mathcal{A}}$ is the standard model of $\mathcal{A}$ (see Definition 12). The formula $q'(x)$ is called an *FO-rewriting of q and $\mathcal{T}$*.

This idea of reducing CQ answering over knowledge bases to database query answering, first formulated by Calvanese et al. (2005), may sound too good to be applicable in all cases. In fact, there are a few issues in realising this idea.

A minor one is that, from a practical point of view, if an FO-rewriting $q'(x)$ is to be executed by a relational database engine then $q'(x)$ must be a domain-independent query (Abiteboul et al., 1995). This is the case, in particular, for FO-rewritings that contain only conjunction, disjunction and existential quantifiers. Such rewritings (and formulas) are called *positive existential rewritings* (PE-rewritings, for short).

A more serious issue is that not all DL constructs can guarantee FO-rewritability of all CQs. To understand why, let us recall (Libkin, 2004) that the problem of evaluating a first-order formula in a given interpretation belongs the class AC^0 for *data complexity*. Data complexity is a complexity measure that only takes account of the size of the data (the interpretation in this case) and regards the query to be fixed. This measure was suggested by Vardi (1982) who tried to find a theoretical explanation of the practical efficiency of database management systems. It is also known from the complexity theory that AC^0 is a *proper* subclass of LOGSPACE and that LOGSPACE $\subseteq$ NLOGSPACE $\subseteq$ P (Papadimitriou, 1994; Arora and Barak, 2009). It follows that if the problem '$(\mathcal{T}, \mathcal{A}) \models q$?' is

NLogSpace- or P-hard, for some fixed q and $\mathcal{T}$, then these q and $\mathcal{T}$ cannot be FO-rewritable. This observation allows us to identify the DL constructs that can ruin FO-rewritability. Here we give two simple examples illustrating this technique; for more consult, e.g., (Calvanese et al., 2006; Artale et al., 2009).

Example 28. A typical example of an NLogSpace-complete problem is the *reachability problem* for directed graphs: given a directed graph $G = (V, E)$ with vertices V and arcs E and two distinguished vertices $s, t \in V$, decide whether there is a directed path from s to t in G. We represent the graph and the target vertex by means of an ABox $\mathcal{A}_{G,t}$ comprising

$$\mathsf{edge}(v_1, v_2), \quad \text{for } (v_1, v_2) \in E,$$
$$\mathsf{ReachableFromTarget}(t).$$

Consider now a TBox containing concept inclusion

$$\exists\mathsf{edge}.\mathsf{ReachableFromTarget} \sqsubseteq \mathsf{ReachableFromTarget}$$

and the Boolean CQ

$$q = \mathsf{ReachableFromTarget}(s).$$

It is readily seen that $(\mathcal{T}, \mathcal{A}_{G,t}) \models q$ if and only if there is a directed path from s to t in G. Therefore, the problem '$(\mathcal{T}, \mathcal{A}_{G,t}) \models q$?' is NLogSpace-hard. Since q and $\mathcal{T}$ are fixed (and do not depend on G or t), q and $\mathcal{T}$ cannot be FO-rewritable. In other words, TBoxes capable of computing the transitive closure of some relations in ABoxes do not allow FO-rewritability.

Example 29. Next, we consider an example of a P-complete problem. Let (V, E) be a pair that consists of a finite set of vertices V and a relation $E \subseteq V \times V \times V$. A vertex $v \in V$ is said to be *accessible* from a set $S \subseteq V$ of source vertices in (V, E) if either $v \in S$ or $(v_1, v_2, v) \in E$, for some v_1 and v_2 that are accessible from S in (V, E) (v_1 and v_2 are called inputs and v the output; such a triple can also be thought of as an implication of the form $v_1 \wedge v_2 \to v$). The *path system accessibility* problem is defined as follows: given (V, E) as above, source vertices $S \subseteq V$ and a terminal vertex $t \in V$, decide whether t is accessible from S in (V, E). This problem is known to be P-complete (Garey and Johnson, 1979). The path system (V, E) and source vertices S can be encoded by an ABox $\mathcal{A}_{V,E,S}$ in the following way:

$\mathsf{Accessible}(v)$,	for $v \in S$,
$\mathsf{input}_1(e, v_1)$, $\mathsf{input}_2(e, v_2)$ and $\mathsf{output}(v, e)$,	for $e = (v_1, v_2, v) \in E$.

Consider now a TBox $\mathcal{T}$ containing

$$\exists\mathsf{input}_1.\mathsf{Accessible} \sqcap \exists\mathsf{input}_2.\mathsf{Accessible} \sqsubseteq \mathsf{BothInputsAccessible},$$
$$\exists\mathsf{output}.\mathsf{BothInputsAccessible} \sqsubseteq \mathsf{Accessible}$$

and the Boolean CQ

$$q = \mathsf{Accessible}(t).$$

It should be clear that $(\mathcal{T}, \mathcal{A}_{V,E,S}) \models \mathsf{Accessible}(v)$ if and only if v is accessible from S in (V, E); and $(\mathcal{T}, \mathcal{A}) \models \mathsf{BothInputsAccessible}(e)$ if and only if *both* inputs of e are accessible, that is, both are instances of $\mathsf{Accessible}$. Therefore, the answer to q is 'yes' if and only if t is accessible from S in (V, E). Thus, the problem '$(\mathcal{T}, \mathcal{A}_{V,E,S}) \models q$' is P-hard, and so these fixed q and $\mathcal{T}$ cannot be FO-rewritable.

The OWL 2 QL profile of OWL 2 was designed so that problems such as graph reachability and path system accessibility above could not be expressed in it (on the other hand, observe that both of the TBoxes above belong to RL and EL, which proves the lower complexity bounds in Theorems 16 and 23). A number of various rewriting techniques have been proposed and implemented for OWL 2 QL: PerfectRef (Poggi et al., 2008), Presto / Prexto (Rosati and Almatelli, 2010; Rosati, 2012), as well as for extensions of OWL 2 QL to datalog$^{\pm}$ and existential rules: Nyaya (Gottlob et al., 2011) and PURE (König et al., 2012) and more expressive DLs: Requiem / Blackout (Pérez-Urbina et al., 2009, 2012), Rapid (Chortaras et al., 2011) and Clipper (Eiter et al., 2012), which go beyond FO-rewritability.

In this section, we discuss the tree-witness rewriting (Kikot et al., 2012b). We require the following definitions in the sequel. Whenever convenient, we write $S(z)$ for either a unary atom $A(z_1)$ or a binary atom $P(z_1, z_2)$; we also identify $P^-(z_2, z_1)$ with $P(z_1, z_2)$. Any CQ $q(x) = \exists y \, \varphi(x, y)$ is regarded as the set of atoms in φ, so we can write $S(z) \in q$ (when referring to the query as a set of atoms, we often omit the answer variables). Any set q of atoms can also be viewed as an interpretation over the domain of its terms (variables and individual names) such that an atom $S(z)$ is true in this interpretation just in case $S(z) \in q$. We slightly abuse notation and denote by q both the set of atoms and the corresponding interpretation. The reason behind these definitions and notations is as follows: it is not hard to see that $\mathcal{I} \models q(a)$ if and only if there is a homomorphism from $q(a)$ to $\mathcal{I}$ (see Definition 14).

4.1   PE-Rewriting for Flat *QL* (and RDFS)

We first consider an important special case of *flat QL* TBoxes that do not contain existential quantifiers on the right-hand side of concept inclusions. In other words, flat QL TBoxes in normal form can only contain concept and role inclusions of the form

$$A \sqsubseteq A', \qquad \exists R \sqsubseteq A \quad \text{and} \quad R \sqsubseteq R',$$

for concept names A and A' and roles R and R'. Note that the language of flat QL TBoxes differs from the language of RDFS[15] only in that QL allows inverse roles in role inclusions whereas RDFS restricts role inclusions to just role names.

---

[15] www.w3.org/TR/rdf-schema

Let $\mathcal{T}$ be a flat QL TBox and $q(x)$ a conjunctive query. By Theorem 27, $(\mathcal{T}, \mathcal{A}) \models q(a)$ if and only if $q(a)$ is true in the canonical model $\mathcal{C}_{\mathcal{T}, \mathcal{A}}$. Since the TBox is flat, the generating relation $\leadsto_{\mathcal{T}, \mathcal{A}}$ is empty, the canonical model $\mathcal{C}_{\mathcal{T}, \mathcal{A}}$ contains no labelled nulls, and so, by the definition of $\mathcal{C}_{\mathcal{T}, \mathcal{A}}$, we have

$$\mathcal{C}_{\mathcal{T}, \mathcal{A}} \models A(a) \quad \text{if and only if} \quad \mathcal{I}_{\mathcal{A}} \models B(a) \text{ and } \mathcal{T} \models B \sqsubseteq A, \text{ for some } B,$$
$$\mathcal{C}_{\mathcal{T}, \mathcal{A}} \models P(a, b) \quad \text{if and only if} \quad \mathcal{I}_{\mathcal{A}} \models R(a, b) \text{ and } \mathcal{T} \models R \sqsubseteq P, \text{ for some } R.$$

Define a PE-formula $q_{\text{ext}}(x)$ to be the result of replacing every atom $A(z)$ in $q(x)$ with $A_{\text{ext}}(z)$ and every atom $P(z_1, z_2)$ in $q(x)$ with $P_{\text{ext}}(z_1, z_2)$, where

$$A_{\text{ext}}(u) = \bigvee_{\mathcal{T} \models B \sqsubseteq A} ST_u(B), \qquad P_{\text{ext}}(u, v) = \bigvee_{\mathcal{T} \models R \sqsubseteq P} ST_{u,v}(R),$$

and ST is the standard translation defined in Section 3.1. It is not hard to see that, for any ABox $\mathcal{A}$ and any tuple a from $\text{ind}(\mathcal{A})$, we have $\mathcal{C}_{\mathcal{T}, \mathcal{A}} \models q(a)$ if and only if $\mathcal{I}_{\mathcal{A}} \models q_{\text{ext}}(a)$.

Proposition 30. *For any CQ $q(x)$ and any flat QL TBox $\mathcal{T}$, $q_{\text{ext}}(x)$ is a PE-rewriting of $q(x)$ and $\mathcal{T}$.*

Thus, in the case of flat QL TBoxes, it is really easy to construct PE-rewritings.

Example 31. Consider the CQ

$$q(x, y) \quad = \quad \text{Student}(x) \land \text{takesCourse}(x, y) \land \text{teacherOf}(\text{p0}, y)$$

and a flat QL TBox $\mathcal{T}$ with the following concept and role inclusions:

$$\text{UndergraduateStudent} \sqsubseteq \text{Student},$$
$$\text{enrolledAt} \sqsubseteq \text{Student},$$
$$\text{teaches}^- \sqsubseteq \text{teacherOf}.$$

We then define the following formulas for concept and role names from the query:

$$\text{Student}_{\text{ext}}(u) \ = \ \text{Student}(u) \lor \text{UndergraduateStudent}(u) \lor$$
$$\exists v \, \text{enrolledAt}(u, v),$$
$$\text{takesCourse}_{\text{ext}}(u, v) \ = \ \text{takesCourse}(u, v),$$
$$\text{teacherOf}_{\text{ext}}(u, v) \ = \ \text{teacherOf}(u, v) \lor \text{teaches}(v, u),$$

and we obtain the following PE-rewriting of $q(x, y)$ and $\mathcal{T}$:

$$q_{\text{ext}}(x, y) \ = \ \big(\text{Student}(x) \lor \text{UndergraduateStudent}(x) \lor \exists v \, \text{enrolledAt}(x, v)\big) \ \land$$
$$\text{takesCourse}(x, y) \ \land \ \big(\text{teacherOf}(\text{p0}, y) \lor \text{teaches}(y, \text{p0})\big).$$

Next, we turn to the case of general QL TBoxes.

4.2   Tree-Witness PE-Rewriting for Full QL

Suppose $\mathcal{T}$ is a QL TBox in normal form. By Theorem 27, to compute certain answers to $q(x)$ over $(\mathcal{T}, \mathcal{A})$, for some $\mathcal{A}$, it is enough to find answers to $q(x)$ in the canonical model $\mathcal{C}_{\mathcal{T},\mathcal{A}}$. To do this, we have to check, for every tuple a of elements in $\mathsf{ind}(\mathcal{A})$, whether there exists a homomorphism from $q(a)$ to $\mathcal{C}_{\mathcal{T},\mathcal{A}}$. Thus, as in the case of flat TBoxes, the answer variables take values from $\mathsf{ind}(\mathcal{A})$. However, the existentially quantified variables in $q(x)$ can be mapped both to $\mathsf{ind}(\mathcal{A})$ and to the labelled nulls in $\mathcal{C}_{\mathcal{T},\mathcal{A}}$. In order to define the rewriting that does not depend on a particular ABox, we need to have a closer look at the structure of the canonical models $\mathcal{C}_{\mathcal{T},\mathcal{A}}$ with fixed $\mathcal{T}$ and varying $\mathcal{A}$.

Let $\exists R.D$ be a concept occurring positively in $\mathcal{T}$ (recall that D is either a concept name or $\top$). For an individual name a, we define the $\exists R.D$-*generated $\mathcal{T}$-tree on a* as the restriction of the canonical model of the KB $(\mathcal{T}, \{(\exists R.D)(a)\})$ to the domain that consists of a and the labelled nulls with the prefix $aw_{\exists R.D}$. We denote this tree by $\mathcal{C}_{\mathcal{T}}^{\exists R.D}(a)$. (Note that $\mathcal{C}_{\mathcal{T}}^{\exists R.D}(a)$ is not necessarily a model of $\mathcal{T}$.) Take now any ABox $\mathcal{A}$ and any $a \in \mathsf{ind}(\mathcal{A})$. By the definition of the canonical model, if $a \leadsto_{\mathcal{T},\mathcal{A}} w_{\exists R.D}$ then $\mathcal{C}_{\mathcal{T},\mathcal{A}}$ contains a sub-tree that is isomorphic to the $\exists R.D$-generated $\mathcal{T}$-tree on a, excluding possibly the root. Moreover, such sub-trees may intersect only on their common root a. For instance, the canonical model in Fig. 7 contains the $\exists\mathsf{worksOn}.\mathsf{Project}$-generated $\mathcal{T}$-tree on chris and the $\exists\mathsf{isManagedBy}.\mathsf{Prof}$-generated $\mathcal{T}$-tree on dyn. The following example illustrates a more complex configuration.

Example 32. Consider a TBox $\mathcal{T}$ with the following concept inclusions:

$$A \sqsubseteq \exists R.D, \qquad\qquad D \sqsubseteq \exists P_1, \qquad\qquad D \sqsubseteq \exists P_2,$$
$$B \sqsubseteq \exists S.C$$

and suppose that an ABox $\mathcal{A}$ contains $A(a), P_1(a, b), A(b), B(b), P_2(b, c)$. The canonical model $\mathcal{C}_{\mathcal{T},\mathcal{A}}$ is depicted in Fig. 8. The individual a in this canonical model has a single $\mathcal{T}$-tree generated by $\exists R.D$. The individual b has two $\mathcal{T}$-trees, one generated by $\exists R.D$ and another by $\exists S.C$. These two $\mathcal{T}$-trees intersect only on their common root b.

For a more formal treatment, we require the following opertation. Given interpretations $\mathcal{I}_1$ and $\mathcal{I}_2$ (under the standard name assumption), we define their *join*, $\mathcal{I}_1 \oplus \mathcal{I}_2$, by taking

$$\Delta^{\mathcal{I}_1 \oplus \mathcal{I}_2} = \Delta^{\mathcal{I}_1} \cup \Delta^{\mathcal{I}_2},$$

$$a^{\mathcal{I}_1 \oplus \mathcal{I}_2} = a, \qquad\qquad \text{for an individual } a \text{ in } \mathcal{I}_1 \text{ or } \mathcal{I}_2,$$

$$A^{\mathcal{I}_1 \oplus \mathcal{I}_2} = A^{\mathcal{I}_1} \cup A^{\mathcal{I}_2}, \qquad\qquad \text{for a concept name } A,$$

$$P^{\mathcal{I}_1 \oplus \mathcal{I}_2} = P^{\mathcal{I}_1} \cup P^{\mathcal{I}_2}, \qquad\qquad \text{for a role name } P.$$

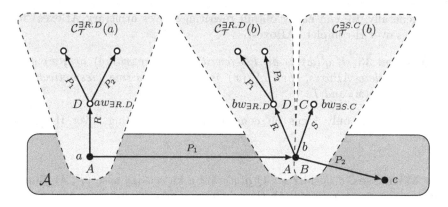

Fig. 8. The canonical model $\mathcal{C}_{\mathcal{T},\mathcal{A}}$ from Example 32

Then the canonical model $\mathcal{C}_{\mathcal{T},\mathcal{A}}$ of any QL knowledge base $(\mathcal{T},\mathcal{A})$, with $\mathcal{T}$ in normal form, can be represented as the following join:

$$\mathcal{C}_{\mathcal{T},\mathcal{A}} \;=\; \mathcal{I}_{\mathcal{A}}^* \;\oplus\; \bigoplus_{\substack{a\in\mathsf{ind}(\mathcal{A}) \\ B\sqsubseteq\exists R.D\in\mathcal{T}\text{ with }\mathcal{I}_{\mathcal{A}}^*\models B(a)}} \mathcal{C}_{\mathcal{T}}^{\exists R.D}(a), \qquad (11)$$

where $\mathcal{I}_{\mathcal{A}}^*$ is a model of $\mathcal{A}$ with domain $\mathsf{ind}(\mathcal{A})$, which will be called the *ABox part* of $\mathcal{C}_{\mathcal{T},\mathcal{A}}$; the join of the $\mathcal{C}_{\mathcal{T}}^{\exists R.D}(a)$ will be called the *anonymous part* of $\mathcal{C}_{\mathcal{T},\mathcal{A}}$. We are now fully equipped to present the tree-witness rewriting of a CQ $q(x)$ and a QL TBox $\mathcal{T}$.

Following the divide and conquer strategy, we show how the process of constructing FO-rewritings can be split into two steps: the first step considers only the flat part of the TBox and uses the formulas $A_{\mathsf{ext}}(u)$ and $P_{\mathsf{ext}}(u,v)$ defined in Section 4.1; the second step (to be described below) takes account of the remaining part of the TBox, that is, inclusions of the form $B\sqsubseteq\exists R.D$.

H-completeness. Let $\mathcal{T}$ be a (not necessarily flat) QL TBox. A simple ABox $\mathcal{A}$ is said to be *H-complete with respect to* $\mathcal{T}$ if, for all concept names A and role names P, we have

$$A(a) \in \mathcal{A} \quad \text{if} \quad \mathcal{I}_{\mathcal{A}} \models B(a) \text{ and } \mathcal{T} \models B \sqsubseteq A, \text{ for some } B = A' \text{ or } B = \exists R,$$
$$P(a,b) \in \mathcal{A} \quad \text{if} \quad \mathcal{I}_{\mathcal{A}} \models R(a,b) \text{ and } \mathcal{T} \models R \sqsubseteq P, \text{ for some } R.$$

We say that a first-order formula $q'(x)$ is an *FO-rewriting of $q(x)$ and $\mathcal{T}$ over H-complete ABoxes* if (10) holds for any ABox $\mathcal{A}$ that is H-complete with respect to $\mathcal{T}$ and any tuple a from $\mathsf{ind}(\mathcal{A})$; as before, a PE-rewriting is an FO-rewriting that contains only conjunction, disjunction and existential quantification.

Observe that if an ABox $\mathcal{A}$ is H-complete with respect to $\mathcal{T}$ then the ABox part of $\mathcal{C}_{\mathcal{T},\mathcal{A}}$, that is, $\mathcal{I}_{\mathcal{A}}^*$ in (11), coincides with $\mathcal{I}_{\mathcal{A}}$. Thus, if $\mathcal{T}$ is flat then $q(x)$ itself is clearly a PE- and FO-rewriting of $q(x)$ and $\mathcal{T}$ over H-complete ABoxes.

More generally, we can easily obtain rewritings (over arbitrary ABoxes) from rewritings over H-complete ABoxes:

Proposition 33. *If $q'(x)$ is an FO-rewriting (PE-rewriting) of $q(x)$ and $\mathcal{T}$ over H-complete ABoxes, then $q'_{\text{ext}}(x)$ is an FO-rewriting (respectively, PE-rewriting) of $q(x)$ and $\mathcal{T}$.*

Thus, we can only focus on constructing PE-rewritings over H-complete ABoxes.

Tree Witnesses. Consider a CQ $q(x)$ and a knowledge base $(\mathcal{T}, \mathcal{A})$. Suppose that, for some tuple a in $\text{ind}(\mathcal{A})$, there is a homomorphism h from $q(a)$ to $\mathcal{C}_{\mathcal{T},\mathcal{A}}$. Then h partitions $q(a)$ into the atoms mapped by h to the ABox part and atoms mapped by h to the $\exists R.D$-generated $\mathcal{T}$-trees of the anonymous part of $\mathcal{C}_{\mathcal{T},\mathcal{A}}$. The tree-witness rewriting of $q(x)$ and $\mathcal{T}$ we are going to present now lists all possible partitions of the atoms of $q(x)$ into such subsets. We begin with an example illustrating this idea.

Example 34. Consider the QL TBox $\mathcal{T}$ from Example 26 with the concept and role inclusions

$$\text{RA} \sqsubseteq \exists\text{worksOn.Project}, \tag{12}$$
$$\text{Project} \sqsubseteq \exists\text{isManagedBy.Prof}, \tag{13}$$
$$\text{worksOn}^- \sqsubseteq \text{involves}, \tag{14}$$
$$\text{isManagedBy} \sqsubseteq \text{involves} \tag{15}$$

and the CQ asking to find those who work with professors:

$$q(x) \;=\; \exists y, z \,\big(\text{worksOn}(x,y) \wedge \text{involves}(y,z) \wedge \text{Prof}(z)\big).$$

Recall that if the canonical model $\mathcal{C}_{\mathcal{T},\mathcal{A}}$, for some ABox $\mathcal{A}$, contains some individuals $a \in \text{RA}^{\mathcal{C}_{\mathcal{T},\mathcal{A}}}$ and $b \in \text{Project}^{\mathcal{C}_{\mathcal{T},\mathcal{A}}}$, then $\mathcal{C}_{\mathcal{T},\mathcal{A}}$ must also contain the $\exists\text{worksOn.Project}$-generated $\mathcal{T}$-tree on a and the $\exists\text{isManagedBy.Prof}$-generated $\mathcal{T}$-tree on b; see Fig. 7, where such an a is chris and such a b is dyn. Let us consider all possible ways of obtaining certain answers to the query, that is, all possible homomorphisms from atoms of $q(x)$ to $\mathcal{C}_{\mathcal{T},\mathcal{A}}$ such that the answer variable x is mapped to $\text{ind}(\mathcal{A})$. First, x, y and z can be mapped to ABox individuals. Alternatively, x and y can be mapped to ABox individuals, a and b, and if b belongs to $\text{Project}^{\mathcal{C}_{\mathcal{T},\mathcal{A}}}$, then there is a homomorphism h_1 from the last two atoms of $q(a)$ to the anonymous part; see Fig. 9. Another option is to map only x to an ABox individual, a, and if a belongs to $\text{RA}^{\mathcal{C}_{\mathcal{T},\mathcal{A}}}$ then the whole $q(a)$ can be homomorphically mapped to the anonymous part; see h_2 in Fig. 9. Finally, another homomorphism, h_3 in Fig. 9, maps both x and z to a provided that a is in $\text{RA}^{\mathcal{C}_{\mathcal{T},\mathcal{A}}}$ and $\text{Prof}^{\mathcal{C}_{\mathcal{T},\mathcal{A}}}$ at the same time. The possible ways of mapping subsets of a query to the anonymous part of the canonical model are called *tree*

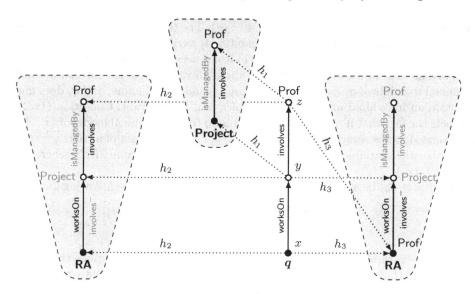

Fig. 9. Three homomorphisms from subsets of q to $\mathcal{T}$-trees

witnesses. The three tree witnesses for $q(x)$ and $\mathcal{T}$ found above give rise to the following PE-rewriting $q_{\text{tw}}(x)$ of $q(x)$ and $\mathcal{T}$ over H-complete ABoxes:

$$q_{\text{tw}}(x) \;=\; \exists y, z \left[\bigl(\mathsf{worksOn}(x,y) \wedge \mathsf{involves}(y,z) \wedge \mathsf{Prof}(z)\bigr) \vee \right.$$
$$\bigl(\mathsf{worksOn}(x,y) \wedge \mathsf{Project}(y)\bigr) \vee$$
$$\left. \mathsf{RA}(x) \vee \bigl(\mathsf{RA}(x) \wedge \mathsf{Prof}(z) \wedge (x = z)\bigr) \right].$$

We now give a general definition of the tree-witness rewriting over H-complete ABoxes. Let $\mathcal{T}$ be a *QL* TBox in normal form and $q(\boldsymbol{x})$ a CQ. Consider a pair $\mathsf{t} = (\mathsf{t_r}, \mathsf{t_i})$ of disjoint sets of terms in $q(\boldsymbol{x})$, where $\mathsf{t_i}$ is non-empty and contains only existentially quantified variables ($\mathsf{t_r}$, on the other hand, can be empty and can contain answer variables and individual names). Set

$$q_{\mathsf{t}} \;=\; \bigl\{ \, S(\boldsymbol{z}) \in q \mid \boldsymbol{z} \subseteq \mathsf{t_r} \cup \mathsf{t_i} \text{ and } \boldsymbol{z} \nsubseteq \mathsf{t_r} \, \bigr\}.$$

We say that t is a *tree witness for $q(\boldsymbol{x})$ and $\mathcal{T}$ generated by $\exists R.D$* if the following two conditions are satisfied:

(tw1) there exists a homomorphism h from q_{t} to $\mathcal{C}_{\mathcal{T}}^{\exists R.D}(a)$, for some a, such that $\mathsf{t_r} = \{z \mid h(z) = a\}$ and $\mathsf{t_i}$ contains the remaining variables in q_{t},

(tw2) q_{t} is a *minimal* subset of q such that, for any $y \in \mathsf{t_i}$, every atom in q containing y belongs to q_{t}.

Note that unary atoms with arguments in $\mathsf{t_r}$ or binary atoms with *both* arguments in $\mathsf{t_r}$ do not belong to q_{t} and, therefore, condition **(tw1)** does not require them to be homomorphically mapped into $\mathcal{C}_{\mathcal{T}}^{\exists R.D}(a)$. The terms in t_r (if any) are called the *roots* of t and the (existentially quantified) variables in t_i the *interior* of t. The homomorphism h in condition (**tw1**) is not necessarily unique; however, it is important that all roots are mapped to a and all variables of the interior are *not* mapped to a. Thus, $\boldsymbol{q}_t$ can contain at most one individual name, a; if $\boldsymbol{q}_t$ does not contain an individual name then the choice of a is irrelevant. Condition (**tw2**) reflects the fact that if a homomorphism from $\boldsymbol{q}$ to the canonical model of $(\mathcal{T}, \mathcal{A})$, for some $\mathcal{A}$, maps a variable y of an atom $R(y, z)$ to a non-root of a tree $\mathcal{C}_{\mathcal{T}}^{\exists R.D}(a)$ then the other variable of the atom must be mapped to the same $\exists R.D$-generated $\mathcal{T}$-tree on a.)

Let $t = (t_r, t_i)$ be a tree witness for $\boldsymbol{q}(\boldsymbol{x})$ and $\mathcal{T}$. Consider the following formula

$$\mathsf{tw}_t \;\; = \;\; \exists u \left[\bigwedge_{x \in t_r} (x = u) \quad \wedge \bigvee_{\substack{B \sqsubseteq \exists R.D \in \mathcal{T} \\ \text{t generated by } \exists R.D}} ST_u(B) \right], \tag{16}$$

whose free variables are the roots, t_r, of t. The formula tw_t describes the ABox individuals that root the trees in the anonymous part of $\mathcal{C}_{\mathcal{T},\mathcal{A}}$ into which the atoms $\boldsymbol{q}_t$ of the tree witness t can be homomorphically mapped. More formally, if $\mathcal{I}_\mathcal{A} \models \mathsf{tw}_t(a, \ldots, a)$, for some $a \in \mathsf{ind}(\mathcal{A})$, then $\mathcal{C}_{\mathcal{T},\mathcal{A}}$ contains the $\exists R.D$-generated $\mathcal{T}$-tree on a, and so there is a homomorphism from $\boldsymbol{q}_t$ to $\mathcal{C}_{\mathcal{T},\mathcal{A}}$ that maps all the roots of t to a. Conversely, if there is a homomorphism from $\boldsymbol{q}_t$ to $\mathcal{C}_{\mathcal{T},\mathcal{A}}$ such that all the roots of t are mapped to a (but all the variables from the interior, t_i, of t are mapped to labelled nulls) then $\mathcal{I}_\mathcal{A} \models \mathsf{tw}_t(a, \ldots, a)$.

Let $\Theta_{\mathcal{T}}^q$ be the set of tree witnesses for $\boldsymbol{q}(\boldsymbol{x})$ and $\mathcal{T}$. Tree witnesses t and t' are said to be *conflicting* if $\boldsymbol{q}_t \cap \boldsymbol{q}_{t'} \neq \emptyset$ (in other words, the interior of one tree witness, say, t, contains a root or an interior variable of the other, t', or the other way round, which makes it impossible to have both tree witnesses mapped into the anonymous part of $\mathcal{C}_{\mathcal{T},\mathcal{A}}$ at the *same time*). A set $\Theta \subseteq \Theta_{\mathcal{T}}^q$ of tree witnesses is said to be *independent* if any two distinct tree witnesses in Θ are non-conflicting. If Θ is independent then we can 'cut' the query $\boldsymbol{q}(\boldsymbol{x})$ into independent subqueries in the following way. Consider a homomorphism that, for each $t \in \Theta$, maps the subset $\boldsymbol{q}_t$ of $\boldsymbol{q}$ to the $\exists R.D$-generated $\mathcal{T}$-tree on some a (provided that t is generated by $\exists R.D$) and maps the remaining atoms in $\boldsymbol{q}$ to the ABox part of $\mathcal{C}_{\mathcal{T},\mathcal{A}}$. By (11), such a homomorphism is possible if there is a tuple $\boldsymbol{a}$ in $\mathsf{ind}(\mathcal{A})$ such that the formula

$$\boldsymbol{q}_{\mathsf{cut}}^\Theta(\boldsymbol{x}) \;\; = \;\; \exists \boldsymbol{y} \left((\boldsymbol{q} \setminus \boldsymbol{q}_\Theta) \wedge \bigwedge_{t \in \Theta} \mathsf{tw}_t \right) \tag{17}$$

holds in $\mathcal{I}_\mathcal{A}$ on $\boldsymbol{a}$, where $\boldsymbol{q} \setminus \boldsymbol{q}_\Theta$ is the conjunction of all the atoms in $\boldsymbol{q}$ that do not belong to $\boldsymbol{q}_t$, for any $t \in \Theta$. (Recall that due to H-completeness of the ABox, $\mathcal{I}_\mathcal{A}^* = \mathcal{I}_\mathcal{A}$.) Conversely, if there is a homomorphism from $\boldsymbol{q}(\boldsymbol{a})$ to $\mathcal{C}_{\mathcal{T},\mathcal{A}}$ then there exists an independent set Θ of tree witnesses such that $\mathcal{I}_\mathcal{A} \models \boldsymbol{q}_{\mathsf{cut}}^\Theta(\boldsymbol{a})$.

The following PE-formula $\boldsymbol{q}_{\mathsf{tw}}(\boldsymbol{x})$ is called the *tree-witness rewriting* of $\boldsymbol{q}(\boldsymbol{x})$ and $\mathcal{T}$ over H-complete ABoxes:

$$\boldsymbol{q}_{\mathsf{tw}}(\boldsymbol{x}) \;\; = \bigvee_{\Theta \subseteq \Theta_{\mathcal{T}}^q \text{ independent}} \boldsymbol{q}_{\mathsf{cut}}^\Theta(\boldsymbol{x}). \tag{18}$$

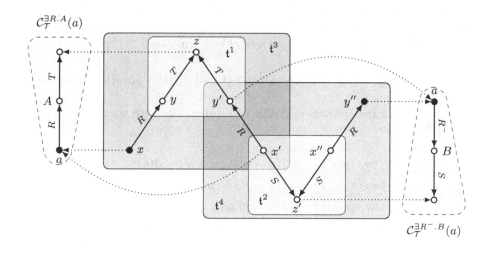

Fig. 10. Tree witnesses in Example 35

Example 35. Consider a TBox with the following concept inclusions:

$$A_0 \sqsubseteq \exists R.A, \qquad\qquad A \sqsubseteq \exists T,$$
$$B_0 \sqsubseteq \exists R^-.B, \qquad\qquad B \sqsubseteq \exists S$$

and the following CQ

$$q(x, y'') = \exists y, z, y', x', z', x'' \, (R(x, y) \wedge T(y, z) \wedge T(y', z) \wedge$$
$$R(x', y') \wedge S(x', z') \wedge S(x'', z') \wedge R(x'', y''))$$

shown in Fig. 10 alongside the $\exists R.A$-generated $\mathcal{T}$-tree and the $\exists R^-.B$-generated $\mathcal{T}$-tree. There are four tree witnesses for $q(x, y'')$ and $\mathcal{T}$:

– $\mathfrak{t}^1 = (\mathfrak{t}^1_r, \mathfrak{t}^1_i)$ generated by $\exists T$ with $\mathfrak{t}^1_r = \{y, y'\}$ and $\mathfrak{t}^1_i = \{z\}$ and

$$q_{\mathfrak{t}^1} = \{\, T(y, z),\ T(y', z)\,\};$$

– $\mathfrak{t}^2 = (\mathfrak{t}^2_r, \mathfrak{t}^2_i)$ generated by $\exists S$ with $\mathfrak{t}^2_r = \{x', x''\}$ and $\mathfrak{t}^2_i = \{z'\}$ and

$$q_{\mathfrak{t}^2} = \{\, S(x', z'),\ S(x'', z')\,\};$$

– $\mathfrak{t}^3 = (\mathfrak{t}^3_r, \mathfrak{t}^3_i)$ generated by $\exists R.A$ with $\mathfrak{t}^3_r = \{x, x'\}$ and $\mathfrak{t}^3_i = \{y, y', z\}$ and

$$q_{\mathfrak{t}^3} = \{\, R(x, y),\ T(y, z),\ T(y', z),\ R(x', y')\,\};$$

– $\mathfrak{t}^4 = (\mathfrak{t}^4_r, \mathfrak{t}^4_i)$ generated by $\exists R^-.B$ with $\mathfrak{t}^4_r = \{y', y''\}$ and $\mathfrak{t}^4_i = \{x', x'', z'\}$ and

$$q_{\mathfrak{t}^4} = \{\, R(x', y'),\ S(x', z'),\ S(x'', z'),\ R(x'', y'')\,\}.$$

Clearly, t^3 and t^4 are conflicting; t^3 is also conflicting with t^1 but not with t^2 despite sharing a common root; symmetrically, t^4 is conflicting with t^2. Thus, we have the following 8 independent sets of tree witnesses:

$$\emptyset, \quad \{t^1\}, \quad \{t^2\}, \quad \{t^3\}, \quad \{t^4\}, \quad \{t^1,t^2\}, \quad \{t^1,t^4\}, \quad \{t^2,t^3\},$$

which result in a tree-witness rewriting of 8 subqueries with the following tree-witness formulas:

$$\begin{aligned}
\mathsf{tw}_{t^1}(y, y') &= \exists u \left((u = y) \wedge (u = y') \wedge A(u)\right), \\
\mathsf{tw}_{t^2}(x', x'') &= \exists u \left((u = x') \wedge (u = x'') \wedge B(u)\right), \\
\mathsf{tw}_{t^3}(x, x') &= \exists u \left((u = x) \wedge (u = x') \wedge A_0(u)\right), \\
\mathsf{tw}_{t^4}(y', y'') &= \exists u \left((u = y') \wedge (u = y'') \wedge B_0(u)\right).
\end{aligned}$$

Theorem 36 (Kikot et al. (2012b)). *Let $\mathcal{T}$ be a QL TBox and $q(x)$ a CQ. For any ABox $\mathcal{A}$ that is H-complete with respect to $\mathcal{T}$ and any tuple a in $\mathsf{ind}(\mathcal{A})$, we have*

$$\mathcal{C}_{\mathcal{T},\mathcal{A}} \models q(a) \quad \text{if and only if} \quad \mathcal{I}_{\mathcal{A}} \models q_{\mathsf{tw}}(a).$$

By Proposition 33, to obtain a PE-rewriting of $q(x)$ and $\mathcal{T}$ over *arbitrary* ABoxes, it is enough to take the tree-witness rewriting $q_{\mathsf{tw}}(x)$ over H-complete ABoxes and replace every atom $S(z)$ in it with $S_{\mathsf{ext}}(z)$.

The number of tree witnesses, $|\Theta_{\mathcal{T}}^q|$, is bounded by $3^{|q|}$. On the other hand, there is a sequence of queries q_n and ontologies $\mathcal{T}_n$ with exponentially many (in $|q_n|$) tree witnesses (Kikot et al., 2012b). The length of q_{tw} is $O(2^{|\Theta_{\mathcal{T}}^q|} \cdot |q| \cdot |\mathcal{T}|)$. It is to be noted that there exist CQs q and QL TBoxes $\mathcal{T}$ any PE-rewritings of which are of exponential size in $|q|$ provided that the rewritings use the same symbols as in q and $\mathcal{T}$ (Kikot et al., 2012a). One can always reduce the size of PE-rewritings to polynomial by employing two new constants that do not occur in q; for details and further references, consult (Gottlob et al., 2014).

If any two tree-witnesses for $q(x)$ and $\mathcal{T}$ are *compatible*—that is, they are either non-conflicting or one is included in the other—then $q_{\mathsf{tw}}(x)$ can be equivalently transformed into the PE-rewriting

$$q'_{\mathsf{tw}}(x) = \exists y \bigwedge_{S(z) \in q} \left(S(z) \vee \bigvee_{t \in \Theta_{\mathcal{T}}^q \text{ with } S(z) \in q_t} \mathsf{tw}_t \right)$$

of size $O(|\Theta_{\mathcal{T}}^q| \cdot |q|^2 \cdot |\mathcal{T}|)$; for details we refer the reader to (Kikot et al., 2012b).

As we saw in Example 29, CQ entailment over *RL* and *EL* knowledge bases is P-hard for data complexity, and so some CQs over such knowledge bases do not have first-order rewritings. In the next two sections, we show that one can always rewrite CQs over *RL* or *EL* TBoxes into datalog queries of polynomial size.

4.3   Datalog Rewriting for *RL*

Recall from Section 3.1 that a *datalog program* is a set of Horn clauses with one positive literal, that is, universally quantified sentences of the form

$$\gamma_0(\boldsymbol{x}) \leftarrow \gamma_1(\boldsymbol{x}) \wedge \cdots \wedge \gamma_n(\boldsymbol{x}),$$

where each variable of the head, $\gamma_0(\boldsymbol{x})$, occurs in at least one of the atoms in the body, $\gamma_1(\boldsymbol{x}), \ldots, \gamma_n(\boldsymbol{x})$. (Following the datalog tradition, we omit the universal quantifiers and write the implication from right to left.) Given a datalog program Π, a set of ground atoms D and a ground atom $Q(\boldsymbol{a})$, we write $(\Pi, D) \models Q(\boldsymbol{a})$ if $Q(\boldsymbol{a})$ is true in every interpretation satisfying D and all clauses of Π, or, equivalently, if $Q(\boldsymbol{a})$ is true in the minimal (or canonical) model of (Π, D), which is constructed in the same way as the canonical models of *RL* knowledge bases (in general, however, the arity of predicates is not bounded by 2).

We say that a CQ $\boldsymbol{q}(\boldsymbol{x})$ and a TBox $\mathcal{T}$ are *datalog-rewritable* if there exist a datalog program Π and a predicate $Q(\boldsymbol{x})$ such that, for any ABox $\mathcal{A}$ and any tuple $\boldsymbol{a}$ of individuals in $\mathcal{A}$, we have

$$(\mathcal{T}, \mathcal{A}) \models \boldsymbol{q}(\boldsymbol{a}) \qquad \text{if and only if} \qquad (\Pi, \mathcal{A}) \models Q(\boldsymbol{a}). \tag{19}$$

(In the following two sections we view any ABox as a set of ground atoms: each concept assertion is a unary ground atom and each role assertion is a binary ground atom.) In this case, the pair $(\Pi, Q(\boldsymbol{x}))$ is called a *datalog rewriting of* $\boldsymbol{q}(\boldsymbol{x})$ *and* $\mathcal{T}$.

Let $\mathcal{T}$ be a *positive RL* TBox, that is, an *RL* TBox without negative concept inclusions of the form $B \sqsubseteq \bot$ (see Section 3.1). Denote by $\Pi_{\mathcal{T}}$ the datalog program that contains the standard translations of all concept and role inclusions in $\mathcal{T}$:

$$ST_u(A) \leftarrow ST_u(B), \qquad \text{for each } B \sqsubseteq A \text{ in } \mathcal{T},$$
$$ST_{u,v}(R_2) \leftarrow ST_{u,v}(R_1), \qquad \text{for each } R_1 \sqsubseteq R_2 \text{ in } \mathcal{T}.$$

(Note that B can be a complex *RL* concept, constructed using $\sqcap$ and $\exists R.C$ with possibly inverse roles.) By Theorem 15, we then obtain the following result:

Corollary 37. *For any positive RL TBox* $\mathcal{T}$ *and any CQ* $\boldsymbol{q}(\boldsymbol{x}) = \exists \boldsymbol{y} \, \varphi(\boldsymbol{x}, \boldsymbol{y})$,

$$(\Pi_{\mathcal{T}} \cup \{Q(\boldsymbol{x}) \leftarrow \varphi(\boldsymbol{x}, \boldsymbol{y})\}, \ Q(\boldsymbol{x}))$$

is a datalog rewriting of $\boldsymbol{q}(\boldsymbol{x})$ *and* $\mathcal{T}$, *where* Q *is a fresh predicate symbol.*

Note that the size of this datalog rewriting is the sum of the sizes of the TBox and the query (thus, it is linear in both).

4.4   Tree-Witness Datalog Rewriting for *EL*

Let $\mathcal{T}$ be an *EL* TBox in normal form (Definition 19). As we saw in Section 3.2, the canonical model of $(\mathcal{T}, \mathcal{A})$ can be defined by unravelling the cycles in the generating model $\mathcal{G}_{\mathcal{T},\mathcal{A}}$. So, the domain of the canonical model consists of $\rightsquigarrow_{\mathcal{T},\mathcal{A}}$-paths of the form $aw_{\exists P_1.D_1} \cdots w_{\exists P_n.D_n}$, $n \geq 0$, such that $a \in \text{ind}(\mathcal{A})$ and, if $n > 0$, then

$$a \rightsquigarrow_{\mathcal{T},\mathcal{A}} w_{\exists P_1.D_1} \quad \text{and} \quad w_{\exists P_i.D_i} \rightsquigarrow_{\mathcal{T},\mathcal{A}} w_{\exists P_{i+1}.D_{i+1}}, \text{ for } i < n.$$

Similarly to the case of QL, we can represent the canonical model as the join of its ABox and anonymous parts. The latter consists of the trees $\mathcal{C}_{\mathcal{T}}^{\exists P.D}(a)$ defined in precisely the same way as in Section 4.2: $\mathcal{C}_{\mathcal{T}}^{\exists P.D}(a)$ is the restriction of the canonical model of $(\mathcal{T}, \{(\exists P.D)(a)\})$ to a and the labelled nulls with the prefix $aw_{\exists P.D}$. More formally, $\mathcal{C}_{\mathcal{T},\mathcal{A}}$ is represented as

$$\mathcal{C}_{\mathcal{T},\mathcal{A}} \;=\; \mathcal{I}_{\mathcal{A}}^* \quad \oplus \quad \bigoplus_{\substack{a \in \text{ind}(\mathcal{A}) \\ A \sqsubseteq \exists P.D \in \mathcal{T} \text{ with } \mathcal{I}_{\mathcal{A}}^* \models A(a)}} \mathcal{C}_{\mathcal{T}}^{\exists P.D}(a), \tag{20}$$

where $\mathcal{I}_{\mathcal{A}}^*$ is a model of $\mathcal{A}$ with domain $\text{ind}(\mathcal{A})$. We again follow the divide and conquer strategy and split the process of query rewiring in two steps: rewriting over H-complete ABoxes and tree witnesses.

H-completeness. Let $\mathcal{T}$ be an EL TBox. A simple ABox $\mathcal{A}$ is said to be *H-complete with respect to* $\mathcal{T}$ if, for all concept names A and role names P, we have

$$\begin{aligned} A(a) \in \mathcal{A} &\quad \text{if} \quad \mathcal{I}_{\mathcal{A}} \models C(a) \text{ and } \mathcal{T} \models C \sqsubseteq A, \text{ for some } EL \text{ concept } C, \\ P(a,b) \in \mathcal{A} &\quad \text{if} \quad \mathcal{I}_{\mathcal{A}} \models R(a,b) \text{ and } \mathcal{T} \models R \sqsubseteq P, \text{ for some role name } R. \end{aligned}$$

(Note that the definition is the same as for QL except that now C can be an arbitrary EL concept, not only A' or $\exists R$.) We say that $(\Pi, Q(\boldsymbol{x}))$, for a datalog program Π and an atom $Q(\boldsymbol{x})$, is a *datalog rewriting of $\boldsymbol{q}(\boldsymbol{x})$ and $\mathcal{T}$ over H-complete ABoxes* if (19) holds for any ABox $\mathcal{A}$ that is H-complete with respect to $\mathcal{T}$ and any tuple $\boldsymbol{a}$ from $\text{ind}(\mathcal{A})$.

Observe that if an ABox $\mathcal{A}$ is H-complete with respect to $\mathcal{T}$ then the ABox part of $\mathcal{C}_{\mathcal{T},\mathcal{A}}$, that is, $\mathcal{I}_{\mathcal{A}}^*$ in (20), coincides with $\mathcal{I}_{\mathcal{A}}$. Thus, if $\mathcal{T}$ is a flat EL TBox in normal form (which does not contain concept inclusions of the form $A \sqsubseteq \exists P.D$) then

$$(\{Q(\boldsymbol{x}) \leftarrow \varphi(\boldsymbol{x},\boldsymbol{y})\}, \; Q(\boldsymbol{x}))$$

is clearly a datalog rewriting of $\boldsymbol{q}(\boldsymbol{x}) = \exists \boldsymbol{y}\, \varphi(\boldsymbol{x},\boldsymbol{y})$ and $\mathcal{T}$ over H-complete ABoxes. Now, any such TBox $\mathcal{T}$ can also be seen as a positive RL TBox, and so, by Corollary 37, the datalog program $\Pi_{\mathcal{T}}$ defined in Section 4.3 describes precisely the conditions of H-completeness of $\mathcal{A}$:

$$\begin{aligned} A(a) \in \mathcal{A} &\quad \text{if and only if} \quad (\Pi_{\mathcal{T}}, \mathcal{A}) \models A(a), \\ P(a,b) \in \mathcal{A} &\quad \text{if and only if} \quad (\Pi_{\mathcal{T}}, \mathcal{A}) \models P(a,b). \end{aligned}$$

It follows then that we can easily obtain datalog rewritings (over arbitrary ABoxes) from datalog rewritings over H-complete ABoxes:

Proposition 38. *If $(\Pi, Q(\boldsymbol{x}))$ is a datalog rewriting of $\boldsymbol{q}(\boldsymbol{x})$ and $\mathcal{T}$ over H-complete ABoxes, then $(\Pi \cup \Pi_{\mathcal{T}}, Q(\boldsymbol{x}))$ is a datalog rewriting of $\boldsymbol{q}(\boldsymbol{x})$ and $\mathcal{T}$ over arbitrary ABoxes.*

Thus, we can only concentrate on constructing datalog rewritings over H-complete ABoxes.

Tree Witnesses. Let $\mathcal{T}$ be an *EL* TBox in normal form and let $\boldsymbol{q}(\boldsymbol{x})$ be a CQ. Similarly to the case of *QL*, to construct a rewriting of $\boldsymbol{q}(\boldsymbol{x})$ and $\mathcal{T}$, we need to consider all possible subsets of $\boldsymbol{q}$, the atoms of the query, that can be homomorphically mapped to the ABox part of the canonical model $\mathcal{C}_{\mathcal{T},\mathcal{A}}$ and subsets of $\boldsymbol{q}$ that can be homomorphically mapped to the anonymous part of $\mathcal{C}_{\mathcal{T},\mathcal{A}}$. Tree witnesses for $\boldsymbol{q}(\boldsymbol{x})$ and $\mathcal{T}$ are defined in absolutely the same way as in Section 4.2. A major difference, however, is that *EL* does not contain inverse roles, and so each $\mathcal{T}$-tree in the anonymous part is generated by a concept of the form $\exists P.D$, where P is a role name. It follows that if a variable, say y, of any CQ belongs to the interior of some tree witness and the CQ contains an atom of the form $P(y, y')$, then y' must also be in the interior of the same tree witness. In particular, we have the following:

Proposition 39. *Let $\mathcal{T}$ be an EL TBox and $\boldsymbol{q}(\boldsymbol{x})$ a CQ. Then, for any binary atom $P(z_1, z_2)$ in $\boldsymbol{q}$, where P is a role name,*

- *there is no tree witness for $\boldsymbol{q}(\boldsymbol{x})$ and $\mathcal{T}$ with $P(z_1, z_2) \in \boldsymbol{q}_{\mathsf{t}}$, $z_2 \in \mathsf{t}_{\mathsf{r}}$, $z_1 \in \mathsf{t}_{\mathsf{i}}$;*
- *there is at most one tree witness t for $\boldsymbol{q}(\boldsymbol{x})$ and $\mathcal{T}$ such that $P(z_1, z_2) \in \boldsymbol{q}_{\mathsf{t}}$, $z_1 \in \mathsf{t}_{\mathsf{r}}$ and $z_2 \in \mathsf{t}_{\mathsf{i}}$.*

These observations suggest a simple algorithm for constructing all tree witnesses for any given CQ and *EL* TBox, which we first illustrate by a concrete example.

Example 40. Let $\mathcal{T}$ be an *EL* TBox containing the following concept and role inclusions:

$$A \sqsubseteq \exists S.B, \qquad B \sqsubseteq \exists R.C, \qquad R \sqsubseteq T.$$

Consider the CQ

$$\boldsymbol{q}(x) = \exists y, z, u, v \left(S(x, y) \wedge T(y, z) \wedge R(u, z) \wedge T(u, v) \wedge C(v) \right).$$

The algorithms begins with the smallest tree witnesses. By **(tw2)**, each tree witness t is uniquely defined by its interior (a non-empty set of existentially quantified variables): the roots are all the terms that do not belong to t_{i} but occur in atoms with an argument in t_{i}. The smallest tree witnesses are thus induced by singleton sets t_{i}. For $\mathsf{t}_{\mathsf{i}} = \{v\}$, we have $\mathsf{t}_{\mathsf{r}} = \{u\}$, which gives the tree witness t^1 with

$$\boldsymbol{q}_{\mathsf{t}^1} = \{\, T(u, v), \ C(v) \,\},$$

which is generated by $\exists R.C$; see h_1 in Fig. 11. For $\mathsf{t}_{\mathsf{i}} = \{u\}$, we have $\mathsf{t}_{\mathsf{r}} = \{v, z\}$ but, since *EL* contains no inverse roles, there can be no homomorphism h that

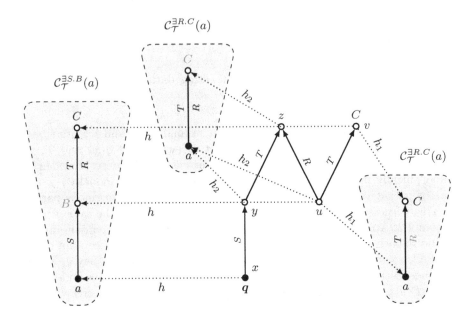

Fig. 11. Tree witnesses in Example 40

maps the set of atoms $\{\, T(y,z),\ R(u,z)\,\}$ into a $\mathcal{T}$-tree in such a way that h takes t_r to an ABox individual and t_i to a labelled null. The same argument applies to $t_i = \{y\}$. However, $t_i^2 = \{z\}$ gives rise to another tree witness, t^2, with

$$q_{t^2} = \{\, T(y,z),\ R(u,z)\,\},$$

which is again generated by $\exists R.C$; see h_2 in Fig. 11 (note that both variables in $t_r^2 = \{y,u\}$ are mapped to a, the root of the $\exists R.C$-generated $\mathcal{T}$-tree $\mathcal{C}_{\mathcal{T}}^{\exists R.C}(a)$). Thus, we have considered all singleton subsets of the existentially quantified variables and constructed all possible tree witnesses of *depth 1*. Next, we observe that larger tree witnesses must contain smaller tree witnesses in their interior. So, suppose that t_i contains both the roots and the interior of tree witness t^2, that is, $\{y,z,u\} \subseteq t_i$. Then, since EL has no inverse roles, t_i must also contain v (and thus, the whole of tree witness t^1). In this way, we obtain a tree witness t of *depth 2* with $t_i = \{y,u,z,v\}$, $t_r = \{x\}$ and

$$q_t = \{\, S(x,y),\ T(y,z),\ R(u,z),\ T(u,v),\ C(v)\,\},$$

which is generated by $\exists S.B$; see h in Fig. 11. We have covered all possible subsets of the existentially quantified variables and in this way obtained all tree witnesses for $q(x)$ and $\mathcal{T}$.

A general algorithm constructing all tree witnesses for any given CQ $q(x)$ and EL TBox $\mathcal{T}$ in normal form works as follows. It begins by identifying tree witnesses that have a single interior variable (these are tree witnesses of depth 1).

The algorithm then considers each set of tree witnesses $t^1, \ldots, t^k$ sharing common roots (provided that all their roots are existentially quantified variables)—the roots and interiors will become the interior of a potential new, larger, tree witness. In order to satisfy **(tw2)**, the algorithm extends the set of atoms in $q_0 = q_{t^1} \cup \cdots \cup q_{t^k}$ by all atoms incident on the variables in q_0 and then, to satisfy **(tw1)**, checks whether this extended set of atoms can be homomorphically mapped to a $\mathcal{T}$-tree. Since EL contains no inverse roles, any two tree witnesses t^i and t^j that share a common root must become part of the *interior* of a larger tree witness (if it exists at all) and therefore, the number of sets of tree witnesses that need consideration is bounded by the number of (existentially quantified) variables in q. Therefore, this algorithm constructs all tree witnesses and runs in polynomial time in the size of q and $\mathcal{T}$. (We note in passing that the presented algorithm resembles the construction of the equivalence relation $\sim_q$ defined by Lutz et al. (2009) except that the equivalence relation does not take account of the TBox and the distinction between answer variables and existentially quantified variables.)

It follows that the number of tree witnesses for any $q(x)$ and $\mathcal{T}$ does not exceed the number of atoms in q. Moreover, each pair, t and t', of tree witnesses for $q(x)$ and $\mathcal{T}$ is compatible, that is,

$$\text{either} \quad q_t \cap q_{t'} = \emptyset \quad \text{or} \quad q_t \subseteq q_{t'} \quad \text{or} \quad q_t \supseteq q_{t'}.$$

(In other words, the tree witnesses are partially ordered by the $\subseteq$ relation on their sets of atoms.) It follows that we can use the 'modified' tree-witness rewriting $q'_{tw}(x)$ over H-complete ABoxes defined at the end of Section 4.2, or rather its datalog representation. Let $Q_{S(z)}$, for each atom $S(z)$ in q, and D be fresh k-ary predicate symbols, for $k = |x| + |y|$, and let D_1 be a fresh unary predicate symbol. Intuitively, the $Q_{S(z)}$ are the rewritings of individual atoms of the query, the interpretation of D_1 consists of individuals from the ABox that are relevant to the query and the interpretation of D of all tuples of such individuals. Formally, let $\Omega_{\mathcal{T}}^q$ comprise the rule

$$Q(x) \leftarrow \bigwedge_{S(z) \in q} Q_{S(z)}(x, y),$$

the following rules, for each atom $S(z)$ in q:

$$Q_{S(z)}(x, y) \leftarrow D(x, y) \wedge S(z),$$
$$Q_{S(z)}(x, y) \leftarrow D(x, y) \wedge \mathsf{tw}_t(t_r), \qquad \text{for } t \in \Theta_{\mathcal{T}}^q \text{ with } S(z) \in q_t,$$

and the following rules defining D and D_1:

$$D(z_1, \ldots, z_k) \leftarrow D_1(z_1) \wedge \ldots D_1(z_k),$$
$$D_1(z) \leftarrow A(z), \qquad \text{for a concept name } A \text{ in } q \text{ or } \mathcal{T},$$
$$D_1(z) \leftarrow P(z, y), \qquad \text{for a role name } P \text{ in } q \text{ or } \mathcal{T},$$
$$D_1(z) \leftarrow P(y, z), \qquad \text{for a role name } P \text{ in } q \text{ or } \mathcal{T}.$$

(Strictly speaking, D_1 is not the same as the set of individuals in the ABox because concept and role names that occur in the ABox but do not occur in the query or the TBox are not included in the definition above: any individual that belongs only to such a concept or role is simply not visible to the query.) Thus we obtain a datalog rewriting $(\Omega_{\mathcal{T}}^q, Q(\boldsymbol{x}))$ of $\boldsymbol{q}(\boldsymbol{x})$ and $\mathcal{T}$ over H-complete ABoxes:

Theorem 41. *Let $\mathcal{T}$ be an EL TBox and $\boldsymbol{q}(\boldsymbol{x})$ a CQ. For any ABox $\mathcal{A}$ that is H-complete with respect to $\mathcal{T}$ and any tuple $\boldsymbol{a}$ in* $\mathsf{ind}(\mathcal{A})$*, we have*

$$\mathcal{C}_{\mathcal{T},\mathcal{A}} \models \boldsymbol{q}(\boldsymbol{a}) \quad \text{if and only if} \quad (\Omega_{\mathcal{T}}^q, \mathcal{I}_{\mathcal{A}}) \models Q(\boldsymbol{a}).$$

Finally, since the number of tree witnesses is linear in the size of $\boldsymbol{q}$, this datalog rewriting is of polynomial size in the size of $\boldsymbol{q}$ and $\mathcal{T}$. We also note in passing that the datalog rewriting over H-complete ABoxes is nonrecursive (none of the predicates is defined, even indirectly, in terms of itself) and the only recursive component of the rewriting over arbitrary ABoxes is the rules ensuring H-completeness of the ABox.

5   OBDA with Ontop and Databases

In the final section of this chapter, we briefly describe the ontology-based data access (OBDA) system *Ontop*[16] (Rodríguez-Muro et al., 2013) implemented at the Free University of Bozen-Bolzano and available as a plugin for the ontology editor Protégé 4, a SPARQL end-point and OWLAPI and Sesame libraries. *Ontop* is the first system to support the W3C recommendations OWL 2 QL, R2RML, SPARQL and the OWL 2 QL direct semantics entailment regime.

We illustrate how *Ontop* works using an example from (Rodríguez-Muro et al., 2013), which involves a (simplified) database IMDb[17] (in a typical OBDA scenario data comes from a relational database rather than an ABox). From a logical point of view, a *database schema* (Abiteboul et al., 1995) contains predicate symbols (with their arity) for both stored database relations (also known as tables) and views (with their definitions in terms of stored relations) as well as a set Σ of *integrity constraints* (in the form of functional and inclusion dependencies; for example, primary and foreign keys): any instance $\boldsymbol{I}$ of the database schema must satisfy its integrity constraints Σ.

The schema of IMDb contains relations title$[m, t, y]$ with information about movies (ID, title, production year), and castinfo$[p, m, r]$ with information about movies' cast (person ID, movie ID, person role). Thus, a data instance $\boldsymbol{I}_{\text{IMDb}}$ of this schema may contain the tables

<table>
<tr><td colspan="3" align="center">title</td></tr>
<tr><td>m</td><td>t</td><td>y</td></tr>
<tr><td>728</td><td>'Django Unchained'</td><td>2012</td></tr>
</table>

<table>
<tr><td colspan="3" align="center">castinfo</td></tr>
<tr><td>p</td><td>m</td><td>r</td></tr>
<tr><td>n37</td><td>728</td><td>1</td></tr>
<tr><td>n38</td><td>728</td><td>1</td></tr>
</table>

---

[16] ontop.inf.unibz.it
[17] www.imdb.com/interfaces

The integrity constraints Σ_{IMDb} of IMDb include the following foreign key (an inclusion dependency):

$$\forall m\,\big(\exists p, r\,\mathsf{castinfo}(p, m, r) \to \exists t, y\,\mathsf{title}(m, t, y)\big) \qquad (21)$$

('each tuple in $\mathsf{castinfo}$ must refer to an existing title') and the following primary key (a functional dependency with determinant m):

$$\forall m \forall t_1 \forall t_2\,\big(\exists y\,\mathsf{title}(m, t_1, y) \wedge \exists y\,\mathsf{title}(m, t_2, y) \to (t_1 = t_2)\big), \qquad (22)$$

$$\forall m \forall y_1 \forall y_2\,\big(\exists t\,\mathsf{title}(m, t, y_1) \wedge \exists t\,\mathsf{title}(m, t, y_2) \to (y_1 = y_2)\big) \qquad (23)$$

('each title is uniquely determined by its ID m').

In the framework of OBDA, the users are not supposed to know the structure of the database. Instead, they are given an ontology, e.g., MO[18], which describes the application domain in terms of concepts and roles. In our example we have concepts $\mathsf{mo{:}Movie}$ and $\mathsf{mo{:}Person}$, and roles $\mathsf{mo{:}cast}$, $\mathsf{mo{:}title}$ and $\mathsf{mo{:}year}$ related by OWL 2 QL TBox $\mathcal{T}_{\mathrm{MO}}$ containing, in particular, the following inclusions:

$$\mathsf{mo{:}Movie} \sqsubseteq \exists\mathsf{mo{:}title}, \qquad \mathsf{mo{:}Movie} \sqsubseteq \exists\mathsf{mo{:}cast},$$
$$\mathsf{mo{:}Movie} \sqsubseteq \exists\mathsf{mo{:}year}, \qquad \cdot\,\exists\mathsf{mo{:}title} \sqsubseteq \mathsf{mo{:}Movie},$$
$$\exists\mathsf{mo{:}cast} \sqsubseteq \mathsf{mo{:}Movie}, \qquad \exists\mathsf{mo{:}cast}^- \sqsubseteq \mathsf{mo{:}Person}.$$

The vocabularies of the database schema and the given OWL 2 QL TBox are linked together by means of mappings produced by a domain expert or extracted (semi)automatically. There are different known types of mappings: LAV (local-as-views), GAV (global-as-views), GLAV, etc.; consult, e.g., (Lenzerini, 2002) for an overview. Here we concentrate on GAV mappings because they guarantee low complexity of query answering (in what follows we call them simply mappings)— *Ontop* uses R2RML[19] to specify them. A *mapping*, $\mathcal{M}$, is a set of rules of the form

$$S(\boldsymbol{x}) \leftarrow \varphi(\boldsymbol{x}, \boldsymbol{z}),$$

where S is a concept or role name in the ontology and $\varphi(\boldsymbol{x}, \boldsymbol{z})$ is a conjunction of atoms with database relations (both stored and views) and a *filter*, that is, a Boolean combination of built-in predicates such as $=$ and $<$. (Note that, by including views in the schema, we can express any SQL query in mappings, which is important from the practical point of view.) In our example, a mapping $\mathcal{M}_{\mathrm{MO}}$ that relates the terms of MO to the schema of IMDb contains the following rules:

$$\mathsf{mo{:}Movie}(m) \leftarrow \mathsf{title}(m, t, y), \qquad (24)$$
$$\mathsf{mo{:}title}(m, t) \leftarrow \mathsf{title}(m, t, y), \qquad (25)$$
$$\mathsf{mo{:}year}(m, y) \leftarrow \mathsf{title}(m, t, y), \qquad (26)$$
$$\mathsf{mo{:}cast}(m, p) \leftarrow \mathsf{castinfo}(p, m, r), \qquad (27)$$
$$\mathsf{mo{:}Person}(p) \leftarrow \mathsf{castinfo}(p, m, r). \qquad (28)$$

---

[18] www.movieontology.org
[19] www.w3.org/TR/r2rml

Given a mapping $\mathcal{M}$ from a database schema to an OWL2QL TBox $\mathcal{T}$ and an instance $\boldsymbol{I}$ of this schema, the ground atoms

$$S(\boldsymbol{a}), \quad \text{for } S(\boldsymbol{x}) \leftarrow \varphi(\boldsymbol{x}, \boldsymbol{z}) \text{ in } \mathcal{M} \text{ and } \boldsymbol{I} \models \exists \boldsymbol{z}\, \varphi(\boldsymbol{a}, \boldsymbol{z}),$$

comprise the ABox denoted by $\mathcal{A}_{\boldsymbol{I},\mathcal{M}}$ and called the *virtual ABox* for $\mathcal{M}$ over $\boldsymbol{I}$ (Rodríguez-Muro and Calvanese, 2011). This ABox is just a convenient presentational tool and does not have to be materialised by the system. Then the virtual ABox for $\mathcal{M}_{\mathrm{MO}}$ over $\boldsymbol{I}_{\mathrm{IMDb}}$ consists of the ground atoms

mo:Movie(728), mo:title(728, 'Django Unchained'), mo:year(728, 2012),

mo:Person(n37), mo:cast(728, n37),

mo:Person(n38), mo:cast(728, n38).

The *certain answers* to a CQ $\boldsymbol{q}(\boldsymbol{x})$ over $\mathcal{T}$ linked by $\mathcal{M}$ to $\boldsymbol{I}$ are defined as the certain answers to $\boldsymbol{q}(\boldsymbol{x})$ over $(\mathcal{T}, \mathcal{A}_{\boldsymbol{I},\mathcal{M}})$. In order to find certain answers, one could first construct a PE-rewriting $\boldsymbol{q}'(\boldsymbol{x})$ of $\boldsymbol{q}(\boldsymbol{x})$ and $\mathcal{T}$ over *arbitrary* ABoxes (in the sequel, it will convenient to represent such a rewriting as a non-recursive datalog program). The rewriting $\boldsymbol{q}'(\boldsymbol{x})$ could then be *unfolded* into an SQL query using the so-called *partial evaluation* (Lloyd and Shepherdson, 1991), which exhaustively applies SLD-resolution to $\boldsymbol{q}'(\boldsymbol{x})$ and the mapping $\mathcal{M}$ and returns those rules whose bodies contain only database atoms. Consider, for example, CQ $\boldsymbol{q}(x) = \text{mo:Movie}(x)$. An obvious rewiring of $\boldsymbol{q}(x)$ and the TBox $\mathcal{T}_{\mathrm{MO}}$ (over arbitrary ABoxes) contains the following three rules:

$$\boldsymbol{q}'(x) \leftarrow \text{mo:Movie}(x), \tag{29}$$
$$\boldsymbol{q}'(x) \leftarrow \text{mo:title}(x, y), \tag{30}$$
$$\boldsymbol{q}'(x) \leftarrow \text{mo:cast}(x, y). \tag{31}$$

The unfolding applies the SLD-resolution procedure to these three rules and the mapping $\mathcal{M}_{\mathrm{MO}}$ and produces the rules

$$\boldsymbol{q}'(x) \leftarrow \text{title}(x, t, y), \tag{29+24}$$
$$\boldsymbol{q}'(x) \leftarrow \text{title}(x, t, y), \tag{30+25}$$
$$\boldsymbol{q}'(x) \leftarrow \text{castinfo}(p, x, r). \tag{31+27}$$

The resulting union of SELECT-PROJECT-JOIN queries could then be forwarded for execution to a relational database management system (RDBMS).

The same result can be achieved by using the tree-witness rewriting $\boldsymbol{q}_{\mathrm{tw}}(\boldsymbol{x})$ of $\boldsymbol{q}(\boldsymbol{x})$ and $\mathcal{T}$ over H-complete ABoxes introduced in Section 4.2. An obvious way to construct H-complete ABoxes is to take the *composition* of $\mathcal{M}$ and the inclusions in $\mathcal{T}$, that is, a mapping $\mathcal{M}^{\mathcal{T}}$ given by

$$
\begin{aligned}
A(x) &\leftarrow \varphi(x, \boldsymbol{z}), & &\text{if } A'(x) \leftarrow \varphi(x, \boldsymbol{z}) \in \mathcal{M} \text{ and } \mathcal{T} \models A' \sqsubseteq A, \\
A(x) &\leftarrow \varphi(x, y, \boldsymbol{z}), & &\text{if } R(x, y) \leftarrow \varphi(x, y, \boldsymbol{z}) \in \mathcal{M} \text{ and } \mathcal{T} \models \exists R \sqsubseteq A, \\
P(x, y) &\leftarrow \varphi(x, y, \boldsymbol{z}), & &\text{if } R(x, y) \leftarrow \varphi(x, y, \boldsymbol{z}) \in \mathcal{M} \text{ and } \mathcal{T} \models R \sqsubseteq P.
\end{aligned}
$$

(Recall that we do not distinguish between $P^-(y,x)$ and $P(x,y)$.) Thus, for any I and any tuple $\boldsymbol{a}$ of individuals in $\mathcal{A}_{I,\mathcal{M}}$, we have:

$$(\mathcal{T},\mathcal{A}_{I,\mathcal{M}}) \models \boldsymbol{q}(\boldsymbol{a}) \quad \text{if and only if} \quad \mathcal{A}_{I,\mathcal{M}^{\mathcal{T}}} \models \boldsymbol{q}_{\mathsf{tw}}(\boldsymbol{a}). \tag{32}$$

So, to compute the answers to $\boldsymbol{q}(\boldsymbol{x})$ over $\mathcal{T}$ linked by $\mathcal{M}$ to I, one can unfold the tree-witness rewriting $\boldsymbol{q}_{\mathsf{tw}}(\boldsymbol{x})$ over H-complete ABoxes with the help of the composition $\mathcal{M}^{\mathcal{T}}$. However, the resulting query will produce duplicating answers if the ontology axioms express the same properties of the application domain as the integrity constraints of the database. For example, the IMDb schema Σ_{IMDb} contains foreign key (21): movie ID in castinfo references movie ID in title, and therefore the unfolded rewriting above will return the same movie many times— once from title and once for each of the cast members of the movie in castinfo. Such a duplication is clearly an undesirable feature of this straightforward approach.

For this reason, before applying $\mathcal{M}^{\mathcal{T}}$ to unfold the tree-witness rewriting, *Ontop* optimises the mapping using the database integrity constraints Σ. This allows *Ontop* to reduce redundancy in answers and substantially shorten the SQL queries, which makes the OBDA system more efficient.

5.1 $\mathcal{T}$-mappings

We say that a mapping $\mathcal{M}$ is a *$\mathcal{T}$-mapping over dependencies* Σ if the ABox $\mathcal{A}_{I,\mathcal{M}}$ is H-complete with respect to $\mathcal{T}$, for any data instance I satisfying Σ. The composition $\mathcal{M}^{\mathcal{T}}$ defined above is trivially a $\mathcal{T}$-mapping over any Σ. *Ontop* starts with $\mathcal{M}^{\mathcal{T}}$ and then applies a series of optimisations to construct a simpler $\mathcal{T}$-mapping.

Inclusion Dependencies. Suppose $\mathcal{M} \cup \{S(\boldsymbol{x}) \leftarrow \psi_1(\boldsymbol{x},\boldsymbol{z})\}$ is a $\mathcal{T}$-mapping over Σ. If there is a more specific rule than $S(\boldsymbol{x}) \leftarrow \psi_1(\boldsymbol{x},\boldsymbol{z})$ in $\mathcal{M}$, then $\mathcal{M}$ itself will also be a $\mathcal{T}$-mapping. To discover such 'more specific' rules, we run the standard query containment check (Abiteboul et al., 1995) taking account of the inclusion dependencies. For example, since $\mathcal{T}_{\mathrm{MO}} \models \exists\mathsf{mo:cast} \sqsubseteq \mathsf{mo:Movie}$ in our running example, the composition of mapping $\mathcal{M}_{\mathrm{MO}}$ and ontology $\mathcal{T}_{\mathrm{MO}}$ contains the following rules for mo:Movie:

$$\mathsf{mo:Movie}(m) \;\leftarrow\; \mathsf{title}(m,t,y),$$
$$\mathsf{mo:Movie}(m) \;\leftarrow\; \mathsf{castinfo}(p,m,r).$$

As we observed above, the latter rule is redundant because Σ_{IMDb} contains inclusion dependency (21), which is repeated here for reference:

$$\forall m \left(\exists p, r\, \mathsf{castinfo}(p,m,r) \to \exists t, y\, \mathsf{title}(m,t,y)\right).$$

Disjunctions in SQL. Another way to reduce the size of a $\mathcal{T}$-mapping is to identify pairs of rules whose bodies are equivalent up to *filters with respect to*

concept	index	interval
mo:Actor	1	$[1,1]$
mo:Artist	2	$[1,2]$
mo:Director	3	$[3,3]$
mo:Person	4	$[1,4]$

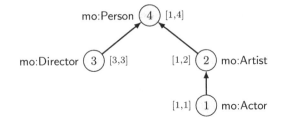

Fig. 12. Semantic Index example

constant values. This optimisation deals with the rules introduced due to the so-called type (discriminating) attributes (Elmasri and Navathe, 2010) in database schemas. For example, the mapping $\mathcal{M}_{MO}$ contains six rules for sub-concepts of mo:Person:

$$\text{mo:Actor}(p) \leftarrow \text{castinfo}(c, p, m, r), (r = 1),$$
$$\text{mo:Actress}(p) \leftarrow \text{castinfo}(c, p, m, r), (v = 2),$$
$$\cdots$$
$$\text{mo:Editor}(p) \leftarrow \text{castinfo}(c, p, m, r), (r = 6).$$

Thus, the composition of $\mathcal{M}_{MO}$ and $\mathcal{T}_{MO}$ contains six rules for mo:Person that differ only in the last condition $(r = k)$, $1 \le k \le 6$. These can be reduced to a single rule:

$$\text{mo:Person}(p) \leftarrow \text{castinfo}(c, p, m, r), \ \big((r = 1) \vee \cdots \vee (r = 6)\big).$$

Note that such disjunctions lend themselves to efficient evaluation by RDBMSs.

Materialised ABoxes and Semantic Index. In addition to working with proper relational data sources, *Ontop* also supports ABox storage in the form of structureless *universal tables*: a binary relation CA[*id, concept-id*] and a ternary relation RA[$id_1, id_2, role\text{-}id$] represent concept and role assertions. The universal tables give rise to trivial mappings, and *Ontop* implements a technique, the *semantic index* (Rodríguez-Muro and Calvanese, 2011), that takes advantage of SQL features in $\mathcal{T}$-mappings for this scenario. The key observation is that, since the IDs in the universal tables CA and RA can be chosen by the system, each concept and role in the TBox $\mathcal{T}$ can be assigned a numeric *index* and a set of numerical *intervals* in such a way that the resulting $\mathcal{T}$-mapping contains simple SQL queries with interval filter conditions. For example, in $\mathcal{T}_{MO}$, we have

$$\text{mo:Actor} \sqsubseteq \text{mo:Artist},$$
$$\text{mo:Artist} \sqsubseteq \text{mo:Person},$$
$$\text{mo:Director} \sqsubseteq \text{mo:Person},$$

so we can choose indexes and intervals for these concepts as in Fig. 12. It can be seen that these intervals respect the concept inclusions of the TBox: for instance,

[1,1] for mo:Actor is a subset of [1,2] for mo:Artist. This will generate a $\mathcal{T}$-mapping with

$$\begin{aligned}
\text{mo:Actor}(p) &\leftarrow \text{CA}(p, \textit{concept-id}), & (\textit{concept-id} = 1), \\
\text{mo:Artist}(p) &\leftarrow \text{CA}(p, \textit{concept-id}), & (1 \leq \textit{concept-id} \leq 2), \\
\text{mo:Director}(p) &\leftarrow \text{CA}(p, \textit{concept-id}), & (\textit{concept-id} = 3), \\
\text{mo:Person}(p) &\leftarrow \text{CA}(p, \textit{concept-id}), & (1 \leq \textit{concept-id} \leq 4).
\end{aligned}$$

Thus, by choosing appropriate concept and role IDs, we effectively construct H-complete ABoxes *without* the expensive forward chaining procedure (and the need to store large amounts of the derived assertions and the extra complications with updating the data). On the other hand, the semantic index $\mathcal{T}$-mappings are based on range expressions that can be evaluated efficiently by RDBMSs using standard B-tree indexes (Elmasri and Navathe, 2010).

5.2 Unfolding with Semantic Query Optimisation (SQO)

Ontop applies the Semantic Query Optimisation (Chakravarthy et al., 1986) to rules obtained at the intermediate steps of unfolding. In particular, this eliminates redundant JOIN operations caused by reification of database relations by means of concepts and roles. Consider, for example, the CQ

$$q(t, y) \leftarrow \text{mo:Movie}(m),\ \text{mo:title}(m, t),\ \text{mo:year}(m, y),\ (y > 2010).$$

It has no tree witnesses, and so $q_{\text{tw}}(t, y) = q(t, y)$. By straightforwardly applying the unfolding to $q_{\text{tw}}(t, y)$ and the $\mathcal{T}$-mapping $\mathcal{M}_{\text{MO}}$, we obtain the query

$$q'_{\text{tw}}(t, y) \leftarrow \text{title}(m, t_0, y_0),\ \text{title}(m, t, y_1),\ \text{title}(m, t_2, y),\ (y > 2010),$$

which requires two (potentially) expensive JOIN operations. However, by using functional dependencies (22) and (23) for the primary key m of title, which are repeated below:

$$\forall m \forall t_1 \forall t_2 \left(\exists y\, \text{title}(m, t_1, y) \wedge \exists y\, \text{title}(m, t_2, y) \to (t_1 = t_2) \right),$$
$$\forall m \forall y_1 \forall y_2 \left(\exists t\, \text{title}(m, t, y_1) \wedge \exists t\, \text{title}(m, t, y_2) \to (y_1 = y_2) \right),$$

we can reduce two JOIN operations in the first three atoms of $q'_{\text{tw}}(t, y)$ to a single atom $\text{title}(m, t, y)$:

$$q''_{\text{tw}}(t, y) \leftarrow \text{title}(m, t, y),\ (y > 2010).$$

Note that these two JOIN operations were introduced to reconstruct the ternary relation from its reification by means of the roles mo:title and mo:year.

The role of SQO in OBDA systems appears to be much more prominent than in conventional RDBMSs, where it was initially proposed to optimise SQL queries. While some of SQO techniques reached industrial RDBMSs, it never had a strong impact on the database community because it is costly compared to statistics- and heuristics-based methods, and because most SQL queries are written by highly-skilled experts (and so are nearly optimal anyway). In OBDA scenarios, in contrast, SQL queries are generated automatically, and so SQO becomes the only tool to avoid redundant and expensive JOIN operations.

References

Abiteboul, S., Hull, R., Vianu, V.: Foundations of Databases. Addison-Wesley (1995)

Arora, S., Barak, B.: Computational Complexity: A Modern Approach, 1st edn. Cambridge University Press, New York (2009)

Artale, A., Calvanese, D., Kontchakov, R., Zakharyaschev, M.: The DL-Lite family and relations. Journal of Artificial Intelligence Research (JAIR) 36, 1–69 (2009)

Baader, F., Brandt, S., Lutz, C.: Pushing the EL envelope. In: Kaelbling, L.P., Saffiotti, A. (eds.) Proceedings of the 19th Int. Joint Conf. on Artificial Intelligence, IJCAI-2005, pp. 364–369. Professional Book Center (2005)

Baader, F., Brandt, S., Lutz, C.: Pushing the EL envelope further. In: Clark, K., Patel-Schneider, P.F. (eds.) Proceedings of the OWLED 2008 DC Workshop on OWL: Experiences and Directions (2008)

Baget, J.-F., Leclère, M., Mugnier, M.-L., Salvat, E.: On rules with existential variables: Walking the decidability line. Artificial Intelligence 175(9–10), 1620–1654 (2011)

Brandt, S.: Polynomial time reasoning in a description logic with existential restrictions, GCI axioms, and—what else? In: Proc. of the 16th European Conf. on Artificial Intelligence, ECAI-2004, pp. 298–302. IOS Press (2004)

Calì, A., Gottlob, G., Kifer, M.: Taming the infinite chase: Query answering under expressive relational constraints. J. of Artificial Intelligence Research 48, 115–174 (2013)

Calì, A., Gottlob, G., Lukasiewicz, T.: A general datalog-based framework for tractable query answering over ontologies. J. of Web Semantics 14, 57–83 (2012)

Calvanese, D., De Giacomo, G., Lembo, D., Lenzerini, M., Rosati, R.: DL-Lite: Tractable description logics for ontologies. In: Proc. of AAAI, pp. 602–607. AAAI Press / The MIT Press (2005)

Calvanese, D., De Giacomo, G., Lembo, D., Lenzerini, M., Rosati, R.: Data complexity of query answering in description logics. In: Proc. of the 10th Int. Conf. on the Principles of Knowledge Representation and Reasoning, KR 2006, pp. 260–270 (2006)

Calvanese, D., De Giacomo, G., Lembo, D., Lenzerini, M., Rosati, R.: Tractable reasoning and efficient query answering in description logics: The DL-Lite family. J. of Automated Reasoning 39(3), 385–429 (2007)

Ceri, S., Gottlob, G., Tanca, L.: What you always wanted to know about datalog (and never dared to ask). IEEE Trans. Knowl. Data Eng. 1(1), 146–166 (1989)

Chagrov, A., Zakharyaschev, M.: Modal Logic. Oxford Logic Guides, vol. 35. Clarendon Press, Oxford (1997)

Chakravarthy, U.S., Fishman, D.H., Minker, J.: Semantic query optimization in expert systems and database systems. Benjamin-Cummings Publishing Co., Inc. (1986)

Chortaras, A., Trivela, D., Stamou, G.: Optimized query rewriting for OWL 2 QL. In: Björner, N., Sofronie-Stokkermans, V. (eds.) CADE 2011. LNCS, vol. 6803, pp. 192–206. Springer, Heidelberg (2011)

Eiter, T., Lutz, C., Ortiz, M., Šimkus, M.: Query answering in description logics: The knots approach. In: Ono, H., Kanazawa, M., de Queiroz, R. (eds.) WoLLIC 2009. LNCS, vol. 5514, pp. 26–36. Springer, Heidelberg (2009)

Eiter, T., Ortiz, M., Šimkus, M., Tran, T.-K., Xiao, G.: Query rewriting for Horn-SHIQ plus rules. In: Proc. of AAAI 2012. AAAI Press (2012)

Elmasri, R., Navathe, S.: Fundamentals of Database Systems, 6th edn. Addison-Wesley (2010)

Garey, M., Johnson, D.: Computers and Intractability: A Guide to the Theory of NP-Completeness. W. H. Freeman (1979)

Gottlob, G., Kikot, S., Kontchakov, R., Podolskii, V.V., Schwentick, T., Zakharyaschev, M.: The price of query rewriting in ontology-based data access. Artificial Intelligence 213, 42–59 (2014)

Gottlob, G., Orsi, G., Pieris, A.: Ontological queries: Rewriting and optimization. In: Proc. of ICDE 2011, pp. 2–13. IEEE Computer Society Press (2011)

Grosof, B.N., Horrocks, I., Volz, R., Decker, S.: Description logic programs: Combining logic programs with description logic. In: Proc. of the 12th Int. World Wide Web Conference, WWW 2003, pp. 48–57 (2003)

Horrocks, I., Kutz, O., Sattler, U.: The even more irresistible SROIQ. In: Proc. of the 10th Int. Conf. on Principles of Knowledge Representation and Reasoning, KR 2006, pp. 57–67. AAAI Press (2006)

Horrocks, I., Motik, B., Wang, Z.: The HermiT OWL reasoner. In: Proc. of ORE, CEUR Workshop Proceedings, vol. 858, CEUR-WS.org (2012)

Johnson, D.S., Klug, A.C.: Testing containment of conjunctive queries under functional and inclusion dependencies. J. Comput. Syst. Sci. 28(1), 167–189 (1984)

Kikot, S., Kontchakov, R., Podolskii, V., Zakharyaschev, M.: Exponential lower bounds and separation for query rewriting. In: Czumaj, A., Mehlhorn, K., Pitts, A., Wattenhofer, R. (eds.) ICALP 2012, Part II. LNCS, vol. 7392, pp. 263–274. Springer, Heidelberg (2012a)

Kikot, S., Kontchakov, R., Zakharyaschev, M.: Conjunctive query answering with OWL 2 QL. In: Proc. of KR 2012, AAAI Press (2012b)

König, M., Leclère, M., Mugnier, M.-L., Thomazo, M.: A sound and complete backward chaining algorithm for existential rules. In: Krötzsch, M., Straccia, U. (eds.) RR 2012. LNCS, vol. 7497, pp. 122–138. Springer, Heidelberg (2012)

Kontchakov, R., Lutz, C., Toman, D., Wolter, F., Zakharyaschev, M.: The combined approach to ontology-based data access. In: Proceedings of the 20th Int. Joint Conf. on Artificial Intelligence, IJCAI-2011, pp. 2656–2661. AAAI Press (2011)

Kozen, D.: Theory of Computation. Springer (2006)

Lenzerini, M.: Data integration: A theoretical perspective. In: Proc. of the 21st ACM SIGACT-SIGMOD-SIGART Symposium on Principles of Database Systems, PODS 2002, pp. 233–246. ACM (2002)

Libkin, L.: Elements Of Finite Model Theory. Springer (2004)

Lloyd, J., Shepherdson, J.: Partial Evaluation in Logic Programming. The Journal of Logic Programming 11(3-4), 217–242 (1991)

Lutz, C., Seylan, İ., Toman, D., Wolter, F.: The combined approach to OBDA: Taming role hierarchies using filters. In: Alani, H., et al. (eds.) ISWC 2013, Part I. LNCS, vol. 8218, pp. 314–330. Springer, Heidelberg (2013)

Lutz, C., Toman, D., Wolter, F.: Conjunctive query answering in the description logic EL using a relational database system. In: Proceedings of the 21st Int. Joint Conf. on Artificial Intelligence, IJCAI 2009, pp. 2070–2075 (2009)

Lutz, C., Wolter, F.: Conservative extensions of the lightweight description logic EL. In: Pfenning, F. (ed.) CADE 2007. LNCS (LNAI), vol. 4603, pp. 84–99. Springer, Heidelberg (2007)

Motik, B.: On the properties of metamodeling in OWL. J. Log. Comput. 17(4), 617–637 (2007)

Papadimitriou, C.: Computational Complexity. Addison-Wesley (1994)

Pérez-Urbina, H., Motik, B., Horrocks, I.: A comparison of query rewriting techniques for DL-Lite. In: Proc. of DL 2009, vol. 477, CEUR-WS (2009)

Pérez-Urbina, H., Rodríguez-Díaz, E., Grove, M., Konstantinidis, G., Sirin, E.: Evaluation of query rewriting approaches for OWL 2. In: Proc. of SSWS+HPCSW 2012, vol. 943, CEUR-WS (2012)

Poggi, A., Lembo, D., Calvanese, D., De Giacomo, G., Lenzerini, M., Rosati, R.: Linking data to ontologies. J. on Data Semantics, X:133–X:173 (2008)

Rodríguez-Muro, M., Calvanese, D.: Dependencies: Making ontology based data access work. In: Proc. of AMW 2011, vol. 749, CEUR-WS.org (2011)

Rodríguez-Muro, M., Kontchakov, R., Zakharyaschev, M.: Ontology-based data access: Ontop of databases. In: Alani, H., et al. (eds.) ISWC 2013, Part I. LNCS, vol. 8218, pp. 558–573. Springer, Heidelberg (2013)

Rosati, R.: Prexto: Query rewriting under extensional constraints in DL-Lite. In: Simperl, E., Cimiano, P., Polleres, A., Corcho, O., Presutti, V. (eds.) ESWC 2012. LNCS, vol. 7295, pp. 360–374. Springer, Heidelberg (2012)

Rosati, R., Almatelli, A.: Improving query answering over DL-Lite ontologies. In: Proc. of KR 2010. AAAI Press (2010)

Schaerf, A.: On the complexity of the instance checking problem in concept languages with existential quantification. J. of Intelligent Information Systems 2, 265–278 (1993)

Sirin, E., Parsia, B., Cuenca Grau, B., Kalyanpur, A., Katz, Y.: Pellet: A practical OWL-DL reasoner. J. of Web Semantics 5(2), 51–53 (2007)

Steigmiller, A., Liebig, T., Glimm, B.: Konclude: System description. J. of Web Semantics (2014)

ter Horst, H.J.: Completeness, decidability and complexity of entailment for RDF Schema and a semantic extension involving the OWL vocabulary. J. of Web Semantics 3(2-3), 79–115 (2005)

Tobies, S.: Complexity results and practical algorithms for logics in knowledge representation. PhD thesis, LuFG Theoretical Computer Science, RWTH-Aachen, Germany (2001)

Tsarkov, D., Horrocks, I.: FaCT++ description logic reasoner: System description. In: Furbach, U., Shankar, N. (eds.) IJCAR 2006. LNCS (LNAI), vol. 4130, pp. 292–297. Springer, Heidelberg (2006)

Vardi, M.: The complexity of relational query languages (extended abstract). In: Proc. of the 14th ACM SIGACT Symp. on Theory of Computing, STOC 1982, pp. 137–146 (1982)

An Introduction to Ontology-Based Query Answering with Existential Rules

Marie-Laure Mugnier[1] and Michaël Thomazo[2]

[1] Université Montpellier 2, France
`mugnier@lirmm.fr`
[2] TU Dresden, Germany
`michael.thomazo@tu-dresden.de`

Abstract. The need for an ontological layer on top of data, associated with advanced reasoning mechanisms able to exploit ontological knowledge, has been acknowledged in the database, knowledge representation and Semantic Web communities. We focus here on the ontology-based data querying problem, which consists in querying data while taking ontological knowledge into account. To tackle this problem, we consider a logical framework based on existential rules, also called Datalog$^\pm$.

In this course, we introduce fundamental notions on ontology-based query answering with existential rules. We present basic reasoning techniques, explain the relationships with other formalisms such as lightweight description logics, and review decidability results as well as associated algorithms. We end with ongoing research and some challenging issues.

1 Ontology-Based Query Answering

Novel intelligent methods are required to manage and exploit the huge amounts of data nowadays available. The interest of considering *ontological knowledge* when accessing data has been widely acknowledged, both in the database and knowledge representation communities. Indeed, ontologies[1], which typically encode general domain knowledge, can be used to infer data that are not explicitly stored, hence palliating incompleteness in databases. They can also be used to enrich the vocabulary of data sources, which allows a user to abstract from the specific way data are stored. Finally, when several data sources use different vocabularies, ontologies can be used to unify these vocabularies.

Example 1. In this simple example, we consider data on movies, described with unary relations *MovieTitle* (titles of movies) and *MovieActor* (movie actors), and a binary relation *Play*, encoding that a given person plays a role in a movie identified by its title. Let q be a query asking if a given person, whose identifier is B, plays in a movie. If the data do not explicitly contain the information that B plays in a movie, the answer to q will be no. Now, assume that the

---

[1] We will reserve the term "ontology" to general domain knowledge—also called terminological knowledge—in order to clearly distinguish it from the data—or assertional knowledge—called here facts.

M. Koubarakis et al. (Eds.): Reasoning Web 2014, LNCS 8714, pp. 245–278, 2014.

data contain the information that B is a movie actor (B is in the extension of *MovieActor* relation) and we have the knowledge that "every movie actor plays a role in some movie". We can infer that B plays in a movie. Hence, the answer to q should be yes. In the following, we will encode knowledge in First-Order logic. Then, the query will be encoded as $q = \exists y\ Play(B, y)$ and the piece of ontological knowledge as the following rule:

$$R = \forall x (MovieActor(x) \rightarrow \exists y (Play(x, y) \wedge MovieTitle(y)))$$

We can check that the ground atom *MovieActor(B)* and the rule R entail q, hence the positive answer to q.

The issue of proposing formalisms able to express ontological knowledge, associated with querying mechanisms able to exploit this knowledge when accessing data, is known as ontology-based data access. In this paper, we will more precisely consider the following problem, called *ontology-based query answering*: given a knowledge base composed of an ontology and facts, and a query, compute the set of answers to the query on the facts, while taking implicit knowledge represented in the ontology into account. We will consider the basic queries called conjunctive queries.

In the Semantic Web, ontological knowledge is usually represented with formalisms based on *description logics* (DLs). However, DLs are restricted in terms of expressivity, in the sense that terminological knowledge can only be expressed by tree-like structures. Moreover, only unary and binary predicates are generally supported. Historically, DLs focused on reasoning tasks about the terminology itself, for instance classifying concepts; querying tasks were restricted to ground atom entailment [BCM+07]. Conjunctive query answering with classical DLs appeared to be extremely complex (e.g., for the classical DL $\mathcal{ALCI}$, it is 2ExpTime-complete, and still NP-complete in the size of the data). Hence, less expressive DLs specially devoted to conjunctive query answering on large amounts of data have been designed, beginning with the DL-Lite family. Another family of lightweight DLs used for query answering is the $\mathcal{EL}$ family, which was originally designed for polynomial time terminological reasoning. These DLs form the core of so-called tractable profiles of the Semantic Web language OWL 2, namely OWL 2 QL and OWL2 EL (the third tractable profile being OWL 2 RL, which is closely related to the rule-based language Datalog).

On the other hand, querying large amounts of data is the fundamental task of databases. Therefore, the challenge in this domain is now to access data while taking ontological knowledge into account. The deductive database language *Datalog* allows to express some ontological knowledge. However, in Datalog rules, variables are range-restricted, i.e., all variables in the rule head necessarily occur in the rule body. Therefore, these rules can produce knowledge about already known individuals, but cannot infer the existence of unknown individuals, a feature sometimes called "value invention" in databases. This feature has been recognized as crucial in an open-domain perspective, where it cannot be assumed that all individuals are known in advance.

Existential rules have been proposed to meet these two requirements, i.e., value invention and the ability to express complex structures. Existential rules extend First-Order Horn clauses, i.e., plain Datalog rules, by allowing to introduce new existentially quantified variables. They are also known as Datalog$^{\pm}$ family, in reference to Datalog. More preciselly, an existential rule is a positive rule of the form *body* $\rightarrow$ *head*, where *body* and *head* are any conjunctions of atoms, and variables occurring only in the *head* are existentially quantified. The rule in Example 1 is an existential rule; it allows to infer the existence of a movie in which B plays a role, even if this movie is not identified.

This paper provides an introduction to ontological query answering with existential rules. In Section 2, we present basic logical foundations for representing and reasoning with facts, conjunctive queries and plain Datalog rules. Section 3 is devoted to existential rules and their relationships with other formalisms (tuple-generating dependencies in databases, conceptual graph rules, positive logic progams via skolemization, lightweight description logics). Section 4 introduces the main approaches to solve the problem. Entailment with general existential rules being undecidable, Section 5 presents the main decidability criteria currently known, as well as associated algorithmic techniques. Section 6 ends with ongoing research and open issues.

We purposely omitted bibliographical references in this introductive section. References will be given later, in the appropriate sections.

2 Fundamental Notions on Conjunctive Query Answering and Positive Rules

Data can be stored in various forms, for instance in a relational database, an RDF triple store or a graph database. We abstract from a specific language or technology by considering first-order logic (FOL). Ontological knowledge will also be expressed as first-order logical formulas. In this section, we present basic theoretical notions for representing and reasoning with facts, conjunctive queries, as well as simple positive rules, namely Datalog rules.

2.1 Basic Logical Notions

We consider first-order vocabularies with constants but no other function symbols. A *vocabulary* is a pair $\mathcal{V} = (\mathcal{P}, \mathcal{C})$, where $\mathcal{P}$ is a finite set of predicates (or relations) and $\mathcal{C}$ is a possibly infinite set of constants. Each predicate has an *arity*, which is its number of arguments. A *term* (on $\mathcal{V}$) is a variable or a constant (in $\mathcal{C}$). An *atom* (on $\mathcal{V}$) is of the form $p(t_1, \ldots, t_k)$ where p is a predicate of arity k (from $\mathcal{P}$) and the t_i are terms (on $\mathcal{V}$). An atom is *ground* if it has no variable. A formula *on* $\mathcal{V}$ has all its atoms on $\mathcal{V}$. A variable in a formula is *free* if it is not in the scope of a quantifier. A formula is *closed* if it has no free variable.

Given a formula F, we note *terms*(F) (respectively vars(F), csts(F)) the set of terms (respectively variables, constants) that occur in F. In the following, we always assume that distinct formulas (representing facts, queries or rules) have *disjoint sets of variables*.

An *interpretation* I of a vocabulary $\mathcal{V} = (\mathcal{P}, \mathcal{C})$ is a pair $(D, .^I)$, where D is a non-empty (possibly infinite) set, called the *domain* of I, and $.^I$ defines the semantics of the elements in $\mathcal{V}$ with respect to D:

- $\forall c \in \mathcal{C},\ c^I \in D$
- $\forall p \in \mathcal{P}$ with arity k, $p^I \subseteq D^k$.

An interpretation I of $\mathcal{V}$ is a *model* of a formula F on $\mathcal{V}$ if F is true in I. A formula G *entails* a formula F (we also say that F is a *semantic consequence* of G) if every model of G is a model of F, which is denoted by $G \models F$. We note $G \equiv F$ if $G \models F$ and $F \models G$.

2.2   The Positive Existential Conjunctive Fragment of FOL

The *positive existential conjunctive* fragment of first-order logic, denoted by $\text{FOL}(\wedge, \exists)$, is composed of formulas built with the single connector $\wedge$ and the single quantifier $\exists$. Without loss of generality, we consider that these formulas are in prenex form, i.e., all existential quantifiers are in front of the formula. Then, it is often convenient to see them as *sets of atoms*. As we will see later on, this fragment allows to represent facts and conjunctive queries.

A fundamental notion in $\text{FOL}(\wedge, \exists)$ is that of a homomorphism. We recall that a *substitution* s of a set of variables V by a set of terms T is a mapping from V to T. Given a set of atoms F, $s(F)$ denotes the set obtained from F by applying s, i.e., by replacing each variable $v \in V$ with $s(v)$.

Definition 1 (Homomorphism, notation $\geq$). *Given two sets of atoms F and G, a homomorphism h from F to G is a substitution of $\text{vars}(F)$ by $\text{terms}(G)$ such that, for all atom $p(t_1 \ldots t_k) \in F$, $p(h(t_1)) \ldots h(t_k)) \in G$, i.e., $h(F) \subseteq G$. We note $F \geq G$ if there is a homomorphism from F to G, and say that F is more general than G.*

Example 2. Let us consider the facts $F_1 = \{p(x_1, y_1), p(y_1, z_1), p(z_1, x_1)\}$ and $F_2 = \{p(x_2, y_2), p(y_2, z_2), p(z_2, u_2)\}$, where all terms are variables. There are three homomorphisms from F_2 to F_1. For instance, $h = \{x_2 \mapsto x_1, y_2 \mapsto y_1, z_2 \mapsto z_1, u_2 \mapsto x_1\}$.

Homomorphism can also be defined among interpretations. Given two interpretations $I_1 = (D_1, .^{I_1})$ and $I_2(D_2, .^{I_2})$ of a vocabulary $\mathcal{V} = (\mathcal{P}, \mathcal{C})$, a homomorphism from I_1 to I_2 is a mapping from D_1 to D_2 such that:

- for all $c \in \mathcal{C}$, $h(c^{I_1}) = c^{I_2}$;
- for all $p \in \mathcal{P}$ and $(t_1 \ldots t_k) \in p^{I_1}$, $(h(t_1) \ldots h(t_k)) \in p^{I_2}$.

We first point out that an interpretation I is a model of a $\text{FOL}(\wedge, \exists)$ formula, if and only if there is a mapping v from $\text{terms}(F)$ to D such that:

- for all $c \in consts(F)$, $v(c) = c^I$;
- for all atom $p(e_1 \ldots e_k) \in F$, $(v(e_1) \ldots v(e_k)) \in p^I$.

Such a mapping is called a *good assignment* of F to I.

A nice property of FOL($\wedge, \exists$) is that each formula has a *canonical model*, which is a representative of all its models, and can be used to check entailment, as we will see below. This model has the same structure as F, hence the name "isomorphic model".

Definition 2 (Isomorphic model). *Let F be a FOL($\wedge, \exists$)-formula built on the vocabulary $\mathcal{V} = (\mathcal{P}, \mathcal{C})$. The* isomorphic model *of F, denoted by $M(F)$, :*

- *D is in bijection[2] with terms$(F) \cup \mathcal{C}$ (to simplify notations, we consider that this bijection is the identity);*
- *for all $c \in \mathcal{C}$, $M(c) = c$;*
- *for all $p \in \mathcal{P}$, $M(p) = \{(t_1 \ldots t_k)|p(t_1 \ldots t_k) \in F\}$ if p occurs in F, otherwise $M(p) = \emptyset$.*

We check that $M(F)$ is indeed a model of F, by choosing the identity as good assignment.

Property 1. For any FOL($\wedge, \exists$) formula F, $M(F)$, the model isomorphic to F, is a universal model, i.e., for all model M' of F, it holds that $M(F) \geq M'$.

Proof. If M' is a model of F, then there is a good assignment v from F to M'. Since $M(F)$ is isomorphic to F, v defines a homomorphism from $M(F)$ to M'.

Given two interpretations I_1 and I_2, with $I_1 \geq I_2$, if I_1 is a model of F, then I_2 also is. Indeed, the composition of a homomorphism from I_1 to I_2 and of a good assignment from F to I_1 yields a good assignment. Hence, to check if G entails F, it is sufficient to check that $M(G)$ is a model of F, i.e., there is a good assignment from F to $M(G)$.

Note that a good assignment from F to $M(G)$ defines a homomorphism from F to G. Reciprocally, a homomorphism from F to G defines a good assignment from F to $M(G)$. It follows that checking entailment in the FOL($\wedge, \exists$) fragment amounts to a homomorphism check:

Theorem 1. *Let F and G be two FOL($\wedge, \exists$) formulas. It holds that $G \models F$ iff there is a homomorphism from F to G (i.e., $F \geq G$).*

Proof. Follows from previous definitions and Property 1.

If $F \geq G$ and $G \geq F$, we say that F and G are (homomorphically) *equivalent*. According to the preceding theorem, this equivalence notion corresponds to logical equivalence.

Definition 3 (Core). *Given a set of atoms F, the* core *of F is a minimal subset of F equivalent to F.*

---

[2] A bijection is a one-to-one correspondence.

It is well-known that among all equivalent sets of atoms on a vocabulary, there is a unique core, up to variable renaming (where a *variable renaming*, or *isomorphism*, from F to F', is a bijective substitution s of vars(F) by vars(F') such that $F = F'$).

2.3   Facts and Conjunctive Queries

Classically, a fact is a ground atom. We extend this notion, so that a fact may contain existentially quantified variables and not only constants. Hence, a fact becomes a closed FOL($\wedge, \exists$) formula. This allows to represent in a natural way null values in relational databases or blank nodes in RDF. Moreover, this is in line with existential rules, which produce existential variables. It follows that a conjunction of facts can be seen as a single fact when it is put in prenex form.

Example 3. Let $F_1 = \exists x \exists y(p(x,y) \wedge q(y,a))$, where a is a constant, and $F_2 = \exists x p(x,x)$. F_1 and F_2 are facts. The formula $F_1 \wedge F_2$ can be seen as a single fact obtained by considering a prenex form, which involves renaming the variable x in F_1 or in F_2. One obtains for instance $\exists x \exists y \exists z(p(x,y) \wedge q(y,a) \wedge p(z,z))$, which can also be seen as the set of atoms $\{p(x,y), q(y,a), p(z,z)\}$.

Conjunctive queries are the basic and more frequent queries in databases. There can be expressed in FOL($\wedge, \exists$). They correspond to SELECT-FROM-WHERE queries in SQL and to basic pattern queries in SPARQL.

Definition 4 (Facts, queries, answers). *A* fact *is an existentially closed conjunction of atoms. A* conjunctive query *(CQ) is an existentially quantified conjunction of atoms with possibly free variables. A* Boolean conjunctive query *(BCQ) has no free variable. Let $\{x_1 \ldots x_k\}$ be the free variables in a CQ q; an* answer *to q in a fact F is a substitution s of $\{x_1 \ldots x_k\}$ by constants in F, such that $F \models s(q)$ (in other words, s is the restriction to $\{x_1 \ldots x_k\}$ of a homomorphism from q to F). Given an ordering $(x_1 \ldots x_k)$ of the free variables in q, we often denote an answer s by $(s(x_1) \ldots s(x_k))$. A Boolean query q has only the empty substitution as possible answer, in which case q is said to have a positive answer, otherwise q has a negative answer.*

Several equivalent basic decision problems can be considered. Let $\mathcal{K}$ be a knowledge base (composed of facts for now, but later enriched with rules); then the following decision problems are polynomially equivalent (see e.g. [BLMS11]):

- CQ ANSWERING decision problem: given a KB $\mathcal{K}$ and a CQ q, is there an answer to q in $\mathcal{K}$?
- CQ EVALUATION decision problem: given a KB $\mathcal{K}$, a CQ q and a list of constants t, is t an answer to q in $\mathcal{K}$?
- BCQ ANSWERING problem: given a KB $\mathcal{K}$ and a BCQ q, is () an answer to q in $\mathcal{K}$?
- BCQ ENTAILMENT problem: given a KB $\mathcal{K}$ and a BCQ q, is q entailed by $\mathcal{K}$?

In the following, we consider BCQ ENTAILMENT as a reference problem.

Checking homomorphism is an NP-complete problem. Hence, BCQ ENTAILMENT is NP-complete. Instead of the classical complexity measure, also called combined complexity, we may also consider *data complexity*, in which case only the data are part of the problem input. Then, BCQ ENTAILMENT becomes polynomial: indeed, a naive algorithm for checking if there is a homomorphism from q to F is in $\mathcal{O}(|F|^{|q|})$.

2.4   Adding Positive Range-Restricted Rules

A basic kind of ontological knowledge is that of *range-restricted* positive rules, where "range-restricted" means that all variables in the head of a rule also occur in the body of this rule [AHV95]. It follows that such rules allows to entail knowledge on individuals that *already exist* in the data. In ontologies, such rules typically express taxonomies (like a schema in RDFS), or properties of relations (like symmetry or transitivity). We will also refer to these rules as *Datalog rules*, as they exactly correspond to plain Datalog rules (i.e., without negation).

Definition 5 (Range-restricted rule, Datalog rule). *A* range-restricted *(positive) rule, or (plain) Datalog rule, is a formula* $R = \forall \boldsymbol{x} \forall \boldsymbol{y}(B[\boldsymbol{x}, \boldsymbol{y}] \to H[\boldsymbol{y}])$, *where* $\boldsymbol{x}, \boldsymbol{y}$ *are sets of variables, B and H are conjunctions of atoms, respectively called the* body *and the* head *of R, also denoted by body(R) and head(R).*

A rule R is *applicable* to a fact F if there is a homomorphism h from body(R) to F. Applying R to F with respect to h consists in adding $h(head(R))$ to F. By iteratively applying rules in all possible ways, one obtain a unique fact, called the *saturation* of F, and denoted by F^*. The process stops in finite time since no new variable is created.

Let us now consider a knowledge base composed of facts (seen as a single fact) and range-restricted rules, $\mathcal{K} = (F, \mathcal{R})$. To check if $\mathcal{K} \models q$, we can rely on notions similar to the positive existential case. Indeed, the model isomorphic to F^* is a model of $(F, \mathcal{R})$ and it keeps the property of being a universal model.

Hence, $\mathcal{K} \models q$ if and only if there is a homomorphism from q to F^*. In combined complexity, this test is still NP-complete if the arity of the predicates is bounded (then the size of F^* is polynomial in the size of F), otherwise it is EXPTIME-complete [AHV95]. It is polynomial with respect to data complexity.

In the next section, we extend positive rules to existential rules, by relaxing the constraint of being range-restricted.

3   Existential Rules

In this section, we present existential rules, as well as their relationships to other database or KR formalisms.

3.1   The Framework of Existential Rules

Definition 6 (Existential rule). *An* existential rule *(or simply a* rule *hereafter) is a formula* $R = \forall \boldsymbol{x} \forall \boldsymbol{y}(B[\boldsymbol{x}, \boldsymbol{y}] \rightarrow \exists \boldsymbol{z} H[\boldsymbol{y}, \boldsymbol{z}])$, *where* $\boldsymbol{x}, \boldsymbol{y}$ *and* $\boldsymbol{z}$ *are sets of variables,* B *and* H *are conjunctions of atoms, respectively called the* body *and the* head *of* R, *also denoted by* body(R) *and* head(R). *The* frontier *of* R, *denoted by* fr(R), *is the set* vars$(B) \cap$ vars$(H) = \boldsymbol{y}$. *The set of* existential variables *in* R *is the set* vars$(H) \setminus$ fr$(R) = \boldsymbol{z}$.

In the following, we will omit quantifiers in rules since there is no ambiguity. For instance, $p(x, y) \rightarrow q(y, z)$ denotes the rule $R = \forall x \forall y \ (p(x, y) \rightarrow \exists z \ q(y, z))$.

Example 4. Consider the following predicates, with their arity mentioned in parentheses; unary predicates can be seen as concept names, i.e. types of entities, and the other predicates as relation names: Area(1), Project(1), Researcher(1), isProject(3), hasExpertise(2), isMember(2)
Here are some examples of existential rules composing the ontology:
"The relation isProject associates a project, the area of this project and the leader of this project, who is a researcher" [signature of isProject]
$R_0 = isProject(x, y, z) \rightarrow Project(x) \wedge \ Area(y) \wedge \ Researcher(z)$
"Every leader of a project is a member of this project"
$R_1 = isProject(x, y, z) \rightarrow isMember(z, x)$
"Every researcher expert in an area is member of a project in this area"
$R_2 = Researcher(x) \wedge hasExpertise(x, y) \rightarrow isProject(u, y, z) \wedge isMember(x, u)$
"Every researcher is expert in an area"
$R_3 = Researcher(x) \rightarrow hasExpertise(x, y)$
R_0 *and* R_1 *are range-restricted, but not* R_2 *and* R_3.

Definition 7 (Application of an existential rule). *An existential rule* R *is applicable to a fact* F *if there is a homomorphism* h *from* body(R) *to* F; *the result of the application of* R *to* F *with respect to* h *is a fact* $\alpha(F, R, \pi) = F \cup \pi^{\text{safe}}(\text{head}(R))$ *where* π^{safe} *is a substitution of* head(R), *that replaces each* $x \in$ fr(R) *with* $h(x)$, *and each other variable with a "fresh" variable, i.e., not introduced before.*

Example 5. We consider the vocabulary and rules from Example 4. Let $F = \{Researcher(a), Researcher(b), hasExpertise(a, \text{"}KR\text{"}), Area(\text{"}KR\text{"})\}$ be a fact. R_2 is applicable to F with respect to $h_0 = \{(x, a), (y, \text{"}KR\text{"})\}$, which yields atoms $\{isProject(u_0, \text{"}KR\text{"}, z_0), isMember(a, u_0)\}$, where u_0 and z_0 are fresh existential variables. R_3 is applicable to F as well, with $h_1 = \{(x, b)\}$, which produces the atom $hasExpertise(b, y_0)$. Then, R_2 could be applied again, to the obtained fact, with respect to $h_2 = \{(x, b), (y, y_0)\}$, which would produce atoms $\{isProject(u_1, y_0, z_1), isMember(b, u_1)\}$.

Existential rules have a double origin. On the one hand, they can be seen as an extension of plain Datalog to enable value invention, yielding the Datalog$^\pm$ family [CGK08, CGL09]. It is important to note, however, that rules make a query in Datalog, while, in Datalog$^\pm$ (and in the present framework), they form an ontology, and the query itself does not embed deductive knowledge. On the other hand, existential rules come from earlier studies on a graph-based knowledge representation framework, inspired by conceptual graphs [CM09]; indeed, the logical translation of conceptual graph rules yields exactly existential rules, as defined in [SM96].

We also point out that existential rules have the same form as a very general kind of dependencies, which has long been studied in databases, namely *Tuple-Generating Dependencies* (TGD) [AHV95]. Intuitively, a database instance D satisfies a TGD t if, each time the body of t is found in D, the head of t is found in D as well; formally, if t is applicable to D by homomorphism h, then h has to be extensible to a homomorphism h' from $head(t)$ to D, i.e., such that $h(x) = h'(x)$ for each $x \in fr(t)$. Existential rules benefit from theoretical results obtained on TGDs (such as results on the chase and on decidability issues, see Sections 4 and 5).

Note that an existential rule is not a Horn clause because of existential variables in its head. However, both are closely related, since by *skolemisation*, an existential rule can be transformed into a set of Horn clauses with functions. The skolemization of a rule R is a rule *skolem*(R) built from R by replacing each occurrence of an existential variable y with a functional term $f_y^R(\boldsymbol{x})$, where $\boldsymbol{x} = fr(R)$. We remind that skolemization does not produce an equivalent formula, however a formula is (un)satisfiable if and only if its skolem form is.

Example 6 (Skolemization). Let $R = Researcher(x) \land hasExpertise(x, y) \rightarrow isProject(u, y, z) \land isMember(x, u)$ (Rule R_2 in Example 4). The frontier of R_2 is $\{x, y\}$. Then, skolem$(R) = Researcher(x) \land hasExpertise(x, y) \rightarrow isProject(f_u^R(x, y), y, f_z^R(x, y)) \land isMember(x, f_u^R(x, y))$, which yields two Horn clauses.

A set of skolemized existential rules can be seen as a specific positive logic program, hence nonmonotonic negation can be added while benefitting from results obtained in logic programming. For instance, if nonmonotonic negation is added with stable model semantics, one obtains a specific case of Answer Set Programming.

This framework can be extended to *equality rules* and *negative constraints*. An equality rule is a rule of the form $B \rightarrow x = t$, where x and t are distinct terms, $x \in vars(B)$ and $t \in vars(B)$ or is a constant. When the unique name assumption is made, i.e., distinct constants refer to distinct individuals, the application of an equality rule is said to fail if it leads to set the equality between distinct constants. This kind of failure corresponds to an inconsistency of the knowledge base. Equality rules generalize functional dependencies, which are widely used in conceptual modeling.

Constraints are another kind of construct specifically devoted to the definition of the consistency or inconsistency of the knowledge base. A *negative* constraint is a rule of the form $C \rightarrow \bot$, where $\bot$ denotes the absurd symbol (i.e., a propositional atom whose value is false). It is satisfied if C is not entailed by $(F, \mathcal{R})$. Negative constraints are typically used to express disjointness of concepts/classes or incompatibility of relations. See [CGL09] and [BLMS11] for the integration of equality rules and negative constraints in the existential rule framework.

3.2 Relationships to Lightweight Description Logics

Interestingly, existential rules generalize lightweight description logics. We focus here on $\mathcal{EL}$ [BBL05, LTW09] and DL-Lite [CGL$^+$07, ACKZ09]. For instance, DL-Lite$_\mathcal{R}$, which underlines OWL2 QL profile [OWL09], can be expressed by linear existential rules (whose body and head are restricted to a single atom) and negative constraints, see e.g. [CGL09]. Other DL-Lite fragments allow to declare functional roles, which can be translated by equality rules. Table 1 summarizes the translation from DL-Lite axioms to existential rules. Example 7 illustrates this translation on a concrete case. The DL $\mathcal{EL}$ can be expressed by "pure" existential rules, as shown in Table 2.

Table 1. Translation of DL-Lite axioms

DL-Axiom	Translated rule
$A \sqsubseteq B$	$A(x) \rightarrow B(x)$
$A \sqsubseteq \exists R$	$A(x) \rightarrow R(x,y)$
$\exists R \sqsubseteq \exists S^-$	$R(x,y) \rightarrow S(z,x)$
$B \sqsubseteq \exists R.C$	$B(x) \rightarrow R(x,y) \wedge C(y)$
$R \sqsubseteq S$	$R(x,y) \rightarrow S(x,y)$
$funct(R)$	$R(x,y) \wedge R(x,z) \rightarrow y = z$
$B \sqsubseteq \neg C$	$B(x) \wedge C(x) \rightarrow \bot$

Table 2. Translation of (normal) $\mathcal{EL}$-axioms

DL-Axiom	Translated rule
$B \sqcap C \sqsubseteq D$	$B(x) \wedge C(x) \rightarrow D(x)$
$B \sqsubseteq C$	$B(x) \rightarrow C(x)$
$B \sqsubseteq \exists R.C$	$B(x) \rightarrow R(x,y) \wedge C(y)$
$\exists R.B \sqsubseteq C$	$r(x,y) \wedge B(y) \rightarrow C(x)$

Example 7. This example borrows a DL-Lite$_\mathcal{R}$ TBox from [CGL$^+$07]. Consider the atomic concepts *Professor* and *Student*, and the roles *TeachesTo* and *Has-Tutor*. The TBox is listed below with its translation into existential rules.

DL-Lite$_\mathcal{R}$ TBox	Existential rules
$Professor \sqsubseteq \exists TeachesTo$	$Professor(x) \rightarrow TeachesTo(x,y)$
$Student \sqsubseteq \exists HasTutor$	$Student(x) \rightarrow HasTutor(x,y)$
$\exists TeachesTo^- \sqsubseteq Student$	$TeachsTo(y,x) \rightarrow Student(x)$
$\exists HasTutor^- \sqsubseteq Professor$	$HasTutor(y,x) \rightarrow Professor(x)$
$Professor \sqsubseteq \neg Student$	$Professor(x) \wedge Student(x) \rightarrow \bot$
$HasTutor^- \sqsubseteq TeachesTo$	$HasTutor(y,x) \rightarrow TeachesTo(x,y)$

In DL-Lite$_\mathcal{F}$, the role *HasTutor* could be declared functional (by the statement (*funct* (*HasTutor*)), which would be translated into the following equality rule: $HasTutor(x, y) \wedge HasTutor(x, z) \rightarrow y = z$.

More generally, existential rules allow to overcome some limitations of light-weight DLs. First, they have unrestricted predicate arity (while DLs consider unary and binary predicates only), which allows for a natural coupling with database schemas, in which relations may have any arity. Moreover, adding pieces of information, for instance to take contextual knowledge into account, such as data provenance for instance, is made easy by the unrestricted predicate arity, since these pieces of information can be added as new predicate arguments. Second, the body and the head of a rule may have any structure, and there is no constraint on frontier variables, hence rules allow to represent cyclic structures, while DLs are fundamentally restricted to tree-like structures.

Example 8. The following rule cannot be expressed in DLs:

$$p(x, y) \rightarrow q(x, z) \wedge q(y, z)$$

Unsurprisingly, there is a price to pay for this expressivity. Indeed, BCQ ENTAILMENT is undecidable for general existential rules (e.g., [BV81, CLM81] for an equivalent problem on TGDs, and [BM02] for fact entailment with conceptual graph rules). However, many classes of rules for which it remains decidable have been studied. The main classes are reviewed in Section 5.

4   Main Approaches to Ontology-Based Query Answering

We now consider a knowledge base (KB) $\mathcal{K} = (F, \mathcal{R})$, composed of a set of facts, seen as a single fact F, and a finite set of existential rules $\mathcal{R}$. We recall that the BCQ ENTAILMENT PROBLEM takes as input a KB $\mathcal{K} = (F, \mathcal{R})$ and a BCQ q, and asks if $\mathcal{K} \models q$ holds, where $\mathcal{K}$ is seen as the conjunction of F and the rules in $\mathcal{R}$.

To solve this problem, there are two main approaches, which are related to the classical paradigms for processing rules, namely *forward chaining* and *backward chaining*. In databases, these paradigms are also called *bottom-up* and *top-down*, respectively. Forward chaining consists in iteratively applying the rules starting from the initial fact, while trying to produce a fact to which the query can be mapped by homomorphism. Backward chaining consists in iteratively using the rules to rewrite the query, starting from the initial query, while trying to produce a query that can be mapped to the initial fact by homomorphism.

In the OBQA context, these two paradigms are recast as follows. Forward chaining is used to *materialize* all inferences in the data, then the query is evaluated against this materialization. Backward chaining is decomposed into two steps as well. First, the query is rewritten into another query using the rules. Then, the rewritten query is evaluated against the initial data. Both approaches can be seen as ways of integrating the rules, respectively into the data and into the query, in order to come back to a classical database query evaluation problem.

Materialization has the advantage of enabling efficient query answering but may be not appropriate, because the saturated data may be too large, but also because of data access rights or data maintenance reasons. Query rewriting has the advantage of avoiding changes in the data, however its drawback is that the rewritten query may be large, even exponential in the size of initial query, hence less efficiently processed, at least with current database techniques.

Since BCQ ENTAILMENT is not decidable, none of these techniques leads to a procedure that terminates in *all* cases. Various conditions on rules ensuring the decidability of BCQ ENTAILMENT have been exhibited. These conditions ensure the termination of algorithms based on materialization or on query rewriting, or on a combination of both. See the next section for an overview.

We now present the main notions and results that underlie these two approaches.

4.1   Materialization-Based Approach

We already pointed out that existential rules have the same form as TGDs. Forward chaining on TGDs is known as the *chase*. It was initially designed to repair a database that violates some TGDs. Indeed, when the database does not satisfy a TGD (according to homomorphism h), this TGD can be applied to the database (according to h) to add missing data. However, these local repairs may lead to a new TGD violation, hence the forward chaining process.

Definition 8 (Derivation Sequence). *Let F be a fact, and $\mathcal{R}$ be a set of rules. An $\mathcal{R}$-derivation of F is a finite sequence $(F_0 = F), \ldots, F_k$ such that for all $0 \leq i < k$, there is $R_i \in \mathcal{R}$ and a homomorphism h from $body(R_i)$ to F_i such that $F_{i+1} = \alpha(F_i, R_i, h)$.*

Theorem 2 (Soundness and completeness of $\mathcal{R}$-derivation). *Let $\mathcal{K} = (F, \mathcal{R})$ be a KB and q be a Boolean conjunctive query. Then $\mathcal{K} \models q$ iff there exists an $\mathcal{R}$-derivation $(F_0 = F), \ldots, F_k$ such that $F_k \models q$.*

It follows that a breadth-first forward chaining mechanism yields a positive answer in finite time when $\mathcal{K} \models q$. This mechanism, called the *saturation* hereafter (and the *chase* in databases) works as follows. Let $F_0 = F$ be the initial fact. Each step is as follows: (1) check if q maps to the current fact, say F_{i-1} at step i $(i > 0)$: if it is the case, q has a positive answer; (2) otherwise, produce a fact F_i from F_{i-1}, by computing all new homomorphisms from each rule body to F_{i-1}, then performing all corresponding rule applications. A homomorphism to F_{i-1} is said to be *new* if it has not been already computed at a previous step, i.e., it uses at least an atom added at step $i - 1$. The fact F_k obtained after the step k is called the k-saturation of F and is denoted by $\alpha_k(F, \mathcal{R})$. Formally: let $\alpha(F, \mathcal{R}) = F \cup \{\pi_{safe}(head(R)), \forall R \in \mathcal{R}$ and homomorphism $\pi : body(R) \to F\}$; then, $\alpha_0(F, \mathcal{R}) = F$ and for $i > 0$, $\alpha_i(F, \mathcal{R}) = \alpha(\alpha_{i-1}(F, \mathcal{R}), \mathcal{R})$.

We define $\alpha_\infty(F, \mathcal{R}) = \cup_{k \geq 0} \alpha_k(F, \mathcal{R})$ and we denote it by $F_{\mathcal{R}}^*$, and simply F^* when there is no doubt on $\mathcal{R}$. F^* can be infinite, as illustrated by the following example.

Example 9. Let $F = p(a)$ and $R = p(x) \rightarrow q(x, y) \wedge p(y)$. $\alpha_\infty(F, \mathcal{R})$ is infinite, since each application of R leads to a new application of R. Note that for all $i \geq 0$, $\alpha_{i+1}(F, \mathcal{R})$ is not equivalent to $\alpha_i(F, \mathcal{R})$.

We recall the nice property that holds for range-restricted rules: M^*, the interpretation isomorphic to F^*, is a representative of all models of $(F, \mathcal{R})$. More precisely, M^* is a *universal* model of $(F, \mathcal{R})$. This property is kept for existential rules. The difference with the range-restricted rule case is that M^* can be infinite.

Theorem 3 (Soundness and completeness of saturation). *Let $(F, \mathcal{R})$ be a KB and q be a Boolean conjunctive query. Let $F^* = \alpha_\infty(F, \mathcal{R})$. The following four statements are equivalent:*

- *$F, \mathcal{R} \models q$;*
- *M^* is a model of q;*
- *there is a homomorphism from q to F^**
- *there is an integer $k \geq 0$ and a homomorphism from q to $\alpha_k(F, \mathcal{R})$.*

Obviously, the saturation terminates when F^* is finite. Further work has proposed mechanisms related to forward chaining to build a finite representation of F^*, even when F^* is infinite, for restricted classes of existential rules [CGK08, TBMR12]. The developed techniques are close in spirit to blocking techniques in DL tableau procedures [BCM+07].

4.2 Query Rewriting Approach

In the OBQA context, query rewriting was first proposed for DL-Lite [CGL+05]: the ontology is used to rewrite the initial conjunctive query into a union of conjunctive queries, which can then be passed to a relational database management system. More generally, the input query can be rewritten into a *first-order query* (e.g., a union of semi-conjunctive queries [Tho13]). First-order queries are exactly the logical counterpart of SQL queries. Query rewriting has been further generalized by considering rewriting into a *Datalog query* (a UCQ can be seen as a specific case of such a query). See the last section for more details.

We focus here on the basic rewriting technique, which outputs a UCQ, seen as a set of CQs. We present a conceptually simple and generic approach to query rewriting with existential rules, namely piece-based query rewriting, which can be applied to any kind of existential rule (but, of course, it is ensured to stop only for some classes of rules). This technique has been introduced in [BLMS09] (and [BLMS11] for the journal version). A slightly different technique has been proposed in [GOP11].

For simplicity reasons, we focus on Boolean conjunctive queries hereafter. To be applicable to arbitrary CQs, the definitions should be extended to process free variables in a special way. However, considering BCQs only is not a restriction, since we can use a simple transformation from any CQ to a BCQ: let q be a CQ with free variables $x_1 \ldots x_q$; q is translated into a BCQ q' by adding an atom $ans(x_1 \ldots x_q)$, where ans is a special predicate not occurring in the knowledge base; the technique presented hereafter ensures that, if we rewrite q' into a UCQ q'', then remove from q'' the atoms with predicate ans (and consider their arguments as free variables), we get the UCQ that should be obtained by rewriting q.

Example 10. Consider again Example 4. Let $q = \exists x_1 \ isProject(x_1, \text{``}KR\text{''}, x_2)$ asking for the leaders of projects in KR. The associated Boolean query is $q' = \exists x_1 \exists x_2 (ans(x_2) \wedge isProject(x_1, \text{``}KR\text{''}, x_2))$. The key point is that the predicate ans does not appear in the knowledge base, hence the added atom will never be rewritten and its variables will be correctly processed (as detailed in following Example 15).

Query rewriting relies on the notion of a *unification* between a query and a rule head. We first recall here the usual definition of unification, used for instance in plain Datalog (or range-restricted rules), then explain why it has to be extended in the case of existential rules.

Definition 9 (Datalog Unification). *Let q be a Boolean conjunctive query, and R be a Datalog rule. A* unifier *of q with R is a pair $\mu = (a, u)$, where a is an atom of q and u is a substitution of vars$(a) \cup$ vars$(head(R))$ by terms$(head(R)) \cup$ consts(a) such that $u(a) = u(head(R))$.*

When a query and a rule unify, it is possible to rewrite the query with respect to that unification, as specified in Definition 10.

Definition 10 (Datalog rewriting). *Let q be a Boolean conjunctive query, R be a Datalog rule and $\mu = (a, u)$ be a unifier of q with R. The* rewriting *of q according to μ, denoted by $\beta(q, R, \mu)$, is $u(body(R) \cup \bar{q}')$, where $\bar{q}' = q \setminus q'$.*

Please note that these classical notions have been formulated in order to stress similarities with the notions we introduce hereafter.

Example 11 (Datalog Unification and Rewriting). Let us consider $q_e = t(x_1, x_2) \wedge s(x_1, x_3) \wedge s(x_2, x_3)$ and $R = s_1(x, y) \rightarrow s(x, y)$. A Datalog unifier of q_e with R is $\mu_d = (s(x_1, x_3), \{u(x_1) = x, u(x_3) = y\})$. The rewriting of q_e according to μ is the following query:

$$t(x, x_2) \wedge s_1(x, y) \wedge s(x_2, y).$$

Let us stress that this query is equivalent to the following query:

$$t(x_1, x_2) \wedge s_1(x_1, x_3) \wedge s(x_2, x_3),$$

where x has been renamed by x_1 and y by x_3. In the following, we will allow ourselves to use such a variable renaming without prior notice.

Applying the same steps without paying attention to the existential variables in existential rule heads would lead to erroneous rewritings, as shown by Example 12.

Example 12 (Wrong Unification). Let us consider $q_e = t(x_1, x_2) \wedge s(x_1, x_3) \wedge s(x_2, x_3)$ and $R = f(x) \rightarrow s(x, y)$. A Datalog unification of q_e with R is $\mu_{error} = (s(x_1, x_3), \{u(x_1) = x, u(x_3) = y\})$. According to Definition 10, the rewriting of q_e with R would be q_r:

$$q_r = t(x, x_2) \wedge f(x) \wedge s(x_2, y).$$

However, q_r is not a sound rewriting of q_e, which can be checked by considering the following fact (obtained by instantiating q_r):

$$F = t(a, b) \wedge f(a) \wedge s(b, c).$$

We have $F \models q_r$, however $F, \mathcal{R} \not\models q_e$. Indeed, $F_{\mathcal{R}}^* \equiv F$ and q_e cannot be mapped by homomorphism to F.

For that reason, the notion of *piece unifier* has been introduced, originally in the context of conceptual graph rules [SM96], then recast in the framework of existential rules [BLMS09]. Instead of unifying only one atom at once, one may have to unify a whole "piece", that is, a set of atoms that should have been created by the same rule application. The following definitions and the algorithm are mainly taken from [KLMT12]. Alternative definitions can be found in [KLMT13]. Given a Boolean conjunctive query q and $q' \subseteq q$, we call *separating variables* of q' (w.r.t. q) the set of variables that belong to both q' and $q \setminus q'$, and we denote this set by $sep_q(q')$. The other variables of q' are said to be non-separating variables.

Definition 11 (Piece Unifier). *Let q be a Boolean conjunctive query and R be an existential rule. A piece unifier of q with R is a pair $\mu = (q', u)$ with $q' \subseteq q, q' \neq \emptyset$, and u is a substitution of $\text{fr}(R) \cup \text{vars}(q')$ by $\text{terms}(\text{head}(R)) \cup \text{consts}(q')$ such that:*

1. *for all $x \in \text{fr}(R)$, $u(x) \in \text{fr}(R)$ or $u(x)$ is a constant (for technical convenience, we allow $u(x) = x$);*
2. *for all $x \in sep_q(q'), u(x) \in \text{fr}(R)$ or $u(x)$ is a constant;*
3. *$u(q') \subseteq u(\text{head}(R))$;*

It follows from this definition that existential variables from R can only be unified with non-separating variables of q'. In other words, when a variable x of q' is unified with an existential variable of R, all the atoms in which x occur must be part of the unification (i.e., x cannot be a separating variable).

Let us consider the unification attempted in Example 12 from this point of view.

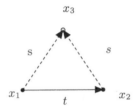

Fig. 1. Since x_3 is unified with an existential variable (Example 13), dashed atoms must be part of the unification

Example 13 (Piece Unifier). We consider again $q_e = t(x_1, x_2) \wedge s(x_1, x_2) \wedge s(x_2, x_3)$ and $R = f(x) \rightarrow s(x, y)$. $\mu error = (q' = \{s(x_1, x_3)\}, \{u(x_1) = x, u(x_3) = y\})$ is not a piece unifier. Indeed, x_3 belongs to $sep_{q_e}(q')$ since it appears in $s(x_2, x_3)$, which does not belong to q', hence violating the second condition of the piece unifier definition.

A correct choice of piece is illustrated by Figure 1. Indeed, let us define μ by $((\{s(x_1, x_3), s(x_2, x_3)\}, \{u(x_1) = x, u(x_3) = y, u(x_2) = x\})$. μ is a piece unifier of q_e with R, which can be checked by verifying that Conditions 1 to 3 are fulfilled.

Given the above definition of piece unifiers, the definition of rewritings remains syntactically the same as in the Datalog case.

Definition 12 (Rewriting). *Given a Boolean conjunctive query q, an existential rule R and a piece unifier $\mu = (q', u)$ of q with R, the* direct rewriting *of q according to μ, denoted by $\beta(q, R, \mu)$ is $u(body(R) \cup \bar{q}')$, where $\bar{q}' = q \setminus q'$.*

Example 14 (Direct rewriting). Let μ be the unifier of q_e with R defined in Example 13. The direct rewriting of q_e with respect to μ is:

$$\beta(q_e, R_2, \mu) = t(x, x) \wedge f(x).$$

The notion of $\mathcal{R}$-rewriting allows to denote queries that are obtained thanks to successive rewriting operations.

Definition 13 ($\mathcal{R}$-rewriting of q). *Let q be a Boolean conjunctive query and $\mathcal{R}$ be a set of existential rules. An $\mathcal{R}$-rewriting of q is a conjunctive query q_k obtained by a finite sequence $q_0 = q, q_1, \ldots, q_k$ such that for all i such that $0 \leq i < k$, there is $R_i \in \mathcal{R}$ and a piece unifier μ_i of q_i with R_i such that $q_{i+1} = \beta(q_i, R, \mu_i)$.*

We are now able to illustrate how non-Boolean queries can be processed by translation into Boolean queries, thus avoiding to consider answer variables in a specific way (see the discussion associated with Example 10).

Example 15. Consider the set of rules $\mathcal{R}$ from Example 4.
Let $q = \exists x_1 isProject(x_1, \text{“}KR\text{”}, x_2)$, which asks for the leaders of projects in KR. Let $q' = \exists x_1 \exists x_2 (ans(x_2) \wedge isProject(x_1, \text{“}KR\text{”}, x_2))$ be the Boolean query

obtained from q. The only rule that contains an atom with predicate $isProject$ is $R_2 = Researcher(x) \land hasExpertise(x, y) \rightarrow isProject(u, y, z) \land isMember(x, u)$. However, q' cannot be piece-unified with the head of R_2 because x_2 would be unified with the existential variable z, whereas it also appears in $ans(x_2)$ which cannot be unified. In this case, the only $\mathcal{R}$-rewriting of q' with the rules from Example 4 is q' itself. Hence, the only rewriting of the original query q would be q itself, obtained from q' by removing the ans atom and making x_2 free.

We now present the fundamental theorem justifying the notion of $\mathcal{R}$-rewriting. This theorem was originally written in the framework of conceptual graph rules [SM96]. Since the logical translation of conceptual graph rules is exactly existential rules, it can be immediately recast in the framework of existential rules.

Theorem 4 (Soundness and completeness of $\mathcal{R}$-rewriting). *Let F be a fact, $\mathcal{R}$ be a set of existential rules, and q be a Boolean conjunctive query. Then $F, \mathcal{R} \models q$ iff there is an $\mathcal{R}$-rewriting q' of q such that $F \models q'$.*

Of course, this does not always provide a halting procedure since there may be an infinite number of $\mathcal{R}$-rewritings, as illustrated by the following example. Note that this example actually considers a Datalog rule.

Example 16. Let $R = p(x, y) \land p(y, z) \rightarrow p(x, z)$. Let $q = p(a, b)$, where a and b are constants. Hence q is a ground atom. A direct rewriting of q with R is $q_1 = p(a, y) \land p(y, b)$. Each atom of q_1 unifies with $head(R)$, which yields two isomorphic queries. Let us consider $q_2 = p(a, y') \land p(y', y) \land p(y, b)$. The same process can be repeated indefinitely, producing increasingly longer "paths" from a to b. Hence, the set of $\{R\}$-rewritings of q is infinite.

For some classes of rules, there exists a *finite* set of $\mathcal{R}$-rewritings (in other words a UCQ), which is both sound and complete, as formally defined below:

Definition 14 (Sound and complete set of $\mathcal{R}$-rewritings). *Let $\mathcal{R}$ be a set of existential rules and q be a Boolean conjunctive query. Let $\mathcal{Q}$ be a set of BCQs. $\mathcal{Q}$ is said to be* sound *with respect to q and $\mathcal{R}$ if, for all fact F, and all $q' \in \mathcal{Q}$, if $F \models q'$ then $F, \mathcal{R} \models q$. Reciprocally, $\mathcal{Q}$ is said to be* complete *with respect to q and $\mathcal{R}$ if, for all fact F, if $F, \mathcal{R} \models q$, then there is $q' \in \mathcal{Q}$ such that $F \models q'$.*

See the next section for conditions on rules ensuring that a finite sound and complete set of rewritings exists, whatever the input conjunctive query is.

5   Decidable Classes of Rules and Algorithmic Techniques

In this section, we present several criteria that ensures decidability of BCQ ENTAILMENT. First, we consider the case where the saturation introduced in Section 4 is equivalent to a finite fact. This allows to apply classical forward chaining techniques. However, sets of rules ensuring such a property are not recognizable, hence the definition of several recognizable sufficient conditions, also known as "concrete" classes. In this paper, we present two of them, and we provide links to other relevant work. Similarly, we consider the case where query rewriting into a union of conjunctive queries can be performed, by presenting a generic algorithm and several concrete cases where it is applicable. Last, we briefly mention and provide relevant links to other decidable cases.

5.1 Finite Expansion Sets

We have already seen how to compute a saturation by applying rules in a breadth-first fashion. A set of rules that produces new information in only a finite number of steps for every initial fact F is called a *finite expansion set*, as formalized in Definition 15.

Definition 15 (Finite Expansion Set). *A set of rules $\mathcal{R}$ is called a* finite expansion set *(fes) if and only if, for every fact F, there exists an integer $k = f(F, \mathcal{R})$ such that $\alpha_k(F, \mathcal{R}) \equiv \alpha_\infty(F, \mathcal{R})$.*

Since one can not decide if a given set of rules is a *fes*[3], it is crucial to design expressive specific cases. All the cases known so far are based on some notion of acyclicity. Several of them have been proposed, and we present here two incomparable notions of acyclicity.

Weak-Acyclicity. The first notion is based on the notion of *position* of a predicate.

Definition 16 (Position). *Let p be a predicate of arity k. A position of p is a pair (p, i), with i from 1 to k.*

We now present the graph of position dependencies. The vertices of this graph are all the positions that appear in a rule set. Intuitively, it tracks how variables are propagated from one position to another one. Moreover, it also tracks how new existentially quantified variables are introduced, and in which positions. Definition 17 formalizes this intuition.

Definition 17 (Graph of Position Dependencies [FKMP05]). *Let $\mathcal{R}$ be a set of rules. The (oriented) graph of position dependencies $(V, A \cup A^*)$ of $\mathcal{R}$ is defined as follows:*

- *V is the set of all positions for all predicates appearing in $\mathcal{R}$;*
- *there is an arc from (p, i) to (q, j) in A if there exist a rule $R \in \mathcal{R}$, and a variable $x \in \text{fr}(R)$ such that x appears in position (p, i) in the body of R and in position (q, j) in the head of R;*
- *there is an arc from (p, i) to (q, j) in A^* if there exist a rule $R \in \mathcal{R}$ and a variable $x \in \text{fr}(R)$ such that x appears in position (p, i) in the body of R and an existentially quantified variable appears in position (q, j) in the head of R. The arcs of A^* are called special arcs.*

---

[3] We say that *fes* is an *abstract class.*

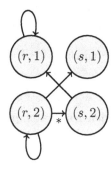

Fig. 2. The graph of position dependencies associated with $\mathcal{R}$ (Example 17)

The rank of a position is the maximum number (possibly infinite) of special arcs on a path leading to that position.

Example 17 illustrates the construction of the graph of position dependencies.

Example 17. Let $\mathcal{R}$ be a set containing the following rules:

- $r(x, y) \rightarrow s(y, z)$
- $s(x, y) \rightarrow r(y, x)$
- $r(x, y) \wedge r(y, z) \rightarrow r(x, z)$

The graph of position dependencies of $\mathcal{R}$ is shown in Figure 2. Special arcs are labelled by a star.

The graph of position dependencies is used to defined "weak-acyclicity", where some cycles are forbidden.

Definition 18 (Weak-Acyclicity [FKMP05]). *Let $\mathcal{R}$ be a set of rules. $\mathcal{R}$ is said to be* weakly-acyclic *if there is no cycle in the graph of position dependencies of $\mathcal{R}$ that goes through a special arc.*

Let us point out that a set of rules containing no existentially quantified variables in rule heads is trivially weakly acyclic (because there is no special arc). Such sets of rules (which can be seen as Datalog programs) are sometimes called *range-restricted*.

Property 2. A weakly-acyclic set of rules is a finite expansion set.

The proof is done by upper-bounding for any fact F and any weakly-acyclic set of rules $\mathcal{R}$ the number of fresh existential variables in the core of the saturation of F with $\mathcal{R}$ (by a double exponential with respect to $\mathcal{R}$; the upper-bound is polynomial if $\mathcal{R}$ is fixed).

Example 18. In the graph of Figure 2 (Example 17), no cycle goes through a special edge, thus $\mathcal{R}$ is weakly acyclic. As such, $\mathcal{R}$ is a finite expansion set.

This condition is sufficient to ensure the finiteness of forward chaining, but not necessary, as witnessed by the following example.

Example 19. Let R be the following rule:

$$r(x, y) \wedge s(x, y) \rightarrow r(x, v) \wedge r(w, y) \wedge s(x, w) \wedge s(v, y).$$

The graph of position dependencies is a clique of special edges, but an application of R cannot trigger a novel application of R —hence, $\{R\}$ is a finite expansion set.

Acyclic Graph of Rule Dependency. The latter example motivates the notion of *rule dependency* [BLMS11], which has originally been introduced for conceptual graph rules [Bag04]. The main idea here is to *characterize* which rule can effectively lead to trigger another rule. Preventing such cycles of dependencies naturally ensures the finiteness of forward chaining.

Definition 19 (Dependency). *Let R_1 and R_2 be two existential rules. R_2 depends on R_1 if there exist a fact F, a homomorphism π_1 from body(R_1) to F and a homomorphism π_2 from body(R_2) to $\alpha(F, R_1, \pi_1)$ such that π_2 is not a homomorphism from body(R_2) to F.*

This definition means that an application of R_1 may, on some fact, trigger a *new* application of R_2. All rule dependencies are summarized in the graph of rule dependencies, whose definition is given below. It is possible to decide if a rule depends on another, by using the notion of piece-unifier introduced in Section 4 [SM96, BLMS11]. The associated decision problem is NP-complete.

Definition 20 (Graph of Rule Dependencies). *Let $\mathcal{R}$ be a set of rules. The graph of rule dependencies of $\mathcal{R}$, denoted by GRD$(\mathcal{R})$ is defined as follows:*

- *its vertices are the rules of $\mathcal{R}$,*
- *there is an arc from R_1 to R_2 if and only if R_2 depends on R_1.*

A set of rules $\mathcal{R}$ is said to have an acyclic graph rule of dependencies (aGRD) if GRD$(\mathcal{R})$ is acyclic. This is in particular the case for Example 20.

Example 20. Let us consider the following two rules:

- $R_1 = p(x) \rightarrow r(x, y) \wedge r(y, z) \wedge r(z, x)$,
- $R_2 = r(x, y) \wedge r(y, x) \rightarrow p(x)$.

Their graph of rule dependencies is given Figure 3.

Let us last notice that Examples 17 and 20 show that weak-acyclicity and aGRD are incomparable criteria.

Fig. 3. The graph of rule dependencies of Example 20

Related Work. The two presented notions are only two examples of the various acyclicity notions that have been introduced so-far. They have indeed been generalized in a variety of ways, such as super-weak acyclicity [Mar09], join-acyclicity [KR11], aGRD$_k$ [BMT11], as well as model-summarizing acyclicity and model-faithful acyclicity [GHK+12]. The interested reader is invited to consult [GHK+13], which among others contains a nice overview of the introduced acyclicity notions.

5.2   Finite Unification Sets

As already noticed in Section 4, materializing the saturation, even when it is theoretically possible, may not be practical due to its large size. Approaches based on query reformulation have thus been proposed. We rely here on piece-based query rewriting, presented in Section 4.

We recall that $q_2 \models q_1$ if and only if there is a homomorphism from q_1 to q_2, which we denote by $q_1 \geq q_2$. Let q be a BCQ, and $\mathcal{Q}$ be a sound and complete UCQ-rewriting of q. If there exist q_1 and q_2 in $\mathcal{Q}$ such that $q_1 \geq q_2$, then $\mathcal{Q} \setminus \{q_2\}$ is also a sound and complete rewriting of q. This observation motivates the definition of *cover* of a set of first-order queries.

Definition 21 (Cover). *Let $\mathcal{Q}$ be a set of Boolean conjunctive queries. A* cover *of $\mathcal{Q}$ is a set $\mathcal{Q}^c \subseteq \mathcal{Q}$ such that:*

1. for any $q \in \mathcal{Q}$, there is $q' \in \mathcal{Q}^c$ such that $q' \geq q$,
2. elements of $\mathcal{Q}^c$ are pairwise incomparable with respect to $\geq$.

Example 21. Let $\mathcal{Q} = \{q_1 = r(x, y) \wedge t(y, z), q_2 = r(x, y) \wedge t(y, y), q_3 = r(x, y) \wedge t(y, z) \wedge t(u, z)\}$. A cover of $\mathcal{Q}$ is $\{q_1\}$. Indeed, $q_1 \geq q_2$ and $q_1 \geq q_3$, because for $i \in \{2, 3\}$, $\pi_{1 \rightarrow i}$ is a homomorphism from q_1 to q_i where:

- $\pi_{1 \rightarrow 2}(x) = x, \pi_{1 \rightarrow 2}(y) = \pi_{1 \rightarrow 2}(z) = y$, and
- $\pi_{1 \rightarrow 3}(x) = x, \pi_{1 \rightarrow 3}(y) = y, \pi_{1 \rightarrow 3}(z) = z$.

We now define the class of finite unification sets, which is the main focus of this section.

Definition 22 (Finite unification set). *Let $\mathcal{R}$ be a set of existential rules. $\mathcal{R}$ is a finite unification set if it holds for any Boolean conjunctive query q that the set of $\mathcal{R}$-rewritings of q admits a finite cover.*

Algorithm 1 is a generic breadth-first rewriting algorithm, that generates for any query q and any finite unification set $\mathcal{R}$ a sound and complete UCQ-rewriting of q with respect to $\mathcal{R}$. Generated queries are queries that belong to $\mathcal{Q}_t$ at some point; explored queries are queries that belong to $\mathcal{Q}_E$ at some point, and thus, for which all one-step rewritings are generated. At each step, a cover of explored and generated queries is computed. This means that only most general queries are kept, both in the set of explored queries and in the set of queries remaining to be explored. If two queries q_1 and q_2 are homomorphically equivalent, and only q_1 has already been explored, then q_1 is kept and q_2 is discarded. This is done in order not to explore two queries that are comparable by the most general relation – which ensures the termination of Algorithm 1.

Algorithm 1. A BREADTH-FIRST REWRITING ALGORITHM

Data: A *fus* $\mathcal{R}$, a Boolean conjunctive query q
Result: A cover of the set of $\mathcal{R}$-rewritings of q
$\mathcal{Q}_F := \{q\}$; // *resulting set*
$\mathcal{Q}_E := \{q\}$; // *queries to be explored*
while $\mathcal{Q}_E \neq \emptyset$ **do**
    $\mathcal{Q}_t := \emptyset$; // *queries generated at this rewriting step*
    for $q_i \in \mathcal{Q}_E$ **do**
        for $R \in \mathcal{R}$ **do**
            for μ *piece-unifier of* q_i *with* R **do**
                $\mathcal{Q}_t := \mathcal{Q}_t \cup \beta(q_i, R, \mu)$;

    $\mathcal{Q}^c := cover(\mathcal{Q}_F \cup \mathcal{Q}_t)$;
    $\mathcal{Q}_E := \mathcal{Q}^c \backslash \mathcal{Q}_F$; // *select unexplored queries from the cover*
    $\mathcal{Q}_F := \mathcal{Q}^c$;
return $\mathcal{Q}_F$

Let us provide a step by step application of Algorithm 1.

Example 22. Let $\mathcal{R}_e = \{R_1, R_2, R_3, R_4, R_5\}$, defined as follows:

- $R_1 : p(x) \wedge h(x) \rightarrow s(x, y)$;
- $R_2 : f(x) \rightarrow s(x, y)$;
- $R_3 : f_1(x) \rightarrow s_1(x, y)$;
- $R_4 : t(x, y) \rightarrow t(y, x)$;
- $R_5 : s_1(x, y) \rightarrow s(x, y)$;

and q_e be the following Boolean query:

$$q_e = t(x_1, x_2) \wedge s(x_1, x_3) \wedge s(x_2, x_3)$$

Initially, $\mathcal{Q}_F = \mathcal{Q}_E = \{q_e = t(x_1, x_2) \wedge s(x_1, x_3) \wedge s(x_2, x_3)\}$. Since $\mathcal{Q}_E$ is not empty, we initialize $\mathcal{Q}_t$ to the empty set, and consider every element of $\mathcal{Q}_E$. The only element of $\mathcal{Q}_E$ is q_e, so we add to $\mathcal{Q}_t$ all possible rewritings of q_e. These are:

- $q_1 = t(x,x) \wedge p(x) \wedge h(x)$, by unifying with respect μ_1, which is defined by $(\{s(x_1,x_3), s(x_2,x_3)\}, u_1(x_1) = u_1(x_2) = x, u_1(x_3) = y)$, and is a unifier of q_e with R_1;
- $q_2 = t(x,x) \wedge f(x)$, with respect to $\mu_2 = (\{s(x_1,x_3), s(x_2,x_3)\}, u_2(x_1) = u_2(x_2) = x, u_2(x_3) = y)$, unifier of q_e with R_2;
- $q_3 = t(x_2,x_1) \wedge s(x_1,x_3) \wedge s(x_2,x_3)$ with respect to $\mu_3 = (\{t(x_1,x_2), u_3(x_1) = y, u_3(x_2) = x)$, unifier of q_e with R_4;
- $q_4 = t(x_1,x_2) \wedge s_1(x_1,x_3) \wedge s(x_2,x_3)$ with respect to $\mu_4 = (\{s(x_1,x_3)\}, u_4(x_1) = x, u_4(x_3) = y)$, unifier of q_e with R_5;
- $q_5 = t(x_1,x_2) \wedge s(x_1,x_3) \wedge s_1(x_2,x_3)$ with respect to $\mu_5 = (\{s(x_2,x_3)\}, u_5(x_2) = x, u_5(x_3) = y)$, unifier of q_e with R_5;
- $q_6 = t(x,x) \wedge s_1(x,x_3)$, with respect to $\mu_6 = (\{s(x_1,x_3), s(x_2,x_3)\}, u_6(x_1) = u_6(x_2) = x, u_6(x_3) = y)$, unifier of q_e with R_5;

Thus $\mathcal{Q}_t = \{q_1, q_2, q_3, q_4, q_5, q_6\}$. $\mathcal{Q}^c$ is set to $\{q_e, q_1, q_2, q_3, q_4, q_5, q_6\}$, since none of the generated queries are comparable. $\mathcal{Q}_E$ is set to $\{q_1, q_2, q_3, q_4, q_5, q_6\}$ and $\mathcal{Q}_F$ to $\mathcal{Q}^c$.

Algorithm 1 performs once more the while loop. $\mathcal{Q}_t$ is reinitialized to the empty set, and all rewritings of $\mathcal{Q}_E$ are rewritten. We thus explore every q_i for $i \le 5$. q_1 and q_2 are not unifiable with any rule. We then explore rewritings of q_3. The following queries can be obtained by a one step rewriting of q_3:

$$q_1^3 = t(x,x) \wedge p(x) \wedge h(x),$$

$$q_2^3 = t(x,x) \wedge f(x),$$

$$q_3^3 = t(x_1,x_2) \wedge s(x_1,x_3) \wedge s(x_2,x_3),$$

$$q_4^3 = t(x,x) \wedge s_1(x,x_3),$$

$$q_5^3 = t(x_2,x_1) \wedge s_1(x_1,x_3) \wedge s(x_2,x_3),$$

$$q_6^3 = t(x_2,x_1) \wedge s(x_1,x_3) \wedge s_1(x_2,x_3).$$

As for q_4, the following rewritings are generable:

$$q_1^4 = t(x_2,x_1) \wedge s_1(x_1,x_3) \wedge s(x_2,x_3),$$
$$q_2^4 = t(x_1,x_2) \wedge s_1(x_1,x_3) \wedge s_1(x_2,x_3).$$

From q_5:

$$q_1^5 = t(x_2,x_1) \wedge s(x_1,x_3) \wedge s_1(x_2,x_3),$$
$$q_2^5 = t(x_1,x_2) \wedge s_1(x_1,x_3) \wedge s_1(x_2,x_3).$$

And from q_6:

$$q_1^6 = t(x, x) \wedge f_1(x).$$

As illustrated by Figure 4, which explicits subsumption relations among queries, a cover of the queries is $\{q_e, q_1, q_2, q_3, q_4, q_5, q_5^3, q_6^3, q_2^4, q_1^6\}$, which is the new value of $\mathcal{Q}^c$. Note that q_6 does not belong to $\mathcal{Q}^c$, because the newly generated query q_2^4 is strictly more general than q_6. $\mathcal{Q}_E$ is set to $\{q_5^3, q_6^3, q_2^4, q_1^6\}$, $\mathcal{Q}_F$ to $\mathcal{Q}^c$, and $\mathcal{Q}_E$ is explored, entering a new iteration of the while loop. Two queries are generated:

$$q' = t(x_2, x_1) \wedge s_1(x_1, x_3) \wedge s_1(x_2, x_3),$$

and

$$q'' = t(x, x) \wedge f_1(x).$$

At the end of this while loop, we have $\mathcal{Q}_E = \{q'\}$ and

$$\mathcal{Q}_F = \{q_e, q_1, q_2, q_3, q_4, q_5, q_5^3, q_6^3, q_2^4, q_1^6, q'\}.$$

Since all queries generable from q' are covered by $\mathcal{Q}_F$, the algorithm halts and outputs:

$$\{q_e, q_1, q_2, q_3, q_4, q_5, q_5^3, q_6^3, q_2^4, q_1^6, q'\}.$$

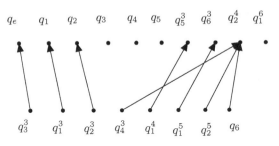

Fig. 4. There is an arrow from q to q' if and only if q' is more general than q

The following lemma is crucial for the completeness of Algorithm 1. It ensures that for any queries q and q' such that $q' \geq q$, any rewriting that can be obtained in one step from q is less general than a rewriting that can be obtained in one step from q'. A detailed discussion of what can happen when considering rewriting procedures where this lemma does not hold can be found in [KLMT13].

Lemma 1 ([KLMT12]). *Let q_1 and q_2 be two Boolean conjunctive queries such that $q_1 \geq q_2$. For any rewriting q_2' of q_2 such that $q_1 \not\geq q_2'$, there exists a rewriting q_1' of q_1 such that $q_1' \geq q_2'$.*

Theorem 5. *The output of Algorithm 1 is a sound and complete set of $\mathcal{R}$-rewritings of q.*

Proof. We define a 1-rewriting of q as a direct rewriting, and a k-rewriting of q as a direct rewriting of a $(k-1)$-rewriting for any $k \geq 2$. We prove by induction on k that for any $i \leq k$, for any q_i that is an i-rewriting of q, there is $q_i^* \in \mathcal{Q}_{F_i}$, that is, Q_F after the ith loop such that $q_i^* \geq q_i$. The only 0-rewriting of q is q, which initially belongs to $\mathcal{Q}_F$, which proves the claim for $k = 0$. Let assume that the claim is true for k, and let us show it for $k+1$. Let q_{i+1} be a $i+1$-rewriting of q. If $i < k$, q_{i+1} is covered by an element of $Q_{F_{i+1}}$ by induction assumption. Otherwise, let q_i be a k-rewriting such that q_{i+1} is a 1-rewriting of q_i. There exists $q_i^* \in Q_{F_i}$ such that $q_i^* \geq q_i$. Lemma 1 ensures that there exists q_{i+1}^* a 1-rewriting of q_i^* such that $q_{i+1}^* \geq q_{i+1}$, which ends the proof.

Backward-Shyness. As for finite expansion sets, the problem of recognizing finite unification sets is undecidable. Several concrete classes of finite unification sets are known, the most famous ones being the class of linear rules ([CGK08] and also [BLMS09], under the name of atomic-hypothesis rules) and the class of sticky sets of rules [CGP10]. We present both classes of rules under the unifying concept of "backward shy"[4] class of rules. To define that notion, we need the notion of *original* and *generated* variables.

Definition 23 (Original and Generated Variables). *Let q be a Boolean conjunctive query, $\mathcal{R}$ be a set of rules, and q' be an $\mathcal{R}$-rewriting of q, obtained by a rewriting sequence $q = q_0, q_1, \ldots, q_n = q'$. Original variables of q' (with respect to q) are inductively defined as follows:*

- *all variables of q are original;*
- *if q_i has original variables X, and q_{i+1} is the rewriting of q_i with respect to $\mu = (q_i', u)$, the original variables of q_{i+1} are the images of the elements of X by u.*

A variable that is not original is generated.

Backward shyness of a set of rules $\mathcal{R}$ ensures that any query q admits a finite set of $\mathcal{R}$-rewritings.

Definition 24 (Backward Shyness). *Let $\mathcal{R}$ be a set of rules. $\mathcal{R}$ is to be said backward shy if for any Boolean conjunctive query q, for any $\mathcal{R}$-rewriting q' of q, no generated variable of q' appears in two atoms.*

Property 3 provides an upper bound on the number of most general rewritings of a query q with respect to a backward shy set of rules.

---

[4] The term "backward shy" is not standard, and inspired from shy rules [LMTV12]. However, there is no inclusion between shy and backward shy rules.

Property 3 (Backward Shy Rules are fus). Let $\mathcal{R}$ be a set of backward shy rules, and q a Boolean conjunctive query. There are at most $2^{p(|terms(q)|+w)^w}$ $\mathcal{R}$-rewritings of q that are not equivalent up to isomorphism, where w is the maximum arity of a predicate and p is the number of predicates appearing in the rules.

Proof. The number of distinct atoms with arguments the terms of q and at most w other terms is upper bounded by $p(|terms(q)| + w)^w$. Since a term that is not a term of q cannot appear in two different atoms, we obtain the claimed upper bound.

Linear rules [CGK08, BLMS09] are rules whose body contains only one atom. Let us observe that linear rules are backward shy.

Property 4. Any set of linear rules is backward shy.

Proof. The claim follows from the following two remarks:

- when a generated variable is introduced by a rewriting step, it appears in exactly one atom;
- if x appears in k atoms of a query q before a rewriting with respect to $\mu = (q', u)$, then $u(x)$ appears in at most k atoms in the rewriting of q with respect to μ.

We now present sticky rules, which have been introduced as a decidability criterion that may deal with non-guarded rules.

Definition 25 (Sticky Sets of Rules [CGP10]). *Let $\mathcal{R}$ be a set of rules. We iteratively mark the variables of the rule bodies of $\mathcal{R}$ according to the following marking procedure. First, for each rule $R \in \mathcal{R}$, and each variable $v \in body(R)$, we mark v if there is an atom a of $head(R)$ such that v is not an argument of a. We then apply until a fixpoint is reached the following step: for each rule R, if a marked variable appears in $body(R)$ at position (p, i), then we mark for each rule R' each occurrence of the variables of $body(R')$ that appear in $head(R')$ at position (p, i). $\mathcal{R}$ is said to be sticky if there is no rule R such that a marked variable appears more than once in $body(R)$.*

Example 23 provides an example of sticky and non-sticky rules.

Example 23. Let $\mathcal{R}_1$ be a set of rules containing the following rule:

- $r(x, y) \wedge t(y, z) \rightarrow s(x, z)$

$\mathcal{R}_1$ is not sticky, since y is marked by the marking procedure, and appears twice in a rule body. On the other hand, the set containing the following two rules is sticky:

- $r(x_1, y_1) \wedge t(y_1, z_1) \rightarrow s(y_1, u_1)$
- $s(x_2, y_2) \rightarrow r(y_2, x_2)$

Indeed, x_1 and z_1 are marked at the initialization step. The propagation step marks y_2, because y_2 appears at the first position of r in the head of the second rule, as x_1 which is already marked. Finally, x_1, z_1 and y_2 are marked, and are the only marked variables. Since none of these variables appears twice in a rule body, this set of rules is sticky.

Property 5. Any sticky set of rules is backward shy.

Proof. We show Property 5 by induction on the length of the derivation. If q' is a one-step rewriting of q, then a generated variable is a variable that has been created at this rewriting step. By the initialization step of the sticky marking, such a variable appears at exactly one position, which is marked. Let assume that the induction assumption holds for any k-rewriting of q, and let q' be a $k+1$-rewriting of q. Let q_k be the k-rewriting of q from which q' has been rewritten. A generated variable of q' may appear for two different reasons: either it has been generated at the last rewriting step, and the same reasoning as before can be applied. Or it is a generated variable with respect to q_k. By induction assumption, it appears at a marked position. The stickiness property implies that it appears also only once in q', and at a marked position.

Related Work. The rewriting algorithm we presented in this section is only one among several. We give here some pointers to several other rewriting algorithms or rewriting tools. Among implemented tools, we can cite Clipper [EOS+12], Kyrie [MC13], QuOnto [ACG+05], Nyaya [GOP11], Rapid [CTS11], Iqaros [VSS12], or the piece-based rewriting algorithm presented in [KLMT12].

5.3   Other Decidable Cases

Presenting algorithms that allow to deal with sets of rules ensuring neither the finiteness of the canonical model nor the existence of a sound and complete first-order rewriting is out of the scope of that short course. We give however a quick overview of topics that have been studied and relevant references.

Bounded Treewidth Sets. Most of the known decidable cases that are neither finite unification sets nor finite expansion sets are *bounded treewidth sets*. This class of rules, once again not recognizable, is based on the structural property of the facts that are generated starting from any fact. Definition 26 introduces formally this notion.

Definition 26 (Bounded treewidth set). *A set of rules $\mathcal{R}$ is called a bounded-treewidth set (bts) if for any fact F, there exists an integer $b = f(F, \mathcal{R})$ such that for any $\mathcal{R}$-derivation F' of F, the treewidth of $core(F')$ is less or equal to b.*

The most prominent example of a bounded treewidth set of rules is that of a set of guarded rules. A rule is guarded if its body contains a guard, that is, an atom that contains all the body variables. The original algorithm for conjunctive query answering under guarded sets of rules performs a traditional forward chaining and stops it after a number of steps which is a function of the sizes of the rule set and the query [CGK08]. Several extensions of the notion of guarded rules have been proposed in the literature, for instance by exploiting the graph of position dependencies (Definition 17) in order to restrict the set of body variables that needs to be guarded. The interested reader can consult [CGK08, KR11, TBMR12] for more details about these restrictions and associated algorithms.

Outside of the Classification and Combinations. Even if the three introduced classes cover most of the known decidable class so far, some classes are outside of this classification. It is in particular the case for *parsimonious* sets of rules [LMTV12], which is an abstract class in its own right. Another popular way of getting sets of rules that do not fall in the afore mentioned classification is to *combine* decidable classes of rules. "Raw" combination usually leads to undecidability, but several restrictions have been proposed in the literature. One can distinguish two kinds of combinations: generic combination, which relies on abstract properties of rule sets and interaction between them, and "built-in" combination, which looks at specific classes and restrict the way they interact. In the first case, the already seen graph of rule dependencies may be used to split the study of a rule set into the study of the sets that are formed by its strongly connected components. In the second category, weakly-sticky sets of rules [CGP10] and tameness [GMP13] have been proposed, allowing to combine (under some restrictions) sticky sets of rules with weakly-acyclic sets of rules for the former, and with guarded rules for the latter.

6   Ongoing Research and Open Issues

We finish this course by presenting two current research issues, that both need to be tackled in order to obtain practical systems. The first one deals with the shortcomings of current query rewriting techniques. Indeed, experiments made with the first rewriting tools have shown the rewritings to be of enormous size, which could not even be passed to an RDMS for execution. How to circumvent that problem? This is an intricate issue, that raises both theoretical and practical work, and that we will touch upon in Section 6.1.

Then, we will consider the important topic of inconsistent data. Given the usually cited Semantic Web application area, it is highly probable that the data a user will want to use is inconsistent with respect to an ontology encompassing both existential rules and negative constraints. This raises a non-trivial problem, since the classical semantics of first-order logic does not allow to draw meaningful, or at least intuitive, results in the presence of any inconsistency. We will present some alternative semantics in Section 6.2.

6.1   Query Rewriting: Any Useful in Practice?

Behind this rather provocative title hides a serious question: how efficient can query answering systems based on query rewriting be in practice? It is widely accepted that RDMS are well optimized and efficient in practice. However, the use of ontologies in order to perform query rewriting modifies the scope of what can be called a real-world query. We first quickly exhibit what the problem is, and present some of the approaches that have been proposed in order to overcome it. Last, we touch upon benchmarking problems.

Large Size of First-Order Rewritings. Since the evaluation of Boolean conjunctive queries is a NP-hard problem, stating that RDMS are efficient means that they are efficient on real-world queries, that is, queries that a user may try to evaluate. In particular, such queries are usually of easy structure and of small size. When adding an ontology, even when starting from a simple ontology and a simple query, one may be led to evaluate a huge union of conjunctive queries, as can be noticed with the following example.

Example 24. Let $\mathcal{R} = \{R_i\}_{1 \leq i \leq n}$, where $R_i : r_i(x, y) \rightarrow r_{i-1}(x, y)$. Let q be the following query:

$$r_0(x_1, x_2) \wedge r_0(x_2, x_3).$$

q has a UCQ-rewriting with $(n+1)^2$ conjunctive queries, which are $\{r_i(x_1, x_2) \wedge r_j(x_2, x_3)\}_{0 \leq i,j \leq n}$.

Example 24 can be generalized by taking a query of k atoms and classes/roles having n subclasses/subroles. This would yield an optimal UCQ-rewriting with $(n+1)^k$ conjunctive queries. This cannot be considered as a small query anymore, and existing systems are not able to deal with such huge queries. Moreover, it has been shown that the exponential size of the rewritings also holds for so-called pure first-order rewritings. The interested reader is invited to consult, among others, [KKPZ12].

Alternative Approaches. Two approaches have been proposed in order to escape from this problem of rewriting size, with the additional constraint of not changing the data. First, changing the target language in which rewritings are expressed. Instead of unions of conjunctive queries, one may use other forms of first-order formulas [Tho13], or Datalog rewritings [RA10]. This may allow to reduce the size of the rewritings in some common cases (such as for large class hierarchies), or for a whole class of ontologies. In particular, it was shown that for a wide class of ontologies, which in particular include linear and sticky rules, there exists a polynomial non-recursive Datalog rewriting for any query [GS12]. These rewritings, however, are not claimed to be efficiently evaluable.

Another approach is to reduce the scope of the rewritings: that is, instead of providing sound and complete answers on any database, the rewriting technique will provide sound and complete answers only on databases that fulfill some additional constraints. In particular, it may be possible in some settings to assume that the database is already complete with respect to some database dependencies. In the case of a rewriting taking the form of a set of conjunctive queries, this would imply that some of the conjunctive queries that are part of this set are not required, and one could ignore them. The interested reader is invited to consult [Ros12, RMC12] for more details.

Benchmarking Problems. An additional problem when one wants to evaluate or compare different approaches is the current lack of benchmarks. Ideally, a test case would contain an ontology, some data, and a conjunctive query. Unfortunately, such trios are not widely available. The benchmark classically used since [PUHM09] to evaluate query rewriting algorithms is composed of five ontologies, with five queries each, and no associated data. The most used ontology is LUBM [5], and several adaptations of it have been proposed [RMC12, LSTW12], together with data generators. The small number of queries in the benchmark is already a serious weakness. This has already been noticed, and a recent paper proposed an automatic generation of relevant queries in order to test soundness and completeness of algorithms [ISG12]. Recently, more expressive real-world ontologies (expressed thanks to Description Logics) have been used for the evaluation of query rewriting [TSCS13]. However, once again queries are hand-crafted and no data are available.

6.2   Dealing with Inconsistent Data

In a setting where data come from several heterogeneous and possibly unchecked sources, it is highly probable for the knowledge base to be inconsistent. An example of inconsistent knowledge base is presented in Example 25.

Example 25. Let us consider the following fact:

$$F = \{cat(Tom), barks(Tom)\},$$

and the following rules:

- $barks(x) \rightarrow dog(x)$
- $cat(x) \rightarrow animal(x)$
- $dog(x) \rightarrow animal(x)$

Last, let us specify that the classes *dog* and *cat* are disjoint, thanks to the following negative constraint:

$$dog(x) \wedge cat(x) \rightarrow \bot.$$

According to the classical first-order semantics, the answer to any Boolean query is yes, since the given knowledge base is inconsistent. This is somehow counterintuitive, and alternative semantics have been proposed in order to provide a more intuitive behavior [LLR+10, LMS12]. We present two of them in the following, which are based on the notion of *repair*.

---

[5] http://swat.cse.lehigh.edu/projects/lubm/

Definition 27 (Repair). *Let $\mathcal{R}$ be a set of rules, $\mathcal{C}$ be a set of constraints, and F be a fact. A repair of F (with respect to $\mathcal{R}$ and $\mathcal{C}$) is a maximal subset F' of F such that $F', \mathcal{R}, \mathcal{C} \not\models \bot$.*

Given this definition of a repair, one can define a semantics for consistent query answering as follows: the query should be entailed by any repair together with the set of rules.

Definition 28 (AR semantics). *Let $\mathcal{R}$ be a set of rules, $\mathcal{C}$ be a set of constraints, F be a fact and q be a Boolean conjunctive query. $\mathcal{K}$ entails q for the AR semantics if for every repair F' of F with respect to $\mathcal{R}$ and $\mathcal{C}$, it holds that $F', \mathcal{R} \models q$.*

A more conservative semantics requires for the query to be entailed by the *intersection* of all the repairs together with the set of rules. Intuitively, this means that any atom that may lead to some contradiction is ignored during the reasoning.

Definition 29 (IAR semantics). *Let $\mathcal{R}$ be a set of rules, $\mathcal{C}$ be a set of constraints, F be a fact and q be a Boolean conjunctive query. $\mathcal{K}$ entails q for the AR semantics if it holds that $F_\cap, \mathcal{R} \models q$, where $F_\cap$ is the intersection of all the repairs of F with respect to $\mathcal{R}$ and $\mathcal{C}$.*

Let us exhibit the difference in the behavior of the two semantics on an example.

Example 26. Let us consider again the knowledge base of Example 25. There are two repairs: $F_1 = \{cat(Tom)\}$ and $F_2 = \{barks(Tom)\}$. Let us consider the query $q = animal(Tom)$. According to the AR semantics, q is entailed by the knowledge base, since q is entailed by F_1 and $\mathcal{R}$ as well as by F_2 and $\mathcal{R}$. However, since the intersection between F_1 and F_2 is empty, q is not entailed by $\mathcal{K}$ according to the IAR semantics.

Let us note that the problem of consistent conjunctive query answering under AR semantics is intractable (i.e., not polynomial) with respect to data complexity [LLR+10, Bie12], even for ontology languages as inexpressive as DL-Lite$_{core}$. An idea to overcome this hardness result has been to develop "approximation schemes" for AR-semantics, that is, to provide two families of efficiently computable semantics that upper and lower bound AR-semantics, while converging towards it [BR13]. However, the design and implementation of efficient consistent query answering algorithms remains an open issue.

References

[ACG+05] Acciarri, A., Calvanese, D., De Giacomo, G., Lembo, D., Lenzerini, M., Palmieri, M., Rosati, R.: Quonto: Querying ontologies. In: AAAI, pp. 1670–1671 (2005)

[ACKZ09]   Artale, A., Calvanese, D., Kontchakov, R., Zakharyaschev, M.: The DL-Lite family and relations. J. Artif. Intell. Res (JAIR) 36, 1–69 (2009)

[AHV95]   Abiteboul, S., Hull, R., Vianu, V.: Foundations of Databases. Addison-Wesley (1995)

[Bag04]   Baget, J.-F.: Improving the forward chaining algorithm for conceptual graphs rules. In: KR 2004, pp. 407–414. AAAI Press (2004)

[BBL05]   Baader, F., Brandt, S., Lutz, C.: Pushing the $\mathcal{EL}$ envelope. In: IJCAI, pp. 364–369 (2005)

[BCM$^+$07]   Acciarri, A., Calvanese, D., De Giacomo, G., Lembo, D., Lenzerini, M., Palmieri, M., Rosati, R.: Quonto: Querying ontologies. In: AAAI, pp. 1670–1671 (2005)

[Bie12]   Bienvenu, M.: On the complexity of consistent query answering in the presence of simple ontologies. In: AAAI (2012)

[BLMS09]   Baget, J.-F., Leclère, M., Mugnier, M.-L., Salvat, E.: Extending Decidable Cases for Rules with Existential Variables. In: IJCAI, pp. 677–682 (2009)

[BLMS11]   Baget, J.-F., Leclère, M., Mugnier, M.-L., Salvat, E.: On Rules with Existential Variables: Walking the Decidability Line. Artif. Intell. 175(9-10), 1620–1654 (2011)

[BM02]   Baget, J.-F., Mugnier, M.-L.: The Complexity of Rules and Constraints. J. Artif. Intell. Res (JAIR) 16, 425–465 (2002)

[BMT11]   Baget, J.-F., Mugnier, M.-L., Thomazo, M.: Towards farsighted dependencies for existential rules. In: Rudolph, S., Gutierrez, C. (eds.) RR 2011. LNCS, vol. 6902, pp. 30–45. Springer, Heidelberg (2011)

[BR13]   Bienvenu, M., Rosati, R.: Tractable approximations of consistent query answering for robust ontology-based data access. In: IJCAI (2013)

[BV81]   Beeri, C., Vardi, M.: The implication problem for data dependencies. In: Even, S., Kariv, O. (eds.) ICALP 1981. LNCS, vol. 115, pp. 73–85. Springer, Heidelberg (1981)

[CGK08]   Calì, A., Gottlob, G., Kifer, M.: Taming the Infinite Chase: Query Answering under Expressive Relational Constraints. In: KR, pp. 70–80 (2008)

[CGL$^+$05]   Calvanese, D., De Giacomo, G., Lembo, D., Lenzerini, M., Rosati, R.: Dl-lite: Tractable description logics for ontologies. In: AAAI, pp. 602–607 (2005)

[CGL$^+$07]   Calvanese, D., De Giacomo, G., Lembo, D., Lenzerini, M., Rosati, R.: Tractable reasoning and efficient query answering in description logics: The DL-lite family. J. Autom. Reasoning 39(3), 385–429 (2007)

[CGL09]   Calì, A., Gottlob, G., Lukasiewicz, T.: A General Datalog-Based Framework for Tractable Query Answering over Ontologies. In: PODS, pp. 77–86. ACM (2009)

[CGP10]   Calì, A., Gottlob, G., Pieris, A.: Query rewriting under non-guarded rules. In: AMW (2010)

[CLM81]   Chandra, A.K., Lewis, H.R., Makowsky, J.A.: Embedded implicational dependencies and their inference problem. In: STOC, pp. 342–354 (1981)

[CM09]   Chein, M., Mugnier, M.-L.: Graph-based Knowledge Representation: Computational Foundations of Conceptual Graphs, 1st edn. Springer (2009)

[CTS11]   Chortaras, A., Trivela, D., Stamou, G.: Optimized query rewriting for OWL 2 QL. In: Bjørner, N., Sofronie-Stokkermans, V. (eds.) CADE 2011. LNCS, vol. 6803, pp. 192–206. Springer, Heidelberg (2011)

[EOS$^+$12]   Eiter, T., Ortiz, M., Simkus, M., Tran, T.-K., Xiao, G.: Query rewriting for horn-shiq plus rules. In: AAAI (2012)

[FKMP05] Fagin, R., Kolaitis, P.G., Miller, R.J., Popa, L.: Data Exchange: Semantics and Query Answering. Theor. Comput. Sci. 336(1), 89–124 (2005)

[GHK+12] Grau, B.C., Horrocks, I., Krötzsch, M., Kupke, C., Magka, D., Motik, B., Wang, Z.: Acyclicity conditions and their application to query answering in description logics. In: KR (2012)

[GHK+13] Grau, B.C., Horrocks, I., Krötzsch, M., Kupke, C., Magka, D., Motik, B., Wang, Z.: Acyclicity notions for existential rules and their application to query answering in ontologies. J. Artif. Intell. Res (JAIR) 47, 741–808 (2013)

[GMP13] Gottlob, G., Manna, M., Pieris, A.: Combining decidability paradigms for existential rules. TPLP 13(4-5), 877–892 (2013)

[GOP11] Gottlob, G., Orsi, G., Pieris, A.: Ontological queries: Rewriting and optimization. In: ICDE, pp. 2–13 (2011)

[GS12] Gottlob, G., Schwentick, T.: Rewriting ontological queries into small non-recursive datalog programs. In: KR (2012)

[ISG12] Imprialou, M., Stoilos, G., Grau, B.C.: Benchmarking ontology-based query rewriting systems. In: AAAI (2012)

[KKPZ12] Kikot, S., Kontchakov, R., Podolskii, V.V., Zakharyaschev, M.: Long rewritings, short rewritings. In: Description Logics (2012)

[KLMT12] König, M., Leclère, M., Mugnier, M.-L., Thomazo, M.: A sound and complete backward chaining algorithm for existential rules. In: Krötzsch, M., Straccia, U. (eds.) RR 2012. LNCS, vol. 7497, pp. 122–138. Springer, Heidelberg (2012)

[KLMT13] König, M., Leclère, M., Mugnier, M.-L., Thomazo, M.: On the exploration of the query rewriting space with existential rules. In: Faber, W., Lembo, D. (eds.) RR 2013. LNCS, vol. 7994, pp. 123–137. Springer, Heidelberg (2013)

[KR11] Krötzsch, M., Rudolph, S.: Extending decidable existential rules by joining acyclicity and guardedness. In: IJCAI, pp. 963–968 (2011)

[LLR+10] Lembo, D., Lenzerini, M., Rosati, R., Ruzzi, M., Savo, D.F.: Inconsistency-tolerant semantics for description logics. In: Hitzler, P., Lukasiewicz, T. (eds.) RR 2010. LNCS, vol. 6333, pp. 103–117. Springer, Heidelberg (2010)

[LMS12] Lukasiewicz, T., Martinez, M.V., Simari, G.I.: Inconsistency handling in datalog+/- ontologies. In: ECAI (2012)

[LMTV12] Leone, N., Manna, M., Terracina, G., Veltri, P.: Efficiently computable datalog; programs. In: KR (2012)

[LSTW12] Lutz, C., Seylan, İ., Toman, D., Wolter, F.: The combined approach to OBDA: Taming role hierarchies using filters. In: Alani, H., et al. (eds.) ISWC 2013, Part I. LNCS, vol. 8218, pp. 314–330. Springer, Heidelberg (2013)

[LTW09] Lutz, C., Toman, D., Wolter, F.: Conjunctive Query Answering in the Description Logic $\mathcal{EL}$ Using a Relational Database System. In: IJCAI, pp. 2070–2075 (2009)

[Mar09] Marnette, B.: Generalized schema-mappings: from termination to tractability. In: PODS, pp. 13–22 (2009)

[MC13] Mora, J., Corcho, Ó.: Engineering optimisations in query rewriting for obda. In: I-SEMANTICS, pp. 41–48 (2013)

[OWL09] W3C OWL Working Group. OWL 2 Web Ontology Language: Document Overview. W3C Recommendation (2009), http://www.w3.org/TR/owl2-overview/

[PUHM09] Pérez-Urbina, H., Horrocks, I., Motik, B.: Efficient query answering for OWL 2. In: Bernstein, A., Karger, D.R., Heath, T., Feigenbaum, L., Maynard, D., Motta, E., Thirunarayan, K. (eds.) ISWC 2009. LNCS, vol. 5823, pp. 489–504. Springer, Heidelberg (2009)

[RA10]   Rosati, R., Almatelli, A.: Improving query answering over dl-lite ontologies. In: KR (2010)

[RMC12]   Rodriguez-Muro, M., Calvanese, D.: High performance query answering over DL-lite ontologies. In: KR (2012)

[Ros12]   Rosati, R.: Prexto: Query rewriting under extensional constraints in $DL-lite$. In: Simperl, E., Cimiano, P., Polleres, A., Corcho, O., Presutti, V. (eds.) ESWC 2012. LNCS, vol. 7295, pp. 360–374. Springer, Heidelberg (2012)

[SM96]   Salvat, E., Mugnier, M.-L.: Sound and complete forward and backward chainingd of graph rules. In: ICCS, pp. 248–262 (1996)

[TBMR12]   Thomazo, M., Baget, J.-F., Mugnier, M.-L., Rudolph, S.: A generic querying algorithm for greedy sets of existential rules. In: KR (2012)

[Tho13]   Thomazo, M.: Compact rewriting for existential rules. In: IJCAI (2013)

[TSCS13]   Trivela, D., Stoilos, G., Chortaras, A., Stamou, G.B.: Optimising resolution-based rewriting algorithms for dl ontologies. In: Description Logics, pp. 464–476 (2013)

[VSS12]   Venetis, T., Stoilos, G., Stamou, G.B.: Incremental query rewriting for OWL 2 QL. In: Description Logics (2012)

Ontology Based Data Access on Temporal and Streaming Data*

Özgür Lütfü Özçep and Ralf Möller

Institute for Softwaresystems (STS)
Hamburg University of Technology
Hamburg, Germany
{oezguer.oezcep,moeller}@tu-harburg.de

Abstract. Though processing time-dependent data has been investigated for a long time, the research on temporal and especially stream reasoning over linked open data and ontologies is reaching its high point these days. In this tutorial, we give an overview of state-of-the art query languages and engines for temporal and stream reasoning. On a more detailed level, we discuss the new language STARQL (Reasoning-based Query Language for Streaming and Temporal ontology Access). STARQL is designed as an expressive and flexible stream query framework that offers the possibility to embed different (temporal) description logics as filter query languages over ontologies, and hence it can be used within the OBDA paradigm (Ontology Based Data Access in the classical sense) and within the ABDEO paradigm (Accessing Big Data over Expressive Ontologies).

Keywords: Ontology Based Data Access, streams, temporal logics, rewriting, unfolding, semantic web.

1 Introduction

Ontology based data access (OBDA) [20] stands for a paradigm of accessing huge data sets through an interface query language that relies on a signature for which constraints are modeled in a knowledge base called ontology. Skimming the publications of conferences/journals on description logics, extended database management systems or the semantic web shows that OBDA has become an important topic with various subtopics and new slightly deviating research aims— in particular, widening its original scope from lightweight representation languages to more expressive ones (e.g., [58] describes an approach for accessing big data with expressive ontologies (ABDEO)). Moreover, OBDA seems to have found its way into industrial applications. In the EU funded FP7 project OPTIQUE [22], an OBDA based software platform is developed to fulfill the needs of the two industrial stakeholders STATOIL and SIEMENS.

* This work has been supported by the European Commission as part of the FP7 project Optique http://www.optique-project.eu/

M. Koubarakis et al. (Eds.): Reasoning Web 2014, LNCS 8714, pp. 279–312, 2014.
© Springer International Publishing Switzerland 2014

A look into recent publications [15,8,18] reveals that OBDA is ripe for the integration of formal approaches dealing with the processing of temporal and streaming data. Upcoming research in temporalizing and streamifying OBDA is going to push OBDA's industrial attractiveness because use cases with some or other form of processing temporal and/or streaming data abound—be it event recognition, monitoring, sensor networking, text processing, video processing, time-series applications, just to name a few.

The rich literature on temporal logics and stream processing on the level of sensor data and relational stream data management systems (see the following sections) provide good directions for the actual venture of temporalizing and streamifying OBDA. The neat semantics of temporal logics combined with the practical and well-proven sliding window operator for streams founds the basis on which to built high-level query languages fitting to the OBDA paradigm and related paradigms such as ABDEO.

Next to a discussion of recent approaches for temporal and streamified OBDA we are also going to illustrate a new query language framework called STARQL which can be used within the classical OBDA as well as the ABDEO paradigm. It heavily relies on a window operator for building sequences of ABoxes; the sequence structure is used to combine classical intra-ABox reasoning/rewriting with temporal inter-ABox reasoning.

The paper is structured as follows. Section 2 introduces the paradigm of ontology based data access. Discussing in detail classical OBDA centered around the family of description logics DL-Lite in Sect. 3, we also discuss OBDA in a broader sense for more expressive logics in Sect. 4. Approaches introducing a temporal dimension into OBDA are discussed in 5, and, in a more detailed manner, approaches introducing streams into OBDA are discussed in Section 6. Section 7 before the conclusion contains an overview of the new stream-temporal language STARQL framework.

2   Ontology Based Data Access

Ever since its introduction, Ontology Based data Access (OBDA) has become a widely accepted research topic in different areas such as the semantic web, database theory, and the description logics, and, moreover, it finds its way into industrial applications, two of which are the STATOIL and the SIEMENS use cases in the FP7 framework OPTIQUE http://www.optique-project.eu/.

The driving idea behind ontology based data access is to keep the source data where they are and access them with a query interface over a declarative knowledge base called ontology. In description logic speak, the ontology is made up of a TBox, which models the terminological part of the domain by general subconcept and subrole axioms and perhaps additional constraints such as functionality assertions, and an ABox, which is the logical presentation of the data as assertional axioms produced my mappings from the data sources.

In the classical OBDA approach, the ABox representation of the data by mappings is just for the purpose of defining the semantics of queries w.r.t. an ontology. So, the ABox is not materialized for the purpose of query answering; instead, complete and correct answering w.r.t. the ontology is handled by compiling the knowledge TBox into the given query. Afterwards, the compiled query, also called the rewritten query, is unfolded w.r.t. the mappings into a query over the data sources, e.g., an SQL query over a relational database.

What are the benefits of OBDA querying over direct querying within the language of the data sources? The first aspect is that one has a declarative language w.r.t. a model described in the TBox and the data in the ABox, thereby allowing to distinguish between a neat representation of intensional knowledge and factual knowledge.

The second aspect is that of semantic integration [63]. Different heterogeneous sources can be accessed under a common ontological interface. Users of the query language on the ontological have to consider/use only the language of the ontology and the associated query language, but do not have to deal with possibly different languages of different sources. Additionally, different models can be implemented by different TBoxes without the need to recompile queries. This offers to set up test scenarios, in which different models (represented by the TBox) can be tested with the same queries (as long as the TBoxes use the same signature.) Following this line, if a TBox has proven to be good or useful, it can be used with various data sources, as long as the mappings are adapted to the various data source in different use cases.

The OBDA approach offers a way to deal with the indefiniteness and incompleteness in data that differs radically from the NULL value approach in relational databases. OBDA abandons the closed world approach by considering many possible models of the ontology. The role of the axioms in the ontology then is to minimize the indefiniteness in the data by axioms constraining all possible models to the intended and most likely ones.

In the classical OBDA approach one has, moreover, the benefit of the rewriting approach, namely that the huge data set does not have to be transformed into the working memory; so, one can rely on the optimization and index mechanisms of the secondary memory data sources, as a query can be compiled directly into a query over the datasources. Clearly a caveat is that the rewritten query may be exponentially bigger than the original query, so that additional optimizations already during the rewriting steps may be necessary. Some optimization strategies are discussed in [73].

As of the time of writing, OBDA related research has diverged into different investigations that cannot be labelled as OBDA in the classical sense. So, we propose the following distinctions in order to get a clear picture. There is, first, OBDA in a narrow sense by which we mean that there is an access to data with mappings producing only a virtual or materialized ABox but with no TBox at all or of expressiveness on the level of RDFS++. Second, OBDA in the classical sense uses logics in the DL-Lite family that allow for the generation of objects (true existentials on the right hand sides of general inclusion axioms) but still allow for a reduction of reasoning w.r.t. the TBox to answering of rewritten first order logic queries on the original data. For some applications even the expressiveness of the classical OBDA paradigm is not sufficient, and hence there is a need for the even more challenging paradigm of accessing big data w.r.t. expressive ontologies (ABDEO).

Orthogonally to these categorization one can also observe that the source data not necessarily have to be relational databases but can equally be RDF triple sources or other non-relational DBs. More radically, in some approaches the data of the original sources are imported into an own DB, which then is the proper source w.r.t. which the queries on the ontological level are queried. A benefit of this approach is the fact that one can define index structures and optimization strategies which are more appropriate for the domain and also for the rewriting strategy one is going to apply. In general, the data may even be preprocessed. The strategy to actually use the data underlying the ABox during the rewriting process is also part of a different rewriting strategy called *combined rewriting* [48].

Next to this hierarchy of OBDA related approaches one has to consider the ontology based access on stream data (OBSA) as an extra paradigm category. The idea of this paradigm is to make the access on big data feasible by first partitioning the data into small chunks (modules), then, second, ordering them w.r.t. some priority criterion and third streaming these into the query answering w.r.t. the fixed ordering (compare the survey [78]). One particular but also the most common case of (OBSA) is the one where the ordering is given by a temporal ordering so that the streams are timestamped data.

3   Classical OBDA

We recapitulate the most important notions related to classical OBDA. For a more detailed view, the reader is referred to [20]. Classical OBDA investigates query answering over an ontology, using mappings to get the data from the sources to the ontology level—the main aim being the reduction of the demanding query answering problem to a model checking/query answering problem over the data sources, which are in many cases relational databases.

The idea of aiming at this reduction is motivated by the demand to enable computationally feasible reasoning services over large ABoxes. Because the size of the TBox (and the queries) is small with respect to the size of the ABoxes, computational feasibility is measured with respect to the size of the ABox alone, thereby fixing all other parameters (TBox, query respectively). The resulting type of complexity is called *data complexity*. Aiming at the reduction, which is also called first order logic (FOL) rewritability and which is explained in detail below, is indeed a successful venture with respect to computational feasibility. This is due to the fact that the data complexity of answering first order logic queries w.r.t. DL-Lite ontologies is in the low boolean circuits complexity class AC^0, which, roughly, is the class of problems that can be decided in constant time with the help of polynomially many processors.

3.1   DL-Lite

Descriptions logics [11] have proven to be an adequate representation language for ontologies, as they have a formal semantics and show good computation properties at least w.r.t. various standard reasoning services such as subsumption testing, satisfiability testing, query answering etc. In the center of classical OBDA stands query answering and also, related to it, satisfiability testing of ontologies. An ontology is defined as a triple $\mathcal{O} = (Sig, \mathcal{T}, \mathcal{A})$ over signature, a TBox and an ABox. In all DLs the signature is made up by subsets of a set of concept symbols N_C, a set of role symbols N_R, and a set of individual constant symbols N_i. DLs with concrete domains or datatypes also allow for additional constants (and predicates) with fixed meanings over the concrete domain. The DLs differ in the set of concept/role constructors they offer and in the constraints for building TBox and ABox axioms. Typically TBox axioms are concept subsumptions $C \sqsubseteq D$ or role subsumptions $R \sqsubseteq S$ and ABox axioms have the form $C(a)$ or $R(a, b)$, where C, D stand for concept descriptions, R, S for role descriptions and a, b for individual constants.

In the focus of of OBDA stands the family of DLs called DL-Lite [6] as it is tailored towards FOL rewritability. DL-Lite is the language family underlying the OWL 2 QL profile of the W3C recommend web ontology language OWL http://www.w3.org/TR/owl2-profiles/#OWL_2_QL. As FOL rewritability is a very strong property it should be no surprise that only lightweight logics such as DL-Lite are considered as representation language for the ontology and moreover that there are also limitations on the query language, which in this case is unions of conjunctive queries (UCQs). (But note, that the limits of expressivity under FOL rewriting can still be pushed a little bit further as shown by the extended family of Datalog$^\pm$ family [19].)

To make the discussion more concrete we give the syntax of a DL-Lite language and its semantics in Fig. 1. The TBox axioms are additionally constrained by the demand that functional roles are not allowed to occur on the right hand side of role axioms. The semantics of concept descriptions is.defined recursively on the basis of an interpretations $\mathcal{I} = (\Delta^\mathcal{I}, \cdot^\mathcal{I})$, which consists of a domain $\Delta^\mathcal{I}$ and a denotation function $\cdot^\mathcal{I}$. The denotation of concept symbols (atomic concepts) A are subsets $A^\mathcal{I} \subseteq \Delta^\mathcal{I}$ of the domain; role symbols P are denoted by binary relations $P^\mathcal{I} \subseteq \Delta^\mathcal{I} \times \Delta^\mathcal{I}$, and constants a are denoted by elements of the domain $a^\mathcal{I} \in \Delta^\mathcal{I}$. The modeling relation is denoted by $\models$ and one defines that $\mathcal{I}$ models or makes true an axiom ax iff $\mathcal{I} \models ax$. An ontology is called satisfiable if there is an interpretation $\mathcal{I}$ makes all axioms in the TBox and the ABox true. An ontology $\mathcal{O}$ entails an axiom ax, shortly: $\mathcal{O} \models ax$ iff all models of $\mathcal{O}$ are also models of ax.

3.2   Query Answering and Rewritability

An *FOL query* $Q = \psi(\boldsymbol{x})$ is a first-order logic formula $\psi(\boldsymbol{x})$ whose free variables are the ones in the n-ary vector of variables $\boldsymbol{x}$; the variables in $\boldsymbol{x}$ are called *distinguished variables.* If $\boldsymbol{x}$ is empty, the query is called boolean. Let $\boldsymbol{a}$ be a

$$\begin{aligned}
&& (P^-)^{\mathcal{I}} &= \{(d,e) \mid (e,d) \in P^{\mathcal{I}}\} \\
R &\longrightarrow P \mid P^- & (\exists R)^{\mathcal{I}} &= \{d \in \Delta^{\mathcal{I}} \mid \exists e.(d,e) \in R^{\mathcal{I}}\} \\
B &\longrightarrow A \mid \exists R & (\neg C)^{\mathcal{I}} &= \Delta^{\mathcal{I}} \setminus C^{\mathcal{I}} \\
C &\longrightarrow B \mid \neg B & \mathcal{I} \models B \sqsubseteq C &\text{ iff } B^{\mathcal{I}} \subseteq C
\end{aligned}$$

$$\begin{aligned}
\text{TBox:} \quad & B \sqsubseteq C, (\text{func } R), & \mathcal{I} \models R_1 \sqsubseteq R_2 &\text{ iff } R_1^{\mathcal{I}} \subseteq R_2 \\
& R_1 \sqsubseteq R_2 & \mathcal{I} \models B(a) &\text{ iff } a^{\mathcal{I}} \in B^{\mathcal{I}} \\
\text{ABox:} \quad & A(a), R(a,b) & \mathcal{I} \models R(a,b) &\text{ iff } (a^{\mathcal{I}}, b^{\mathcal{I}}) \in R^{\mathcal{I}} \\
& & \mathcal{I} \models (\text{func } R) &\text{ iff } R^{\mathcal{I}} \text{ is a (partial) function}
\end{aligned}$$

Fig. 1. DL-Lite

vector of constants from the signature of the ontology. The semantics of n-ary FOL queries with respect to an interpretation $\mathcal{I}$ is given by the set $Q^{\mathcal{I}}$ of n-ary tuples $\boldsymbol{d}$ over the domain $\Delta^{\mathcal{I}}$ such that $\mathcal{I}_{[\boldsymbol{x} \mapsto \boldsymbol{d}]} \models \psi(\boldsymbol{x})$. Here, $\mathcal{I}_{[\boldsymbol{x} \mapsto \boldsymbol{d}]}$ extends $\mathcal{I}$ by interpreting the variables in $\boldsymbol{x}$ by the elements in $\boldsymbol{d}$.

The crucial notion of answers w.r.t. an ontology is handled by an *certain answer semantics* also known from database theory. We are not going to discuss the appropriateness of this kind of semantics but just state its definition. (For an adequateness discussion of certain answer semantics in particular w.r.t aggregation we refer the reader to [49]). Given an ontology $(Sig, \mathcal{T}, \mathcal{A})$, the set of certain answers is denoted $cert(Q, \mathcal{T} \cup \mathcal{A})$ and it consists of n-ary tuples of constants $\boldsymbol{a}$ from Sig such that $\psi[\boldsymbol{x}/\boldsymbol{a}]$ (i.e. the formula resulting from $\psi(\boldsymbol{x})$ by applying the substitution $[\boldsymbol{x}/\boldsymbol{a}]$) is entailed by the ontology.

$$cert(\psi(\boldsymbol{x}), \mathcal{T} \cup \mathcal{A}) = \{\boldsymbol{a} \mid \mathcal{T} \cup \mathcal{A} \models \psi[\boldsymbol{x}/\boldsymbol{a}]\}$$

FOL queries are too complex to be used as queries on the ontological level. Hence, in order to guarantee FOL rewritability two well known weaker subclasses of FOL queries are considered, *conjunctive queries (CQ)* and *unions of conjunctive queries (UCQ)*. A CQ is a FOL query in which $\psi(\boldsymbol{x})$ is an existentially quantified conjunction of atomic formulas $at(\cdot)$, $\psi(\boldsymbol{x}) = \exists \boldsymbol{y} \bigwedge_i at_i(\boldsymbol{x}, \boldsymbol{y})$. The UCQs allow disjunctions of CQs, i.e., $\psi(\boldsymbol{x})$ can have the form $\exists \boldsymbol{y_1} \bigwedge_{i_1} at_{i_1}(\boldsymbol{x}, \boldsymbol{y_1}) \vee \cdots \vee \exists \boldsymbol{y_n} \bigwedge_{i_n} at_{i_n}(\boldsymbol{x}, \boldsymbol{y_n})$. Note that the existential quantifiers in UCQs are interpreted in the same way as for FOL formulas (*natural domain semantics*) and not with respect to a given set of constants mentioned in the signature (*active domain semantics*). This is the strength of this query language and the critical place for weakening it if the OBDA application at hand demands TBox languages stronger than DL-Lite.

In the following, let the canonical model of an ABox $\mathcal{A}$, denoted $DB(\mathcal{A})$, be the minimal Herbrand model of $\mathcal{A}$, i.e. the model, where the domain is made up by all constants occurring in the ABox, all constants are interpreted by themselves, and where $a^{DB(\mathcal{A})} \in A^{DB(\mathcal{A})}$ iff $A(a) \in \mathcal{A}$ and $(a^{DB(\mathcal{A})}, b^{DB(\mathcal{A})}) \in R^{DB(\mathcal{A})}$ iff $R(a,b) \in \mathcal{A}$. *Checking the satisfiability of ontologies is FOL rewritable* iff for all TBoxes $\mathcal{T}$ there is a boolean FOL query $Q_{\mathcal{T}}$ such that for all $\mathcal{A}$ it is the case that the ontology $\mathcal{T} \cup \mathcal{A}$ is satisfiable just in case the query $Q_{\mathcal{T}}$ evaluates to false in the model $DB(\mathcal{A})$. *Answering queries from a subclass $\mathcal{C}$ of FOL queries w.r.t. to ontologies is FOL rewritable iff for all TBoxes $\mathcal{T}$ and queries $Q = \psi(\boldsymbol{x})$ in $\mathcal{C}$ there is a FOL query $Q_{\mathcal{T}}$ such that for all ABoxes $\mathcal{A}$ it is the case that* $cert(Q, \mathcal{T} \cup \mathcal{A}) = Q_{\mathcal{T}}^{DB(\mathcal{A})}$.

For members of the DL-Lite family it can be shown [20] that the satisfiability check is FOL rewritable. As an example take $\mathcal{T} = \{A \sqsubseteq \neg B\}$ and $\mathcal{A} = \{A(a), B(a)\}$, then satisfiability is tested by answering the query $Q_{\mathcal{T}} = \exists x.A(x) \wedge B(x)$ w.r.t. $DB(\mathcal{A})$, resulting in the answer yes and indicating that $\mathcal{T} \cup \mathcal{A}$ is unsatisfiable. Moreover, answering UCQs can be shown to be FOL rewritable [20]. The rewriting technique used in [20] is called *perfect rewriting*. It considers the (positive) axioms as rules and uses a backward-chaining method to blow up the query with new CQ covering the rules' additional implications. FOL rewritability of satisfiability is a prerequisite for answering queries because in case the ontology is not satisfiable the set of certain answers is identical to all tuples of constants in the signature.

In what sense is the fact that DL-Lite provides existential quantification with natural domains semantics a benefit over those approaches such as the very narrow OBDA approaches using RDFS++? Having such existential quantification operators means that one can ask for objects which are not mentioned in the ABox but whose existence is guaranteed w.r.t. the TBox. Let us illustrate this strength with a risk management scenario for measurement data and event data from sensors and control units of turbines. The TBox is assumed to contain a (predictive) subsumption that says that if a turbine shows some anomaly in some fixed sensor, then there is a risk of a can flame failure.

$$\exists showsAnomalyInTempSens \sqsubseteq \exists risk.canFlameFailure$$

These observations have direct consequences for possible queries. For example, the engineer might be interested in all turbines for which there is a risk for can flame failure. This could be formulated in following conjunctive query

$$Q = \exists y.risk(x, y) \wedge canFlameFailure(y)$$

The variable y cannot be bound to an object within the data. But nonetheless, this query may have positive answers due to the predictive subsumption above which would lead to a reformulation of the query, adding a CQ and giving the UCQ

$$Q_{rew} = (\exists y.risk(x, y) \wedge canFlameFailure(y)) \vee showsAnomalyInTempSens(x)$$

Without the subsumption (resulting from the time series analysis), some turbines wold not have been identified as being in a risk to run in a can flame failure.

3.3   Mappings

In the classical OBDA setting, the ABox is not given in advanced but produced by mappings [71]. These are formally represented as rules with queries of the

```
SENSOR(SID, CID, Sname, TID, description)
SENSORTYPE(TID, Tname)
COMPONENT(CID, superCID, AID, Cname)
ASSEMBLY(AID, AName, ALocation)
MEASUREMENT(MID, MtimeStamp, SID, Mval)
MESSAGE(MesID, MesTimeStamp, MesAssemblyID,
        catID, MesEventText)
CATEGORY(catID, catName)
```

Fig. 2. Part of the relational schema in a measurement DB

ontological level, called the target, as the head of the rule (here the left-hand side) and queries in the the data source language (in many cases SQL) as the body of the rule, which is noted here always on the right-hand side. We are going to present mappings in the logical notation. A recent W3C recommended mapping language in machine readable form is R2RML, a mapping language from relational databases to RDF (http://www.w3.org/TR/r2rml/). As constructing mappings is a non-trivial task recent research considers also bootstrapping mappings, see, e.g., the technical report [28] and the papers to be fond therein.

We illustrate mappings within a sensor measurement scenario, assuming that there is one central DB with sensor measurement data and also sensor descriptions w.r.t. the DB schema in Fig 2. The ontology is assumed to model sensors, measurements, events etc. in the same manner as the nearly standard semantic sensor networks (SSN) ontology authored by the members of the W3C Sensor Network Incubator Group [27]. (See also the final report at http://www.w3.org/2005/Incubator/ssn/XGR-ssn-20110628/.) A general ontology of this kind can be extended for specific sensor measurement scenarios by introducing new names to the signature of the ontology and adding new ontology axioms. Here, we assume that there is a concept symbol $Sens$ (for sensors) and an attribute symbol $name$. ABox assertions saying which element is a sensor and what their names are, are produced by the following mapping:

$$m : Sens(x) \land name(x, y) \longleftarrow$$
$$\text{SELECT f(SID) as x, Sname as y FROM SENSOR}$$

The information in the row of the measurement table is mapped to unary facts $(Sens(x))$ and binary atomic facts $(name(x, y))$. If the table SENSOR contains a row

$$\text{(123, comp45, TC255, TempSens, 'A temperature sensor')}$$

then the mapping produces the conjunction of ABox assertions $Sens(f(123)) \land name(f(123), TempSens123)$.

In the DL-Lite setting, mappings have in general on their left-hand side CQs and on their right-hand side SQL queries. The mappings are safe in the sense that all variables used on the left-hand side must occur on the right-hand side as columns; but the source query may contain additional variables.

The term f(SID) denotes an individual constant, constructed as a functional term indicating the value of the attribute SID of the sensor. All expressions f(SID) could be mapped to the more convenient atomic names of the form, e.g., s_i. If the ontology language allows for datatypes or concrete domains—as we assume here—then we can use attribute values directly without the need of an additional functional symbol. This is demonstrated above for the column Sname containing strings.

For different purposes mappings can be split up into a simpler form where the target consist of an atomic query only. Within the splitting the source query is projected to the variables occurring in the atom; in the case of the query above the resulting split mappings would be as follows:

$m_1 : Sens(x)$ ⟵ SELECT f(SID) as x,FROM SENSOR
$m_2 : name(x, y)$ ⟵ SELECT f(SID) as x, Sname as y FROM SENSOR

For a given database DB and a set of mappings M, the induced ABox $\mathcal{A}(M, DB))$ is just the union of the ABox assertions produced by the mappings in M over the DB. The semantics of query answering w.r.t. a set of mappings over a DB and a TBox is just the certain answer semantics introduced above and applied to the ontology $(Sig, \mathcal{T}, \mathcal{A}(M, DB))$.

Now the important point is that the induced ABox is not materialized for query answering but is kept virtual. Queries over the induced ABox are *unfolded* to queries over the DB. So, in the classical approach a UCQ over a TBox and the induced ABox of mappings w.r.t. a DB is first rewritten into a FOL query, then this query is unfolded into an SQL query over the DB (using the mappings) and then the unfolded query is evaluated over the DB, given the set of answers to the original query.

There is no canonical way for unfolding a UCQ into a SQL query, and, indeed, different strategies for unfolding a UCQ w.r.t DL-Lite ontologies are discussed in the literature, e.g., one strategy is introduced in[71], another in [74]. The common idea of both strategies is to view the mappings as logical rules and use logical programming ideas such as resolution to get the unfolded query. We do not spell out the procedure but only mention very roughly, that unfolding an atomic query q results in an SQL query which is a union of all the source queries Ψ_i from mappings $m_i : q$ ⟵ Ψ_i with q as their target. Recursively, if two queries q_1, q_2 are unfolded to SQL queries Ψ_1 and Ψ_2, then conjunctive query $q_1 \wedge q_2$ is mapped to a join of Ψ_1 and Ψ_2. The disjunction $q_1 \vee q_2$ (if it corresponds to a UCQ) is unfolded to the union of Ψ_1 and Ψ_2.

As the rewriting of queries may lead to an exponential blow-up, optimizations on different levels (rewriting, unfolding and mappings) are a must for OBDA systems. Different optimization strategies are discussed in [73], [75] and implemented, e.g., in the -ontop- OBDA system (http://ontop.inf.unibz.it/).

4   OBDA in the Broad Sense: ABDEO

Though DL-Lite provides existential quantification with natural domain semantics in the TBox and in the query language, for many use cases it does not have sufficient representation capabilities. For example, qualified existential quantification on the left-hand side of TBox axioms is not allowed, though such constructors are necessary for identifying interesting (though still tree-shaped) patterns and using them to deduce new knowledge.

Another logical constructor which cannot be handled with DL-Lite are transitive declarations for roles because transitive roles lead directly to non-FOL rewritability. Transitive relations are useful modeling means for modeling part-of-relations of components in a complex system such as a turbine. The typical entity-relationship modeling methodology for representing chains or tree-like structures by a self-referencing foreign key is illustrated with the COMPONENT schema of Fig. 2 and picked up here again.

COMPONENT(<u>CID</u>, superCID, AID, Cname)
ASSEMBLY(<u>AID</u>, AName, ALocation)

The superCID column specifies the next upper component at which the component with identifier CID is attached (foreign key to attribute CID of COMPONENT itself). The turbine assembly at which the component is (indirectly) attached is given by AID (foreign key from COMPONENT to ASSEMBLY).

Every component has a reference to a top component, which again has a reference to a top component, and so on until the upper most component on the level directly under the assembly level. A useful qualitative modeling of the component hierarchy relies on the part-of relation. A mapping, generating the direct part-of relation between components would be as follows:

$partOf(x, y) \longleftarrow$ SELECT f(CID) AS x, g(superCID) AS y FROM COMPONENT

That the part-of relation is transitive can be declared by using a TBox axiom inducing further tuples in the part-of relation that are not directly visible in the SQL schema. So, if for example there are two ABox assertions $partOf(comp1, comp2)$, $partOf(comp2, comp3)$ induced by the mappings, then the transitivity condition entails $partOf(comp1, comp3)$. A Boolean query w.r.t. the ABox and the extended TBox asking whether $comp1$ is a part of $comp3$ would thus have to be answered with yes. A similar query could not directly be formulated in pure SQL, which does not support recursion.

As a resume, many use cases demand transitive roles, qualified existentials on the left-hand side and also disjunctions, hence there are more than one good reasons to consider more expressive logics such as $\mathcal{SHI}$ [44]. Of course, FOL rewritability does not hold for $\mathcal{SHI}$ ontologies, so a different strategy has to be invented in order to deal with really large ABoxes. A promising approach is ABox modularization [79], which uses relevant information from the TBox in order to built small modules of ABoxes. The relevant TBox information is stored in a data structure called $\forall$-info structure. This information is propagated along the role edges of the ABox as long as necessary. Modules consist of subgraphs induced by an individual constant and those individuals that are reached by the propagation.

The benefit of the modularization approach is that reasoning services such as instance retrieval (asking queries of the form $C(x)$) over the whole ABox can be reduced to a small set of ABox modules, which in turn are small in many practical applications. In [58], the approach is extended to the reasoning service of answering grounded CQs, i.e., CQs where the existentials adhere to the active domain semantics.

5   Temporalizing OBDA

Inspecting the whole life cycle of the query from being issued by a user until its being answered by an OBDA query answering system hints to the possible components for extensions w.r.t. temporal or streaming aspects. Though this observation does not say anything about which components' extension is appropriate for which use case, it provides a good aid which may help in categorizing the different approaches. So, the approaches may be distinguished w.r.t. the extensions of the TBox language, the ABox language, the query language, the language of the mappings, and the presupposed language of the data sources. In all this cases, the extension concerns syntactical aspects and also semantical aspects as well as ontological aspects in the original philosophical sense.

Processing time-dependent data has been investigated for a long time. Starting from early approaches in computer vision [61,62,72], *temporal data processing* using declarative techniques has been an important research topic in artificial intelligence (e.g., [50,51,41,40,13,9]). All these approaches use some form of temporal logic. Here we are going to discuss shortly the relevant notions for temporal extensions of OBDA based on the main ideas of temporal logics and then give pointers to the state of the art for temporal OBDA. In later sections we go more into detail w.r.t. the processing of temporal streams.

The simplest way to deal with temporal aspects is to refer to time points just with a simple attribute (as, e.g., done in the temporal extension of OWL called tOWL [57]). This is the most conservative strategy where the extension of non-temporal OBDA concerns only the domain of the models with objects to which time is attributed. Taking, e.g., the measurement scenario, a time attribute is attached to measurement (and message event) objects. Consider the following mapping producing assertions that describe measurements, their attached measured values and the times attached to them.

$$
\left\{
\begin{array}{l}
meas(x) \wedge \\
val(x,y) \wedge \\
time(x,z)
\end{array}
\right\}
\longleftarrow
\begin{array}{l}
\texttt{SELECT f(MID) AS m, Mval AS y, MtimeStamp AS z} \\
\texttt{FROM MEASUREMENT}
\end{array}
$$

The mapping is a classical mapping and the assertions induced by it are ordinary ABox assertions. The crucial point is that there have to be proper objects that reify temporal events (there was a something measured at that and that time). This is discussed in the literature under the term *temporal reification* (e.g. [2]).

Though reification means less adaptation needs, it leads to less control on the time aspects, as these are hidden in some objects of the domain. Moreover, reification has in many cases a higher ontological commitment than in the measurement scenario, where the presumption of measurements objects is plausible. For a discussion of these points we refer the reader to [38].

Non-reified extensions of OBDA consider time as a necessary dimension in the model semantics for assertions. Time is modelled with a structure $(T, \leq)$, also called *flow of time*. Depending on the needs of the use case, the set of time points T may have different properties, being discrete, such as the natural numbers, being dense, such as the rational numbers, being (left, right) bounded, being continuous such as the real numbers, being linear vs. branching etc. For an in-depth discussion of axiomatization and model theoretic aspects of the time domain the reader is referred to the early monograph [12].

A very general way to combine the flow of time into a logic is described in the literature on first-order temporal logic [43]. Instead of considering one single interpretation, the semantics rests now on a family of interpretations $\mathcal{I}_t$, one for each time point $t \in T$ on which a formula can be evaluated.[1] In many applications, it is assumed that the domains of all $\mathcal{I}_t$ are the same and that the individual constants are rigid, i.e., interpreted with the same object in all $\mathcal{I}_t$.

The decision which semantical objects are becoming temporal (non-sentential objects such as roles and concept as done in [8] vs. sentential objects such as ABox and TBox axioms (as done implicitly in [15] or explicitly in [54]) differs w.r.t. the needs of the use case. In first-order temporal logic one can refer directly to the time points and express further conditions, in the more state oriented approach of modal temporal logics, it is possible to talk about the validity of a formula in some state, referring to other states by modal operators such "In some state before ", "In some state in the future" etc.

Referring to the time argument as a time tag, one could formulate that the assertion of a sensor s_0 showing the value 90° is true at second 3 as the timestamped ABox assertion $val(s_0, 90°)\langle 3s \rangle$. Such an ABox assertion would be true in the given family of interpretations $(\mathcal{I}_t)_{t \in T}$ if $\mathcal{I}_{3s} \models val(s_0, 90°)\langle 3s \rangle$.

Approaches for temporalizing OBDA in the very narrow sense can be found in particular in [77], [68], [39], [54], all describing temporal extensions for RDF triples. In [54], the W3C recommend query language SPARQL is extended to work with RDF quadruples, where the fourth component is not only a time point but may be an interval, the intended meaning being that the interval describes the time period at which the fact expressed in the RDF triple is valid.

Two recent examples for temporalizing classical OBDA are described in [15] and [8]. The authors of [15] use a classical temporal logic inspired approach. The TBox is a classical DL-Lite TBox, in which all axioms are assumed to hold at all time points. The temporalized ABox is a finite sequence of pure DL-Lite ABoxes. The real temporal extension concerns the query language TCQ, which is a combination of embedded CQs with an outer propositional linear temporal logic template (LTL). To illustrate TCQ, assume, e.g. that there is an information need for turbines that have been at least two times in a critical situation the last three time units before, one would formulate a CQ $critical(x, y)$ formalizing the critical property and use previous operators $\bigcirc^{-1}$ and the some

---

[1] An alternative approach is to extend one interpretation to a two-sorted interpretation with a sort for the objects of the domain and a sort for the time points, cf. [43].

time in the future operator $\diamond$ within an LTL outer template given the TCQ denoted $Q(x, y)$.

$$Critical(x, y) = Turbine(x) \wedge showsMessage(x, y) \wedge FailureMessage(y)$$
$$Q(x, y) = \bigcirc^{-1} \bigcirc^{-1} \bigcirc^{-1} (\diamond (Critical(x, y) \wedge \bigcirc \diamond Critical(x, y)))$$

The authors [15] extend the notion of rewritability to sequences of ABoxes, which is in essence local rewritability w.r.t. each time point, and demonstrate two different algorithms for answering queries. Mapping aspects are not discussed in the article.

In the approach of [8], the temporal extension mainly concerns the TBox language, which allows to use modal logical operators in the front of concept descriptions and role descriptions. For example, on can express the fact that if a turbine shows an anomaly at some time, then some time in the future it will shut down itself:

$$showsAnomaly \sqsubseteq \diamond UnplanedShutDown$$

ABox assertions are extended with a time argument, so that one can formulate $val(s_0, 90°, 3s)$; the query language is an UCQ language, where the atoms have also time arguments and where one can quantifiy over the time argument and also formulate constraints using the ordering relation on the time flow. For example, one may ask whether there was a time between 3s and 6s where some turbine showed an anomaly: $\exists x \exists t. 3s \leq t \leq 6s \wedge showsAnomaly(x, t)$. The authors show, that under some completeness assumption regarding ABox assertions, FOL rewritability for consistency checking and query answering holds. As in [15], mapping and unfolding aspects are not discussed.

Research on temporalizing ABDEO is in the beginning and still there have to be invented approaches that do 1) temporal query answering over very expressive TBoxes and 2) very large ABoxes that are 3) either virtually constructed or at least materialized w.r.t. some set of declarative mappings. So we can only mention approaches that fulfill a subset of the three conditions above. Similar to [15], the approach of [10] uses LTL operators in the query language but this time using TBoxes in the more expressive DL $\mathcal{ALC}$. Mappings and the largeness of ABoxes are not discuessed. A general overview of temporal DLs can be found in [7]. OWL related temporalizations are discussed in [42,67,60,57].

6   Stream Processing

Stream processing has strong connections to the processing of temporal data in a temporal DB using temporal (logic) operators; nonetheless, the scenarios, the objects of interest, the theoretical and practical challenges are different from those of temporal logics/ temporal DBs. While query answering on temporal DBs is a one-step activity on static historical data, answering queries on streams is a reactive, continuous activity (hence the notion of a continuous query).

A challenging fact of stream processing is the high frequency of the data in some application contexts. A second challenging fact is the changing frequency (burstiness) of incoming data, which is quite a natural phenomenon for event messages, which are produced in the moment the related events occur. Furthermore, in contrast to temporal DBs settings, stream scenarios come up with multiple queries as there may be many streams corresponding, e.g., to different sensors and control units, and as there are many features that one wants to query, such as different statistical and time-series features.

6.1 Stream Definition

Though there exist various stream definitions over various research communities, and even even within researcher of the same community, a common aspect of all streams is that they are constituted by a (potentially infinite) sequence of data elements from some domain. The sequence is thought to be ordered-isomorphic to the natural numbers, so that there is always a least element of a subset of the stream (and additionally there is always a unique predecessor and successor of an element in the stream). Following usual notation, we will represent streams in set notation, it being understood that there is an ordering isomorphic to the ordering of the natural numbers. We denote this ordering by $\leq_{ar}$, where ar stands for "arrival".

Though not restricted to, temporal streams are one of the most common stream types to occur in applications. A *temporal stream* is defined to be a set of timestamped domain elements $d\langle t \rangle$. The first argument is instantiated by an object d from a domain D, which we call the domain of streamed objects. The second argument is instantiated by a timestamp t from a linear time flow $(T, \leq)$, i.e., $\leq$ is a transitive, reflexive, antisymmetric, and total order on T. In the examples introduced below, we work with a discrete time flow T, e.g., natural numbers with the usual ordering. But our model introduced is also applicable to dense time domains such as the rational numbers $\mathbb{Q}$ or even continuos time domains such as the the real number $\mathbb{R}$, the crucial point being the fact, that streams have the isomorphism-type of the natural numbers.

According to the definition, a temporal stream may contain two different objects d_1 and d_2 with the same timestamp t, and even many different occurrences of the same time tagged tuple $d\langle t \rangle$. Moreover, it may be the case that there are timestamps which do not occur in the stream; the latter is useful in particular for those situations where there is no information at some time point from T—and hence this representation is also useful to model varying frequencies of stream element occurrences.

The elements of the stream are thought to be arriving at the query answering system in some order, which is inherent in the definition of streams as sequences. In a *synchronized stream setting*, one demands that the timestamps in the arrival ordering make up a monotonically increasing sequence, so that $\leq$ is conform with $\leq_{ar}$. In an *asynchronous stream setting*, it may be the case that elements with earlier timestamps arrive later than data with later timestamps. In particular, in this latter case, the order needed for a stream to be isomorphic to the natural numbers does not have to adhere to the order $\leq$ of the flow of time $(T, \leq)$.

The distinction regarding synchronicity hints to possible layers of streams. For example, in [53], the authors distinguish between raw, physical, and logical streams. Raw streams correspond to temporal streams according to our definition and are intended to model the streams arriving at a data stream management system (DSMS). Logical streams are abstractions of raw streams where the order of the sequence is ignored, so they can be defined as multi-sets of timestamped tuples.[2] Physical streams allow not only for timestamps but also half-open intervals $[t_s, t_e)$ as time annotations, the ordering of the stream being non-decreasing w.r.t. the start timestamps t_s.

The semantics for the relational stream query language CQL [5] is defined on the basis of synchronized streams. The new query language STARQL (see below) in its full version also allows asynchronous streams. But here for ease of exposition, we will assume that STARQL operates on synchronous streams, and even simpler logical streams (as we do not discuss sequence depending operators in this paper). It should be stressed, that though a layered approach as that of [53], where all synchronization is handled on the levels below, is in principle adequate it is not a must when designing a stream processing system on the abstraction level of ontologies. Regarding the synchronicity aspect, e.g., it is a matter of flexibility to give also the user of the ontological query language a means to specify the way he wants to handle asynchronous streams directly, and even doing the specification for each stream query—independently of the other queries.[3]

Orthogonally to these layered distinction of stream types, streams are categorized according to the type of the domains. In the context of OBDA for streams, at least two different domains D of streamed objects have to be taken into consideration. The first domain consists of relational tuples from some schema; in this case, we call the stream a *relational* stream. The second domain is made up by data facts, either represented as ABox assertions or as RDF triples. In this case we just talk of a stream of ABox assertions, RDF streams resp. In case of relational streams all tuples adhere to the same schema, hence relational streams are homogeneous, whilst in the case of streams of ABox assertions/RDF triples the used logical vocabulary must not be restricted to some relation symbols. In so far, these streams are inhomogeneous. Nonetheless, one may restrict the signature of the assertions to a specific signature, thereby replacing the role of the relational schema in relational streams by a signature.

6.2   Query Constructors over Streams

The idea of a sliding window over a stream is a useful constructor abstraction for processing streams. In the following, we are going to discuss the window

---

[2] Note that the original definition in [53] would also consider uncountable sets as streams, if one chooses $\mathbb{R}$ as time domain, so that the intuition of a stream as a set ordered as the natural numbers cannot be applied here.

[3] A possibility for this is the use of a slack parameter. And indeed STARQL as defined in the technical report [66] is intended to handle also these.

operator and more generally the usual constructs for query languages over relational streams—focussing on one of the early relational query languages, the
continuous query language CQL [5]. As a side effect of this focussing strategy
we will have laid the ground for understanding the unfolding method for transforming STARQL queries into CQL queries.

CQL is a query language for relational streams. Next to streams, CQL presupposes a data structure called *relation*; this data structure lifts relations of
classical relational algebra to the temporal setting; formally, let be given a classical relational schema, then a (temporal) relation R is a total function from
the time domain T to the set of finite bags (multi-sets) of tuples over the given
schema. The (classical) relation at time point $t \in T$ is called *instantaneous
relation*.

CQL defines operators that map streams to relations (the most important
being the window operator), operators that map relations to streams, and moreover relation-to-relation operators, which adapt the usual relational algebra operators to the temporal setting. Stream-to-stream operators can be simulated by
the given operators.

The most important stream-to-relation construct is that of a sliding window.
Let S denote a stream and wr be an element of the time domain T. The time-
based sliding window operator with window range wr is denoted by [Range wr]
and attached to stream arguments in post-fix notation. The relation R denoted
by S [Range wr] is defined for every $t \in T$ as follows:

$$R(t) = \{s \mid (s, t') \in S \text{ and } (t' \leq t) \text{ and } t' \geq max\{t - wr, 0\}\}$$

So the bag of tuples at time point t consists of all tuples from S whose timestamps
are in the interval $[t - wr, t]$—with an intuitive handling of the cases of all t with
$t \leq wr$. The special case of a window with zero window range is also denoted by
[Now]; the case of an unbounded window by [Unbound].

The following example illustrates the effects of time sliding windows. Let be
given a stream S of timestamped tuples having the form $(sensor, value)\langle time \rangle$.
The smallest time granularity of time measurements is seconds, so we can presuppose that T is given by the natural numbers standing for time points measured
in seconds. Now let the stream S start as follows:

$$S = \{(s_0, 80°)\langle 0 \rangle, (s_1, 93°)\langle 0 \rangle, (s_0, 81)\langle 1 \rangle, (s_0, 82°)\langle 2 \rangle, (s_0, 83°)\langle 3 \rangle,$$
$$(s_0, 85°)\langle 5 \rangle, (s_0, 86°)\langle 6 \rangle....\}$$

Then the relation $R = $ S [Range 2] is given by:

t :	0	1	2	3	4	5	6
$R(t)$:	$\{(s_0, 80),$	$\{(s_0, 80),$	$\{(s_0, 80),$	$\{(s_0, 81),$	$\{(s_0, 82),$	$\{(s_0, 82),$	$\{(s_0, 83),$
	$(s_1, 93)\}$	$(s_1, 93),$	$(s_1, 93),$	$(s_0, 82),$	$(s_0, 83)\}$	$(s_0, 83),$	$(s_0, 85),$
		$(s_0, 81)\}$	$(s_0, 81),$	$(s_0, 83)\}$		$(s_0, 85)\}$	$(s_0, 86)\}$
			$(s_0, 82)\}$				

Please note, that the bag-approach for defining the relation is not unproblematic; the bags are timestamp agnostic, i.e., the tuples within a bag do not contain timestamps anymore. Formulating functionality constraints then becomes a demanding issue as these are not formulated w.r.t. a specific schema but directly over the domain. Take, for example, in a measurement scenario the functionality dependency (fd) constraint on measurement tuples with the content that a sensor can have maximally one value for every time point, resp. Applying a window operator to the stream measurement may lead to a bag of tuples where the same sensor has more than one value. So, streaming these tuples out again (with e.g. the RStream operator below) may lead to a stream of tuples violating the fd constraint.

A generalized version of the sliding window allows the specification of the sliding parameter, i.e. the frequency at which the window is slided forward in time. The semantics of the relation R = S [Range wr Slide sl] is as follows:

$$R(t) = \begin{cases} \emptyset & \text{if } t < sl \\ \{s \mid (s,t') \in S \text{ and } max\{\lfloor t/sl \rfloor \cdot sl - wr, 0\} \leq t' \leq \lfloor t/sl \rfloor \cdot sl\} & \text{else} \end{cases}$$

So the sliding window operator takes snapshots of the stream every sl second; for all time points in between multiples of sl the snapshot is the same. The relation of the window range parameter wr and the slide parameter sl determines the effects of the sliding window; if $twr = sl$, then the window is tumbling, if $wr > sl$, then the window contents are overlapping, an if $sl > wr$, then the operator has a sampling effect. For other stream-to-relation operators such as the tuple based window operators or partition operators, the reader is referred to the original article [5].

Relation-to-relation operations are the usual ones known form SQL adapted to the new temporal relation setting by using them time-point wise on the instantaneous relations. In particular, the join of (temporal) relations is done pointwise. For example, the CQL expression in Listing 1.1 joins the relations of the window application results to a measurement and an event stream, filters a subset out according to a condition and projects out the sensor IDs.

```
1  SELECT m.sensorID
2  FROM Msmt[Range 1] as m, Events[Range 2] as e
3  WHERE m.val > 30 AND e.category = Alarm AND
4          m.sensorID = e.sensorID
```

Listing 1.1. Example relation-to-relation operators in CQL

As relation-to-stream operators, the authors of [5] define *Istream* (giving a stream of newly inserted tuples w.r.t. the last time point), *Dstream* (giving a stream of newly deleted tuples w.r.t. the last point) and *Rstream* (returning all elements in the relation). Assuming that for $t < 0$ one specifies $R(t) = \emptyset$ for $t < 0$ the formal definitions are:

$$Istream(R) = \bigcup_{tinT} (R(t) \setminus R(t-1)) \times \{t\}$$

$$Dstream(R) = \bigcup_{t \in T} (R(t-1) \setminus R(t)) \times \{t\}$$

$$Rstream(R) = \bigcup_{t \in T} R(t) \times \{t\}$$

6.3   Streamifying OBDA

Streamified OBDA approaches, in which the OBDA is to be understood in the classical sense, presuppose some stream engine on the level below ontologies which are accessed by mappings. So we first give an overview of the non-ontological stream processing systems and then discuss higher level (OBDA) stream processing.

Within stream processing on the level below ontologies two different perspective exist, the sensor perspective (semantic sensor networks) and the database perspective used in data stream management systems (DSMS). The sensor perspective of stream-based data processing pursues the idea of pushing data processing to the sensors and, as a consequence, investigates approximations for statistical data analysis operations in order to cope with memory and power limitations of sensors [29]. Query languages for sensor networks are investigated in [16,37,36,35]. Also here, data processing is pushed to the sensor level.

Stream processing on the level of data management systems has been an active research field which emerged ten years ago. A well known stream data management system is the academic prototype STREAM from Stanford which is based on the relational stream query language CQL [5] discussed above. Other academic data stream management systems (DSMS) with SQL like query languages are TelegraphCQ (Berkeley) [26], Aurora/Borealis (Brandeis, Brown and MIT) [45], or PIPES (Marburg University) [52,24,25,23,53]. To complete the list with commercial systems, we mention the stand-alone systems StreamBase, Truviso (extension of TelegraphCQ incorporated into Cisco products), or the stream add-ons for well known relational DBMSs (MySQL, PostgreSQL, DB2 etc.). Also PIPES now has a commercial successor developed by Software AG. Though much progress has been achieved on data stream management systems, there is still no agreement on a common (SQL) standard query language over streams. (Some first steps are discussed in [46]).

Much of the ideas and methods used in relational have inspired the recent streamified OBDA systems. Various systems extending the SPARQL language http://www.w3.org/TR/rdf-sparql-query/ have been developed—prominent ones being, next to C-SPARQL, the SPARQL$_{stream}$ system [17,18], or CQELS [69,70]. C-SPARQL and SPARQLstream use a black box approach w.r.t. the underlying streaming engine, whilst CQELS has whitebox approach.

All these systems use a window operator inspired from CQL, where the window's semantics is a bag semantics with tuples of bindings for the query, sub-queries resp. Hence, as the time attribute is not contained within the tuples all the approaches have to cope with similar (functional) constraint issues as discussed for CQL.

The SRBenchmark [81] and also the benchmarks provided in [55] show that the 2012 versions of the stream engines offer only basic functionalities. In particular w.r.t. the OBDA related properties one may state that only C-SPARQL is attributed to incorporate entailments of the TBox represented in an RDFS+ ontology. Only [17,18] discusses mappings, resulting in a new mapping language S2O, which is applied to map low sensor streams (using the source language Snee [35]) to RDF streams. But the exact semantics of the produced time stamps in the RDF streams is not laid out in [18], so that it is not clear how a time stamped tripled would interact with a temporal ABox and lead to further entailments. In contrast to the use of time as in STARQL (see below), time is referred to in a reified manner.

Somewhat related to streamified OBDA but at least clearly to be coined as high-level stream processing approaches are those using ideas of *complex event processing*. Examples are EP-SPARQL/ETALIS [4,3], T-REX using the event specification language TESLA [30,31,32], or Commonsens [76] and its open source successor ESPER (esper.codehaus.org). The approach by [56] is more on the OBDA line; it tries to compute predictions on streams (using autocorrelation of ontologies) over the lightweight description logic $\mathcal{EL}$; query answering is not in the focus of the approach.

7 A New Stream Temporal Query Language: STARQL

STARQL (Streaming and Temporal ontology Access with a Reasoning-based Query Language, pronounced Star-Q-L) is a query language framework in the intersection of classical OBDA, ABDEO and OBSA. Considering the fact that there are already many streaming languages, that, more or less, fit to the OBDA paradigm for query answering over streams [33,17,18,69], it is a justified question why to define another query language?

All of the mentioned approaches for stream processing on the RDF level model the window contents as a multi-set (bag) of variable bindings for the open variables in the query. But this solution has three main problems. First, the semantics based on the variable-binding solution presupposes mixed interim states in which the constraints and consequences of the ontologies (in particular the inconsistencies) are faded out. Second, such solutions do not adhere to the requirements of an orthogonal query language, according to which the inputs and interim-outputs are data structures in the same categories. And last but not least, if one considers KBs that allow for the formulation of persistency assumptions—which should be possible in the ABDEO paradigm—then one has to keep track of the time points in the window operators, as facts on previous time points may lead to consequences on later time points. For example, if a female person gives birth to a child at some time point, then it is a mother at all following time points.

The resume of these observations is that there is a good justification for defining a new query language and semantics with a necessary extension on the window concepts, fitting better into the OBDA/ABDEO paradigms. The main idea of STARQL, described in detail in the technical reports [66,64], is to provide ABox sequence constructors that group timestamped ABox assertions into ABoxes. The sequence sets up a nearly standard context in which OBDA (or ABDEO) reasoning services can be applied.

7.1   An Example from the Measurement Scenario

We are going to illustrate the STARQL constructs in a sensor measurement scenario where a stream S_{Msmt} of timestamped ABox assertions gives the values of a sensor s_0. The initial part up to second 5 is denoted $S_{Msmt}^{\leq 5}$.

$$S_{Msmt}^{\leq 5} = \{val(s_0, 90°)\langle 0s\rangle, val(s_0, 93°)\langle 1s\rangle, val(s_0, 94°)\langle 2s\rangle$$
$$val(s_0, 92°)\langle 3s\rangle, val(s_0, 93°)\langle 4s\rangle, val(s_0, 95°)\langle 5s\rangle\}$$

The stream may be materialized or virtual. The latter case will be illustrated below with mappings for timestamped ABox assertions from the stream query language CQL generating the upper level stream.

Assume that an engineer wants to express his information need for the fact whether the temperature value in sensor s_0 grew monotonically in the last 2 seconds, the information being updated every one second. In STARQL this can be formulated as follows.

```
1   CREATE STREAM S_out_1 AS
2   SELECT { s0 rdf:type RecentMonInc }<NOW>
3   FROM S_Msmt [NOW-2s, NOW]->1s
4   SEQUENCE BY StdSeq AS SEQ
5   HAVING
6     FORALL i < j IN SEQ,?x,?y:
7     IF ({ s0 val ?x }<i>  AND { s0  val ?y }<j>) THEN ?x <= ?y
```

Listing 1.2. Basic STARQL example

STARQL uses a mixed SQL and domain calculus notation for the realization of the information need. The window operator works like the window operator of CQL, but in one important point it differs from it: it does not delete the timestamps of the incoming ABox assertions. Moreover, the window operator it is syntactically represented with a suggestive interval notation containing a variable NOW for the evolving time. The slide parameter of one second is given by the forward arrow notation ->. The output of the query is a stream of RDF tuples { s0 rdf:type RecentMonInc }<NOW> (or written as ABox assertion $RecentMonInc(s_0)\langle NOW\rangle$) where the evolving time variable NOW is instantiated with the actual time.

The output of the window operators is a stream of temporal ABoxes, i.e., for every time point in the time domain T, here the natural numbers, one has a set

Time (in seconds)	Temporal ABox
$0s$	$\{val(s_0, 90°)\langle 0s\rangle\}$
$1s$	$\{val(s_0, 90°)\langle 0s\rangle, val(s_0, 93°)\langle 1s\rangle\}$
$2s$	$\{val(s_0, 90°)\langle 0s\rangle, val(s_0, 93°)\langle 1s\rangle, val(s_0, 94°)\langle 2s\rangle\}$
$3s$	$\{val(s_0, 93°)\langle 1s\rangle, val(s_0, 94°)\langle 2s\rangle, val(s_0, 92°)\langle 3s\rangle\}$
$4s$	$\{val(s_0, 94°)\langle 2s\rangle, val(s_0, 92°)\langle 3s\rangle, val(s_0, 93°)\langle 4s\rangle\}$
$5s$	$\{val(s_0, 92°)\langle 3s\rangle, val(s_0, 93°)\langle 4s\rangle, val(s_0, 95°)\langle 5s\rangle\}$

Fig. 3. Temporal ABoxes produced by the window operator

of timestamped ABox assertions (resp. timestamped RDF tuples.) The result is illustrated in Figure for the time up to second 5.

So far, the STARQL query does not quite differ from the stream extended SPARQL query languages CSPARQL, SPARQL$_{Stream}$ or CQELS. The main difference is the new SEQUENCE BY constructor, which at every time point t merges the assertions in the temporal ABox for time point t according to a method given by keyword directly after the constructor, here StdSeq, which denotes the standard sequencing method. The standard sequencing method gathers all ABox assertions with the same timestamp into the same (pure) ABox.

The result, here and for other sequencing strategies, is a sequence of pure ABoxes at every evolving time point NOW. In the example above the sequence at time point 5 seconds is depicted in Fig. 7.1. In this case, the sequencing is trivial as there is only one ABox assertion for the timestamps 3s, 4s, 5s, resp.

In STARQL the ABoxes in the sequence are not represented by timestamps but state numbers in the order of the timestamps. These states can be referred to by specific variables $(i, j$ above). In case of the ABox sequence above, the resulting ABox sequencing is depicted in Fig. 7.1. The reason for choosing the state annotated representation is, first, that it provides the ground for incorporating temporal logics in the modal logic traditions such as LTL, which have proven to be useful specification checking tools. The semantics of modal

Time (in seconds)	ABox sequence (with time stamp annotated ABoxes)
$5s$	$\{val(s_0, 92°)\}\langle 3s\rangle, \{val(s_0, 93°)\}\langle 4s\rangle, \{val(s_0, 95°)\}\langle 5s\rangle$

Fig. 4. Sequence of ABoxes at time point 5s

Time (in seconds)	ABox sequence (with state annotated ABoxes)
$5s$	$\{val(s_0, 92°)\}\langle 0\rangle, \{val(s_0, 93°)\}\langle 1\rangle, \{val(s_0, 95°)\}\langle 2\rangle$

Fig. 5. Sequence of ABoxes at time point 5 with state annotation

temporal logics such as LTL are based on states. In particular, it is also possible to incorporate the LTL approach for temporal DL-Lite knowledge bases [15,14] into the HAVING clause fragment. (We note, here, that the semantics of the HAVING clause is slightly different from the semantics of the query language TCQ in [15]. But actually, the fragment of HAVING clauses that uses only operators of [15] is as expressive as TCQ.)

The second reason is that for other sequencing strategies the time annotations are not unique. For example, in STARQL we foresee sequencing strategies based on arbitrary equivalence relations over the time domain—with an additional constraint requiring that the equivalence classes are connected intervals. (So the equivalence relation can be thought of doing a time roughening.) All time points in an equivalence class are equally good candidates for the annotation hence there is no unique timestamp choice. Clearly, one can choose a canonical candidate (such as the left interval point) or even the whole interval by itself. But then one has to choose the HAVING language very carefully. Adding, e.g., time annotations to states in LTLs leads to highly complex logics known as metric temporal logics [59].

The expressive strength of STARQL lies in its HAVING clause language which allows to use FOL for querying the ABox sequence. In the example above, the formula realizes the known condition of monotonicity. The HAVING clause allows for embedding pure (non-temporal) CQs, here represented by binary graph patterns, and attaches a state to them. Here and in the following we call those queries occurring with a state tag *embedded conditions* and the language in which the are formulated the *embedded condition language*. In this example, the embedded conditions are $val(s_0, ?x)$ and $val(s_0, ?y)$ and the embedded condition language is UCQ.

The intended meaning of the expression $val(s_0, ?x)\langle i \rangle$ is that one wants to find all $?x$ that are certain answers of the query $Q = val(s_0, ?x)$ w.r.t. the ith ABox—and also the TBox and the static ABox (see below)— that is, in the notation introduced above, one calculates $cert(Q, \mathcal{A}_i \cup \mathcal{A}_{static} \cup \mathcal{T})$. Similarly, $val(s0, ?y)\langle j \rangle$ finds the values $?y$ w.r.t. to the jth ABox in the sequence. These steps in evaluating the HAVING clause are intra-ABox steps, as they are done locally w.r.t. (pure) ABoxes in the sequence. Though regarding the semantics intra-ABox query answering is just the one for UCQS over pure DL-Lite ontologies, the crucial difference is the fact that the ABoxes are not static but are updated dynamically. On the top of the intra-ABox step one has an inter-ABox step, which is realized by the FOL formula around the embedded conditions; in the case of this example, the FOL formula constrains the variables stemming from the intra-ABox evaluations to those fulfilling $?x <= ?y$.

Already in this example we see the subtleties of the HAVING clause language. For example, if we replaced $i < j$ by $i <= j$, then the HAVING clause would also test for every time point $i = j$ whether all values i are smaller or equal than all values at $j = i$, which amounts to saying that there can be at most one value for $s0$ at every state within the sequence.

The STARQL semantics, which we have sketched here is similar to the epistemic semantics of the query language EQL [21]: At every time point (state) i one considers only those bindings for which it is (certainly) known that they make the embedded CQs true. In contrast to EQL, in STARQL we have an explicit temporal domain, and we have an explicit safety mechanism for the formulas [65].

7.2   Extended Examples

The information need of the engineer may be more complex in that he asks for all temperature sensors that show a monotonic increase in the last two seconds. Temperature sensors are assumed to be declared in a static ABox, which is produced by classical mappings of the data sources (e.g. SQL databases). Temperature sensors found in the static ABox are delegated to the HAVING clause to specify the monotonicity condition. The sources to be used (such as the static ABox) are specified after keyword USING.

```
1   CREATE STREAM S_out_2 AS
2
3   SELECT  { ?s rdf:type RecentMonInc }<NOW>
4   FROM S_Msmt [NOW-2s, NOW]->1s
5   USING   STATIC ABOX <http://Astatic>,
6           TBOX <http://TBox>
7   WHERE { ?s:type TempSens }
8   SEQUENCE BY StdSeq AS SEQ
9   HAVING
10   FORALL i < j IN SEQ,?x,?y:
11   IF ({ ?s val ?x }<i>  AND { ?s  val ?y }<j>) THEN ?x <= ?y
```

Listing 1.3. STARQL example for using ABox and TBox

Due to possible inferences of the TBox together with the ABox, the query refers also to the TBox. For example, assume that the TBox contains the axiom $BurnerTipTempSens \sqsubseteq TempSens$. A complete answer to the STARQL query would first have to rewrite the embedded CQs. The embedded $TempSens(?s)$ would result in the new embedded $TempSens(?s) \lor BurnerTipTempSens(?s)$. This type of rewriting uses the rewriting technique appropriate for the underlying chosen embedded condition language, here perfect rewriting for UCQs. Perfect rewriting is possible, as in the framework of STARQL, the TBox is assumed to be a classical TBox without any additional temporal constructors. All subsumptions in the TBox hold at every time point.

If we were considering a different embedded condition language, for example grounded CQs within the ABDEO approach [58], then query answering could not be realized with rewriting but would have to use, e.g., an ABox modularization approach.

A more compact formulation of the extended monotonicity query uses a library entry for the monotonicity condition; after the keyword `CREATE  AGGREGATE OPERATOR` is given the name of the library entry `monInc`.

```
1   CREATE STREAM S_out_3 AS
2
3   SELECT   { ?s rdf:type RecentMonInc }<NOW>
4   FROM S_Msmt [NOW-2s, NOW]->1s
5   USING    STATIC ABOX <http://Astatic>,
6            TBOX <http://TBox>
7   WHERE { ?s :type TempSens }
8   SEQUENCE BY StdSeq AS SEQ
9   HAVING monInc(SEQ, {?s val *})
10
11  CREATE AGGREGATE OPERATOR monInc(seq,  f(*)) AS
12     FORALL i <= j in SEQ,x,y:
13     IF   (f(x)<i>  AND  f(y)<j>) THEN  x <= y
```

Listing 1.4. STARQL example for aggregation definition

The variables that can be selected in the `SELECT` line (line 3) are not restricted to those specified within the `WHERE` clause but may also refer to (open) variables in the `HAVING` clause. If, e.g., one wants to know at every second the value for the sensor s_0 in the last two seconds, than this can be queried in STARQL as depicted in 1.5.

```
1   CREATE STREAM S_out_4 AS
2   SELECT { s0 :val ?x }<NOW>
3   FROM S_Msmt [NOW-2s, NOW]->1s
4   SEQUENCE BY StdSeq AS SEQ
5   HAVING   EXISTS i IN SEQ ({ s0 val ?x }<i>
```

Listing 1.5. Using variables from the `HAVING` clause

Let us give an example with a more complex condition in the `HAVING` clause using a further constructor, multiple streams and the average operator (Listing 1.6). We are interested in those temperature sensors with a recent monotonic increase which are known to be in an operational mode (not service maintenance mode) in the last 2s. Furthermore we want to get the average of the values in the last 2s. Next to the monotonicity condition we have a further condition using the `FORALL` operator. It evaluates the boolean condition in its scope on all ABoxes in the sequence and outputs the truth value true if the condition holds in all ABoxes.

```
1   CREATE STREAM S_out_5 AS
2
3   SELECT   { ?s rdf:type RecentMonInc }<NOW>,
4            { ?s hasMean AVG(?sens val *) }<NOW>
5   FROM SMsmt NOW-2s, NOW]->1s
6   USING    STATIC ABOX <http://Astatic>,
7            TBOX <http://TBox>
8   WHERE { ?s rdf:type TempSens }
9   SEQUENCE BY StdSeq as SEQ
10  HAVING   monInc(?s val *) AND
11           FORALL i IN SEQ   { ?s rdf:type InOperationalMode }<i>
```

Listing 1.6. STARQL example for complex filter condition

The STARQL stream query language fulfills the desirable orthogonality property as it takes streams of timestamped assertions as input and produces again streams of timestamped assertions. This approach is motivated by the idea that getting answers to queries is not only an activity of GUI client programs (it is not only variable bindings that one wants to determine by queries), but query outcomes are going to be used as input to other queries as well as the generation of (temporal) ABox assertions in the application scenario itself. The expressions following the SELECT clause are templates for generating further timestamped ABox assertions (based on the intended interpretations within the query). The produced ABox assertions hold only within the output stream in which they are generated—and not universally. Otherwise we would have to handle recursion in queries—which, though possible using some kind of fixpoint operator, might lead to bad performance due to theoretically high complexity of the query answering problem. Hence the stream of ABox assertions generated by a query is in a different "category" than the assertions in the static ABox and the historical ABox. This is a kind of a locality principle.

Though the ABox assertions are limited to hold in the output streams, they may interact with the TBox, leading to entailed assertions. Assume that the TBox contains the following axiom stating that a sensor with a recent monotonic increase is a sensor in a critical mode:

$$RecMonInc \sqsubseteq Critical$$

The engineer could ask for those temperature sensors in a critical mode at every second on the stream S_{out_3} generated by one of our queries above. The components at which the temperature sensors had been in a critical state are declared as those ones that have to be removed in the next service maintenance in 10^4 seconds (see Listing 1.7).

The query is evaluated on the stream S_{out_3} which contains assertions of the form $RecMonInc(sens)\langle t \rangle$. At every second only the actual assertion is put into the temporal ABox (window range = 0s) so that the sequence contains only a trivial sequence of length 1 (at most). The EXISTS operator just tests whether the

```
1   CREATE STREAM S_out_6 AS
2
3   SELECT { ?comp removeDueToSensor   ?s}<NOW + 10^4s>
4   FROM S_out_3  [NOW, NOW]->1s
5   USING    STATIC ABOX <http://Astatic>,
6            TBOX <http://TBox>
7   WHERE { ?s rdf:type TempSens . ?sens partOf ?comp }
8   SEQUENCE BY StdSeq AS SEQ
9   HAVING EXISTS i IN SEQ { ?sens rdf:type Critical }<i>
```

Listing 1.7. STARQL example for scope locality

condition $Critical(sens)$ holds in some ABox in the sequence. Now, the stream S_{out_3} does not contain any ABox assertions with the concept symbol $Critical$, but such assertions are entailed by assertions of the form $RecMonInc(sens)\langle t\rangle$ in S_{out_3} and the TBox. Hence, the query above will indeed find those components that have to be removed due to a critical sensor. The example might use oversimplification but the reader should be able to understand the main idea.

Changing the stream from S_{out_3} to S_{Msmt} and thereby keeping everything else the same, will lead to a query which does not find any components—as the TBox and the assertions in S_{Msmt} do not entail assertions of the form $Critical(sens)$. Hence, the answers of a query really depend on the streams to which the queries are issued.

The general motivation of this approach is similar to the CONSTRUCT operator in the SPARQL query language, which provides the means to prescribe the format in which the bindings of the variables should be outputted. But in contrast, our approach also considers the outputs as ABox assertions that are part of an ontology. The idea of viewing the query head as a template for general ABox assertions was described already in the query language nRQL [80] coming with the Racer system.

7.3   Unfolding STARQL into CQL

We are going to illustrate the unfolding mechanism for the monotonicity example. Let be given a CQL stream of measurements $Msmt$, where the tuples adhere to the schema Msmt(MID, MtimeStamp, SID, Mval). A mapping takes a CQL query over this stream and produces a stream of timestamped ABox assertions of the from $val(x, y)\langle t\rangle$.

$val(x, y)\langle z\rangle \longleftarrow$
```
            SELECT Rstream(f(SID) as x, Mval as y, MtimeStamp as t)
            FROM Msmt[NOW]
```

For this example we assume that s_0 is a shortcut for the compound individual constant $f(TC255)$, i.e., s_0 is the abstract representation of the sensor named TC255 in the data.

The stream query language STARQL follows a locality principle that allows to choose static ABoxes, TBoxes, and also the streams w.r.t. which the query is evaluated. This means in particular that the streams referred to in a query must be defined either by mappings or on a higher level by another STARQL query. So, assume that an input stream S is defined by the following mappings:

$$ax_1\langle t\rangle \leftarrow \Psi_1, ax_2\langle t\rangle \leftarrow \Psi_2, \ldots, ax_n\langle t\rangle \leftarrow \Psi_n$$

where for all i ax_i is an ABox assertion templates (in RDF speak: basic graph patterns) and Ψ_i is a CQL query containing all variables in ax_i within its Select head. The virtual stream consists of the time wise union of time tagged instantiations of the templates $ax_i\langle t\rangle$. Note, that this definition fixes only a logical stream. If one wants to work with streams having an arrival ordering, than one has either to fix the ordering according to some method or work with an indeterminism given by the query answering system which chooses the exact ordering. For all our examples, the exact arrival sequence is not relevant as we do not discuss stream operators that depend on the exact ordering. Hence, we can safely assume that the stream of timestamped ABox assertions/RDF tuples fixed by the mappings is a logical stream.

We assume that we have an input stream S_{msmt} defined exactly by the mapping above and take the basic monotonicity query in Listing 1.2.

The main problem for an unfolding strategy for STARQL queries is new data structure of an ABox sequence, which is not directly representable in CQL. A further demanding aspect is the fact that the HAVING clause is quite complex. Regarding the former, we therefore assume that the STARQL queries only use the standard sequencing, so that for every time point t_{NOW} from every state i in the sequence associated with t_{NOW} one can reconstruct the timestamps of the tuples occurring in the ABox $\mathcal{A}_i$.

A second assumption is that all tuples in the input stream contain an attribute timestamp the value of which is the same as the value of the timestamp. Such a method is also discussed in [5], in order to do computations directly on the timestamps. So, we may assume a default stream-to-stream operator implemented into the CQL answering system and applied directly after every window-to-stream operator. It takes elements $d\langle t\rangle$ of a stream and returns an element $(d, t)\langle t\rangle$, thereby extending the schema of the tuples in the input stream by a time attribute for the output schema. If d already contains a time attribute, then it is overwritten by the new values. In the definition of the mapping for $val(x, y)\langle t\rangle$, we applied this assumption, where we refer to the time attribute MtimeStamp of the input stream Msmt. Note that this assumption mitigates the weakness of time-ignoring bag semantics in the window operators of CQL.

Regarding the complexity of the HAVING clause, the STARQL grammar (see [64,65]) uses a safety mechanism that restricts the use of variables by adornments. For example, in the HAVING clause $?y > 3$, the variable $?y$ is not safe, as the set

```
1   NOT EXISTS   i,j in SEQ ?x,?y:
2   ({ s0 val ?x }<i>   AND { s0   val ?y }<j>) AND   ?x > ?y
```

Listing 1.8. Normalized monotonicity condition

```
1   CREATE VIEW windowRelation as
2   SELECT *  FROM Msmt[RANGE 2s Slide 1s];
3
4   SELECT
5   Rstream('{ s0 rdf:Type RecMonInc }'||'<'||timestamp||'>'
        )
6   FROM windowRel
7   WHERE windowRel.SID = 'TC255'  AND
8   NOT EXISTS (
9     SELECT * FROM
10    (SELECT timestamp as i, value as x FROM windowRelation)
      ,
11    (SELECT timestamp as j, value as y FROM windowRelation)
12    WHERE   i < j AND x > y );
```

Listing 1.9. Monotonicity STARQL query unfolded into CQL

of certain answers with bindings for $?y$ would be infinite. On the other hand, in $val(s_0, ?y)\langle i\rangle \land (?y > 3)$ the variable $?y$ is safe, as it is bounded by $val(s_0, ?y)\langle i\rangle$, which gives a finite set of bindings. Actually, safety has not only to guarantee the finiteness of the non-bounded variables but also the domain independence [1], as the target language CQL (as a SQL extension) is also domain independent. Domain independence ensures that the query language can be evaluated only on the basis of the constants in the query and the database/streams (thus using only the active domain) and does not have to incorporate the whole domain.

The safety conditions guarantee, that the HAVING clause can be transformed into a FOL formula which is in so called *safe range normal form*. Such formulas can further be transformed to relational algebraic normal form (RANF), for which a direct translation into the relational algebra and so also into SQL is possible. This SQL query depends on the states in the sequence associated with the evolving time point t_{NOW}. But the association of states and timestamps is unique: we can refer to states i just by the timestamps stored in the attribute value of the tuple.

The HAVING clause in the STARQL query of Listing 1.2 is given in relational algebraic normal form in Listing 1.8. The whole unfolded CQL query for the STARQL query of Listing 1.2 is given in Listing 1.9. Here, the view windowRelation creates a temporal relation of measurements according to the time window specified in the mapping. The expression after the RStream constructs (as a string) the RDF triple as expected by the STARQL query.

8   Conclusion

Research on temporal and streamified OBDA has just begun. It can profit by the many ideas, formalisms, and techniques known from the vast literature on temporal logics and relational stream processing. But as the benchmarks in particular w.r.t. OBDA streaming engines [81] show, the theoretical formalization has still not settled—not to speak of the implementation and optimization aspects, in particular the demanding scalability issues for stream processing (number of continuous queries, number of streams, frequency, size of the static ABox etc.)

As part of a possible theoretical formalization, we introduced the STARQL query language that uses the crucial data structure of streams of ABox sequences. The ABox sequencing strategy can be considered as syntactic sugar only for those cases where the chosen sequencing strategy is as simple as that of standard sequencing. For non-standard sequencing strategies, such building only consistent ABoxes which are queried, a reduction to the standard window operator is not possible. As of now, STARQL is implemented and tested in the OPTIQUE project within a prototype that uses a stream extended version of ADP [47], a highly distributed data management system, as the data source to which STARQL queries are unfolded.

Next to the in-depth theoretical foundation of streamifying classical OBDA, further relevant research is going to be in the direction of streamifying and temporalizing ABDEO. The idea of modularization has to be adapted to handle fast importing of modules for intra-ABox reasoning, using time as a special modularization parameter.

References

1. Abiteboul, S., Hull, R., Vianu, V.: Foundations of Databases. Addison-Wesley (1995)
2. Allen, J.F.: Towards a General Theory of Action and Time. Artificial Intelligence 23(2), 123–154 (1984)
3. Anicic, D., Fodor, P., Rudolph, S., Stojanovic, N.: Ep-sparql: a unified language for event processing and stream reasoning. In: Srinivasan, S., Ramamritham, K., Kumar, A., Ravindra, M.P., Bertino, E., Kumar, R. (eds.) WWW, pp. 635–644. ACM (2011)
4. Anicic, D., Rudolph, S., Fodor, P., Stojanovic, N.: Stream reasoning and complex event processing in etalis. Semantic Web 3(4), 397–407 (2012)
5. Arasu, A., Babu, S., Widom, J.: The CQL continuous query language: semantic foundations and query execution. The VLDB Journal 15, 121–142 (2006)
6. Artale, A., Calvanese, D., Kontchakov, R., Zakharyaschev, M.: The DL-Lite family and relations. J. Artif. Intell. Res (JAIR) 36, 1–69 (2009)
7. Artale, A., Franconi, E.: A survey of temporal extensions of description logics. Annals of Mathematics and Artificial Intelligence 30(1-4), 171–210 (2001)
8. Artale, A., Kontchakov, R., Wolter, F., Zakharyaschev, M.: Temporal description logic for ontology-based data access. In: Proceedings of the Twenty-Third International Joint Conference on Artificial Intelligence, IJCAI 2013, pp. 711–717. AAAI Press (2013)

9. Artikis, A., Skarlatidis, A., Portet, F., Paliouras, G.: Logic-based event recognition. Knowledge Eng. Review 27(4), 469–506 (2012)
10. Baader, F., Borgwardt, S., Lippmann, M.: Temporalizing ontology-based data access. In: Bonacina, M.P. (ed.) CADE 2013. LNCS (LNAI), vol. 7898, pp. 330–344. Springer, Heidelberg (2013)
11. Baader, F., Nutt, W.: Basic description logics. In: Baader, F., Calvanese, D., McGuinness, D., Nardi, D., Patel-Schneider, P. (eds.) The Description Logic Handbook, pp. 43–95. Cambridge University Press (2003)
12. van Benthem, J.: The Logic of Time: A Model-Theoretic Investigation into the Varieties of Temporal Ontology and Temporal Discourse, 2nd edn. Reidel (1991)
13. Bohlken, W., Neumann, B., Hotz, L., Koopmann, P.: Ontology-based realtime activity monitoring using beam search. In: Crowley, J.L., Draper, B.A., Thonnat, M. (eds.) ICVS 2011. LNCS, vol. 6962, pp. 112–121. Springer, Heidelberg (2011)
14. Borgwardt, S., Lippmann, M., Thost, V.: Temporal query answering in dl-lite. In: Eiter, et al. (eds.) [34], pp. 80–92
15. Borgwardt, S., Lippmann, M., Thost, V.: Temporal query answering in the description logic dl-lite. In: Fontaine, P., Ringeissen, C., Schmidt, R.A. (eds.) FroCoS 2013. LNCS (LNAI), vol. 8152, pp. 165–180. Springer, Heidelberg (2013)
16. Brenninkmeijer, C.Y.A., Galpin, I., Fernandes, A.A.A., Paton, N.W.: A semantics for a query language over sensors, streams and relations. In: Gray, A., Jeffery, K., Shao, J. (eds.) BNCOD 2008. LNCS, vol. 5071, pp. 87–99. Springer, Heidelberg (2008)
17. Calbimonte, J.-P., Corcho, O., Gray, A.J.G.: Enabling ontology-based access to streaming data sources. In: Patel-Schneider, P.F., Pan, Y., Hitzler, P., Mika, P., Zhang, L., Pan, J.Z., Horrocks, I., Glimm, B. (eds.) ISWC 2010, Part I. LNCS, vol. 6496, pp. 96–111. Springer, Heidelberg (2010)
18. Calbimonte, J.P., Jeung, H., Corcho, O., Aberer, K.: Enabling query technologies for the semantic sensor web. Int. J. Semant. Web Inf. Syst. 8(1), 43–63 (2012)
19. Calì, A., Gottlob, G., Lukasiewicz, T.: Datalog+/-: A unified approach to ontologies and integrity constraints. In: Proceedings of the 12th International Conference on Database Theory, pp. 14–30. ACM Press (2009)
20. Calvanese, D., De Giacomo, G., Lembo, D., Lenzerini, M., Poggi, A., Rodriguez-Muro, M., Rosati, R.: Ontologies and databases: The DL-Lite approach. In: Tessaris, S., Franconi, E., Eiter, T., Gutierrez, C., Handschuh, S., Rousset, M.-C., Schmidt, R.A. (eds.) Reasoning Web. LNCS, vol. 5689, pp. 255–356. Springer, Heidelberg (2009)
21. Calvanese, D., De Giacomo, G., Lembo, D., Lenzerini, M., Rosati, R.: Epistemic first-order queries over description logic knowledge bases. In: Proc. of the 19th Int. Workshop on Description Logics (DL 2006). CEUR Electronic Workshop Proceedings, vol. 189, pp. 51–61 (2006), http://ceur-ws.org/
22. Calvanese, D., et al.: Optique: Obda solution for big data. In: Cimiano, P., Fernández, M., Lopez, V., Schlobach, S., Völker, J. (eds.) ESWC 2013. LNCS, vol. 7955, pp. 293–295. Springer, Heidelberg (2013)
23. Cammert, M., Heinz, C., Kramer, J., Seeger, B., Vaupel, S., Wolske, U.: Flexible multi-threaded scheduling for continuous queries over data streams. In: 2007 IEEE 23rd International Conference on Data Engineering Workshop, pp. 624–633 (April 2007)
24. Cammert, M., Heinz, C., Krämer, J., Seeger, B.: Sortierbasierte joins über datenströmen. In: Vossen, G., Leymann, F., Lockemann, P.C., Stucky, W. (eds.) BTW. LNI, vol. 65, pp. 365–384. GI (2005)

25. Cammert, M., Krämer, J., Seeger, B., Vaupel, S.: An approach to adaptive memory management in data stream systems. In: Liu, L., Reuter, A., Whang, K.Y., Zhang, J. (eds.) ICDE, p. 137. IEEE Computer Society (2006)
26. Chandrasekaran, S., Cooper, O., Deshpande, A., Franklin, M.J., Hellerstein, J.M., Hong, W., Krishnamurthy, S., Madden, S., Raman, V., Reiss, F., Shah, M.A.: Telegraphcq: Continuous dataflow processing for an uncertain world. In: CIDR (2003)
27. Compton, M., Barnaghi, P., Bermudez, L., GarcÃa-Castro, R., Corcho, O., Cox, S., Graybeal, J., Hauswirth, M., Henson, C., Herzog, A., Huang, V., Janowicz, K., Kelsey, W.D., Phuoc, D.L., Lefort, L., Leggieri, M., Neuhaus, H., Nikolov, A., Page, K., Passant, A., Sheth, A., Taylor, K.: The {SSN} ontology of the {W3C} semantic sensor network incubator group. Web Semantics: Science, Services and Agents on the World Wide Web 17, 25–32 (2012)
28. Console, M., Horrocks, I., Jimenez-Ruiz, E., Kharloamov, E., Lenzerini, M., Rosati, R., Ruzzi, M., Santarelli, V., Savo, D.F., Soylu, A., Thorstensen, E., Zheleznyakov, D.: Deliverable D4.1 – WP4 Year 1 progress report (ontology and mapping management). Deliverable FP7-318338, EU (October 2013)
29. Cormode, G.: The continuous distributed monitoring model. SIGMOD Record 42(1), 5–14 (2013)
30. Cugola, G., Margara, A.: Tesla: A formally defined event specification language. In: Proceedings of the Fourth ACM International Conference on Distributed Event-Based Systems, DEBS 2010, pp. 50–61. ACM, New York (2010)
31. Cugola, G., Margara, A.: Complex event processing with t-rex. Journal of Systems and Software 85(8), 1709–1728 (2012)
32. Cugola, G., Margara, A.: Processing flows of information: From data stream to complex event processing. ACM Comput. Surv. 44(3), 15 (2012)
33. Della Valle, E., Ceri, S., Barbieri, D., Braga, D., Campi, A.: A first step towards stream reasoning. In: Domingue, J., Fensel, D., Traverso, P. (eds.) FIS 2008. LNCS, vol. 5468, pp. 72–81. Springer, Heidelberg (2009)
34. Eiter, T., Glimm, B., Kazakov, Y., Krötzsch, M. (eds.): Informal Proceedings of the 26th International Workshop on Description Logics, Ulm, Germany, July 23-26. CEUR Workshop Proceedings, vol. 1014. CEUR-WS.org (2013)
35. Galpin, I., Brenninkmeijer, C., Gray, A., Jabeen, F., Fernandes, A., Paton, N.: Snee: a query processor for wireless sensor networks. Distributed and Parallel Databases 29, 31–85 (2011), doi:10.1007/s10619-010-7074-3
36. Galpin, I., Brenninkmeijer, C.Y., Jabeen, F., Fernandes, A.A., Paton, N.W.: Comprehensive optimization of declarative sensor network queries. In: Winslett, M. (ed.) SSDBM 2009. LNCS, vol. 5566, pp. 339–360. Springer, Heidelberg (2009)
37. Galpin, I., Brenninkmeijer, C.Y.A., Jabeen, F., Fernandes, A.A.A., Paton, N.W.: An architecture for query optimization in sensor networks. In: Alonso, G., Blakeley, J.A., Chen, A.L.P. (eds.) ICDE, pp. 1439–1441. IEEE (2008)
38. Galton, A.: Reified temporal theories and how to unreify them. In: Proceedings of the 12th International Joint Conference on Artificial Intelligence, IJCAI 1991, vol. 2, pp. 1177–1182. Morgan Kaufmann Publishers Inc., San Francisco (1991)
39. Gutierrez, C., Hurtado, C.A., Vaisman, A.A.: Temporal rdf. In: Gómez-Pérez, A., Euzenat, J. (eds.) ESWC 2005. LNCS, vol. 3532, pp. 93–107. Springer, Heidelberg (2005)
40. Heintz, F., Kvarnström, J., Doherty, P.: Stream-based reasoning support for autonomous systems. In: Coelho, H., Studer, R., Wooldridge, M. (eds.) ECAI. Frontiers in Artificial Intelligence and Applications, vol. 215, pp. 183–188. IOS Press (2010)

41. Heintz, F., Rudol, P., Doherty, P.: From images to traffic behavior - a uav tracking and monitoring application. In: FUSION, pp. 1–8. IEEE (2007)

42. Hobbs, J.R., Pan, F.: An ontology of time for the semantic web. ACM Transactions on Asian Language Information Processing 3(1), 66–85 (2004)

43. Hodkinson, I., Reynolds, M.: Temporal logic. In: Blackburn, P., van Benthem, J., Wolter, F. (eds.) Handbook of Modal Logic, ch. 11, vol. 6, pp. 655–720. Elsevier Science (2006)

44. Horrocks, I., Sattler, U.: A description logic with transitive and inverse roles and role hierarchies. Journal of Logic and Computation 9(3), 385–410 (1999)

45. Hwang, J.H., Xing, Y., Çetintemel, U., Zdonik, S.B.: A cooperative, self-configuring high-availability solution for stream processing. In: ICDE, pp. 176–185 (2007)

46. Jain, N., Mishra, S., Srinivasan, A., Gehrke, J., Widom, J., Balakrishnan, H., Çetintemel, U., Cherniack, M., Tibbetts, R., Zdonik, S.: Towards a streaming sql standard. In: Proc. VLDB Endow., vol. 1(2), pp. 1379–1390 (2008)

47. Kllapi, H., Bilidas, D., Ioannidis, Y., Koubarakis, M.: Deliverable D7.1: Techniques for distributed query planning and execution: One-time queries. Deliverable, Optique (2013)

48. Kontchakov, R., Lutz, C., Toman, D., Wolter, F., Zakharyaschev, M.: The combined approach to ontology-based data access. In: Walsh, T. (ed.) IJCAI, pp. 2656–2661. IJCAI/AAAI (2011)

49. Kostylev, E.V., Reutter, J.: Answering counting aggregate queries over ontologies of the DL-Lite family. In: Proceedings of the 27th AAAI Conference on Artificial Intelligence (AAAI 2013), Bellevue, Washington (2013)

50. Kowalski, R.A., Sadri, F.: Towards a logic-based unifying framework for computing. CoRR abs/1301.6905 (2013)

51. Kowalski, R.A., Toni, F., Wetzel, G.: Towards a declarative and efficient glass-box CLP language. In: WLP, pp. 138–141 (1994)

52. Krämer, J., Seeger, B.: A temporal foundation for continuous queries over data streams. In: Haritsa, J.R., Vijayaraman, T.M. (eds.) COMAD, pp. 70–82. Computer Society of India (2005)

53. Krämer, J., Seeger, B.: Semantics and implementation of continuous sliding window queries over data streams. ACM Trans. Database Syst. 34(1), 1–49 (2009)

54. Kyzirakos, K., Karpathiotakis, M., Koubarakis, M.: Strabon: A Semantic Geospatial DBMS. In: International Semantic Web Conference, Boston, USA (November 2012)

55. Le-Phuoc, D., Dao-Tran, M., Pham, M.-D., Boncz, P., Eiter, T., Fink, M.: Linked stream data processing engines: Facts and figures. In: Cudré-Mauroux, P., et al. (eds.) ISWC 2012, Part II. LNCS, vol. 7650, pp. 300–312. Springer, Heidelberg (2012), http://dx.doi.org/10.1007/978-3-642-35173-0_20

56. Lecue, F., Pan, J.Z.: Predictive learning in sensor networks. Submitted to IJCAI

57. Milea, V., Frasincar, F., Kaymak, U.: tOWL: A Temporal Web Ontology Language. IEEE Transactions on Systems, Man and Cybernetics 42(1), 268–281 (2012)

58. Möller, R., Neuenstadt, C., Özçep, Ö.L., Wandelt, S.: Advances in accessing big data with expressive ontologies. In: Timm, I.J., Thimm, M. (eds.) KI 2013. LNCS (LNAI), vol. 8077, pp. 118–129. Springer, Heidelberg (2013), http://dx.doi.org/10.1007/978-3-642-40942-4_11

59. Montanari, A., Policriti, A.: Decidability results for metric and layered temporal logics. Notre Dame Journal of Formal Logic 37, 37–260 (1996)

60. Motik, B.: Representing and querying validity time in RDF and OWL: a logic-based approach. In: Patel-Schneider, P.F., Pan, Y., Hitzler, P., Mika, P., Zhang,

L., Pan, J.Z., Horrocks, I., Glimm, B. (eds.) ISWC 2010, Part I. LNCS, vol. 6496, pp. 550–565. Springer, Heidelberg (2010)

61. Neumann, B., Novak, H.J.: Event models for recognition and natural language description of events in real-world image sequences. In: Bundy, A. (ed.) IJCAI, pp. 724–726. William Kaufmann (1983)

62. Neumann, B., Novak, H.J.: Noas: Ein system zur natürlichsprachlichen beschreibung zeitveränderlicher szenen. Inform., Forsch. Entwickl. 1(2), 83–92 (1986)

63. Noy, N.F.: Semantic integration: a survey of ontology-based approaches. SIGMOD Record 33(4), 65–70 (2004)

64. Özçep, O.L., Möller, R., Neuenstadt, C.: Obda stream access combined with safe first-order temporal reasoning. Technical report, Hamburg University of Technology (2014)

65. Özçep, O.L., Möller, R., Neuenstadt, C.: A stream-temporal query language for ontology based data access. To be published in Proceedings of the 7th International Workshop on Description Logics (2014)

66. Özçep, Ö.L., Möller, R., Neuenstadt, C., Zheleznyakov, D., Kharlamov, E.: Deliverable D5.1 – a semantics for temporal and stream-based query answering in an OBDA context. Deliverable FP7-318338, EU (October 2013)

67. Papadakis, N., Stravoskoufos, K., Baratis, E., Petrakis, E.G.M., Plexousakis, D.: Proton: A prolog reasoner for temporal ontologies in owl. Expert Syst. Appl. 38(12), 14660–14667 (2011)

68. Perry, M.: A Framework to Support Spatial, Temporal and Thematic Analytics over Semantic Web Data. Ph.D. thesis, Wright State UNiversity (2008)

69. Le-Phuoc, D., Dao-Tran, M., Xavier Parreira, J., Hauswirth, M.: A native and adaptive approach for unified processing of linked streams and linked data. In: Aroyo, L., Welty, C., Alani, H., Taylor, J., Bernstein, A., Kagal, L., Noy, N., Blomqvist, E. (eds.) ISWC 2011, Part I. LNCS, vol. 7031, pp. 370–388. Springer, Heidelberg (2011)

70. Phuoc, D.L., Nguyen-Mau, H.Q., Parreira, J.X., Hauswirth, M.: A middleware framework for scalable management of linked streams. J. Web Sem. 16, 42–51 (2012)

71. Poggi, A., Lembo, D., Calvanese, D., Giacomo, G.D., Lenzerini, M., Rosati, R.: Linking data to ontologies. Journal of Data Semantics 10, 133–173 (2008)

72. Rist, T., Herzog, G., André, E.: Ereignismodellierung zur inkrementellen highlevel bildfolgenanalyse. In: Buchberger, E., Retti, J. (eds.) ÖGAI. Informatik-Fachberichte, vol. 151, pp. 1–11. Springer (1987)

73. Rodriguez-Muro, M., Calvanese, D.: High performance query answering over dl-lite ontologies. In: Brewka, G., Eiter, T., McIlraith, S.A. (eds.) KR. AAAI Press (2012)

74. Rodriguez-Muro, M., Calvanese, D.: Quest, an owl 2 ql reasoner for ontology-based data access. In: Klinov, P., Horridge, M. (eds.) OWLED. CEUR Workshop Proceedings, vol. 849. CEUR-WS.org (2012)

75. Rodriguez-Muro, M., Kontchakov, R., Zakharyaschev, M.: Query rewriting and optimisation with database dependencies in ontop. In: Eiter, et al. (eds.) [34], pp. 917–929

76. Søberg, J., Goebel, V., Plagemann, T.: Deviation detection in automated home care using commonsens. In: PerCom Workshops, pp. 668–673. IEEE (2011)

77. Tappolet, J., Bernstein, A.: Applied temporal rdf: Efficient temporal querying of rdf data with sparql. In: Aroyo, L., Traverso, P., Ciravegna, F., Cimiano, P., Heath, T., Hyvönen, E., Mizoguchi, R., Oren, E., Sabou, M., Simperl, E. (eds.) ESWC 2009. LNCS, vol. 5554, pp. 308–322. Springer, Heidelberg (2009)

78. Valle, E.D., Schlobach, S., Krötzsch, M., Bozzon, A., Ceri, S., Horrocks, I.: Order matters! harnessing a world of orderings for reasoning over massive data. Semantic Web 4(2), 219–231 (2013)
79. Wandelt, S., Möller, R.: Towards abox modularization of semi-expressive description logics. Applied Ontology 7(2), 133–167 (2012)
80. Wessel, M., Möller, R.: A high performance semantic web query answering engine. In: Horrocks, I., Sattler, U., Wolter, F. (eds.) Description Logics. CEUR Workshop Proceedings, vol. 147. CEUR-WS.org (2005)
81. Zhang, Y., Duc, P.M., Corcho, O., Calbimonte, J.-P.: Srbench: A Streaming RDF/SPARQL Benchmark. In: Cudré-Mauroux, P., et al. (eds.) ISWC 2012, Part I. LNCS, vol. 7649, pp. 641–657. Springer, Heidelberg (2012)

Querying and Learning
in Probabilistic Databases

Maximilian Dylla[1], Martin Theobald[2], and Iris Miliaraki[3]

[1] Max Planck Institute for Informatics, Saarbrücken, Germany
[2] University of Antwerp, Antwerp, Belgium
[3] Yahoo Labs, Barcelona, Spain

Abstract. Probabilistic Databases (PDBs) lie at the expressive inter-section of databases, first-order logic, and probability theory. PDBs employ logical deduction rules to process Select-Project-Join (SPJ) queries, which form the basis for a variety of declarative query languages such as Datalog, Relational Algebra, and SQL. They employ logical consistency constraints to resolve data inconsistencies, and they represent query answers via logical lineage formulas (aka. "data provenance") to trace the dependencies between these answers and the input tuples that led to their derivation. While the literature on PDBs dates back to more than 25 years of research, only fairly recently the key role of lineage for establishing a closed and complete representation model of relational operations over this kind of probabilistic data was discovered. Although PDBs benefit from their efficient and scalable database infrastructures for data storage and indexing, they couple the data computation with probabilistic inference, the latter of which remains a #P-hard problem also in the context of PDBs.

In this chapter, we provide a review on the key concepts of PDBs with a particular focus on our own recent research results related to this field. We highlight a number of ongoing research challenges related to PDBs, and we keep referring to an information extraction (IE) scenario as a running application to manage uncertain and temporal facts obtained from IE techniques directly inside a PDB setting.

Keywords: Probabilistic and Temporal Databases, Deduction Rules, Consistency Constraints, Information Extraction.

1 Introduction

Over the past decade, the demand for managing structured, relational data has continued to increase at an unprecedented rate, as we are crossing the "Big Data" era. Database architectures of all kinds play a key role for managing this explosion of data, thus aiming to provide efficient storage, querying, and update functionalities at scale. One of the main initial assumptions in databases, however, is that all data stored in the database is deterministic. That is, a data item (or "tuple") either holds as a real-world piece of truth or it is absent from

M. Koubarakis et al. (Eds.): Reasoning Web 2014, LNCS 8714, pp. 313–368, 2014.
© Springer International Publishing Switzerland 2014

the database. In reality, a large amount of the data that is supposed to be captured in a database is inherently noisy or otherwise uncertain. Example applications that deal with uncertain data range from scientific data management and sensor networks to data integration and knowledge management systems. Any sensor, for example, can only provide a limited precision, and hence its measurements are inherently uncertain with respect to the precise physical value. Also, even the currently most sophisticated information extraction (IE) methods can extract facts with particular degree of confidence. This is partly due to the ambiguity of sentences formulated in natural language, but mainly due to the heuristic nature of many extractions tools which often rely on hand-crafted regular expressions and various other forms of rule- or learning-based extraction techniques [9,6,62,33].

As a result of the efforts for handling uncertain data directly inside a scalable database architecture, the field of probabilistic databases (PDBs) has evolved as an established area of database research in recent years [63]. PDBs lie in the intersection of database systems [2,32] (for handling large amounts of data), first-order logic [60,65] (for formulating expressive queries and constraints over the captured data items), and probability theory [25,58] (for quantifying the uncertainty and coupling the relational operations with different kinds of probabilistic inference). So far, most research efforts in the field of PDBs have focused on the representation of uncertain, relational data on the one hand, thus designing appropriate data models, and on efficiently answering queries over this kind of data on the other hand, thus proposing suitable methods for query evaluation. Regarding the data model, a variety of approaches for compactly representing data uncertainty have been presented. One of the most popular approaches, which forms also the basis for this chapter, is that of a *tuple-independent PDB* [15,63], in which a probability value is attached to each tuple in the database, and all tuples are assumed to be independent of each other. More expressive models, such as *pc-tables* [31], have been proposed as well, where each tuple is annotated by a logical formula that captures the tuple's dependencies to other tuples in the database. Finally, there are also more sophisticated models which capture *statistical correlations* among the database tuples [37,52,56].

Temporal-Probabilistic Databases. Besides potentially being uncertain, data items can also be annotated by other dimensions such as time or location. Such techniques are already partly supported by traditional database systems, where temporal databases (TDBs) [35] have been an active research field for many years. To enable this kind of temporal data and temporal reasoning also in a PDB context, the underlying probabilistic models need to be extended to support additional data dimensions. As part of this chapter, we thus also focus on the intersection of temporal and probabilistic databases, i.e., capturing data that is valid during a specific time interval with a given probability. In this context, we present a *unified temporal-probabilistic database* (TPDB) *model* [21] in which both time and probability are considered as first-class citizens.

Top-k Query Processing. Query evaluation in PDBs involves—apart from the common data computation step, found also in deterministic databases—an additional probability computation step for computing the marginal probabilities of the respective query answers. While the complexity for the data computation step for any given SQL query is polynomial in the size of the underlying database, even fairly simple Select-Project-Join (SPJ) queries can involve an exponential cost in the probability computation step. In fact, the query evaluation problem in PDBs is known to be #$\mathcal{P}$-hard [16,30]. Thus, efficient strategies for probability computations and the early pruning of low-probability query answers remains a key challenge for the scalable management of probabilistic data. Recent works on efficient probability computation in PDBs have addressed this problem mostly from two ends. The first group of approaches have restricted the class of queries, i.e., by focusing on *safe query plans*[16,14,17], or by considering a specific class of tuple-dependencies, commonly referred to as *read-once functions* [57]. In particular the second group of approaches allows for applying *top-k style pruning methods* [49,48,8,23] at the time when the query is processed. This alternative way of addressing probability computations aims to efficiently identify the top-k most probable query answers. To achieve this they rely on lower and upper bounds for the probabilities of these answers, to avoid an exact computation of their probabilities.

Learning Tuple Probabilities. While most works in PDBs assume that the initial probabilities are provided as input along with the data items, in reality, an update or estimation of the tuple's input probabilities often is highly desirable. To this end, enabling such a learning approach for tuple probabilities is an important building block for many applications, such as creating, updating, or cleaning a PDB. Although this has already been stated as a key challenge by Dalvi et al. [13], to date, only very few works [61,41] explicitly tackle the problem of creating or updating a PDB. Our recent work [22], which is also presented in the context of this chapter, thus can be seen as one of the first works that addresses the *learning of tuple probabilities* in a PDB setting.

In brief, this chapter aims to provide an overview of the key concepts of PDB systems, the main challenges that need to be addressed to efficiently manage large amounts of uncertain data, and the different methods that have been proposed for dealing with these challenges. In this context, we provide an overview of our own recent results [23,20,22] related to this field. As a motivating and running example, we continue to refer to a (simplified) IE scenario, where factual knowledge is extracted from both structured and semistructured Web sources, which is a process that inherently results in large amounts of uncertain (and temporal) facts.

1.1   Running Application: Information Extraction

As a guiding theme for this chapter, we argue that one of the main application domains of PDBs—and in fact a major challenge for scaling these techniques to very large relational data collections—is *information extraction* [68]. The goal

WonPrizeExtraction

	Subject	Object	Pid	Did	p
I_1	Spielberg	AcademyAward	1	1	1.0
I_2	Spielberg	AcademyAward	2	1	1.0

BornInExtraction

	Subject	Object	Pid	Did	p
I_3	Spielberg	Cincinnati	3	1	1.0
I_4	Spielberg	LosAngeles	3	2	1.0

UsingPattern					FromDomain		
	Pid	Pattern	p		Did	Domain	p
I_5	1	Received	0.8	I_8	1	Wikipedia.org	0.9
I_6	2	Won	0.5	I_9	2	Imdb.com	0.8
I_7	3	Born	0.9				

Fig. 1. An Example Probabilistic Database for an Information Extraction Setting

of IE is to harvest factual knowledge from semistructured sources, and even from free-text, to turn this knowledge into a more machine-readable format—in other words, to "turn text into database tuples". For example, the sentence "Spielberg won the Academy Award for Best Director for Schindler's List (1993) and Saving Private Ryan (1998)" from Steven Spielberg's Wikipedia article[1], entails the fact that *Spielberg* won an *AcademyAward*, which we could represent as *WonAward(Spielberg, AcademyAward)*.

Due to the many ways of rephrasing such statements in natural language, an automatic machinery that mines such facts from textual sources will inherently produce a number of erroneous extractions. Thus, the resulting knowledge base is never going to be 100% clean but rather remains to some degree uncertain. Since the Web is literally full of text and facts, managing the vast amounts of extracted facts in a *scalable way* and at the same time providing *high-confidence query answers* from potentially noisy and uncertain input data will remain a major challenge of any knowledge management system, including PDBs.

For an illustration, we model a simple IE workflow in a PDB. Usually, candidates for facts in sentences are detected by textual patterns [9,42]. For instance, for winning an award, the verb "won" might indeed be a good indicator. In our PDB, we want to capture the different ingredients that lead to the extraction of a fact. Besides the textual pattern, this could also involve the Web domain (such as *Wikipedia.org*), where we found the sentence of interest. Hence, we store these in separate probabilistic relations as shown in Figure 1. Therefore, the probabilities of the tuples of each domain and each pattern reflect our trust in this source and pattern, respectively. To reconcile the facts along with their resulting probabilities from the PDB of Figure 1, we employ two deduction rules. In essence, they formulate a natural join on the *Pid* and *Did* columns of the underlying relations to connect an extraction pattern and an extraction domain to the actual fact:

---

[1] http://en.wikipedia.org/wiki/Steven_Spielberg (as of December, 2013).

$$WonPrize(S,O) \leftarrow \begin{pmatrix} WonPrizeExtraction(S,O,Pid,Did) \\ \wedge \ UsingPattern(Pid,P) \\ \wedge \ FromDomain(Did,D) \end{pmatrix} \tag{1}$$

$$BornIn(S,O) \leftarrow \begin{pmatrix} BornInExtraction(S,O,Pid,Did) \\ \wedge \ UsingPattern(Pid,P) \\ \wedge \ FromDomain(Did,D) \end{pmatrix} \tag{2}$$

If we execute a query on the resulting *WonPrize* or *BornIn* relations, then the probabilities of the pattern and domain establish the probability of each answer fact with respect to the relational operations that were involved to obtain these query answers.

1.2   Challenges and Outline

A number of PDB systems have been released as open-source prototypes recently. These include systems like *MayBMS* [5], *MystiQ* [8], *Orion* [59], *PrDB* [56], *SPROUT* [46], and *Trio* [7], which all allow for storing and querying uncertain, relational data and meanwhile found a wide recognition in the database community. However, in order to make PDB systems as broadly applicable as conventional database systems, we would like to highlight the following challenges.

1. Apart from being uncertain, data can be annotated by other dimensions such as time or location. These techniques are partly already supported by traditional DBs, but to enable this kind of data in PDBs, we need to extend the probabilistic data models to support additional data dimensions.
2. Allowing a wide range of expressive queries, which can be executed efficiently, was one of the ingredients that made traditional database systems successful. Even though the query evaluation problem has been studied intensively in PDBs, for many classes of queries efficient ways of computing answers along with probabilities are not established yet.
3. Most importantly, the field of creating and updating PDBs still is in an early stage, where only very few initial results exist so far. Nevertheless, we believe that supporting the learning or updating of tuple probabilities from labeled training data and selective user inputs will be a key building block for future PDB approaches.

The remainder of this chapter thus is structured as follows. In Section 2, we establish the basic concepts and definitions known from relational databases which form also the basis for defining PDBs in Section 3. Next, in Section 4, we describe a closed and complete data model for both temporal and probabilistic databases (TPDBs), thus capturing data that is not only uncertain but also is annotated with time information. Section 5 discusses query evaluation in PDBs and describes an efficient top-k style evaluation strategy in this context. Last, in Section 6, we introduce the problem of learning tuple probabilities from labeled query answers, which allows also for updating and cleaning a PDB. Section 7 summarizes and concludes this chapter.

2   Relational Databases

The primary purpose of our first technical section is to establish the basic concepts and notations known from *relational databases*, which will form also the basis for the remainder of this chapter. We use a Datalog-oriented notation to represent intensional knowledge in the form of logical rules. Datalog thus fulfills two purposes in our setting. On the one hand, we employ Datalog to write *deduction rules*, from which we derive new intensional tuples from the existing database tuples for query answering. On the other hand, we also employ Datalog to encode *consistency constraints*, which allow us to remove inconsistent tuples from both the input relations and the query answers. For a broader background on the theoretical foundations of relational databases, including the relationship between Datalog, Relational Algebra and SQL, we refer the interested reader to one of the two standard references [2,32] in this field.

2.1   Relations and Tuples

We start with the two most basic concepts of relational databases, namely relations and tuples. We consider a *relation* R as a logical predicate of arity $r \geq 1$. Together with a finite set of *attributes* $A_1, \ldots, A_m \in \mathcal{A}$ and a finite set of (potentially infinite) *domains* $\Omega_1, \ldots, \Omega_m \in \mathcal{O}$, we refer to $R(A_1, \ldots, A_r)$ also as the *schema* of relation R, where $dom : \mathcal{A} \to \mathcal{O}$ is a *domain mapping function* that maps the set of attributes onto their corresponding domains.

For a fixed universe of constants $\mathcal{U} = \bigcup_{\Omega_i \in \mathcal{O}} \Omega_i$, a *relation instance* $\mathcal{R}$ then is a finite subset $\mathcal{R} \subseteq \mathcal{U}^r$. We call the elements of $\mathcal{R}$ *tuples*, and we write $R(\bar{a})$ to denote a tuple in $\mathcal{R}$, where $\bar{a}$ is a vector of constants in $\mathcal{U}$. Furthermore, for a fixed set of variables $\mathcal{V}$, we use $R(\bar{X})$ to refer to a first-order literal over relation R, where $\bar{X} \subseteq \mathcal{U} \cup \mathcal{V}$ denotes a vector consisting of both variables and constants. We will use $Var(\bar{X}) \subseteq \mathcal{V}$ to refer to the set of variables in $\bar{X}$.

Definition 1. *Given relations $R_1, \ldots, R_n$, a relational database comprises the relation instances $\mathcal{R}_i$ whose tuples we collect in the single set of* extensional *tuples $\mathcal{T} := \mathcal{R}_1 \cup \cdots \cup \mathcal{R}_n$.*

In other words, a relation instance can simply be viewed as a table. A tuple thus denotes a row (or "record") in such a table. For convenience of notation, we collect the sets of tuples stored in all relation instances into a single set $\mathcal{T}$. In a deterministic database setting, we can thus say that a tuple $R(\bar{a})$ that is composed of a vector of constants in $\mathcal{U}$ is *true* iff $R(\bar{a}) \in \mathcal{T}$ (which we will also refer to as a "database tuple" in this case). As a shorthand notation, we will also employ $\mathcal{I} = \{I_1, \ldots, I_{|\mathcal{T}|}\}$ as a set of unique tuple identifiers.

Example 1. We consider a database with two relation instances from the movie domain, which capture information about the directors of movies and the awards that various movies may have won.

Directed	
Director	Movie
I_1 Coppola	ApocalypseNow
I_2 Coppola	Godfather
I_3 Tarantino	PulpFiction

WonAward	
Movie	Award
I_4 ApocalypseNow	BestScript
I_5 Godfather	BestDirector
I_6 Godfather	BestPicture
I_7 PulpFiction	BestPicture

For example, the tuple *Directed(Coppola, ApocalypseNow)*, which we also abbreviate by I_1, indicates that *Coppola* directed the movie *ApocalypseNow*. Thus, the above database contains two relation instances with tuples $\mathcal{T} = \{I_1, \ldots, I_7\}$.

2.2   Deduction Rules

To derive new tuples (and entire relations) from an existing relational database, we employ deduction rules. These can be viewed as generally applicable "if-then-rules". That is, given a condition, its conclusion follows. Formally, we follow Datalog [2,10] terminology but employ a more logic-oriented notation to express these rules. Each deduction rule takes the shape of a logical implication, with a conjunction of both positive and negative literals in the body (the "antecedent") and exactly one positive head literal (the "consequent"). Relations occurring in the head literal of a deduction rule are called *intensional relations* [2]. In contrast, relations holding the database tuples, i.e., those from $\mathcal{T}$, are also called *extensional relations*. These two sets of relations (and hence logical predicates) must not overlap and are used strictly differently within the deduction rules.

Definition 2. *A deduction rule is a logical rule of the form*

$$R(\bar{X}) \leftarrow \bigwedge_{i=1,\ldots,n} R_i(\bar{X}_i) \ \wedge \ \bigwedge_{j=1,\ldots,m} \neg R_j(\bar{X}_j) \ \wedge \ \Phi(\bar{X}_A)$$

where

1. *R denotes the intensional relation of the head literal, whereas R_i and R_j may refer to both intensional and extensional relations;*
2. *$n \geq 1$, $m \geq 0$, thus requiring at least one positive relational literal;*
3. *$\bar{X}$, $\bar{X}_i$, $\bar{X}_j$, and $\bar{X}_A$ denote tuples of both variables and constants, such that $Var(\bar{X}) \cup Var(\bar{X}_j) \cup Var(\bar{X}_A) \subseteq \bigcup_i Var(\bar{X}_i)$;*
4. *$\Phi(\bar{X}_A)$ is a conjunction of arithmetic predicates such as "=" and "$\neq$".*

We refer to a set of deduction rules $\mathcal{D}$ also as a Datalog *program.*

By the second condition of Definition 2, we require each deduction rule to have at least one positive literal in its body. Moreover, the third condition ensures *safe* deduction rules [2], by requiring that all variables in the head, $Var(\bar{X})$, in negated literals, $Var(\bar{X}_j)$, and in arithmetic predicates, $Var(\bar{X}_A)$, occur also in at least one of the positive relational predicates, $Var(\bar{X}_i)$, in the body of each rule. As denoted by the fourth condition, we allow a conjunction of arithmetic comparisons such as "=" and "$\neq$". All variables occurring in a deduction rule are implicitly universally quantified.

Example 2. Imagine we are interested in famous movie directors. To derive these from the tuples in Example 1, we can reason as follows: "if a director's movie won an award, then the director should be famous." As a logical formula, we express this as follows.

$$FamousDirector(X) \leftarrow Directed(X, Y) \wedge WonAward(Y, Z) \qquad (3)$$

The above rule fulfills all requirements of Definition 2, since (1) all relations in the body are extensional, (2) there are two positive predicates, $n = 2$, and no negative predicate, $m = 0$, and (3) the single variable X of the head is bound by a positive relational predicate in the body.

For the remainder of this chapter, we consider only *non-recursive* Datalog programs. Thus, our class of deduction rules coincides with the core operations that are expressible in Relational Algebra and in SQL [2], including *selections*, *projections*, and *joins*. All operations in Datalog (just like in Relation Algebra, but unlike SQL) eliminate duplicate tuples from the intensional relation instances they produce.

2.3   Grounding

The process of applying a deduction rule to a database instance, i.e., employing the rule to derive new tuples, is called *grounding*. In the next step, we thus explain how to instantiate the deduction rules, which we achieve by *successively substituting* the variables occurring a rule's body and head literals with constants occurring in the extensional relations and in other deduction rules [2,65].

Definition 3. *A substitution $\sigma : \mathcal{V} \rightarrow \mathcal{V} \cup \mathcal{U}$ is a mapping from variables $\mathcal{V}$ to variables and constants $\mathcal{V} \cup \mathcal{U}$. A substitution σ is applied to a first-order formula Φ as follows:*

Definition	Condition
$\sigma(\bigwedge_i \Phi_i) := \bigwedge_i \sigma(\Phi_i)$	
$\sigma(\bigvee_i \Phi_i) := \bigvee_i \sigma(\Phi_i)$	
$\sigma(\neg\Phi) := \neg\sigma(\Phi_i)$	
$\sigma(R(\bar{X})) := R(\bar{Y})$	$\sigma(\bar{X}) = \bar{Y}$

In general, substitutions can rename variables or replace variables by constants. If all variables are substituted by constants, then the resulting rule or literal is called *ground*.

Example 3. A valid substitution is given by $\sigma(X) = Coppola, \sigma(Y) = Godfather$, where we replace the variables X and Y by the constants *Coppola* and *Godfather*, respectively. If we apply the substitution to the deduction rule of Equation (3), we obtain

$$FamousDirector(Coppola) \leftarrow \begin{pmatrix} Directed(Coppola,\ Godfather) \\ \wedge\ WonAward(Godfather, Z) \end{pmatrix}$$

where Z remains a variable.

We now collect all substitutions for a first-order deduction rule which are possible over a given database or a set of tuples to obtain a set of propositional formulas. These substitutions are called *ground rules* [2,10].

Definition 4. *Given a set of tuples $\mathcal{T}$ and a deduction rule D*

$$R(\bar{X}) \leftarrow \bigwedge_{i=1,\ldots,n} R_i(\bar{X}_i) \wedge \bigwedge_{j=1,\ldots,m} \neg R_j(\bar{X}_j) \wedge \Phi(\bar{X}_A)$$

the ground rules $G(D, \mathcal{T})$ *are all substitutions σ where*

1. *σ's preimage coincides with $\bigcup_i Var(\bar{X}_i)$;*
2. *σ's image consists of constants only;*
3. *$\forall i : \sigma(R_i(\bar{X}_i)) \in \mathcal{T}$;*
4. *$\sigma(\Phi(\bar{X}_A)) \equiv true$.*

The first and second condition requires the substitution to bind all variables in the deduction rule to constants. In addition, all positive ground literals have to match a tuple in $\mathcal{T}$. In the case of a deterministic database, negated literals must not match any tuple. Later, in a probabilistic database context, however, they may indeed match a tuple, which is why we omit a condition on this case. The last condition ensures that the arithmetic literals are satisfied.

Example 4. Let the deduction rule of Equation (3) be D. For the tuples of Example 1, there are four substitutions $G(D, \{I_1, \ldots, I_7\}) = \{\sigma_1, \sigma_2, \sigma_3, \sigma_4\}$, where:

$$\sigma_1(X) = Coppola \qquad \sigma_2(X) = Coppola$$
$$\sigma_1(Y) = ApocalypseNow \quad \sigma_2(Y) = Godfather$$
$$\sigma_1(Z) = BestScript \qquad \sigma_2(Z) = BestDirector$$

$$\sigma_3(X) = Coppola \qquad \sigma_4(X) = Tarantino$$
$$\sigma_3(Y) = Godfather \qquad \sigma_4(Y) = PulpFiction$$
$$\sigma_3(Z) = BestPicture \qquad \sigma_4(Z) = BestPicture$$

All substitutions provide valid ground rules according to Definition 4, because (1) their preimages coincide with all variables of D, (2) their images are constants only, (4) there are no arithmetic literals, and (3) all positive body literals match the following database tuples:

Literal	Tuple	Literal	Tuple
$\sigma_1(Directed(X,Y))$	I_1	$\sigma_1(WonAward(Y,Z))$	I_4
$\sigma_2(Directed(X,Y))$	I_2	$\sigma_2(WonAward(Y,Z))$	I_5
$\sigma_3(Directed(X,Y))$	I_2	$\sigma_3(WonAward(Y,Z))$	I_6
$\sigma_4(Directed(X,Y))$	I_3	$\sigma_4(WonAward(Y,Z))$	I_7

Finally, we employ the groundings of a deduction rule to derive new tuples by instantiating the head literal of the rule.

Definition 5. *Given a single deduction rule $D := (R(\bar{X}) \leftarrow \Psi) \in \mathcal{D}$ and a set of extensional tuples $\mathcal{T}$, the* intensional tuples *are created as follows:*

$$IntensionalTuples(D, \mathcal{T}) := \{\sigma(R(\bar{X})) \mid \sigma \in G(D, \mathcal{T})\}$$

We note that the same new tuple might result from more than one substitution, as it is illustrated by the following example.

Example 5. Let D be the deduction rule of Equation (3). Continuing Example 4, there are two new intensional tuples:

$$IntensionalTuples(D, \{I_1, \ldots, I_7\}) = \begin{cases} FamousDirector(Coppola), \\ FamousDirector(Tarantino) \end{cases}$$

The first tuple originates from σ_1, σ_2, σ_3 of Example 4, whereas the second tuple results only from σ_4.

2.4   Queries and Query Answers

We now move on to define queries and their answers over a relational database with deduction rules. Just like the antecedents of the deduction rules, our queries consist of conjunctions of both positive and negative literals.

Definition 6. *Given a set of deduction rules $\mathcal{D}$, which define our intensional relations, a* query *Q is a conjunction:*

$$Q(\bar{X}) := \bigwedge_{i=1,\ldots,n} R_i(\bar{X}_i) \; \wedge \; \bigwedge_{j=1,\ldots,m} \neg R_j(\bar{X}_j) \wedge \Phi(\bar{X}_A)$$

where

1. *all R_i, R_j are intensional relations in $\mathcal{D}$;*
2. *$\bar{X}$ are called* query variables *and it holds that $Var(\bar{X}) = \bigcup_{i=1,\ldots,n} Var(\bar{X}_i)$;*
3. *all variables in negated or arithmetic literals are bound by positive literals such that $Var(\bar{X}_A) \subseteq \bigcup_{i=1,\ldots,n} Var(\bar{X}_i)$, and for all $j \in \{1, \ldots, m\}$ it holds that $Var(\bar{X}_j) \subseteq \bigcup_{i=1,\ldots,n} Var(\bar{X}_i)$;*
4. *$\Phi(\bar{X}_A)$ is a conjunction of arithmetic predicates such as "=" and "≠".*

The first condition allows us to ask for head literals of any deduction rule. The set of variables in positive literals are precisely the query variables. The final two conditions ensure safeness as in deduction rules. We want to remark that for a theoretical analysis, it suffices to have only one intensional literal as a query, since the deduction rules allow us to encode any combination of relational operations such as projections, selections or joins. However, for practical purposes, it is often useful to combine more than one literal into a query via a conjunction.

Example 6. Extending Examples 1 and 2, we can formulate the query

$$Q(X) := \textit{FamousDirector}(X) \wedge (X \neq \textit{Tarantino})$$

which asks for all famous directors except *Tarantino*. Thus, the only query variable in this example is X.

Since queries have the same shape as the antecedents of the deduction rules, we apply Definition 4 also for grounding the queries. Assuming that $\mathcal{T}'$ comprises all database tuples and all new intensional tuples resulting from grounding the deduction rules, we may again rely on $G(Q(\bar{X}), \mathcal{T}')$ to define the query answers.

Definition 7. *For a set of tuples $\mathcal{T}'$ and a query $Q(\bar{X})$, the set of query answers is given by:*

$$QueryAnswers(Q(\bar{X}), \mathcal{T}') := \{\sigma(Q(\bar{X})) \mid \sigma \in G(Q(\bar{X}), \mathcal{T}')\}$$

Thus, each answer provides a distinct binding of (all of its) query variables to constants in $\mathcal{U}$.

Example 7. For the query $Q(X)$ of Example 6 and the deduction rule of Example 2, there exists only one answer, namely *FamousDirector(Coppola)*.

Again, in a deterministic database setting, we can thus say that a tuple $R(\bar{a})$ (which may now refer to either a "database tuple" or a "derived tuple") is *true* iff $R(\bar{a}) \in \mathcal{T}'$. This assumption will be relaxed in the next section.

3   Probabilistic Databases

We now move on to present a model for probabilistic databases. This model extends the one for relational databases by using probabilities.

3.1   Possible Worlds

In this subsection, we relax the common assumption in deterministic databases, namely that all tuples, which are captured in both the extensional and intensional relations of the database, are certainly *true*. Depending on the existence (i.e., the "correctness") of the tuples, a database can be in different states. Each such state is called a *possible world* [3,63].

Definition 8. *For a relational database with extensional tuples $\mathcal{T}$, a* possible world *is a subset $\mathcal{W} \subseteq \mathcal{T}$.*

The interpretation of a possible world is as follows. All tuples in $\mathcal{W}$ exist (i.e., they are *true* in $\mathcal{W}$), whereas all tuples in $\mathcal{T} \backslash \mathcal{W}$ do not exist (i.e., they are *false* in $\mathcal{W}$). In the absence of any constraints that would restrict this set of possible worlds (see Subsection 3.6), any subset $\mathcal{W}$ of tuples in $\mathcal{T}$ forms a valid possible world (aka. "possible instance") of the probabilistic database. Hence, there are $2^{|\mathcal{T}|}$ possible worlds.

Example 8. Considering the relational database of Example 1, a possible world is $\mathcal{W} := \{I_2, I_4, I_6\}$, which hence has only one tuple in the *Directed* relation and two tuples in the *WonAward* relation.

3.2   Probabilistic Database Model

Based on the possible worlds semantics, we can now formally introduce probabilistic databases [63], which—in their most general form—simply impose a probability distribution over the set of possible worlds.

Definition 9. *Given a set of tuples $\mathcal{T}$ with possible worlds $\mathcal{W}_1, \ldots, \mathcal{W}_n$, a probabilistic database (PDB) assigns a probability $P : 2^{\mathcal{T}} \to [0,1]$ to each possible world $\mathcal{W} \subseteq \mathcal{T}$, such that:*

$$\sum_{\mathcal{W} \subseteq \mathcal{T}} P(\mathcal{W}) = 1$$

In other words, in a PDB the probabilities of the possible worlds $P(\mathcal{W})$ form a probability distribution. Thus, each possible world can be seen as the outcome of a probabilistic experiment.

Example 9. If we allow only two possible worlds $\mathcal{W}_1 := \{I_1, I_3, I_5, I_7\}$ and $\mathcal{W}_2 := \{I_2, I_4, I_6\}$ over the tuples of Example 1, we can set their probabilities to $P(\mathcal{W}_1) = 0.4$ and $P(\mathcal{W}_2) = 0.6$ to obtain a valid PDB.

We remark that the above possible-worlds semantics, which is the predominant data model of virtually any recent PDB approach [63], is a very expressive representation formalism for probabilistic data. By defining a probability distribution over the possible instances of the underlying deterministic database, it in principle allows us to represent any form of correlation among the extensional tuples. In practice, however, it is usually not permissible to store an exponential amount of possible worlds over the set of extensional tuples $\mathcal{T}$. We thus now move on to the concept of *tuple independence*.

3.3   Tuple Independence

Since there are exponentially many possible worlds, it is prohibitive to store every possible world along with its probability in an actual database system. Instead, we opt for a simpler method by annotating each individual tuple with a probability value. By assuming that the probabilities of all tuples are independent [25,58], we obtain the representation model of *tuple-independent PDBs* [15,63].

Definition 10. *For a set of extensional tuples $\mathcal{T}$, a tuple-independent PDB $(\mathcal{T}, p)$ is a pair, where*

1. *p is a function $p : \mathcal{T} \to (0,1]$, which assigns a non-zero probability value $p(I)$ to each tuple $I \in \mathcal{T}$;*
2. *the probability values of all tuples in $\mathcal{T}$ are assumed to be independent;*
3. *every subset $\mathcal{W} \subseteq \mathcal{T}$ is a possible world and has probability:*

$$P(\mathcal{W}, \mathcal{T}) := \prod_{I \in \mathcal{W}} p(I) \cdot \prod_{I \in \mathcal{T} \setminus \mathcal{W}} (1 - p(I))$$

The probability $p(I)$ of a tuple I denotes the confidence in the existence of the tuple in the database where a higher value $p(I)$ denotes a higher confidence in I being valid. However, the probabilities of different tuples do not depend on each other; that is, they are assumed to be probabilistically *independent*. This allows us to multiply the probabilities of the tuples to obtain the probability of the possible world. From a probabilistic perspective, each extensional tuple corresponds to an independent binary random variable.

Example 10. Assuming we are unsure about the existence of each of the tuples in Example 1, we may now annotate them with probabilities as follows.

<table>
<tr><td colspan="4" align="center">*Directed*</td></tr>
<tr><td></td><td>*Director*</td><td>*Movie*</td><td>*p*</td></tr>
<tr><td>I_1</td><td>*Coppola*</td><td>*ApocalypseNow*</td><td>0.7</td></tr>
<tr><td>I_2</td><td>*Coppola*</td><td>*Godfather*</td><td>0.5</td></tr>
<tr><td>I_3</td><td>*Tarantino*</td><td>*PulpFiction*</td><td>0.2</td></tr>
</table>

<table>
<tr><td colspan="4" align="center">*WonAward*</td></tr>
<tr><td></td><td>*Movie*</td><td>*Award*</td><td>*p*</td></tr>
<tr><td>I_4</td><td>*ApocalypseNow*</td><td>*BestScript*</td><td>0.1</td></tr>
<tr><td>I_5</td><td>*Godfather*</td><td>*BestDirector*</td><td>0.8</td></tr>
<tr><td>I_6</td><td>*Godfather*</td><td>*BestPicture*</td><td>0.9</td></tr>
<tr><td>I_7</td><td>*PulpFiction*</td><td>*BestPicture*</td><td>0.5</td></tr>
</table>

Here, *Coppola* directed the movie *Godfather* only with probability 0.5. In addition, the possible world $\mathcal{W} := \{I_1, I_3, I_5, I_7\}$ has the probability:

$$P(\mathcal{W}, \{I_1, \dots, I_9\}) = 0.7 \cdot (1 - 0.5) \cdot 0.2 \cdot (1 - 0.1) \cdot 0.8 \cdot (1 - 0.9) \cdot 0.5 = 0.00252$$

In Subsection 3.2, we required a PDB to form a probability distribution over its possible worlds. For a tuple-independent PDB, we can now prove that this condition also holds.

Proposition 1. *Given a tuple-independent PDB $(\mathcal{T}, p)$, then $P(\mathcal{W}, \mathcal{T})$ of Definition 10 forms a probability distribution over the possible worlds $\mathcal{W} \subseteq \mathcal{T}$, such that:*

$$\sum_{\mathcal{W} \subseteq \mathcal{T}} P(\mathcal{W}, \mathcal{T}) = 1$$

Proof. We prove the proposition by induction over the cardinality of $\mathcal{T}$.

Basis $i = 1$:
$$\sum_{\mathcal{W} \subseteq \{I_1\}} P(\mathcal{W}, \{I_1\}) = p(I_1) + (1 - p(I_1)) = 1$$

Step $(i - 1) \to i$:

Let $\mathcal{T} := \{I_1, \dots, I_i\}$ where I_i is the new tuple.

$$\sum_{\mathcal{W} \subseteq \mathcal{T}} P(\mathcal{W}, \mathcal{T})$$
$$\stackrel{=}{} \sum_{\mathcal{W} \subseteq \mathcal{T}} \prod_{I \in \mathcal{W}} p(I) \cdot \prod_{I \in \mathcal{T} \setminus \mathcal{W}} (1 - p(I))$$
$$= \underbrace{(p(I_i) + (1 - p(I_i)))}_{=1} \cdot \underbrace{\sum_{\mathcal{W} \subseteq \mathcal{T} \setminus \{I_i\}} \prod_{I \in \mathcal{W}} p(I) \cdot \prod_{I \in \mathcal{T} \setminus \mathcal{W}} (1 - p(I))}_{=1 \text{ by hypothesis}}$$

In the remaining parts of this chapter, we will always consider a tuple-independent PDB when we refer to a PDB.

3.4 Propositional Lineage

In this subsection, we introduce how to trace the derivation history of intensional tuples. In database terminology, this concept is commonly referred to as *data lineage* [7,12,54], which we represent via propositional (Boolean) formulas. More specifically, lineage relates each newly derived tuple in $\mathcal{T}'\backslash\mathcal{T}$ with the extensional tuples in $\mathcal{T}$ via the three Boolean connectives $\wedge$, $\vee$ and $\neg$, which reflect the semantics of the relational operations that were applied to derive that tuple.

Definition 11. *We establish* lineage *inductively via the function*

$$\lambda : GroundLiterals \rightarrow Lineage$$

which is defined as follows:

1. *For tuples $\mathcal{T}$ and $R(\bar{a})$ with R being extensional and $R(\bar{a}) \in \mathcal{T}$, we have*

$$\lambda(R(\bar{a})) := I$$

   where I is a Boolean (random) variable representing the tuple $R(\bar{a})$.
2. *For tuples $\mathcal{T}$, deduction rules $\mathcal{D}$, and $R(\bar{a})$ with R being intensional, lineage is defined as*

$$\lambda(R(\bar{a})) := \bigvee_{\substack{D \in \mathcal{D}, \\ \sigma \in G(D,\mathcal{T}), \\ \sigma(\bar{X})=\bar{a}}} \left(\bigwedge_{i=1,\ldots,n} \lambda(\sigma(R_i(\bar{X}_i))) \ \wedge \bigwedge_{\sigma(R_j(\bar{X}_j)) \in \mathcal{T}} \neg\lambda(\sigma(R_j(\bar{X}_j))) \right)$$

   where D is a deduction rule having R as its head literal:

$$R(\bar{X}) \leftarrow \bigwedge_{i=1,\ldots,n} R_i(\bar{X}_i) \ \wedge \bigwedge_{j=1,\ldots,m} \neg R_j(\bar{X}_j) \wedge \Phi(\bar{X})$$

3. *If there is no match to $R(\bar{a})$ in both $\mathcal{T}$ and $\mathcal{D}$:*

$$\lambda(R(\bar{a})) := false$$

In the first case, we simply replace a ground literal $R(\bar{a})$ by a Boolean random variable I that represents this database tuple. The second case however is slightly more involved. The ground literal $R(\bar{a})$ is replaced by the disjunction over all deduction rules and all groundings of thereof, where the ground head literal matched $R(\bar{a})$. Likewise, negative literals are only traced if they occur in the tuples. In the third case, all literals not being matched at all are replaced by the constant *false*, which resembles a *closed world assumption* that is common in databases and is known as "negation-as-failure" in Datalog [2]. Finally, arithmetic literals do not occur in the lineage formulas, since a successful grounding replaces them with the constant *true* (see Definition 4). Similarly, because a query has the same shape as the body of a deduction rule, we write $\lambda(Q(\bar{a}))$ to refer to the lineage formula associated with a query answer.

Example 11. Building on Examples 4 and 5, we determine the lineage of the tuple *FamousDirector(Coppola)*, which was produced by the three substitutions σ_1, σ_2, and σ_3. The second case of Definition 11 delivers a disjunction ranging over both substitutions:

$$\lambda(FamousDirector(Coppola)) =$$
$$\left(\begin{array}{c} \lambda(Directed(Coppola, ApocalypseNow)) \\ \wedge\ \lambda(WonAward(ApocalypseNow, BestScript)) \end{array} \right) \quad \text{from } \sigma_1$$
$$\vee$$
$$\left(\begin{array}{c} \lambda(Directed(Coppola, Godfather)) \\ \wedge\ \lambda(WonAward(Godfather, BestDirector)) \end{array} \right) \quad \text{from } \sigma_2$$
$$\vee$$
$$\left(\begin{array}{c} \lambda(Directed(Coppola, Godfather)) \\ \wedge\ \lambda(WonAward(Godfather, BestPicture)) \end{array} \right) \quad \text{from } \sigma_3$$

Then, the first case of Definition 11 replaces all ground literals by their tuple identifiers:

$$\underbrace{(I_1 \wedge I_4)}_{\text{from } \sigma_1} \vee \underbrace{(I_2 \wedge I_5)}_{\text{from } \sigma_2} \vee \underbrace{(I_2 \wedge I_6)}_{\text{from } \sigma_3}$$

Next, we study the computational complexity of lineage tracing. It is known that grounding non-recursive Datalog rules, which coincides with our class of deduction rules, has polynomial data complexity [39]. Now, we extend this result to lineage tracing.

Lemma 1. *For a fixed set of deduction rules $\mathcal{D}$, grounding with lineage as of Definition 11 has polynomial data complexity in $|\mathcal{T}|$.*

Proof. We have to show that, according to Definition 11, lineage creates an overhead which is polynomial in $|\mathcal{T}|$. In the first and third case of the definition, we can see that we solely rely on a look-up in $\mathcal{D}$ or $\mathcal{T}$, which is computable in polynomial time. The second case iterates over all deduction rules $D \in \mathcal{D}$. For each deduction rule D, it performs a number of look-ups which is upper-bounded by $|G(D, \mathcal{T})| \cdot |D|$. Since grounding has polynomial data complexity, $G(D, \mathcal{T})$ is of polynomial size in $\mathcal{T}$. Thus, also the third case has polynomial data complexity.

We next introduce a normal form of propositional lineage formulas, which is very common in logic [60]. Assuming lineage formulas to be in a normal form will simplify proofs that follow later on.

Definition 12. *A propositional lineage formula ϕ is in* Disjunctive Normal Form *(DNF) if $\phi = \psi_1 \vee \cdots \vee \psi_n$ and each clause ψ_i is of the form $\bigwedge_j I_j \wedge \bigwedge_k \neg I_k$.*

As an illustration, the lineage formula of Example 11 is in DNF. In general, any propositional formula can be transformed into DNF [60], which we rely on in order to show the following statement.

Proposition 2. *The deduction rules of Definition 2 allow us to express any propositional lineage formula.*

Proof. Consider a probabilistic database $(\mathcal{T}, p)$ and an arbitrary propositional formula ϕ connecting tuple identifiers. Without loss of generality, let the formula ϕ be in DNF and range over only one relation R. First, we introduce one additional tuple $R(0)$ and set $p(R(0)) = 1$. Then, for each clause $\psi_i = \bigwedge_j I_j \wedge \bigwedge_k \neg I_k$ of ϕ, we create exactly one deduction rule:

$$R'(0) \leftarrow R(0) \wedge \bigwedge_j R(j) \wedge \bigwedge_k \neg R(k)$$

The lineage formula of the intensional tuple $R'(0)$ thus is ϕ. The reason is that each rule creates one clause. Then, these clauses are connected by a disjunction that originates from the second case of Definition 11.

From the above consideration, it follows that the lineage formulas considered in our context may take more general forms than lineage formulas resulting from (unions of) conjunctive queries (UCQs) [14,16], which produce only formulas which are restricted to positive literals.

3.5   Computing Probabilities

Since in a probabilistic database each tuple exists only with a given probability, we can now quantify the probability that each answer exists. Based on [28,54,63], we compute probabilities of query answers via their lineage formulas. To achieve this, we interpret the propositional lineage formulas over a possible world of a probabilistic database $(\mathcal{T}, p)$ as follows. We say that a possible world $\mathcal{W}$ is a *model* [65] for a propositional lineage formula ϕ, denoted as $\mathcal{W} \models \phi$, if, by setting all tuples in $\mathcal{W}$ to *true* and all tuples in $\mathcal{T} \backslash \mathcal{W}$ to *false*, $\mathcal{W}$ represents a truth assignment that satisfies ϕ. Moreover, let the set $\mathcal{M}(\phi, \mathcal{T})$ contain all possible worlds $\mathcal{W} \subseteq \mathcal{T}$ being a model for a propositional lineage formula ϕ.

$$\mathcal{M}(\phi, \mathcal{T}) := \{\mathcal{W} \mid \mathcal{W} \subseteq \mathcal{T}, \mathcal{W} \models \phi\} \tag{4}$$

If it is clear from the context, we drop $\mathcal{T}$ as an argument of $\mathcal{M}$. We compute the *probability* of any Boolean formula ϕ over tuples in $\mathcal{T}$ as the sum of the probabilities of all the possible worlds that are a model for ϕ:

$$P(\phi) := \sum_{\mathcal{W} \in \mathcal{M}(\phi, \mathcal{T})} P(\mathcal{W}, \mathcal{T}) \tag{5}$$

Here, $P(\mathcal{W}, \mathcal{T})$ is as in Definition 10. We can interpret the above probability as the marginal probability of the lineage formula ϕ. The above sum can range over exponentially many terms. However, in practice, we can—at least in many cases—compute the probability $P(\phi)$ directly via the structure of the lineage formula ϕ. Let $Tup(\phi) \subseteq \mathcal{T}$ denote the set of tuples occurring in ϕ. Then, the following computations can be employed:

Definition	Condition
$P(I) := p(I)$	$I \in \mathcal{T}$
$P(\bigwedge_i \phi_i) := \prod_i P(\phi_i)$	$i \neq j \Rightarrow Tup(\phi_i) \cap Tup(\phi_j) = \emptyset$
$P(\bigvee_i \phi_i) := 1 - \prod_i (1 - P(\phi_i))$	$i \neq j \Rightarrow Tup(\phi_i) \cap Tup(\phi_j) = \emptyset$
$P(\phi \vee \psi) := P(\phi) + P(\psi)$	$\phi \wedge \psi \equiv false$
$P(\neg\phi) := 1 - P(\phi)$	
$P(true) := 1$	
$P(false) := 0$	

$$(6)$$

The first line captures the case of an extensional tuple I, for which we return its attached probability value $p(I)$. The next two lines handle *independent-and* and *independent-or* operations for conjunctions and disjunctions over tuple-disjoint subformulas ϕ_i, respectively. In the fourth line, we address disjunctions for subformulas ϕ and ψ that denote disjoint probabilistic events (*disjoint-or*). The fifth line handles negation. Finally, the probability of *true* and *false* is 1 and 0, respectively.

Example 12. Let us compute the probability $P(I_1 \wedge I_2 \wedge \neg I_3)$ over the tuples of Example 10. First, the second line of Equation (6) is applicable, which yields $P(I_1) \cdot P(I_2) \cdot P(\neg I_3)$. Next, we can replace the negation to obtain $P(I_1) \cdot P(I_2) \cdot (1 - P(I_3))$. Now, looking up the tuples' probability values in Example 10 yields $0.7 \cdot 0.5 \cdot (1 - 0.2) = 0.28$.

The definition of $P(\phi)$ presented in Equation (6) can be evaluated in linear time in the size of ϕ. However, for general lineage formulas, computing $P(\phi)$ is known to be $\#\mathcal{P}$-hard [16,15,45]. Here, $\#\mathcal{P}$ [66] denotes a class of counting problems. Its prototypical problem, $\#\mathcal{SAT}$, asks for the number of satisfying assignments of a propositional formula and may thus have to consider a number of satisfying assignment that is exponential in the number of variables in the formula.

We next present a number of deduction rules which are known to yield lineage formulas that may exhibit computationally hard instances in terms of probability computations.

Lemma 2. *Let a probabilistic database* $(\mathcal{T}, p)$ *and the following deduction rules be given:*

$$H(0) \leftarrow R(X) \wedge S(X,Y) \wedge T(Y)$$

$$H(1) \leftarrow R(X) \wedge S(X,Y)$$
$$H(1) \leftarrow S(X,Y) \wedge T(Y)$$

$$H(2) \leftarrow R(X) \wedge S_1(X,Y)$$
$$H(2) \leftarrow S_1(X,Y) \wedge S_2(X,Y)$$
$$H(2) \leftarrow S_2(X,Y) \wedge T(Y)$$

$$H(3) \leftarrow R(X) \wedge S_1(X,Y)$$
$$H(3) \leftarrow S_1(X,Y) \wedge S_2(X,Y)$$
$$H(3) \leftarrow S_2(X,Y) \wedge S_3(X,Y)$$
$$H(3) \leftarrow S_3(X,Y) \wedge T(Y)$$

$$\cdots$$

Then, for each $H(k)$ the corresponding computations of the probabilities $P(\lambda(H_k))$ are #$\mathcal{P}$-hard in $|\mathcal{T}|$.

In the lemma above, k is a constant, hence $H(0)$ is a ground literal resembling a Boolean query. A formal proof for the above statement can be found in [17].

To be able to address also these hard cases, we employ the following equation, called *Shannon expansion*, which is applicable to any propositional lineage formula:

$$P(\phi) := p(I) \cdot P(\phi_{[I/true]}) + (1 - p(I)) \cdot P(\phi_{[I/false]}) \qquad (7)$$

Here, the notation $\phi_{[I/true]}$ for a tuple $I \in Tup(\phi)$ denotes that we replace all occurrences of I in ϕ by *true*. Shannon expansion is based on the following logical equivalence:

$$\phi \equiv (I \wedge \phi_{[I/true]}) \vee (\neg I \wedge \phi_{[I/false]}) \qquad (8)$$

The resulting disjunction fulfills the *disjoint-or* condition (see Equation (6)) with respect to I. Repeated applications of Shannon expansions may however increase the size of ϕ exponentially, and hence do not circumvent the computational hardness of the problem.

Example 13. We calculate the probability of the lineage formula of Example 11 as follows:

$$P((I_1 \wedge I_4) \vee (I_2 \wedge I_5) \vee (I_2 \wedge I_6))$$

The top-level operator is a disjunction where the third line of Equation (6) is not applicable, since I_2 occurs in two subformulas. Hence, we first apply a Shannon expansion for I_2:

$$p(I_2) \cdot P((I_1 \wedge I_4) \vee I_5 \vee I_6) + (1 - p(I_2)) \cdot P(I_1 \wedge I_4)$$

Now, we can resolve the disjunction and the conjunction by independent-or and independent-and, respectively:

$$p(I_2) \cdot (1 - (1 - p(I_1) \cdot p(I_4)) \cdot (1 - p(I_5)) \cdot (1 - p(I_6))) + (1 - p(I_2)) \cdot p(I_1) \cdot p(I_4)$$

Partial Derivatives. As introduced in [38,50], we can quantify the impact of the probability of a tuple $p(I)$ on the probability $P(\phi)$ of a propositional lineage formula ϕ by its partial derivative, which has many applications to sensitivity analysis [38] and gradient-based optimization methods [43] (see also Section 6.4).

Definition 13. *Given a propositional lineage formula ϕ and a tuple $I \in Tup(\phi)$, the partial derivative of $P(\phi)$ with respect to $p(I)$ is*

$$\frac{\partial P(\phi)}{\partial p(I)} := \frac{P(\phi_{[I/true]}) - P(\phi_{[I/false]})}{P(true) - P(false)} = P(\phi_{[I/true]}) - P(\phi_{[I/false]})$$

Again, $\phi_{[I/true]}$ means that all occurrences of I in ϕ are replaced by *true* (and analogously for *false*).

Example 14. We may determine the derivative of the probability of the propositional lineage formula $\phi := I_1 \wedge I_4$ with respect to the tuple I_4 as follows:

$$\begin{aligned} \frac{\partial P(\phi)}{\partial p(I_4)} &= P((I_1 \wedge I_4)_{[I_4/true]}) - P((I_1 \wedge I_4)_{[I_4/false]}) \\ &= p(I_1) - P(false) \\ &= p(I_1) \end{aligned}$$

3.6 Consistency Constraints

To rule out instances (i.e., possible worlds) of the probabilistic database, which would be inconsistent with assumptions we may make about the real world, we support *consistency constraints*. For instance, if for the same person two places of birth are stored in the database, then we may intend to remove one of them by a consistency constraint. In general, we consider the constraints to be presented in the form of a single propositional lineage formula ϕ_c, which connects different tuple identifiers. Intuitively, the constraint formula ϕ_c describes all possible worlds that are valid. In contrast, all possible worlds that do not satisfy the constraint will be dropped from the probability computations. Because it is tedious to manually formulate a propositional formula over many database tuples, we allow ϕ_c to be induced by deduction rules $\mathcal{D}_c$ and two sets of queries $\mathcal{C}_p$ and $\mathcal{C}_n$ as follows. For simplicity, we assume $\mathcal{C}_p \cap \mathcal{C}_n = \emptyset$ and $\mathcal{D}_c \cap \mathcal{D}_q = \emptyset$, where $\mathcal{D}_q$ are the deduction rules related to the query.

Definition 14. *Let a set of deduction rules $\mathcal{D}_c$ and two sets $\mathcal{C}_p$ and $\mathcal{C}_n$ of intensional literals from $\mathcal{D}_c$ be given. If $\mathcal{T}$ contains all tuples deducible by $\mathcal{D}_c$, then the constraint formula ϕ_c is obtained by:*

$$\phi_c := \bigwedge_{\substack{C_p(\bar{X}) \in \mathcal{C}_p, \\ C_p(\bar{a}) \in Answers(C_p(\bar{X}), \mathcal{T})}} \lambda(C_p(\bar{a})) \quad \wedge \bigwedge_{\substack{C_p(\bar{X}) \in \mathcal{C}_n, \\ C_n(\bar{a}) \in Answers(C_n(\bar{X}), \mathcal{T})}} \neg\lambda(C_n(\bar{a}))$$

Hence, based on the above definition, we create constraints on probabilistic databases directly via deduction rules. All answers from literals in $\mathcal{C}_p$ yield propositional lineage formulas which must always hold, whereas the lineage formulas being derived from literals in $\mathcal{C}_n$ must never hold. We connect all these ground constraints, i.e., their lineage formulas, by a conjunction to enforce all of them together. It is important to note that the deduction rules of the constraints do not create any new tuples, but merely serve the purpose of creating the propositional constraint formula ϕ_c.

Example 15. Let us formalize that every movie is directed by only one person. Suppose we create the following deduction rule

$$Constraint(P_1, P_2, M) \leftarrow (Directed(P_1, M) \wedge Directed(P_2, M) \wedge P_1 \neq P_2)$$

and insert $Constraint(P_1, P_2, M)$ into $\mathcal{C}_n$, which hence disallows the existence of two persons P_1 and P_2 that both directed the same movie.

Due to the logical implication, we may also abbreviate constraints consisting of a single deduction rule by the body of the deduction rule only. That is, we may just omit the head literal in these cases.

Example 16. We can write the constraint of Example 15 without the head literal as follows:

$$\neg(Directed(P_1, M) \wedge Directed(P_2, M) \wedge P_1 \neq P_2)$$

Here, the negation indicates that the former head literal was in $\mathcal{C}_n$.

With respect to the probability computations, constraints remove all the possible worlds from the computations, which violate the constraint. This process is called *conditioning* [41], which can be formally defined as follows.

Definition 15. *Let constraints be given as a propositional lineage formula ϕ_c over a probabilistic database $(\mathcal{T}, p)$. If ϕ_c is satisfiable, then the probability $P(\psi)$ of a propositional lineage formula ψ over $\mathcal{T}$ can be conditioned onto ϕ_c as follows:*

$$P(\psi \mid \phi_c) := \frac{P(\psi \wedge \phi_c)}{P(\phi_c)} \tag{9}$$

In the above definition, ψ can represent any lineage formula, in particular also that of a query answer. After removing the possible worlds violating a constraint from the probabilistic database, conditioning (re-)weights the remaining worlds such that they again form a probability distribution.

Example 17. We consider the lineage formula $\psi = I_2 \wedge (I_5 \vee I_6)$ over the tuples of Example 10. Without any constraints, its probability is computed by Equation (6) as $P(\psi) = 0.5 \cdot (1 - (1 - 0.8) \cdot (1 - 0.9)) = 0.49$. If we set $\phi_c = I_2$ as a constraint, we remove all possible worlds that exclude I_2. Consequently, the probability is updated to:

$$P(\psi \mid I_2) = \frac{P(I_2 \wedge (I_5 \vee I_6))}{P(I_2)} = \frac{p(I_2) \cdot P(I_5 \vee I_6)}{p(I_2)} = P(I_5 \vee I_6) = 0.98$$

In the following, we characterize a useful property of constraints. If a number of constraints do not share any tuple with a lineage formula ψ, then the probability $P(\psi)$ is not affected by the constraints.

Proposition 3. *If the constraints ϕ_c and the lineage formula ψ are independent with respect to their database tuples, i.e., $Tup(\psi) \cap Tup(\phi_c) = \emptyset$, then it holds that:*

$$P(\psi \mid \phi_c) = P(\psi)$$

Proof. Due to the second line of Equation (6) and $Tup(\psi) \cap Tup(\phi_c) = \emptyset$, we can write $P(\psi \wedge \phi_c) = P(\psi) \cdot P(\phi_c)$. Therefore, the following equation holds:

$$P(\psi \mid \phi_c) = \frac{P(\psi \wedge \phi_c)}{P(\phi_c)} = P(\psi) \cdot \frac{P(\phi_c)}{P(\phi_c)} = P(\psi)$$

Hence, if we have the constraint $\phi_c \equiv true$, the standard unconditioned probability computations of Section 3.5 arise as a special case. Finally, since Equation (9) invokes probability computations on the constraint ϕ_c, constraints may also yield #$\mathcal{P}$-hard computations, which we capture next.

Observation 11. *Constraints can cause #$\mathcal{P}$-hard probability computations.*

The reason is that one of the lineage formulas described in Lemma 2 could occur in ϕ_c.

Expressiveness of Constraints. The deduction rules of Definition 14, which we employ to induce the constraints, may yield an arbitrary propositional lineage formula when grounded. This is formally shown in Proposition 2. We note that restrictions on the shape of the constraints, i.e., to avoid the #$\mathcal{P}$-hard instances of Observation 11, should follow work on tractable probability computations in probabilistic databases. The reason is that the computational complexity arises from the probability computations. In contrast, when solving constraints over deterministic databases, the complexity mainly results from finding a single consistent subset of the database, rather than from counting all of these subsets.

4   Temporal-Probabilistic Databases

In recent years, both temporal and probabilistic databases have emerged as two intensively studied areas of database research. So far, the two fields have however been investigated largely only in isolation. In this section, we describe a *closed* and *complete* temporal-probabilistic database (TPDB) model [21], which provides the expressiveness of the afore defined probabilistic database model, but augments this model with temporal annotations for tuples and temporal predicates for the rules. To the best of our knowledge, prior to [21], only Sarma et al. [55] have explicitly modeled time in PDBs. However in the former work time refers to the "transaction-time" of a tuple insertion or update, thus focusing on versioning a probabilistic database. Rather, we consider time as the actual temporal validity of a tuple in the real world (e.g., the time interval of a marriage in the IE scenario).

Example 18. This time, our running example is centered around the actors "Robert De Niro" and "Jane Abott" about whom the TPDB of Figure 2 captures a number of facts. Tuple I_1 expresses that *DeNiro* was born in *Greenwich* (New York) on August 17th, 1943, which is encoded into the time interval [1943-08-17, 1943-08-18) using an ISO style date/time format. The time and probability

BornIn

	Subject	Object	Valid Time	p
I_1	DeNiro	Greenwich	[1943-08-17, 1943-08-18)	0.9
I_2	DeNiro	Tribeca	[1998-01-01, 1999-01-01)	0.6

Wedding

	Subject	Object	Valid Time	p
I_3	DeNiro	Abbott	[1936-11-01, 1936-12-01)	0.3
I_4	DeNiro	Abbott	[1976-07-29, 1976-07-30)	0.8

Divorce

	Subject	Object	Valid Time	p
I_5	DeNiro	Abbott	[1988-09-01, 1988-12-01)	0.8

Fig. 2. Example Temporal-Probabilistic Database with Tuple Timestamping

annotations together express that this tuple is *true* for the given time interval with probability 0.9, and it is *false* (i.e., it does not exist in the database) for this interval with probability 0.1. Furthermore, tuples are always *false* outside their attached time intervals. Notice that another tuple, I_2, states that *DeNiro* could have also been born in *Tribeca* in the interval [1998-01-01, 1999-01-01) with probability 0.6. In the remainders of this section, we investigate how to evaluate queries over this kind of data, i.e., how to propagate time and probabilities from the database to the query answers. We also discuss consistency constraints. For instance, the two tuples of *BornIn* state different birth places of *DeNiro* and create an inconsistency we should rule out by the use of constraints.

4.1 Time

We start with the most important point, namely our model of time. As in a calendar, there are a number of choices to make. First, we have to decide on the granularity of time, which could be days, hours or minutes, for instance. Also, we should determine whether time is finite, and, if so, when it starts or ends, e.g., at the first or the last day of a year, respectively.

Technically, we adopt the view of time as points which then can be coalesced to form intervals [35,67]. We consider the *time universe* $\mathcal{U}^T$ as a linearly ordered finite sequence of *time points*, e.g., days, minutes or even milliseconds. Considering time to be finite and discrete later ensures that there are finitely many possible worlds. A *time interval* consists of a contiguous and finite set of ordered time points over $\mathcal{U}^T$, which we denote by a half-open interval $[t_b, t_e)$ where $t_b, t_e \in \mathcal{U}^T$ and $t_b < t_e$. For instance, a day can be viewed as an interval of hours. Moreover, we employ the two constants t_{min}, t_{max} to denote the earliest and latest time point in $\mathcal{U}^T$, respectively. Finally, temporal variables are written as T or $[T_b, T_e)$, if we refer to a time interval.

At this point, we want to remark that we do not consider the finiteness of $\mathcal{U}^T$ to be any limitation of the above model for time in practice, since we can always choose t_{min}, t_{max} as the earliest and latest time points we observe among the tuples and deduction rules. Also, discrete time points of fixed granularity do not present any restraint, as we could resort to employing time points of smaller granularity than the ones observed in the input data if needed. The complexity of the following operations, which we define over this kind of temporally and probabilistically annotated tuples, will in fact be independent of the granularity of the underlying time universe $\mathcal{U}^T$.

Example 19. Regarding the database of Figure 2, $\mathcal{U}^T$ comprises the sequence of days starting at $t_{min} := $ 1936-11-01 and ending at $t_{max} := $ 1999-01-01. We could equally choose any more fine-grained unit for the time points, but for presentation purposes, we select days.

4.2   Temporal Relations and Tuples

We now relate data to time, that is, tuples are considered to be valid during a specific time interval, only, and they are invalid outside their attached time intervals. For this, we extend the relations introduced in Section 2.1 to temporal relations, following work by [1,35,64]. We annotate each tuple by a time interval specifying the validity of the tuple over time—a technique, which is commonly referred to as *tuple timestamping* [35]. More specifically, a *temporal relation* R^T is a logical predicate of arity $r \geq 3$, whose latter two arguments are temporal. Hence, an instance of a temporal relation is a finite subset $\mathcal{R}^T \subseteq \mathcal{U}^{r-2} \times \mathcal{U}^T \times \mathcal{U}^T$. Therein, we interpret the temporal arguments t_b, t_e of a tuple $R^T(\bar{a}, t_b, t_e)$ to form a time interval $[t_b, t_e)$. Choosing intervals over time points has the advantage that the storage costs are independent of the granularity of the time points.

Example 20. The tuple $BornIn(DeNiro, Greenwich, $ 1943-08-17, 1943-08-18$)$ is valid only at one day, namely on August 17th, 1943.

In general, a temporal relation instance can contain several tuples with equivalent non-temporal arguments $\bar{a}$, but with varying temporal arguments. For instance, assume we have two tuples describing *DeNiro*'s birthday, one timestamped with the year 1943 and one by the day 1943-08-18. Then, a database engine might conclude that he was born twice on August 18th, 1943 with different probabilities. To resolve this issue, we enforce the time intervals of tuples with identical, non-temporal arguments to be disjoint. A relation instance that adheres to this condition is going to be termed *duplicate-free* [19].

Definition 16. *A temporal relation instance* $\mathcal{R}^T$ *is called* duplicate-free, *if for all pairs of tuples* $R^T(\bar{a}, t_b, t_e), R^T(\bar{a}', t_b', t_e') \in \mathcal{R}^T$ *it holds that:*

$$\bar{a} = \bar{a}' \quad \Rightarrow \quad [t_b, t_e) \cap [t_b', t_e') = \emptyset$$

We remark that the above definition does not affect tuples of different, non-temporal arguments or with non-overlapping temporal arguments.

Example 21. In Figure 2 the temporal relation instance *Wedding* is duplicate-free, as both tuples have equivalent non-temporal arguments, but their time intervals are non-overlapping.

4.3   Temporal-Probabilistic Database Model

In this section, we extend tuple-independent probabilistic databases of Definition 10 to temporal data as in [21]. Intuitively, each tuple has two annotations: a temporal and a probabilistic one. Hence, each tuple exists only during a given time and with a given probability. Supporting both probability and time annotations allows to represent data, where we are unsure whether a tuple is valid at a given set of time points or during an entire time interval, respectively.

Definition 17. *For temporal relations $R_1^T, \ldots, R_n^T$ a tuple-independent temporal-probabilistic database (TPDB) $(\mathcal{T}, p, \mathcal{U}^T)$ is a triple, where*

1. *$\mathcal{T} := \mathcal{R}_1^T \cup \cdots \cup \mathcal{R}_n^T$ is a finite set of tuples;*
2. *$\forall i \in \{1, \ldots, n\} : \mathcal{R}_i^T$ is duplicate-free;*
3. *all tuples $R_i^T(\bar{a}, t_b, t_e)$ of all relation instances $\mathcal{R}_i^T$ share the time universe $\mathcal{U}^T$, that is, $t_b, t_e \in \mathcal{U}^T$;*
4. *p is a function $p : \mathcal{T} \to (0, 1]$ which assigns a non-zero probability value $p(I)$ to each tuple $I \in \mathcal{T}$;*
5. *the probability values of all tuples in $\mathcal{T}$ are assumed to be independent.*

In the above definition, the first, fourth and fifth condition are analogous to Definition 10. Still, we here consider *temporal* relation instances $\mathcal{R}_i^T$ and require them to be duplicate-free (see Definition 16). Additionally, all time points occurring in any relation instance $\mathcal{R}_i^T$ must be contained in the time universe $\mathcal{U}^T$. We highlight that the probabilities of two tuples $R(\bar{a}, t_b, t_e)$ and $R(\bar{a}, t_b', t_e')$, even if they share $\bar{a}$, are independent due to the fifth condition. In the remaining parts of this chapter, we will thus again drop the attribute "tuple-independent" when we refer to a TPDB. As in Section 3, dependencies among tuples will be induced by constraints and queries.

Example 22. The temporal relation instances of Figure 2, together with their time universe defined in Example 19 form the TPDB $(\{I_1, I_2, I_3, I_4, I_5\}, p, \langle 1936\text{-}11\text{-}01, \ldots, 1999\text{-}01\text{-}01 \rangle)$.

Since tuple probabilities here are defined as in PDBs, and $\mathcal{U}^T$ is finite as well as discrete, the possible-worlds semantics of Subsection 3.1 applies to TPDBs as well. Next, we thus more formally characterize the relationship between TPDBs and (non-temporal) PDBs.

Proposition 4. *Every PDB instance $(\mathcal{T}, p)$ can be encoded in a TPDB instance $(\mathcal{T}', p, \mathcal{U}^T)$.*

Proof. To achieve the encoding, we create the time universe $\mathcal{U}^T := \langle 1, 2 \rangle$, expand each relation R in $\mathcal{T}$ by two temporal arguments, and set $\mathcal{T}' := \{R^T(\bar{a}, 1, 2) \mid R(\bar{a}) \in \mathcal{T}\}$.

4.4 Temporal Arithmetic Predicates

To express temporal statements, it is necessary to be able to compare temporal annotations in the form of time points. Hence, we support two temporal-arithmetic predicates "$=^T$" and "$<^T$" [27,44], which each check for the equality and precedence of two time points, respectively.

Definition 18. *For $t_1, t_2 \in \mathcal{U}^T$ the temporal-arithmetic predicates $=^T$ and $<^T$ are evaluated as follows:*

$$t_1 =^T t_2 \equiv \begin{cases} \text{true} & \text{if } t_1 = t_2, \\ \text{false} & \text{otherwise}, \end{cases}$$

$$t_1 <^T t_2 \equiv \begin{cases} \text{true} & \text{if } t_1 \text{ strictly before } t_2 \text{ in } \mathcal{U}^T, \\ \text{false} & \text{otherwise}. \end{cases}$$

In other words, "$=^T$" is satisfied, whenever two time points are identical, whereas "$<^T$" compares the order of two time points in $\mathcal{U}^T$.

Example 23. Since 1998-01-01 is before 1999-01-01, we have 1998-01-01 $<^T$ 1999-01-01 $\equiv$ *true*.

By utilizing conjunctions of "$<^T$" and "$=^T$" predicates over the temporal arguments, we are able to express all of the 13 relationships between time intervals defined in the seminal work of Allen [4], such as *overlaps*, *disjoint* or *starts*.

Proposition 5. *We can express all the 13 relationships between two time intervals as defined by Allen [4] by relying solely on conjunctions of "$=^T$" and "$<^T$".*

Proof.

Allen's Relation	Encoding
$[T_b, T_e)$ before $[T_b', T_e')$	$T_e <^T T_b'$
$[T_b, T_e)$ equal $[T_b', T_e')$	$T_b =^T T_b' \wedge T_e =^T T_e'$
$[T_b, T_e)$ meets $[T_b', T_e')$	$T_e =^T T_b'$
$[T_b, T_e)$ overlaps $[T_b', T_e')$	$T_b <^T T_b' \wedge T_b' <^T T_e \wedge T_e <^T T_e'$
$[T_b, T_e)$ during $[T_b', T_e')$	$T_b' <^T T_b \wedge T_e <^T T_e'$
$[T_b, T_e)$ starts $[T_b', T_e')$	$T_b =^T T_b' \wedge T_e <^T T_e'$
$[T_b, T_e)$ finishes $[T_b', T_e')$	$T_b' <^T T_b \wedge T_e =^T T_e'$

The remaining 6 relationships are the inverse of one of the above ones, except for equality which is symmetric.

4.5 Temporal Deduction Rules

Next, we devise temporal deduction rules, that is, general "if-then" rules which mention time. Formally, our temporal deduction rules [21] are logical implications over temporal relations and temporal arithmetic predicates, defined as follows.

Definition 19. *A temporal deduction rule is a logical rule of the form*

$$R^T(\bar{X}, T_b, T_e) \leftarrow \bigwedge_{i=1,\dots,n} R_i^T(\bar{X}_i, T_{i,b}, T_{i,e}) \ \wedge \ \bigwedge_{j=1,\dots,m} \neg R_j^T(\bar{X}_j, T_{j,b}, T_{j,e}) \ \wedge \Phi(\bar{X}_A, \bar{T}_A)$$

(10)

where

1. *all requirements of Definition 2 hold;*
2. T_b, T_e, $T_{i,b}$, $T_{i,e}$, $T_{j,b}$, $T_{j,e}$ *and* $\bar{T}_A$ *are temporal constants and variables, where* $Var(T_b, T_e)$, $Var(T_{j,b}, T_{j,e})$, $Var(\bar{T}_A) \subseteq \bigcup_i Var(T_{i,b}, T_{i,e})$;
3. $\Phi(\bar{X}_A, \bar{T}_A)$ *is a conjunction of literals over the arithmetic predicates, such as* "$=$" *and* "$\neq$", *and the temporal arithmetic predicates* "$=^T$" *and* "$<^T$".

With respect to non-temporal arguments, all restrictions of non-temporal deduction rules (see Definition 2) hold. Combining this observation with the second requirement above, we conclude that temporal deduction rules are *safe* [2]. Furthermore, the third condition allows the temporal-arithmetic predicates of Definition 18 to occur in temporal deduction rules. Of course, also non-temporal relations are allowed in temporal deduction rules, hence inducing mixtures of temporal and non-temporal rules. We note that the above class of temporal deduction rules is very expressive, as it allows T_b, T_e to be constants or to be variables from different literals R_i^T. As before, we assume also the temporal deduction rules to be *non-recursive*.

Example 24. Given the tuples of Figure 2 about both *DeNiro*'s wedding and divorce with *Abbott*, we aim to deduce the time interval of their marriage by temporal deduction rules. The first rule states that a couple stays married from the begin time point of their wedding (denoted by the variable $T_{b,1}$) until the last possible time point we consider (denoted by the constant t_{max}), unless there is a divorce tuple.

$$Marriage^T(P_1, P_2, T_{b,1}, t_{max}) \leftarrow \left(\begin{array}{c} Wedding^T(P_1, P_2, T_{b,1}, T_{e,1}) \ \wedge \\ \neg Divorce(P_1, P_2) \end{array} \right)$$

(11)

Here, the existence of a divorce independent of time is modeled by the following projection:

$$Divorce(P_1, P_2) \leftarrow Divorce^T(P_1, P_2, T_b, T_e)$$

The second rule states that a couple stays married from the begin time point of their wedding till the end time point of their divorce.

$$Marriage^T(P_1, P_2, T_{b,1}, T_{e,2}) \leftarrow \left(\begin{array}{c} Wedding^T(P_1, P_2, T_{b,1}, T_{e,1}) \ \wedge \\ Divorce^T(P_1, P_2, T_{b,2}, T_{e,2}) \ \wedge \\ T_{e,1} <^T T_{b,2} \end{array} \right)$$

(12)

Thereby, we consider only weddings that took place before divorces as stated by the condition $T_{e,1} <^T T_{b,2}$.

4.6 Lineage and Deduplication

As in Section 3.4, we trace the deduction history of tuples via lineage, however, with the additional twist that lineage may now also vary over time. Since temporal deduction rules are safe, the groundings $G(D, \mathcal{T})$ of Definition 4 and the new tuples $IntensionalTuples(D, \mathcal{T})$ of Definition 5 apply to temporal deduction rules as well. Hence, at first glance lineage tracing according to Definition 11 works in a temporal context, but with one random variable for each tuple with its time interval. However, if we execute temporal deduction rules, the newly derived tuples may not necessarily define a duplicate-free relation instance. We illustrate this issue by the following example.

Example 25. Let the deduction rules of Example 24 and the tuples of Figure 2 be given. Now, in Figure 3, we visualize both the tuples from database (at the bottom) and the deduced tuples (in the middle). Inspecting the deduced tuples, we realize that they have equivalent non-temporal arguments, i.e., *DeNiro* and *Abbott*, but their time intervals are overlapping, which contradicts Definition 16 of duplicate-free relation instances.

Hence, in order to convert a temporal relation instance with duplicates (as shown in the middle of Figure 3) into a duplicate-free temporal relation (as shown on the top of Figure 3), we provide the following definition.

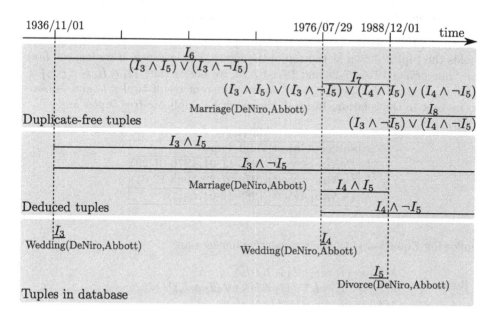

Fig. 3. Deducing and Deduplicating Tuples with Time Intervals

Definition 20. *Let a temporal relation R^T, non-temporal constants $\bar{a}$, a time point $t \in \mathcal{U}^T$, and a set of tuples $\mathcal{T}$ be given. Then, L is defined as the set of lineages of tuples $R^T(\bar{a}, t_b, t_e)$ that are valid at time point t:*

$$L(R^T, \bar{a}, t, \mathcal{T}) := \{\lambda(I) \mid I = R^T(\bar{a}, t_b, t_e) \in \mathcal{T}, t_b \leq t < t_e\}$$

We create duplicate free tuples $I' = R^T(\bar{a}, t_b, t_e)$ such that for any pair of time points $t_0, t_1 \in [t_b, t_e)$ it holds that:

$$L(R^T, \bar{a}, t_0, \mathcal{T}) = L(R^T, \bar{a}, t_1, \mathcal{T}) \tag{13}$$

Furthermore, we define the new tuples' lineage to be:

$$\lambda(I') := \bigvee_{\phi_i \in L(R^T, \bar{a}, t_b, \mathcal{T})} \phi_i \tag{14}$$

In short, for each time point t, we create the disjunction of all tuples being valid at t (see Equation 14). More detailed, for a given relation instance and the non-temporal arguments of a tuple, L is the set of all tuples' lineages that share the same non-temporal arguments and which are valid at time point t. Hence, consecutive time points for which L contains the same lineage formulas form the new intervals (see Equation (13)).

We remark that for the equality of Equation (13), we focus on syntactical equivalence checks between the lineage formulas. We thus refrain from full (i.e., logical) equivalence checks, as they are known to be *co-$\mathcal{NP}$-complete* [11].

Example 26. Applying Definition 20 to the tuples in the middle of Figure 3 yields the tuples shown at the top of the figure. For instance, if we inspect L at the time points 1976-07-28 and 1976-07-29, we notice that $\{I_3 \wedge I_5, I_3 \wedge \neg I_5\} \neq \{I_3 \wedge I_5, I_3 \wedge \neg I_5, I_4 \wedge I_5, I_4 \wedge \neg I_5\}$, so two different result tuples I_6 and I_7 have to be kept in the relation. In total, the resulting duplicate-free tuples are:

Marriage

	Subject	Object	Valid Time
I_6	*DeNiro*	*Abbott*	[1936-11-01, 1976-07-29)
I_7	*DeNiro*	*Abbott*	[1976-07-29, 1988-12-01)
I_8	*DeNiro*	*Abbott*	[1988-12-01, t_{max})

Following Equation (14), their respective lineages are:

$$\lambda(I_6) = (I_3 \wedge I_5) \vee (I_3 \wedge \neg I_5)$$
$$\lambda(I_7) = (I_3 \wedge I_5) \vee (I_3 \wedge \neg I_5) \vee (I_4 \wedge I_5) \vee (I_4 \wedge \neg I_5)$$
$$\lambda(I_8) = (I_3 \wedge \neg I_5) \vee (I_4 \wedge \neg I_5)$$

Hence, for temporal deduction rules the combination of Definitions 11 and 20 creates the lineage formulas. We want to remark that these lineage formulas are guaranteed to yield purely propositional formulas, as it is captured by the following observation.

Observation 12. *Temporal deduction rules and temporal deduplication produce propositional lineage formulas without any explicit mentioning of time.*

Hence, any work on PDBs with lineage can be applied to TPDBs as well, especially also works on efficient probability computations (see Section 3.5).

4.7 Queries and Query Answers

As a final step, we introduce temporal queries which extend Definition 6 by a temporal component. Thus, in analogy to the atemporal case, a temporal query again resembles the body of a temporal deduction rule.

Definition 21. *Given temporal deduction rules $\mathcal{D}$ with their intensional relations a temporal query Q is a conjunction:*

$$Q(\bar{X}, \bar{T}) := \bigwedge_{i=1,\ldots,n} R_i^T(\bar{X}_i, T_{i,b}, T_{i,e}) \wedge \bigwedge_{j=1,\ldots,m} \neg R_j^T(\bar{X}_j, T_{j,b}, T_{j,e}) \wedge \Phi(\bar{X}_A, \bar{T}_A)$$

where

1. *all requirements of Definition 6 hold;*
2. *$\bar{T}$, $T_{i,b}$, $T_{i,e}$, $T_{j,b}$, $T_{j,e}$ and $\bar{T}_A$ are temporal constants and variables, which satisfy:*
   (a) *$Var(\bar{T}) = \bigcup_{i=1,\ldots,n} Var(T_{i,b}, T_{i,e})$;*
   (b) *$Var(\bar{T}_A) \subseteq \bigcup_{i=1,\ldots,n} Var(T_{i,b}, T_{i,e})$;*
   (c) *for all $j \in \{1, \ldots, m\}$ it holds that*
       $Var(T_{j,b}, T_{j,e}) \subseteq \bigcup_{i=1,\ldots,n} Var(T_{i,b}, T_{i,e})$;
3. *$Var(\bar{X}) \cup Var(\bar{T})$ denote the query variables;*
4. *$\Phi(\bar{X}_A, \bar{T}_A)$ is a conjunction of (temporal) arithmetic literals.*

Temporal queries thus inherit all properties from their non-temporal counterparts (see Definition 6), in particular that all relations occurring in the query are intensional. The first and second condition above ensure *safe queries* [2]. In this section, the query variables are formed by both the variables in $\bar{X}$ and in $\bar{T}$. With respect to arithmetic predicates, we support both non-temporal ones as in Section 2.4 and additionally the temporal ones from Definition 18.

Example 27. If we are interested in people who were married before 1980, we write the query

$$Marriage(P_1, P_2, T_b, T_e) \wedge T_b <^T 1980\text{-}01\text{-}01$$

where the intensional relation *Marriage* is defined as in Example 24.

Since the restrictions on variables of Definition 6 and Definition 21 coincide, query answers can be obtained as in the non-temporal case of Definition 7.

4.8   Temporal Consistency Constraints

In Subsection 3.6, we introduced constraints as propositional lineage formula ϕ_c. Following Definition 14, we can create constraints via deduction rules. For this, we keep two sets of literals C_p and C_n which again relate to constraints that must always hold and must never hold, respectively. Then, the literals of both sets induce the lineage formula ϕ_c (see Definition 14). Hence, in this section constraints are formulated as temporal deduction rules. As we support temporal-arithmetic predicates (see Definition 18) in the temporal deduction rules, we can express any temporal precedence (i.e., ordering) constraint, and any temporal disjointness or containment constraint.

Example 28. If we intend to enforce that persons are born before their marriage starts, we write

$$Constraint(P_1, P_2, T_b, T_e, T_b', T_e') \leftarrow \left(\begin{array}{c} Born^T(P_1, T_b, T_e) \wedge \\ Marriage^T(P_1, P_2, T_b', T_e') \wedge \end{array} T_b' <^T T_e \right) \tag{15}$$

and add $Constraint(P_1, P_2, T_b, T_e, T_b', T_e')$ to C_n. To abbreviate this notation, we also write the above constraint as:

$$\neg(Born^T(P_1, T_b, T_e) \wedge Marriage^T(P_1, P_2, T_b', T_e') \wedge T_b' <^T T_e)$$

Here, the negation resembles that the head literal of Equation (15) is in C_n, i.e., it should never hold. When we ground the above constraint, all pairs of $Marriage^T$ and $Born^T$ tuples contradicting the correct temporal ordering are excluded by ϕ_c.

4.9   Closure and Completeness

Generally, a representation formalism is called *complete* [31] if it can represent any finite instance of data, which in our case is temporal and probabilistic. Furthermore, a representations system is *closed* [31] if all query results can be expressed in the representation itself.

Theorem 1. *A TPDB* $(\mathcal{T}, p, \mathcal{U}^T)$ *with lineage is closed and complete under all relational operations which are expressible by the temporal deduction rules* $\mathcal{D}$.

Because completeness is the stronger requirement, which also implies closure, we next provide a proof for the completeness of our TPDB model.

Proof. We show that, when given any finite instance $\mathcal{T}$ of temporal and probabilistic relational data, we can represent it in our TPDB model. Without loss of generality, we are given only one relation instance $\mathcal{R}^T$ along with its possible worlds $\mathcal{W}_1, \ldots, \mathcal{W}_n$ and a probability $P(\mathcal{W}_i)$ for each of them. Now, to encode these in a TPDB $(\mathcal{T}, p, \mathcal{U}^T)$, there are three points to show, namely (1) setting $\mathcal{U}^T$, (2) ensuring that $\mathcal{R}^T$ is duplicate free, and (3) determining $\mathcal{T}$ and p.

First, we select the earliest and latest time points t_{min} and t_{max}, respectively, which occur in $\mathcal{R}^T$. From this, we create the sequence $\mathcal{U}^T := \langle t_{min}, \ldots, t_{max} \rangle$ where each time point is of the smallest granularity of time points that occurs in $\mathcal{R}^T$. Second, to guarantee that each $\mathcal{R}^T$ is duplicate-free (see Definition 16), we create a new relation instance $\mathcal{R}^{T'}$ which extends each tuple by a unique id, e.g., if $R^T(\bar{a}, t_b, t_e) \in \mathcal{R}^T$, then $R^{T'}(id, \bar{a}, t_b, t_e) \in \mathcal{R}^{T'}$. Third, regarding the probabilistic data, we follow [7,63] by proving the statement via induction over the number of possible worlds. Let the possible worlds $\mathcal{W}_i$ range over $\mathcal{R}^{T'}$.

<u>Basis $n = 1$:</u>

In this case, there is only one possible world $\mathcal{W}_1$ with $P(\mathcal{W}_1)$. We store $\mathcal{W}_1$ in the deterministic relation $R_1^{T',d}$ and create an uncertain relation $R^u(X)$ holding exactly one tuple $R^u(1)$ with $p(R^u(1)) = 1$. Then, the rule

$$R_1^{T'}(\bar{X}) \leftarrow R_1^{T',d}(\bar{X}) \wedge R^u(1)$$

along with $\mathcal{T}_1 := \mathcal{W}_1$ encodes the TPDB. Now, queries posed on $R_1^{T'}$ deliver the correct semantics.

<u>Step $n \rightarrow n+1$:</u>

We want to extend the TPDB by a possible world $\mathcal{W}_{n+1}$ which should have $P(\mathcal{W}_{n+1}) = p_{n+1}$. For this, we create the deterministic relation $R_{n+1}^{T',d}$ containing the tuples of $\mathcal{W}_{n+1}$. Then, we insert the tuple $R^u(n+1)$ into R^u and set its probability value to p_{n+1}. Now, we add the rules:

$$R_{n+1}^{T'}(\bar{X}) \leftarrow R_{n+1}^{T',d}(\bar{X}) \wedge R^u(n+1)$$
$$R_{n+1}^{T'}(\bar{X}) \leftarrow R_n^{T'}(\bar{X}) \wedge \neg R^u(n+1)$$

Next, we set $\mathcal{T}_{n+1} := \mathcal{T}_n \cup \mathcal{W}_{n+1}$ to finalize the construction of the resulting TPDB. Again, queries formulated on $R_{n+1}^{T'}$ yield the intended semantics.

5   Top-k Query Processing

Motivated by queries whose probability computations entail #$\mathcal{P}$-hard [16,15] instances, the query evaluation problem in PDBs has been studied very intensively [16,15,17,36,40,51,57]. Except for two works [48,49], which we are aware of, each of these approaches aims for computing all answers along with their probabilities. Still, among these answers many of them may exhibit low probabilities, thus indicating, for example, that we are not very confident in them or that they are unlikely to exist. To avoid this, in our recent work [23], we opt for returning only the *top-k query answers*, ranked by their probabilities. Besides the benefit of presenting only the high-probability answers to the user, top-k approaches allow for significant runtime speed-ups. The reason is that we can save on computations for the neglected low-probability answers. Thus, an algorithmic approach for bounding the probabilities of the top-k answers represented via a novel notion of *first-order lineage* formulas is developed in this section.

Example 29. Figure 4 depicts a probabilistic database in the movie domain. By the given deduction rules we intend to derive actors and directors who are known for working on movies in the crime genre as expressed by the query $KnownFor(X, Crime)$.

Query:

$$KnownFor(X, Crime)$$

Deduction Rules:

$KnownFor(X, Y) \leftarrow BestDirector(X, Z) \wedge Category(Z, Y)$
$KnownFor(X, Y) \leftarrow WonAward(Z, BestPicture) \wedge ActedOnly(X, Z) \wedge Category(Z, Y)$
$BestDirector(X, Z) \leftarrow Director(X, Z) \wedge WonAward(Z, BestDirector)$
$ActedOnly(X, Z) \leftarrow ActedIn(X, Z) \wedge \neg Directed(X, Z)$

Probabilistic Database Tuples:

Directed

	Director	Movie	p
I_1	Coppola	ApocalypseNow	0.8
I_2	Coppola	Godfather	0.9
I_3	Tarantino	PulpFiction	0.7

ActedIn

	Actor	Movie	p
I_4	Brando	ApocalypseNow	0.6
I_5	Pacino	Godfather	0.3
I_6	Tarantino	PulpFiction	0.4

WonAward

	Movie	Award	p
I_7	ApocalypseNow	BestScript	0.3
I_8	Godfather	BestDirector	0.8
I_9	Godfather	BestPicture	0.4
I_{10}	PulpFiction	BestPicture	0.9

Category

	Movie	Category	p
I_{11}	ApocalypseNow	War	0.9
I_{12}	Godfather	Crime	0.5
I_{13}	PulpFiction	Crime	0.9
I_{14}	Inception	Drama	0.6

Fig. 4. Example PDB with a Query and Deduction Rules

When we execute the query, we obtain the following three answers together with their lineages:

Answer	Lineage	Probability
$KnownFor(Coppola, Crime)$	$I_2 \wedge I_8 \wedge I_{12}$	0.36
$KnownFor(Tarantino, Crime)$	$I_{10} \wedge I_6 \wedge \neg I_3 \wedge I_{13}$	0.10
$KnownFor(Pacino, Crime)$	$I_9 \wedge I_5 \wedge I_{12}$	0.06

Now, imagine we are not interested in all answers, as in the table above, but rather in the most probable answer, e.g., $KnownFor(Coppola, Crime)$. This is the setting of the present section. We will elaborate on how to compute the k most likely answers efficiently by (1) not fully computing lineage and (2) pruning other less probable answers, such as $KnownFor(Tarantino, Crime)$ and $KnownFor(Pacino, Crime)$, as early as possible.

5.1   First-Order Lineage

To handle partial grounding states, we next extend the definition of propositional lineage from Subsection 3.4 to a new notion of first-order lineage [23], which hence can contain variables and quantifiers. In contrast to propositional lineage, a first-order lineage formula does not necessarily represent a single query answer, but may rather represent entire sets of answers via variables that have not been bound to constants by the grounding procedure yet. Each distinct query answer in such a set will thus be characterized by constants once the query variables become bound by the grounding procedure.

Throughout this section, we assume the extensional relations to be duplicate-free. That is, there is no pair of tuples having the same arguments. This assumption facilitates the theoretical analysis which follows. Still, in practice, we could always remove potential duplicates by an *independent-or* projection over the input relations as a preprocessing step.

Deduction Rules with Quantifiers. To facilitate the construction of first-order lineage, we will write out the existential quantifiers that occur only in the bodies of the deduction rules explicitly, which is captured more precisely by the following definition.

Definition 22. *A first-order deduction rule is a logical rule of the form*

$$R(\bar{X}) \leftarrow \exists \bar{X}_e \bigwedge_{i=1,\ldots,n} R_i(\bar{X}_i) \wedge \bigwedge_{j=1,\ldots,m} \neg R_j(\bar{X}_j) \wedge \Phi(\bar{X}_A)$$

where

1. *all requirements of Definition 2 hold;*
2. $\bar{X}_e = (\bigcup_{i=1,\ldots,n} Var(\bar{X}_i)) \setminus Var(\bar{X})$

The difference to Definition 2 might seem subtle, but we this time explicitly enforce all variables $\bar{X}_e$, which occur in positive literals $R_i(\bar{X}_i)$, but not in the head $R(\bar{X})$, to be existentially quantified. This still is in accordance to standard Datalog semantics [2]. Later however, when constructing first-order lineage formulas, we will need to trace and maintain the existential quantifiers in the lineage formulas explicitly.

Example 30. Let us adapt the deduction rules of Figure 4 to Definition 22 by writing the quantifiers explicitly:

$$
\begin{aligned}
KnownFor(X,Y) &\leftarrow \exists Z \; BestDirector(X,Z) \wedge Category(Z,Y) \\
KnownFor(X,Y) &\leftarrow \exists Z \left(\begin{array}{c} WonAward(Z, BestPicture) \wedge ActedOnly(X,Z) \\ \wedge \, Category(Z,Y) \end{array} \right) \\
BestDirector(X,Z) &\leftarrow Director(X,Z) \wedge WonAward(Z, BestDirector) \\
ActedOnly(X,Z) &\leftarrow ActedIn(X,Z) \wedge \neg Directed(X,Z)
\end{aligned}
$$

Top-Down Grounding with First-Order Lineage. Our main observation for this section is that first-order lineage can be constructed from a top-down grounding procedure in Datalog and can thus capture any intermediate state in this process. In a top-down approach, we start at the query literals and iteratively expand the deduction rules until we reach the database tuples. In Section 3.4, the direction was reversed, since we started at the database until we ended up at the query. As first theoretical tool, we establish consistent vectors of constants $\bar{a}$ and mixtures of variables and constants $\bar{X}$. This technique enables us to match first-order literals against database tuples.

Definition 23. *Let X_i and a_i denote the i-th entry in the vector of variables and constants $\bar{X}$ and the vector of constants $\bar{a}$, respectively. We call $\bar{X}$ and $\bar{a}$ consistent, if*

$$\forall X_i \in \bar{X} : X_i \text{ is a constant} \Rightarrow X_i = a_i$$

In other words, all constants in the vector $\bar{X}$ have to match the constant in $\bar{a}$ at the respective position.

Example 31. The vectors $(X, Crime)$ and $(Coppola, Crime)$ are consistent, as the constant in the second entry occurs in both vectors.

Based on consistent vectors, we gather all constants binding a variable in a set of tuples. Later, this allows us to collect all tuples from the database, which match a first-order literal.

Definition 24. *Let $\mathcal{T}$ be a set of tuples and $R(\bar{X})$ be a literal with extensional relation R. Then, the set of constants from $\mathcal{T}$, which bind the variable X_i in $\bar{X}$ is:*

$$Bindings(X_i, R(\bar{X}), \mathcal{T}) := \{a_i \mid R(\bar{a}) \in \mathcal{T}, \bar{X} \text{ and } \bar{a} \text{ consistent}\}$$

We note that a_i and X_i refer to i-th entry of $\bar{a}$ and $\bar{X}$, respectively. In general, the above set can be empty or reach the same cardinality as $\mathcal{T}$.

Example 32. Let the tuples of Figure 4 establish $\mathcal{T}$. Then, considering the literal $Directed(Coppola, Y)$ we obtain the following bindings for the variable Y:

$$Bindings(Y, Directed(Coppola, Y), \mathcal{T}) = \{ApocalypseNow, Godfather\}$$

The last technical prerequisite before introducing the construction of first-order lineage are logical equivalences which eliminate quantifiers. For this, assuming that $a_1, \ldots, a_n$ are all possible constants for the variable X, then the following two equivalences [2,65] hold:

$$\exists X \Phi \equiv \sigma_{a_1}(\Phi) \vee \cdots \vee \sigma_{a_n}(\Phi)$$
$$\forall X \Phi \equiv \sigma_{a_1}(\Phi) \wedge \cdots \wedge \sigma_{a_n}(\Phi) \tag{16}$$

Here, σ_{a_i} is shorthand for $\sigma(X) = a_i$. Finally, we establish the top-down counterpart to Definition 11 for first-order lineage. We create first-order lineage by starting with the query literals and then by iteratively replacing the first-order literals by the bodies of the respective deduction rules and, finally, by tuples from the database.

Definition 25. *Let a set of tuples $\mathcal{T}$, a set of deduction rules $\mathcal{D}$, a first-order lineage formula Φ, and a literal $R(\bar{X})$ which occurs in Φ be given. We define the expansion of $R(\bar{X})$ in Φ by a function:*

$$SLD : Literals \times FirstOrderLineage \rightarrow Set[FirstOrderLineage]$$

In detail:

1. *If R is* intensional, *then:*

$$SLD(R(\bar{X}), \Phi) := \left\{ \Phi[R(\bar{X}) / \bigvee_{(R(\bar{X}') \leftarrow \Psi) \in \mathcal{D}} \sigma_{\bar{X}}(\Psi)] \right\}$$

   where $\sigma_{\bar{X}}$'s image coincides with $\bar{X}$.
2. *If R is* extensional, *we initialize:*

$$S_0 := \{\Phi\}$$

   and then iterate over all variables $X \in Var(\bar{X})$:
   (a) *If X is a query variable:*

$$S_i := \{\sigma_a(\Phi') \mid \Phi' \in S_{i-1}, a \in Bindings(X, R(\bar{X}), \mathcal{T})\}$$

   where $\sigma_a(X) = a$.
   (b) *If X is bound by $\exists X$, then we replace the subformula $\exists X \; \Psi$ of Φ in S_i by $\sigma_{a_1}(\Psi) \vee \cdots \vee \sigma_{a_n}(\Psi)$ where all $a_i \in Bindings(X, R(\bar{X}), \mathcal{T})$.*
   (c) *If X is bound by $\forall X$, then we replace the subformula $\forall X \; \Psi$ of Φ in S_i by $\sigma_{a_1}(\Psi) \wedge \cdots \wedge \sigma_{a_n}(\Psi)$ where all $a_i \in Bindings(X, R(\bar{X}), \mathcal{T})$.*
   Finally, we replace all ground literals $R(\bar{a})$ in the last S_i by their tuple identifier I and assign $SLD(R(\bar{X}), \Phi) := S_i$.
3. *If there is* no *match to $R(\bar{X})$, neither in $\mathcal{T}$ nor in $\mathcal{D}$, then:*

$$SLD(R(\bar{X}), \Phi) := \{\Phi_{[R(\bar{X})/false]}\}$$

4. *If R is* arithmetic *and $Var(\bar{X}) = \emptyset$, then we evaluate $R(\bar{X})$ to a constant truth value V (thus assigning* true *or* false*), and we set:*

$$SLD(R(\bar{X}), \Phi) := \{\Phi_{[R(\bar{X})/V]}\}$$

The above definition is admittedly more involved than the previous definition of propositional lineage. In the first case, we address *intensional literals* $R(\bar{X})$, where we exchange $R(\bar{X})$ for the disjunction of the deduction rules having R in their head literal. Since $\bar{X}$ can contain constants, we propagate them to the rules' bodies by writing $\sigma_{\bar{X}}(\Psi)$. *Extensional literals*, which are the subject of the second case, can yield sets of first-order lineage formulas. We proceed by considering each variable individually and distinguish between query variables (see Definition 6), existentially bound variables, and universally bound variables. If X is a *query variable*, then each constant a that yields a valid binding to X produces a new distinct set of query answers represented by the lineage formula $\sigma_a(\Phi')$.

Conversely, if X is *existentially quantified*, we apply Equation (16) to expand the formula by introducing a disjunction ranging over the constants $a_1, \ldots, a_n$ which bind X. Analogously, a *universally quantified* X yields the conjunction over the constants $a_1, \ldots, a_n$. The third case again reflects a closed-world assumption [2], where we replace a literal with *no match* by the constant *false*. Finally, if we have an *arithmetic* literal that has only constants as arguments, we evaluate it to its truth value. We can safely assume that all arguments of the arithmetic literal are finally going to be bound to constants, because these must be bound to at least one positive, relational literal (see Definition 2). What we omitted for brevity are constants in the head literal of a deduction rule. Since these constants bind variables as in extensional literals (the second case), a mixture of the first and second case arises.

Example 33. We illustrate Definition 25 by providing an example for each case. As for $\mathcal{T}$ we assume it to comprise all tuples of Figure 4.

1. We expand the formula $\Phi := KnownFor(X, Crime)$ over the deduction rules of Example 30. Since *KnownFor* is an intensional relation, we start with the first case of Definition 25. There, the substitution $\sigma_{\bar{X}}$ binds the second argument to *Crime*:

$$\sigma_{\bar{X}}(Y) = Crime$$

   Since there are two rules having *KnownFor* in the head literal we apply the substitution to both bodies which then yields:

$$\left\{ \begin{array}{c} (\exists Z \; BestDirector(X, Z) \wedge Category(Z, Crime)) \\ \vee \\ \left(\exists Z \; \begin{array}{c} WonAward(Z, BestPicture) \wedge \\ ActedOnly(X, Z) \wedge Category(Z, Crime) \end{array} \right) \end{array} \right\}$$

2. (a) Imagine we are given the first-order lineage formula

$$\Phi := BestDirector(X, Z) \wedge Category(Z, Crime)$$

   and we intend to expand the literal $Category(Z, Crime)$. Here, *Category* is an extensional relation. First, we determine the bindings of Z, which are *Godfather* and *PulpFiction*. Since Z is not quantified, but a query variable, we obtain several formulas, one for each of the constants:

$$\left\{ \begin{array}{l} (BestDirector(X, Godfather) \wedge Category(Godfather, Crime)), \\ (BestDirector(X, PulpFiction) \wedge Category(PulpFiction, Crime)) \end{array} \right\}$$

   (b) In this case, we quantify Z existentially and otherwise keep the previous formula:

$$\Phi := \exists Z \; BestDirector(X, Z) \wedge Category(Z, Crime)$$

Then, we expand the *Category* literal by case 2(b) of Definition 25 which results in a disjunction over the two constants *Godfather* and *PulpFiction*:

$$\left\{ \begin{array}{c} (BestDirector(X, Godfather) \wedge Category(Godfather, Crime)) \\ \vee \\ (BestDirector(X, PulpFiction) \wedge Category(PulpFiction, Crime)) \end{array} \right\}$$

(c) Let us consider a universal quantifier instead:

$$\Phi := \forall Z \; BestDirector(X, Z) \wedge Category(Z, Crime)$$

When applying a SLD step to the *Category* literal, we instantiate Z by the two constants *Godfather* and *PulpFiction* to obtain the conjunction:

$$\left\{ \begin{array}{c} (BestDirector(X, Godfather) \wedge Category(Godfather, Crime)) \\ \wedge \\ (BestDirector(X, PulpFiction) \wedge Category(PulpFiction, Crime)) \end{array} \right\}$$

3. Trying to resolve the second literal of

$$\Phi := \exists Z \; BestDirector(X, Z) \wedge Category(Z, Comedy)$$

over $\mathcal{T}$ delivers no result. Hence, we replace it by *false* which yields:

$$\{\exists Z \; BestDirector(X, Z) \wedge false\}$$

4. In the last case, we have an arithmetic literal, for example

$$I_1 \wedge I_2 \wedge ApocalypseNow \neq Godfather$$

which we then evaluate to $I_1 \wedge I_2 \wedge true$.

Analogously to the Disjunctive Normal Form (DNF) for propositional formulas, any first-order formula can equivalently be transformed into prenex form by pulling all quantifiers in front of the formula. The remaining formula can again be transformed into DNF, which is then called Prenex Disjunctive Normal Form (PDNF) [65].

Next, we devise two formal properties of first-order lineage formulas. First, the existence of at least one proof implies that all query variables are bound. Second, unbound query variables imply that a first-order lineage formula represents a set of query answers.

Proposition 6. *Expanding a query $Q(\bar{X})$ with query variables $\bar{X}$ to first-order lineage by repeatedly applying Definition 25 has the following properties:*

1. *If at least one clause in the disjunctive normal form of the lineage formula is propositional, then all query variables $\bar{X}$ are bound to constants.*
2. *If at least one query variable $X \in \bar{X}$ is unbound a lineage formula represents a (potentially empty) set of query answers.*

Proof. We prove both statements separately.

1. Without loss of generality, we assume the formula to be in PDNF. Then, every clause stands for one proof of the answer candidate. When one of these clauses is propositional, all query variables within this clause were bound and hence become bound in the entire formula.
2. Since a query variable can be bound to many constants, each representing a different query answer, the first-order lineage formula represents all these answers.

5.2   Probability Bounds for Lineage Formulas

In this section, we develop lower and upper bounds for the probability of any query answer that can be obtained from grounding a first-order lineage formula. We proceed by constructing two propositional lineage formulas ϕ_{low} and ϕ_{up} from a given first-order lineage formula Φ. Later, the probabilities of ϕ_{low} and ϕ_{up} serve as lower and upper bounds on the probabilities of all query answers captured by Φ. More formally, if $\phi_1, \ldots, \phi_n$ represent all query answers we would obtain by fully grounding Φ, then it holds that:

$$\forall i \in \{1, \ldots, n\} : \ P(\phi_{low}) \leq P(\phi_i) \leq P(\phi_{up})$$

Building upon results of [26,47,53], we start by considering bounds for propositional formulas, from which we extend to the more general case of first-order lineage. Then, we show that these bounds converge monotonically to the probabilities $P(\phi_i)$ of each query answer ϕ_i, as we continue to ground Φ.

Bounds for Propositional Lineage. Following [47], we relate the probability of two propositional lineage formulas ϕ and ψ via their sets of models $\mathcal{M}(\phi)$ and $\mathcal{M}(\psi)$ (see Equation (4)), i.e., the sets of possible worlds over which ϕ and ψ evaluate to *true*.

Proposition 7. *For two propositional lineage formulas ϕ and ψ it holds that:*

$$\mathcal{M}(\phi) \subseteq \mathcal{M}(\psi) \ \Rightarrow \ P(\phi) \leq P(\psi)$$

Proof.

$$
\begin{aligned}
P(\phi) \ &\overset{\text{Equation (5)}}{=} \ \sum_{\mathcal{W} \in \mathcal{M}(\phi)} P(\mathcal{W}) \\
&\leq \ \sum_{\mathcal{W} \in \mathcal{M}(\phi)} P(\mathcal{W}) + \sum_{\mathcal{W} \in \mathcal{M}(\psi) \setminus \mathcal{M}(\phi)} P(\mathcal{W}) \\
&\overset{\mathcal{M}(\phi) \subseteq \mathcal{M}(\psi)}{=} \ \sum_{\mathcal{W} \in \mathcal{M}(\psi)} P(\mathcal{W}) \\
&\overset{\text{Equation (5)}}{=} \ P(\psi)
\end{aligned}
$$

Since we assume $\mathcal{M}(\phi) \subseteq \mathcal{M}(\psi)$, the possible worlds satisfying ϕ fulfill ψ as well. However, there might be more worlds satisfying ψ but not ϕ. This might yield more terms over which the sum of Equation (5) ranges, and thus we obtain $P(\phi) \leq P(\psi)$.

Example 34. Consider the two propositional formulas $\phi \equiv I_1$ and $\psi \equiv I_1 \vee I_2$. From $\mathcal{M}(I_1) \subseteq \mathcal{M}(I_1 \vee I_2)$ it follows that $P(I_1) \leq P(I_1 \vee I_2)$, which we can easily verify by Equation (5).

To turn Proposition 7 into upper and lower bounds, we proceed by considering *conjunctive clauses* in the form of conjunctions of propositional literals. Then, following a result from [47], we obtain the following proposition.

Proposition 8. *Let ϕ, ψ be two propositional, conjunctive clauses. It holds that:*

$$\mathcal{M}(\phi) \subseteq \mathcal{M}(\psi) \quad \Leftrightarrow \quad Tup(\phi) \supseteq Tup(\psi)$$

The above statement expresses that adding literals to a conjunction ϕ removes satisfying worlds from $\mathcal{M}(\phi)$.

Example 35. For the two clauses $I_1 \wedge I_2$ and I_1 it holds that $Tup(I_1 \wedge I_2) \supseteq Tup(I_1)$ and thus Proposition 8 yields $\mathcal{M}(I_1 \wedge I_2) \subseteq \mathcal{M}(I_1)$.

We now establish a relationship between two formulas in Disjunctive Normal Form (DNF) (see Definition 12) via their conjunctive clauses as in [47,53]. Since any propositional formula can be transformed equivalently into DNF, this result is generally applicable.

Lemma 3. *For two propositional DNF formulas $\phi \equiv \phi_1 \vee \cdots \vee \phi_n$ and $\psi \equiv \psi_1 \vee \cdots \vee \psi_n$, it holds that:*

$$\forall \phi_i \exists \psi_j : \mathcal{M}(\phi_i) \subseteq \mathcal{M}(\psi_j) \Rightarrow \mathcal{M}(\phi) \subseteq \mathcal{M}(\psi)$$

If we can map all clauses ϕ_i of a formula ϕ to a clause ψ_j of ψ with more satisfying worlds, i.e., $\mathcal{M}(\phi_i) \subseteq \mathcal{M}(\psi_j)$, then ψ has more satisfying worlds than ϕ. This mapping of clauses is established via Proposition 8.

Example 36. For the propositional DNF formula $\phi \equiv (I_1 \wedge I_2) \vee (I_1 \wedge I_3) \vee I_4$, we can map each conjunctive clause in ϕ to a clause in $\psi \equiv I_1 \vee I_4$. Hence, ψ has more models than ϕ, i.e., $\mathcal{M}(\phi) \subseteq \mathcal{M}(\psi)$.

Thus, Lemma 3 enables us to compare the probabilities of propositional formulas in DNF based on their clause structure.

Converting Formulas to DNF. When transforming any propositional formula into DNF, we can first iteratively apply De Morgan's law [65] which pushes negations down in a formula:

$$\begin{aligned} \neg \bigwedge\nolimits_i \Phi_i \equiv \bigvee\nolimits_i \neg \Phi_i \\ \neg \bigvee\nolimits_i \Phi_i \equiv \bigwedge\nolimits_i \neg \Phi_i \end{aligned} \tag{17}$$

Thereafter, we apply the distributive law which allows the following observation.

Observation 13. *If a tuple I occurs exactly once in a propositional formula ϕ, then all occurrences of I in the DNF of ϕ have the same sign.*

The reason is that the sign of a tuple I changes only when De Morgan's law is applied. However, when applying De Morgan's law, no tuples are duplicated. When utilizing the distributive law, tuples are duplicated but preserve their signs.

Example 37. Applying the distributive law to $(I_1 \vee I_2) \wedge \neg I_3$ yields $(I_1 \wedge \neg I_3) \vee (I_2 \wedge \neg I_3)$. Now, I_3 occurs twice, but its sign was preserved.

Bounds for First-Order Lineage. For our following constructions on first-order formulas, we assume the first-order formulas to be given in PDNF. Next, given a first-order lineage formula Φ, we construct two propositional formulas ϕ_{low} and ϕ_{up} whose probabilities then serve as lower and upper bound on Φ, respectively.

Definition 26. *Let Φ be a first-order lineage formula.*

1. *We construct the propositional lineage formula ϕ_{up} by substituting every literal $R(\bar{X})$ in Φ with*
   - *true if $R(\bar{X})$ occurs positive in the PDNF of Φ, or*
   - *false if $R(\bar{X})$ occurs negated in the PDNF of Φ.*
2. *We construct the propositional lineage formula ϕ_{low} by substituting every literal $R(\bar{X})$ in Φ with*
   - *false if $R(\bar{X})$ occurs positive in the PDNF of Φ, or*
   - *true if $R(\bar{X})$ occurs negated in the PDNF of Φ.*

The idea of the above definition is as follows. If we replace a positive literal by *true*, we add models to the resulting formula. Hence, due to Proposition 7 the resulting formula can serve as an upper bound on the probability, which we show formally later. The remaining three cases are analogous. We note that R can be intensional, extensional and even arithmetic.

Example 38. We consider Figure 4 and the first-order lineage formula:

$$\Phi := I_1 \wedge \exists X \, WonAward(X, BestPicture)$$

Then, the upper bound is given by $P(\phi_{up}) = P(I_1 \wedge true) = p(I_1) = 0.8$ and the lower bound is $P(\phi_{low}) = P(I_1 \wedge false) = P(false) = 0$. If we execute one SLD step (see Definition 25) on Φ we obtain $I_1 \wedge (I_9 \vee I_{10})$. Its probability is $P(I_1 \wedge (I_9 \vee I_{10})) = 0.8 \cdot (1 - (1 - 0.4) \cdot (1 - 0.9)) = 0.752$ which is correctly captured by the upper and lower bound.

As a next step, we discuss the application of Definition 26 to general first-order lineage formulas which do not necessarily adhere any normal form.

Proposition 9. *By first exhaustively applying De Morgan's law of Equation (17) on a first-order lineage formula Φ, we can apply Definition 26 to Φ, even if Φ is not in PDNF. Hence, constructing ϕ_{up} and ϕ_{low} can be done in $O(|\Phi|)$.*

Proof. We can implement De Morgan by traversing the formula once, which thus is in $O(|\Phi|)$. Subsequently, we traverse the formula again and replace all first-order literals by *true* or *false* as devised in Definition 26. Observation 13 ensures the replacements to be unique for each literal.

Convergence of Bounds. Our last step is to show that, when constructing first-order lineage Φ (see Definition 25) for a fixed query answer ϕ resulting from Φ, the probability bounds converge monotonically to the probability of the propositional lineage formula $P(\phi)$ with each SLD step.

Theorem 2. *Let $\Phi_1, \ldots, \Phi_n$ denote a series of first-order formulas obtained from iteratively grounding a conjunctive query via the form of SLD resolution provided in Definition 25 until we reach the propositional formula ϕ. Then, rewriting each Φ_i to $\phi_{i,low}$ and $\phi_{i,up}$ according to Definition 26 creates a monotonic series of lower and upper bounds $P(\phi_{i,low})$, $P(\phi_{i,up})$ for the probability $P(\phi)$. That is:*

$$0 \leq P(\phi_{1,low}) \leq \cdots \leq P(\phi_{n,low}) \leq P(\phi)$$
$$\leq P(\phi_{n,up}) \leq \cdots \leq P(\phi_{1,up}) \leq 1$$

Proof. The proof proceeds inductively over the structure of Definition 25, where we show that each SLD step preserves the bounds. We assume the observed literal $R(\bar{X})$ to occur positively in the PDNF of Φ_i. The negated version is handled analogously.

1. We have an intensional literal $R(\bar{X})$ which was substituted in Φ_i by the disjunction of deduction rules' bodies, which we call Ψ here, to yield Φ_{i+1}. Because there are only literals and no tuple identifiers in Ψ, Definition 26 yields $\psi_{low} \equiv false$ and $\psi_{up} \equiv true$. Hence, the bounds of Φ_{i+1} are not altered, which reads as $P(\phi_{i+1,up}) = P(\phi_{i,up})$ and $P(\phi_{i+1,low}) = P(\phi_{i,low})$.

2. As in Definition 25, we separate the cases of different variables.

   (a) In this case we consider an extensional literal $R(\bar{X})$ where $Var(\bar{X})$ are query variables. Now, $SLD(R(\bar{X}), \Phi_i)$ delivers a set of formulas. Let Φ_{i+1} be an arbitrary formula in this set. We obtain Φ_{i+1} by replacing $R(\bar{X})$ in Φ_i by a tuple identifier I. Hence, in the DNF of $\phi_{i+1,up}$ we added I to the clauses, whereas in the DNF of $\phi_{i,up}$ we replace $R(\bar{X})$ by $true$. Thus, Lemma 3 applies and we have $P(\phi_{i+1,up}) \leq P(\phi_{i,up})$. The reasoning for lower bounds is analogous.

   (b) Again, we have an extensional literal $R(\bar{X})$, but all variables $Var(\bar{X})$ are bound by an existential quantifier. As a result, each Φ_{i+1} in the set $SLD(R(\bar{X}, \Phi_i)$ is constructed from Φ_i by the first line of Equation (16). Now, the DNF of $\phi_{i,up}$ has clauses where $R(\bar{X})$ was substituted by $true$. Then, in $\phi_{i+1,up}$ each clause featuring a new tuple identifier I can be mapped to one of these clauses in the DNF of $\phi_{i,up}$. Therefore, Lemma 3 gives us $P(\phi_{i+1,up}) \leq P(\phi_{i,up})$. Again, lower bounds are handled analogously.

   (c) If the variables $\bar{X}$ in the extensional literal $R(\bar{X})$ are universally quantified, then $R(\bar{X})$ in Φ_i is replaced by a conjunction (as given in the second line of Equation (16)) to yield Φ_{i+1}. In the DNF of $\phi_{i,up}$, we employed $true$ whenever $R(\bar{X})$ occurred. Conversely, in $\phi_{i+1,up}$ we replaced $R(\bar{X})$ by a conjunction of tuple identifiers. The resulting extended clauses of $\phi_{i+1,up}$ can be mapped to a clause of $\phi_{i,up}$, so Lemma 3 applies: $P(\phi_{i+1,up}) \leq P(\phi_{i,up})$. The lower bounds are addressed analogously.

3. Here, a literal $R(\bar{X})$ was replaced in Φ_i by *false* to yield Φ_{i+1}. Hence, for the lower bounds constructed according to Definition 26, we have $P(\phi_{i,low}) = P(\phi_{i+1,low})$. For the upper bounds Lemma 3 delivers $P(\phi_{i+1,up}) \leq P(\phi_{i,up})$, since the PDNF of Φ_{i+1} has fewer clauses as the PDNF of Φ_i.

4. In the last case, $R(\bar{X})$ is arithmetic and $\bar{X}$ consists of constants only. Now, if $R(\bar{X})$ evaluates to *true*, we have $\phi_{i,up} = \phi_{i+1,up}$ and hence also $P(\phi_{i,up}) = P(\phi_{i+1,up})$. For the lower bound, the DNF of $\phi_{i+1,low}$ can have more clauses than the DNF of $\phi_{i,low}$ and so Lemma 3 comes to our rescue again: $P(\phi_{i,low}) \leq P(\phi_{i+1,low})$. Conversely, if $R(\bar{X})$ evaluates to *false*, the reasoning for the upper and lower bounds is inverted.

The resulting lower and upper bounds for all answer candidates can be plugged into any top-k algorithm (see [34] for an extensive overview) that—in our case—will then iteratively refine these lower and upper bounds via SLD resolution until a termination condition is reached. The seminal line of threshold algorithms proposed by Fagin, Lotem and Naor [24], for example, iteratively maintains two disjoint sets of top-k answers and remaining answer candidates, coined *top-k candidates*, respectively, and it terminates when:

$$\min\{P(\phi_{i,low}) \mid \phi_i \in \text{top-}k\} \geq \max\{P(\phi_{i,up}) \mid \phi_i \in candidates\}$$

6   Learning Tuple Probabilities

Most works in the context of PDBs assume the database tuples along with their probabilities to be given as input. Also the preceding sections of this chapter followed this route. Nevertheless, when creating, updating or cleaning a PDB, the tuple probabilities have to be altered or even be newly created—in other words: they have to be *learned*. Learning the probability values of databases tuples from labeled lineage formulas thus is the subject of the present section and is also discussed in more detail in [22].

Example 39. Our running example resembles the information-extraction setting of Section 1.1, in which we employ a set of textual patterns to extract facts from various Web domains. However, instead of knowing all probabilities of all tuples the respective values in the *UsingPattern* and *FromDomain* relations are missing as indicated by the question marks in Figure 5. We thus are unsure about the reliability—or "trustworthiness"—of the textual patterns and the Web domains that led to the extraction of our remaining facts, respectively. Grounding the deduction rules of Equation (1) and Equation (2) against the database tuples of Figure 5 yields the new tuples *BornIn(Spielberg, Cinncinati)*, *BornIn(Spielberg, LosAngeles)*, and *WonPrize(Spielberg,AcademyAward)*. Figure 6 shows these new tuples along with their propositional lineage formulas.

WonPrizeExtraction

	Subject	Object	Pid	Did	p
I_1	Spielberg	AcademyAward	1	1	0.6
I_2	Spielberg	AcademyAward	2	1	0.3

BornInExtraction

	Subject	Object	Pid	Did	p
I_3	Spielberg	Cinncinati	3	1	0.7
I_4	Spielberg	LosAngeles	3	2	0.4

UsingPattern

	Pid	Pattern	p
I_5	1	Received	?
I_6	2	Won	?
I_7	3	Born	?

FromDomain

	Did	Domain	p
I_8	1	Wikipedia.org	?
I_9	2	Imdb.com	?

Fig. 5. Example Probabilistic Database with Missing Probability Values

A closer look at the new tuples reveals, however, that not all of them are correct. For instance, *BornIn(Spielberg,LosAngeles)* is wrong, so we might rather label it with the probability of 0.0. Moreover, *WonPrize(Spielberg,AcademyAward)* is likely correct, but we are unsure, hence we label it with the probability of 0.7, as shown on top of Figure 6. Given the probability labels of the query answers, the goal of the learning procedure is to learn the database tuples' unknown probability values for *UsingPattern* and *FromDomain*, such that the lineage formulas again produce the given probability labels. The probabilities of the tuples of *WonPrizeExtraction* and *BornInExtraction*, on the other hand, should remain unchanged.

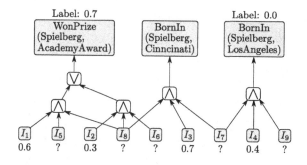

Fig. 6. Partially Labeled Lineage Formulas

6.1   Encoding Propositional Lineage into Polynomials

For the theoretical analysis of the learning problem presented in this section, we devise an alternative way of computing probabilities of lineage formulas via polynomial expressions. First, we reduce the number of terms in the sum of Equation (5) by considering just tuples $Tup(\phi)$ that occur in the propositional lineage formula ϕ.

Proposition 10. *We can compute $P(\phi)$ relying on tuples in $Tup(\phi)$, only, by writing:*

$$P(\phi) = \sum_{\mathcal{V} \in \mathcal{M}(\phi, Tup(\phi))} \underbrace{P(\mathcal{V}, Tup(\phi))}_{\text{Definition } 10} \tag{18}$$

Proof.

$$P(\phi) = \sum_{\mathcal{W} \in \mathcal{M}(\phi, \mathcal{T})} P(\mathcal{W}, \mathcal{T})$$
$$= \left(\sum_{\mathcal{V} \in \mathcal{M}(\phi, Tup(\phi))} P(\mathcal{V}, Tup(\phi)) \right) \cdot \underbrace{\left(\sum_{\mathcal{V} \subseteq (\mathcal{T} \setminus Tup(\phi))} P(\mathcal{V}, \mathcal{T} \setminus Tup(\phi)) \right)}_{=1 \text{ by Proposition } 1}$$

Thus, Equation (18) expresses $P(\phi)$ as a polynomial. Its terms are defined as in the third item of Definition 10, and the variables are $p(I)$ for $I \in Tup(\phi)$. The degree of the polynomial is limited as follows.

Corollary 1. *The probability $P(\phi)$ of a propositional lineage formula ϕ can be expressed by a multi-linear polynomial over variables $p(I)$, for $I \in Tup(\phi)$, with a degree of at most $|Tup(\phi)|$.*

Proof. By inspecting Proposition 10, we note that the sum ranges over subsets of $Tup(\phi)$ only, hence each term has a degree of at most $|Tup(\phi)|$.

Example 40. Considering the propositional lineage formula $\phi \equiv I_1 \vee I_2$, the occurring tuples are $Tup(\phi) = \{I_1, I_2\}$. Then, it holds that $\{I_1, I_2\} \models \phi$, $\{I_1\} \models \phi$, and $\{I_2\} \models \phi$. Hence, we can write $P(\phi) = p(I_1) \cdot p(I_2) + p(I_1) \cdot (1 - p(I_2)) + (1 - p(I_1)) \cdot p(I_2)$. Thus, $P(\phi)$ is a polynomial over the variables $p(I_1)$, $p(I_2)$ and has degree $2 = |Tup(\phi)| = |\{I_1, I_2\}|$.

6.2   Learning Problem

We now move away from the case where the probability values of all database tuples are known, which was a basic assumption we made for the previous sections. Instead, we intend to learn the unknown probability values of (some of) these tuples (e.g., of I_5–I_9 in Example 39). More formally, for a tuple-independent PDB $(\mathcal{T}, p)$, we consider $\mathcal{T}_l \subseteq \mathcal{T}$ to be the set of base tuples for which we learn their probability values. That is, initially $p(I)$ is unknown for all $I \in \mathcal{T}_l$. Conversely, $p(I)$ is known and fixed for all $I \in \mathcal{T} \setminus \mathcal{T}_l$. To be able to complete $p(I)$, we are given labels in the form of pairs (ϕ_i, l_i), each containing a propositional lineage formula ϕ_i (i.e., a query answer) and its desired probability l_i. We formally define the resulting learning problem as follows.

Definition 27. *We are given a probabilistic database* $(\mathcal{T}, p)$, *a set of tuples* $\mathcal{T}_l \subseteq \mathcal{T}$ *with unknown probability values* $p(I_l)$ *and a multi-set of given labels* $\mathcal{L} = \langle (\phi_1, l_1), \ldots, (\phi_n, l_n) \rangle$, *where each* ϕ_i *is a propositional lineage formula over* $\mathcal{T}$ *and each* $l_i \in [0, 1] \subset \mathbb{R}$ *is a probability for* ϕ_i. *Then, the learning problem is defined as follows:*

$$\text{Determine: } p(I_l) \in [0, 1] \subset \mathbb{R} \text{ for all } I_l \in \mathcal{T}_l$$
$$\text{such that: } P(\phi_i) = l_i \text{ for all } (\phi_i, l_i) \in \mathcal{L}$$

Intuitively, we aim to set the probability values of the base tuples $I_l \in \mathcal{T}_l$ such that the labeled lineage formulas ϕ_i again yield the probability l_i. We want to remark that all probability values of tuples in $\mathcal{T} \backslash \mathcal{T}_l$ remain unaltered. Also, we note that the Boolean labels *true* and *false* can be represented as $l_i = 0.0$ and $l_i = 1.0$, respectively. Hence, Boolean labels resolve to a special case of the labels of Definition 27.

Example 41. Formalizing the problem setting of Example 39, we obtain $\mathcal{T} := \{I_1, \ldots, I_9\}$, $\mathcal{T}_l := \{I_5, \ldots, I_9\}$ with labels $((I_1 \wedge I_5 \wedge I_8) \vee (I_2 \wedge I_6 \wedge I_8), 0.7)$, and $((I_3 \wedge I_7 \wedge I_9), 0.0)$.

6.3   Properties of the Learning Problem

We next discuss the complexity of solving the learning problem. Unfortunately, it exhibits hard instances. First, computing $P(\phi_i)$ may be #$\mathcal{P}$-hard (see Lemma 2), which would require many Shannon expansions to compute an exact probability $P(\phi_i)$. But even for cases when all $P(\phi_i)$ can be computed in polynomial time (i.e., when Equation (6) is applicable), there are combinatorially hard cases of the above learning problem.

Lemma 4. *For a given instance of the learning problem of Definition 27, where all* $P(\phi_i)$ *with* $(\phi_i, l_i) \in \mathcal{L}$ *can be computed in polynomial time, deciding whether there exists a solution to the learning problem is* $\mathcal{NP}$-*hard.*

Proof. We encode the 3-Satisfiability Problem (3SAT) [29] for a Boolean formula $\psi \equiv \psi_1 \wedge \cdots \wedge \psi_n$ in Conjunctive Normal Form (CNF) into the learning problem of Definition 27. For each variable $X_i \in Var(\psi)$, we create two tuples I_i, I_i' whose probability values will be learned. Hence, $2 \cdot |Var(\psi)| = |\mathcal{T}_l| = |\mathcal{T}|$. Then, for each X_i, we add the label $((I_i \wedge I_i') \vee (\neg I_i \wedge \neg I_i'), 1.0)$. The corresponding polynomial equation $p(I_i) \cdot p(I_i') + (1 - p(I_i)) \cdot (1 - p(I_i')) = 1.0$ has exactly two possible solutions for $p(I_i), p(I_i') \in [0, 1]$, namely $p(I_i) = p(I_i') = 1.0$ and $p(I_i) = p(I_i') = 0.0$. Next, we replace all variables X_i in ψ by their tuple I_i. Now, for each clause ψ_i of ψ, we introduce one label $(\psi_i, 1.0)$. Altogether, we have $|\mathcal{L}| = |Var(\psi)| + n$ labels for the problem of Definition 27. Each labeled lineage formula ϕ has at most three variables, hence $P(\phi)$ takes at most 8 steps. Still, Definition 27 solves 3SAT, where the learned values of each pair of $p(I_i)$, $p(I_i')$ (either 0.0 or 1.0) correspond to a truth value of all X_i for a satisfying assignment of ψ. From this, it follows that the decision problem formulated in Lemma 4 is $\mathcal{NP}$-hard.

After discussing the complexity of the learning problem, we characterize its solutions. First, there might also be *inconsistent* instances of the learning problem. That is, it may be impossible to define $p : \mathcal{T}_l \rightarrow [0,1]$ such that all labels are satisfied.

Example 42. If we consider $\mathcal{T}_l := \{I_1, I_2\}$ with the labels $\mathcal{L} := \langle (I_1, 0.2), (I_2, 0.3), (I_1 \wedge I_2, 0.9) \rangle$, then it is impossible to fulfill all three labels at the same time.

From a practical point of view, there remain a number of questions regarding Definition 27. First, how many labels do we need in comparison to the number of tuples for which we are learning the probability values (i.e., $|\mathcal{L}|$ vs. $|\mathcal{T}_l|$)? And second, is there a difference in labeling lineage formulas that involve many tuples or very few tuples (i.e., $|Tup(\phi_i)|$)? These questions are addressed by the following theorem. It is based on the computation of probabilities of lineage formulas via their polynomial representation as in Corollary 1. We write the conditions of the learning problem $P(\phi_i) = l_i$ as polynomials over variables $p(I_l)$ of the form $P(\phi_i) - l_i$, where $I_l \in \mathcal{T}_l$ and the probability values $p(I)$ for all $I \in \mathcal{T} \backslash \mathcal{T}_l$ are fixed and hence represent constants.

Theorem 3. *If the labeling is consistent, the problem instances of Definition 27 can be classified as follows:*

1. *If $|\mathcal{L}| < |\mathcal{T}_l|$, the problem has infinitely many solutions.*
2. *If $|\mathcal{L}| = |\mathcal{T}_l|$ and the polynomials $P(\phi_i) - l_i$ have common zeros, then the problem has infinitely many solutions.*
3. *If $|\mathcal{L}| = |\mathcal{T}_l|$ and the polynomials $P(\phi_i) - l_i$ have no common zeros, then the problem has at most $\prod_i |Tup(\phi_i) \cap \mathcal{T}_l|$ solutions.*
4. *If $|\mathcal{L}| > |\mathcal{T}_l|$, then the polynomials $P(\phi_i) - l_i$ have common zeros, thus reducing this to one of the previous cases.*

Proof. The first case is a classical under-determined system of equations. In the second case, without loss of generality, there are two polynomials $P(\phi_i) - l_i$ and $P(\phi_j) - l_j$ with a common zero, say $p(I_k) = c_k$. Setting $p(I_k) = c_k$ satisfies both $P(\phi_i) - l_i = 0$ and $P(\phi_j) - l_j = 0$, hence we have $\mathcal{L}' := \mathcal{L} \backslash \langle (\phi_i, l_i), (\phi_j, l_j) \rangle$ and $\mathcal{T}_l' := \mathcal{T}_l \backslash \{I_k\}$ which yields the first case of the theorem again ($|\mathcal{L}'| < |\mathcal{T}_l'|$). Regarding the third case, Bezout's theorem [18], a central result from algebraic geometry, is applicable: for a system of polynomial equations, the number of solutions (including their multiplicities) over variables in $\mathbb{C}$ is equal to the product of the degrees of the polynomials. In our case, the polynomials are $P(\phi_i) - l_i$ with variables $p(I_l)$ where $I_l \in \mathcal{T}_l$. So, according to Corollary 1 their degree is at most $|Tup(\phi_i) \cap \mathcal{T}_l|$. Since our variables $p(I_l)$ range only over $[0,1] \subset \mathbb{R}$, and Corollary 1 is an upper bound only, $\prod_i |Tup(\phi_i) \cap \mathcal{T}_l|$ is an upper bound on the number of solutions. In the fourth case, the system of equations is over-determined, such that redundancies like common zeros reduces the problem to one of the previous cases. ∎

Example 43. We illustrate the theorem by providing examples for each of the four cases.

1. In Example 41's formalization of Example 39, we have $|\mathcal{T}_l| = 5$ and $|\mathcal{L}| = 2$. So, the problem is under-specified and has infinitely many solutions, since assigning $p(I_7) = 0.0$ enables $p(I_9)$ to take any value in $[0,1] \subset \mathbb{R}$.
2. We assume $\mathcal{T}_l = \{I_5, I_6, I_7\}$, and $\mathcal{L} = \langle (I_5 \wedge \neg I_6, 0.0), (I_5 \wedge \neg I_6 \wedge I_7, 0.0), (I_5 \wedge I_7, 0.0) \rangle$. This results in the equations $p(I_5) \cdot (1 - p(I_6)) = 0.0$, $p(I_5) \cdot (1 - p(I_6)) \cdot p(I_7) = 0.0$, and $p(I_5) \cdot p(I_7) = 0.0$, where $p(I_5)$ is a common zero to all three polynomials. Hence, setting $p(I_5) = 0.0$ allows $p(I_6)$ and $p(I_7)$ to take any value in $[0,1] \subset \mathbb{R}$.
3. Let us consider $\mathcal{T}_l = \{I_7, I_8\}$.
   (a) If $\mathcal{L} = \langle (I_7, 0.4), (I_8, 0.7) \rangle$, then there is exactly one solution as predicted by $|Tup(I_7)| \cdot |Tup(I_8)| = 1$.
   (b) If $\mathcal{L} = \langle (I_7 \wedge I_8, 0.1), (I_7 \vee I_8, 0.6) \rangle$, then there are two solutions, namely $p(I_7) = 0.2$, $p(I_8) = 0.5$ and $p(I_7) = 0.5$, $p(I_8) = 0.2$. Here, $\prod_i |Tup(\phi_i) \cap \mathcal{T}_l| = |Tup(I_7 \wedge I_8)| \cdot |Tup(I_7 \vee I_8)| = 4$ is an upper bound.
4. We extend the second case of this example by the label $(I_5, 0.0)$, thus yielding the same solutions but having $|\mathcal{L}| > |\mathcal{T}_l|$.

In general, a learning problem instance has many solutions, where Definition 27 does not specify a precedence, but all of them are equivalent. The number of solutions shrinks by adding labels to $\mathcal{L}$, or by labeling lineage formulas ϕ_i that involve fewer tuples in $\mathcal{T}_l$ (thus resulting in a smaller intersection $|Tup(\phi_i) \cap \mathcal{T}_l|$). Hence, to achieve more uniquely specified probabilities for all tuples $I_l \in \mathcal{T}_l$, in practice we should obtain the same number of labels as the number of tuples for which we learn their probability values, i.e., $|\mathcal{L}| = |\mathcal{T}_l|$, and label those lineage formulas with fewer tuples in $\mathcal{T}_l$.

Now that we characterized the number of solutions, we furthermore provide an insight on their nature. We give conditions on learning problems which imply the existence of an integer solution, i.e., that assigns only 0 or 1 as tuple probabilities. Hence, the resulting tuples are either non-existent or deterministic as in conventional databases.

Proposition 11. *For a learning problem, where*

1. $\forall I \in \mathcal{T} \backslash \mathcal{T}_l : p(I) \in \{0,1\}$
2. $(\phi_i, l_i) \in \mathcal{L} : l_i \in \{0,1\}$
3. $\bigwedge_{(\phi_i,1) \in \mathcal{L}} \phi_i \wedge \bigwedge_{(\phi_i,0) \in \mathcal{L}} \neg \phi_i$ *is satisfiable,*

there exists an integer solution p', *that is for all* $I_l \in \mathcal{T}_l : p'(I_l) \in \{0,1\}$.

Proof. Due to the first requirement we can remove all tuples in $\mathcal{T} \backslash \mathcal{T}_l$ from the labels' formulas ϕ, since these tuples correspond to either *true* or *false*. Likewise, the second condition allows the construction of the formula $\bigwedge_{(\phi_i,1) \in \mathcal{L}} \phi_i \wedge \bigwedge_{(\phi_i,0) \in \mathcal{L}} \neg \phi_i$. As we require the existence of a satisfying assignment for this formula, precisely this assignment is the integer solution.

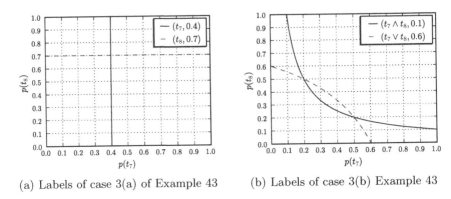

(a) Labels of case 3(a) of Example 43   (b) Labels of case 3(b) Example 43

Fig. 7. Visualization of the Learning Problem

Visual Interpretation. Based on algebraic geometry, the learning problem allows for a visual interpretation. All possible definitions of probability values for tuples in $\mathcal{T}_l$, that is, $p : \mathcal{T}_l \to [0, 1]$, span the hypercube $[0, 1]^{|\mathcal{T}_l|}$. In Example 43, cases 3(a) and 3(b), the hypercube has two dimensions, namely $p(I_7)$ and $p(I_8)$, as depicted in Figures 7(a) and 7(b). Hence, one definition of p specifies exactly one point in the hypercube. Moreover, all definitions of p that satisfy a given label define a curve (or plane) through the hypercube (e.g., the two labels in Figure 7(a) define two straight lines). Also, the points, in which all labels' curves intersect, represent solutions to the learning problem (e.g., the solutions of Example 43, case 3(b), are the intersections in Figure 7(b)). If the learning problem is inconsistent, there is no point in which all labels' curves intersect. Furthermore, if the learning problem has infinitely many solutions, the labels' curves intersect in curves or planes, rather than points.

6.4   Gradient Based Solutions

We formally characterized the learning problem and devised the basic properties of its solutions. From a visual perspective, Definition 27 established curves and planes whose intersections represent the solutions (see, e.g., Figure 7(b)). We now introduce different objective functions that describe surfaces whose optima correspond to these solutions. For instance, the problem of Figure 7(b) has the surface of Figure 8(a) if we the employ mean squared error (MSE) as the objective, which will be defined in this section. Calculating a gradient on such a surface thus allows the application of an optimization method to solve the learning problem.

Desired Properties. Before we define objective functions for solving the learning problem, we establish a list of desired properties of these (which we do not claim to be complete). Later, we judge different objectives based on these properties.

Definition 28. *An objective function to the learning problem should satisfy the following three* desired properties:

1. *All instances of the learning problem of Definition 27 can be expressed, including inconsistent ones.*
2. *If all $P(\phi_i)$ are computable in polynomial time, then also the objective is computable in polynomial time.*
3. *The objective is stable, that is $\mathcal{L} := \langle (\phi_1, l_1), \ldots, (\phi_n, l_n) \rangle$ and $\mathcal{L} \cup \langle (\phi_i', l_i) \rangle$ with $\phi_i' \equiv \phi_i$, $(\phi_i, l_i) \in \mathcal{L}$ define the same surface.*

Here, the first case ensures that the objective can be applied to all instances of the learning problem. We insist on including inconsistent instances, because they occur often in practice. The second property restricts a blow-up in computation, which yields the following useful characteristic: if we can compute $P(\phi)$ for all labels, e.g., for labeled query answers, then we can also compute the objective function. Finally, the last of the desiderata reflects an objective function's ability to detect dependencies between labels. Since $\phi_i \equiv \phi_i'$ both $\mathcal{L}$ and $\mathcal{L} \cup \langle (\phi_i', l_i) \rangle$ allow exactly the same solutions, the surface should be the same. Unfortunately, including convexity of an objective as an additional desired property is not possible. For example Figure 7(b) has two disconnected solutions, which induce at least two optima, thus prohibiting convexity. In the following, we establish two objective functions, which behave very differently with respect to the desired properties.

Logical Objective. If we restrict the probability labels of the learning problem to $l_i \in \{0.0, 1.0\}$, we can define an objective function based on computing probabilities of lineage formulas as follows.

Definition 29. *Let an instance of the learning problem of Definition 27 be given by a probabilistic database $(\mathcal{T}, p)$, tuples with unknown probability values $\mathcal{T}_l \subseteq \mathcal{T}$, and labels $\mathcal{L} = \langle (\phi_1, l_1), \ldots, (\phi_n, l_n) \rangle$ such that all $l_i \in \{0.0, 1.0\}$. Then, the logical objective is formulated as follows:*

$$Logical(\mathcal{L}, p) := P \left(\bigwedge_{(\phi_i, l_i) \in \mathcal{L}, l_i = 1.0} \phi_i \land \bigwedge_{(\phi_i, l_i) \in \mathcal{L}, l_i = 0.0} \neg \phi_i \right) \tag{19}$$

The above definition is a maximization problem, and its global optima are identified by $Logical(\mathcal{L}, p) = 1.0$. Moreover, from Definition 13, we may obtain its derivative.

Example 44. Let $\mathcal{T} = \mathcal{T}_l := \{I_1, I_2\}$ and $\mathcal{L} := \langle (I_1 \lor I_2, 1.0), (I_1, 0.0) \rangle$ be given. Then, $Logical(\mathcal{L}, p)$ is instantiated as $P((I_1 \lor I_2) \land \neg I_1) = P(\neg I_1 \land I_2)$. Visually, this defines a surface whose optimum lies in $p(I_1) = 0.0$ and $p(I_2) = 1.0$, as shown in Figure 8(b).

With respect to Definition 28, the third desired property is fulfilled, as $P(\phi_i' \land \phi_i) = P(\phi_i)$. Hence, the surface of the logical objective, shown for instance in

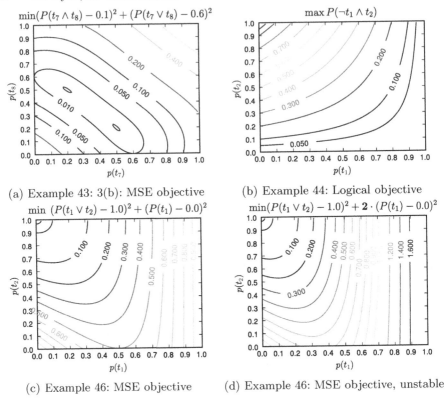

(a) Example 43: 3(b): MSE objective

(b) Example 44: Logical objective

(c) Example 46: MSE objective

(d) Example 46: MSE objective, unstable

Fig. 8. Visualization of the MSE and Logical Objective Functions

Figure 8(b), is never altered by adding equivalent labels. Still, the first property is not given, since the probability labels are restricted to $l_i \in \{0.0, 1.0\}$ and inconsistent problem instances collapse Equation (19) to $P(false)$, thus rendering the objective non-applicable. Also, the second property is violated, because in the spirit of the proof of Lemma 4, we can construct an instance where for each label $P(\phi_i)$ on its own is computable in polynomial time, whereas the computation of the probability for Equation (19) is again #P-hard.

Mean Squared Error Objective. Another approach, which is also common in machine learning, lies in using the mean squared error (MSE) to define the objective function.

Definition 30. *Let an instance of the learning problem of Definition 27 be given by a probabilistic database* $(\mathcal{T}, p)$, *tuples with unknown probability values* $\mathcal{T}_l \subseteq \mathcal{T}$, *and labels* $\mathcal{L} = \langle (\phi_1, l_1), \ldots, (\phi_n, l_n) \rangle$. *Then, the* mean squared error objective *is formulated as:*

$$MSE(\mathcal{L}, p) := \frac{1}{|\mathcal{L}|} \sum_{(\phi_i, l_i) \in \mathcal{L}} (P(\phi_i) - l_i)^2$$

Moreover, its partial derivative with respect to the probability value $p(I)$ of the tuple is:

$$\frac{\partial MSE(\mathcal{L}, p)}{\partial p(I)} := \frac{1}{|\mathcal{L}|} \sum_{(\phi_i, l_i) \in \mathcal{L}, I \in Tup(\phi_i)} 2 \cdot (P(\phi_i) - l_i) \cdot \underbrace{\frac{\partial P(\phi_i)}{\partial p(I)}}_{Definition\ 13}$$

The above formulation is a minimization problem whose solutions have 0.0 as the target value of the objective function.

Example 45. Example 43, case 3(b), is visualized in Figure 7(b). The corresponding surface induced by the MSE objective is depicted in Figure 8(a) and has its minima at the solutions of the learning problem.

Judging the above objective by means of Definition 28, we realize that the first property is met, as there are no restrictions on the learning problem, and inconsistent instances can be tackled (but deliver objective values larger than zero). Furthermore, since the $P(\phi_i)$'s occur in separate terms of the sum of the objective, the second desired property is maintained. However, the third desired property is violated, as illustrated by the following example.

Example 46. In accordance to Example 44 and Figure 8(b), we set $\mathcal{T} = \mathcal{T}_l := \{I_1, I_2\}$ and $\mathcal{L} := \langle(I_1 \vee I_2, 1.0), (I_1, 0.0)\rangle$. Then, the MSE objective defines the surface in Figure 8(c). However, if we replicate the label $(I_1, 0.0)$, thus resulting in Figure 8(d) (note the "times two" in the objective), its surface becomes steeper along the $p(I_1)$-axis, but has the same minimum. Thus, MSE's surface is not stable. Instead, it becomes more ill-conditioned [43].

Discussion. Both the logical objective and the MSE objective have optima exactly at the solutions of the learning problem of Definition 27. With respect to the desired properties of Definition 28, we summarize the behavior of both objectives in the following table:

	Properties		
Objective	1.	2.	3.
Logical	×	×	✓
MSE	✓	✓	×

The two objectives satisfy opposing desired properties, and it is certainly possible to define other objectives behaving similarly to one of them. Unfortunately, there is little hope for an objective that will be adhering to all three properties. The second property inhibits computational hardness. However, Lemma 4 and the third property's logical tautology checking (i.e., $\models \phi_i \leftrightarrow \phi_i'$, which is *co-$\mathcal{NP}$-complete*) require this. In this regard the logical objective addresses both computationally hard problems by computing probabilities, whereas the MSE objective avoids the latter form of tautology checking.

7   Conclusions

In recent years, the need to efficiently manage large amounts of uncertain data has become evident as more and more data arise from various applications such as information extraction, sensor networks, and scientific data management. As a result, PDBs have evolved as an establish field of research in recent years [63]. In this chapter, we provide an overview of the key concepts of PDBs and the main challenges than need to be addressed. Specifically, we begin by describing the main characteristics of probabilistic databases assuming tuple independence, and we present the respective data model and query evaluation strategies. Apart from being uncertain, data can be annotated by other dimensions such as time and location. In this regard, we describe a closed and complete temporal-probabilistic database model [21], coined TPDB, which allows us to cope with data that is variable over time as well as uncertain. Complementary to the basics, we review state-of-the-art methods in this field and also describe some of our own recent research results including a top-k style evaluation strategy [23]. The latter attempts to tackle the increased complexity of the probability computation step involved in query evaluation in PDBs. This is achieved by pruning answer candidates without fully grounding the lineage formula and hence saving also on the data computation step. Last, although most works assume the probabilities are provided as input along with the data, this assumption often does not hold and a learning approach is required. As we consider learning to be a key building block for future probabilistic database engines, we conclude this chapter by discussing such a learning approach [22] for creating, updating and cleaning of PDBs.

Acknowledgements. This article is based on the doctoral dissertation by Maximilian Dylla: "Efficient Querying and Learning in Probabilistic and Temporal Databases", Saarland University, February 2014." [20]

References

1. Abiteboul, S., Herr, L., den Bussche, J.V.: Temporal Connectives versus Explicit Timestamps in Temporal Query Languages. In: Clifford, J., Tuzhilin, A. (eds.) Recent Advances in Temporal Databases, Proceedings of the International Workshop on Temporal Databases, Zürich, Switzerland, September 17-18. Workshops in Computing, pp. 43–57. Springer, New York (1995)
2. Abiteboul, S., Hull, R., Vianu, V. (eds.): Foundations of Databases, 1st edn. Addison-Wesley, Boston (1995)
3. Abiteboul, S., Kanellakis, P., Grahne, G.: On the representation and querying of sets of possible worlds. SIGMOD Record 16(3), 34–48 (1987)
4. Allen, J.F.: Maintaining knowledge about temporal intervals. Communications of the ACM 26(11), 832–843 (1983)
5. Antova, L., Jansen, T., Koch, C., Olteanu, D.: Fast and Simple Relational Processing of Uncertain Data. In: Proceedings of the 24th International Conference on Data Engineering, ICDE, pp. 983–992. IEEE Computer Society, Washington, DC (2008)

6. Auer, S., Bizer, C., Kobilarov, G., Lehmann, J., Cyganiak, R., Ives, Z.G.: DBpedia: A Nucleus for a Web of Open Data. In: Aberer, K., et al. (eds.) ISWC/ASWC 2007. LNCS, vol. 4825, pp. 722–735. Springer, Heidelberg (2007)
7. Benjelloun, O., Das Sarma, A., Halevy, A., Theobald, M., Widom, J.: Databases with uncertainty and lineage. VLDB Journal 17(2), 243–264 (2008)
8. Boulos, J., Dalvi, N., Mandhani, B., Mathur, S., Re, C., Suciu, D.: MYSTIQ: a system for finding more answers by using probabilities. In: Proceedings of the International Conference on Management of Data, SIGMOD, pp. 891–893. ACM, New York (2005)
9. Brin, S.: Extracting Patterns and Relations from the World Wide Web. In: Atzeni, P., Mendelzon, A.O., Mecca, G. (eds.) WebDB 1998. LNCS, vol. 1590, pp. 172–183. Springer, Heidelberg (1999)
10. Ceri, S., Gottlob, G., Tanca, L.: What You Always Wanted to Know About Datalog (And Never Dared to Ask). IEEE Transactions on Knowledge and Data Engineering 1(1), 146–166 (1989)
11. Cormen, T.H., Leiserson, C.E., Rivest, R.L., Stein, C.: Introduction to Algorithms, 3rd edn. MIT Press, Cambridge (2009)
12. Cui, Y., Widom, J., Wiener, J.L.: Tracing the Lineage of View Data in a Warehousing Environment. ACM Transactions on Database Systems 25(2), 179–227 (2000)
13. Dalvi, N., Ré, C., Suciu, D.: Probabilistic Databases: Diamonds in the Dirt. Communications of the ACM 52(7), 86–94 (2009)
14. Dalvi, N., Schnaitter, K., Suciu, D.: Computing Query Probability with Incidence Algebras. In: Proceedings of the Twenty-ninth ACM SIGMOD-SIGACT-SIGART Symposium on Principles of Database Systems, PODS, pp. 203–214. ACM, New York (2010)
15. Dalvi, N., Suciu, D.: Efficient query evaluation on probabilistic databases. VLDB Journal 16(4), 523–544 (2007)
16. Dalvi, N., Suciu, D.: The dichotomy of conjunctive queries on probabilistic structures. In: Proceedings of the Twenty-Sixth ACM SIGMOD-SIGACT-SIGART Symposium on Principles of Database Systems, PODS, pp. 293–302. ACM, New York (2007)
17. Dalvi, N., Suciu, D.: The Dichotomy of Probabilistic Inference for Unions of Conjunctive Queries. Journal of the ACM 59(6), 30:1–30:87 (2013)
18. Dickenstein, A., Emiris, I.Z.: Solving Polynomial Equations: Foundations, Algorithms, and Applications, 1st edn. Springer, Heidelberg (2010)
19. Dignös, A., Böhlen, M.H., Gamper, J.: Temporal alignment. In: Proceedings of the International Conference on Management of Data, SIGMOD, pp. 433–444. ACM, New York (2012)
20. Dylla, M.: Efficient Querying and Learning in Probabilistic and Temporal Databases. Doctoral Dissertation, Saarland University (2014)
21. Dylla, M., Miliaraki, I., Theobald, M.: A Temporal-Probabilistic Database Model for Information Extraction. Proceedings of the VLDB Endowment 6(14), 1810–1821 (2013)
22. Dylla, M., Theobald, M.: Learning Tuple Probabilities in Probabilistic Databases. Research Report MPI-I-2014-5-001, Max-Planck-Institut für Informatik, Stuhlsatzenhausweg 85, 66123 Saarbrücken, Germany (January 2014)
23. Dylla, M., Theobald, M., Miliaraki, I.: Top-k query processing in probabilistic databases with non-materialized views. In: Proceedings of the 29th International Conference on Data Engineering, ICDE, pp. 122–133. IEEE Computer Society, Washington, DC (2013)

24. Fagin, R., Lotem, A., Naor, M.: Optimal Aggregation Algorithms for Middleware. In: Proceedings of the Twentieth ACM SIGMOD-SIGACT-SIGART Symposium on Principles of Database Systems, PODS, pp. 102–113. ACM, New York (2001)

25. Feller, W.: An introduction to probability theory and its applications, 3rd edn. Wiley, Hoboken (1968)

26. Fink, R., Olteanu, D.: On the optimal approximation of queries using tractable propositional languages. In: Proceedings of the 14th International Conference on Database Theory, ICDT, pp. 174–185. ACM, New York (2011)

27. Fisher, M., Gabbay, D., Vila, L.: Handbook of Temporal Reasoning in Artificial Intelligence, 1st edn. Foundations of Artificial Intelligence. Elsevier, Essex (2005)

28. Fuhr, N., Rölleke, T.: A Probabilistic Relational Algebra for the Integration of Information Retrieval and Database Systems. ACM Transactions on Information Systems 15(1), 32–66 (1997)

29. Garey, M.R., Johnson, D.S.: Computers and Intractability: A Guide to the Theory of NP-Completeness. Freeman, New York (1990)

30. Grädel, E., Gurevich, Y., Hirsch, C.: The Complexity of Query Reliability. In: Proceedings of the Seventeenth ACM SIGACT-SIGMOD-SIGART Symposium on Principles of Database Systems, PODS, pp. 227–234. ACM, New York (1998)

31. Green, T.J., Tannen, V.: Models for Incomplete and Probabilistic Information. IEEE Data Engineering Bulletin 29(1), 17–24 (2006)

32. Widom, J., Garcia-Molina, H., Ullman, J.D.: Database systems: the complete book, 1st edn. Prentice-Hall, Upper Saddle River (2002)

33. Hoffart, J., Suchanek, F.M., Berberich, K., Weikum, G.: YAGO2: A Spatially and Temporally Enhanced Knowledge Base from Wikipedia. Artificial Intelligence 194, 28–61 (2013)

34. Ilyas, I.F., Beskales, G., Soliman, M.A.: A Survey of Top-k Query Processing Techniques in Relational Database Systems. ACM Computing Surveys 40(4), 11:1–11:58 (2008)

35. Jensen, C.S.: Temporal Database Management. PhD thesis, Aalborg University, Aalborg, Denmark (April 2000)

36. Jha, A., Suciu, D.: Knowledge Compilation Meets Database Theory: Compiling Queries to Decision Diagrams. Theory of Computing Systems 52(3), 403–440 (2013)

37. Kanagal, B., Deshpande, A.: Lineage processing over correlated probabilistic databases. In: Proceedings of the International Conference on Management of Data, SIGMOD, pp. 675–686. ACM, New York (2010)

38. Kanagal, B., Li, J., Deshpande, A.: Sensitivity analysis and explanations for robust query evaluation in probabilistic databases. In: Proceedings of the International Conference on Management of Data, SIGMOD, pp. 841–852. ACM, New York (2011)

39. Kanellakis, P.C., Kuper, G.M., Revesz, P.Z.: Constraint query languages. In: Proceedings of the Ninth ACM SIGACT-SIGMOD-SIGART Symposium on Principles of Database Systems, PODS, pp. 299–313. ACM, New York (1990)

40. Khanna, S., Roy, S., Tannen, V.: Queries with Difference on Probabilistic Databases. Proceedings of the VLDB Endowment 4(11), 1051–1062 (2011)

41. Koch, C., Olteanu, D.: Conditioning probabilistic databases. Proceedings of the VLDB Endowment 1(1), 313–325 (2008)

42. Nakashole, N., Weikum, G., Suchanek, F.: PATTY: A Taxonomy of Relational Patterns with Semantic Types. In: Proceedings of the 2012 Joint Conference on Empirical Methods in Natural Language Processing and Computational Natural Language Learning, EMNLP-CoNLL, pp. 1135–1145. Association for Computational Linguistics, Stroudsburg (2012)

43. Nocedal, J., Wright, S.J.: Numerical Optimization, 2nd edn. Springer, Heidelberg (2006)
44. Ohrstrom, P.: Temporal Logic: From Ancient Ideas to Artificial Intelligence. Springer, Heidelberg (2009)
45. Olteanu, D., Huang, J.: Using OBDDs for Efficient Query Evaluation on Probabilistic Databases. In: Greco, S., Lukasiewicz, T. (eds.) SUM 2008. LNCS (LNAI), vol. 5291, pp. 326–340. Springer, Heidelberg (2008)
46. Olteanu, D., Huang, J., Koch, C.: SPROUT: Lazy vs. Eager Query Plans for Tuple-Independent Probabilistic Databases. In: Proceedings of the 25th International Conference on Data Engineering, ICDE, pp. 640–651. IEEE Computer Society, Washington, DC (2009)
47. Olteanu, D., Huang, J., Koch, C.: Approximate confidence computation in probabilistic databases. In: Proceedings of the 26th International Conference on Data Engineering, ICDE, pp. 145–156. IEEE Computer Society, Washington, DC (2010)
48. Olteanu, D., Wen, H.: Ranking Query Answers in Probabilistic Databases: Complexity and Efficient Algorithms. In: Proceedings of the 28th International Conference on Data Engineering, ICDE, pp. 282–293. IEEE Computer Society, Washington, DC (2012)
49. Ré, C., Dalvi, N.N., Suciu, D.: Efficient Top-k Query Evaluation on Probabilistic Data. In: Proceedings of the 23rd International Conference on Data Engineering, ICDE, pp. 886–895. IEEE Computer Society, Washington, DC (2007)
50. Ré, C., Suciu, D.: Approximate Lineage for Probabilistic Databases. Proceedings of the VLDB Endowment 1(1), 797–808 (2008)
51. Ré, C., Suciu, D.: The trichotomy of HAVING queries on a probabilistic database. VLDB Journal 18(5), 1091–1116 (2009)
52. Rekatsinas, T., Deshpande, A., Getoor, L.: Local Structure and Determinism in Probabilistic Databases. In: Proceedings of the International Conference on Management of Data, SIGMOD, pp. 373–384. ACM, New York (2012)
53. Sagiv, Y., Yannakakis, M.: Equivalences Among Relational Expressions with the Union and Difference Operators. Journal of the ACM 27(4), 633–655 (1980)
54. Sarma, A.D., Theobald, M., Widom, J.: Exploiting Lineage for Confidence Computation in Uncertain and Probabilistic Databases. In: Proceedings of the 24th International Conference on Data Engineering, ICDE, pp. 1023–1032. IEEE Computer Society, Washington, DC (2008)
55. Das Sarma, A., Theobald, M., Widom, J.: LIVE: a lineage-supported versioned DBMS. In: Gertz, M., Ludäscher, B. (eds.) SSDBM 2010. LNCS, vol. 6187, pp. 416–433. Springer, Heidelberg (2010)
56. Sen, P., Deshpande, A., Getoor, L.: PrDB: managing and exploiting rich correlations in probabilistic databases. VLDB Journal 18(5), 1065–1090 (2009)
57. Sen, P., Deshpande, A., Getoor, L.: Read-once Functions and Query Evaluation in Probabilistic Databases. In: Proceedings of the VLDB Endowment, vol. 3(1-2), pp. 1068–1079 (2010)
58. Shiryaev, A.N.: Probability, 2nd edn. Springer, Heidelberg (1995)
59. Singh, S., Mayfield, C., Mittal, S., Prabhakar, S., Hambrusch, S.E., Shah, R.: Orion 2.0: native support for uncertain data. In: SIGMOD Conference, pp. 1239–1242 (2008)
60. Smullyan, R.M.: First-order logic, 1st edn. Springer, Heidelberg (1968)
61. Stoyanovich, J., Davidson, S., Milo, T., Tannen, V.: Deriving Probabilistic Databases with Inference Ensembles. In: Proceedings of the 27th International Conference on Data Engineering, ICDE, pp. 303–314. IEEE Computer Society, Washington, DC (2011)

62. Suchanek, F.M., Kasneci, G., Weikum, G.: Yago: A Core of Semantic Knowledge. In: Proceedings of the 16th International Conference on World Wide Web, WWW, pp. 697–706. ACM, New York (2007)
63. Suciu, D., Olteanu, D., Christopher, R., Koch, C.: Probabilistic Databases, 1st edn. Morgan & Claypool, San Rafael (2011)
64. Tuzhilin, A., Clifford, J.: A Temporal Relational Algebra As Basis for Temporal Relational Completeness. In: Proceedings of the 16th International Conference on Very Large Data Bases, VLDB, pp. 13–23. Morgan Kaufmann Publishers, San Rafael (1990)
65. Sperschneider, G.A.V.: Logic: A Foundation for Computer Science, 1st edn. Addison-Wesley, Boston (1991)
66. Valiant, L.G.: The Complexity of Computing the Permanent. Theoretical Computer Science 8(2), 189–201 (1979)
67. van Benthem, J.: The Logic of Time: A Model-Theoretic Investigation into the Varieties of Temporal Ontology and Temporal Discourse, 2nd edn. Kluwer Academic Publishers, Dordrecht (1991)
68. Weikum, G., Theobald, M.: From Information to Knowledge: Harvesting Entities and Relationships from Web Sources. In: Proceedings of the Twenty-Ninth ACM SIGMOD-SIGACT-SIGART Symposium on Principles of Database Systems, PODS, pp. 65–76. ACM, New York (2010)

Semantic and Reasoning Systems for Cities and Citizens

Spyros Kotoulas

IBM Research, Dublin, Ireland

Abstract. The Semantic Web is finally leaving the lab. In this article, we examine some practical, industry-oriented Semantic Web systems and discuss the costs and benefits on this disruptive technology. We focus on applications for cities and citizens and present a set of key challenges and solutions made possible using semantics at scale. When applicable, we report on the differentiating factors for Semantic Technologies, showcasing their unique capabilities, as well as the cost of this paradigm shift.

1 Introduction

The Semantic Web is becoming mainstream beyond the research lab. Large organizations and technology companies are using Semantic Technologies to provide global and flexible integration - BBC is using this to connect its online content[1], search engines are using semantics to annotate content on the Web through Schema.org[2]. Major vendors are adding RDF capabilities to their offerings - IBM[3] and Oracle[4] have added SPARQL capability to their databases, Cray markets an appliance for SPARQL processing[5].

The emergence of Semantic Technologies is driven by changes in IT infrastructures, in terms of information networking, and business, in terms of emergent opportunities on a data-driven business:

- *Siloed information is seen as an inhibitor of efficient business.* Enterprises realize that data is not only usable in the context in which it has been produced or collected. It is becoming increasingly common that the business unit responsible for some data collection is not the only consumer of this information. Information sharing within the business is of course nothing new: data warehouses and master data management infrastructures have been in use for at least one decade. What is different is the desire to access information as context, in a setting where the information producer/publisher and information consumer are largely independent.

---

[1] http://www.bbc.co.uk/blogs/internet/posts/Linked-Data-Connecting-together-the-BBCs-Online-Content

[2] http://schema.org

[3] http://www-01.ibm.com/support/knowledgecenter/SSEPGG_10.1.0/com.ibm.swg.im.dbclient.rdf.doc/doc/r0060562.html

[4] http://docs.oracle.com/cd/E11882_01/appdev.112/e11828/sem_jena.htm#RDFRM234

[5] http://www.yarcdata.com/Products/

M. Koubarakis et al. (Eds.): Reasoning Web 2014, LNCS 8714, pp. 369–387, 2014.

- *Data is increasingly seen as an asset.* There is an increasing trend towards data-driven business [1]. In this setting, insights coming from data become the driver for identifying new business opportunities and optimizing execution rather than supplementary tools for traditional business disciplines. The demand for data scientists and executive appointment of chief data officers (CDO's) testifies to this trend.
- *Organizations realize that cross-domain information is more valuable than more-of-the-same information.* Critical information often lies in multiple domains. By merging information across disciplines, organizations can make better informed decisions. A good example is dealing with the Social Determinants of Health[6]: optimizing healthcare delivery is dependent on information coming from local government (e.g. about the environment or safety), transportation (e.g. access to services) and finance (e.g. economic feasibility of treatments), among others [2]. This multi-domain information not only calls for efficient data sharing, but also for fit-for-use knowledge sharing across disciplines.

The rest of this paper is structured as follows: Section 2 provides motivation and background by describing the characteristics of some information resources used by the systems this paper. Section 3 describes a set of approaches focused on the operation of cities. Section 4 describes a set of approaches focused at the citizens. We discuss some key advantages and disadvantages of Semantic Technologies and conclude in Section 5.

2   Information Resources

2.1   Scaling Up the Semantic Web: Linked Data

Over the last years, we have witnessed explosive growth in the publication of Linked Open Data (LOD). This growth happens in multiple dimensions: In terms of domains, LOD covers a broad range, such as general knowledge (DBPedia), public administration (IPSV), bioinformatics (Uniprot) and many more. In terms of size, in 2008, LOD consisted of "several billion" triples[7]; in 2010, it consisted of some 13 billion triples[8]; in 2012, it consisted of some 32 billion triples[9]. The users of LOD also changing: initially limited to academia, with the advent of Linked Enterprise Data, there is an increasing tendency to use Linked Data within the enterprise. We refer the reader to the respective article in the same volume for further information regarding Linked Data.

2.2   Urban Data

Cities are both producers and consumers of vast volumes of information. Urban data comes in many forms, shapes and sizes. Part of this information is

---

[6] http://www.who.int/social_determinants/en/
[7] http://events.linkeddata.org/ldow2008/
[8] http://events.linkeddata.org/ldow2010/
[9] http://events.linkeddata.org/ldow2012/

generally openly accessible while another can be sensitive from a privacy, security or business perspective.

Open Data. Government agencies and other organizations are increasingly making their data accessible to promote transparency and economic growth. Since the first data.gov initiative launched by the US government, many city agencies and authorities have made their data publicly available through content portals: New York City[10], London[11], San Francisco[12], Boston[13], and Dublin[14], to name a few. Sometimes, this data is exposed as Linked Data. Managing Open and Linked data require that publishers put significant resources. A critical question for government agencies is what *return-on-investment* they are getting for resources spent in making their data open. This may come as an increase in economic activity in their constituencies, decrease in administration costs and increased transparency.

User generated content can provide information outside of the scope of traditional data sources. For example, a traffic jam that emerges due to an unplanned protest may be captured through a twitter stream, but missed when examining weather conditions, event databases, reported roadworks, etc. Additionally, weather sensors in the city tend to miss localised events such as flooding. These views of the city combined however, can provide a richer and more complete view of the state of the city, by merging traditional data sources with messy and unreliable social media streams.

Closed Data. Not all data can be made publicly accessible, due to privacy restrictions (e.g. residence occupancy, health-related information), public safety restrictions (e.g. plans for disaster management) or business reasons (e.g. electricity consumption can be used to estimate the levels of production). Many of the systems operating in a city rely on such information - systems for public safety, social security, transportation and public administration systems, to name a few.

More interestingly, for many problems in cities, it is necessary to combine information across systems. An example domain is person-centred care. As a simple motivating example, consider an individual quartered in inappropriate housing while suffering from a relatively minor health issue, aggravated by the housing condition. As a result, the given individual frequently resorts to visiting emergency rooms, resulting in significant cost to the healthcare system and a less effective treatment. By itself, the housing situation does not warrant state intervention. Nevertheless, resolving it would dramatically improve the health situation, resulting in a better quality-of-life for the individual and lower costs for the health system. In addition, a possible conviction for illegally selling prescription medication would strengthen the need to this intervention. Possible

---

[10] http://www.nyc.gov/html/
[11] http://data.london.gov.uk/
[12] http://datasf.org/
[13] http://www.cityofboston.gov/doit/databoston/app/data.aspx
[14] http://www.dublinked.ie

convictions leading to incarceration would weaken it (individual might not be home anyway). The above example makes it obvious that information from multiple domains and systems needs to be combined to achieve better results in a complex environment like a city.

In the following sections, we will focus on how some systems use Semantics to solve challenging problems in cities. Although the discussion will not be limited to efforts from industry, we will only mention systems with a heavy practical focus.

3   City-Centric Systems

There is a large body of literature aiming at providing better insight into the operation of cities. We will focus on two use cases: Open Data management and industry-specific systems using semantics. We will give an overview of some systems in both categories and provide a more detailed description for some examples for traffic and for managing city data as Linked Data.

3.1   Open Data Management

With the advent of Open Data, research organizations, non-profits and software vendors has started looking at scalable ways to manage this information. The problem of managing Open Data is broad, spanning from file-based content management to complex methods aimed at semantically lifting and linking data coming from heterogeneous sources.

Data Cataloguing and Hosting. As soon as cities and other public organizations realised the value of opening up their data, they began investigating technical solutions to make this possible. Initially, most solutions were proprietary (e.g. the original `data.gov` site). Soon enough, data cataloguing and hosting solutions started appearing, both from non-profits (e.g. CKAN[15]) and commercial organizations (e.g. Socrata[16]), .

As these technologies started maturing, additional capability has been added to provide visualizations on top of this data. In Figure 1, one can see the data interaction interface of CKAN for some Open Data from Italy`www.publicdata.eu`. In Figure 2, one can see an example of a simple visualisation: The user is called to select a set of columns from a CSV file (shown in Figure 1) for the information to be plotted on a chart. In this case, it is important to note that (a) the input has no explicit semantics (b) the system relies solely on structure to display this information. In the following paragraphs, we describe some approaches aimed at understanding such data.

---

[15] `http://www.ckan.org`
[16] `http://www.socrata.com`

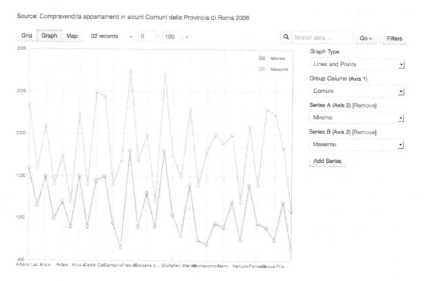

Source: Compravendita appartamenti in alcuni Comuni della Provincia di Roma 2006

Comuni	Tipo Abitazione	Minimo	Massimo
Albano Laziale	Abitazioni parzialmente da ristrutturare	1150	1600
Anzio	Abitazioni nuove o ristrutturate	1500	2100
Anzio	Abitazioni parzialmente da ristrutturare	1000	1400
Ardea	Abitazioni nuove o ristrutturate	1200	1750
Ardea	Abitazioni parzialmente da ristrutturare	900	1200
Ariccia	Abitazioni nuove o ristrutturate	1500	2250
Ariccia	Abitazioni parzialmente da ristrutturare	900	1400
Castel Gandolfo		1450	2500

Fig. 1. Example data from CKAN

Source: Compravendita appartamenti in alcuni Comuni della Provincia di Roma 2006

Fig. 2. Example visualisation from CKAN

From Data to Knowledge. There has been a set of research efforts towards automated approaches for turning tabular data into Semantic Web formats. Pattern-based methods for re-engineering non-ontological resources into ontologies [3] are based on the use of thesauri, lexica and WordNet for making explicit the relations among terms. TARTAR [4] automatically generates knowledge models out of tables. In this system, grounded in the cognitive table model introduced by Hurst [5], a table is handled from a structural, functional and semantic point of view by respectively identifying homogeneous regions (group of cells) in a table, distinguishing between attribute cells and instance cells, and then finding semantic labels for each region content with the help of WordNet. The coverage of these approaches depends on WordNet or an ontology that models the domains of interest. To annotate tables on the Web and improve search, [6] uses a column-based approach. A class label is attached to a column if a sufficient number of the values in the column are identified with that label in some "is-a" databases extracted from the Web.

In [7], a new dataset-specific ontology is constructed for each dataset, representing only the data stored in the particular database. To convert this data into RDF, scripts are developed in correspondence with their manually-designated and built ontologies.

A number of tools for automatically converting tabular data (mostly CSV) into RDF also exist, such as RDF123 [8]. W3C defines a standardised mapping language R2RML[17] and an approach for converting relational databases to RDF. In this W3C candidate recommendation, the first row is used to suggest properties and each other row refers to entities, with one of the columns uniquely identifying the entity. This approach is used, for example, in the Datalift project [9] to automate the conversion from the source format to "raw RDF", before transforming it to "well-formed" RDF by using selected vocabularies and SPARQL construct queries.

The approach presented in [10] is based on Google Refine for data cleaning and a reconciliation service extended with Linked Data capabilities to enable exporting tabular data into RDF, while keeping provenance descriptions represented according to the *Open Provenance Model Vocabulary* [11].

Queriocity. We will go into more detail regarding a system that combines the data storage and management capabilities of data portals and the semantic uplift capabilities of the approaches mentioned above. The novelty of Queriocity [12] lies in the ability of the system to ingest highly heterogenous data and process it in an incremental manner. The cost of entry to the system is minimal (i.e. datasets can be imported as they are), and processing (annotation, linking, integration) can be done incrementally, exploiting semantic technologies. The main purpose of the system, from an industry perspective, is to show that a stack based on semantic technologies can go a long way, without the need for global integration, pre-defined schemas, or even linking the entire input. At the same time, it exploits the Web-wide wealth of resources rich in meaning and structure published as Linked Open Data.

In Queriocity, raw data is ingested, annotated, and transformed into a meaningful and connected structure, in order to be accessed and queried on demand and in context based on space, time and semantic relations to other relevant data. This goes beyond classical document search or entity search, since it largely relies on externally available models to disambiguate, organize and query non-semantic data. To achieve this, data is semantically uplifted and entities and relations between them are extracted and aligned to well-known vocabularies and widely used LOD resources. Different views and exploration paths are exposed according to dynamically chosen models, allowing users to profit from the expressive power of semantic standards while hiding the complexity behind services exposed in an intuitive and easy-to-use interface.

---

[17] http://www.w3.org/TR/r2rml/

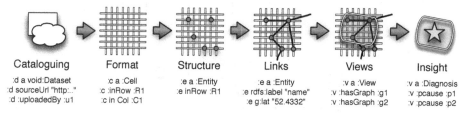

Cataloguing	Format	Structure	Links	Views	Insight
:d a void:Dataset	:c a :Cell	:e a :Entity	:e a :Entity	:v a :View	:v a :Diagnosis
:d sourceUrl "http:.."	:c :inRow :R1	:e inRow :R1	:e rdfs:label "name"	:v :hasGraph :g1	:v :pcause :p1
:d :uploadedBy :u1	:c in Col :C1		:e g:lat "52.4332"	:v :hasGraph :g2	:v :pcause :p2

Fig. 3. Data processing approach in Queriocity

Figure 3 summarizes the steps taken to go from raw data to a useful business result, from a data management perspective:

- Initially, data is catalogued in a semantically interoperable manner, i.e. using existing ontologies such as VOID[18], PROV[19] and IPSV[20].
- Datasets in the system are loaded into a store so that they can be accessed in an uniform manner (i.e. formats are homogeneised). This representation is not intended to capture semantics, but rather to provide a convenient and uniform way to represent the content of files, which are further processed as described in the following sections.
- The next step in the process is to infer, and possibly validate with the user, the structure of the data. For example, a file may contain an entity per row, an entity per column or other combinations.
- The platform leverages semantic data types (geographical coordinates, dates, etc.) and automatically converts units of measurement. In addition, it uses user input or mapping techniques to detect common types and entity co-reference.
- To abstract from the complexity of the domain, Queriocity uses semantic views as a way to expose the relevant information to applications. Instead of being closely coupled to the data layout, applications define how their input should look like and, using a pay-as-you go paradigm, the user helps the platform populate those views.
- Finally, analytics components can be used to infer new knowledge on top of these views. Sometimes, the output of these analytics is stored in the system.

Throughout these steps, Queriocity follows a pay-as-you-go paradigm: the steps above are only performed as required. For example, the cataloguing part is performed for all datasets, format homogenization is performed for datasets with a fixed set of formats (for which there are converters in place), linking is done as required by the views, which are, in turn defined by the applications to be run.

---

[18] http://www.w3.org/TR/void/

[19] http://www.w3.org/TR/prov-o/

[20] http://doc.esd.org.uk/IPSV/

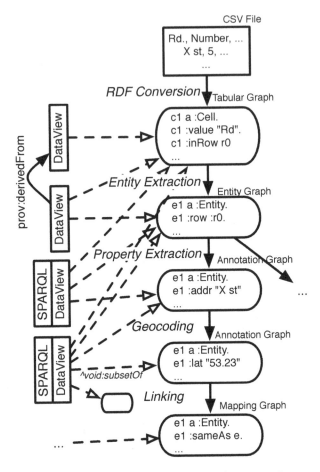

Fig. 4. Support for views and multiple integrations

Figure 4 shows an example for the data model. Data is stored in Graphs. DataViews are the access methods for data in the system, each referring to one or more graphs. Graphs are shared between DataViews (i.e. a Dataset may reference multiple Graphs, and a Graph can be referenced by multiple Datasets), using union semantics. Data manipulation tasks entail creating new Graphs, which are then referenced together with existing graphs. For read-stability reasons, the only operation allowed on Graphs is splitting and re-writing existing references to the graph. The said design avoids data duplication while inducing as little overhead as possible.

Graphs are physically stored as named graphs on the underlying infrastructure. Management information, i.e. the information about DataViews, Graphs etc, is also stored in RDF, on a separate named graph. The system keeps both dataset-level provenance and graph-level provenance, storing *derivedFrom* relationships for both Datasets and Graphs.

3.2   Applications

In the following paragraphs, we will briefly describe some systems that exploit the semantics of data coming for various sources for decision-making.

Cities increasingly rely on information management systems for decision-making. Decision-making can be roughly split into four main categories [13]: *strategic*, operating on long-term and at high aggregation level to evaluate and influence sustainability and growth, such as planning new development areas; *tactical*, targeting goals with a time horizon from days to months, such as preparing for snow in the winter; *operational*, that address events in a time-frame from minutes to hours, such as monitoring occupation of bike-sharing stations around the city or traffic congestion management systems; and *real-time*, time-critical operations on a frame from seconds to minutes, such as monitoring traffic to operate traffic lights.

In particular, we will focus on two applications that reason over traffic data and operate mainly at the operational and tactical levels and one that focuses on real-time information.

TrafficLarKC. TrafficLarKC [14] is probably the first example of a semantics-augmented service for traffic routing. It relies on the pluggable platform developed in the context of the Large Knowledge Collider (LarKC) project[21] to integrate conceptual query answering with statistical learning and operations research algorithms. The service taps on several external resources to get an integrated view of the traffic environment and propose the best routes. The results are visualized on a mobile phone.

Figure 5[22], shows the high-level architecture of TrafficLarKC: a wealth of information is collected from Linked Data, street maps, traffic sensors and web sensors (such as online weather forecasts) and processed in a framework combining multiple techniques. These techniques are arranged in a 5-step approach, largely applicable to most (semantic) systems: *Identify* relevant information, *transform* into an appropriate machine-processeable representation, *select* relevant subsets, *reason* over the combined information and *decide* on an appropriate solution.

STAR-CITY. STAR-CITY [15] is a semantics-based system for traffic. It integrates both human and physical sensors representing information in a variety of formats to perform analysis, diagnosis, exploration and prediction using Semantic Technologies. We explain the main functionality of the system using a screenshot (Figure 6):

- The user is able to make temporal selections for the data being explored (①, ②).
- The user makes a spatial selection using a map ③.
- The environmental context of the current selection is shown. In ④, one can examine key information regarding weather conditions.

---

[21] http://larkc.eu

[22] Figure taken from http://emanueledellavalle.org/Projects/TrafficLarKC.html

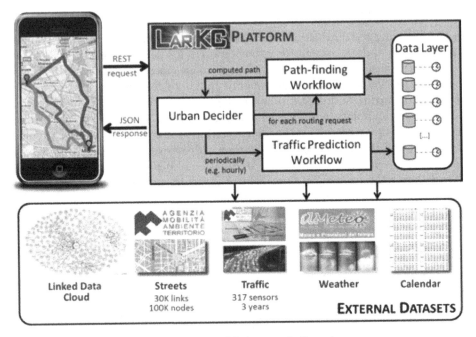

Fig. 5. TrafficLarKC Approach Overview

- At a glance, the user is able to examine travel time vs historical information (⑤). The user can select individual segments to isolate information. Detailed records are also visible (⑥) as well as proportions (⑦).
- Additional views for exploration, diagnosis etc are available as separate tabs (⑧).

Figure 7 shows the main diagnosis approach: The system does an off-line compilation of historic diagnosis information into a deterministic finite state machine, following the structure of the road network[23]. The network is used to both get the connections between roads and for propagating road congested states. This state machine is augmented with events extracted from a variety of sources from the Web (as shown in the figure). In addition, these events are correlated to past observed congestions. Real-time diagnosis is performed by analyzing and matching current states to historical versions.

3.3   Real-Time Monitoring

Streaming semantic data is not limited to traffic scenarios, the system described in [16], a system to process real-time urban information in the public safety domain is presented. One of the problems addressed by this system is selecting the most relevant closed-circuit television (CCTV) cameras.

---

[23] Extracted from http://www.linkedgeodata.org

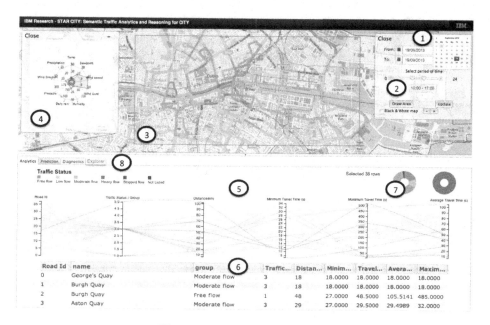

Fig. 6. Interface of STAR-CITY

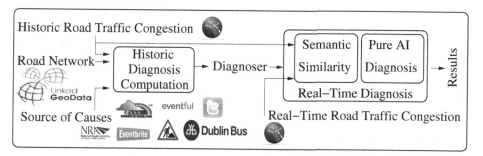

Fig. 7. STAR-CITY Diagnosis Approach Overview

The rationale behind the system is that, complementary to video processing techniques, information about the environment, as detected by sensors, can be used to select the most relevant cameras for a human to monitor. In this scenario, a "sensor" has a very wide meaning ranging from physical sensors capturing noise, to Web sensors producing streams about happenings in a city.

The decision-making process is generally as follows: (i) take into account a number of stream measurements, such as percentage of vehicles entering a region with a traffic congestion, ambient noise beyond a given threshold, etc., and assign a score to each of them, weighted by the distance from the cameras; (ii) assign a weight for the presence of amenities in the area, such as schools and hospitals; (iii) detect changes across three different time spans, called *windows*: a short-window of a few seconds to measure recent changes, a medium-window of tens of seconds to measure the persistence of the state evaluated by the short window,

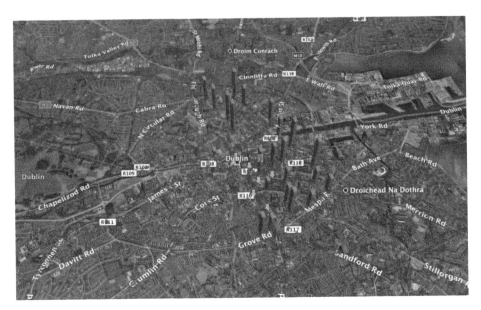

Fig. 8. Real-time camera selection

and a large-window, ending in the past, to account for regular variations, such as daily rush hours.

Figure 8 shows some of the inputs and output of the system, plotted on top of Dublin: yellow arrows represent currently selected CCTV cameras (i.e. the output), bars represent pollution levels, noise levels, utilization of public bikes and pedestrian counts (from footfall sensors), blue dots represent buses in congestion and red dots represent amenities (from LinkedGeoData[24]).

Figure 9 shows the main components of the system, which is similar to other systems in the literature [17,18,19,20,21,22], with a set of extensions to improve performance and deal with heterogeneous input . The system takes as input static or streaming data in heterogeneous formats, in this particular case CSV or RDF input. An optional reasoning step does basic RDFS reasoning over this information. Then, given a set of continuous SPARQL queries, performs the selection, joining, aggregation and other operations.

Figure 10 shows an example query including extensions to SPARQL for processing graph information and information coming from CSV files. Every triple pattern is used to define a single variable of the query: the first element of the triple is the variable that will bound to the value of the specific field of the CSV stream, the second element is a special predicate (*"ibm:csvCol"*) plus a number that is used to specify the field of the CSV record. The last element is the URI reference of the specific CSV input stream. For example, in line 12, in Figure 10 the variable *"?stationid"* will get its bindings for field zero (*"ibm:csvCol_0"*) of the CSV stream identified by the URI *http : //.../csv*.

---

[24] http://linkedgeodata.org/

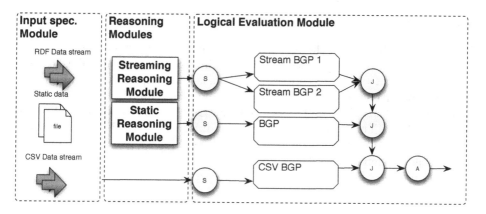

Fig. 9. Real-time camera selection components

```
1   SELECT ?station ?stationid ?stationlat ?stationlong ?address
2                   (AVG( ?bikecount / ?numBike ) AS ?bike)
3   FROM <http://.../rfid>
4   FROM CSV <http://.../csv> 1 [RANGE 20m STEP 20m] AS 'bikestream'
5   WHERE{
6     { ?station dpPedia:agencyStationCode ?stationid.
7       ?station dpPedia:maxNumOfBike ?numBike.
8       ?station wsg84:long ?stationlong.
9       ?station wsg84:lat ?stationlat.
10      ?station address:streetAddress ?address.}
11    CSV 'bikestream' {
12      ?stationid ibm:csvCol_0 <http://.../csv>.
13      ?bikecount ibm:csvCol_2 <http://.../csv>.}
14  } GROUP BY ?station ?stationid ?stationlat ?stationlong ?address
```

Fig. 10. Graph pattern extensions for processing heterogeneous stream information

4   Citizen-Centric Systems

In the following sections, we will describe a set of systems that are centred on
or oriented-towards the individual, rather than a city. We will describe systems
in two extremes: Revyu [23] is one of the first semantic web systems. It relies
on persistent identifiers to allow users to review anything. The system is simple
and completely open (i.e. all information is publicly visible). Link2Outcome [24]
is an enterprise system to improve Care. It aims at collecting and interpreting
personal information from multiple systems. The system is closed and most data
stored therein is sensitive.

4.1   Revyu

Revyu is arguably one of the first Semantic Web systems exploiting the power
of Linked Data. It allows users to review things or people and publishes the
results as RDF. The architecture of the system is very simple (shown in Fig. 11),
consisting of a Web Server and PHP code to issue calls to an RDF store backed by
a MySQL database. The system both consumes and publishes data using Linked
Data principles. This allows already existing information (such as information
from DBpedia) to be mashed-up with user-content. Similarly, the system exposes
data using dereferenceable URIs and a SPARQL endpoint. Revyu is a good
illustration of how little semantics can go a long way.

Fig. 11. Revyu Architecture

4.2   Link2Outcome

A more complicated application scenario arises in the domain of care. Organizations seeking to improve health outcomes and lower costs are facing unique
challenges such as aligning care delivery to population needs, creating and managing holistic, individualized care plans and care coordination to produce positive and sustainable outcomes at reduced cost. In [25], it is reported that 5% of
individuals face complex issues spanning multiple domains and accounting for
50% of the cost. Identifying these individuals early on is key to reducing costs.
The impact of social determinants for health dictates that multi-domain information is needed for holistic and individualized care delivery [26]. Furthermore,
coordination across care agencies and stakeholders requires an integrated view
of the individual, their vulnerabilities and their environment [27].

The common denominator is the need for *fit-for-use* information spanning
multiple domains. In general, needs span six core areas: health, food, shelter,
safety, education and income. Potential information sources are diverse and numerous (e.g. the American Hospital Association numbers 5724[25] members and
the number of homeless shelters surpasses 4000[26]). The complexity of Health
Care data is vast and Social Care systems have a very broad scope.

Relevant use-cases are abundant: In a New York hospital, a survey has shown
that 9.2 minutes out of a 15-minute doctor's visit were spent on social needs,
crowding out clinical care [28] and illustrating that "social context" of individuals
is critical in improving care (for example, consider asthma triggered by
sub-standard housing, depression or chemical dependency affecting medication

---

[25] http://www.aha.org/research/rc/stat-studies/fast-facts.shtml,
retrieved 19/04/2013
[26] http://www.shelterlistings.org/

adherence, lack of food impacting diabetes). A single social worker may be responsible for thousands of people [28]. Providing timely, relevant, multi-dimensional and fit-for-purpose information about vulnerability to all care workers is critical.

Typical Health Care data integration approaches use an all-or-nothing model, i.e. data is either part of the (mediated) model or not accessible at all [29]. In constrast, Link2Outcome uses Linked Data to incrementally integrate and present information coming from distributed sources. A set of reference ontologies is used to map data from enterprise systems and access it in a uniform manner. In addition, the reference ontologies are used to simplify information and make it fit-for-use for the non-experts (for example, one could simplify the name of "Pica Disease" to "Eating Disorder").

As an example use-case, Link2Outcome [30] can provide an overview of the vulnerability in a set of key dimensions. Fig. 12 shows a screenshot from the system:

- The structure shown on Figure 12(α) shows a concise navigational structure of the vulnerabilities of an example individual. The circles represent the relative importance of the vulnerabilities in a set of dimensions that are deemed important in the domain of the user. The user gets an immediate impression of the key weaknesses of an individual (in this case, it would be problems regarding Health and Food) and retains the capability to explore further.
- To get finer-grain information, an exploration pane (Figure 12(β)) is used to navigate the entire space, based on the Linked Data structure and potential ontology overlap. In the example, the user can see that the individual is receiving child benefit amounting to 170 euros weekly.

The architecture of the system (as shown in Fig. 13, taken from [30]) is complex: Web-facing services use a set of REST services, implemented on a custom application running on IBM WebSphere Application Server. The main components for these services are the *Node registry*, which tracks nodes in the *Federated Query Engine*, the *View definitions*, that are used to project information out of the graph model for use by analytics widgets and UI elements. *Data Sources* are exposed as virtual RDF, using SeDA, an IBM technology to execute R2RML mappings. The virtual RDF Data Sources, the Metadata Repository and the Ancillary Indexes are accessed through the *Federated Query Engine*, providing transparent access to the distributed information. All core components in this architecture can be clustered, for high availability and performance.

5 Discussion and Outlook

In this Section, we are discussing some advantages and disadvantages of Semantic Technologies, mainly from an industry perspective.

The global semantics of RDF allow retrieving the relevant information transparently. URI dereferencing and federated query capabilities allow retrieving information regardless of physical infrastructure and location. For contextual retrieval, this is of paramount importance, since which data is important is not

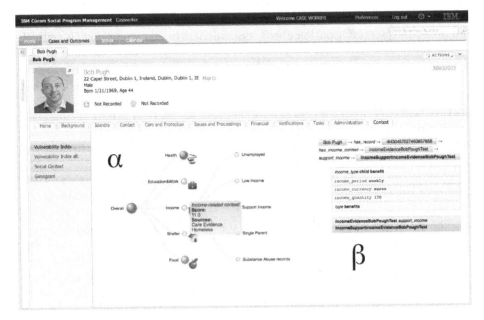

Fig. 12. Interface of Link2Outcome

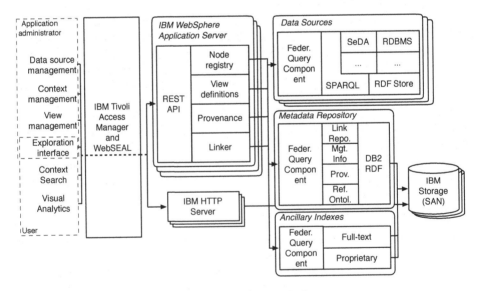

Fig. 13. Architecture for Link2Outcome

always known in advance and we often need to follow connections across entities.

At a high-level, given a complex or dynamic domain, Semantic Technologies are more flexible than Data Warehouses or a Master Data Management (MDM) infrastructures. Traditional Extract-Transform-Load (ETL) or MDM approaches typically require significant up-front investment, since they rely on a (set of) global models, where data is projected on. While such approaches have shown good performance, a Semantic approach is more suitable for dynamic situations requiring partial and extensible integration across multiple sources. Partial integration in relational schemas is very cumbersome: typically, data is either fully integrated or not accessible at all.

This flexibility comes at a cost: The lack of a rigid model means that accessing data is more difficult. Generic graph-based exploration and querying, typical in many Semantic Web approaches, is not attractive from an enterprise application perspective. Use-case specific navigational aids are necessary, hiding the complexity of the graph.

Regarding visualization, tabular-style visualizations are preferred to graph-based visualizations. When dealing with distributed data and inference, methods to capture information provenance are highly desirable, since most semantic approaches abstract from the underlying data.

A particularly challenging requirement for Linked data-based approaches is coping with missing data, or rather knowing whether data is missing. For example, a system that calculates an aggregate score based on all the medical conditions of an individual needs to be able to distinguish between missing data, mis-integration and data not supporting the aggregate. Given the open-world assumption in the Semantic Web, indicating data completeness remains an open challenge and, potentially, a significant drawback.

RDF provides a natural way to implement a consolidated information space within and across organizations, while allowing re-use of assets from the Web. Such assets include reference ontologies and vocabularies to standardize datatypes, define types , ranges etc. In some cases, these ontologies and vocabularies facilitate querying, even when lacking pre-defined and common structures, through common or related (linked) values (e.g., broader or narrower topics in the reference vocabularies).

Core components for RDF-based solutions are finally enterprise-ready. Several systems presented here rely, to a large extent, on enterprise-grade components that can be clustered for robustness and performance. Semantic Web tooling has advanced significantly, although it is still far less developed than similar tools in the relational domain, and in data warehousing and master data management in particular.

The majority of enterprise infrastructures relies on systems of record [31], meaning that there is an authoritative source, in a single system, for a piece of information, in order to cope with the disparity of information. We are witnessing a shift towards systems of engagement [32], where information across systems is connected arbitrarily across systems and users interact with data in a way that is not pre-determined. The Semantic Web plays a critical role in the future of information systems by providing global identifiers, self-describing, reason-able data and an interoperable, machine-understandable format.

Aknowledgements. We would like to thank the following researchers from IBM that have contributed to the systems presented in detail in this paper: Vanessa Lopez, Martin Stephenson, Pierpaolo Tommasi, Marco Luca Sbodio, Pol Mac Aonghusa, Freddy Lecue, Simone Tallevi-Diotallevi, Weijia Shen, Gang Hu, Veli Bicer, Anastasios Kementsietsidis, M. Mustafa Rafique, Jason B. Ellis, Guo Tong Xie, Jer Hayes, Robert Tucker, Anika Schumann, Thomas Erickson, Kavitha Srinivas and Kevin McAuliffe.

References

1. Davenport, T.H., Harris, J.G.: Competing on analytics: the new science of winning. Harvard Business Press (2013)
2. Marmot, M., Wilkinson, R.: Social determinants of health. Oxford University Press (2005)
3. García-Silva, A., Gómez-Pérez, A., Suárez-Figueroa, M.C., Villazón-Terrazas, B.: A pattern based approach for re-engineering non-ontological resources into ontologies. In: Domingue, J., Anutariya, C. (eds.) ASWC 2008. LNCS, vol. 5367, pp. 167–181. Springer, Heidelberg (2008)
4. Pivk, A.: Automatic ontology generation from web tabular structures. AI Communications 19, 2006 (2005)
5. Hurst, M.: Layout and language: Challenges for table understanding on the web, pp. 27–30 (2001)
6. Venetis, P., Halevy, A., Madhavan, J., Paşca, M., Shen, W., Wu, F., Miao, G., Wu, C.: Recovering semantics of tables on the web. VLDB Endow. 4(9), 528–538 (2011)
7. Alani, H., Dupplaw, D., Sheridan, J., O'Hara, K., Darlington, J., Shadbolt, N.R., Tullo, C.: Unlocking the potential of public sector information with semantic web technology. In: Aberer, K., et al. (eds.) ISWC/ASWC 2007. LNCS, vol. 4825, pp. 708–721. Springer, Heidelberg (2007)
8. Han, L., Finin, T.W., Parr, C.S., Sachs, J., Joshi, A.: Rdf123: From spreadsheets to rdf. In: Sheth, A.P., Staab, S., Dean, M., Paolucci, M., Maynard, D., Finin, T., Thirunarayan, K. (eds.) ISWC 2008. LNCS, vol. 5318, pp. 451–466. Springer, Heidelberg (2008)
9. Scharffe, F., Atemezing, G., Troncy, R., Gandon, F., et al.: Enabling linked-data publication with the datalift platform. In (AAAI 2012) Workshop on Semantic Cities (2012)
10. Maali, F., Cyganiak, R., Peristeras, V.: A publishing pipeline for linked government data. In: Simperl, E., Cimiano, P., Polleres, A., Corcho, O., Presutti, V. (eds.) ESWC 2012. LNCS, vol. 7295, pp. 778–792. Springer, Heidelberg (2012)
11. Zhao, J.: Open provenance model vocabulary specification. tech. rep. university of oxford (2010), http://open-biomed.sourceforge.net/opmv/ns.html
12. Kotoulas, S., Lopez, V., Lloyd, R., Sbodio, M.L., Lecue, F., Stephenson, M., Daly, E., Bicer, V., Gkoulalas-Divanis, A., Di Lorenzo, G., et al.: Spud? semantic processing of urban data. Web Semantics: Science, Services and Agents on the World Wide Web (2014)
13. Sandu, D.: Operational and real-time business intelligence. Revista Informatica Economică 3(47), 33–36 (2008)
14. Della Valle, E., Celino, I., Dell'Aglio, D., Grothmann, R., Steinke, F., Tresp, V.: Semantic traffic-aware routing using the larkc platform. IEEE Internet Computing 15(6), 15–23 (2011)

15. Lécué, F., Tallevi-Diotallevi, S., Hayes, J., Tucker, R., Bicer, V., Sbodio, M.L., Tommasi, P.: Star-city: semantic traffic analytics and reasoning for city. In: IUI, pp. 179–188 (2014)

16. Tallevi-Diotallevi, S., Kotoulas, S., Foschini, L., Lécué, F., Corradi, A.: Real-time urban monitoring in dublin using semantic and stream technologies. In: Alani, H., et al. (eds.) ISWC 2013, Part II. LNCS, vol. 8219, pp. 178–194. Springer, Heidelberg (2013)

17. Bolles, A., Grawunder, M., Jacobi, J.: Streaming sparql - extending sparql to process data streams. In: Bechhofer, S., Hauswirth, M., Hoffmann, J., Koubarakis, M. (eds.) ESWC 2008. LNCS, vol. 5021, pp. 448–462. Springer, Heidelberg (2008)

18. Rodriguez, A., McGrath, R.E., Liu, Y., Myers, J.D.: Semantic management of streaming data. In: International Workshop on Semantic Sensor Networks at ISWC (2009)

19. Anicic, D., Fodor, P., Rudolph, S., Stojanovic, N.: Ep-sparql: a unified language for event processing and stream reasoning. In: WWW, pp. 635–644 (2011)

20. Le-Phuoc, D., Dao-Tran, M., Xavier Parreira, J., Hauswirth, M.: A native and adaptive approach for unified processing of linked streams and linked data. In: Aroyo, L., Welty, C., Alani, H., Taylor, J., Bernstein, A., Kagal, L., Noy, N., Blomqvist, E. (eds.) ISWC 2011, Part I. LNCS, vol. 7031, pp. 370–388. Springer, Heidelberg (2011)

21. Barbieri, D.F., Braga, D., Ceri, S., Valle, E.D., Grossniklaus, M.: C-sparql: Sparql for continuous querying. In: WWW, pp. 1061–1062 (2009)

22. Ren, Y., Pan, J.Z.: Optimising ontology stream reasoning with truth maintenance system. In: CIKM, pp. 831–836 (2011)

23. Heath, T., Motta, E.: Revyu: Linking reviews and ratings into the web of data. Web Semantics: Science, Services and Agents on the World Wide Web 6(4), 266–273 (2008)

24. Kotoulas, S., Lopez, V., Sbodio, M.L., Tommasi, P., Stephenson, M., Aonghusa, P.M.: Improving cross-domain information sharing in care coordination using semantic web technologies. In: IUI, pp. 347–352 (2014)

25. Conwell, L.J., Cohen, J.W.: Characteristics of persons with high medical expenditures in the US civilian noninstitutionalized population, 2002. Medical Expenditure Panel Survey, Agency for Healthcare Research and Quality (2005)

26. Marmot, M., Wilkinson, R.: Social determinants of health. Oxford University Press (2009)

27. Kodner, D.L., Spreeuwenberg, C.: Integrated care: meaning, logic, applications, and implications–a discussion paper. International journal of integrated care 2 (2002)

28. Onie, R., Farmer, P., Behforouz, H.: Realigning health with care. Stanford Social Innovation Review 10, 28–35 (2012)

29. Nodine, M., Hee, A., Ngu, H., Bohrer, W.: Semantic brokering over dynamic heterogeneous data sources in infosleuth. In: Proc. of the 15th Inter. Conference on Data Engineering, pp. 358–365. IEEE Computer Society (1999)

30. Kotoulas, S., Lopez, V., Stephenson, M., Tommasi, P., Shen, W., Hu, G., Sbodio, M.L., Bicer, V., Kementsietsidis, A., Rafique, M.M., Ellis, J.B., Erickson, T., Srinivas, K., McAuliffe, K., Xie, G.T., Aonghusa, P.M.: Coordinating social care and healthcare using semantic web technologies. In: International Semantic Web Conference (Posters & Demos), pp. 169–172 (2013)

31. Inmon, W.H.: Building the data warehouse. John Wiley & Sons (2005)

32. Moore, G.: Systems of engagement and the future of enterprise it-a sea change in enterprise it. AIIM, Silver Spring (2011)

Author Index